F 2395

D0985932

CHRONICLES
OF THE
CRUSADES

a ce faire seront ordenes et les dits clers representeront
les dictes escriptures devant le Prince et son conseil et
celles qui au dit Prince et conseil sembleront estre din,
gnes de ramentevoir les dits clers les mettront en escri
pt dedens un liure le quel sappellera le liure des auene
mens aus cheualiers de la compagnie du saint esperit
au droit desir: Et demorra le dit liure tous iours en la
dicte chappelle.

Item se la sainte eglise de roume ou au i
cuns Princeps des crestiens en preist le
uoyage doultre mer pour la terre sainte
la ou est le sepulcre de nostre seignour i
recourer et le getter hors des mains des
mescrans chascun cheualier de la dicte i
compaigne sera tenus dy estre en propre
personne si pourront bonnement et se chose
feist que le Prince de la dicte compaignie
de qui le dit heritage doit estre raisonnable
ment empreist le dit uoyage ou passage alaide de la i
sainte eglise et des autres Princeps crestiens ou le dit
Prince y alast personnelment en la compaignie dautru
chascuns des dits cheualiers seront tenu de aler personne
lment et di demorer continuelment tant comme le i
dit Prince y demorra salue se aucune expresse et appa
rant necessite ne le contredeist. ✝

CHRONICLES
OF THE
CRUSADES

EYE-WITNESS ACCOUNTS
OF THE WARS BETWEEN
CHRISTIANITY AND ISLAM

EDITED BY ELIZABETH HALLAM

Welcome Rain
NEW YORK

FAMILY HISTORY RESOURCE CENTER

First Welcome Rain edition 2000
by arrangement with Salamander Books
Copyright © 2000 Salamander Books
All rights reserved
1-56649-193-2
M 10 9 8 7 6 5 4 3 2 1

Maps: Jeff Edwards

Phototypesetting: Tradespools Ltd, Frome, Somerset

Origination: Scantrans Pte Ltd, Singapore

Printed and bound in Portugal by:
Printer Portuguesa Industria Grafica, LDA

Frontispiece: *Crusaders load up their
vessels prior to departure for the Holy Land.*

Created and Produced by Phoebe Phillips Editions

Editorial Director: Tessa Clark

Editorial

Project Editor: Cecilia Walters

Hilary Bird
Fred Gill
Paul Mackintosh
Jenny Overton
Liliane Reichenbach

Kevin Tongue
Timothy Probart

Picture Research:
Dr Margaret M. Condon

Design

Harry Green

Production

Roger Multon
Tim Scott

General Editor

Dr Elizabeth Hallam, *Assistant Keeper of Public Records, Head of Museum Section, Public Record Office, London*

Preface

Jonathan Riley-Smith, *Professor of History, Royal Holloway and Bedford New College, University of London, U.K.*

Special Acknowledgement

Professor Aziz al-Azmeh, *Department of Arabic and Islamic Studies, University of Exeter, United Kingdom*

Consultant Editors

Dr Malcolm Barber, *Department of History, Reading University, United Kingdom*

Dr Richard G. Eales, *Lecturer in History, University of Kent, Canterbury, United Kingdom*

Susan Edgington, *The Huntingdonshire College, United Kingdom*

Dr Norman J. Housley, *Department of History, Leicester University, United Kingdom*

Dr Graham A. Loud, *School of History, Leeds University, United Kingdom*

Michael Parkinson, *Head of History Department, Rochester Grammar School, United Kingdom*

Dr Elizabeth Siberry, *Surbiton, United Kingdom*

Translators

Translation Editor: Michael Parkinson

Anna Sapir Abulafia
Sarah Baker
Matthew Bennet
Karen Brookfield
Anthony Calderbank
Linda Campbell
Percy Denton
Susan Edgington
Monica Gale
Diana Gallagher
Roy Gibson
Ruth Harvey
James Masters

Jim Neville
Andy Orchard
Avril Powell
Alison Sharrock
Janet Shirley
Peter Singer
Sylvia Trott
Leslie Turano
Roderick Vassie
Pamela Waley
Geoffrey West
Kate Westoby

Special thanks to

M. Boggan
Professor Peter M. Holt
Michael Jenner
David Nicolle

Contributors

Dr Anna Sapir Abulafia, *Laura Ashley Research Fellow, Lucy Cavendish College, Cambridge, United Kingdom*

Dr David Abulafia, *Lecturer in Medieval History, Gonville and Caius College, Cambridge, United Kingdom*

Reuven Amitai-Preiss, *Institute of Asian and African Studies, Hebrew University, Israel*

Dr Benjamin Arnold, *Lecturer in History, University of Reading, United Kingdom*

Dr Malcolm Barber, *Senior Lecturer in History, Department of History, University of Reading, United Kingdom*

Brenda Bolton, *Senior Lecturer in History, Westfield College, London, United Kingdom*

Dr Michael Brett, *Lecturer in the History of North Africa, School of Oriental and African Studies, University of London, United Kingdom*

Dr Patrick Donabedian, *art historian, Paris, France*

Susan Edgington, *Senior Lecturer, The Huntingdonshire College, United Kingdom*

Dr Bruno Figliuoli, *Associate Professor of Social and Economic History, University of Molise, Italy*

Dr John France, *Lecturer in History, Department of History, University College, Swansea, United Kingdom*

Dr Carole Hillenbrand, *Lecturer in Arabic and Islamic History, Department of Islamic and Middle Eastern Studies, The Muir Institute, Edinburgh, United Kingdom*

Dr Robert Irwin, *writer and historian, London, United Kingdom*

Dr Peter Jackson, *Lecturer in History, Department of History, University of Keele, United Kingdom*

Sarah Lambert, *London, United Kingdom*

Dr Graham A. Loud, *Lecturer in Medieval History, University of Leeds, United Kingdom*

Dr Anthony Luttrell, *Research Officer of the Venerable Order of St John of Jerusalem, London, United Kingdom*

Dr Christopher J. Marshall, *London, United Kingdom*

Dr Sophia Menache, *Senior History Lecturer, Department of General History, University of Haifa, Israel*

Dr Rosemary Morris, *Lecturer in Medieval History, University of Manchester, United Kingdom*

Dr Alan V. Murray, *Assistant Editor, International Medieval Bibliography, University of Leeds, United Kingdom*

Professor Mahmoud Said Omran, *Department of Middle Ages History, Faculty of Arts, University of Alexandria, Egypt*

Dr Denys Pringle, *Edinburgh, United Kingdom*

Associate Professor John H. Pryor, *Department of History, University of Sydney, Australia*

Professor Jean Richard, *Académie des Inscriptions et Belles-Lettres, Paris, France*

Dr Elizabeth Siberry, *Surbiton, United Kingdom*

Tom Sinclair, *Centre for Byzantine Studies, University of Birmingham, United Kingdom*

Dr Robert Somerville, *Professor of Religion and History, Columbia University, New York City, U.S.A.*

Peter Stocks, *Supervisor, Oriental Reading Room, British Library, London, United Kingdom*

Dr Frank Tallett, *Lecturer in European History, History Department, University of Reading, United Kingdom*

Sister Benedicta Ward, *Tutor in Medieval History, Centre for Medieval and Renaissance Studies, Oxford, United Kingdom*

Dr Geoffrey West, *Curator, Hispanic Section, British Library, London, United Kingdom*

William G. Zajac, *Queens College, Cambridge, United Kingdom*

EDITOR'S NOTE

'Jerusalem is the navel of the world, a land fruitful above all others, like a second paradise of delights. This royal city is now held captive by her enemies . . ., so she asks and prays to be liberated, and calls on you unceasingly to come to her aid'. So, according to one chronicler, Robert the Monk, spoke Pope Urban II at the council of Clermont in November 1095. 'Everyone,' Robert continues, 'moved by the same feeling, shouted "God wills it, God wills it". And the venerable pope raised up his eyes to heaven and gave thanks to God'. In his speech Urban fused together two potent ideals of 11th-century Christendom – pilgrimage to Jerusalem and holy war against the Moslems – and the crusades were born.

In this book we take crusades to be holy wars authorized by the papacy, and waged in the name of Christ against the internal or external enemies of Christendom, to recover Christian lands or to defend the Church; indulgences giving remission from penance or from sins were granted by the pope to reward the participants. Although Jerusalem remained the principal inspiration, the crusades were from the outset fought over a wider field. By 1098 crusaders were combating the Muslim Almoravids in Spain as well as fighting in the East, and over the next 150 years were also active in the Baltic, Italy, Greece, north Africa and southern France. After the fall of Acre in 1291 crusades continued to be preached and fought for another three hundred years, despite mounting criticism, growing scepticism about their value, and after the Reformation, fewer people on whom to draw. Crusading ideas and rhetoric lingered yet longer, into the 18th century, and even found a place in writings about the conquest of the New World.

The exciting diversity of the crusades is here captured in the words of contemporary or near contemporary writers, chosen to represent the often conflicting points of view of the western crusaders (collectively described as 'Franks' or 'Latins' in the sources); of the Byzantines (generally called the 'Greeks' by the crusaders and the 'Romans' by themselves); and, more unusually in such a compilation, of the crusaders' Muslim opponents.

Specialist chapter consultants have selected and introduced the extracts – many of which are here translated for the first time – and with other leading scholars from many different parts of the world, have contributed short essays tying in with ideas and occurrences in the narrative. Certain names, dates and titles have been modernized or supplied where elucidation is required, and explanatory linking text has been added. Otherwise editorial intervention has been kept to a minimum, bringing each reader into direct contact with the many different peoples, cultures and outlooks caught up in the long unfolding drama of the crusades.

The Christian chronicler
William of Tyre writing his
account of the crusades

CONTENTS

Preface
Jonathan Riley-Smith
11

PREFACE

In 1099 a crusader called Guy of Bré, a castellan from the Limousin in France, lay dying at Lattakieh in Syria. Seven neighbours from the Limousin, one of them another castellan, a relative of his by marriage, witnessed the gifts Guy made in his last agony to two local religious communities at home. At about the same time, another crusader, a canon of Le Puy called Bertrand of Bas, fell ill at sea and renounced tithes he had held illegally back in France. His deed of renunciation was witnessed by six companions, all from the same region as he.

Scenes of dying crusaders in an alien environment, thinking of home and surrounded by men they had probably known all their lives, crop up again and again in the archives of the religious houses which benefited from crusaders' wills. And the suffering, disorientation and waste of life which are illustrated in this book caused some men to question the wisdom of crusading to the east since it put such a great number of lives at risk and deprived Christianity of many great and good men.

On this sort of pilgrimage against the Muslims countless people die, sometimes from sickness at sea, sometimes in battle, sometimes from a lack or excess of food; not only the common people, but also kings and princes and persons who do great service to Christianity. How much harm was done through the death of King Louis [IX of France], whose life was so beneficial to the Church of God, and through the deaths of many others!

The luxurious existence of a Muslim prince in his harem, a contrast to the spartan and relatively primitive Franks.

11

The blunt reply of an experienced crusade preacher in the late 13th century, Humbert of Romans, a former master general of the Dominican Order, that 'the aim of Christianity is not to fill the earth but to fill heaven', although unanswerable, is not of much help to us when we ask ourselves why men and women were prepared to expose themselves to the discomfort and danger so often described in the pages that follow, in such widely dispersed theatres of war, from the Atlantic and the Baltic to the eastern Mediterranean, and over so many generations, from the late 11th to the 16th century, and perhaps beyond.

Of course in a martial society the call to war had more positive resonances than it has for us; and although a knight had plenty of opportunities for displaying his prowess in western Europe, crusading had a prestige which made reputations. Crusaders who performed adequately and did not run away – many did – gained honour, which enhanced their status at home and probably helped their daughters to make better marriages. But, on the other hand, their experiences were generally very unpleasant. They were often very frightened – they particularly dreaded a sea-crossing – and they rapidly became disorientated. Apart from the risks of injury or death in combat, they were exposed to starvation and disease. And they were involved in something that was very expensive.

A reasonable method of estimating the cost to an early 12th-century knight of joining an expedition to the east would be to multiply his income by four times; and as the price of equipment rose in the 13th and 14th centuries, the outgoings must have increased considerably. Crusading in Spain or along the Baltic would have been cheaper, but only relatively so, because the same capital outlay in horses, arms and armour would have been needed. At first these expenses had to be met entirely out of an individual's own pocket, which is why the surviving archives of European cathedrals and monasteries are full of the records of crusaders' sales and unredeemed mortgages. The disposal of land, patrimony in which all relatives had an interest, involved a crusader's family in a collective sacrifice; and the decision would have been a grave one at the time of a major crusade when the land market was being flooded with properties and prices were falling. The returns were negligible. Very few crusaders ever planned to settle in a region which was a theatre of war; conquered territories tended to be colonized once crusades were over. And although the narrative accounts contain many references to looting, this was usually a reaction to crisis

of men desperately short of food and fodder and forced to live off the land, often operating outside Christian territory, far from supply points and without any system of regular provisioning. It is not surprising that one theme in crusade history is that of the raising of finance by kings and by popes, who from 1199 onwards resorted to taxing the Church to subsidize crusaders. Even with subsidies, as John of Joinville's experiences show, a crusader always had to commit his own substance to the enterprise.

So what made them do it?

The response to appeals to crusade should be put into perspective. Early crusade armies were often swollen by large numbers of unsuitable and unwarlike men and women who could not be prevented from joining, since crusades were preached as pilgrimages, and a pilgrimage confined to young, healthy, upper-class males was a contradiction in terms; later they contained many mercenaries, who were paid soldiers and not volunteers. Although general goodwill was needed for crusading to flourish, the number of nobles and knights who actually took crusade vows – and they are the only crusaders we can discuss since little or nothing is known of the motives of the masses – can be exaggerated. There were, of course, many who did not join because they were not attracted, but even an enthusiast needed more than zeal for the crusade to be a realistic option for him. He had, as we have seen, to raise cash; he required assurances about the security of his family and property in his absence; he may well have felt the need to be attached to a patron who could subsidize him and give some protection in the dangerous years ahead; and he usually had to have the support and encouragement of family and neighbours. As the decades went by, the obstacles to recruitment multiplied and at no time did more than a fraction of the able-bodied knights available take the cross.

At first, moreover, commitment tended to be concentrated in certain families. Probably no more than 7,000 nobles and knights joined the three waves of the First Crusade which left Europe between 1096 and 1101; 17 of them were from the closely related families of Le Puiset and Montlhéry, six were from the family of Poissy and five from the family of Aalst. I could go on multiplying examples. The reasons why some family nexuses were more responsive than others are not yet clear, but may be associated with domestic traditions of pilgrimage, devotional practice and religious politics; the influence of women as promoters of crusading within family circles is certainly discernible. Over time, sympathy for the movement within kin groups was reinforced by the tradition of crusading itself: of John of Joinville's ancestors, Geoffrey III had taken part in the Second Crusade, Geoffrey IV had died on the Third Crusade, Geoffrey V had gone on the Third and had died on the Fourth Crusade, and Simon, John's father, had taken the cross for the Albigensian and Fifth Crusades.

The influence of family, which tended to be supraregional as chains of blood-relationships straggled across western Europe, remained powerful in the 13th century, but by then it was being supplanted by more local and regional forces, characterized by feudal ties and networks of patronage, which worked in the same way. In 1270 Robert Bruce IV, Robert Bruce V, Alan of Lascelles, Eustace of Balliol, John of Romundeby, Adam of Jesmond, Ralph of Cotun, Gilbert of Middleton, Thomas of Fenwick, Walter of Cambo, John of Vescy, Richard of Stiveton, William le Latimer and William fitzRalph were all crusaders from northern England, who were bound together and possibly propelled into the movement by very complex ties of kinship, local interest and vassalage.

But, again, why did these family and local nexuses encourage an activity that tended to undermine their wealth and deprived them for a time at least of the contribution of active members? It must be remembered that crusading took root in communities obsessed with their own sinfulness in a way which our own relatively self-satisfied society can barely comprehend. The nobles and knights lived lives which they perceived to be immoral. Starved of privacy and books, they could never engage in private devotions, which is why their acts of piety tended to be public ones, like attendance at Mass or participation in pilgrimages. Until the late 12th century many young men's lives were frustrated by a general family policy of allowing only one son to marry and expecting the rest to hang around as loyal supporters of the breeder. In a martial society, in which the kin and its interests were paramount, they had to take part in acts of violence engendered by blood-feuds, and the extravagant social generosity expected of them was often tempered by intransigence over rights unjustly claimed and exercised by force. Meanwhile, the Church was making demands on them which required for their fulfilment a heroism quite beyond most men and women: married couples, for instance, were supposed to abstain from sexual relations on 'forbidden days', which filled up more than half the year. Living in a world which they recognized was permeated by sin and unable to avoid the sinfulness that coiled around them

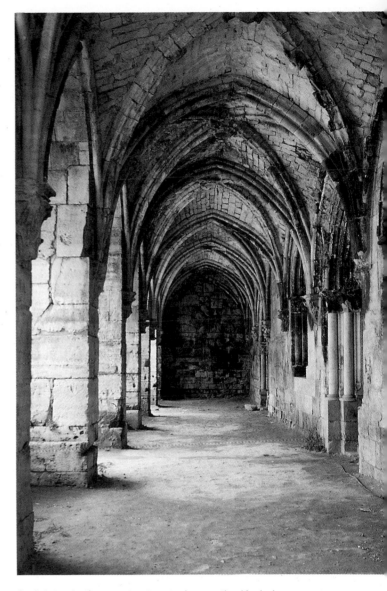

A cloister in the greatest crusader castle, Krak des Chevaliers, built for the Knights Hospitaller.

like the snake round the tree in the Garden of Eden, they generally accepted that the only way out was escape into the religious life. But that route was not necessarily open, even to the pious, because oblates and postulants were supposed to bring with them entry-gifts to the communities concerned; a family was always keen to have one member in a local abbey or priory so that it could benefit directly from the stream of intercessory prayer that flowed upwards to God from within the walls, but it was obviously not in its interest to allow too many relatives to join, because this would have led to a dispersal of land.

With the preaching of the crusades the Church provided morally vulnerable men with a glimmer of hope, paving the way for the recognition in the 12th century of the lay condition as a kind of vocational life in itself. It became no longer necessary for a man to escape to a monastic dormitory or cell to save his soul; here in the world, functioning as he had been trained, he could engage in an activity he understood – often, it must be admitted, in terms of a vendetta – and could contribute to his own salvation. And the extraordinary achievement of the First Crusade, made up largely of untrained pilgrims, with no overall command, with inadequate or no provisioning, led by knights most of whose horses were dead before they reached Syria, in marching thousands of miles from western Europe into Asia and liberating Jerusalem, could be explained only in terms of divine approval. It demonstrated to participants and observers alike, who were not fools and could find no other explanation for its success, that it really was Christ's own war: one contemporary even went so far as to claim that the crusade was the clearest manifestation of divine intervention after the creation and the incarnation.

There are plenty of examples of the devotional appeal of the movement in the 13th century, when it was at its height, but as crusading in all theatres of war became embedded in class and family traditions there was a shift to a more secular, though still religious, ethos, which became an important element in chivalric culture, its early history glimmering in a hazy golden penumbra, and still an inspiration to the 16th-century crusaders in the victorious Christian fleet at Lepanto.

But by 1571, the movement was dying on its feet. The idea of crusading had lost its hold on public opinion. There had been few people in medieval Europe, of course, who had not been touched directly by the movement, even if they only listened to sermons or contributed to crusade taxes, and the popularity of the accounts of many of the chroniclers, commentators and letter-writers quoted in this book demonstrated the insatiable interest of contemporaries. Stories about crusading appealed to a very wide audience indeed – much wider than the circles which produced crusaders – and drew responses on many levels: devotional, practical, romantic, incredulous and critical. The ebbing of mass enthusiasm is discernible from the late 14th century onwards. It was when public interest began to fade that the roots of crusading started to wither.

JONATHAN RILEY-SMITH

The Holy Land after the First Crusade, 1100

Black Sea

• Sinope

• Trebizond

Manzikert •

• Amasia

Bithynia

nstantinople •

• Nicomedia

• Nicaea

• Brusa

• Dorylaeum

• Angora

• Sebastea

D a n i s h m e n d

Melitene •

Halys

SELDJUK SULTANATE

OF RUM

(ICONIUM)

Edessa •

COUNTY OF EDESSA

• Aintab

Harran •

Armenians

• Sis

LORDSHIP OF
JOSCELIN

• Hierapolis

• Antiochi

• Iconium

Cilicia Mamistra

Heraclea •   • Adana

Tarsus •

T a u r u s

Alexandretta •

Harenc •   • Aleppo

Euphrates

BYZANTINE EMPIRE

Taurus Mountains

Antioch •

St Symeon •

PRINCIPALITY
OF ANTIOCH

Orontes

• Ma'arra

• Ephesus

• Laodicea

• Attalia

Lattakieh •

Caesarea •

• Hama

Assassins

• Homs

S E L D J U K

Rhodes

• Famagusta

Tortosa •

Mount Lebanon

E M P I R E

• Nicosia

Cyprus

Tripoli •   • Arqa

COUNTY OF TRIPOLI

Byblos •   • Baalbek

Beirut •

EMIRS

Litani

Sidon •

• Damascus

Lebanon   Beaufort

OF

Tyre •

Crusader States
Edessa
Antioch
Tripoli
Jerusalem

Acre •   Hattin •

• Tiberias

DAMASCUS

Haifa •   Nazareth •

Jordan

Belvoir

0   100   200 km

Mount Carmel   • Belvoir

Caesarea •

Arsuf •   Nablus •

Jaffa •   Lydda •

Ibelin •   Ramleh •   Jericho •

Bethlehem •   **Jerusalem**

Ascalon •

Gaza •   Hebron •

Dead Sea

Mediterranean Sea

• Damietta

KINGDOM OF
JERUSALEM

• Alexandria

Eilat •

• Cairo

FATIMID CALIPHATE   **Sinai**

Nile

Europe at the time of the First Crusade, *c.* 1100

When in 1095 the Byzantine emperor, Alexius I Comnenus, appealed to the Council of Piacenza for help from the west against the inroads of the Seldjuk Turks, Pope Urban II called on nobles, knights and ordinary people from north of the Alps as well as Italy to liberate the holy places from the Muslims. Of the great number who responded – modern estimates suggest that between 100,000 and 140,000 took crusading vows – the great majority came from France, Italy, and southern and western Germany. They took a variety of routes to Constantinople, from where, in 1097, most of the army set off together for the arduous march on Jerusalem.

Estonians
Novgorod
Lithuanians
Moscow
ussians
R U S
ow
Vistula
AND
Kiev
Dnieper
P e c h e n e g s
Black Sea
Belgrade
Sinope
Trebizond
erbs
Varna
B U Z A N T I N E
Bulgarians
Nissa
Sardica
Philippopolis
Constantinople
gusa
Adrianople
Skodra
Rodosto
Nicomedia
Sebastea
ro
Durazzo Okhrida
Nicaea
Salonica
Abydos
Dorylaeum
SELDJUK
Caesarea
County of
isi
Valona
E M P I R E
SULTANATE OF
Edessa
RUM(ICONIUM)
Armenians
Mosul
Corfu
Smyrna
Heraclea
Edessa
Iconium
Hierapolis
Euphrates
Tarsus
Aleppo
Ephesus
Seleucia
Antioch
Baghdad
Lattakieh
Principality
Rhodes
Cyprus
Famagusta
of Antioch
SELDJUK
County
of Tripoli
Tripoli
Sidon
Damascus
EMPIRE
Beirut
Crete
Tyre
JERUSALEM
Acre
Jordan
S e a
Jaffa
Jerusalem
e a n
Ascalon
Damietta
Barka
Alexandria
Eilat
B a r k a
Cairo
FATIMID CALIPHATE
Nile
N o m a d s
Athens
Tigris

— 1 —

THE MUSLIM WORLD BEFORE 1096

The crusades were the long-term result of the rise of Islam. Within the space of a generation, Islam had developed into the third of the world's great monotheistic religions, rivalling Christianity and Judaism. It also became an aggressive and successful military movement. When its founder, the Prophet Mohammed, died in 632, he controlled the Hijaz (the western coast of the Arabian peninsula) and his role as a religious and political leader was acknowledged by most of Arabia. A decade after his death, his disciples had conquered Iraq and Syria, and ten years after that Egypt and most of Persia had fallen to their swords. By the end of the seventh century Islam had conquered the whole of the North African coast. Islamic forces invaded Spain in 711 and within two decades had overcome all but the mountain fastnesses of the north. In the ninth century Sicily also fell to the Muslim troops.

The caliphs, the successors to the authority of the Prophet, were both religious leaders and secular rulers. But, although Islam was a proselytizing, and in the early centuries a conquering, religion, it was not intolerant. Christians and Jews, who remained the majority of the population until the tenth or eleventh century, were seen as 'people of the Book', adherents of religions which were in some way, however imperfect, the product of divine guidance. As such they ought to be protected peoples (*djimmi*), albeit showing their inferior status to Muslims by the payment of a capitation tax (the *jizya*). As in many other institutions, and in concepts of practical and social organization, Muslims here adopted norms prevalent under Byzantine rule.

The tranquil life of the
Muslim east, soon to be
shattered by the onslaught
of Christian crusaders.

By the middle of the eighth century, however, the unity of the early Islamic period had started to break down. The replacement of the Ummayad line of caliphs by the 'Abbasids in 750 led to the creation of an independent emirate in Spain, ruled by descendants of the Ummayads, one of whom, in 929, arrogated to himself the title of caliph, with all its connotations of supreme religious authority. And from the 10th century the 'Abbasid caliphate became increasingly enfeebled, hostage to praetorian troops, financial problems and the rise of religious tension as Shi'ism began to challenge the unity of the faith. The Fatimid conquest of Egypt created a Shi'ite caliphate in the Near East that rivalled the Sunnite 'Abbasid one in Baghdad, a situation made more serious for the Sunnites by Egypt's economic prosperity coinciding with the decline of Iraq, the 'Abbasid power base.

In the mid-11th century, the Turks, originally from the steppes of central Asia, migrated south-westwards, conquered Persia in the 1040s and then invaded Armenia and Iraq, capturing Baghdad in 1055. Their systematic patronage of Sunni religious institutions and their reunification of eastern Muslim domains shifted the geo-political balance again in favour of the east and provided a counterweight to the Fatimids of Egypt, now themselves hostages to military adventurers.

Their arrival also dealt a nearly mortal blow to the Byzantine Empire, the chief Christian power in the Mediterranean region. Despite the loss of Egypt and Syria in the seventh century, Byzantium had been able to withstand the Arabs, and the rule of the emperors of Constantinople had been consolidated in Asia Minor. As 'Abbasid authority weakened and Islamic unity declined in the 10th century, the empire went on the offensive and imperial troops penetrated into Syria. Antioch was captured by the Emperor Nikephoros Phokas in 969.

The Byzantines saw themselves as the heirs of the old Roman Empire and Constantinople, their capital, as the New Rome. Their emperor was the legitimate successor to the rulers of pagan Rome, and also the instrument of God's chosen people, themselves, and his particular representative on earth, 'the 13th apostle'. Their fellow Christians in the west regarded their belief in the god-given status of their empire as unwarranted arrogance, and ridiculed the claims of the 'king of the Greeks' to be the successor to Roman authority. By the 11th century theological differences had emerged between the western Christians, whose liturgy and culture were Latin, and those of the Greek-speaking Byzantine Empire. Problems developed about the use of leavened (the Latins) or unleavened (the Greeks) bread at the Eucharist, about the proper interpretation of the Trinity in the Creed, and – in the long run perhaps the most significant issue – about the nature and extent of papal authority.

To the Byzantines the pope was only one, albeit the most senior, of the five patriarchs, the senior churchmen of the Christian world, who together with the emperor and councils of bishops should govern the Church. To Latin churchmen and an increasing number of western laymen the pope was St Peter's successor as God's chosen minister on earth. 'Thou art Peter, and upon this rock [petra] I will build my Church … and I will give unto thee the keys of the kingdom of heaven: and whatsoever thou shalt bind on earth shall be bound in heaven: and whatsoever thou shalt loose on earth shall be loosed in heaven' (Matt. 16. 18–19). In the 11th century such scriptural justification was the basis for burgeoning claims of papal authority in the movement known as the Gregorian Reform, after Pope Gregory VII (1073–85), its most conspicuous proponent, whose attempts to reform the Church led him into a holy war against the Holy Roman Emperor, Henry IV.

The reforming clerics, many from the Rhineland area, who dominated the papacy from the late 1040s onwards, wished to eliminate long-standing abuses within the Church and restore what they saw as 'right order in the world'. A crucial part of their programme was to free the Church from the evils of control by laymen, above all from the sin of simony – the sale and purchase of clerical offices. But the more ambitious reformers also wanted to improve the moral tone of lay society, partly by enlisting the support of the laity in Church reform, and by encouraging laymen to perform meritorious spiritual exercises such as pilgrimage. They developed the Peace and Truce of God, to limit internecine warfare within Christendom.

The Peace of God had first been promulgated in France in the last quarter of the 10th century, and was an attempt to protect non-combatants (women, children, the poor, and above all clerics) from the violence of the warrior class. The Truce of God was intended to prevent fighting on Sundays and the great feast days of the Church and, increasingly, periods of particular religious significance, such as Lent and Advent. For much of the 11th century it was a French phenomenon; significantly the first pontiff to promulgate the Truce of God, Urban II, was a Frenchman. He proclaimed it among the Normans of southern Italy in 1089, and, six years later, at the Council of Clermont. At the same time, he called for the First Crusade, preaching that the knightly class should direct its warlike energies against the infidel, and exercise its propensity for violence in a higher cause than warfare against fellow Christians. He begged them: 'Let those who have long been robbers now be soldiers of Christ. Let those who once fought against brothers and relatives now rightfully fight against barbarians.'

Western Christians had already been successfully wielding their swords against the unbeliever, and the frontiers of Christendom were expanding. In Spain, after the death of al-Mansur, the great vizier of Cordoba, in 1002, the unity of the caliphate had disintegrated. Muslim Spain divided into a series of increasingly quarrelsome petty kingdoms, and the Christian principalities of the north, Castile, León, Aragon and Navarre, for the first time had opportunities for expansion. By c. 1040 Christian settlers were moving into the hitherto largely deserted frontier region in the valley of the river Duero, and by the 1080s the Castilian frontier had advanced south to the river Tagus. The great city of Toledo was captured from the Muslims in 1085. In 1094 a Castilian freelance general, Rodrigo Diaz de Vivar, more usually known by his nickname of El Cid, conquered Valencia. The Muslims of Spain were reinforced by Berber tribesmen from North Africa and after El Cid's death Valencia was once again lost. It was not recaptured by the Christians until 1236, but Christianity was on the advance and in 1089 Urban II proclaimed that those who assisted in rebuilding the recently captured city of Tarragona should enjoy the same reward as pilgrims to Jerusalem.

Sicily's recovery from Muslim rule was set in motion in 1059 when Pope Nicholas II recognized the Norman Robert Guiscard as duke of Apulia and Calabria in southern Italy and as the 'future duke of Sicily'. From 1060 onwards, Robert, and more particularly his younger brother Roger, undertook the island's conquest. Although Palermo was captured only in 1072, and the conquest was not complete until 1091, it was a signal victory for Christianity.

To Christendom and to the papacy, the campaigns in Spain and Sicily appeared as models of holy warfare against the infidel. And in both areas, and in the genesis of the crusades proper, pilgrimage was an important factor. Many Frenchmen who campaigned in Spain the the 11th century had originally gone as pilgrims to the shrine of St James at Compostella in the remote province of Galicia in the north-west. Pilgrims to Rome, or the shrine of St Michael at Monte Gargano, and even those heading for, or returning from, Jerusalem, played a part in the Norman conquest of southern Italy. But Jerusalem, the site of Christ's passion and his tomb, was by far the most compelling destination. Its attraction was enhanced when Hungary's conversion to Christianity, and the incorporation of the hitherto backward and much fought-over kingdom of Bulgaria into the Byzantine Empire, made it possible to travel overland from the west to the Holy Land. By the late 11th century Jerusalem was much more important in the religious outlook of western Christendom than it had been in the early Middle Ages when pilgrims had been few and far between.

At precisely this period Turkish invasions threatened to disrupt the passage of the increasing numbers of pilgrims. Palestine became the frontier zone between the newly emergent power of the (Sunnite) Turks in the north and the strongest Arab state, (Shi'ite) Egypt in the south. It was also ravaged by wandering Turcoman nomads and fought over by Turkish officers keen to found independent principalities and escape from the authority of the Seldjuk sultans.

Byzantium, which had previously exercised an unofficial, but none the less effective, protectorate over pilgrims and the native Christians of Palestine, was powerless to intervene. From the early 1060s it had been under attack by the Turks and in 1071, when the Emperor Romanus IV Diogenes decided to crush the Turkish threat, his counter-attack met with a catastrophic defeat at the hands of Sultan Alp-Arslan at the battle of Manzikert – during which the emperor was captured. The empire's governing class tore itself apart in internecine quarrels and the Turks overran almost all of Asia Minor, as much by infiltration as by conquest. When an ambitious and able general, Alexius Comnenus, seized the imperial throne in 1081 only a few coastal towns in the north were left in Byzantine hands.

Alexius was able to halt the Turkish invasions, but his treasury was all but bankrupt, his army had to be rebuilt from scratch, and his attention was distracted, first by Robert Guiscard's attacks in Albania in the 1080s and then by threats posed to the empire's Danube frontier by the Pecheneg and Cuman nomads from the Russian steppe. It was 1094 before Alexius defeated these tribes and was able to turn his attention to the recovery of the Asiatic territories; but he needed outside assistance and in February 1095, Byzantine envoys appeared at Pope Urban II's Council of Piacenza, requesting help.

That help was the First Crusade.

Hail then, holy city, sanctified by the Highest as his own temple so that this generation might be saved in and through you! Hail, city of the great King, source of so many blest and indescribable marvels! Hail, mistress of nations and queen of provinces, heritage of patriarchs, mother of apostles and prophets, source of the faith and glory of Christendom!

Hail, promised land, fount of milk and honey for your venerable people, now grown the source of healing grace and vital nourishment for the whole earth! Yes, I say, you are that good and excellent soil which received into its fertile depths the heavenly seed from the heart of the eternal Father. Those who have seen you are most happily filled with the great abundance of your sweetness and are well nourished on your munificent bounty. Everywhere they go, they publish the fame of your great goodness and relate the splendours of your glory to those who have never seen it, proclaiming the marvels accomplished in you even to the ends of the earth.

Indeed, glorious things of thee are spoken, city of God! Now we will set forth some of the delights you abound in for the praise and glory of your name.

Despite its distance from western Europe, Jerusalem remained the ultimate goal for Christian pilgrims. In the above passage St Bernard meditates on the significance of the holy places.

The career of Caliph al-Hakim

Muslims and Christians in Palestine enjoyed a peaceful coexistence during the 10th century. But in 1009 this harmony was shattered when the caliph of Egypt, al-Hakim, destroyed the church of the Holy Sepulchre and began to persecute Christians and Jews. Al-Maqrizi, a 15th-century Egyptian scholar, describes al-Hakim's behaviour and his final descent into madness.

In the year 1009 the caliph of Egypt, Syria and Palestine, al-Hakim, ordered the Jews and Christians to wear sashes round their waists and distinguishing badges on their clothes. He also forbade people to eat mulukhiyya, roquette, mutawakkiliyya, or tellina [herbs and shellfish], or to slaughter a healthy cow except for the feast of sacrifices. He forbade outright the sale and making of beer. He gave orders that no one should enter the public baths without wearing a loincloth, that women should not uncover their faces in the street or in a funeral procession and should not bedeck themselves, and that no fish without scales should be sold or caught by any fisherman. He enforced all these rules with the utmost rigour, and many persons were flogged for disobeying his orders and prohibitions.

Al-Hakim also caused notices to be placed on the doors of the mosques, and on the doors of shops, barracks and cemeteries, abusing and cursing the early Muslims. He forced his subjects to write and inscribe these curses in different colours in all these places. Then people came from every side to enter the *da'wa*. He appointed two days in the week for them, and the crowd was so great that many people died.

Two years later, al-Hakim gave orders to erase the curses against the early Muslims, and all these writings were duly erased. Prices rose because of the low Nile – it was down to only eighty metres and then dropped even lower.

Since the Nile was not flooding, public prayers for water were held twice, and the caliph abolished several taxes. Bread became so dear and so scarce that it was difficult to find. Al-Hakim forbade people to hold public musical performances or to indulge in pleasure cruises on the river. He prohibited the sale of intoxicating drinks and would not allow anyone whatsoever to go out into the streets before daybreak or after nightfall. Times were hard for everybody.

Sickness spread, deaths multiplied and medicines became scarce. Taxes which had been abolished were reimposed, the churches which were on the Makas road [in Cairo] were destroyed, as was also a church which was in the street of the Greeks, and its contents were pillaged. Many eunuchs, scribes and slaves were put to death, after some of the scribes had had their hands cut off from mid-arm with a chopper on a block.

Caliph al-Hakim orders the destruction of the church of the Holy Sepulchre in Jerusalem, in 1009. The church was later rebuilt by Christians after al-Hakim's death.

On 4 October 1009, al-Hakim wrote to Jerusalem ordering the destruction of the church of the Holy Sepulchre. He also established a new register office to register property seized from executed people and others. He destroyed the monastery known as Dayr al-Qasr and strictly enforced the rule against Christians and Jews, requiring them to wear the special mark.

Al-Hakim forbade people to sail on the canal on boats and had the doors and windows of houses overlooking the canal blocked up. Several taxes were abolished, music and games were forbidden, as also were the sale of singing girls, and pleasure parties in the desert.

Sunnites and Shi'ites

The Sunnites, often seen as the orthodox part of Islam, were attached not just to the Koran but to the *sunna*, the corpus of Mohammed's salutary examples, both words and deeds. They believed that the Ummayad and 'Abbasid lines of caliphs were legitimate. The Shi'ites (literally 'partisans of Ali') began as followers of 'Ali, the Prophet's cousin and son-in-law and the fourth caliph, who had been murdered in 661, after a civil war with the Ummayads. His descendants and their supporters, often aristocratic, at first mainly in southern Iraq, were an ever-present source of legitimist claims.

The Shi'ites developed into a messianic sect, who expected the miraculous appearance of a leader or teacher, an *Imam*, who with direct divine inspiration would destroy tyranny and re-establish godly order. They held that the *Imams* were descended from 'Ali and his younger son al-Husayn and, by the mid-tenth century, one group, the 'Twelvers', believed that the redeemer *Imam* would be the 12th in line from the Prophet Mohammed, who would reappear as the redeeming Messiah (the *Mahdi*). The Shi'ites were hostile to the memory of the first three caliphs, Abu Bakr, 'Umar and especially 'Uthman (held to have usurped the position properly belonging to 'Ali), venerated the tombs of the latter and his descendants and celebrated certain special festivals, notably a day of mourning for al-Husayn on the anniversary of his death in battle, which became a festival in the tenth century.

The 'Twelvers' were only one of the groups among the Shi'ites. Another, the Ismailis, believed the reincarnated *Imam* would be Ismail, seventh in line from the Prophet. In 969, the Ismailis conquered Egypt and set up a rival Fatimid caliphate to the Sunnite one in Baghdad. Like the 'Twelvers' they execrated the memory of the Prophet's immediate successors, and in 1004 al-Hakim, caliph of Egypt, ordered his subjects to inscribe ritual curses against them on the doors of public buildings.

A third Shi'ite group, the 'Assassins', emerged from the Ismailis in Persia in the late 11th century. It quickly gained recruits in the main Syrian cities, but was largely concentrated in remote mountain fastnesses of Syria and Persia. An extremist Ismaili sect, hostile to the orthodox, it murdered prominent Sunnite leaders, and so contributed greatly to the divisions within Islam which so hampered resistance to the fledgeling crusader states.

Al-Hakim persecutes Christians and Jews

The Christians were ordered to dress in black and to hang wooden crosses from their necks, half a metre long, half a metre wide, weighing five ratls, and uncovered so that people could see them. They were forbidden to ride horses and allowed to ride only mules or donkeys, with wooden saddles and black girths without any ornament. They had to wear the *zunnar* sash, and could not employ any Muslim or buy any slave of either sex. These orders were so strictly enforced that many of them became Muslims.

Several people were flogged for playing chess. Churches were destroyed and their contents pillaged as also were their tenement houses and the houses pertaining to them.

On the 'Id al-Fitr [feast, following the Ramadan fast], al-Hakim rode on horseback to the place of prayer without adornment, sumpter animals, or any pomp, save only ten led horses with saddles and bridles adorned with light white silver, with plain flags and with a white parasol without any golden adornment. He was dressed in white without embroidery or gold braid; there were no jewels on his turban and no carpets on his pulpit. He forbade people to curse the first Muslims and had those who disobeyed flogged and publicly reviled.

In the year 1013 the Jews were compelled to wear bells round their necks when they entered the public baths. Al-Hakim forbade people to talk about the stars, and astrologers disappeared from the streets. They were pursued, hid themselves, and were banished. Al-Hakim gave many gifts, much charity, and freed many slaves. He ordered the Christians and the Jews to leave Egypt.

Al-Hakim now began to ride about in a white woollen cloak, with a piece of cloth as turban and with Arab sandals tied with cord to his feet. He went to excess in his gifts and returned to their owners all estates and properties that had been confiscated. He abolished a number of taxes, had all the dogs killed, and rode out much by night. He forbade women to walk in the streets; the public baths for women were closed; and shoemakers were forbidden to make women's shoes, and their shops fell into disuse.

The strange end of al-Hakim

On 13 February 1021, al-Hakim disappeared. It was said that his sister had killed him, but this is untrue. He was thirty-six years and seven months old and had reigned for twenty-five years and one month. He was generous but a shedder of blood, who killed numberless victims. His way of life was the strangest that can be. He studied the sciences of the ancients and observed the stars. He made astronomical observations, and he had a house on Mount Muqattam, to which he used to retire alone for this purpose. It is said that he was afflicted with a dryness in his brain and that this was the cause of his many contradictions. It was well said of him that 'His actions were without purpose and the dreams of his imaginings without interpretation.'

Al-Musabbihi says that in April 1024 they arrested a man of the house of Husayn who had started a rising in the remotest part of Upper Egypt. This man confessed that it was he who had killed al-Hakim. He said that he had had four accomplices, who had fled to different countries. He displayed a piece of the skin of al-Hakim's head and a piece of the head-cloth which he had been wearing. He was asked, 'Why did you kill him?' and replied, 'Out of zeal for God and Islam.' He was asked, 'How did you kill him?' and he drew a dagger, struck himself to the heart and killed himself, saying, 'That is how I killed him.'

His head was cut off and sent to the caliph, together with the things which were found with him. This is the truth regarding the murder of al-Hakim and not the story the easterners tell about his sister killing him.

The first Christian call to arms

Al-Hakim's persecution of the Christians had made an impression on the west. At the end of the 11th century, the monks of Moissac Abbey, in southern France, forged an encyclical, purportedly sent out by Pope Sergius IV (1004–12) to the faithful, calling for an army from the west to be launched against al-Hakim. Crusading rhetoric is here exemplified.

Let all Christians know that news has come from the east to the seat of the apostles that the church of the Holy Sepulchre has been destroyed from roof to foundations at the impious hands of the pagans. This destruction has plunged the entire church and the city of Rome into deep grief and distress.

The whole world is in mourning, and the people tremble, breathing deep sighs. Never should our eyes be blessed with sleep, or our heart with joy, if we ever read in the prophets, in the Psalms or in the fathers that the Redeemer's tomb would be destroyed.

Therefore, let this Christian intention be known: that we, personally, if it pleases the Lord, desire to set out from these shores with any Romans, Italians or Tuscans who wish to come with us.

With the Lord's help we intend to kill all these enemies and to restore the Redeemer's Holy Sepulchre. Nor, my sons, are you to fear the sea's turbulence, nor dread the fury of war, for God has promised that whoever loses the present life for the sake of Christ will gain another life which he will never lose. For this is not a battle for an earthly kingdom, but for the eternal Lord.

It is our part to begin the enterprise, the Lord's to see it to a successful conclusion.

It seems right that we should have your help and advice, inspired as it is by divine mercy.

For all of us Italians – whether we are Venetians or Genoese – with your financial help, wish to prepare a fleet of a thousand ships to travel across the sea to Syria to claim back the Redeemer's tomb.

Look out across the sea. Think of the day of judgement when you will possess all the joys of Christ if you act well here on earth. Come, my sons, defend God and win an everlasting kingdom.

The miracle of the dove

In Abbot Richard's immediate retinue were a father and son called Hubert and Godfrey from the city of Bayeux. They had joined the expedition in the following circumstances: Hubert had been stricken with illness for some considerable time, so much so that for an entire year he had been unable either to rise from his bed or even turn himself over unaided. One day an angel appeared in the form of a dove as he was sleeping in his cubicle. The angel addressed him like this:

'Go forth; make the necessary preparations. Go to Jerusalem for it is the Lord's command that you do.'

To this he replied: 'How can I do this since I am unable to get up?'

The angel spoke again: 'Prepare what is necessary and go forth, for it is the will of the Lord.'

And Hubert got up and set out with thanks on the journey he had longed to begin.

From Hugh of Flavigny, *Chronicon*

Cultivation in the Holy Land

Writing in the late tenth century, the geographer al-Muqaddasi divided Syria (including Palestine) into four topographical zones. The first, bordering the Mediterranean, was flat with sandy tracts alternating with cultivated land. The second was the hill country, well wooded with many springs, villages and cultivated fields. The third was the Jordan Valley, where there were palm groves, fields and indigo plantations, and, like the hill country, villages. The fourth, the mountain country between the Jordan and the desert, was also well populated, with springs and woods.

In al-Muqaddasi's time, the number of villages had fallen significantly since the mid-eighth century. It had been particularly dramatic in the low-lying, less fertile areas, such as the coastal plain, the Jezreel Valley and the Jordan Valley. In Palestine, in addition to 600–700 peasant villages (*casalia*) recorded there in crusader documents, there were also some 200 deserted sites (*gastinae*), whose lands were often used seasonally by inhabitants of neighbouring villages.

Unlike in the west, it was unusual for landowners in the east to live on their lands, or take much interest in their management. In general, the incoming Franks followed this example and were absentee landlords, leaving the running of their estates to native estate officials. Rents were collected in kind as a proportion of a village's annual harvest.

In the hills, olives, fruits, goats and honey probably predominated, as in later times, over corn and legumes; in the plains the opposite was the case. All villages, however, required the basic necessities of life: corn (wheat and barley), legumes (lentils, chick peas, beans, vetches, peas) and olive oil. Most practised a two-year rotation, with the half of the village lands which had just produced the main winter corn crop being left fallow for the summer, before being ploughed and planted again, one half with winter legumes and the other with summer crops (sesame, chick peas, sorghum, vegetables). Village houses were surrounded by gardens, orchards and enclosures for stock and fowl; there was grazing for sheep and goats farther afield.

Crusaders, struck by the fertility of the land, marvelled at products like bananas (trees of paradise), dates, oranges, lemons and sugar cane. Rice was grown around Baisan in Galilee, and cotton for export in the area around Acre.

Abbot Richard's pilgrimage, 1026

In reality, under al-Hakim's successors, pilgrims to Jerusalem were given protection and support. In 1026 Richard, abbot of Saint-Vannes (in Verdun, France), led a large group of pilgrims to Jerusalem. His preparations and journey were described by the French chronicler, Hugh of Flavigny.

Richard, abbot of Saint-Vannes, was rejoicing at the prospect of setting out to the east where he might contemplate God without hindrance since, as things were, the world had encroached upon his heart. It was then generally believed that those who had died in the east slept blessedly in Christ.

Abbot Richard was affected by the same desire to display holy devotion. Exultant at the prospect of visiting the tomb of the Lord, he sought and obtained, only with difficulty, the consent of Robert the Pious, king of France, the bishops and the nobles of the realm and the neighbouring vassals. Then he arranged for the monks of his monastery to be looked after and cared for in all respects, so that he could undertake his pilgrimage with the goodwill of all.

In this way the hoped-for pilgrimage was launched. Abbot Richard, that man of God, led seven hundred pilgrims and adequately catered for their sustenance from his own resources. They came to the land of the Saracens, and when Abbot Richard entered their cities he preached Jesus Christ to all. He trusted in his Lord God because there was no guile in his personality.

The pilgrims came to Constantinople, where Abbot Richard was received by the emperor, Constantine VIII, with honour, and weighed down with gifts. From there they continued overland to Jerusalem, arriving in the spring of 1027.

On his entry through the city gate of Jerusalem, Abbot Richard chanted sweetly with his companions the response for Palm Sunday, *'As the Lord was entering the Holy City'*, adoring Christ crucified who is the Blessed God of all worlds, and cherishing his place of burial with the eyes of faith. He devoutly visited all the places associated with Christ's birth, passion and resurrection and when not sating his eyes in contemplating them, he was feasting upon them in his heart. He was filled with joy and unspeakable gladness at the wonderful sights associated with the Lord.

The patriarch of Jerusalem came out to meet Abbot

كنت بلد الحوا، من وفاها فاتت عليه فاتت عليه وعضت اهامه ما قدر لحوا

اها وجعها

اخرج شكينا

وقطع ابهام

واغلي زينا وكواها

ها الي الضيعه

وية بدصبي

هافقال ت

جود عند كم

قال اعشي ما قدر

ها ان هذا

قوم اهل التاور قالت واقامت الاصمع بلك كال، على، و، فاتر، ته من الله فجعا يفضد وسه، وآكله

Careful cultivation supported the lush stands of sugar-cane, groves of trees and other crops recorded by Nasir-i Khosrau.

Richard, for he had heard of his fame from all. They exchanged greetings and the kiss of peace and rejoiced together in the Lord. The patriarch looked upon him as if he were an angel, with his modest speech, his mild manner, his distinguished grey hair and the characteristics of old age which are to be respected by everyone. He greeted him like this: 'As we have heard, so have we seen.'

In this way Abbot Richard was introduced into Holy Zion, and celebrated Mass with the patriarch and clergy assisting. He revisited the sepulchre of the Lord with love in his heart, and wandered devoutly about the holy place. Never did he miss a celebration of Mass, nor cease from expounding the word of the Lord.

On Palm Sunday once again he entered Jerusalem and spent every night of Holy Week in praising God. Even when sword-girt pagans rushed through the church, he showed neither doubt nor hesitation. He stayed awake rendering God his due in continual prayer and fasting so that even the pagans marvelled at his devotion and were deeply impressed by his steadfastness. On Maundy Thursday he acted on the Lord's command and gave refreshment to the poor, washing their feet and giving them clothing and whatever else they needed.

Journey through the Holy Land

In 1045 Nasir-i Khosrau, a Muslim from Persia, had a dream in which a holy figure admonished him to repent of his iniquities (he was over-fond of wine) and go on a pilgrimage to the holy places of Islam. In 1046 he set off for Palestine en route for Mecca, and kept a diary of his impressions of the cities he visited.

Aleppo [in northern Syria] appeared to me a fine city with great walls – I estimated their height to be about twelve metres – and an immense citadel, with foundations entirely of stone. The town acts as a custom-house for trade between the lands of Syria, Byzantium, the Mesopotamian region, Egypt and Iraq, with merchants from all these countries staying there.

By the road we took, the distance from Aleppo to Tripoli [on the coast of Lebanon] was about one hundred and twenty miles. We arrived there on Saturday 6 February 1047. All around the city were fields, gardens and trees. There was sugar-cane in abundance, as well as orange, lime, banana, lemon and date trees. At that time they were extracting sugar-cane juice.

The city of Tripoli itself has been built in such a way that the sea surrounds it on three sides, and when the sea is whipped up, some of the waves reach up to the city walls. On the side which faces dry land, they have dug a vast ditch and they have also placed a solid iron gate. These eastern-facing ramparts are of hewn stone with turrets and crenellations; and along the top of the walls they have placed military catapults; they fear the Byzantines, who often attack the place by ship. The hostelries are of four, five and even six storeys high. The narrow streets and bazaars are so fine and clean, one would think each were a palace, all decorated; and every kind of food or fruit which I had seen in Persia could be found here, although a hundred times more abundant.

In the middle of the city lies the Friday mosque. It is very clean, well adorned and soundly built. In the middle of its courtyard stands a large dome underneath which is a bronze fountain set in the middle of a marble tank. In the main bazaar they have built a watering-place, out of whose five spouts flows much water which the people use, the rest runs along the ground and into the sea. They say that there are twenty thousand people in this city. It also has many outlying districts and villages. They produce good-quality paper there, similar to the paper in Samarkand only better still.

A garrison from the sultan is always stationed there with a

Next we went to the city of Sidon, which is also by the sea. They were cultivating sugar-cane extensively. The city has strong stone walls with three gates, and it has a fine, excellently situated Friday mosque, the interior of which is completely covered with patterned mats. The market-place was so well laid out that, when I saw it, I imagined they were preparing for the arrival of the sultan, or else that some good news had reached them. When I asked them, they said, 'It has always been the custom in the town.' The garden there with its trees was arranged in such a way that one might say some king had had it done to please him; and in it had been erected a small villa. Most of the trees were fruit-bearing.

Travelling on, we reached the town of Acre [in Palestine]. The town stands on an eminence, part of which slopes, the rest being level. Along the coast, where there are no promontories, they do not build towns for fear of the sea and the waves which strike the shore. The Friday mosque is in the middle of the town and it stands taller than anything else. Its columns are all of marble, and the main expanse of the mosque is partly paved in stone and partly sown with grass. It is said that Adam – on whom be peace – had farmed there. The west and south side face the sea, and to the south there is

The little honeyed reeds

In that place the people sucked little honeyed reeds, found in plenty throughout the plains, which they call 'sukkar'; they enjoyed this reed's wholesome sap, and because of its sweetness once they had tasted it they could scarcely get enough of it. This kind of grass is cultivated every year by extremely hard work on the part of the farmers. Then at harvest time the natives crush the ripe crop in little mortars, putting the filtered sap into their utensils until it curdles and hardens with

the appearance of snow or white salt. They shave pieces off and mix them with bread or with water and take them as a relish, and it seems to those who taste it sweeter and more wholesome even than a comb of honey. Some say that it is a sort of that honey which Jonathan, son of King Saul, found on the face of the earth and disobediently dared to taste. The people, who were troubled by a dreadful hunger, were greatly refreshed by these little honey-flavoured reeds during the sieges of Albara, Ma'arra and Arqa.

From Albert of Aachen, *Historia Hierosolymitana*

general in command, to protect Tripoli from enemies. There is a custom-house, where ships which come from Byzantium, the Franks, al-Andalus and the Maghreb pay a tithe to the sultan. The garrison is paid for out of this money.

The sultan also keeps ships here, which trade with Byzantium, Sicily and the west.

The people of this city are all Shi'ites. The Shi'ites have built fine mosques in all the towns. There, one also finds houses built like caravanserais, except that no one stays in them, and they call them shrines.

There are no houses outside the city of Tripoli.

the harbour, which is built to safeguard ships, rather like a stable, with its back to the town and its walls reaching into the sea. They leave a distance of twenty-five metres without any wall, only chains which they stretch from one wall to the other.

When they want a ship to enter the harbour, they slacken off the chains, letting them drop enough for the ship to pass over them. Then they draw them up once more, so that no strange vessel may get at the ships.

By the eastern gate, there is a spring where one must descend twenty-six steps to reach the water. They say that

Adam – on whom be peace – discovered that spring and watered his bull there, and for that reason it is called the 'Bull's Spring'.

Jerusalem – a holy place because it was where Mohammed ascended into heaven – was the highlight of Nasir-i Khosrau's visit.

By 5 March 1047 I was in Jerusalem. The people of Syria call Jerusalem the Holy City. Anyone of that province who cannot perform the pilgrimage to Mecca will visit Jerusalem, and there perform the statutory rites and offer a sacrifice on the feast, according to custom. Some years, more than twenty thousand people are present there. They also bring children to be circumcised. From the Byzantine and other regions come Christians and Jews in large numbers to worship at the church and synagogue there.

Jerusalem, with its surrounding districts and villages, is a mountainous region given over to the cultivation of olives, dates, and so on. Although it is entirely without water, crops are abundant and inexpensive. The village chiefs fill up their wells and tanks with seventy-five thousand tons of olive oil, which they export all over the world. They say that the Prophet – upon him be peace and benediction – saw a saint in a dream, who said, 'Prophet of God, help me gain my daily bread'; and the Prophet – upon whom be peace – replied, 'By the bread and oil of Syria, trust in me.'

I shall now describe the Holy City. It is a city set on a hill, and it receives no water except from rainfall. Strong walls of stone and mortar with gates of iron surround the city. It is a populous place which, when I saw it, contained twenty thousand people. There are fine bazaars and many tall buildings, and all the streets are paved in stone. Wherever there was a hill or slight rise they cut and levelled it off, so that when it rains the whole place is washed clean.

Whatever rain falls does not flow away to be wasted but collects in the tanks for people to draw from. Pipes of lead have been constructed for the water to flow down. Below these pipes are stone tanks with holes at the bottom so that the water, in flowing down the channels to the main tank, is not polluted or lost. About nine miles from the city I saw the huge reservoir to collect the water which runs down from the mountains. From there they have built an aqueduct which leads to the central mosque, and in the whole city it is here that water is most plentiful. Even so every building has tanks for rain-water, since there is no other kind. Everyone collects water from his own roof. In the hot baths as everywhere else only rain-water is used. The water of Jerusalem is sweeter and purer than any other.

The Dome of the Rock

The great Dome stands on twelve pillars around the Rock. When you look at it from a distance of three miles, the dome appears like the pinnacle of a mountain: this is because the dome from top to bottom is fifteen metres. The roof and ceiling of the building are clothed in carved wood, and the pillars and walls are of a style rarely seen elsewhere. The Rock itself exceeds the height of a man, and around it they have made a marble balustrade to stop people touching it. The Rock is of a blue-coloured stone. No one has ever stepped on it.

People are to be found in the building which houses the Rock at all times, be they pilgrims or worshippers. The building is laid with fine carpets of silk and other materials, and from its centre above the Rock hangs a silver lamp on a silver chain. There are many silver lamps in that place, and on each is inscribed its weight. The sultan of Egypt had these lamps made. According to my calculations all the silver utensils there together must have weighed about one and a half tons.

They say that the Prophet – upon him be benediction and peace – on the night of his ascent into heaven prayed first on the Rock, then he placed his hand on it. On account of his splendour the Rock began to rise so the Prophet – upon whom be peace – laid his hand upon the Rock a second time to return it and fix it in its place.

Bishop Lietbert's pilgrimage, 1056

In 1055 the Seldjuk Turks assumed power over the caliph of Baghdad's lands and in that year conditions in Syria and Palestine became increasingly disturbed. The following year Lietbert, bishop of Cambrai, set off for Jerusalem; but, as a 12th-century chronicler from the monastery of St Andrew at Cambrai relates, he could get no further than Lattakieh, in Syria.

Since the city of Cambrai, in northern France, enjoyed great peace and prosperity, its bishop, Lietbert, had a holy longing to go Jerusalem. Everyone approved of the self-sacrifice involved; so he made the necessary preparations, selected companions for the journey, and set off in 1056.

They crossed the inhospitable homelands of the Huns. Beyond the Danube, they came to the vast wilderness called the desert of Bulgaria, which is inhabited by Scythian bandits. These men behave like wild animals and have no laws to tame them. Nor do they dwell in cities but live by day

The church of the Holy Sepulchre

The Christians have a church in Jerusalem which they call the church of the Holy Sepulchre. Every year many Byzantines come here on pilgrimage. Even the emperor comes secretly so as not to be recognized.

During the time of the Glory of Egypt, the Caliph al-Hakim ordered that that church be plundered and destroyed. And for a while it remained in ruins. Then in 1027 Emperor Constantine VIII sent ambassadors with gifts and offers of service in order to seek a treaty which would allow them to rebuild the church.

This church is large enough to hold eight thousand people. Great attention has been paid to the entire building, with coloured marbles, ornamentation and sculptures. From inside the church is decked in Byzantine brocade and murals, and much use has been made of gold. In several places they have made images of Jesus – upon him be peace – sitting on an ass, and images of other prophets also, such as Abraham, Ishmael, Isaac, and Jacob and his children – upon them be peace. They have varnished the images with oil of sandarac and made thin sheets of an extremely transparent glass, the size of each image, to place over them; and so the images are never covered over. And every day the servants come and clean the glass.

In this church there is a picture which is divided in two, made to represent heaven and hell. One half describes heaven and its inhabitants, and the other half represents the inhabitants of hell and what happens there. There can be no other place like this in the whole world. The church is full of priests and monks, seated either reading the gospel or at prayer, and night and day they are engrossed in worship.

From Nasir-i Khosrau, *Journey through Syria and Palestine*

wherever they happen to have spent the night and prey on travellers by killing those who get in their way and robbing the rest. The bishop and his companions – quaking at heart – passed through many potentially deathly places where they might be ambushed by their beastly enemies.

On the seventh day, in the thickest of the forests, they came across men wearing cloaks, naked beneath them, with crested head-dresses and enormous boots. From their shoulders hung quivers and they carried unstrung bows and long spears. The others were terrified when they saw these men, but Bishop Lietbert, because of his lionlike bravery, remained cheerful. The enemy's fury was so abated by the sight of the

bishop that, wonderful to tell, they let him go through and even showed the pilgrims the way. It was like this that the bishop and his companions passed through a deadly, bandit-infested region and entered Greece, where the Roman emperor Diocletian had long before caused the deaths of Christian martyrs by various punishments while they worked on the construction of his baths. The pilgrims then changed course and reached Corinth; when they heard that the body of the famous Christian martyr Demetrius was buried there, they went to his tomb.

From Corinth they travelled to Lattakieh, in Syria, where they found that Christians had been forcibly ejected from the church of the Lord's Sepulchre, on orders from Toghrul Beg, the Seldjuk Turkish king of Baghdad and Babylon. As the pilgrims feared pagans, the way forward was closed to them so they stayed for three months in Lattakieh.

Now that all hope of travelling through by land had been lost, Bishop Lietbert decided to take the sea route to Jerusalem. When ships and captains had been found to make the voyage, naval weapons were installed and necessary food supplies prepared. The weather was now suitable for sailing and the bishop embarked with his companions. Endangered by a violent storm, they landed on Cyprus, where they made preparations to continue to Jerusalem; but instead they were

The Dome of the Rock: a Muslim holy place in Jerusalem, built probably with Byzantine help, c. AD700.

transported back to Lattakieh. As there was now no hope of going on to Jerusalem, on the advice of the bishop of Lattakieh they began their sad journey home.

Bishop Lietbert, on his return from his uncompleted journey during which he had been so longing to reach Jerusalem, and had been diverted by so many different dangers, decided to carry out his intention in some other way: so he vowed to build a church dedicated to the Holy Sepulchre just outside the walls of Cambrai.

The rise of Islam

By 750 the Arabs presided over a vast empire, which stretched from Spain in the west to central Asia and the river Indus in the east, regions in which their religion, Islam, gradually prevailed.

Islam originated with the Prophet Mohammed (d. 632), an inhabitant of the Arabian city of Mecca. At the heart of the Muslim faith is his receipt of a series of revelations from God's messenger, Gabriel, which established him as the emissary of God. The principal emphasis in the revelations received by Mohammed was the oneness and majesty of God; the inevitability of the last judgement; the duty to show charity to the less fortunate; and the mercy of God to those who submit to his will. In Arabic, *muslim* denotes one who submits, and 'submission' is *islam*.

The revelations were preserved, collected and committed to writing after the Prophet Mohammed's death. They constitute Islam's holy book, the Koran (*Qur'an*, literally 'reading'), which for Muslims is the word of God.

Both Christianity and Judaism had penetrated the environment in which Mohammed was raised, and the Koran contains elements of the Old Testament, together with a few references to events in the New. Islam regards itself as the last and most definitive true revelation in a line of prophets from Abraham through the Jewish prophets and Jesus to, finally, Mohammed, the Seal of the Prophets. Jesus is seen as the last great prophet before Mohammed, but his divinity and his death on the cross are flatly rejected. Nevertheless, Muslims regarded Christians and Jews as 'peoples of the book', possessed of their own incomplete revelation, and under Muslim rule they were protected. They were allowed to continue practising their religion, but were forbidden to seek converts, and they were subject to a poll tax (*jizya*) not payable by Muslims, who instead paid the *zakat*, a tithe which was roughly comparable.

After Mohammed's death in 632, Abu Bakr became his successor (*khalifa*, 'caliph') and the majority of Muslims have upheld the legitimacy of his rule, as also that of the Ummayad (661–750) and 'Abbasid (750 – 1258) dynasties which followed. This is the Sunnite position. For a minority, however, the Prophet's true heir was his cousin and son-in-law 'Ali, who became fourth caliph (656–61), only to be outmanoeuvred by the Ummayads and assassinated by a dissident from within his own camp. The supporters of the legitimist 'dynastic' claims of 'Ali's line are known as the Shi'ites.

In the 1050s the Byzantine emperors began to levy tolls on the pilgrims and their horses as they passed through imperial territory. In 1087, Pope Victor III wrote from Rome to the empress-mother, Anna Dalassena, complaining about these practices.

Bishop Victor, servant of the servants of God, to his glorious and beloved daughter the Empress Anna Augusta.

Dearest daughter in Christ, we are compelled by what is owed to the Holy See not to waive a single command, be it to the great or the small. Therefore, the more we know that the mighty are able to injure the poor of Christ in worldly things, the more heavily we must bear down upon them. And so, desiring that your highness be not in future condemned for the oppression of pilgrims and the poor in this world, but rather made glorious for your efforts to ameliorate their plight, we denounce the extortionate and intolerable tax imposed by your officials on those who visit and pray at the glorious and holy sepulchre of the Lord Jesus, and beseech you in his name to put a stop to it.

We forbear to mention other things suffered in all parts of your empire; but in two places in particular it is reported that three gold coins are levied for each horse, and the same for every two pedestrians. In addition, your officials interfere with the horses of those who have come to pray, violently snatching them away and keeping them at will.

Unless you drive this evil from your kingdom as soon as possible by an imperial edict, you must know that it will become a stain on your soul – which God forbid.

We esteem highly yourself and your noble lineage, as indeed we ought. We desire and pray that your excellency enjoy perpetual might and that you remember, as you should, the Roman Church, your first and rightful mother, and we exhort you always to venerate her. May she likewise always regard you favourably and esteem your grandfather's successors.

Byzantine patriarch excommunicated, 1054

Relations between Byzantium and the west were made worse by clashes between Michael Cerularius, patriarch of Constantinople, and Leo IX, a reforming pope. In 1054 Leo sent a legation to Constantinople to discuss points of theology and ecclesiastical allegiance. The legates' meetings with their Byzantine hosts ended in their excommunication of Michael as this letter reports.

Humbert, by the grace of God, cardinal bishop of the Holy Roman Church; Peter, archbishop of Amalfi; Frederick, deacon and chancellor: to all the sons of the Catholic Church.

How excessive are the tares of false doctrine which Michael Cerularius, unworthily called the patriarch, and his supporters, daily sow in Constantinople! Simoniacs sell the gifts of God; Valerii castrate their guests and not only make them priests, but even bishops. The Manichaeans say among much other nonsense that whatever is fermented has a soul; the Nazarenes keep the Jewish hygiene laws so rigidly that they would deny baptism to babies dying within eight days of birth, would forbid the sacraments to menstruating women or those who have just given birth, would not baptize these if they were pagans.

They refuse communion to those who shave, cut their hair, or have a Roman-style tonsure.

In the matter of these errors and many others, the patriarch himself ignored letters of warning from our lord pope, Leo IX. Moreover, he refused to admit papal ambassadors to his presence, or allow them to attempt to correct his errors by reasoned arguments. He also forbade celebrations of Mass in the churches, just as he had earlier shut down the Latins' churches, taking issue with their use of unleavened bread in the Eucharist and persecuting them in every way. He has persisted to the extent of anathematizing the Apostolic See, and maintaining that he is the chief bishop over all churches of both east and west.

For all these reasons, we do not tolerate this unheard-of outrage and injury against the Holy See.

By the authority of the Holy and Undivided Trinity and Apostolic See whom we represent, by the authority of all the orthodox fathers, and on pain of anathema by the whole Catholic Church, our most reverend pope has excommunicated Michael and all his successors, unless they come to their senses.

Michael Cerularius attacks the Latin religious practices in a letter to his fellow patriarch, Peter of Antioch.

Rumour has reached me that the patriarchs of Alexandria and Jerusalem are following the teachings of the pope in Rome.

Not only do they accept people who eat unleavened bread, but sometimes they themselves celebrate the divine mystery with unleavened bread. In addition, they prohibit the marriage of priests; that is, those who have wives may not receive the dignity of priesthood, but those who wish to be ordained must be unmarried.

Two brothers may marry two sisters.

Bishops wear rings on their fingers, as though they take the churches as wives; they say they wear them as a token. They go out into battle and pollute their hands with blood: because of this, they destroy lives and are destroyed. According to some reports we have received, when celebrating holy baptism they baptize with one immersion, calling on the name of the Father, the Son and the Holy Ghost.

What is more, they even fill the mouths of those being baptized with salt.

They do not allow the veneration of relics of saints, and some exclude veneration of holy images. They do not include among the other saints our great and holy fathers, the teachers and high priests – I mean Gregory the Theologian, the great Basil and the divine Chrysostom – nor do they fully accept their teaching.

We have nobody to hand through whom we may make enquiries on this matter and, further, have no confidence in other people on such matters.

We entrust the whole business of the enquiry to you, so that your excellency may make careful investigation into the matter and inform us.

The great German pilgrimage

Despite the hazards of travel and the doctrinal wranglings among the Latins and Greeks, there were groups of pilgrims who managed to reach Jerusalem.

In 1064–5 a pilgrimage consisting of some 7,000 Germans set out from Germany to Palestine. Their tribulations and ultimate triumph are recounted in several sources; the early stages are here described in the annals of the Bavarian monastery of Niederaltaich, written between 1073 and 1076.

In the year 1065 a great multitude flocked to Jerusalem to worship at Christ's sepulchre. Who would believe the crowd of nations who went there? Since much might fittingly be said about this expedition, I hope that nobody will find it tedious if I mention in passing one or two details.

Among those who undertook the journey were its leaders: Siegfried, archbishop of Mainz, William, archbishop of Trier, Otto, bishop of Regensburg, and Bishop Gunther of Bamberg. This last was at that time regarded as the glory and pillar of the entire German kingdom. Those who knew him intimately were wont to claim that he embodied many virtues to perfection.

The *jihad* and the holy war

The first campaigns of the Islamic holy war (*jihad*, literally 'striving') were waged by the Prophet Mohammed and his followers as a reaction to aggression and to secure booty for the infant Muslim community. But the *jihad* soon went on the offensive – to extend Muslim dominions. There was no question of forced conversion, although, in time, the growth of territory under Muslim rule led to the spread of the faith. During the Muslim expansion, participation in the holy war was made the duty of all adult male Muslims; those who perished were assured of paradise, and the idea entered Muslim tradition.

After the early eighth century, Islamic conquest waned and enthusiasm for holy war was only intermittent, in response to local events such as the Frankish invasion of Syria and Palestine.

Christian holy war had its roots in the Just War, first defined by St Augustine of Hippo in *c.* 400, which enabled Christians to reconcile Christ's rejection of violence with the need to uphold justice and order in an imperfect world. The influence of Germanic warrior converts to Christianity, and the threat to Christendom posed in the ninth and tenth centuries by the attacks of pagan Vikings, Magyars and Muslims, also modified the Church's attitude towards war. The idea of the Christian knight, who fought for the Church or on behalf of the poor and defenceless, was nurtured by churchmen who gave some measure of sanction to the pursuit of arms.

Pope Gregory VII (1073–85) was responsible for a dramatic shift of emphasis. In conflict with the Holy Roman Emperor, Henry IV, about lay investiture, he spoke of the 'warfare of Christ' – a phrase which had formerly denoted the spiritual struggle of the monk – in physical, military terms; and it now became meritorious for Christian warriors, far from retreating into the cloister, to remain instead in the world and establish right order there by force. This period also saw the burgeoning counter-offensive against Muslim powers in the Mediterranean, and the recovery of former Christian territory, notably in Spain and Sicily.

Penitential pilgrimages had grown in popularity and when, in 1095, Pope Urban II launched an expedition to aid eastern Christians against the Muslims, he specifically couched the journey in terms of a great armed penitential pilgrimage. In fusing the elements of holy war and pilgrimage, he fathered that kind of holy war known as the crusade.

Such a huge multitude of counts and princes, rich and poor, came in the train of these leaders that the number probably exceeded twelve thousand. Once they had crossed the river Danube the danger of robbery and capture beset them on all sides, but they avoided it by their skill and watchfulness and at length reached the city of Constantinople. Bishop Gunther made such a good showing that the Byzantines gaped at him in wonder; they imagined that he was not a bishop but the king of the Romans [Holy Roman Emperorelect] disguised as a bishop, since only in disguise would he have been able to travel to the Lord's sepulchre through the Byzantine Empire.

After some days' journey the pilgrims reached Lattakieh, travelling along various narrow and dangerous routes, which Bishop Gunther described when he wrote to his friends at home: 'In truth, brethren, we passed through fire and water, and at length the Lord led us to the place which holy scripture calls Lattakieh, in Syria. We took on those faithless servants the Ungrians and those devious bandits the Bulgars. We put to flight those shameless debauchers the *Uzi* and encountered the proud and imperious Greeks of Constantinople. We suffered the Romanians, whose raging was beyond the fury of man or beast; we have endured difficulties indeed, but greater trials lie ahead.'

Having stayed for a few days in Lattakieh, they set out to meet the large numbers who were returning daily from Jerusalem. These men reported the deaths of innumerable companions and disasters endured by themselves and displayed wounds still gory. They declared loudly that nobody could possibly pass by that route, since the most savage race of Arabs occupied the whole territory, thirsting for human blood.

So what were they to do? Where were they to turn? They swiftly decided to lay aside their fears and trust in the Lord, knowing that whether alive or dead they were of the Lord, and with eager hearts they set out for the holy city through pagan lands.

In his chronicle written soon after 1077, Lambert, a monk belonging to the abbey of Hersfeld (on the borders between Thuringia and Franconia), describes the ordeals which faced the German pilgrim band in Syria and Palestine.

While the German pilgrims and their bishops were journeying towards Jerusalem, they ill-advisedly revealed the extent of their wealth to the people among whom their journey lay. They would have laid themselves open to extreme danger, had not divine mercy restored what had been lost through human indiscretion. For the barbarians, who had poured out from their towns and fields to see such famous men, were driven by a great hope and desire for plunder. So when the pilgrims were just a short distance from Rama, on Good Friday around the third hour of the day they were attacked by marauding Arabs. These Arabs had learned of the approach of a company of famous men and so attacked them in an armed throng to see what spoils they might plunder.

Many of the Christians, thinking they might rely on their religion for assistance and salvation, had trusted in God's protection rather than in weapons when they had set out for foreign parts. They were, as a result of the first attack, brought down by many wounds and robbed. Among them was William, archbishop of Trier, whose arm was almost paralysed by wounds. He was left naked and half-dead.

The other Christians did their best by throwing stones – in

relays, they might attack without respite. They suspected that since vital supplies were running out, it would not take them too long to finish their task.

The Christians, for the whole of Friday and Saturday nights, right up to the third hour of Easter Day, were attacked without a break. Nor did their wicked enemy allow them a single second during which they might refresh themselves by snatching a little sleep. Because the spectre of death was always before their eyes, they wanted neither food nor drink, but took whatever they could since they had almost no resources.

On the third day, exhausted by toil and hunger, they had reached the point of desperation, their courage and strength tested beyond endurance by unbroken fasting. One of the priests with them cried out that they had gone wrong by relying on their weapons rather than on the God of hope and strength, and by trying to avert by their own resources the

The rape of the abbess

On this pilgrimage a memorable event happened which I include as an example, so that those who obstinately oppose the counsels of the wise might take it as a dreadful warning.

One of the pilgrims was a noble abbess, physically imposing and spiritually minded. Against all the best advice she resigned the care of the sisters committed to her and undertook this pilgrimage which was fraught with danger. She was captured by pagans and, in the sight of all, raped by a band of licentious men until she died. This event was a scandal to all Christian people. Brought low by incidents like this and other humiliations in the name of Christ, the pilgrims won high regard everywhere, by men and by angels, because they chose to enter the kingdom of God suffering many tribulations.

From Life of Bishop Altmann of Passau

plentiful supply owing to the nature of the territory – not so much to drive away danger as a desperate measure to escape imminent death. Gradually retreating, they descended to a farmhouse which lay some distance from their path. From the sound of the name they guessed that they must be near Capernaum. They went inside, and the bishops all occupied the main room on the upper floor, because the enclosure wall was so old, low and rickety that it might easily fall down. The house was in the middle of the enclosure, and its upper room was sufficiently high above the ground to act as a base for defence, almost as if it had been been designed for that very purpose.

Since the Arabs could not keep up their attack by superiority of position or in a pitched battle, they changed their policy from one of lightning attacks to one of siege, and used the weapons of starvation and exhaustion where the sword had proved futile. They divided their only too plentiful forces into units of about twelve thousand men, so that, operating in

disaster that had befallen them. For this reason, he went on, they should give themselves up to God, especially since three days' starvation had made them quite incapable of resistance. It would not be difficult for God to show them mercy and take them from under the yoke of the enemy, for God had many times miraculously freed his people in the very last hour of their need. They might further conclude that the barbarians had launched so great an offensive to rob them, not to kill them. If they managed to take their goods they would release them untouched.

On 27 March 1065 Bishop Gunther turned the tables on his assailants during a skirmish.

During the fighting, one of the Saracen leaders seized the piece of cloth which he wore around his head after the custom of his race, and made it into a lasso which he threw

Armenia and the crusades

An independent kingdom during the heyday of the Roman Empire, Armenia – the mountainous enclave bounded by Georgia, present-day Azerbaijan and Turkey – had converted early to Christianity, in the fourth century. But the Armenian Church rejected the decrees of the Council of Chalcedon in 451, and, from the sixth century onwards, distanced itself from the Byzantine Church, adopting its own language and developing its own alphabet. The sense of religious unity thus created survived a period of Arab overlordship from 653 to 886, when the independence of Armenia under the leadership of the Bagratid dynasty was recognized by the Byzantine emperors of Constantinople and the 'Abbasid caliphs at Baghdad. Armenian culture, which had flowered from the fifth to the seventh centuries, enjoyed a renaissance from the ninth to the 11th centuries, when Armenia was dotted with churches and monasteries. Literature flourished, and cattle-breeding, agriculture, trading in textiles and commerce also thrived.

However, Armenia was divided internally between the kingdoms of Ani, Kars and Lorri in the north and the kingdom of Vaspuracan in the south; the Byzantine Empire coveted its territories and, in 966, annexed the principality of Tyana. During the 11th century it also took Vaspuracan (1021), Ani (1045) and Kars (1065). Deprived of its defensive system, Armenia was invaded by the Seldjuk Turks who, under the leadership of Alp Arslan, occupied the capital city, Ani, in 1064. After taking Manzikert in 1071, Alp Arslan occupied the whole of Asia Minor.

Large numbers of Armenians emigrated towards the Black Sea, Cappadocia, where their kings were in exile, and Cilicia, forming a solid Christian bloc well disposed towards the crusaders, who thereby gained access to the eastern shores of the Mediterranean Sea. These people of Lower Armenia greeted the arrival of the First Crusade favourably and supplied many contingents to the Frankish army occupying Edessa. Most notable was Prince Roupen, who had since 1080 been establishing a solid base for an Armenian state in Cilicia, and who formed alliances with the Normans of Antioch, for defence against the Byzantines and the Turks. During the 12th century, Roupen's descendants made marriage alliances with the ruling families of Outremer and extended their domination to include the whole of Cilicia.

around Bishop Gunther's neck. The bishop was not prepared to put up with such a disgrace and gave his assailant a hefty blow in the face which sent him sprawling to the ground. As the man fell, the bishop shouted to him that he would pay him back for his impiety in having the audacity to raise his unclean, idolatrous hands against a priest of Christ. At once clerics and laymen rushed at this man, and at others who had climbed into the upper room. They bound the Saracen's hands so tightly behind his back that blood burst through his skin and nails.

News of this bold deed reached those who were in the lower part of the farmhouse and the men there treated the Arab leaders in the same way. At this point all the laymen clamoured to their maker for his assistance and took up arms again. They seized the enclosure wall and with a concerted effort expelled and then routed the guards around the gate. Their actions were so vigorous, and met with such unexpected success on all fronts, that you would never have guessed they had endured three days of hunger and toil.

Indeed their vitality was such that the Arabs, exceedingly disturbed by this alarming turn of events, lost heart. They then began to suspect that their own leaders had made supplies available to the Christians; this revived their hostility and they rushed into battle. They made a wall of arms and prepared to burst through the men in the enclosure. And they would have succeeded, had not the Christians speedily adopted the stratagem of placing the Arab leaders whom they had bound where the enemy pressed most fiercely, and where the weapons fell most thickly. Above their heads stood a Christian wielding a drawn sword. He shouted to the Arabs by means of an interpreter that unless they halted their attack the Christians would use not arms in retaliation, but the heads of their princes.

At this the Arab princes themselves, already uncomfortable from the tightness of their bonds, were alarmed by the swords hanging over their heads. They screamed out at their men to act with circumspection, lest in their obstinacy to continue the battle they might, when all hope of mercy had died, inspire their deaths.

Thus the pilgrims crushed a great force massed against them in a pitched battle. In this way they experienced no difficulty on the outward journey to Jerusalem. There they offered thanks to God for returning them alive after such an ordeal. Then they returned through Christian lands as planned. Finally they reached Hungary, where, alas, Bishop Gunther of Bamberg was struck down by an early death and thus brought a sad end to a successful and joyful return. He died on 23 July 1065, having enjoyed the rewards of this world. He was a man of high moral and spiritual standing and well endowed with worldly goods.

Massacre of the Armenians, 1059

In Persia, the Seldjuk Turkish ruler Toghrul Beg, a Sunnite, had carved out a powerful kingdom. In 1059 his troops ravaged the Armenian town of Sebastea, in Byzantine territory. Matthew of Edessa, an Armenian chronicler who wrote before 1136, describes the shocking effects of their attacks upon his people.

In March 1059 a dreadful disaster befell the Christian faithful. Words cannot express the tribulations they had to suffer; for the Turkish people of Persia, numerous as the sands of the sea, launched attacks against the Christians of Armenia. Many provinces were put to the sword and delivered into slavery by three ferocious beasts issued from the couch of Sultan Toghrul, men more cruel than wild animals. They advanced on the populous and noble city of Sebastea, in Armenia, at the head of their black troops, flying their standards, signs of death. Their roars rolled out like thunder, proclaiming their desire to satisfy their rage.

On Sunday 6 August 1059 the siege of Sebastea began, as did the slaughter; thousands of corpses littered the ground. What a dreadful scene! The bodies of highly renowned men were piled in a heap as if a forest of trees had been felled, and the ground was soaked with their blood. At first, although Sebastea had no ramparts, the infidels had not dared to enter the city; they had mistaken the white domes of the churches which they saw rising over the horizon for their enemies' tents. But as soon as they realized their mistake, they gave vent to their rage in full and became the instruments of God's anger against the Christians.

They ruthlessly massacred an immense number of people, carried off a large amount of booty and took untold numbers of captives, men and women, young boys and girls, whom they sold into slavery. It would be impossible to work out how much gold and silver and how many precious stones, pearls and brocades they seized, for this city was the residence of the Armenian rulers. Fateful day! In a matter of minutes Sebastea and the surrounding plain were bathed in blood. The clear waters of the river Kizil Irmak which cuts through the city walls suddenly flowed red. The infidels stayed for a week, then went back home.

It would be impossible to recall in detail all the misfortunes which befell the Armenians, the grief and the tears, everything they suffered at the hands of the Turks, those ferocious blood-drinking beasts, in the days when our kingdom was without its rightful rulers, who had been seized by its false protectors, the powerless, effeminate and ignoble Byzantine Greeks!

The Greeks, whose claim to fame and glory rests on the speed with which they take to their heels, had overturned our throne and demolished the protective wall formed by our brave militia and our fearless warriors. They placed the guardianship of our country in the hands of eunuch generals and soldiers, so that eventually the Persian Turks realized that the whole of the east was without a master. Not meeting any obstacle to their progress, they poured in, and in the space of a year they reached the gates of Constantinople itself, they took control of all the Armenian provinces, the coastal towns and the islands which belonged to the Byzantines and shut the latter up, prisoners, in the fortress of their capital.

Overleaf: Yilanlikale Castle in Armenia; a bastion of the Armenians in their long struggle against the Turks. Like many Armenian forts, the castle later fell to the crusaders. Below: Turkish cavalry pursue fleeing civilians.

After the Persians had subjugated Armenia, the Greeks found a new way to renew the war against the Armenians: they set to work stirring up religious controversy, hastily abandoning all resistance against the Persians. Their efforts were limited to turning faithful believers away from the true faith and annihilating them. In the case of renowned warriors they blinded them or drowned them in the sea.

Throughout, the Greeks were at particular pains ceaselessly to remove from the east all great-hearted men and valiant war leaders of Armenian origin and to distance them by making them live with them. They transformed the young boys into eunuchs and instead of strong breastplates, the adornment of the brave, they gave them garments with full, floating pleats; instead of steel helmets they covered their heads with bonnets; and they encased their shoulders, not with coats of mail but with wide shawls. Like women, they whisper and talk in secret; they are forever plotting the ruin of brave warriors; and it is thanks to the Greeks that the faithful have been driven into slavery among the Persians.

After Toghrul Beg's death in 1063 his nephew, Alp-Arslan, intensified the raids on Armenia. His aim was conquest.

In the year 1064 the ruler of Persia, Sultan Alp-Arslan, Toghrul's nephew and successor, levied troops from among the Persians and the Turks as well as from all Kurdistan and Sakasdan and started out in a rage. He was like a heaving sea spewing up angry waves, or the tempestuous waters of a river in flood; he was like a savage and maddened beast giving free rein to his cruel instincts.

He made his way towards Armenia and entered the country; the inhabitants were put to the sword and driven into slavery. The infidels were so numerous that they covered the plains far off and closed off all the escape routes. Then he invaded Georgia, bringing death and slavery wherever he went. Having pitched his camp in the area called Dchavalkhs he attacked the town of Akhal and took it by assault.

The Turks exterminated all the inhabitants, men, women, priests, monks and nobles; the young boys and girls were taken away captive into Persia. Countless piles of gold, silver, precious stones and pearls fell into the hands of the conquerors. That very same year the sultan, the dragon of Persia, proud of this success, swooped on Armenia.

As threatening as a black cloud, the sultan arrived at the walls of the royal capital of Ani and surrounded it on all sides like a serpent coiled up on itself. The inhabitants trembled at the sight of him; nevertheless they prepared to defend themselves strenuously. The infidels, though, launched their first attack with terrifying force and threw the Armenian troops back *en masse* inside the walls. Their non-stop assaults drove the defenders to death's door and, frightened out of their wits, they started to weep; fathers wept for their sons, sons for fathers, mothers for daughters, daughters for mothers, brothers for brothers, friends for their friends. Their situation was desperate and the enemy was all the while redoubling his efforts. Faced with such prolonged attacks the inhabitants resorted to fasting and prayer; their voices rose in unison to God in supplication, begging him, through their tears and sighs, to save them from the savage hordes.

When the cock crows at sunset

Who would be strong enough to tell the story of Armenia's plight? Blood flowed everywhere and the mountains and hills were trampled underfoot as the hooves of the infidels' horses destroyed them. The smell given off by the dead bodies spread infection far and wide. Persia overflowed with captives; carnivores feasted on corpses. Plunged into mourning and sadness the children of men dissolved into tears because the Creator had turned his gaze far away from them.

Having eaten their fill of blood and booty, the infidels led their crowd of captives into Persia, massed together in groups like flocks of birds. As they looked at them they were full of amazement and said to them: 'Why did you let yourselves be taken by surprise when you had such excellent defences? How is it that you did not foresee what was going to happen and take flight when you learned of our approach or when all the indications were that we were coming?' The captives replied: 'There was no way we could learn of it.'

The infidels' wives, in turn, said to them: 'There were omens pointing to your downfall; when your cockerel crowed in the evening, when your cattle or your sheep squatted to make their droppings, those were signs of the calamities in store for you.' The captives replied: 'That sort of thing often happened with us and we did not know that it was a bad omen.'

From Matthew of Edessa, *Chronicle*

The battle of Manzikert, 1071

By 1067 the Turks had secured Armenia, and they began to raid even further into Byzantine territory. The next year the dowager empress of Byzantium, Eudocia, ruling on behalf of her young son Michael VII Ducas, married the commander of her army, Romanus Diogenes, and raised him to the imperial throne in Michael's stead.

In 1071 Romanus decided to fight back against the Seldjuk advance. With the aim of recapturing Armenia, he raised a massive army – some estimates put it at 100,000 men.

But his force was weakened by treachery and poor equipment, and he was defeated by Alp-Arslan at Manzikert on 19 August. Nicephorus Bryennius, the son-in-law of the later Byzantine emperor, Alexius Comnenus, wrote this account of the débâcle, in which his grandfather, whose name he bore, had taken part.

After the emperor, Romanus IV Diogenes, had arrived in Cappadocia, he called the best generals to council and submitted to discussion the plan to be followed. The question to be decided was whether it was necessary to continue the march towards Persia and give battle to the Turks there, or if it was enough to wait for their arrival in Byzantine territory. It was known that the sultan had already left Persia and was advancing by short stages against the Roman Empire.

Some, those who were at once most bold and most anxious to curry favour, argued that there was no point in temporizing, and that they should march into the field and offer battle to the sultan, who had just penetrated into the region of Vatona in Armenia. But the Greek Joseph Tarchionites, then commanding a large section of the troops, and Nicephorus Bryennius, thought this plan totally erroneous, and begged the emperor, if possible, to wait for and to harass the enemy, fortifying the neighbouring towns and setting the countryside to the torch, in order that the enemy might lack victuals. In default of such tactics, those wise generals counselled at least to head for Theodosiopolis, to encamp there, and to wait there for the enemy in conditions which would oblige the sultan, whose supplies would soon be running short, to engage in battle with the Byzantines on terrain favourable to our armies.

But there is no value, as the proverb says, in singing to the ears of a deaf man, and the party of the flatterers won the day. Although he should have listened to the heroes who threw into the balance the weight of their personal valour, Emperor Romanus IV Diogenes followed the advice of the flatterers in preference to that of his wise counsellors. So then, with all his troops, he marched towards Persia, straight at his adversaries.

At Manzikert, a Byzantine general, Basiliakis, came to the rendezvous, bringing considerable reinforcements from Syria and Armenia. Basiliakis was full of force: his arm was valiant, but his character was rash, and he was not master of his generous impulses. Wanting to flatter the emperor, when his advice was asked, he made no worthwhile reply. For the Vestarch Leo Diobatenus had written a letter to the emperor, announcing that the sultan, informed of his march, and doubting his own power, had left Persia and fled towards Babylon. Persuaded by these reports, Emperor Romanus split his army into two, kept a part of his troops where they were, and sent the rest to Khleat, putting at their head the magister Joseph Tarchionites.

Alp-Arslan sets a trap

The sultan, Alp-Arslan, was by then very close to the Byzantine camp, busy taking clever measures in preparation for battle – completely unknown to the emperor. Alp-Arslan, wishing to lure the emperor on, incited him to risk an advance in order to draw him into a trap; he sent forward some horsemen who, as fast their horses could go, hurled themselves at the outskirts of the Byzantine camp, and then turned about as though in flight. By repeating this manoeuvre, they drew out some of the Byzantine generals, the first of whom was Basiliakis, who launched an ill-considered charge against the enemy. The Turks feigned flight. But once they had drawn a considerable distance away from the camp, they turned about and, falling on their dispersed enemies, crushed them. The loss among our soldiers was such that, as the saying goes, no messenger remained even to announce a disaster, and Basiliakis himself was captured.

The emperor now conveyed his army in line of battle. The Turks remained quiet because they had no intention of accepting a pitched battle with the Byzantine army. But the sultan, whose headquarters was a good distance to the rear, gave (against the wish of his troops) the signal for combat. He entrusted the bulk of his forces to a eunuch called Taranges, who enjoyed his full confidence, and made him commander for this action.

Taranges divided the Turkish army into several groups, organized advance reconnaissance parties and ambuscades, and ordered his men to surround the Byzantine regiments and to shoot a shower of arrows against them from all sides. The Byzantines, seeing their cavalry as an archery target, were forced to follow and support it. They therefore advanced, while the enemy pretended to flee. But they suffered great losses in securing advanced positions and in the ambushes which the enemy had prepared to the rear.

Emperor Romanus is captured

The Emperor Romanus IV Diogenes himself resolved to accept the decisive battle and advanced with the infantry, hoping to find somewhere a body of Turkish footmen, fight a full engagement with it, and thus to secure the victory. But the Turks, instead of massing together, spread out in proportion, which did not prevent them from suddenly turning about, charging back with fury and savage cries and forcing the people of our right wing to flee. That immediately also brought about the retreat of the rearguard. The emperor, surrounded by the Turks, saw himself and his men overwhelmed by projectiles raining in from all sides. He wanted to call his left wing to the rescue. But the Turks prevented this movement, since, having arrived at the back of the Byzantine army, and also commencing to encircle the left wing, they forced it to flee. The result was that the emperor was completely isolated and deprived of reinforcement. Then he charged, his sword bare, killed more than one Turk and forced others to flee. But finally, surrounded by a mass of enemies, he was wounded in the hand. Recognized by the enemy, hemmed in on all sides, he was captured when an arrow wounded his horse, which slipped and lost its footing, felling its rider at the same time.

So it was that Emperor Romanus became a prisoner of war and was led bound to Sultan Alp-Arslan, divine providence having arranged this last act to the drama – I don't know with what end. A large number of senior officers were captured at the same time as the emperor. As to the rest, some were slaughtered, others managed to save themselves. The whole camp was taken, along with the imperial tent, the treasure and the most beautiful among the crown jewels, including the famous pearl called the Orpheline. The soldiers who escaped from this battle dispersed in all directions, each rushing to return home.

A very few days passed before one of the fugitives arrived at Constantinople as bearer of the evil tidings, and then there was another, then a third and a fourth, having nothing precise to announce except the catastrophe itself, of which each gave a different version. Some said that the emperor was dead, others that he was a prisoner, others affirmed that they had seen him wounded and lying on the ground, others then that they had seen him taken, clad in irons, to the enemy camp. The matter was discussed in council by Empress Eudocia, Romanus's wife, who was asking what she had to do. Everyone agreed that it was necessary provisionally to abandon Romanus to his fate, whether he was prisoner or dead, and that the empress must secure the power for herself and her sons. Everything was still in suspense when it was decided that the empress-mother and Michael Ducas, the eldest of her sons, should share the empire under the following conditions: Eudocia should have the honours due to the mother of the emperor, but she should share with her son the reality of supreme power. The Emperor Michael VII Ducas was of the same opinion and approved his mother's plan. But other men desirous of enjoying power hastened to immerse themselves in the government, for purely personal motives, and began to intrigue, urging the dowager empress to exercise power without sharing it, and the son to rise up against his mother.

But in the enemy camp, meanwhile, the chief of the Persians, Sultan Alp-Arslan, although Emperor Romanus was his prisoner-of-war, did not allow himself to be intoxicated by his victory, but rather showed a moderation in his triumph which nobody could have imagined. He comforted the prisoner, admitted him to his table, gave liberty to all the other prisoners in whose favour the emperor interceded, and even gave liberty to the emperor himself.

Antioch falls to the Turks, 1085

After Alp-Arslan's death in 1072 his son and successor, Malik Shah, sent Suleyman ibn Kutulmish, his son-in-law, into Anatolia to complete its conquest. By 1081 the Seldjuks had secured all but the coastal strip, and Suleyman turned his attention back towards the east.

Matthew of Edessa describes the fall to the Turks, in 1085, of Antioch in northern Syria. Suleyman took it from Philaretes, formerly governor of Marash in the service of the Byzantines, who had profited from disputes at court to carve himself out a principality in Cilicia, in southern Turkey. In 1078 the citizens of Antioch had asked him for protection against Suleyman's army; now Philaretes, in Matthew's eyes, was to betray them to the Turks.

In the year 1085 Antioch was captured from the [Byzantine] Christians. Emir Suleyman, who lived at Nicaea in Bithynia, at the far end of the Mediterranean, made his way secretly to the very walls of Antioch, getting there without being noticed. He found the town without any defences or garrison and launched a surprise night attack on it from the side facing Aleppo, while Philaretes was at Edessa and his cavalry far away. Suleyman entered the town with three hundred men.

The next day the inhabitants were dismayed to see the infidels in their midst for, in addition to the fact that they had no troops, they were as easily frightened and as ill-fitted to defend themselves as women. They ran immediately to the citadel. Meanwhile, more Turks were flooding in but were not doing anyone any harm; they blockaded the citadel and completely cut off its food and water supplies. In the end the besieged townspeople asked the emir to swear that they would not be killed if they came out; he agreed to their request, guaranteed them safe conduct and they went back quietly to their homes.

Philaretes heard of this surprise attack but there was nothing he could do to help Antioch; all he could do was breathe bitter sighs of regret in silence. After this victory Suleyman extended his sway over all Cilicia.

Left: Byzantine treasure of the time of Emperor Romanus: a turquoise bowl from Iran or Iraq, adorned by Byzantine craftsmen with a bejewelled gold mounting.
Below left: A Byzantine votive panel encrusted with jewels.
Below: A Byzantine chalice of sardonyx mounted in silver-gilt, decorated with pearls and cloisonné enamel.

Thus it was that the populous city of Antioch was captured, thanks to the cowardice and pusillanimity of the infamous Byzantine nation, which claims to be of the Christian faith but whose deeds and words show it to be Muslim: it is a people of blasphemers who profane the orthodox faith, who hate the holy life, who oppose fasting, apply themselves solely to evil, and persecute the Armenian faith. They are like weak, morbid women who have nothing better to do than sit in the road, gossip and talk rubbish.

Not only the Byzantines were weakened by internal feuds. As Matthew of Edessa shows, Tutush, a powerful rival of Suleyman, seized Antioch from him within a year of its conquest. He was subsequently killed fighting his nephew Barkiyaruq in 1095.

Tutush, sultan of Damascus, was the son of Alp-Arslan and the brother of the sultan Malik Shah. In 1079 he had seized Damascus. He had killed the great emir of Persia, Atsiz, who had made himself master of the town and all the coastal strip. This Atsiz, a Turk by nationality, was a worthy warrior; he had beaten the Egyptians, conquered their king Aziz and expelled him from his lands. Tutush had also captured the holy city of Jerusalem, Damascus and the coastal towns.

In the year 1085 Tutush attacked Suleyman, now the emir of Antioch, with a very large army. The war between them was terrible; there was a battle fought on the territory separating Aleppo from Antioch. On both sides the troops were commanded by royal princes and they massacred each other mercilessly. But at the height of battle the sultan had the upper hand and Suleyman fled in defeat. He was killed by Tutush's soldiers and was buried by his own men. Antioch was captured along with all its dependencies and passed into the control of Tutush.

The expansion of Christendom: Spain, 1065–99

Much of the Spanish peninsula was captured by the Moors during the eighth century, and in the ninth the Ummayad caliphs established a powerful and sophisticated kingdom in the area known as al-Andalus. Muslim armies continued to push north against the Christian kingdoms; but the disintegration of al-Andalus into a series of petty kingdoms saved the kingdom of León from almost certain extinction. In the second half of the 11th century the leading Christian ruler was Alfonso VI of León and Castile (1065–1109), whose dominions included an overlordship over the Moorish rulers of Saragossa, Seville and Toledo. Rodrigo Diaz de Vivar, better known as El Cid, was glamorized in Spanish heroic literature as the leader of the epic struggles against the Moors. The reality was rather different, as is shown by the *Gesta Roderici Campi Docti*, an early 12th-century compilation of biographical fragments which may have been written before his death in 1099. The *Gesta* finds El Cid in 1079 fighting with the army of Alfonso's tributary, al-Mu'tamid of Seville, against Abdullah of Granada – on whose side was ranged Count Garcia Ordonez, a favourite of Alfonso VI.

When Rodrigo Diaz, El Cid, came to al-Mu'tamid, king of Seville, he was immediately informed that Abdullah, king of Granada, was advancing with Christian support upon al-Mu'tamid and his kingdom. El Cid then sent word to the king of Granada and the Christians with him, saying that for love of his lord, Alfonso VI, king of León and Castile, they should not attack the king of Seville nor enter his kingdom. However, the king of Granada and his forces were confident in their great number; not only did they refuse to heed his entreaties but scorned them entirely; they advanced and devastated the land as far as the castle which is called Cabra.

When Rodrigo Diaz heard of this, he immediately set out with his army to intercept them. A fierce battle was joined, which lasted from three until six o'clock. A very great number of the army of Abdullah were slaughtered, both Saracens and Christians alike; all the rest were finally defeated and fled in disorder before El Cid. In the battle Count Garcia Ordonez was captured; El Cid held his captives for three days following this victory, but he let them go free after taking their tents and all their armour.

El Cid returned victorious to Seville. Al-Mu'tamid gave him tribute for King Alfonso, adding to it many gifts and presents.

So Rodrigo Diaz, El Cid, returned in triumph to Castile and his king. As a result of this triumphant victory which God had bestowed upon him, many people, both kinsmen and foreigners, made false accusations to the king concerning him, out of envy.

Following El Cid's glorious return to Castile, King Alfonso advanced immediately into the territory of some rebellious Saracens under the rule of Toledo, with the intention of subduing them and of enlarging and bringing peace to his kingdom. Meanwhile, El Cid, who was sick, remained in Castile. The Saracens, however, attacked and overran a castle called

Gormaz, where a small quantity of plunder was taken. When he heard of this, Rodrigo was exceedingly angry and saddened, saying: 'I shall pursue this band, and perhaps I shall overtake them.' He gathered together his army and, with all his knights well armed, he pillaged and laid waste Saracen lands in the Toledo region. He took back to Castile with him seven thousand prisoners, both men and women, and boldly seized all their property and wealth.

When Alfonso and the leading nobles of his court heard of Rodrigo's action they viewed it with displeasure and annoyance. Speaking with one accord before the king, the jealous courtiers accused Rodrigo thus: 'Lord king, your highness should know that El Cid carried out this action so that all of us who were laying waste Saracen lands should be killed by those Saracens and should die there.' The king was unjustly roused to anger by this accusation based on envy and banished El Cid from his kingdom; El Cid returned to Saragossa, where al-Mu'tamid received him fittingly.

After these events King Alfonso was accorded a very great victory, by divine mercy, when he boldly captured Toledo, the most celebrated city in Spain. He had been attacking and besieging it for all of seven years, and brought it under his rule, together with its outlying districts and land.

Meanwhile, King al-Mu'tamid ordered El Cid to rally his forces so that together they might invade and ravage the Christian kingdom of Aragon. This indeed is what happened. They pillaged the land of Aragon and stripped it of its wealth and took prisoner a great number of the inhabitants. After five days they returned victorious to the castle of Monzon. At the time King Sancho of Aragon was there in the kingdom, but he did not dare to resist.

After these events Rodrigo Diaz attacked the land of al-Hayib, al-Mu'tamid's brother, and laid it waste. He inflicted considerable loss and damage, especially in the mountains which are called Morella and the surrounding area. There was no home left standing, no property that he did not carry off. He attacked the castle of Morella, advancing as far as the gates and causing the greatest possible damage.

Indeed, al-Hayib, who was then ruler of that region, sent word from there to El Cid seeking peace. When the treaty had been agreed and signed, the Saracen ambassadors returned to al-Hayib. El Cid also withdrew his army, and went off to the Valencia region, which he had long wanted for himself.

This 11th-century Spanish illustration shows the relatively primitive trappings of El Cid's Christian armies and allies.

El Cid and the Christian kingdoms of Spain

The caliphate of Cordoba disintegrated during the first decades of the 11th century and Muslim kingdoms, the *taifas*, emerged across al-Andalus. Their disagreements benefited the Christian kingdoms to the north. Ferdinand I, king of Castile and León (1035–65), conquered considerable lands in the western peninsula, and also imposed tribute on the Muslims, weakening them still further. For the *taifa* rulers, the payments ensured peace with the Christian king and protection from rivals. Pope Alexander II (1061–73) saw the reconquest as a war against infidels as exemplified by the spiritual indulgences he granted to the besiegers of Barbastro in 1064.

During the first half of the reign of Alfonso VI of León (1065–1109) and Castile (1072–1109), pressure on the Muslims increased, and in May 1085 Alfonso took the well-nigh impregnable city of Toledo. Toledo's loss was calamitous for the Muslims and the king of Seville sought aid from the North African emir, Yusuf Ibn Tashfin, leader of a newly founded and expanding Muslim state, a move that introduced the element of holy war into the conflict. Yusuf's Almoravid armies inflicted two major defeats on Alfonso: at Sagrajas (1086) and Uclés (1108).

Only one man withstood the challenge: Rodrigo Díaz de Vivar (1043–99), 'El Cid' (Arabic *al-Sayyid*, 'the lord'). A supreme tactician, a born leader, practical and humane in his treatment of defeated enemies, he was the stuff of epic legend. Appointed a commander by Sancho II of Castile in 1065, and prominent in Sancho's campaign against Alfonso VI, his influence waned when the latter came to the throne in 1072. Although the king arranged Rodrigo's marriage to his own cousin, Jimena Díaz, in 1074, he remained mistrustful of El Cid.

Exiled by Alfonso after leading an unauthorized raid on Toledo in 1081, Rodrigo served the Muslim king of Saragossa as a mercenary, and fought for him with Christian forces. Recalled by the king in 1087, he fought under his banner to subjugate the Moorish kingdom of Valencia (1089–94), emerging as a semi-independent ruler in his own right. At Cuarte in 1094, El Cid defeated a large Almoravid army, and he was similarly successful at the battle of Bairén in 1097.

Until his death in 1099, El Cid acted as a Christian bulwark against Muslim penetration into the eastern peninsula.

When al-Qadir, who was then king of Valencia, heard that al-Hayib had made peace with El Cid, he was greatly afraid and alarmed. After taking counsel with his men, he immediately sent messengers with countless large gifts of money to El Cid. They brought these to El Cid and thus they made peace between him and the king of Valencia. El Cid also received considerable tribute and similar gifts from all the castles that were in revolt against the king of Valencia and were refusing to obey his authority. When King al-Hayib heard that al-Qadir had made peace with El Cid, he was struck with great fear and withdrew from Murviedro in the middle of the night and fled in terror from that region.

El Cid captures Valencia, 1094

In 1086 al-Qadir and other Muslim kings invited Yusuf Ibn Tashfin, the king of the Almoravids of Morocco and Algeria, to bring an army to their aid against the advancing Christians. Yusuf soon turned from an ally into a master: by 1094 he had deposed several petty rulers including al-Mu'tamid, and had won a dominance over the whole south of al-Andalus. His first reverses were at the hands of El Cid, whom Alfonso VI, king of León and Castile, had licensed to build for himself a principality out of the Muslim lands. Valencia was the key.

El Cid vigorously attacked and captured that part of Valencia called Villanueva, stripping it totally of all the riches and wealth that he found there. In the mean time, he successfully stormed another part of the city, called Alcudia. The inhabitants of that area surrendered and submitted themselves immediately to his rule and authority. Those who surrendered he resettled in peace and freedom in their own homes and neighbourhood with all their property.

When other citizens of Valencia saw this, they were greatly afraid. They immediately expelled the Almoravids from the city in accordance with El Cid's decree and submitted to his rule. He allowed them to remain and live in peace and freedom as far as Denia.

Shortly before, Yusuf, king of the Almoravids [at that time in North Africa], sent El Cid a letter absolutely forbidding him to enter the kingdom of Valencia. When he heard this, El Cid

Christians versus Moors in Spain: Moors scout a city, then attack and surround a Christian force bearing crosses and an image of the Virgin, who fight their way free.

was greatly angered. Incensed by the flame of anger, he scorned him and addressed him with mocking words, sending letters to all the lords and rulers of al-Andalus declaring that Yusuf would not dare cross the sea and come to Valencia out of fear of him. When Yusuf heard this, he immediately ordered a huge army to be assembled and then instructed it to cross the straits of Gibraltar without delay.

Meanwhile, Rodrigo addressed the citizens of Valencia in favourable terms: 'Men of Valencia, I shall willingly grant you a truce until the end of August. If in the mean time Yusuf should come to your aid and drive me in defeat from these lands and free you from my rule, serve him and recognize his rule. If, however, he should fail to do this, serve me and be my vassals.'

The Valencians were pleased at this speech. They immediately sent letters to Yusuf and all the rulers of al-Andalus who were under Yusuf's rule telling them to come to Valencia with a large army and free them from Rodrigo's rule and informed the rulers also that, if they refused to come before August, the Valencians would most certainly rather obey Rodrigo's command and serve him in all things.

El Cid seizes enormous booty

When August had come and gone, the Valencians received a reliable report that the Almoravids were definitely coming with Yusuf's huge army, to aid them and free them from Rodrigo's rule. They withdrew straightaway from the agreement that they had with Rodrigo and, failing to honour their pledge, declared themselves in open rebellion. Rodrigo was fully aware of this and laid siege to Valencia, mounting a strong and vigorous attack on it from all sides; it was soon clear that a serious famine was spreading in the city.

Meanwhile, the Almoravid army which was hurrying to the aid of Valencia reached the city. However, the Almoravids did not dare join battle with Rodrigo: terrified and struck with fear they fled under cover of darkness and retreated in confusion to their own territory.

After maintaining a typically vigorous campaign against Valencia on all sides for some considerable time, Rodrigo heroically stormed and captured the city by force, plundering it immediately after its fall. There he discovered and seized an immeasurable quantity of money, an immense and priceless horde of gold and silver, precious necklaces, jewels heavily decorated with gold, many different kinds of ornaments, and silk garments embroidered with fine gold. In that city he acquired such a quantity of wealth that he and his men became richer and wealthier than it is possible to describe.

The battle of Cuarte, 1094

When Yusuf, king of the Almoravids, heard that Rodrigo had courageously captured and pillaged Valencia, he was full of anger and grief. After taking counsel of his men, he made one of his own kinsmen, his nephew Mohammed, general of al-Andalus. He sent him with a large number of Berbers, Almoravids and Saracens living in al-Andalus to lay siege to Valencia, and to bring Rodrigo to him a prisoner.

When these forces came to a place called El Cuarte, some four miles from Valencia, they pitched camp. The inhabitants of the surrounding region immediately came to them with supplies of food and essential provisions; some of the foodstuffs they offered, the rest they sold. There were almost one hundred and fifty thousand horsemen, plus three thousand infantry. El Cid was much amazed at the sight of so great and so immense an army that had come to do battle with him.

The huge Almoravid army remained above Valencia for ten days and nights. The Almoravids would encircle the city daily, howling and shouting many different war-cries and roaring mightily. They frequently let fly arrows at the tents and shelters of Rodrigo and his men and pressed them hard with their attacks. Rodrigo, however, gave stout heart and encouragement both to himself and his men by virtue of his customary fighting spirit. He also offered ceaseless sincere prayers for divine assistance to the Lord Jesus Christ.

One day the Almoravids were circling the city, strong in the belief that they were powerful enough to capture it, all the while uttering howls and cries as they attacked. Rodrigo, that invincible soldier of the Lord, putting his faith in divine mercy with all his heart, set out boldly with his troops well armed, uttering war-cries and terrifying the Almoravids with threats.

Robert Guiscard's call for a holy war

'Our trust in God is worth more than mere numbers. Fear not, the Lord Jesus Christ is with us! As he said: "If your faith is only the size of a mustard seed it is still enough to move mountains." Through the steadiness of our faith, the flame of the Holy Spirit, and in the name of the Blessed Trinity, we shall drive away this mountain, composed not of stones and earth but a filth of heresy and like corruption. Let us now purge ourselves of sin through confession and penitence, and receive the body and blood of our Lord Jesus Christ, and prepare our souls. Because the strength of God will

He fell upon them and engaged them in a mighty battle.

With the aid of divine mercy he defeated all the Almoravids and thus won over them a victory granted to him by God.

The defeated Almoravids turned and fled, but many of them were cut down. Others were captured and led to Rodrigo's camp, together with their wives and children. All their encampments and tents were seized: they were stripped entirely of all the wealth found in them; Rodrigo and his men were greatly enriched and well supplied with much gold and silver, valuable garments, horses and palfreys, mules and weapons of various sorts, supplies of food and indescribable wealth. This victory occurred in June 1094.

Interest in the Christian campaigns in Spain was felt throughout the west: in 1089 Pope Urban II promised in a letter spiritual benefits to those who assisted in the rebuilding of Tarragona, recently recaptured from the Moors, and equated such support with the Jerusalem pilgrimage.

We command that you Christians, in penitence and for the remission of your sins, apply your power and wealth most devoutly, and with utmost zeal, to restore the church [in Tarragona]. And we urge those proposing to set out for Jerusalem or other destinations, in the spirit of penitence or prompted by religious ardour, to direct instead all their resources for the journey to the restitution of the church of Tarragona.

And we promise that when, with God's help, the bishop's seat is securely held and the city itself, harbouring within and without its walls Christian people, and standing opposed to

enable us, a small but faithful band, to overcome the multitude of the faithless.'

And so it was done. Everyone crossed themselves, raised their standards on high and began to fight. But God fought for the Norman, Christian host. He was their salvation, overthrowing and destroying the infidels. And the Saracens began to flee, much heartening the Christians who pursued the pagans vigorously. It was a marvellous thing, never heard of before, for there was not a knight or foot-soldier killed or wounded on the Christian side. Yet so many Saracens were killed that no man might tell their number.

From Amatus of Montecassino, *History of the Normans*

the Saracens, they will enjoy God's mercy no less than if they had reached their intended destinations.

The expansion of Christendom: Sicily, 1061–91

In March 1041, Norman and Italian adventurers seized Melfi in Apulia, in southern Italy, then under Byzantine rule, and founded a petty state. Among their leaders were two of the many sons of a Norman knight, Tancred of Hauteville, at least six of whom eventually went to Italy. In 1059 Pope Nicholas II recognized Robert Guiscard, the eldest surviving brother, as duke of Apulia and Calabria – and of Sicily. That island had, however, been in Muslim hands since the ninth century, and Robert's younger brother, Roger, set about its conquest. The chronicler Geoffrey of Malaterra, a Norman monk from the monastery of St Agatha in the Sicilian city of Catania, describes the long and ultimately successful war.

While he was at Reggio with his brother, Duke Robert Guiscard, following the conquest of Calabria, Count Roger of Calabria, a most civilized young man, learned that Sicily was in the hands of unbelievers. Seeing it from close at hand, with only a short stretch of sea lying between, he was seized by the desire to capture it, for he was always eager for conquest. He perceived two benefits for himself, one for his spiritual, the other for his material, good, if he brought back to the worship of God that land which had yielded to idolatry. Turning over these ideas in his mind, he moved rapidly to carry out his intention. With just sixty knights he set sail upon the short but most dangerous sea, between Scylla and Charybdis. He reconnoitred Sicily and set off on the expedition, having ferried across his army of followers.

The populous city near the harbour where they landed is called Messina. The many citizens of the town were greatly angered when they learned that enemies had invaded them, especially because there appeared to be so few of them. They sprang forth from the city gates and went out to engage them. Count Roger, who was most cunning and experienced in battle, first feigned fear. Then, when he had led them some distance from the city, he counter-attacked, mounting a fierce charge against them, and put them to flight. After cutting down the stragglers he returned, while those who had fled made the long way back to the city gates under his threatening and terrible gaze. When he had seized their

The Normans in Sicily

The Normans, the 'men from the north', were a race of intrepid sailors and ruthless pirates from Scandinavia who, at the end of the ninth century, settled in the lower Seine basin, the area known as Normandy.

In 999, a group returning from a pilgrimage to the Holy Land arrived in Salerno, in time to help the inhabitants defend the city from an Arab attack. Attracted by the country's mild climate and, especially, the gold of the local princes, they were ready to serve the highest bidder as mercenaries.

At the beginning of the 11th century southern Italy was divided between several powers: the Arab emirate of Sicily; the Byzantine dominions; the Lombard principalities; and three duchies, Byzantine in name but in fact autonomous. Within this fluid configuration the Normans created an independent political role for themselves and, by 1076, had in effect conquered the whole of South Italy, their leader Robert of Hauteville, called Guiscard, becoming its principal ruler as count of Apulia. By 1091 Sicily was likewise reduced by Robert's brother, Roger I. Both political and military factors played a part in Norman success. Political fragmentation and local loyalties in the regions involved enabled the Normans to attack one enemy at a time, and they could often count on a friendly faction within the cities they besieged.

In 1127, Roger II of Hauteville, son of Roger I and count of Sicily, claimed the vacant duchy of Apulia. He met strong opposition, but in 1130, Roger succeeded in persuading Pope Anacletus II, whom much of Christendom considered to be the anti-pope, to crown him king of Sicily in Palermo; he immediately crushed a revolt by the Apulian barons.

The Norman monarchy he set up in Sicily preserved the concept of the public function of power, exercised by the king through his salaried officials. Few Normans had any administrative experience – or were even literate – and for the most part they kept the existing public institutions founded in Roman law, and the old class of local officials. Roger showed the same caution and tolerance towards the ecclesiastical institutions of the Muslims and the Greek Orthodox Church, and revived the authority of the Roman Church only very gradually and without using force. The Normans soon became integrated and assimilated into the local population.

equipment and the horses that they had left, he boarded his ships and returned to Reggio and his brother, Robert Guiscard.

After the fall of Messina, on the north-east tip of Sicily, Roger proceeded to drive the Muslims out of the island.

By 1063 he had captured Troina, 50 miles south-west of Messina, and came to Cerami, where he inflicted a decisive defeat on the Muslims, which secured north-east Sicily for the invader.

In the year 1063 it was made known that the Berbers and the Arabs, together with the Sicilians, had arrived with a large army to wage war on Count Roger. The latter readily set out with his forces to engage them and ascended to the summit of the mountain above the river Cerami in order to have a better view of them. He could see them on the other side of the river on another mountain-top, looking at him in their turn.

And so for three days they stared at one another with the river in between, neither side wanting to be the first to cross the river. On the fourth day, however, our forces, unwilling to allow the enemy to stay so close with impunity, made their confession before God with the utmost devotion in the presence of the priests and, having received absolution, advanced to attack the enemy, entrusting themselves to God's mercy and confident of his aid. But when they had advanced halfway, they received a message that Cerami had been attacked. The count dispatched his army in that direction, and sent ahead Serlo, his nephew, with thirty-six men so that he might penetrate the camp and hold out there until he himself should arrive with some one hundred knights, for he had no more.

Serlo invaded the camp at Cerami and, not waiting for his uncle to arrive within the walls, burst upon the enemy like a raging lion and inflicted great slaughter among them, although they numbered three thousand, not to mention the infantry, of whom there were an infinite number. A truly extraordinary event, for he with just thirty-six knights put them all to flight. This event enables us to recognize that God was our protector.

When the count, who was following his nephew with one hundred knights, came to Cerami, he realized that the enemy had already been defeated. While he considered whether to press on and inflict a greater defeat, some men were losing heart out of fear and were saying that the victory achieved by God through his nephew should suffice, lest changing fortune might turn for the worse if they were to continue the pursuit.

Miraculous appearance of a saint

When the count heard all this, he was angry and sternly reprimanded the faint-hearted. He quickly advanced towards the enemy's camp, where they had taken refuge, to engage them in battle. But when he saw that his men were more afraid than usual because of the enemy's great number, which was truly terrifying, he gave them words of encouragement: 'Keep up your spirits, you brave soldiers in Christ's army. We all bear the emblem of Christ, who will not desert his emblem, unless he is wronged. Our God, the God of gods, is all-powerful. Nor is it right to have doubts, for it is certain that, with God going before us, resistance is impossible.'

The count's men were hastening into battle when there appeared a knight, splendidly armed, mounted on a white horse and carrying on the point of his spear a white banner bearing a splendid cross. He was advancing before our front line in order to make our men more resolute in battle, when with a most powerful charge he attacked the enemy where they were thickest. When our men saw this, they were overjoyed and cried out repeatedly to God and St George. Overcome, they burst into tears of joy at such a sight and readily followed the figure advancing before them. Many saw hanging from the count's spear the banner with the cross which cannot have been placed there except by divine power.

Urging on his front line, the count clashed with Arcadius of Palermo who, clad in a breastplate of shining mail, was resolutely leading his company in order to test our men. Felling him with his spear in a powerful struggle, the count killed him, thereby striking fear into the rest of the troops. Arcadius was an outstanding soldier, thought to be invincible in battle.

When the enemy saw that we were scattering the dense formation, made up of both heathens and Sicilians, that was confronting and surrounding us – just as thick clouds are broken up by a furious wind and swift hawks scatter a helpless flock of birds – they were unable to withstand our attack any longer and endeavoured to flee, rather than fight. Our forces pursued them boldly as they retreated and, now victorious, killed as many as fifteen thousand of the enemy.

The following day, they attacked the twenty thousand infantry who had fled to the rocks and crags of the mountain, killing most of them. They sold the defeated survivors for a huge sum of money. However, after delaying there a while, they were overcome by the smell of the rotting bodies of the slain and, recoiling from the stench, they returned to Troina.

Out of gratitude to God and St Peter, whose protection he knew had brought him so great a victory, the count sent one of his men, called Meledius, to present to Pope Alexander, as a sign of his victory, four camels which he had taken from the enemy. The pope was pleased, more at the victory granted by God over the heathen than at the gifts, and he sent his papal blessing and, by the power he exercised, absolution from their sins – provided they were repentant in the future – to the count and all those assisting in winning Sicily from the heathen and in keeping it for ever for the Christian faith. He also sent a standard endowed with papal authority by the see of Rome.

With this reward and trusting in St Peter's protection, they would be able to attack the Saracens in greater safety.

The capture of Palermo, 1072

Despite spirited Muslim resistance, by 1072 Robert Guiscard and his brother Roger had reached Palermo, capital of Sicily.

After making ready supplies and all the other things appropriate to the expedition, the duke, Robert Guiscard, followed his brother Roger and reached the port of Catania [fifty miles south of Messina], where Count Roger had been sent under the pretence of attacking Malta and of not being concerned with Palermo. Urged on by his brother, he set off with a large cavalry force, ships, infantry and supplies and came to Palermo, where he laid siege to the city from the sea.

After five months of siege, Duke Robert secretly entered the gardens with three hundred knights to storm the city from the side where the fleet was, while he instructed his brother to do likewise from his side. At a given signal, they forced their way in without delay, making a tremendous noise. The entire city hastily took up arms, terrified by the noise the assailants were making, and rushed to defend the city. One section, where they had taken fewer precautions, had been imprudently evacuated. Here, the duke's forces placed ladders against the walls and scaled them. The suburbs fell and the iron gates of the city were opened for their comrades to enter. The duke and his brother, Count Roger, took quarters inside the walls together with the whole army.

Having thus been tricked and knowing that the enemy was at their backs within the walls, the inhabitants of Palermo retreated. Night put an end to the conflict. The next morning a truce was agreed, and the leaders of the city came to speak with the two brothers, saying that because their present situation obliged them to do so, they promised to surrender the city, to be faithful vassals, to pay tribute and to ratify this on oath according to their law.

The duke and the count gladly accepted the terms of the

Robert Guiscard

Robert of Hauteville, a younger brother of Drogo, the powerful leader of the Apulian Normans, arrived in southern Italy in 1047. He was called 'Guiscard' (astute, shrewd) because, according to a chronicler, he was more subtle than Cicero, more wily than Ulysses. A strong personality, he was respected even by his enemies, and the Byzantine princess Anna Comnena, daughter of the Emperor Alexius and a deadly foe, described him as fierce and ruthless, but also handsome, tall, agile, strong and daring.

He arrived in Italy with only five horsemen and 30 foot-soldiers, and his kinsmen, already well established there, received him coldly. At first, Robert was driven by poverty to live as a brigand, pillaging and raiding Byzantine Calabria, until he carved out for himself an extensive domain in the south of the region.

His prestige and fortune grew considerably after the battle of Civitate in 1053. His contribution was decisive in defeating the papal and German imperial forces under the personal command of Pope Leo IX, who had determined to put an end to the intrusive Norman dominance in South Italy. In 1059, Robert and Pope Nicholas II worked out a political solution to the conflict: the Norman leaders swore an oath of fealty to the pope, promising him military support in exchange for recognition of the legitimacy of their rule in southern Italy.

Designated count of Apulia in 1057, Guiscard completed his conquest of southern Calabria with a campaign in which he was assisted by his younger brother, Roger I of Hauteville. The brothers now turned their attention to Arab Sicily, and by 1072 had conquered the island, which was left almost entirely in Roger's hands while Robert imposed his rule on the Apulian lords. By 1076, with the occupation of Salerno, he had completed his conquest of the southern part of the Italian peninsula.

In May 1081, Robert embarked upon an ambitious military campaign against Byzantium itself, and defeated the Byzantine army under the command of the Byzantine emperor, Alexius Comnenus, outside the city of Durazzo on 18 October. However, Alexius incited the Apulian barons to rebellion, and Guiscard was compelled to return to Italy in April 1082. Two years later, in the autumn of 1084 Robert embarked on his second campaign against the Byzantine Empire, but died at Cephalonia on 17 July 1085.

offer. It was the year 1072. Having achieved this, as faithful observers of the scriptures which say 'But seek ye first the kingdom of God, and all shall be added unto you' [Matt. 6.33], with great devotion they first restored to the Catholic religion the church of Santa Maria, which had formerly been a cathedral, but had since been profaned by the godless Saracens and had become a temple of superstition. They enriched it with an endowment and church ornaments. They brought back the archbishop who had been expelled by the heathen and who, although a Greek and a timid man, was still observing Christian worship as best he could in the poor church of St Cyriacus.

Byzantium and the west, 1080–95

Robert Guiscard had gradually conquered southern Italy from the Byzantines (1040–71), and in 1091 the last Muslim stronghold of Noto in Sicily fell to his brother. In 1078 Michael VII Ducas, the Byzantine emperor, was forced to abdicate and the empire degenerated into anarchy. This gave Guiscard a good opportunity to attack Constantinople. His motives are recounted by Anna Comnena – daughter of Alexius Comnenus, who became emperor in 1081. Her *Alexiad* was written in the 1140s.

Robert Guiscard, duke of Calabria, became famous from totally obscure circumstances. He mustered a great force about him, and even aimed at becoming emperor of Constantinople, concocting excuses – which sounded reasonable enough – for his hatred of and hostility towards the Byzantines. It is said that he was totally unscrupulous, and was thirsting for war against the Byzantines. He had been making preparations for war for a long time, but was prevented from doing so by the good advice of some of the most reputable men around him, and by his wife Sichelgaita herself. They argued that he would be starting unjust wars against Christians, and he was frequently prevented from undertaking such an attack. Yet he still wanted to devise a plausible excuse for war.

A monk called Raiktor sought shelter at Robert Guiscard's court, and presented himself as the Byzantine emperor, Michael VII Ducas, Robert's ally (through the betrothal of Robert's daughter to Michael's infant son), who had been deposed in 1078.

Robert staged a grand deception on stage pretending that Raiktor was the Emperor Michael; that he had been ousted from his throne; that his wife and children had been taken from him, along with all his property, and that, unjustly, they had bestowed on him a monk's habit instead of the imperial crown.

'He has now come to us,' said Robert, 'as a suppliant.'

Robert made this statement publicly, and urged that the kingdom should be restored to the supposed Michael, as he was a relative.

He treated him every day as though he really was Emperor Michael, giving him a seat above all others, higher thrones and greater honour. He worked on the public assemblies in different ways on different occasions: sometimes he stirred up pity for what the so-called emperor was suffering; and sometimes he spurred on and incited the barbarian crowd around him by cunningly promising them heaps of gold, which he undertook to obtain for them from the Roman Empire.

Thus Robert led them all by the nose.

Palermo, Robert Guiscard's prize, with its citizens. The city's population reflected the various races in Sicily: a mixture of Arabs, Greeks, Italians and (later) Normans.

The siege of Durazzo, 1081

On the Norman side, William of Apulia, a chronicler probably of French origin, described Robert's siege of Durazzo (in present-day Albania) in 1081. His *Gesta Roberti Wiscardi* written in 1094–9, is an early and valuable source for Robert's victory over the new emperor, Alexius I Comnenus, and his death four years later.

The duke besieged Durazzo in the spring of 1081. The citizens were very afraid, and they posted sentinels; a loyal guard was set up through the city; they notified the Emperor Alexius that the duke was besieging them; and they went about the task of requesting aid through ambassadors. The duke struggled to attack the city by every means, and a remarkable wooden tower was built. On top of it was erected a huge catapult which could shoot a great distance so as to destroy the walls of the city. The citizens, seeing that the duke's camp was being continuously enlarged, that everything was being destroyed, that the enemy were making off with a great amount of plunder, and that houses were being built to deal with the onset of the winter cold, began of necessity to abandon their vain and illusory hopes that the enemy would return home.

They sent ambassadors to ask him why he had come. The duke said that he had come in order to restore the Emperor Michael VII, who had been undeservedly deposed from the Byzantine throne, to his position of honour. They promised him that they would not deny him entry into the city, as he had asked, if they could see Michael. To the sound of horns, trumpets and lyres, the monk Raiktor who pretended to be Michael was brought in, crowned like an emperor, surrounded by chanting crowds. All the citizens together, when they saw this man, laughed and cackled at the sight, saying, 'He used to serve bowls full of wine at tables; he is a bartender, and one of the worst.'

Arrival of the Venetian fleet

The Emperor Alexius I Comnenus, fearing that the duke might capture Durazzo, prepared to move against him with a large army, and asked allies to join him. These allies were highly skilled in naval warfare, and brave; they had been sent, at Alexius's request, from populous Venice, rich in resources and rich in men, which lies at the northern edge of the Adriatic gulf. The Venetians' walls are surrounded by sea; no person can cross from his own house to another person's house unless he is conveyed in a boat. They live permanently on water; and no people is more pre-eminent than they in marine warfare and in guiding ships over the seas.

Alexius urged them to bring help to the besieged citizens, to bring their own ships and fight against the duke's ships, so that when the enemy had been worsted by them, it would be an easy task to wage war on land as the duke's forces would have been reduced. The Venetians obeyed the emperor, and hurriedly moved off to fight against the duke's fleet.

When the duke learned that the enemy was about to arrive, and had found out the size of the forces with which Alexius was attacking, he called together all the chieftains under his command and told them everything he knew. And so he put all his men in order wisely and cleverly, and saw to all the necessary preparations.

Alexius had given orders to all the people of Durazzo that they should try to attack the enemy's rear; Duke Robert therefore would be left with no refuge either in front or behind. At daybreak the duke, anticipating this, burned the camp, so that no one would be able to attack it when he was gone. First he himself moved his cohorts into battle.

Alexius attacked him with a larger force. The duke's forces were terrified, everyone turned and fled.

The imperial army, believing that the enemy had been conquered, and the Venetian fleet, which was sailing close by hoping to capture the defeated men, started on their plunder, greedy for spoils. Horses and all kinds of other things were seized, which the duke's army had left behind.

Meanwhile, part of the duke's army managed to rejoin the duke. The duke was happy that his men were with him, and encouraged them with a few brief words, shouting out that their only safety would be in arms. He also warned them that if they ran from the Greeks, they would all be butchered like sheep; for those captured, he declared, there would be a life no better than death. Robert inflamed the hearts of his men, and although he could see the innumerable troops on Alexius's side rushing forward, he had faith in the banner which the pope had given him in honour of the supreme priest Peter, and in the merits of St Matthew, whose cathedral [in Salerno] he had built; so he charged confidently against the enemy, and fiercely joined battle not far from the besieged city of Durazzo.

Alexius was overcome, his men fled; more than five thousand of the Greek army were killed in this battle, a large proportion of the Turks perished along with the Greeks, shining arms and sleek horses were captured, and so too were various Greek banners of honour. Of the duke's army, barely thirty dead knights could be seen. Alexius wept to think that the enemy had proved stronger than he, especially since they were not his equals in numbers of troops or in wealth. He withdrew, himself wounded, and was compelled to return home inglorious, weeping – he who had once vainly hoped for the glory of a triumph.

Death of Robert Guiscard, 1085

Robert Guiscard's occupation of Durazzo – and Corfu – gave him an important toehold in Byzantine territory. But in 1082 he was recalled to Italy to rescue Pope Gregory VII, besieged in the castle of Sant'Angelo by the Holy Roman Emperor Henry IV. In 1085 Robert, having extricated Gregory, took ship for Cephalonia, which one of his younger sons, Roger Borsa, was trying to capture on his behalf. His death followed soon afterwards.

In 1085, it was proposed that Robert should make for the island of Cephalonia, which he had sent his son Roger Borsa to capture. Robert embarked on a ship, but before he could see his son again he was taken with fever. The seething dog-star had begun to flame, that star which, when it burns most savagely during the summer season, is always harmful to mortal men. Robert's wife Sichelgaita had come from Italy not long before, and when she found out that Robert was ill – Robert, on whom all her hopes were founded, such a magnificent husband – she tore her clothes, wept, and ran quickly to be with him; and seeing that her husband had all but succumbed, she slashed at her cheeks with her fingernails, tore at her dishevelled hair, and lamented.

Who could watch with dry eyes the tears of the people standing by? Who is so enduring, so iron-hearted, that he would not suffer alongside these sufferers?

Surrounded by tears, Robert received the body and blood of Christ, and, giving up his well-loved life, he died. Thus the spirit of the robust prince left the body, he who had always been one to strengthen the spirits of others, and had never allowed his men to fear so long as he was present.

With Robert gone, his army was struck with fear so powerful that they lost hope of ever managing to escape, as if they had been denied life and salvation. The death of this man was the cause of fear for many: those who had regularly defeated armies of enormous size while the duke was alive, were afraid, now that the duke was dead, to put up a struggle against even a small force.

New east–west relations

By 1089 relations between Rome and Constantinople had improved. Pope Urban II lifted the excommunication on the Byzantine emperor and asked that the Latin churches in his empire be reopened. The Byzantine synod sent a cautiously favourable response.

Long ago the Roman Church came together again into a single community with our Holy Catholic Church and with the other most holy patriarchs. Since then, a schism has occurred [1054], right down the middle of the churches, and the name of the pope is no longer mentioned along with the names of the other patriarchs; and this situation has prevailed up until now. Yet Urban II, who presides over the Church in Rome, has written to Byzantium asking for peace and harmony, and requests the restoration of his name in the holy diptych [i.e. his recognition] – not that it was through the decision and decree of the synod that the Church of Rome was separated from our communion, but, it would seem, through error.

The most holy patriarchs of Constantinople and Antioch have been summoned and been asked to discover whether anything included in writings from the pope tends, in the opinion of our most great and holy Church, to constitute a gulf between the Church of Rome and ourselves.

The patriarchs agreed that these writings were not suspect. They added that the enquiries between both churches had been canonical, and that they wanted the reconciliation to be accepted in these matters too. The patriarchs concluded that the ancient privilege of a mention in the diptych should be restored to the pope. Even if any other ambiguity be found, it should not be lawful or canonical for the pope's name to be struck off without a full canonical condemnation.

The easing of relations between the eastern and western churches paved the way for Alexius, still beleaguered by the Turks, to appeal to a papal council, at Piacenza, for help, in February 1095. As the monk Bernold of Constance, an ardent supporter of clerical reform, relates, Pope Urban II agreed. Soon afterwards, the First Crusade was preached.

An embassy of the emperor of Constantinople came to the synod, and humbly begged the lord pope and all the faithful of Christ to send some help to him for the defence of the Holy Church against the pagans. For these pagans were then ravaging those parts, and had conquered almost all the lands up to the walls of Constantinople.

The lord pope encouraged many to give this help. Indeed, Urban II asked them to promise, on oath, that they would go and bring faithful aid to the emperor to the best of their ability, with God's help.

The emperor of Constantinople, with attendants bearing the 'S.P.Q.R.' banner of the old Roman Empire.

2

THE FIRST CRUSADE
1096–1099

Jerusalem was the inspiration and objective of the first crusade. When Urban II exhorted Christendom to go to war for the Holy Sepulchre, at the Council of Clermont, it was apparently his reference to the Holy City which inspired thousands of men, women and even children to undertake the journey to the Holy Land.

Although it is certain that such an extraordinary migration was not in the pope's mind, his precise expectations are impossible to recapture; accounts of his speech and of subsequent events were written after the capture of Jerusalem and the memories – or imaginations – of the writers were coloured by that achievement. Urban's letters mention Jerusalem, but speak also of the liberation of the eastern Church, a reminder that the expedition was conceived in response to the request from the Byzantine emperor, Alexius I Comnenus, for aid against the Turks, delivered at Piacenza in March 1095.

The pope did not foresee the wide-ranging response to his appeal, which he directed at the knightly class; his own background, the lesser nobility of Champagne, enabled him to hit exactly the right note. The violence and political fragmentation of 11th-century France had produced a group of men whose purpose in life was fighting, but the Church had reacted with the Peace of God. The Christian warrior embodied a contradiction in terms and at Clermont Urban offered to resolve the conflict: by joining Christ's militia a knight could do what he was good at with the blessing of the Church.

The pillage of Jerusalem by
Christian crusaders.
Although engaged in a holy
war, they frequently looted.

Piety was therefore a major motivating force among the 'upper classes' of crusaders, mixed with the knightly desire for glory and the lure of adventure. The idea that many were landless younger sons seeking their fortune in the east has been abandoned:, it routinely took a knight around two years' income to equip himself; much more for an expedition to the Holy Land. Furthermore most crusaders returned home when they completed their pilgrimage, and charters show that they envisaged either dying on the expedition or returning to reclaim their lands. Men who carved out careers for themselves in the east, including Godfrey of Bouillon and Raymond of Toulouse, were by no means lacking in prospects in the west. This is not to say that greed played no part in crusaders' motives: it drove the German count, Emich of Leisingen, who superintended the merciless attacks on the Rhineland Jews; and the genuine piety of Bohemund I of Taranto, later prince of Antioch, was mixed with powerful ambition.

Complex though their motives were, it is easier to understand why knights joined the First Crusade than to explain the participation of hordes of peasant. The poor were not the target of Urban's appeal. Rather they were the audience of itinerant preachers like Peter the Hermit, whose eloquence persuaded generations of historians that he was the instigator of the crusade. Those who heard him preach were receptive to his message for all sorts of reasons.

The theme of Jerusalem was all-important to them. They undertook the expedition not as a military campaign but as a pilgrimage, an important feature of 11th-century life. People prayed at local shrines and travelled far afield to centres that housed holy relics, to seek help and health in an uncertain world. A journey to a major shrine like Rome or the church of St James at Compostella was an adventure, but could also be undertaken as a penance and earn forgiveness for past sins. The most important place of pilgrimage was Jerusalem, the scene of Christ's passion and resurrection. Its very stones were holy relics. The Holy City maintained a centuries-old tradition of welcoming pilgrims, but when Peter and other popular preachers told of alleged Muslims' ill-treatment of Christians, they aroused the anger of their listeners. For many, the crusade was a massive pilgrimage blessed by the pope and with powerful armed protection.

Jerusalem had a resonance beyond its status as a shrine, however. It was also the heavenly city and would be the scene of the Last Days, as told in the book of Revelation. One of the underlying beliefs of the 11th century was that Domesday would arrive at the millennium – its date not known precisely, but believed to be 1,000 years since the completion of the New Testament – and that the scene of Judgement would be Jerusalem, in Christian hands. The poor had a special commitment to this idea because theirs would be the kingdom of heaven, and among the vast numbers who travelled to the Holy Land there were countless non-combatants – women, clerics, the old and the young – as well as able-bodied men who could fight as foot-soldiers.

It was an army such as this which left first for the east, disregarding Urban's announced date of 15 August 1096 and departing in May, even before the harvest. Peter's band included only eight knights, led by Walter Sansavoir of Poissy.

Alexius's feelings can be imagined when he heard of the trouble these unofficial armies caused as they crossed Europe. When they reached Constantinople he shipped them across to Asia Minor and cautioned them to wait. However, they advanced and were destroyed by the Turks.

As the official armies arrived one by one, the Byzantine emperor presented gifts to their leaders and extracted oaths of loyalty. Already suspicious, especially of Bohemund, Robert Guiscard's son, he wanted to ensure that towns liberated from Muslim rule were yielded to him and not kept by westerners. For his part, Alexius promised military and other support for the crusade.

As they travelled through Asia Minor and beyond, the crusaders faced a confused political situation. They had come to fight the Seldjuk Turks but found their power already in decline. Qulij Arslan still held Nicaea, but in Syria the brothers Ridwan of Aleppo and Duqaq of Damascus found it difficult to agree, let alone impose order. The Turkish general Kerbogha threatened to invade from the north, and in the south the Egyptians captured Jerusalem in 1098 and commanded the Mediterranean and Red Seas. Seemingly in every city petty leaders, 'emirs', asserted their independence. There were nomadic tribes whose volatile influence might be exerted almost anywhere; and, not least, there were the urban and peasant natives. Mainly Arab, they included Jews and Christians as well as Muslims.

After the siege of Nicaea, the first major engagement of the campaign, the victorious crusaders yielded the city to Alexius, in June 1097, in accordance with their oath to the emperor. However, Baldwin and Tancred began to strike out on their own account. The Christian inhabitants of Edessa invited Baldwin of Boulogne to be their duke, as much to escape Byzantine domination as to throw off Turkish suzerainty. There was no question of surrendering the city to Alexius, and in 1098 it became the first Latin state in the east.

The siege of Antioch had begun at the end of 1097. An important Byzantine trading centre and frontier town before it fell to the Turks in 1085, its repossession was of prime importance to Alexius. The Byzantine emperor's chief representative and general, Tacitius, who had with a small group of advisers accompanied the army up to that time, was, however, persuaded by Bohemund that his life was in danger; and, when Taticius fled, Bohemund had it put about that the emperor had failed in his part of the bargain, and therefore he had forfeited his claim to Antioch. His fellow princes finally agreed that if the emperor sent no assistance, and if Bohemund could take Antioch, he should keep it. But its governor Yaghi Siyan was prepared for a long blockade. He appealed to his Muslim allies, who were beginning to appreciate the Latin threat and who prepared to relieve the city. Antioch could not be taken by force and the crusaders soon suffered almost as severely as the Antiochenes from shortages of food and disease.

Antioch was taken in June 1098 but the crusaders barely had time to occupy the city before Kerbogha arrived with his relieving army. The Franks desperately needed assistance but Stephen of Blois, one of their leaders who had fled to Constantinople just before the city capitulated, persuaded Alexius that the situation was hopeless. Alexius's consequent inaction lost him any chance of regaining Antioch. The crusaders defeated Kerbogha without his help and when the army resumed its march towards Jersualem, Bohemund was left in charge of Antioch, the second Latin state. In July 1099 Jerusalem itself became the third.

The impact of the First Crusade resulted in a surge of histories. The most precious Latin documents are the few surviving letters from crusaders. These are immediate testimony, not coloured by hindsight, while the other accounts were written after the success of the expedition and to celebrate its achievement. Some writers were eyewitnesses – although not of all the events they recount. It was by chance that they followed the fortunes of different leaders. The anonymous author of the *Gesta Francorum* ('Deeds of the Franks') was a follower of Bohemund I of Antioch, who left his master after Antioch's capture to press on to Jerusalem. Raymond of Aguilers, who left France with Bishop Adhemar of Le Puy and became chaplain to Raymond, count of Toulouse, represents the Provençal view. He was an enthusiastic reporter of visions and a firm believer in the Holy Lance. Fulcher of Chartres went east with Stephen of Blois but accompanied Baldwin of Boulogne to Edessa and remained his chaplain when he became king of Jerusalem. A reliable historian, he was remarkably tolerant of Byzantines and eastern Christians. Radulph of Caen, who did not arrive in Syria until 1108, was fiercely loyal to Tancred, Bohemund's nephew; his violently anti-Provençal chronicle contains interesting anecdotes about his hero.

Albert of Aachen wrote the most detailed account of the crusade even though he never went east. He recorded the reminiscences of pilgrims on their return from the crusade and, although there are occasional mistakes in his chronicle, he is an important purveyor of western perceptions as well as the 'official biographer' of Godfrey of Bouillon. Many of these sources, all written in Latin, are also of value for the Second Crusade. Other western accounts of the First Crusade come from the Genoese Caffaro, the German Ekkehard, the French Guibert and the English historian William of Malmesbury. The Hebrew account of the Rhineland massacres of the Jews gives a unique insight into a dark period of crusading history, and legend creeps in with the Old French *Chanson d'Antioche* and Norse saga.

Inevitably, Muslims viewed the crusade differently and did not chronicle their defeat. Ibn al-Athir, author of a 'Sum of World History', lived in Mosul between 1160 and 1233. He made use of earlier materials and is respected as a historian. Like Sibt Ibn al-Jawsi (d. 1256), he is more informative about his own time. Matthew of Edessa, an Armenian Christian, had first-hand experience of events in his native city and betrays a fierce hatred of the Byzantines. The *Alexiad*, the Greek princess Anna Comnena's biography of her father Alexius I, written 40 years after the crusade when she was an old woman in exile, sheds an invaluable light on events in Constantinople.

These writers chronicle the events of the First Crusade, to the climactic capture of Jerusalem. Godfrey of Bouillon, the city's first ruler, was left with a handful of men to face the hostility of the Muslims, the rivalry of his compeers and the suspicion of Byzantium. After his death in 1100 his brother Baldwin I, king of Jerusalem, extended Latin rule city by city along the coast. Finally, in 1124, Baldwin's regent, Eustace Garnier, captured Tyre; the Muslim citizens were on this occasion not massacred like those of Jerusalem, but allowed to depart unmolested.

et aultres sains lieux la enuiron. rinaultes . Et comment il
Et les xpiens y habitans z demou les tenoient en trop oprobrieuse
rans . z que les aultres par eulx captiuite z seruage . ou tresgrant
tyranniquement z inhumaine deshonneur z oprobre de tous
ment tues . Ilz auoient referue les xpiens . Concluant z non
en infelicieuse vie a fin que sur stant par diuerses raisons tres
eulx en loprobre du saint nom euidentes que ce saint peuple
xpien peussent continuer plus xpien ne debuoit plus souffrir
longuement leurs Infattables nendurer que les sains lieux et

A great commotion arose through all the regions of France, so that if anyone earnestly wished to follow God with pure heart and mind, and wanted to bear the cross faithfully after him, he would hasten to take the road to the Holy Sepulchre. For Pope Urban II began to deliver eloquent sermons and to preach, saying that if anyone wished to save his soul, he should not hesitate to undertake with humble spirit the way of the Lord, and if he did not have a great deal of money, divine mercy would provide for him. For the lord pope said, 'Brothers, you must suffer many things in the name of Christ, wretchedness, poverty, nakedness, persecution, need, sickness, hunger, thirst and other things of this kind, just as the Lord says to his disciples: "You must suffer many things in my name."'

When news of this sermon had spread throughout all the regions of France, the French, hearing such words, straightaway began to sew crosses over their right shoulders, saying that they would all as one follow in the footsteps of Christ, by whom they had been redeemed from the power of hell. And they left their homes straightaway.

The great warrior Bohemund of Taranto, who was besieging Amalfi, hearing that an immense army of French Christians was on its way to the Lord's Sepulchre, began to inquire carefully as to what weapons this army was carrying, what sign they bore on Christ's journey, and what battle-cry they called out in the fight.

He was told, respectively: 'They carry weapons suited for war, they bear the cross of Christ on their right shoulder or between the two shoulders; and with one voice they cry out the words "God wills it, God wills it, God wills it!"'

Then Lord Bohemund went back again to his own land and carefully prepared himself to begin the journey to the Holy Sepulchre.

In the summer of 1095, five months after hearing the appeal for help from Emperor Alexius I Comnenus, Pope Urban II had left Italy and crossed the Alps. He travelled through Provence, across the French border, into Burgundy, and in November he was at Clermont, high in the Massif Central.
At a great gathering outside the eastern gate of the city, he preached the momentous sermon that was to launch the first crusade.
An extract is quoted above in the *Gesta Francorum*, an anonymous chronicle written probably by a follower of Bohemund of Taranto – one of the leaders of the crusade – who describes the excitement that swept through the kingdom of France.

Urban II calls for a crusade

From December 1095 until July 1096 Urban toured France, and in a letter to the people of Flanders he gave reasons for the crusade.

Bishop Urban, servant of the servants of God, to all the faithful waiting in Flanders, both rulers and subjects: greetings, grace and apostolic blessing. We know you have already heard from the testimony of many that the frenzy of the barbarians has devastated the churches of God in the east, and has even – shame to say – seized into slavery the holy city of Christ, Jerusalem. Grieving in pious contemplation of this disaster, we visited France and strongly urged the princes and people of that land to work for the liberation of the Eastern Church.

At the council of Auvergne, we enjoined on them this undertaking for the remission of all their sins, and appointed our dear son Adhemar, bishop of Le Puy, as leader of the journey on our behalf, so that whoever should set out on such a journey should obey his orders as if they were our own. If God calls any of you to this task, know that the bishop will set out, with the aid of God, on 15 August [1096], the feast of the Assumption of the Blessed Virgin.

On his return to Italy in August 1096, the pope spread the word there. In September he wrote to the people of Bologna, taking a more cautious tone than earlier.

We have heard that some of you desire to go to Jerusalem, because you know that this would greatly please us. Know, then, that anyone who sets out on that journey, not out of lust for worldly advantage but only for the salvation of his soul and for the liberation of the Church, is remitted in entirety all penance for his sins, if he has made a true and perfect act of confession. This is because he has dedicated his person and his wealth to the love of God and his neighbour.

But we will not allow priests and monks to go there without the permission of their bishop or abbot. Furthermore, bishops should ensure that parishioners are not left without priests. Attention must be paid also to young married men, to make certain that they do not rashly undertake such a journey without the agreement of their wives.

May Almighty God strengthen you in his love and fear and bring you free from all sins and errors to the contemplation of perfect charity and true piety.

Pope Urban II preaching at Clermont in 1095, exhorting Christendom to liberate Jerusalem from Islam.

Pope Urban II

Urban was born in about 1035, to a noble family in the diocese of Soissons. After studying at Reims he entered the monastery of Cluny where he later served as prior. In 1079/80 Pope Gregory VII appointed him cardinal-bishop of Ostia, which he remained until 1088, when he was elected pope.

As a result of political disputes arising out of the great reform movement, known after Pope Gregory VII as the Gregorian Reform, the Latin Church was beset by schism between Gregorians and supporters of the anti-pope, Clement III. The creature of the Holy Roman Emperor Henry IV, Clement held Rome, while Urban was in southern Italy under the protection of the Normans. Both sides courted European-wide support. Throughout his pontificate Urban laboured, successfully, to rescue the Gregorian party from this precarious situation. But while struggling for diplomatic advantage over his rival, he also promoted the Gregorian reforming programme by repeatedly condemning clerical incontinence, simony and lay involvement in church appointments.

The first five years of Urban's pontificate were occupied with initiatives to establish his claims – in opposition to Clement III – as the legitimate successor of St Peter, to gain access to Rome (which he did at the end of 1093) and to regain support throughout the Church for the Gregorian cause. The last five and a half years were a period of renewed activity for ecclesiastical reform, marked especially by the two great councils convened in 1095, in March at Piacenza, and in November at Clermont. During his decade-long reign Urban also held eight other councils, in locations as disparate as Melfi, Tours, Rome and Bari; no pope since Leo IX half a century earlier had travelled so widely and been so visible throughout Latin Christendom.

From the beginning of his pontificate and the time of his residence in southern Italy, Urban had been concerned about the volatile state of relations between the west and Byzantium, and on 27 November 1095, at the end of the Council of Clermont, he made a public appeal for warriors to wrest Jerusalem from the Saracens. Participants were granted remission of penance owed for confessed sins; their property was to be protected under the Peace of God during their absence.

Urban II died on 29 July 1099, unaware that two weeks earlier his Latin Christian army had successfully stormed and captured the Holy City.

Preparations for the crusade

One of the princes who responded to the pope's call was Robert, duke of Normandy, who, in order to pay for his expedition, pawned his duchy to his rapacious brother, William Rufus, king of England. The English chronicler William of Malmesbury recounts the financial pressures laid by Rufus on clergy and laity alike in his attempts to buy out Robert.

In 1096, Robert, duke of Normandy, suddenly decided to go to Jerusalem at the prompting of Pope Urban II. He pawned his duchy to his brother William Rufus, king of England, for the sum of ten thousand marks; Rufus therefore imposed an insupportable tax throughout the whole of England. Many bishops and abbots came to Rufus's court complaining about its severity, saying that they could not meet so great a tax without driving away their wretched peasants. The courtiers, with their usual sarcasm, replied: 'Do you not have reliquaries made of gold and silver, full of dead men's bones?'

So the ecclesiastics, realizing what the reply meant, stripped saints' caskets, despoiled crucifixes and melted down chalices, not for the benefit of the poor, but for the king's treasury. Almost everything which the holy frugality of our ancestors had saved up, the greed of those robbers spent.

Fulcher of Chartres went on crusade in October 1096, in the entourage of Stephen, count of Blois. His *Historia Hierosolymitana* describes the variety of men and their leaders, and events during the journey.

In the year of our Lord 1096, in the month of March, after the council at Clermont which Pope Urban II held in November 1095, some who prepared sooner than others began the holy journey; others followed in April or May, or in June or July, or even in August or September and October, as each could raise the necessary funds. In that year all areas of the world were blessed with peace and a particularly good harvest of grain and wine, for God so arranged it, lest lack of bread should fail his pilgrims on the road, when they had chosen to take up the cross and follow him according to his teaching.

Hugh of Vermandois, brother of Philip I, king of France, was the first of the heroes to cross the Adriatic sea in August 1096. He then made for the city of Durazzo in Bulgaria with his retinue, but as he travelled carelessly with his army spread out, he was captured by the citizens there and taken to Alexius I Comnenus, the emperor of Constantinople. There he was delayed for a while, not completely at liberty. Hugh was followed by the Norman Bohemund of Taranto, count of Apulia, son of Robert Guiscard. He followed the same path with his army. Then Godfrey of Bouillon, duke of Lower Lorraine, went through Hungary with a large following; next Raymond of St Gilles, count of Toulouse, crossed over through Dalmatia with his Provençaux and Gascons, together with Adhemar, bishop of Le Puy, the leader of the whole expedition.

First of all to make his way through Hungary was Peter the Hermit; he was accompanied by many foot-soldiers but few knights. This group was later led by Walter, called the Penniless, a fine soldier, who was eventually killed by the Turks, along with many of his companions, between Nicaea and Nicomedia in Anatolia.

In October 1096, Robert, duke of Normandy, the son of King William I of England, began the journey, having gathered for himself a great army of Normans, English and British. With him went Stephen, the noble count of Blois, his brother-in-law, and Robert, count of Flanders, and many other noble companions.

With so great a throng proceeding along the road from the west, the army swelled to such a size that one could see an infinite multitude, from many lands and languages. They were not, however, gathered into one force until we reached Nicaea.

What should I say? We can read many things in the prophets about this journey, which would take too long to mention now. Oh what pain! What sighs! What weeping! What laments between friends, when a husband left his dearly beloved wife, his children, whatever possessions he had, his mother and father, brothers and other relatives.

Yet the pilgrims were by no means deterred from leaving everything they possessed for the love of God: for they truly believed that they would receive a hundredfold, as the Lord promised to those who love him. Grief it was for those who remained behind, but joy to those who left.

What can we say about it? 'This is the Lord's doing, it is marvellous in our eyes' [Psalm 118.23].

Fulcher of Chartres goes on to describe their journey south into Italy.

Going through the middle of Campania, we came to Bari, which is a fine city situated on the eastern coast of Italy. We went down to the harbour with the intention of crossing the sea to Durazzo. The local sailors, however, made objections, claiming that winter was fast approaching. Duke Robert of Normandy then decided to go by land to Calabria and winter there [with Stephen of Blois]; Count Robert of Flanders crossed the sea with his men. Then indeed many of the common people in the armies were desolate, fearing future poverty; and so they sold their bows and, taking walking-sticks, the cowards returned to their own homes. This affair made them cheap as much in the eyes of God as of men, and became a reproach for them.

Therefore in the following year, in March [1097], when

Peter the Hermit

While all the princes, who required large funds and great retinues of supporters, were arranging their affairs in an organized and scrupulous fashion before they left for the Holy Land, the common people, who were poor in possessions but rich in numbers, attached themselves to a certain Peter the Hermit.

Unless I am mistaken, he came from the city of Amiens in France, and had led the solitary life, wearing a monk's habit, in some part of northern France – I do not know where. He left, for what purpose I do not know, and travelled through cities and towns to preach. He was surrounded by such throngs of people, given such gifts, acclaimed as such an example of holiness, that I remember no one ever having been held in such honour. For he was generous in the way he made very liberal gifts to the poor out of the things which had been given to him; he bestowed prostitutes as wives and provided their dowries; he settled disputes and restored peace on all sides with wonderful authority. Indeed, whatever he did or said seemed almost godlike, to such a degree that hairs were pulled from his mule as relics. We report this not for love of truth, but to show the common people's love of novelty.

He used to wear the simplest woollen tunic, with a hooded cape over it, both down to his ankles, and over that, without sleeves, a cloak, and he went barefoot. He lived on wine and fish, bread rarely or never. This man, when he had inspired an enormous army of followers, partly from the strength of his reputation, partly by his preaching, decided to travel through Hungary.

From Guibert of Nogent, *Historia Hierosolymitana*

Anna Comnena, royal scholar

Anna Comnena, the daughter of the Byzantine emperor Alexius I Comnenus, who reigned from 1081 to 1118, was 'born to the purple' on 1 December 1083. She wrote the *Alexiad*, the life of her father, in the enforced idleness of a nunnery after attempting unsuccessfully to persuade Alexius on his death-bed to adopt her husband, Nicephorus Bryennius, and not her brother John as his heir. Since 1092, when Alexius had deposed his adopted successor, the rightful heir to the throne, Constantine Ducas – to whom Anna had until then been betrothed – Anna had intrigued against her brother. Nicephorus, whom she married in 1097, was loyal to Alexius and to John, who reigned as John II from 1118 to 1143.

Anna's upbringing made her well equipped to write history; Byzantine society was more literate than that of the west and its aristocracy was cultured. The *Alexiad* reflects her education in the Greek classics, and in its preface she cites Aristotle and Plato, Homer and Aesop. Her Greek is difficult and stilted and, although she protests her impartiality, she flatters Alexius, who is portrayed as a skilful politician. Yet her work is valuable, for it reflects her access to officials of the court and also to the imperial achives.

The *Alexiad* also gives a lively impression of Anna as a forceful and influential personality. She is one of a great tradition of able royal women – of whom her mother, Empress Irene, who plotted with her against John, was not the least – who shaped the destinies of the Byzantine Empire throughout its history. Her interests went beyond the confines of her classical education. She describes herself as 'not altogether untrained' in geometry'; her knowledge of medicine is plain; and she describes weapons and siege-engines in detail. But her world was the Byzantine Empire and she is often ignorant of events beyond its frontiers.

Conventionally pious, despising Islam and even Roman Christianity, Anna depicted as barbarians those western soldiers and pilgrims who arrived at Constantinople in 1096 on the First Crusade, her hostility reflecting contemporary Byzantine fears that these westerners might attack the empire (admittedly she was writing with hindsight, over 40 years after the crusade). Although most of her animosity is directed towards Bohemund, the Norman leader from South Italy, her portrayal of him is ambivalent: in her old age she clearly remembered him as a handsome man of striking personality, and wrote of him with something like affectionate hatred.

spring returned, the duke of Normandy and Count Stephen of Blois took to sea once more with all their followers. When a fleet was finally ready, on 5 April, which happened to be Easter Day, they boarded ship at the harbour of Brindisi on the eastern coast of Italy. Oh how deep and inscrutable are the decisions of God: for before our very eyes, one of the ships suddenly split in the middle, still close to the shore, for no apparent reason.

Four hundred men and women drowned. But all at once, joyous praise to God resounded: for when those who were standing around went to collect the corpses, the sign of the cross was found imprinted in the flesh of some above the shoulder-blades.

Of the remainder who struggled with death, very few survived. The horses and the mules were drowned and a great deal of money was lost.

We were confused and terrified by the sight of this misfortune, to the extent that many who were weak in heart and had not yet boarded ship returned home, giving up the journey, saying they would never trust themselves again to the deceptive and treacherous sea. But we, putting our hope entirely in Almighty God, went to sea with foresails raised and trumpets blasting, wafted by a moderate breeze. Four days later we reached land, about ten miles, I would guess, from the city of Durazzo. Our fleet landed in two harbours and from there, with great joy, we continued on dry land and passed by Durazzo.

Peter the Hermit's crusade

Meanwhile, a very different expedition headed east, inspired by the crusading fervour of the French popular preacher, Peter the Hermit. Peter and his great rabble left Cologne, where they had gathered, in April 1096, and, having robbed and pillaged their way through Hungary, reached Constantinople in August. Anna Comnena, daughter of the Emperor Alexius I Comnenus, describes Byzantine amazement at the sight of this 'army', and chronicles its fate in Anatolia.

As if he had sounded a divine voice in the hearts of all, Peter the Hermit inspired the Franks from everywhere to gather together with their weapons, horses and other military equipment. There was such universal eagerness and enthusiasm that every highway had some of them; along with the soldiers went an unarmed crowd, more numerous than the sand or the stars, carrying palms and crosses on their shoulders, including even women and children who had left their own countries. To look upon them was like seeing rivers flowing together from all sides, and coming against us in full force, for the most part through Hungary.

The emperor of Constantinople, Alexius 1 Comnenus, advised Peter to await the other Christian forces. However, he did not; trusting in the large numbers of his [French, German and Italian] followers, he crossed the Bosporus and pitched camp at a small village called Helenopolis. But as many as ten thousand French crusaders separated from the rest of the army and, with the utmost cruelty, plundered the Turkish territory around Nicaea. They dismembered some of the babies, others they put on spits and roasted over a fire; those of advanced years they subjected to every form of torture. When the people inside the city of Nicaea learned what was happening they opened the gates and went out against the crusaders. A violent encounter ensued, but Peter's followers attacked hard, forcing them to retreat.

The raiders then took all their booty and returned to Helenopolis. An argument broke out between them and those who had stayed behind, as usually happens in such cases,

when envy inflames the mind. Then some audacious Germans separated from the others, went to the castle of Xerigordos and took it by assault. When the Turkish sultan Qilij Arslan learned what had happened, he sent an adequate force against them. He recaptured Xerigordos, put some of the Germans to the sword and took others captive.

At the same time, he devised a plan against those who had remained behind with Peter the Cuckoo. He placed men in ambush at suitable places, so that anyone heading for Nicaea would fall into the trap and be caught. Further, knowing the Franks' love of money, he instructed two energetic men to go to Peter's camp and announce that the forces had captured Nicaea and were dividing up the spoil from the city. When this report reached the men with Peter, it threw them into total confusion. At the news of plunder and money, they immediately set off along the road to Nicaea, with no semblance of order, all forgetting their military skill and the discipline required of those going out to battle.

The race of Latins is generally noted for its love of money; but when it embarks on the invasion of a country, then it becomes totally unbridled, devoid of all reason. Since these

Peter the Hermit at the head of a mob of crusaders, of both sexes, whose headlong enthusiasm led them to disaster in Anatolia.

The People's Crusade and the Jews

The People's Crusade left for Jerusalem in the spring of 1096, some months before the departure of the official princely armies. On their route overland to the east, the crusaders encountered the flourishing Jewish communities of the expanding cities of the Rhineland: Speyer, Worms, Mainz, Cologne and Trier. In all of them except Speyer, where Bishop John was able to avert a catastrophe, there were horrifying scenes of forced baptism, murder and pillage. In many cases the Jews' response to this unprecedented onslaught was mass suicide: on no account were they prepared to fall into the hands of the crusaders.

The massacres did not reflect any official policy of the Church. Forced conversion, for instance, was contrary to canon law, and, although the bishops of the cities involved may have been unwilling to risk their lives for the Jews, this does not mean that any of them favoured their persecution. Contemporary western sources almost invariably condemn the crusaders' actions.

Nevertheless, the massacres were not mindless attacks by an uninformed rabble. First, many of the participants in the People's Crusade were knights of some standing. Second, there were specific reasons why the crusaders behaved as they did.

Greed was one of their motives. Real need, too, made them desperate for supplies. It is likely that they saw the Jews as a medium through which to obtain money and food by whatever means they thought fit. Certainly, Jews paid bribes to the crusaders in the hope of being left alone.

However, Hebrew chroniclers of the First Crusade emphasize another motive: vengeance for the crucifixion of Christ. And some contemporary western writers join them in claiming that the crusaders thought it strange to travel to the east to fight the 'enemies of God' while the Jews, whom they considered to be responsible for the death of Christ, were in their very midst. In addition, 11th-century theologians emphasized the human nature of Christ and his suffering on the cross. When those elements are combined, it becomes apparent that, to the crusaders, it was important to avenge Christ on those who were unfortunate enough to be regarded as his enemies. It was the misfortune of the Jewish communities of the Rhineland that they lay in the path of the crusaders' route to the Holy Land.

men were advancing in no sort of order or discipline, they fell into the Turkish ambushes near Drakon and were miserably wiped out. Such a large number of Franks became the victims of Turkish swords, that when the scattered remains of the slaughtered men were collected, they made not merely a hill or mound or peak, but a huge mountain, deep and wide, most remarkable, so great was the pile of bones.

Massacre of the Jews

Peter's rabble was followed by other, even less reputable bands, some of whom could not wait to reach Jerusalem before they began killing the 'infidel'. The German chronicler, Albert of Aachen, writing after 1100, described their cruel slaughter of Jews in the Rhineland; one of the chief persecutors was the lawless petty lord Emich of Leisingen.

I do not know if it was because of a judgement of God or because of some delusion in their minds, but the pilgrims rose in a spirit of cruelty against the Jews, who were scattered throughout many cities in the Rhineland. They inflicted a most cruel slaughter on them, especially in the kingdom of Lorraine, claiming that this was the beginning of their journey and the killings would be of service against the enemies of Christianity. A massacre of the Jews was first carried out in the city of Cologne by the citizens there. They suddenly attacked a small band of Jews, they decapitated many and inflicted serious wounds, they destroyed their homes and synagogues, and divided a very great sum of looted money among themselves.

When the Jews saw this cruelty, about two hundred started to flee by boat to Neuss in the stillness of the night; but the pilgrims and crusaders discovered them and did not leave a single one alive. Moreover, after they had massacred them all, they robbed them of all their possessions.

After these events the pilgrims continued their journey without delay, as they had vowed, and they arrived in great numbers at the city of Mainz. Here Count Emich of Leisingen, a noble and very powerful man in this region, was waiting with a very great band of Germans for the arrival of the pilgrims.

The Jews of Mainz, indeed, hearing about the slaughter of their brothers, and realizing that they could not escape the hands of so many, took refuge with the bishop Ruothard, placing priceless treasures in his care and his trust, and putting great faith in his protection because he was the bishop of that city. He, moreover, as the most important priest in Mainz, put away carefully the incredible quantity of money which he received from them, and he settled the Jews in the very large hall of his home, out of sight of Count Emich and his followers, so that they might remain there safe and sound.

These precautions were not enough to keep Emich and his followers away. A Jewish chronicler, known as Salomon bar Simson, describes the subsequent massacre in graphic terms and laments the dead.

Count Emich was the enemy of all the Jews – may his bones be crushed to pieces in millstones of iron. He was known as a man who had no mercy on the old, or on young women, who took no pity on babies or sucklings or the sick, who pulverized God's people like the dust in threshing, who slew their young men with the sword and cut open their pregnant women.

Emich decided to attack the bishop's palace at daybreak on Tuesday 27 May 1096.

Each man of Israel armed himself with his weapons, in the inner courtyard, and they all marched to the gatehouse to do battle with the crusaders and the citizens. They fought right into the gatehouse; but on account of our sins, the enemy overpowered them and seized the gatehouse. Then all the Gentiles gathered against the Jews who were in the courtyard of the palace, to annihilate them. Our people were disheartened when they saw that the bishop's men, who until then had ensured the Jews' protection, had fled and so delivered them into the hands of their enemy. Like broken reeds were they unto them [Isaiah 36.6].

The bishop himself also fled since he heard he would be killed too because he had been a spokesman for Israel. The enemy gathered together in the courtyard on that Tuesday, 'a day of darkness and gloominess, a day of clouds and thick darkness' [Zephaniah 1.15].

In the middle of the courtyard, the enemy found some of the pious ones with our rabbi, Isaac ben Moses, a very brilliant scholar. He was the first to stretch out his neck, and they cut off his head. The Jews had enveloped themselves in fringed prayer shawls and they sat in the courtyard to hasten to fulfil the will of their Creator; they did not wish to remain alive an hour longer; they accepted upon themselves the judgement of heaven. The enemy threw stones and arrows at them but they did not think of running away; all who were found there were slaughtered.

When those Jews who were in the chambers of the palace saw what those pious ones had done, and when they saw that the enemy was about to storm them, they all shouted: 'There is none like God and we can do nothing better than to sacrifice our life to him.'

The women slaughtered their sons and daughters, and then themselves. Many of the men too, slaughtered their wives, their sons and children. 'The tender and delicate woman' slaughtered her favourite child [Deut. 28.56]; they all, men and women, stood up and killed each other.

Alexius and the crusaders

Pope Urban II had called on the princes to join forces at Constantinople, before proceeding across Anatolia towards Palestine. One of the last to arrive, in April 1097, was Bohemund of Taranto. Anna Comnena, then a young woman of 14, was both fascinated and repelled by him, as is evident from her description written some 40 years after she met him.

Bohemund was, to put it briefly, like no other man ever seen in the Byzantine Empire, whether barbarian or Greek. The sight of him caused astonishment, the mention of his name occasioned panic. To describe the barbarian's appearance systematically: he was so tall in body that he exceeded even the tallest men by almost fifty centimetres. He was narrow in the belly and flanks, broad in the chest and shoulders and strong in the arms. His whole stature could be described as neither constricted nor over-endowed with flesh, but blended as perfectly as possible, built, so to speak, according to the canon of Polykleitos. His hands were broad, he had a firm stance and was compact in neck and back. If one looked at him carefully and closely, he seemed somewhat stooping – not that the vertebrae of the lower spine had been injured, but he had had this deformity from birth, it seems.

The flesh on his body was very white, that on his face ruddy as well as white. His hair was light brown, and did not hang down as far as his back, as it does on other barbarians; the man was not hirsute, but had his hair cut short around the ears. I cannot say whether his beard was reddish or some other colour, for the razor had removed it and left his face smoother than marble; it did, however, seem reddish. His eyes were greyish, indicating courage and dignity. His nose and nostrils breathed air freely: his broad lungs complemented his nostrils and his nostrils the breadth of his lungs.

Right: The walls of Constantinople. Built by the Byzantine emperor Theodosius II in the fifth century, they formed a four-mile defensive system protecting the city from land attack, with two walls and towers every 60 yards, a complex of fortifications unrivalled in 11th-century Europe. The forces of the First Crusade were billeted outside the walls, by order of Emperor Alexius I Comnenus, and allowed into the city in groups of five or six at a time. Once within the city, they were amazed by its wealth and splendour, the richness of its monasteries and palaces.

Above: A panel of a diptych of the Twelve Feasts: an example of the skilled workmanship which so impressed crusaders visiting Constantinople in the 11th century. This diptych was a portable miniature mosaic for use as an icon, made of tiny cubes of colour and precious metals pressed into wax on wooden boards, illustrating scenes from the life of Christ.

Some charm also manifested itself in this man, but it was obscured by the fear he inspired all around him. For he seemed harsh and wild partly because of his size and partly because of his appearance; even his laughter was a cause of fear in others. In body and soul, his disposition was such that both courage and love welled up inside him, and both looked towards war. His mind ranged over all possibilities, dared anything and rushed into any undertaking. In his conversation he gave responses that were always ambiguous. Such was Bohemund's character, and such his physical size, that only the emperor, through luck, eloquence and other natural advantages, could surpass him.

As the *Gesta Francorum* makes plain, Alexius did not trust Bohemund.

When the Emperor Alexius had heard that Bohemund, that most noble man, had arrived at Constantinople, he gave orders that he should be received honourably, but also, cautiously, that he should be looked after outside the city. When Bohemund had been lodged, the emperor sent a message summoning him to speak in secret with him. Godfrey of Bouillon and his brother Baldwin of Boulogne also went; Raymond, count of Toulouse, was near the city.

The emperor, full of anxiety and boiling with anger, was thinking of how to capture these soldiers of Christ by cunning and fraud. But by divine grace, neither place nor time for mischief was found, either by the emperor or by his men.

Fulcher of Chartres describes how the leaders of the crusade took an oath to the emperor. He also records their amazement at the size and wealth of Constantinople.

Since we could not enter Constantinople, for the Emperor Alexius would not allow it, fearing that we planned some harm to him, we had to buy our daily needs outside the walls. The emperor ordered the citizens to bring these to us. Nor were we permitted to enter the city in groups of more than five or six at a time, and then with an hour between each group; as some came out, others went in to pray in the churches.

Oh what a fine and noble city! What monasteries, what palaces it has, what amazing workmanship! How many marvellous works even in the streets and suburbs! It would take too long to relate the wealth of all manner of goods there, of gold, silver, all types of clothes and holy relics. For merchants sail all the time bringing necessities there. There are, I think, around twenty thousand eunuchs living there always.

When we were sufficiently refreshed and rested, our leaders took counsel with the emperor and made a pledge with him, on oath of fealty, at his insistence. This was done by our leaders Lord Bohemund and Godfrey of Bouillon but Raymond of Toulouse then refused to do it, although Robert of Flanders, like the others, took the oath. Such a pledge was essential to consolidate our friendship with the emperor, without whose counsel and aid we would not be able to expedite our journey.

The emperor provided our leaders with as much coinage and silk clothing as they wanted, and also with horses and money, of which they were very short, sufficient to see them through their journey.

The *Gesta Francorum* gives more details about promises made by the emperor, who hoped to use the crusading army to recapture former Byzantine lands.

The emperor also pledged good faith and security for us all, and swore that he would accompany us with his own army on land and sea, would faithfully give us provisions, and would carefully replace all the things that we had lost; furthermore, he would not cause or allow any of our pilgrims to be disturbed or troubled on their journey to the Holy Sepulchre.

The capture of Nicaea

By the end of April 1097 most of the crusaders had crossed the Bosporus. Their army headed south to Nicaea, only 50 miles from Constantinople, yet the capital of the Seldjuk sultan, Qilij Arslan. From the crusader camp outside Nicaea, Stephen of Blois, William the Conqueror's son-in-law, wrote home to his wife, Adela.

Count Stephen to Countess Adela, his wife and sweetest friend: whatever kindly greetings her mind can imagine.

Let your loving heart know that I have travelled on this blessed journey in all honour and bodily comfort.

I arrived at the city of Constantinople in May 1097 with great joy, by the grace of God. The Emperor Alexius received me like his own son with all kindness and honour, and enriched me with very many precious gifts. In this whole

The unrepentant nun

When the attack at Nicaea had calmed down on both sides, while different discussions were going on about giving up the city, and many of the Christians' prisoners were returned, a certain nun from the convent of St Mary at Trier was set free and returned with the rest into the hands of the Christian army. She claimed she had been captured and taken away from Peter's defeated army, and she complained bitterly that she had been taken in vile and detestable union by a certain Turk and others with scarcely a pause.

While she was uttering her wretched moans about these wrongs in an audience of Christians, she recognized Henry of Castle Ascha among the nobles and soldiers of Christ. Addressing him by name in a tearful and low voice, she appealed to him to come to the aid of her purification. He recognized her at once and was affected by her misfortune, and he employed diligence and every argument of pity with Duke Godfrey, until advice for repentance was given to her by Lord Adhemar, the venerable bishop. At last when advice about such an unchaste act had been received from the priest, she was granted forgiveness for her unlawful liaison with the Turk, and her repentance was made less burdensome, because she had endured this hideous defilement by wicked and villainous men under duress and unwillingly.

A short time after this, only one night, she was invited again very persuasively and with coaxing promises to the unlawful and unchaste union by a messenger of that same Turk who had violated her and had taken her from the rest. For that same Turk had been inflamed with passion for the nun's inestimable beauty, and so he was excessively annoyed at her absence; indeed he had promised to give her rewards which had so possessed her imagination that she would return to her abominable husband. This Turk was even promising to become a Christian himself shortly, if by chance he got out of imprisonment and the emperor's chains. At length this most wretched woman, who may have been forced to do wrong before, now was deceived by flattery and vain hope, and she rushed back to her unlawful bridegroom and her false marriage; no one in the whole army knew what cunning or lewdness could have been used to take her away from them. After this it is known from those who tell the story that she went back to the Turk in exile where he was, but no more is known about her reasons, unless it was because her own lust was too much to bear.

From Albert of Aachen, *Historia Hierosolymitana*

army of God's and ours there is no duke or count or any other powerful person whom he trusts and favours more than me. Indeed, my love, his Imperial Dignity has in the past often advised me (and still does) that we should entrust one of our sons to him, whom he promised to treat with such outstanding honour that he would not miss us at all.

Truly I tell you, in our day there is not another such man living under heaven. For he is most generous to all our leaders, he assists all the knights with gifts and he refreshes all the poor with feasting. I have wanted to write about him to you, so that you might have a glimpse of his character.

I remained in Constantinople for ten days, during which Alexius kept me beside him in the highest honour. My departure from him was like that from a father. He himself gave orders for ships to be made ready for me, and by this aid I was able to travel very quickly through that calm arm of the sea which surrounds the city, the Bosporus. Some people say that the sea at Constantinople is cruel and dangerous, but this is quite untrue. From there we came to another arm, the Hellespont, which is called the Arm of St George. Because we could not find enough ships, we took to horse and headed towards Nicomedia, a city left desolate by the Turks.

From there we hurried to the city of Nicaea, arriving on 3 June, praising God. But Nicaea, my love, is surrounded by more than three hundred towers with the most amazing walls. We found the Turks inside the city bold fighters; for we discovered that the boundless army of God [i.e. the other crusaders] had already been locked in mortal combat with the people of Nicaea for four weeks.

A little before we reached our fellows, Qilij Arslan, who had suddenly returned from campaigning in Armenia, attacked us with a great force, thinking that he would be able to burst through our ranks and into the city and so aid his allies. We got ready with the utmost haste, and met the Turkish attack in a warlike frame of mind; they all, straightaway, turned tail and fled. Our men pursued them closely, killing many of them, and scattering dead and wounded over a wide area. Some of our people were killed, although certainly not many; the only notable knight killed was Baldwin, count of Ghent.

Since God did not deem our leaders worthy to take Nicaea by arms alone, they began the enormous task of constructing high wooden siege-towers with bulwarks and various engines. When the Turks saw this, they were overcome by fear and through envoys handed over their city to the emperor. The condition was that some unarmed men should be granted safe passage to leave the city and become the emperor's hostages.

When the revered Alexius heard this, he came to a nearby island in the sea. All our leaders, except for Raymond of Toulouse and myself, rushed to him there, in order to congratulate him on so great a victory. When he heard that I had remained at the city lest any hostile band of Turks should approach it and our army, he was very pleased. Indeed he was more pleased by my remaining at the city than he would have been if I had given him a mountain of gold.

On the island where he was staying, the great emperor organized the treasures from the spoils of Nicaea so that the gold, jewels, silver, clothes and horses went to the cavalry, while all the foodstuffs were distributed among the infantry. He arranged to enrich all the leaders out of his own treasures.

As I said, God triumphed and great Nicaea was won back on 19 June 1097. I am telling you this, my love, since we will reach Jerusalem from Nicaea in five weeks, if Antioch does not get in our way.

Farewell.

Battle at Dorylaeum, 1097

On 26 June 1097 the crusade left Nicaea in triumph and headed across the Anatolian plateau. It had split into two sections, one of which, the Norman contingent, met Qilij Arslan's forces on 30 June 1097. The *Gesta Francorum* describes the Frankish victory at Dorylaeum, which opened the route to Antioch.

The Turks made a vigorous attack on Bohemund and those who were with him. Suddenly the Turks began to shriek and babble and shout, making with shrill voices some kind of devilish sound in their own language. The wise Bohemund, seeing from afar innumerable Turks shrieking and shouting with their demonic voices, immediately ordered all his knights to dismount and to pitch camp quickly. Before the camp had been pitched, he said again to all his soldiers, 'Gentlemen, brave soldiers of Christ, you can see that a difficult battle is all around us. Therefore let all knights go out like men to meet the enemy, and let the foot-soldiers pitch camp carefully and quickly.'

By the time all this was done, the Turks were surrounding us on all sides, throwing darts and casting javelins and shooting arrows from a surprisingly long distance. Although we were unable to resist them or withstand the weight of so

Painful death from thirst

The army marched into the valley called Malabrunias, where, because of difficulties of the terrain and of narrow passes between the rocks, they shortened their journey during the days, for the sake of the countless multitude and the too great heat of the month of August. Then the day came, a certain Saturday of the same month, when the great shortage of water became acute among the people. And therefore, overwhelmed by the anguish of thirst, as many as around five hundred people of both sexes gave up the ghost on the same day – so they say who were there. Moreover, horses, donkeys, camels, mules, oxen and many animals suffered the same very painful death from thirst.

Very many pregnant women, their throats dried up, their wombs withered, and all the veins of the body drained by the indescribable heat of the sun and that parched region, gave birth and abandoned their own young in the middle of the highway in the view of everyone.

Many men, failing with the exertion and the heat, gaping with open mouths and throats, were trying to catch the thinnest mist to cure their thirst: it could not help them at all. Even the hawks, no less, tame birds and favourites of high-born princes, were dying of that heat and thirst in the hands of their owners who were carrying them. Dogs as well, who were praiseworthy in the hunter's art, panting with the same torment of thirst, were destroyed by the hands of their masters.

Now, while everyone was thus suffering with this affliction, the river they had longed for and searched for was discovered. As they hurried towards it, each was keen because of his excessive longing to get before the rest in the great press. They set no limit to their drinking and went on until very many who had been weakened – as many men as beasts of burden – died from drinking too much.

From Albert of Aachen, *Historia Hierosolymitana*

The Frankish victory at Dorylaeum. The town, shown here, behind the battle, with splendid walls, was actually a small settlement on the trade route from Antioch to Jerusalem.

many of the enemy, none the less we managed to advance as one man. Our women were a great help to us on that day, since they kept on bringing water for our embattled men to drink, and bravely comforted them as they resisted. The wise Bohemund immediately sent a message to the others – that is, to Raymond of Toulouse, Godfrey of Bouillon, Hugh of Vermandois, Adhemar, bishop of Le Puy, and all the other knights of Christ – to make them hurry and come to battle more quickly, saying: 'If they wish to fight today, let them come like men.' So Godfrey of Bouillon, a man of audacity and courage, and Hugh of Vermandois came first, together, with their armies; Bishop Adhemar of Le Puy followed them with his army, and Raymond of Toulouse came next with a large force.

Our men were perplexed as to where so large a number of Turks could have come from, and Arabs and Saracens too, as well as others I cannot list; because almost all the mountains and hills and all the plains inside and outside the hills were covered with these unchristian races. So we held secret discussions among ourselves, praising God and making resolutions, saying: 'Let everyone be of one accord in their faith in Christ and in the victory of the Holy Cross, because today, God willing, we will all be made rich.'

Our battle-lines were immediately put in order. On the left-hand side was the wise Bohemund, with Tancred his nephew and others. Adhemar of Le Puy came over the other mountain, so that the unbelieving Turks would be surrounded on all sides. Also on the left-hand side rode that valiant knight Raymond of Toulouse. On the right-hand side was Godfrey of Bouillon, and that ardent soldier Robert, count of Flanders, as well as Hugh of Vermandois.

As soon as our soldiers attacked, the Turks, Arabs, Saracens and all the barbarians sped away in flight through the mountain passes across the plains. Altogether, the pagans numbered three hundred and sixty thousand, not counting the Arabs, whose numbers no one knows but God alone. They fled very quickly to their camp, but even there they could not stay for long. Again they took flight, and we followed them, killing as we went, for a whole day. We seized much booty, gold, silver, horses and asses, camels, sheep, oxen and many other things which we did not recognize. If God had not been with us in battle and sent us the other army quickly, none of us would have escaped, because the battle lasted from the third hour right up until the ninth.

The crusader states

The westerners who settled in the Holy Land after the First Crusade always referred to it as Outremer – 'the land beyond the sea' – and in many ways it was an extension of their homelands. After early doubts as to whether a king might suitably rule in Jerusalem, since Christ himself had been crowned 'king of the Jews', a monarchy was established and with it came many features familiar from contemporary western society.

Land conquered from the Muslims was granted out in fiefs either of land or, quite commonly, money revenues in return for the provision of military service by the fief-holders. The chief nobles formed the *Haute Cour*, the highest council of the realm, which advised the king and acted as the highest court of justice; the masters of the military Orders, important figures in a kingdom which was consistently involved in military campaigning, were also members of the council. By the beginning of the 12th century, the county of Edessa had become a fief of the kingdom of Jerusalem, but two other regions – the principality of Antioch and the county of Tripoli – retained a considerable degree of independence.

One of the crusaders' first priorities had been to establish Latin bishoprics in the Holy Land, and to this end the Greek patriarchs of Jerusalem and Antioch were expelled by the leaders of the First Crusade, leaving only the lesser Greek clergy in office – a cause of considerable friction with Byzantium. Other western ecclesiastical institutions soon followed and by the mid-12th century monasteries had been set up at all the major holy places.

As a reward for naval assistance in the conquest of such towns as Antioch, Tripoli, Acre and Beirut during the First Crusade and its aftermath, the Italian cities of Genoa, Pisa and Venice were allowed to set up trading communes within them, where trade, services and legislation followed Italian custom and revenues from commerce went mainly to Italian merchants. In all the crusader states there were separate courts for the nobility, townsmen and merchants. Indigenous populations – Muslims, Greeks and other eastern Christians, and Jews – were allowed to observe their own legal practices in matters solely affecting their communities, but all were second-class citizens. In particular, Jews and Muslims were not permitted to take part in the administration of the kingdom and were regarded as potential enemies.

From Dorylaeum, the army marched on across the plateau to Antioch. The crusaders suffered from extremes of heat and cold, as the old French epic poem, the *Chanson d'Antioche* – by Richard the Pilgrim – reveals.

The day dawned bright and clear, increasing to burning heat by midday. Our noble warriors were parched and feeling deserted. Tancred's knights were thirsting for water. Then the women and young girls, their countrywomen, came to them in their hour of need. Rolling up their sleeves and casting aside their long dresses, they carried water to the brave knights in pots, pans and even golden bowls. When they had drunk, the noble warriors were much refreshed.

Starved of supplies, the Christian forces were suffering badly. No one could give aid to another in word or deed. At this time the absence of provisions caused such distress that the Christians were forced to eat their pack-horses in desperation. Through hunger, even fine Spanish war-horses were killed and eaten. Knights and sergeants, fair young girls alike, all rent their garments and cried out in a loud voice:

'God who died on the cross for us, come to our aid!'

Many were weak and fainting through hunger. Winds tore at a land lashed by sleet and hail. Daily there were storms with brilliant lightning. No warrior, no matter how brave or hard-bitten, could forbear to shudder at Nature's violence. The horses and mules stamped and pawed the earth in fear; the hawks and falcons screeched so loudly that they could be heard several miles away. But the Lord God, the king of heaven, gave thought to the holy companionship and delivered it from disaster.

Edessa: the first crusader state

The army rested at Konya, then headed towards Antioch. But Baldwin of Boulogne, with Bohemund's nephew Tancred, headed east, into Cilicia, in search of land and booty. Fulcher of Chartres was with them.

When we were not more than three days away from Antioch in Syria, I, Fulcher, left the army in October 1097, with my lord Baldwin of Boulogne, the brother of Godfrey of Bouillon, and turned towards the west.

Baldwin was a very fine soldier; leaving the army with his train in September, he had captured with great daring the city which is called Tarsus of Cilicia, taking it from Tancred, Bohemund's brother, who had sent in his own men with the agreement of the Turks. Leaving a garrison there he had returned to the army. Now, trusting in God and in his own power, he gathered to himself a few knights and made for the river Euphrates. There he captured many fortified towns by force and by guile. Among those he captured was one particularly fine one called Turbessel. The Armenians who lived there handed it over to him peacefully, and many other forts were subdued by him.

Baldwin's fame travelled far and wide, to the extent that a delegation was sent to him by Thoros, prince of the city of Edessa, a famous city rich in the goods of the earth. It lies in Syrian Mesopotamia, about twenty miles beyond the river Euphrates, and a hundred miles, or perhaps a little further, from Antioch.

Baldwin was requested to go there so that the two men might become friends for as long as both lived, like father and son. If by chance Thoros of Edessa should die, Baldwin would immediately inherit for ever his city and lands, as if he were his son; for Thoros had no children. Since he could not defend himself from the Turks, this Armenian prince wanted Baldwin to defend him and his land, for he had heard that Baldwin and his knights were exceptionally brave fighters.

On hearing this, and believing it on the oath of the delegates, Baldwin set out across the Euphrates in February 1098 with a very small army, a mere eighty knights. After crossing the river, we made our way fearfully and hurriedly all night, past the Saracen towns which lay here and there. But you would have been amazed at what happened when we passed before the towns of the Armenians, for they humbly came out to meet us with crosses and standards and kissed our feet and cloaks for the love of God. This was because they had heard that we would defend them from the Turks, under whose yoke they had been oppressed for a long time. So we came at last to Edessa, where Prince Thoros and his wife, with all the citizens, received us with great joy: and they quickly fulfilled what had been promised to Baldwin.

We had been there for just over a fortnight, when [on 7 March] some citizens hatched a wicked plot to kill their prince, whom they hated, and elevate Baldwin to the palace. It was no sooner said than done. Baldwin and his people were greatly saddened at this, since they were unable to obtain mercy for the prince. Nevertheless, Baldwin received the principality by the gift of the people. Straightaway he took up arms against the Turks in the country, overcoming and killing them in many engagements. Many of our people were also killed by the Turks.

Baldwin of Boulogne had thus set up a principality for himself in the east – the first crusader state. But unlike Fulcher of Chartres, the Armenian chronicler Matthew of Edessa implicates him directly in Thoros's death.

Baldwin discovered evil counsellors in Edessa, traitors who plotted with him to have Thoros killed and promised to hand

The citizens of Edessa do homage to Baldwin I. Their treachery helped Baldwin to supplant Prince Thoros as ruler of Edessa, which subsequently became the first of four crusader states.

Edessa over to him. Baldwin agreed to join them. Thoros certainly did not deserve such a fate, since he had served the city well; it was thanks to his skill, his clever hard work and his bravery that the town had been freed from the thrall of the cruel and ferocious race of Muslims.

On 7 March the traitors began to stir the crowd up against Thoros. The following Sunday the crowd ransacked the houses of the nobles attached to Thoros's household and seized the upper part of the citadel. The following day they gathered to surround the inner building of the place where Thoros had shut himself up and laid vigorous assault to it. Thoros was in desperate straits and said that if the traitors swore to spare him he would hand the citadel over to them and would withdraw with his wife to Melitene. He gave them the cross of Varak and the cross of Mak'enis and Baldwin swore on holy relics, in the middle of the church of the Holy Apostles, that he would not harm him. He called on the angels and archangels, the prophets, the patriarchs, the apostles, the holy pontiffs and all the ranks of martyrs to witness that he would carry out the requests made by Thoros.

Albert of Aachen too, who describes Thoros's last hours, is unable to exonerate Baldwin.

Thoros, prince of Edessa, also revealed to Baldwin his matchless treasure – in purple, in vessels of gold and silver, in plentiful golden bezants – asking him to take them, provided that Baldwin would intercede for Thoros's life and safety with the citizens, and for them to allow him to leave the tower, naked and empty-handed. Baldwin listened to the man's entreaties and was moved to pity by his despair; he pleaded for him resolutely with the people's leaders and urged that they should spare the prince, that there was nothing to stop them dividing among themselves the treasures.

The senate and all the citizens paid little attention to Baldwin's words and the promise of treasures; they were shouting out with one voice that the prince was not to escape alive and well in return for any exchange or gift of things; they were hurling at him the insults and injustices which they had often suffered under him and from the Turks at his instigation.

The prince, therefore, despairing of his life and seeing that neither his entreaties nor any precious gifts would be of any use to him, sent Baldwin from the tower and left it himself, letting himself down from his throne-room through the window on a rope. However, his destroyers immediately shot him down into the middle of the street, with a thousand arrows. And cutting off his head, they carried it fixed on a spear through all the quarters of the city for everyone to mock.

The rest of the army went on to Antioch, a holy city to the Christians, for it was here that St Peter had founded his first bishopric. Antioch was also a formidable fortress, held by the Byzantine emperor until 1085, and in 1097 under the control of the Turkish Yaghi Siyan, an unruly and semi-independent vassal of the emir, Ridwan of Aleppo. On 29 March 1098 Stephen of Blois sent another letter to his wife Adela, waxing enthusiastic about the wealth so far acquired on his travels, and describing the siege of the city.

Written in the camp near Antioch, 29 March 1098.

Count Stephen to Adela, his sweetest and most beloved wife, and to his dear children and all the faithful members of his household, from the greatest to the least: blessing and grace and every greeting.

You may certainly believe, dearest, that this messenger, whom I have sent to your loving heart, left me safe and well, prosperous and honoured, by the grace of God, before Antioch. At that time, the chosen army of Christ had been heading for the land of our Lord Jesus – with his great power attending us – for twenty-three continuous weeks.

Know for certain, my love, that I now have twice the amount of gold, silver and many other riches as your loving heart would have given to me when I departed from you. For all our leaders with the whole army in agreement have placed me as their commander-in-chief, the overseer and helmsman of all their actions, even against my will.

You have heard enough about how after the capture of Nicaea we followed the wicked Turks right across Armenia, pushing them before us in flight right up to the great river Euphrates. When they reached the banks, they dropped all their baggage and pack-animals and fled across the river into Arabia. Some of the bolder Turkish soldiers galloped day and night to reach the royal city of Antioch before our arrival. With great joy we hurried to Antioch and laid siege to it in October 1097. We had frequent engagements with the Turks; seven battles in which we killed an innumerable quantity of them; they also killed many of our Christian brothers, sending their souls to the joys of heaven.

We found Antioch to be enormous beyond belief, and very strong and well fortified. More than five thousand bold Turkish soldiers had flocked together within the city, not to mention the boundless mass of Saracens, Arabs, Turks, Syrians, Armenians and various other peoples who had gathered

The interior of St Peter's church in Antioch. The city was famous for its association with the apostle who had founded his first bishopric there.

there. Many were the trials and countless the evils we bore there by the grace of God in order to overcome these enemies of God and ourselves. Many even spent all they had in this holy passion. Many of our Franks would have suffered death from hunger, had not the mercy of God and our money come to their aid. Throughout the whole winter before Antioch we suffered bitter cold and driving rain for Christ our Lord. Those who say that the heat is the only thing there is to suffer in Syria are wrong: their winter is just like ours in the west.

When Yaghi Siyan the emir of Antioch (that is, the prince and lord), saw how heavily besieged he was by us, he sent his son, Shams ad-Daula by name, to ask for the help of Prince Ridwan of Aleppo and Prince Duqaq of Damascus. As a result, twelve thousand picked Turkish soldiers came immediately to aid Antioch. Being totally ignorant of this, we had sent many of our knights around the cities and fortified towns. We now have one hundred and sixty-five cities and towns throughout Syria under our dominion. But a little before the reinforcements arrived at the city [on 29 December 1097], we met them nine miles away on a plain by the Iron Bridge with seven hundred knights. But God fought for his faithful servants against them; for on that day by the hand of God we conquered them in battle and killed them without number, for God was always battling on our side. Furthermore, we brought back more than two hundred of their heads into the camp, so that the people of Christ could rejoice.

I want to relate to you, dearest, what happened to us in Lent [1098]. Our leaders had decided to set up a fort before a certain gate, which was situated between our camp and the sea; for through that gate each day the Turks would make a sortie and kill our people as they were going down to the sea (the city of Antioch is fifteen miles from the sea). To this end, they sent the peerless Bohemund and Raymond of Toulouse, accompanied by only sixty knights, down to the sea to bring back seamen to assist in this task. While they were returning to camp with the seamen on 8 February 1098, our two leaders were unexpectedly set upon by a massed army of Turks and driven into a dangerous flight. We were ignorant of their misfortune and, as we approached the same city gate, we were attacked by a crowd of people from Antioch, both foot and horse, vaunting themselves in triumphant mode. But Bohemund and Raymond of Toulouse came up with their army and told the story of the misfortune they had suffered. On hearing it our soldiers were incensed against the sacrilegious Turks and engaged in battle. Our enemies and God's straightaway fled before us, trying to enter their city. They were trying to cross by the bridge over the great river, but we were close on their heels. Many we cast into the river, many we killed on top of the bridge, and many we slaughtered in front of the entrance to the gate.

Indeed I tell you, my love, and you may well believe it, that in that battle we killed three hundred emirs, that is, leaders, and another three hundred noble Turkish soldiers, not to mention other Turks and pagans. The number of the dead, Turkish and Saracen, was reckoned at one thousand two hundred and thirty. But on our side we suffered no casualties.

While my chaplain Alexander was writing this letter in

Flying secret agents

The envoys from the emir of Azaz, Omar, to Godfrey of Bouillon at Antioch were very joyful and happy with Godfrey's promise of help in rebelling against their overlord, Ridwan, hostile to the Franks. Without delay they took from their garments two pigeons, nice tame birds which they had brought with them. They wrote Duke Godfrey's replies on paper, tied them to the birds' tails with thread, and sent them forth from their hands to carry the good news.

Godfrey and everyone who was with him wondered at this sending-out of birds. But the reply came at once as to why the messages were sent this way: 'Our lord duke and his supporters should not wonder at these birds we have just sent off. The pigeons were sent for this reason, that they may hasten with rapid and unceasing flight the message of trust which you hold towards the emir of Azaz, and that they may bear assurances concerning your assistance and whatever good luck or hindrance has befallen us. There is yet another reason why these birds were sent ahead with letters: if they were found in our garments by any of our brother Turks, then they would be our death sentence.'

The birds had already flown away with the letters entrusted to them, and they faithfully returned to the palace and home of the emir of Azaz. The emir welcomed the tame birds affectionately, as was his custom, released the written papers from their tails, opened them and read Duke Godfrey's secret messages. And so he learned all about the day of Godfrey's arrival to support him, and with how many thousands the Christian army would relieve him.

From Albert of Aachen, *Historia Hierosolymitana*

haste on the day after Easter, a group of our people ambushed a party of Turks and overcame them, with the Lord as their leader. They killed sixty of their soldiers and took all their heads back to the camp.

I am only telling you snippets of our many doings, dearest, and since I cannot express to you what is in my mind, dearest, I can only say: keep well, manage your estate well, and treat your children and your servants honourably, as befits you, since you will certainly see me as quickly as I can arrange it.

Farewell.

Despite Stephen's apparent enthusiasm, on 2 June 1098 he abandoned his post and returned to France. Fulcher's regrets at his departure were minimally formal.

On 2 June 1098 Count Stephen of Blois left the siege and went to Alexandretta, on his way home to France over the sea. We all grieved at this, since he was a most noble man and strong in arms. On the very day after his departure, 3 June 1098, the city of Antioch was handed over to the Franks. If he had persevered, he would have shared in the joy of this. But instead it became a reproach for him. For to start well is of no use to anyone, unless he also ends well.

The betrayal of Antioch, 1098

Writing about a century later, the Arab historian Ibn al-Athir gives more details about the fall of Antioch to the crusaders, including an incident which provides evidence of treachery. Only its citadel remained in Muslim hands.

The siege of Antioch lasted nine months. Yaghi Siyan, emir of Antioch, displayed unprecedented bravery, presence of mind, wisdom and activity; consequently most of the Franks died there. Yaghi Siyan did not fail to provide for the needs of the families of the Christian men whom he had forced to leave the town, and he prevented those – who would otherwise have been tempted – from doing them wrong. Finally, despite these precautions, the Franks came to an agreement with the commander of one of Antioch's towers, a breastplate-maker called Firouz: they promised him silver and considerable wealth if he would betray the city to them.

The tower which he commanded overlooked the valley; its gates were opened, and a large number of Franks managed to get in by using ropes. When they numbered over fivehundred they began to sound their trumpets.

It was dawn and the garrison was tired out by constant work and vigils.

Yaghi Siyan woke up and asked what all the noise was. His men told him that the trumpet calls were coming from the citadel, which must therefore have been occupied by the enemy. Now the noise was not coming from the citadel but from the tower; nevertheless, Yaghi Siyan was seized with fear and, giving orders for one of the town gates to be opened, he fled, accompanied only by thirty attendants. Meanwhile, his second-in-command had come to consult him on what measures they should take in defence; when he learned that Yaghi Siyan had fled, this man left the town by another gate and ran away himself. This was very fortuitous for the Franks; had Yaghi Siyan held out only for an hour, they would have been unable to take control of the town.

As it was, the Frankish army entered through the open gate, ransacked the town and killed any Muslims that they came across. The capture of Antioch took place in the month of June, 1098.

Albert of Aachen gives a graphic description of Yaghi Siyan's subsequent death.

While Yaghi Siyan, the fleeing emir of Antioch, was wandering alone in the mountains, some Syrians, men of the Christian faith, who were travelling through the mountain regions for supplies, saw him from a long way off and recognized him, and they wondered a great deal why he had turned aside alone from the fortress of the citadel into such out-of-the-way places.

And so the travellers said to one another: 'Look, our lord and king Yaghi Siyan is not journeying through these mountain wildernesses without reason: perhaps the city has been captured and his men killed; he himself is certainly intent on flight. So that he may not escape our hands, let us remember who has inflicted on us so many losses, injustices and sharp practices.'

Although the three Syrians were plotting Yaghi Siyan's death, they hid their feelings and showed him false reverence with heads bowed, greeting him deceitfully; then, coming close to him, they seized and drew his own sword and threw him down from his mule, cutting off his head and putting it in their bag. They soon took it into the city of Antioch, into the view of all the Christians and princes. The head was of enormous size, the ears very wide and hairy. His hair was white and he had a very long beard which flowed from his chin to his navel.

How crusaders paid their way

Although pilgrims to Jerusalem faced a long, arduous and costly journey, this did not deter peasants, the poor, townspeople and other less prosperous crusaders from answering Pope Urban II's call for an armed pilgrimage to the Holy City. Many of them must have set out with the hope that when they exhausted their meagre supplies God would furnish them with the means for survival: alms from the faithful and booty from the infidel. The pogroms and plundering that marked the advance of various contingents of the People's Crusade were partly because substantial numbers of these poorer pilgrims were anxious to obtain funds and provisions that would enable them to continue their march.

A knight who took the cross had to make more careful preparations for the expedition: for the maintenance of arms, horses, servants and pack animals, he could need up to four times his regular income. To raise these large sums, a few knights levied taxes on their dependants and others conceded contested rights in exchange for monetary payments. But the most lucrative and the most common way of raising money was the mortgage or sale of lands.

To take a single example, the knight Achard of Montmerle secured a loan of 2,000 shillings in the money of Lyons and four mules from the abbey of Cluny, in return for a pledge of some properties that only he could redeem, and that would pass to the abbey if he did not return from the crusade or died without heirs. As frequently happened, members of his family sacrificed rights in the property involved to enable him to perform the pilgrimage. Landless knights, often thought to have made up a large proportion of the crusading forces, would have found it difficult to take part unless they were in the service of their richer fellows.

Leaders of the crusade, who had to support retinues of soldiers, chaplains and servants, assist poorer pilgrims and contribute to the general expenses of the crusading army, needed to accumulate even more money before departing for Jerusalem. Their techniques for raising funds, although on a grander scale, were no different from those resorted to by the ordinary knights. Robert, duke of Normandy, for example, pledged the duchy to his brother, William Rufus, king of England, in return for a three-year loan of 10,000 marks of silver.

The crusaders had barely installed themselves in Antioch when a Muslim relief force under Kerbogha, the Turkish ruler of Mosul, arrived, together with further forces under Duqaq of Damascus. On 7 June 1098, this great army installed itself in the very place which the crusading forces had occupied during the previous nine months. Raymond of Aguilers, the chaplain of Raymond of Toulouse, tells of the hardships which afflicted the now besieged crusaders.

Once Kerbogha's army had arrived, there was such a famine in the city that the head of a horse without the tongue would be sold for two or three sous, the innards of a goat for five sous, a hen for eight or nine sous. As to bread I can only say that five sous would not be enough to offset the hunger of one person. Many knights lived on the blood of their horses, since in hope of God's mercy they did not want to kill them yet.

One day, at around noon, about three hundred Turks climbed one of our towers. Our people were able to repulse them, for in this time of danger they strove with God as their aid; they managed to kill some and cause others to fall. In response to this event everyone promised obedience to Bohemund until the fifteenth day after the battle, so that he could make arrangements for the defence of the city and the management of the war.

The beleaguered crusaders pinned their hopes of rescue on Stephen of Blois; but, as the *Gesta Francorum* relates, he proved a broken reed.

The foolish Stephen of Blois, who had been chosen by all the leaders as commander-in-chief, had pretended to be laid low by a serious illness just before the capture of Antioch, and had withdrawn shamefully to Alexandretta. We, who were shut up in the city of Antioch lacking any help to save us, waited for him day after day to come to our aid. But when he heard that the Turkish army was surrounding us and besieging us, he secretly climbed a nearby mountain which was close to Antioch, and saw the immense camp; and was seized with a violent fear, and fled quickly with his army.

He returned to his camp and practically pillaged it, and took the road back home at top speed. When he came across the Emperor Alexius at Philomelium, he took him aside in secret, and said: 'You should know that Antioch has been captured, though the citadel has not been captured yet; all our men are under a state of heavy siege, and I think by now they have been killed by the Turks. So go back home as fast as you can, in case they find you and your army.'

On 27 June, the leaders of the crusade sent envoys to negotiate with Kerbogha – an embassy which failed.

Bohemund and the other Christian leaders chose Peter the Hermit and a Frank called Herluin, and told them: 'Go to the accursed army of the Turks, and ask them why they have so boldly and arrogantly entered the land that belongs to the native Christians and to us.'

When that had been said, the messengers Peter and Herluin went off and came to the unholy company, giving all of the message to Kerbogha and to the others, as follows: 'Our leaders and commanders are amazed – utterly amazed – that you have entered so boldly and arrogantly the land that belongs to the Christians and to themselves. We suppose that perhaps you have come here because you wish at all costs to become Christians; or have you come here in order to afflict the Christians at all costs?

All of our leaders together ask you to withdraw at once from the land of God and the Christians, which the blessed apostle Peter long ago converted by his preaching to the worship of Christ. But they will allow you to take away all your belongings with you.'

Then Kerbogha, the leader of the army of the sultan of the Turks, and all the others, full of arrogance replied fiercely: 'We do not choose or want your God or your Christianity, and we spit them out, and you too. We have come this far because we are amazed at those leaders and commanders you mention, and wonder why land which we captured from an effeminate people they are now claiming as their own.

Do you want to know what we say to you? Return quickly and tell your leaders that if they wish at all costs to become Turks, and are willing to deny the God whom you worship on bended knee, and to cast aside your laws, we will give them this land and plenty more, and cities and castles in such abundance that none of your men will stay foot-soldiers, but will all be knights like us; and we will always consider them the greatest of friends. But if not, let them know that they shall pay the penalty of death, or shall be led in chains to Khorasan [north-eastern Persia], where in perpetual captivity they will serve us and our children for ever.'

Our messengers returned quickly, reporting all the things that the cruel race had replied to them. It is said that Herluin was an interpreter for Peter the Hermit. Meanwhile our army was in a state of panic on two counts, and did not know what to do. On the one hand an excruciating hunger was oppressing them, and on the other was their fear of the Turks.

The miracle of the Holy Lance

At the lowest ebb of their fortunes, the crusaders were heartened by the discovery of the Holy Lance, allegedly used to pierce Christ's side at the crucifixion. The crusader Radulph of Caen – he went to the Holy Land in 1108 – describes 'visions' which enabled a man called Peter Bartholomew to find the Lance.

I n Antioch discord flourished. For while the besieged people were afflicted by the famine, there arose from among Count Raymond's people one Peter Bartholomew, skilled in lies and inventions. He preached the salvation of the people as revealed to him in this way:

'The blessed apostle Andrew appeared to me while I was half asleep and gave me these instructions. "Get up and announce to the struggling people that a source of consolation has fallen from heaven for them, through the finding of the lance which opened the side of our Lord. It lies hidden beneath the earth within the church of St Peter. You must take up the floor right here (and he showed the place); there if you dig you will find the weapon. When the clash of arms threatens, raise it up against your foes, and in it you will conquer."

Jolting awake, I thought I had been deceived by a dream. I did not make it known but kept completely silent, until I had been warned a second time. I spent the whole day and most of the night in prayer and fasting, asking a third visitation

The Holy Lance, borne in battle outside Antioch by Adhemar, bishop of Le Puy (at left, wearing a mitre). Whether genuine or not, it inspired the crusaders in battle.

from God, if the first two had been from him. Twice the cock had heralded the dawn, when, just before it crowed the third time, sleep bound my tired limbs. Straightaway, a third visitation occurred, still more terrible and insistent. "Come on, get up, you lazy mute dog, delayer of salvation, procrastinator of triumph, cause of loss for the citizens and of solace for the enemy. You feared when there was nothing to fear: when there is, you do not fear." These threats and insults remained in my mind when in my terror I pulled myself out of both threat and sleep. I was shaking and sweating by turns; a fire burned one side of me, while the other was hard with cold. Therefore I came to tell you what I have told you. But you, fathers and brothers, do not delay to find out the truth of the matter. It remains only for me to show you the place, and for you to dig.'

When Raymond of Toulouse heard a rumour of this, he called a meeting, and Peter was summoned to the church of St Peter. When he was asked for the place, he indicated that it was behind the altar, for so he had invented it, and he advised them to dig. He even composed his features so as to command credence. They dug, but to no avail. But Peter secretly had with him an Arab spear, which he had found by chance and had kept as useful material for deception. Seeing that it was rusty, eroded, old and different from what we were used to both in appearance and in size, he judged that with this, credence would be given to his imaginings. Therefore, when a convenient moment arose for his deception, seizing his mattock he jumped into the ditch and turned to the corner, saying, 'Dig here. Here lies what we seek. Here is where it will come out.' Then striking blow after blow he fraudulently slipped the lance down from himself as he dug.

At the sound of iron striking iron, the ears of simple people pricked up, and the weaver of lies raised up the lance and filled them with these words: 'See, see what heaven promised, earth preserved, the apostle revealed and the prayers of a contrite people obtained.'

Raymond of Aguilers, who was chaplain to Raymond of Toulouse, gives a more sympathetic account of the discovery and authenticity of the relic.

At that time there were many revelations to our brothers, and we saw a miraculous sign in the heavens. A very great star stood all night above Antioch, and then divided into three parts and fell on the Turkish camp. Our people were comforted by this for a little while. Then, on 15 June 1098, having made the necessary preparations, twelve of us went to the church of St Peter with the man who had told the story of the lance. When everyone else had left the church, we began to

dig. Among the twelve present were the bishop of Orange, Count Raymond's chaplain, who wrote this history, and the count himself. We dug from morning to evening, by which time some began to despair of finding the lance. The count had left to guard the fort. But in the place of him and those who were tired of digging we brought in others who were fresh and who set to the task with a will.

When the young man who had spoken of the lance saw that we were tiring, he disrobed and removed his shoes and, dressed only in a shirt, went down into the pit. There he implored us to pray to God to give us the lance, for the strengthening and the victory of his people. At last, thanks to his piety, God showed us his lance. As the weapon appeared above ground, I kissed it. I cannot express the joy and exultation which filled the city then. The lance was found on 14 June 1098.

Radulph of Caen notes the advantages which accrued to Peter Bartholomew and Raymond, count of Toulouse, once the lance was found.

The people led the lance in procession with hymns and songs, loading Peter with gifts and rolling him in gold and fine clothes. Raymond of Toulouse and those who favoured him did this by design; but the crude simplicity of other sections of our people devoted itself to making offerings. Before the subsequent victory this was done eagerly, but after the victory much more so, as if the triumph were to be ascribed to the fact that the lance was carried into the battle; for this was the story shouted around by the people of Provence. Therefore Raymond's coffers were increased, his spirits were raised and his army grew proud. Others among the leaders favoured him, that is, those whom he had flattered and fawned upon.

But Bohemund, who was no fool, scrutinized the matter carefully: some dreamer had entangled the people in a web of confusion, had indicated the place to the diggers so that he himself could jump in, dig, and find. As soon as he had discovered the trick, he used clever conjectures to falsify the invention and the inventor. 'It is a fine story for blessed Andrew to have appeared to a man who, so I hear, frequents taverns, runs through market-places, loves all manner of trifles, and seems born to be hanged at the crossroads. The holy apostle chose an honourable person to whom to open the secrets of heaven! Let the cupidinous count Raymond and his foolish crowd assign the victory to the lance: but we, in the name of Jesus Christ our Lord and God, have conquered and will conquer.' So spoke Bohemund, and those who were men of judgement.

Cannibalism at Ma'arra

Some of the poorest people in the crusading army always marched barefoot, bore no arms, themselves had absolutely no money; but, entirely filthy in their nakedness and want, marched in advance of all the others, and lived on roots of plants.

There was a certain man of Norman birth, and of not

Cannibalism was more often rumoured than actually practised (as here by Mongols).

low station in life, so they say, who started as a knight but became a foot-soldier; he saw that these men were wandering about without a lord, so he laid down his weapons and clothes, and volunteered to be their king. From then on he was called King Tafur in the barbarian language. For these men were called Tafur by the infidels whom we, if I may speak more colloquially, call Trudennes or tramps: they are so called because they tramp, that is, they do things in a carefree way, travelling hither and thither throughout the years.

When at Ma'arra – and wherever else – scraps of flesh from the pagans' bodies were discovered; when starvation forced our soldiers to the deed of cannibalism (which is known to have been carried out by the Franks only in secret and as rarely as possible), a hideous rumour spread among the infidel: that there were men in the Frankish army who fed very greedily on the bodies of Saracens. When they heard this the Tafurs, in order to impress the enemy, roasted the bruised body of a Turk over a fire as if it were meat for eating, in full view of the Turkish forces.

From Guibert of Nogent, *Historia Hierosolymitana*

Despite doubts as to the authenticity of the Holy Lance, it inspired the crusaders to victory over Kerbogha, as a letter from the leaders of the Christian army to Pope Urban II explains.

On 2 July 1098, when the siege by the Turks had lasted for three weeks and four days, we went out with all our equipment of war, seeking the city gates. After firmly ordering our battle-lines, of both foot and horse, we boldly sought the place where their valour and bravery were greatest. The Holy Lance was with us, and from the very first engagement of the battle we forced the enemy to flee.

According to their custom, they began to scatter in all directions, hoping that, by occupying the hills and making for the roads wherever they could, they would be able to encircle us and so slaughter us all. But we had learned in our many wars with them about their clever tricks, and the grace and mercy of God came to our aid, so that we, who were very few compared with them, still managed, for the right hand of God fought with us, to drive them together and to force them to flee, leaving their camp and all its contents.

Bohemund of Antioch received the citadel and a thousand Muslim men, and so our Lord Jesus Christ transferred the whole city of Antioch to the Roman religion and faith.

From Antioch to Jerusalem

To allow the army to recover after its tribulations, Raymond of Toulouse and the other leaders set a date of 1 November 1098 for the departure for Jerusalem. Fulcher of Chartres describes the early stages of the army's progress south, under the leadership of Bohemund and Raymond of Toulouse.

When we had been at Antioch for four months, and our men and horses, exhausted by their long labour, had regained their strength through rest and food, part of the army took counsel and decided to go to inner Syria, desiring to take the road to Jerusalem.

Bohemund and Count Raymond of Toulouse were the most important men in this group; the other leaders remained in the area of Antioch, but these two left Antioch on 1 November 1098 with their followers, and very quickly captured the city of Banias; they slaughtered all its citizens and seized everything they found in it. Then they hurried off to Ma'arra and besieged it.

But after twenty days, our people suffered a severe

Frankish medicine

Although physicians travelled with the crusading armies, the sparseness of references to them in contemporary chronicles suggests that when faced with patients suffering from wounds, hunger, exhaustion, or epidemics, as at Antioch in 1098, they were largely ineffectual.

The superior medical skills of Arab physicians were recognized by both sides. The Arab anecdotalist Usama describes with disgust two examples of Frankish medicine. A knight with an abscess on his leg was being treated with a poultice by an Arab physician when his Frankish counterpart intervened and insisted on amputating with an axe. The patient died. A female imbecile who was being treated by an Arab doctor according to humoral theory was taken by a Frankish physician to be a case of diabolical possession. He shaved her head, exposed the bone of her skull and rubbed salt on it. She also died.

Usama also describes two cases where Frankish treatment was successful. One was a knight with 14 wounds on his leg: the doctor washed it in strong vinegar (an antiseptic) and the man recovered. The other was a boy with scrofula, for which the Frank prescribed an ointment made of burnt glasswort, oil and vinegar. Usama was so impressed by this cure that he often used it himself.

By the 1160s, as William of Tyre observes, 'the Latin leaders, urged by their womenfolk, scorned Latin medicine and only trusted the Jews, Samaritans, Syrians and Saracens'. The laws of the kingdom of Jerusalem, a little later, provided for the licensing of doctors: Arabs and Franks were tested before the local bishop on exactly the same terms.

The Arabs had well-organized hospitals (Nur ad-Din built a famous one in Damascus), an idea which the crusaders imitated, notably in the great hospital in Jerusalem run by the Knights of St John. It had beds for 2,000 patients, divided into wards. Four doctors and four surgeons were employed. There were detailed regulations for the care of the sick, including diet. Nevertheless, John of Würzburg, writing in the 1170s, reports that 50 patients died there each day.

Amalric I of Jerusalem brought a physician from Egypt in the vain hope of curing his son's leprosy. When he himself succumbed to dysentery in 1174, Greek and Syrian doctors considered he was too weak for bleeding and purging, but the Frankish doctor prevailed and, fatally weakened, Amalric died at the age of 38.

famine. I shudder to speak of it: our people were so frenzied by hunger that they tore flesh from the buttocks of the Saracens who had died there, which they cooked and chewed and devoured with savage mouths, even when it had been roasted insufficiently on the fire. And so the besiegers were more harmed than the besieged. Meanwhile they made siege-engines as well as they could and brought them up to the walls. Then in an assault of great audacity, with God's support, the Franks succeeded in getting themselves in over the top of the wall. On that day and the next they killed all the Saracens from the greatest to the least and seized all their wealth.

When the city had been destroyed in this way, Bohemund returned to Antioch. There he turned out the men of Count Raymond of Toulouse whom the latter had stationed to guard his share. Bohemund thus possessed the city and the whole province.

Bohemund's seizure of Antioch annoyed not only the other crusading leaders, but also the Emperor Alexius, as Raymond of Aguilers relates.

In the spring of 1099 a delegation came to the crusader army from the Emperor Alexius, bearing bitter complaints against Bohemund, because he had retained the city in defiance of the oath of allegiance which he had sworn to the emperor. Bohemund was indeed holding Antioch at the time; for when he heard that Raymond of Toulouse had left Ma'arra for Syria, he violently expelled the count's men from those towers in Antioch which they had been guarding. Alexius also promised to give much gold and silver to our other leaders, and said that he would come to them in Jerusalem. They should wait for him until midsummer 1099. It was then almost Easter.

Fulcher charts the progress of the great army through Syria and Palestine in 1099 as it continued its journey towards Jerusalem.

Raymond of Toulouse, together with Tancred, continued the journey he had begun, and Duke Robert of Normandy joined the army on the day following their departure from Ma'arra. On 13 January 1099 they set out for the fort of Arga, which lies at the base of Mount Lebanon and which was founded, so it is written, by Aracaeus, son of Canaan and grandson of Noah. But since it is very difficult to take, the siege struggled on for about five weeks until they went away having

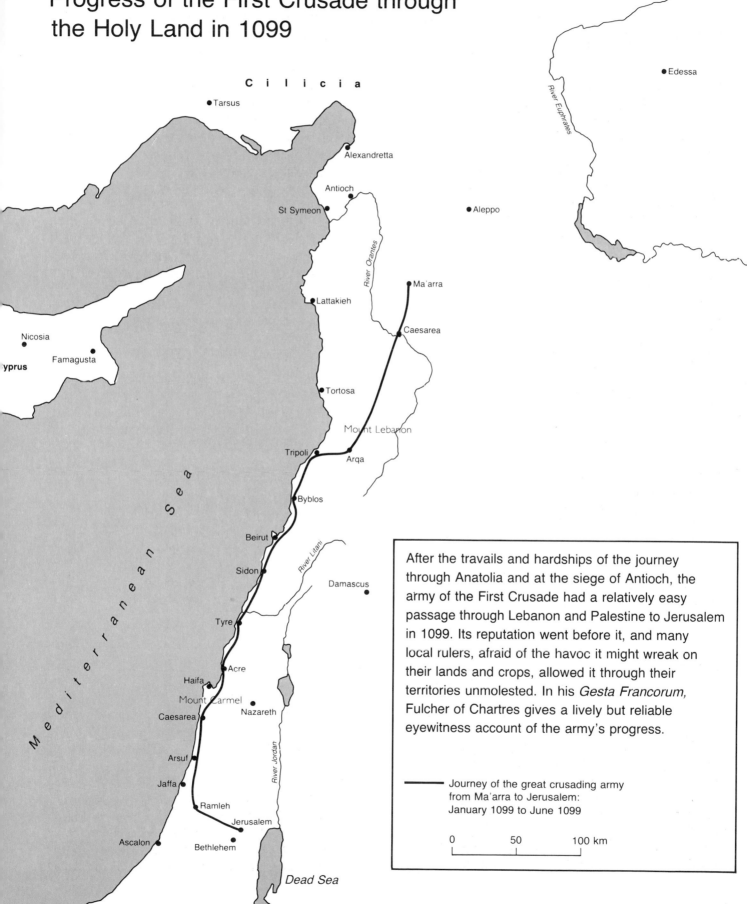

Progress of the First Crusade through the Holy Land in 1099

C i l i c i a

• Tarsus

• Alexandretta

Antioch

St Symeon •

Nicosia
•

Famagusta
•

yprus

River Orontes

• Lattakieh

• Aleppo

• Ma'arra

• Caesarea

• Tortosa

Mount Lebanon

Tripoli • Arqa

• Byblos

M e d i t e r r a n e a n   S e a

Beirut

Sidon

River Litani

Damascus
•

Tyre

Acre
Haifa
Mount Carmel

Caesarea

Nazareth

River Jordan

Arsuf

Jaffa

Ramleh

Jerusalem

Ascalon

Bethlehem

Dead Sea

• Edessa

River Euphrates

After the travails and hardships of the journey through Anatolia and at the siege of Antioch, the army of the First Crusade had a relatively easy passage through Lebanon and Palestine to Jerusalem in 1099. Its reputation went before it, and many local rulers, afraid of the havoc it might wreak on their lands and crops, allowed it through their territories unmolested. In his *Gesta Francorum,* Fulcher of Chartres gives a lively but reliable eyewitness account of the army's progress.

――――― Journey of the great crusading army
from Ma'arra to Jerusalem:
January 1099 to June 1099

0   50   100 km

achieved nothing. Godfrey of Bouillon and Count Robert of Flanders followed the army not much later.

They passed the city of Tripoli on the coast of Lebanon [on 16 May]. Progressing further south, they passed Beirut and came to another city, which we read of as Sidon in the land of Phoenicia. Continuing from there they found the wonderful city of Tyre, and then went on south again, towards Ptolemais, or Acre, standing to the north of Mount Carmel. Passing this by, they left the town of Haifa on their right hand, and then came to Dora and to Caesarea of Palestine, which in antiquity was called the Tower of Strato. Here Herod Agrippa, the grandson of the Herod in whose time Christ was born, was eaten by worms and died miserably. Then they passed on their right the port and town of Arsuf, and then went through the city called Ramleh from which the Saracen inhabitants fled on the day before the Franks arrived. There they found a great deal of food.

In fact the army delayed in Ramleh for four days, and installed a bishop in the church of St George and placed a garrison in the citadels of the city. Then on 6 June 1099 they resumed their journey to Jerusalem. That day, they walked to the fort called Imwas, next to the city of the Maccabees.

That night a hundred of the more noble knights mounted their horses and, passing near Jerusalem as dawn was breaking, hurried to Bethlehem: Tancred was among them, as was Baldwin. When the Christians who lived there, that is, Greeks and Syrians, realized that the Franks had come, they rejoiced greatly. For at first they did not know what people it was who were coming, and thought they were Turks or Arabs. But when they were able to get a close view of them, and no longer doubted that they were Franks, they joyfully raised up their crosses and their banners and came out to meet them, weeping and singing holy songs. There the Franks prayed to God in the basilica of our blessed Lady, visited the place where Christ was born, gave the kiss of peace to the Syrians, and quickly returned to the holy city of Jerusalem. When they approached the city, the standard-bearers showed their raised signs to the citizens, and straightaway the enemy within the city came out to meet them. But those who had hurried out were soon hurried back into the city.

The siege of Jerusalem, 1099

On 7 June the crusader army camped outside Jerusalem, one of the strongest cities in the world. An attempt to storm the walls on 13 June failed, and the army, tortured by thirst in the baking heat as the *Gesta Francorum* relates, settled in to a hard siege.

During the siege we were so oppressed by thirst that we sewed together the hides of oxen and buffalo, which we used to carry water over a distance of about six miles. Because of the vile-smelling water from these vessels and the barley bread, we were in daily distress and affliction, for the Saracens used to lie in wait around the springs and water sources, and would ambush our men, kill them and cut them to pieces, and would also lead off our animals into their own caves and hideouts. We were so distressed by thirst that even for one penny a single man could not buy enough water to quench his thirst.

Then our commanders made arrangements for Jerusalem to be captured with siege-engines, so that our men could enter to worship at the church of the Holy Sepulchre. They made two wooden siege-towers, and many other devices. Godfrey of Bouillon made his own siege-tower with machines in it, and so too did Raymond of Toulouse; the wood for these things had to be dragged from a considerable distance away.

The Saracens inside the city, seeing that our men were making these devices, made remarkable improvements in its fortifications and had the towers nightly increased in height. When our leaders saw which part of the city was the weakest, one Saturday night they brought a wooden siege-tower and a machine up to the eastern side. At the break of dawn they erected them, fitted out the siege-tower and equipped it on Sunday, Monday and Tuesday. Raymond of Toulouse was putting up his own machine on the southern side.

In order to build the siege-towers, the crusaders needed wood. Radulph of Caen describes a near-miracle whereby his lord, Tancred, while on a foraging party, discovered a load of timber in a cave.

The leaders decided to inspect all the hiding-places, to travel along all the paths and to all pathless places, to try to scrape together wood from everywhere for the siege-towers. Tancred was suffering from severe dysentery, but did not spare himself from riding out even though he could barely stay on his horse. This nuisance kept on forcing him to dismount, go away from the group and find a hiding-place. He had been troubled by this many times and he had almost decided to give up the search and return ingloriously when the accustomed trouble struck again. He began to feel weighed down so he pulled away from the others and dismounted. He hoped that by dismounting he would be able to avoid the gaze of his companions, but on looking back he saw that he had not done so.

He therefore sought concealment further away, but again he could see a few men wandering about, so he changed his position a third and a fourth time, until in a deep recess beneath a hollow rock, surrounded by trees and bristling shade he found peace. Good gracious! Who but God? He it was who brought forth water from a rock, speech from an ass, creation from nothing. He it was who healed the army through the illness of one knight, who brought strength out of weakness, and from a vile affliction made a remedy more precious than gold. For while Tancred was relieving himself there, he faced a cave in the rock opposite, where four hundred timbers lay open to view.

Hardly believing his eyes at this sight (such was his joy), he jumped up and went forward, his heart pounding, to inspect them. 'Hey! Companions! Come here quickly!' he shouted. 'Here, here,' he repeated, 'look, God has given us more than we sought. We sought plain wood, but we have found it ready prepared.' His companions came as soon as he called. Their grief was turned into joy; and Tancred hurriedly sent a messenger to bring comfort to the unhappy army. When the joyous news had spread through the people a voice of gladness and exultation was raised in the tents of the Franks, and they went forth to meet the foragers, singing as if in litany.

Raymond of Aguilers describes the making of the siege-engines for the assault on Jerusalem.

The duke and the counts of Normandy and Flanders placed Gaston of Béarn in charge of the workmen who were constructing the siege-engines and were making fascines and earthworks for invading the walls. In the same way Count Raymond placed William Embriaco in charge of his workmen on Mount Zion and the bishop of Albara in charge of the Saracens and others who were bringing wood. The count's men were making the Saracens work like their slaves. Fifty or sixty of them carried on their necks a huge beam, which four pairs of oxen could not bear.

What can I say? Everyone united to further the task, by labour, by construction and by generally helping. No one was lazy and no one slacked. Everyone worked voluntarily, except for the craftsmen, who were paid from a collection taken among the people. But Count Raymond paid his workmen from his own coffers.

The siege of Jerusalem by the crusaders. Siege-engines were so important in this assault that the Franks were forced to build them with the timbers of their own vessels.

The navel of the world

Jerusalem is the navel of the world, a land which is fruitful above all others, like another paradise of delights. The redeemer of the human race illuminated this land by his coming, graced it by his living there, made it holy by his suffering, redeemed it by his death, distinguished it by his burial. This royal city, set in the centre of the world, is now held captive by its enemies and is enslaved in heathen rite by people who do not know God. Therefore the city demands and desires to be set free, and calls upon you without ceasing to come to its assistance. Indeed Jerusalem requires your support in particular, because God has granted to you before all nations outstanding military glory, as we have already said. Therefore take this journey for the remission of your sins, certain of the unfading glory of the kingdom of heaven.

From Robert the Monk, *Historia Hierosolymitana*

Above: A medieval world map; Jerusalem at its hub.

Right: Jerusalem: navel of the world.

The holy city

The city of Jerusalem is situated in a mountainous place, lacking streams, woods and springs, with the sole exception of the spring at Siloam, which is a bow-shot from the town, in the bottom of the valley under Mount Zion. However, there are many cisterns in the city holding plentiful water, which are reserved for the rains of winter. Many are also found outside the city for the refreshment of men and of cattle.

This town offends no one by its smallness or largeness; on the inside from wall to wall it is four bow-shots wide. It has on the west side the Tower of David, forming on both sides part of the city wall; Mount Zion is to the south, a little less than a bow-shot away; to the east is the Mount of Olives, a mile distant from the city.

The church of the Holy Sepulchre is round in shape, and it has never been roofed over, but by means of an aperture devised by the masterly skill of a cunning architect it is always open to view from above.

There is in the same city the Temple of the Lord [the Dome of the Rock], a round structure, built where Solomon previously established a wonderful building, but though it may in no way be compared to that former plan, the present temple is yet of marvellous workmanship and very beautiful appearance.

I am unable, I dare not, I know not how to tell of the many things which are in the temple, some of them indeed still there, some already gone, lest I should fail in some particular those who are reading or hearing these things. In the middle of the temple when we first entered it, and after that for some fifteen years, there was a certain native rock kept there, in which, they said by divine inspiration, the ark of the covenant of the Lord had been sealed up with the urn and Moses' tablets.

They say that on this rock also, an angel of the Lord had stood and had destroyed the people, because of an enumeration made foolishly by David and displeasing to the Lord. However, because that rock disfigured the temple of the Lord it was afterwards covered up and paved over with marble, underneath where the altar is now and the priest performs the service. All the Saracens had held this temple of the Lord in great reverence, and used to say their prayers there according to their law more willingly than anywhere else, although they wasted them on an idol made in the name of Mohammed. Also they used to allow no Christian to enter the temple.

The streets of the city do not lack gutters through which all filth is washed away in winter.

Emperor Aelius Hadrianus adorned this city wonderfully and decorated its quarters and its streets fittingly with pavements. Jerusalem was called Aelia after his name. Because of these and other such things it is a glorious and venerated city.

From Fulcher of Chartres, *Historia Hierosolymitana*

The Genoese chronicler Caffaro, writing in about 1155, describes how the Genoese contingent, arriving to join the army, broke up its ships to provide extra wood.

After the city had been besieged for a month, two Genoese galleys arrived at Jaffa; but because they were afraid of the Saracens at Ascalon the Genoese were unable to keep the galleys there. So they destroyed the galleys, and they had all the wood from them carried to Jerusalem, as it was needed to make siege-engines for the capture of the city. The Christians, indeed, rejoicing greatly at the arrival of the Genoese, welcomed them with honour, and accepted them entirely into their council for the capture of the city.

By the middle of July the crusaders were ready for an all-out attack. The *Gesta Francorum* describes how the Franks at last reached their goal, when Jerusalem fell to them on 15 July.

Before we attacked Jerusalem, the bishops and priests preached to us, telling us to go in a procession in God's honour around Jerusalem, and pray and give alms and fast.

On Friday 15 July 1099, early in the morning, we attacked the city from all sides, but we could make no headway against it, and we were all numb with astonishment and very frightened. Godfrey of Bouillon and his brother, Baldwin, count of Boulogne, were fighting bravely in the siege-tower. Then one of our knights, Lethold by name, climbed up on to the wall of the city. As soon as he had climbed it, all the defenders of the city fled along the walls and through the city, and our men, following Lethold, chased after them, killing them and dismembering them as far as the Temple of Solomon. And in that place there was such slaughter that we were up to our ankles in their blood.

Count Raymond of Toulouse led his army and a siege-tower from the south close up to the wall. But then the emir who was in David's Tower surrendered to the count, and opened up for him the gate where the pilgrims used to pay their taxes.

Our pilgrims entered the city, and chased the Saracens, killing as they went, as far as the Temple of Solomon. There the enemy assembled, and fought a furious battle for the whole day, so that their blood flowed all over the Temple. At last the pagans were overcome, and our men captured a good number of men and women in the Temple; they killed whomsoever they wished, and chose to keep others alive.

Soon our army overran the whole city, seizing gold and silver, horses and mules, and houses full of riches of all kinds.

All our men came rejoicing and weeping for joy, to worship at the church of the Holy Sepulchre.

In the morning our men climbed up cautiously on to the roof of the Temple and attacked the Saracens, both male and female, and beheaded them with unsheathed swords. The other Saracens threw themselves from the Temple.

Then our men held a council, and gave out that everyone should give alms and pray that God would choose whom he wished to reign over the others and rule the city. They further gave orders that all the dead Saracens should be cast out on account of the terrible stench; because nearly the whole city was crammed with their bodies. The Saracens who were still alive dragged the dead ones out in front of the gates, and made huge piles of them, as big as houses. Such a slaughter of pagans no one has ever seen or heard of; the pyres they made were like pyramids. Raymond of Toulouse had the emir and the others with him brought to him at Ascalon, safe and unharmed.

Jerusalem was captured by the Christians on Friday 15 July. On the eighth day after the city was captured, they chose Godfrey of Bouillon as ruler of the city [advocate of the Holy Sepulchre], to subdue the pagans and protect the Christians. So too they chose as patriarch that wise and noble man by the name of Arnulf, on 1 August 1099.

A letter from the leaders of the crusade to the pope, written in September 1099, records the capture of the city, and the defeat at Ascalon of a relief force under the leadership of al-Afdal, vizier of the Fatimid Shi'ite caliph of Cairo.

A letter from Daimbert, archbishop of Pisa, papal legate, Godfrey of Bouillon, advocate of the Holy Sepulchre, and Raymond of Toulouse, and all the army in the land of Israel, to the pope and all the Christian faithful.

Since the army was suffering greatly in this siege from lack of water, a council was held, and the bishops and leaders preached the necessity of walking round the city with bare feet. The Lord was pleased with this act of humility, for on the eighth day after we performed it he handed over to us the city, together with his enemies. This was on 15 July 1099.

If you want to know what was done to the enemies we found in the city, know this: that in the portico of Solomon and in his Temple, our men rode in the blood of the Saracens up to the knees of their horses. Then we made arrangements as to who should hold the city. The others desired to return out of love of home and piety towards their parents. But then the news came that al-Afdal, vizier of Cairo, had come to Ascalon with a multitude of pagans, to take captive the

Godfrey of Bouillon

Born c.1060, Godfrey was the son of Count Eustace II of Boulogne and the saintly Ida, daughter of Godfrey the Bearded, count of Verdun. As a second son, excluded from his paternal inheritance, he was groomed as heir to Ida's childless brother. In 1076 he succeeded to a collection of territories scattered along the valley of the Meuse, centred on the great castle of Bouillon in the Ardennes forest. By 1095, when Urban II called for the First Crusade, Godfrey had spent most of his adult life fighting to preserve this inheritance and attempting to assert his authority as duke of Lower Lorraine.

The crusade therefore represented a new opportunity for Godfrey, and in August 1096 he set off at the head of an army of French and German-speaking Lorrains, many of them his own kinsmen. Financed by the sale or mortgage of his ancestral lands and by levying protection money from the Jewish communities of the Rhineland, he was able to pay for the support of many poorer crusaders. As a result, when Jerusalem fell to the Franks in 1099, Godfrey was the obvious candidate to become its ruler; in addition, most other princes had founded principalities of their own, or were resolved to return to Europe. After his election he preferred to be known as 'advocate of the Holy Sepulchre' or simply 'Prince', shrewdly sidestepping a rival's objection that no one should be called king and wear a crown where Christ had worn a crown of thorns.

The departure of the majority of pilgrims left Godfrey with a mere 300 knights and 2,000 foot-soldiers, and none of the sea power which would be needed to blockade the Muslim cities of the coast. The fleet was provided by the newly arrived Daimbert, archbishop of Pisa, whose price for the alliance was the patriarchate of Jerusalem. Daimbert's ultimate vision, however, was an ecclesiastical state headed by himself, which Godfrey attempted to stave off with concessions of territory – to be implemented in the future. Just before his untimely death in 1100, he established a counterweight to the patriarch through an alliance with the Venetians.

Courageous, astute, ruthless, and more zealous than devout, Godfrey was far removed from the pious paragon of Christian chivalry that legend made him. His one-year reign was an untiring struggle to ensure the survival of the infant Christian state, an achievement upon which his brother Baldwin built the kingdom of Jerusalem.

Franks who were in Jerusalem, and to capture Antioch: so he claimed but the Lord had decided otherwise.

When we had found out for certain that al-Afdal's army was at Ascalon, we set out to meet them, leaving our baggage and our sick with a garrison in Jerusalem. When the two armies caught sight of each other, we knelt and called on God our helper.

In our army there were not more than five thousand cavalry and fifteen thousand infantry, while the enemy could have had a hundred thousand horse and four hundred thousand foot. Then God's doing was marvellous in the eyes of his servants, since, before we entered the conflict, by our charge alone we drove this multitude to flight and tore away all their weapons, so that even if they wanted to fight back they lacked the equipment in which they trusted. More than one hundred thousand Saracens fell there by the sword, but their fear was such that at the gate of the city of Ascalon around two thousand were suffocated in the crush. Countless more died in the sea; thorn-bushes caught many. The world itself clearly fought for us, and had not the spoils of the camp detained many of our people, there would have been very few enemy left.

On the day before the battle the army captured many thousands of camels and cattle and sheep. And when at the princes' command the people let them go, because they were going to fight, wonderful to relate, the camels formed many and multiple squadrons, and the cattle and sheep likewise. Moreover these animals marched in company with us, so that when we halted they halted, when we advanced they advanced, when we charged they charged. Also clouds protected us from the heat of the sun and cooled us down.

This battle took place on 29 July 1099 at Ascalon against al-Afdal. A hundred thousand Egyptian horse and forty thousand foot were conquered by a small army of Christians. Thanks be to God. Here the letter ends.

The death of Godfrey

Godfrey of Bouillon ruled for only one year, during which he struggled to subdue the coastal towns. In 1100 the emir of Caesarea agreed to pay him tribute and invited him to a banquet. A month later, Godfrey died, probably of disease. But Matthew of Edessa, an Armenian chronicler, thought otherwise.

In 1100, Godfrey, leader of the Franks, came with his army to Caesarea of Philippi, a town on the Mediterranean coast. The Muslim leaders went to meet him on the pretext of making peace; they bought supplies and served them in his presence. Godfrey accepted and unsuspectingly ate the dishes they presented, which were poisoned. He died several days later along with forty other people.

Godfrey was buried in Jerusalem, the place of his death, on the hill which is called Golgotha.

Radulph of Caen describes Godfrey's death
in more detail.

One year passed from the beginning of Godfrey's reign to his death. During his fatal illness, he ordered Daimbert of Pisa, who was now patriarch of Jerusalem, and others to be summoned and said to them: 'Listen, I am going on the road to the eternal land. Now, therefore, while I live, let a council be held among you to decide who ought to rule Jerusalem in my stead.' But they replied, 'We would rather put this in your charge. We undertake to be subject to whomever you choose.' So he said, 'If the decision rests with me, I judge my brother Baldwin of Boulogne, count of Edessa, suited to take up this high calling.'

On hearing him name Baldwin, they all earnestly agreed and praised the choice, swearing loyalty to him since they knew him to be liberal with his money, knowledgeable in military matters, modest in address, noble and magnanimous. He had been made count of Edessa and was staying there at that time.

The first Latin kingdom of Jerusalem

After some debate the crusaders agreed with
Godfrey's nomination; Fulcher of Chartres shows that,
unlike his brother, Baldwin was crowned king.

On Christmas Day, in the year of our Lord 1100, in the church of our blessed Lady at Bethlehem, Baldwin was crowned king of Jerusalem. He was anointed king with holy oil, with all due honour, by the patriarch Daimbert in the presence of the bishops, priests and people. They had not done this to his elder brother Godfrey [who had been styled advocate of the Holy Sepulchre], both because he did not wish it and because his assumption of the throne would not have found favour with certain people at that time; but the crusaders decided, on careful consideration, to crown Baldwin king.

Godfrey of Bouillon, one of the greatest crusaders, leading his men. After death he became a near-mythical figure: hero of the poet Tasso's crusading epic *Gerusalemme Liberata*.

Meanwhile, in September 1100, Bohemund of Taranto, prince of Antioch, had been captured by a local Muslim prince, Malik Ghazi the Danishmend.

Bohemund first arrived at Antioch [early in 1100], where he was welcomed joyfully by his men, and ruled his land for six months. But when, in the following July, he was on his way with a few of his men to the city called Malatya (which was going to be delivered to him in accordance with a treaty of mutual friendship already made through ambassadors), a certain emir called Malik Ghazi the Danishmend intercepted Bohemund with a great horde of Turks, as he travelled unawares. Not far from Malatya that wicked horde, lurking in ambush, sprang upon Bohemund from all sides. Our men did not dare join battle because they were few in number; instead they at once took flight and scattered. The Turks killed many of them and took all their money, seized Bohemund and took him off into captivity.

When this unfortunate event was made known by the men who had escaped, great desolation spread among our people. Nevertheless, Duke Baldwin of Edessa assembled as many Franks as he could – Edessans, that is, and Antiochenes – and wasted no time in seeking out the enemy. Bohemund, for his part, cut a lock of hair from his head and sent it as an agreed signal to Duke Baldwin so that he would quickly come to his aid.

When Malik Ghazi the Danishmend heard of this, he became afraid and did not dare to linger before Malatya,

The coronation of Baldwin I, king of Jerusalem, on Christmas Day 1100. He defended his kingdom energetically despite a chronic shortage of Christian fighting men.

which he had surrounded and besieged. Fleeing before us, he succeeded in returning to his own lands. We were very sorry about this, since we pursued them for three days beyond Malatya, and would have fought against them with great goodwill.

When we had retraced our steps, the emir Gabriel, patron of Malatya, delivered the city to Baldwin. Once their alliance was thus sealed, and he had brought his own guards into the city, Baldwin returned to Edessa and the Antiochenes went back to their homes, sorrowing for their captive lord, Bohemund.

Bohemund was held prisoner until 1103, when he was ransomed by the other princes for 100,000 gold bezants. He returned home to Europe to raise a new crusading army which, however, he directed against Constantinople. He was defeated and at last, in 1108, Emperor Alexius forced him to do homage. Bohemund slunk back to Italy where he died in 1111.

Fulcher of Chartres goes on to recount the problems which afflicted the infant kingdom of Jerusalem, emphasizing in particular its lack of manpower.

At the start of his reign, Baldwin possessed only a few cities and people, but he energetically protected his kingdom on all sides during the whole winter. Since his enemies had discovered that he was a most noble knight, even though his people were few, they did not dare to attack him. Indeed, had he had a larger army, he would have gladly gone out to meet them.

At this stage, the road to Palestine by land was completely blocked by the Muslims to western foreigners, who from time to time therefore set sail and came across the sea as far as Jaffa, with the Lord leading them, in great fear as they passed between hostile pirates and before the Saracen cities. Franks and English, Italians and Venetians came, all together in one ship or in three or four. They came to Jaffa because at first this was the only port we had. When we saw these westerners arriving, straightaway we would joyfully run up to them as if to saints. Each of us would question them closely about our countries and families. They would give us the news as far as they knew it. We rejoiced at the prosperity we heard of and grieved at the troubles. They would go to Jerusalem and visit the Holy of Holies, for which they had come. Then some would remain in the Holy Land, while others would return to their homes. For this reason the land around Jerusalem remained rather empty of people, nor was there anyone who could defend it from the Saracens, if only they had dared to attack us.

But why did they not dare? So many people, so many king-doms, why did they fear to invade our little kingdom and handful of people? For we had no more than three hundred horse and as many foot to garrison Jerusalem, Jaffa, Ramleh and even Haifa. Moreover, we hardly dared to bring our knights together when we ambushed the enemy, lest by leaving our defences empty we should suffer losses in the mean time. Truly it was an amazing miracle that we lived at all among so many thousands of thousands, still more that we ruled some and made them pay tribute, and threw others into confusion by plundering them and taking them captive. But where did this valour come from? Whence this power? Indeed from him who is called the Almighty, who does not forget the people who labour for his name's sake.

What historic times! Often indeed we were sad, since we could not have aid from our friends across the sea; and we feared that our enemies would sometime realize the paucity of our number and suddenly attack us from all sides, when no one but God himself would be able to help us.

The crusade of 1101

To alleviate their manpower problems, the crusading leaders sent an appeal to the pope for a new crusade. Caffaro, the Genoese historian, describes the mission.

The Genoese, that is to say William Embriaco and his brother Primus, who in the summer of 1099 had brought two galleys to Jaffa, and had made from their wood the siege-engine with which the city of Jerusalem was captured; these brothers took an enormous quantity of gold and silver and jewels from the vizier of Cairo, when he was conquered by the Frankish army and lost his camp. These brothers, then, with all the money they had taken and one galley which they had bought, crossed the sea and returned to Genoa on Christmas Eve 1099. They took with them letters from Patriarch Daimbert and from Godfrey, lord of the kingdom of Jerusalem, concerning the capture of Jerusalem and the help that was needed.

When the Genoese read the letters they immediately put an end to the wars and disputes among themselves which were the result of a year and a half without a consulate and settled government. They laid down their weapons, and so many of them took the cross that they bravely assembled twenty-six galleys and four ships loaded with pilgrims at the port of Lattakieh, for the service of God and the Holy Sepulchre. Meanwhile the Genoese also sent the letters from Jerusalem throughout the cities and regions of Lombardy. As

a result the people of Lombardy, clerical and lay, Anselm, archbishop of Milan, and Albert, count of Biandrate, together with many counts and marquises, proceeded to Constanti-nople with a great army of knights and foot-soldiers.

Others went or returned to the east for a variety of reasons, among them Stephen of Blois. As Orderic Vitalis relates, his wife Adela nagged him, even in bed, until he went back to the Holy Land.

When the western nobles heard the good news about the famous champions who had set out on pilgrimage and tri-umphed gloriously over the infidels in the east, fighting in Christ's name, they and their relations and neighbours were inspired by the example of such achievement to a similar undertaking. Many were fired by enthusiasm to go on pil-grimage, to see the Saviour's sepulchre and the holy places.

Fear of the pope's curse also forced some to go on pilgrim-age: for Pope Paschal II [pope 1099–1118] had publicly excommunicated and cut off from all Christendom all those who had freely taken the cross of the Lord and come back without completing their journey, unless they retraced their steps and devotedly accomplished their vows.

Therefore in March 1101, William IX, duke of Aquitaine, assembled an enormous army from Aquitaine and Gascony, and set out cheerfully on that journey of holy pilgrimage. He was a bold and honest man and so merry he could beat even the wittiest stage-performers with his many jokes. Three hun-dred thousand men are said to have followed him.

Stephen also, count of Blois, was despised and shamed by almost everyone, because in 1098 he had disgracefully fled from the siege of Antioch and deserted his glorious comrades who were suffering in Christ's martyrdom. He was so often reproached, by so many people, that he was forced to rejoin Christ's army, as much from embarrassment as from fear. His wife Adela also frequently urged him to go, and between caresses of her loving husband she would say: 'Far be it from you, my lord, to deign to suffer the reproaches of such men for long. Recapture the famous vigour of your youth, and take up the weapons of the glorious army for the salvation of many thousands, so that there may be a great rejoicing aris-ing from Christians all over the world, and terror for the heathen, and the public overthrow of their wicked law.'

This wise and proud woman put forward these and many similar words to her husband; but Stephen knew of the dan-gers and difficulties and he was terrified of undergoing the hard labours a second time. At last, he mustered enough spirit and strength; he took the road with many thousands of Franks, and kept going all the way to the Holy Sepulchre.

All three relieving armies of crusaders met disaster and defeat in 1101. The Lombards, who had joined forces with Raymond of Toulouse at Constantinople, were massacred by Malik Ghazi the Danishmend and Qilij Arslan, the Turkish Seldjuk sultan of Rum (Anatolia), at Mersivan in July 1101. The army of William I, count of Nevers, was likewise decimated by Malik Ghazi and Qilij Arslan near Konya at the end of August. A week later, it was the turn of the followers of William, duke of Aquitaine, who were ambushed by the Turks near Heraclea. The Armenian chronicler Matthew of Edessa believed that the Emperor Alexius had betrayed the crusaders by sending them into the Anatolian wilderness in high summer.

In 1101, William, the great Frankish duke of Aquitaine, crossed the Byzantine Empire at the head of an army of three hundred thousand horsemen, and arrived with his troops before Constantinople. He spoke to Alexius with sovereign arrogance, only giving him the title *eparch*, not emperor, although he himself was only a youth of twenty or so years. He terrified Alexius and all his people.

The emperor, along with the nobles of his court, went to the duke of Aquitaine's camp and, finally giving way to William's demands, took him back into the town. Alexius gave him a magnificent reception, loaded him with treasure, held splendid feasts and went to great expense to convey him to the other side of the Bosporus, to Cappadocia. He also gave him Greek troops to accompany him.

Thus the emperor began carrying out his treacherous plan, ordering his officers to lead the Franks across uninhabited parts. For two weeks they made them travel through waterless wilderness, where nothing could be seen but the desert in all its aridity, nothing but the harsh mountain rocks. The only water they found was white, as if it had lime dissolved in it, and salty. Alexius had advised his troops to give the Franks bread in which they had mixed lime. This was an enormous crime before God: after many successive days of hunger and exhaustion the crusaders began to succumb to sickness.

Alexius's behaviour was due to the bitterness he felt towards them for having broken the oath the leaders of the first crusade had originally sworn him in 1097, and for having gone back on their promises. But the Byzantines were none the less guilty in God's eyes for behaving so mercilessly towards the crusaders, for making them the victims of vexation and treachery, and for bringing about their end. Thus the Lord allowed the infidels to march against the Byzantines and make them atone for their sins.

When the Seldjuk sultan, Qilij Arslan, learned of the arrival of the Franks, he wrote to Nicaea to warn Malik Ghazi the Danishmend that he was advancing against the Christians at the head of a huge army. Christians and infidels met in pitched battle near Heraclea. The fighting was fierce and lasted for the greater part of a day; blood ran in rivers. The Franks, overwhelmed and lost in a foreign land, could see no way out of their desperate situation. Confused, they stopped and herded together like frightened animals. It was a bloody and terrible day for them; and while this was going on, the Byzantine leader fled.

From his position on top of a neighbouring hill, the base of which was surrounded by infidels, William, duke of Aquitaine, looked down on his men's defeat. What a sight! The air was full of the harsh sound of arrows thudding from bows, horses reared up in terror and the mountains reverberated with the din of battle. The Frankish duke wept bitterly to see his soldiers massacred.

Then the infidels redoubled their attack and William, driven back on all sides, took flight with four hundred horsemen. His army of three hundred thousand men was completely destroyed. He sought asylum in Antioch, with Tancred [now its regent], and from there he went on to Jerusalem. In October 1101 William of Aquitaine left there to return to France, from whence he had come. He swore a solemn oath to return to fight the Seldjuk Turks again, to be revenged for this failure and to punish the Byzantine emperor's treachery. His soldiers, in fact, were taken off into slavery to Persia by the thousand.

Stephen of Blois also escaped the massacres; but he was prevented from returning home to France by bad weather. Instead, as Fulcher shows, he joined King Baldwin to lift the siege of Ramleh by the Egyptian army. Here, on 18 May 1102, he met his death.

Stephen of Blois then tried to cross the sea with many others, but he was blocked by the sea-winds and returned to Jaffa just as King Baldwin mounted his horse to go out against his enemies who were besieging Ramleh. This was an act of arrogance on the king's part, as he neglected to wait for his people, and did not proceed to war in an orderly fashion.

Baldwin rushed to attack the enemy, until he had unknowingly implanted himself among the Arab hordes. And since he had more faith than he ought in his valour, and thought that there could not be more than seven hundred or a thousand of the enemy, Baldwin was in a great hurry to come up against them before they could flee.

When he caught sight of their army, he was terrified and groaned in his mind, but he assumed the appearance of

Crusader knights charge against their Arab opponents.
At Ramleh such impetuous valour had dire consequences.

strength and looked back at his army, saying piously: 'Soldiers of Christ and my friends, fight manfully, for we are the Lord's. There is now no hope of escaping. If you fight you will conquer, but if you flee you will fall.'

So at once, and bravely, they threw themselves on the Arabs. Our mere two hundred knights were surrounded by twenty thousand; overwhelmed by the press of people, most of our side fell in the space of less than an hour. King Baldwin escaped by the grace of God, together with some of the more noble members of his company to Ramleh.

King Baldwin quickly made a plan and tried to get outside. He took only five companions, and them he did not keep long, for they were stopped by the enemy. Galloping on a

Baldwin I, king of Jerusalem

Baldwin of Boulogne, who ruled the kingdom of Jerusalem as Baldwin I from 1100 to 1118, was tall, with dark brown hair, a beard of the same colour and an aquiline nose. As a youth he had been destined for the Church and throughout his life his dignified manner and sobriety in speech and dress caused him to appear 'more like a bishop than a layman'. He was not, however, a mild and pious figure. His creation of the first crusader principality, the county of Edessa, with only a small body of Frankish supporters showed him to be ambitious, shrewd and ruthless.

While Baldwin's brother Godfrey, Jerusalem's first ruler, had refused to accept a royal title, or to wear a crown where Christ had been crowned with thorns, Baldwin displayed no such scruples and was crowned king on Christmas Day 1100. He ruled his new realm with vigour and determination. Hardly a year passed in which he did not take to the field with the kingdom's troops. On several occasions, he engaged powerful Muslim forces threatening Jerusalem, and in all but two instances he emerged as the victor.

Baldwin worked tirelessly to extend the boundaries of his domain. Enlisting the aid of fleets from Italy and elsewhere, often by promising trading and other concessions in the kingdom, he undertook the conquest of the Muslim coastal towns. At the end of his reign only Tyre and Ascalon remained unconquered. In the interior, he and his vassals worked to secure their hold on lands already in their possession and to extend the realm by military and diplomatic means at the expense of the rulers of Egypt and Damascus, who lost territory to him.

In the latter half of his reign, Baldwin also gave military assistance to the other Latin principalities on several occasions. This vital support, following his successful mediation in a dispute between the heirs of Raymond of Toulouse over the possession of Tripoli in 1109, contributed greatly to the prestige of the crown of Jerusalem and established Baldwin as the pre-eminent leader in the Latin east.

In the spring of 1118, Baldwin launched a campaign against Egypt, but illness forced him to turn back. He died before he reached the Holy City, on 2 April 1118. Although he had married three times, Baldwin left no direct heir and the kingdom of Jerusalem, of which he was the true founder, passed to his cousin, Baldwin of Le Bourg.

very swift horse, Baldwin made for the mountains and escaped. Those who remained in Ramleh could not afterwards leave the city but were besieged by the heathens, until, sad to say, some were killed, and others taken alive. When the bishop in the church of St George heard of this misfortune, he secretly fled to Jaffa.

Alas! how many noble and valiant knights we lost both in the battle and later in the city just mentioned. Stephen, count of Blois, was killed, a wise and noble man, together with the other Stephen, the count of Burgundy.

The reign of Baldwin I

The early part of Baldwin's 18-year reign saw the crusader states involved in constant warfare. The Arab historian Sibt Ibn al-Jawzi gives a terse account of the many sieges, culminating at Sidon in 1110.

In 1101 the Franks conquered several coastal towns, including Jaffa, Arsuf and Caesarea, taking them by brute force and massacring the inhabitants. The Frankish count, Raymond of Toulouse, besieged Tripoli. Its governor, Ibn 'Ammar, requested reinforcements from Damascus: a detachment from the army left Damascus under the command of Djenah ed-Daula, the governor of Imwas, and marched on Tortosa. There was a battle; Djenah ed-Daula sought refuge at Imwas, and the remnants of his army returned to Damascus.

An Egyptian army was sent to the Syrian coast and arrived at Ascalon during April 1102. Immediately Baldwin rushed over from Jerusalem with seven hundred men, horsemen and foot-soldiers alike, and charged the Egyptian army, who put up a strong resistance and killed the greater part of Baldwin's troops.

Baldwin fled with three men towards Ramleh and hid in a thicket of reeds, but the Muslims surrounded him and set light to the reeds. Hidden by the flames which were all around him, he escaped to Jaffa, his body half-covered in burns. His companions were captured and taken to Egypt. From Tripoli, Ibn 'Ammar again sent messages to Damascus and Imwas. With their help he managed to drive off the enemy.

In March 1104 Frankish ships, full of soldiers, merchants and other passengers, arrived at the port of Lattakieh and took up position around the land walls of Tripoli on the coast of Lebanon, under the command of Raymond of Toulouse. After blockading it for several days, the Franks entered the town, promising to spare it; however, they broke their word and massacred the inhabitants.

At that same time, the Turkish lords Sokman, the son of Urtuq, lord of Mardin, and the emir Jekermish, lord of Mosul, moved towards Edessa, intending to join battle with the Franks. Bohemund and Tancred rushed from Antioch to Edessa to help the local commander, but the Muslims, warned of this troop movement, advanced to the area around Edessa to meet the Christians at Harran. God gave them the victory: ten thousand Franks, infantrymen and horsemen alike, were killed; Bohemund and Tancred fled with only a small number of men left. This success did much to restore Muslim confidence.

In this same year Baldwin I, king of Jerusalem, arrived in front of Acre with a fleet composed of more than ninety warships; he threw a tight blockade around the town and exhausted the garrison with his continual attacks. The governor, unable to hold out any longer, requested guarantees of safety for himself and the Muslims; but the Franks refused and took the town by brute force in the month of May or, according to another version, in the month of June, 1104.

Raymond of Toulouse wanted to be able to dominate Tripoli, so he had a fortified castle built above the town which he had equipped with plenty of soldiers, weapons and provisions. But in 1104, the qadi Ibn 'Ammar attacked the castle unexpectedly, killed the garrison, seized all its treasure, weapons and supplies and then destroyed it. He then went back to Tripoli, unscathed and laden with booty.

Raymond of Toulouse died in February 1105 just as he had reached a truce with Ibn 'Ammar, under which the count remained in control of the suburbs of Tripoli provided that he allowed safe passage to travellers and to supplies.

In 1107 Baldwin arrived under the walls of Tyre and built a fort on a hill called Tell al-Ma'shouka, 'the hill of the loved one'. When a month had passed, he concluded an agreement with the governor of Tyre in return for seven thousand dinars, on receipt of which he withdrew.

Montreal, a castle at Shaubak in Jordan: one of the many castles and forts which Baldwin I built.

In spring 1108 Fakhr al-Mulk, lord of Tripoli, hard pressed by the arrival of the Franks and their constant assaults, left the city along with five hundred men, both horsemen and infantrymen, carrying gifts and precious objects which he intended to present to the sultan, Mohammed.

In 1109, Tripoli was captured by the Franks. Bertrand, son of Raymond of Toulouse, prince of Antioch, and Baldwin, the king of Jerusalem, appeared before it with a fleet of sixty ships full of troops. They began hostilities immediately and set up a blockade, maintaining it from 6 March to 10 July 1109. When their mobile towers reached the ramparts of Tripoli the garrison and the citizens gave in to despair and thought there was no hope for them. Moreover, the Egyptian fleet sent by the vizier al-Afdal took a long time to come; every time it started out towards Tripoli it encountered contrary winds which blew it back towards Egypt.

The Franks launched an all-out attack, ransacked the town, took all the people captive, regardless of sex, and seized an enormous amount of booty which they divided among themselves. [Bertrand of Toulouse became its first Frankish count.] Then they made for the town of Byblos, which surrendered on 21 July, but its governor Fakhr al-Mulk got away safely.

At the same time the Egyptian fleet arrived, a far more powerful fleet than any of the previous ones. But finding that Tripoli had been captured, it returned to Egypt.

In 1108, Baldwin, king of Jerusalem, concluded a truce with Tughtikin, lord of Damascus, on the following conditions: that the northern Transjordan should be divided into three zones, one of them to be occupied by the Franks and the other two by the Muslims.

The same year, Tancred left Antioch, seized Tarsus, and exacted a tribute of ten thousand gold pieces to be paid annually.

Baldwin, king of Jerusalem, accompanied by Bertrand, count of Tripoli, the son of Raymond of Toulouse, was threatening the town of Beirut when Jocelin, lord of Tell Bashir, came to their aid and asked for their assistance against Mawdud. This emir Mawdud had just expelled Jawali, the previous governor, from Mosul and had occupied Mesopotamia on Sultan Mohammed's orders. Finally, Mawdud camped in front of Edessa.

The arrival of the Egyptian fleet, which was bringing troops and supplies to Beirut, lifted the spirits of the Muslim inhabitants. But the Genoese, summoned by Baldwin, arrived on the scene with forty warships, enabling the Franks to attack the town by land and sea. They took Beirut by siege and went in fighting, killing, pillaging and reducing the population to slavery, as they had done at Tripoli.

First Baldwin set aside the best share in the booty and pro-visions for himself, and then he set up camp before Sidon, ordering it to open its gates. The inhabitants having agreed to surrender at a predetermined date, Baldwin levied a tax from them and went off to Jerusalem for the pilgrim festivals.

In 1110 a pilgrim from far afield, Sigurd I, joint king of Norway, arrived in Outremer. Fulcher describes how on Baldwin's persuasion he joined in the successful siege of Sidon.

Meanwhile a group of Norwegians, whom God had urged to come from the western sea, put in at Jaffa to make the journey to Jerusalem. Their fleet consisted of fifty-five ships. Their leader, King Sigurd, was a young man of outstanding beauty. When King Baldwin returned to Jerusalem, he was delighted at their arrival and spoke in a very friendly fashion to them, advising and begging them, for the love of God, to remain for a while in the Holy Land and help him to further and augment the Christian cause.

They received his plea kindly, and answered that they had come to Jerusalem for no other purpose, but that wherever the king wanted to go with his army, they would gladly go at the same time by sea, as long as he would provide them with the necessary victuals. This was agreed and acted upon.

At first they arranged to go to Ascalon, but then a better counsel prevailed, and they went to besiege Sidon. King Baldwin moved his army from Acre, while the Norwegians went by ship from Jaffa. At that time the fleet of the emir of Egypt was lying hidden in the port of Tyre; from there the Saracens often attacked in the manner of pirates those Christians new to the land, and they were strengthening the defences of the coastal cities which the Egyptian caliphs still possessed. But when they heard rumours about the Norwegians, they did not dare to leave the port of Tyre or to meet them.

When the crusaders arrived at Sidon, King Baldwin besieged it from the land and the Norwegians from the sea. Then he constructed siege-engines and terrified the enemy within, to the extent that those who were mercenaries requested the king to allow them to leave the city unharmed and, if he wished, to keep the farmers in the city to till the land for his own profit. Their request was granted. The mercenaries left without being paid, and the country-people remained in peace, in accordance with the arrangement.

Right: Soldiers defending a walled city; from an 11th-century manuscript.

Holy Sepulchre and Holy Lance

The departure of so many people on a pilgrimage dedicated to the defence of the holiest place in Christendom against the enemies of the Church seemed to contemporaries in itself a miracle, a sign of God's blessing on the enterprise. Their goal was the land in which the miracles recorded in the Bible had taken place, and specifically the tomb of Christ, now enclosed in the church of the Holy Sepulchre in Jerusalem, the place of the 'great miracle' of the resurrection.

Since the fourth century, pilgrims had gone to the Holy Sepulchre, above all during the vigil before the celebration of Easter, when all lights were extinguished in the building and the patriarch came out to the waiting crowds bearing new fire, miraculously kindled out of the darkness of the Tomb. It was a ceremony repeated as a liturgical act throughout the west each Easter, but here in Jerusalem it seemed both miracle and reality in a unique sense. This place of wonder was the focus of the crusaders' own pilgrimage, the first place they visited when Jerusalem was taken, the site of the major relic, the True Cross, and of the miraculous fire of the resurrection, the visible sign of the central mystery of Christianity; this church was the crown of the crusaders' endeavour.

During the First Crusade, miraculous visions assured the crusaders of the continued support of God. In particular, during the hardships of the siege of Antioch in 1097–8, the crusaders were encouraged by three such signs. The first was a vision by the priest Stephen, who entered a church dedicated to St Mary; there St Mary and St Peter appeared to him, rebuking the sins of the crusaders but promising help within five days. More widely known were the visions of another priest, Peter Bartholomew, in which he was repeatedly urged by St Andrew to dig up the Lance with which Christ's side had been pierced on the cross, as a visible sign of God's assistance for the besieged crusaders. The subsequent discovery of the Lance by Peter himself was surrounded by intrigue and fraud on the part of interested parties in Antioch, but was hailed as a miracle by the discouraged troops. A further vision emphasized the message of divine assistance: in the same battle, many soldiers saw horsemen in white who rode mysteriously with them, three of whom were identified as St George, St Demetrius and St Mercury, soldier-saints popular in the east.

The pilgrimage of Sigurd also found its way into Norse saga: the *Heimskringla* celebrated his capture of Sidon.

In the summer of 1110 King Sigurd sailed across the Mediterranean to Palestine, then went up to Jerusalem, and there met Baldwin I, king of Jerusalem. King Baldwin greeted King Sigurd particularly well and rode with him up to the river Jordan and back to Jerusalem. The poet Einar Skulason says the following:

> The leader let his sea-cold ship
> Slip through Grecian waters –
> Not few to the songster
> The king's good gifts –
> Before the generous chieftain
> Anchored in expansive Acre;
> All his men made merry
> Then, with the king, that morning.

> I say that the strife-glad king
> Journeyed to Jerusalem –
> Men know of no greater prince
> Under storm-hall's skies;
> Then the glad, gold-giving king
> Could in clean streams
> Of Jordan bathe:
> An action
> Well worth praise.

King Sigurd stayed a long time in Palestine, during the autumn and early winter.

King Baldwin prepared a fine banquet for King Sigurd and for many of his men. Then King Baldwin gave King Sigurd many holy relics and a splinter was taken from the Holy Cross on the orders of King Baldwin and the patriarch, who swore on the holy relic that it was the wood of the Holy Cross on which God himself was crucified. That holy relic was given to King Sigurd on the condition that he, together with twelve other men, swore to promote Christianity with all his power, and to set up an archbishopric in Norway. Also, the Cross was to be kept where St Olaf lay, and Sigurd was to introduce tithes, and pay them himself.

After that King Sigurd returned to his ships at Acre, and King Baldwin prepared his army to go to Syria, to a town called Sidon. The town was infidel. King Sigurd accompanied him on this expedition. When the kings had besieged the town for a short time only, the heathen men gave up. The kings took possession of the town, and their troops of the booty. King Sigurd gave possession of the whole town to King Baldwin.

The poet Halldor Skvaldri says the following:

You took the heathens' town
By force, you she-wolf-feeder:
Each battle was begun with pride,
You gave it away with grace.

Einar Skulason also speaks about this:

The catapults crashed
In the clamour of conflict.
The fierce raven-feeder
Broke down brave walls.
Fair blades became bloodied:
The bold king boasted of victory.

After that King Sigurd went back to his ships and prepared to leave Palestine.

Death of Baldwin

Baldwin and his army, having consolidated their hold on most of Palestine's coastal strip, began to push south. In 1115 they went as far as the Red Sea, where they fortified the town of Eilat, on the gulf of Aqaba. The Franks were increasingly aware that their most dangerous opponent was the Fatimid caliphate, and it was during a raid on Egypt, in 1118, that Baldwin contracted his fatal illness. Albert of Aachen described his death-bed scene.

On 2 April 1118, Baldwin began to suffer worse from his illness, even unto death, in the sight of his faithful nobles.

They realized he was departing this life and, because he was a man of great wisdom, they asked him, while he was still sound, whom he wanted to be appointed and crowned as heir to the kingdom of Jerusalem after his death. Baldwin resolved that the kingdom should go to Eustace, his elder brother, count of Boulogne, if by any chance he came to the Holy Land; if indeed he was unable because of his advanced age, then Baldwin's cousin, Baldwin of Le Bourg, count of Edessa, should be chosen, or any such man who would rule the Christian people, defend the churches, stand firm in the faith, and whom no force of the enemy would frighten, no bribe easily corrupt.

Having said this, Baldwin, a man who was the noblest of noble blood in the land of his birth, Lorraine, most glorious

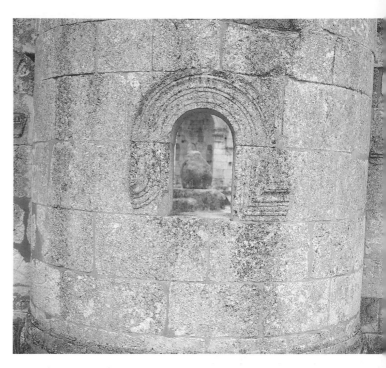

A relic of St Simeon the Stylite inside St Simeon's basilica at Telanissus in Syria: the stump of the column on top of which he lived for 36 years. Relic-hunters stole most of its length.

and victorious king in the kingdom of Jerusalem, bravest champion of God, breathed his last, steadfast in the faith of Christ, purified by confession, fortified by partaking of the Lord's body and blood.

Now, on 2 April 1118, their most famous prince was dead in the land of the barbarians. The foremost nobles and fellow-soldiers, cavalry and infantry, burst into great floods of tears on account of their grief, with a great wailing and lamentation: and they would have redoubled their weeping, but for the fear they felt in losing so great a prince in a land which was everywhere hostile.

Because of this they hid his death and all their sadness. And just as he resolutely asked, his stomach was cut; his internal organs were taken out and buried; his body was salted inside and out, also embalmed with spices and balsam in the eyes, mouth, nostrils and ears; sewn in a hide and wrapped in hangings; placed on horseback and firmly tied on. This was done so that the infidels' cunning would not be able to perceive that he had died, which might inspire them to boldness in hunting down the bereaved army.

When the lifeless body had been prepared in this way, they cautiously made their return with the conveyance through the foreign land, escorting it through deserts and out-of-the-way places, through the region of the valley of Hebron, where the fortress and tomb of the holy fathers Abraham, Isaac and Jacob are honoured by the faithful to this

Baldwin organizes his own funeral

Baldwin told all who were present, very insistently and appealing to their good faith, that if he died, they should never bury his body in any grave in the land of the Saracens, lest it should be held in derision and mockery by the infidels, but with all the skill and exertion they could muster, they should carry his corpse back to the land of Jerusalem, and bury it next to his brother Godfrey of Bouillon.

Hearing his speech and scarce restraining themselves from weeping, they replied that he was laying on them a heavy and insupportable burden, for it would be impossible to keep, touch and carry any corpse in those days of extreme summer heat.

Whereupon the king insisted even more, and told them all that because they loved him they should not refuse this task. And after this he entreated them: 'As soon as I die, I entreat you to open up my stomach with a knife, take out my insides, embalm my body with salt and spices and wrap it in a skin or hangings, and in this way it may be taken back to a Christian funeral in Jerusalem and buried next to my brother's grave.'

Without delay he summoned Addo the cook, who was one of his household, and he bound him with an oath concerning the cutting of his stomach and the throwing-out of his internal organs. He also said to him: 'You know that I am shortly to die. On this subject, as you love me, or as you used to love me when I was alive and well, so should you keep faith with me when I am dead. Disembowel me with the knife; rub me inside and outside especially with salt; fill my eyes, nostrils, ears and mouth generously; and be sure to take me back with the rest. In this way know that you are fulfilling my wishes, and believe you are keeping faith with me in this matter.' And so it was arranged.

From Albert of Aachen, *Historia Hierosolymitana*

very day. They travelled for days on end, always keeping a guard of armed knights to the right and the left.

Then arriving on the plains of Ascalon with the king's dead body, they put their faith in military strength alone, with standards flying and in battle formation, and they are reported to have crossed the plains without hindrance or any enemy attack, until finally, on that very holy and honoured day, Palm Sunday, 7 April 1118, they entered as one the mountains of Jerusalem with the royal corpse.

On that same day, the patriarch of Jerusalem had come down from the Mount of Olives with his clergy after the consecration of palms. Brothers met him from the Temple and from all the churches and they assembled for the feast day with hymns and songs of praise. The dead king was carried up in the middle of their singing. At the sight of him, their voices were hushed, their praises were brought low, and a great weeping was heard.

Everyone came in with the dead king through the Golden Gate, through which the Lord Jesus coming to his passion had entered, and it was decided by common consent that the lifeless body should at once be taken to its funeral, because it had been kept for a long time and was now stinking. Without delay, once the Christian burial rites were over, Baldwin was consigned to the earth by the lord patriarch, next to the tomb of his brother, Godfrey of Bouillon.

There a mausoleum, such as befits kings, was built in memory and honour of his name. It was of great and wonderful workmanship, and of white polished marble, grander than the rest of the tombs. His brother Godfrey, too, was honoured by the building of a mausoleum.

Matthew of Edessa found characteristics to praise in Baldwin's successor, Baldwin II, although he regarded Baldwin I as the greater man.

King Baldwin I was a good man, holy of inclination and humble of heart. When those who had accompanied him on his funereal journey back found Baldwin of Le Bourg, count of Edessa, at Jerusalem, they were amazed and delighted at the same time, and considered his arrival to have been caused by Providence. They followed the terms of the king's will, so that on Palm Sunday, 7 April, the count of Edessa was led to the Temple of Solomon and raised to the throne as regent; and at the end of the year he was crowned king.

Prince Baldwin was, by rank, one of the most illustrious of the Franks; he was a brave fighter and his morals were

A cutaway view showing Baldwin's tomb, marked L in the picture, in the chapel of Mount Calvary in Jerusalem.

Cappelle sopra il Móte Caluario.

exemplary, he was the enemy of sin and was both gentle and modest. These qualities, though, were tarnished by greed – he was most ingenious when it came to seizing other people's wealth – by an insatiable love of money and by a lack of generosity. For the rest, he was very orthodox in his faith, very decided in behaviour and personality. So there you have two kings of Jerusalem who both came from Edessa and who were both called Baldwin.

The death of Alexius I

The year 1118 also saw the death of Sultan Mohammed in Persia, and, to Anna Comnena's deep sorrow, the end of her father, the Emperor Alexius, greatest potentate in the eastern Mediterranean, which she movingly retells.

Alexius was attacked by a deadly illness, probably stemming from worry; he was much affected by the burden of affairs and the many concerns of government. I often heard him tell the empress about it; in a way, he was blaming the sickness. 'What on earth is this ailment that troubles my breathing? I want to take a deep, full breath and be rid of this care that oppresses me, but no matter how I try I can't ever once lift a small portion of the burden that troubles me.'

When the empress heard these words and realized what he was enduring, she was most upset; one would imagine that she suffered from the same disease, the same asthmatic condition. She often called the ablest physicians and asked to be told the direct and indirect causes of it. They felt his pulse and conceded that they found in each motion signs of all sorts of irregularities, but they were quite unable to assign a cause for this. They knew the emperor's diet was not rich; it was very moderate and frugal, the type of diet athletes or troops have, so that the possibility of an aggregation of humours from rich food was discounted; they assigned the obstruction in respiration to some other cause and said the principal cause of his sickness was overwork and the ceaseless oppression of his worries. His heart, they said, was inflamed as a result and was accumulating all the excess matter from the rest of his body.

After this the frightful illness gave him no rest at all: it was choking him like a noose. Each day it became worse, assailing him no longer intermittently, but continuously, without respite. He could not lie on either side, and was so weak that every inhalation required great effort.

He had to sit upright to be able to breathe at all; if by acci-dent he lay on his back or side, the suffocation was terrible; to inhale or exhale even a tiny breath of air grew impossible.

Whatever we and the doctors tried was in vain. Eleven days went by when the malady was in its terminal phase; it was at its peak and now endangering his life . . .

At last, after many days I realized that the last of his strength was going and the movement of blood in the arteries had finally ceased. I turned from his bed, exhausted and cold, my head bowed and my hands over my eyes. Without speaking I stepped back and started to weep.

Suddenly in the extremity of her grief the empress uttered a loud, shrill cry. She doffed her empress's veil and with a razor shaved off her beautiful hair. She threw off her purple-dyed shoes and asked for plain black sandals and an un-adorned dark veil.

Then the emperor gave up his soul to God. And my sun went down.

The Field of Blood

The expansion of the principality of Antioch under its ruler Roger of Salerno, Tancred's nephew, had meanwhile increasingly alarmed the Turkish Urtukid ruler Il-Ghazi, and his ally Tughtikin of Damascus. On 28 June 1119 Roger met Il-Ghazi's army in battle south of Aleppo. The Frankish defeat, and the horrible fate which befell Roger's army, are dramatically recounted by his chancellor, Walter.

By some ill omen we were snatched into danger, not waiting for the proud to be brought low according to their deserts and the humble to be exalted. We, as if braver than lions and more inexorable than tigers, forced our way to pitch camp at *Ager Sanguinis*, 'the Field of Blood', near Aleppo – as it is called by the populace in reality and in name – where we stayed for some time, because of the shortage of food and natural drink in those parts.

What happened to us was not the result of the strength of the enemy, but the judgement of a just God for our crimes and wickedness.

Our men, relying on their boldness and disregarding the enemy's ingenuity, drew their shields close to their sides, brandished their lances, sank in their spurs, all these at once as befits knights, and charged into the middle of the enemy. Dealing violent blows in military fashion they threw down some to the ground, with blood pouring forth, and drove others down to hell with fatal wounds.

After this the prince, Roger of Antioch, summoned his

Above: A mosaic portrait of Emperor Alexius in the splendid panoply of a Byzantine Emperor, from Hagia Sophia in Constantinople. His grand effigy belies the slow agony of his death, from an incurable respiratory complaint.

stableman and the public criers, and commanded the entire army to prepare for arms. He ordered it to be announced in a loud voice that, at the first sound of the bugle, everyone should make haste to put on arms and armour; at the second, being ready with battle-lines drawn up, both knights and foot-soldiers should assemble; and, hearing the third, individual battle-lines should advance, approaching at the command of standard-bearers, and present themselves at the sign of the cross of our Lord.

There was no delay: at the first signal our troops were alerted and made ready, at the second they assembled in front of the chapel, where the cross was, in the prince's presence. And at the third the bishop, bearing the cross of our Lord in reverent hands, said: 'What more? Strengthened by the arms of faith, with this health-giving cross going before, let us advance into their midst.'

An initial sortie by the crusader army established the 'intolerable strength' of their opponents; the crusaders formed a defensive ring around their camp and awaited their fate.

What next? Suddenly the flags and standards of the heathens appeared from the mountain-sides among the olives. When he saw them Prince Roger declared: 'Soldiers of Christ, let us not be put off by this many-sided contest; but let us now play our parts. Let us serve today as soldiers for God in a successful battle, whether we end up alive or dead.'

Prince Roger engaged in the struggle with steadfast mind. Although his men lay cut down and dead on all sides, he never retreated or looked back, but, accompanied by a few men, he obeyed the command of God and the bishop by fighting energetically against the force of the entire military might. He was struck by a Saracen's sword through the middle of his nose, right into his brain; and settling his debts in the name of the Lord by death, in the presence of the symbol of the holy cross, he gave up his body to the earth and his soul to heaven.

109

CHRONICLES OF THE CRUSADES

After this attack the priest was killed who was carrying this same cross in his hands; and indeed many of the heathens were seized by greed for the gold and the precious stones and, knowing nothing of the strength of God's power hidden in the cross, they shared it there and then with swift blows and they were stricken by that timber of death, and they passed away to the lower regions.

Then at once and all together, a hundred thousand infidel fighting men attacked our army very fiercely from the four quarters of the world. Some of our men (of whom there were reputed to be seven hundred knights and three thousand foot-soldiers, with many others who had gone to battle for the sake of trade or on account of greed for enemy wealth) were wounded; some were killed, and some who were mutilated with different injuries were brought out for destruction on the battle-field, while some were put in the bounds of most wretched captivity by judgement of the just God.

Some were struck down with stones, some pierced by javelins, and many were mutilated in different ways. Watching this, the wicked heathen was delighted by their torments and he laughed at them. Yet he was not satisfied and was thinking up crueller things. He commanded that everyone at once, however many there were, be brought into the middle of the field. At his order, a thousand or more soldiers were ready, carrying naked swords in their hands, so that by striking out they could both tear the prisoners to pieces and delight their unholy leader.

Il-Ghazi instructed things to be arranged thus: prisoners chosen were put on one side for torture, the rest were left in the field for destruction. Then this most wicked leader said: 'Come on, soldiers! Guardians and agents of the supreme law! Here is a sacrifice of dogs ready for your swords,' and he shouted: 'Hey! Hey! Run at them readily and quickly!' So in one attack, the wicked soldiers struck the condemned men with swords of death, and they did not cease from killing until there was none of the prisoners' parts left whole.

Not yet sated with the slaughter of men, they entreated their prince on bended knee to be able to destroy the prisoners chosen for torture with a like slaughter, at his command. However, his divine majesty refused. He ordered the chosen prisoners to be handed over to his son who brought them into captivity at Aleppo, to torture them.

He received the chosen prisoners and gave them flints for food and hard blows for drink; for a bed he caused halters to be bound on their feet and necks.

On the following day they were led to the pillory in Aleppo, where they suffered repeated blows and different sorts of torture. Some were killed but some were ransomed.

Turkish tortures

Next to the battlefield, five hundred or more prisoners were held bent over to the ground, their hands twisted behind their backs and bound with iron chains, and their feet bound very tightly. In the manner of dogs they were tied together two by two by the neck, waiting in a circle to undergo the death sentence.

The badly wounded and the others, led to execution, suffered agonies from their skin being flayed from their living and half-severed heads before their decapitation at the hands of the heathen. The rest, knowing they were to be tortured thus, spent that dark night in violence and fear, demanding death, and yet often calling for it not to come to them in their unhappiness.

Therefore after a night cramped together in fetters, at sunrise on the following day – sun, I say, which was blacker for them than the dark night – they were ordered to be produced in the tents, so that the prince of wickedness, the Turk Il-Ghazi, could decide what should be done to them.

And this was the abominable prince's pleasure: at the third hour in the morning the naked prisoners, some two or three hundred all tied together by the neck with rope, were led out under swords and cudgels, whips and ropes for the distance of a mile through fields planted with brambles and thistles, into the newly harvested vineyard next to Sarmedan.

It was hot, of course, not only for the wounded and ailing prisoners but even for the healthy, the enemy and free men, so that any one of the prisoners would have given one of his limbs or life itself for a cup of cold water. Certain prisoners, seeing the grapes of the vineyard lying on the ground, rivalled one another in falling face downwards, eagerly gathering even the dirt-covered grapes, and those trodden by feet, into their mouths. When the juice ran from the mouth of someone biting on the grapes, no matter how, it was received by another's mouth. Frequently, thinking to hold the dribbled juice and driven by passion, they would bite their own tongues; some were raging and holding on to others' beards, having seen a wretched little drop of juice.

From Walter the Chancellor, *Bella Antiochena*

Capture of Tyre, 1124

The Christians were fortunate that Il-Ghazi did not follow up his decisive victory over them in the battle of the Field of Blood. The Turkish ruler celebrated instead and allowed the Franks time to recoup their strength. In February 1124 the army of Jerusalem laid siege to Tyre, supported by a powerful Venetian fleet. They were able to cut off supplies of food and water, and the Tyrians' only hope was relief from the Egyptians, which failed to arrive.

After four months of siege the situation was desperate, as William of Tyre shows. Now only Ascalon remained in Muslim hands.

The Tyrians were now suffering most severely from hunger. As they gathered in their meeting-places, they began to discuss how they might put an end to the troubles they were undergoing: saying it was better to surrender the city to the enemy, and to be able to go as free men to other cities of their people, rather than to waste away from hunger; rather than to see their wives and their children be destroyed by famine and to be unable to succour them. At length after discussions of this kind had been held among the common people, by general agreement the matter was reported to the elders and the governors of the city, and to the general public. When the entire city

Christian prisoners about to be decapitated by their Saracen captors. Crusaders and Saracens often beheaded captives.

was assembled, the matter was conscientiously put forward and discussed in a public meeting. Everyone's mind was made up: put an end to so great an evil and arrive at a peace settlement whatever the outcome, and whatever the conditions.

At last, after many arguments, both sides agreed that the city should be handed over to the Christians, with free egress granted to the citizens, their wives and children, and all their wealth.

Moreover, if some of the citizens preferred to stay in the city, their possessions and homes should be preserved intact and a free licence to stay granted to them.

Of course, when the people and the men of the lower class realized what was being discussed among the princes, they took it badly that the city should be surrendered on these terms, and that it would not be available to them to smash up violently for booty and loot, and they unanimously declared that their effort was being betrayed for military necessities, ready entirely to disagree with the princes. Nevertheless, the saner mentality of their superiors prevailed, and when the city was surrendered, freedom to leave was given to the citizens, as had been agreed in the pact.

As a symbol of victory, King Baldwin II of Jerusalem's standard was raised over the tower which is near the gate of the city; with great glory, the standard of the doge of Venice was flown over the tower which is called Viridis, and the standard of Pons, count of Tripoli, Michael Falieri, was flown over that called the tower of Tanaria.

When the citizens of Tyre, tired from the long siege, came out, they hurried to our camp for the sake of relieving their weariness. They considered attentively what sort of people these Christians were – so unyielding, so long-suffering, so skilled in the use of weapons – who had in the space of a few months reduced so glorious a town, so fortified a city, to utmost want, and compelled it to submit to extreme terms. The Tyrians liked to look at the appearance of the siege-engines, the height of the siege-towers, the kind of weapons, the siting of the camp.

They were even keen to discover the names of our leaders and enquired carefully into everything, so that they would be able to compose reliable and detailed histories for their descendants.

In the same way, when our men entered the city they marvelled at its defences, the strength of the buildings, the height of the towers, the massiveness of the walls, the fine appearance of the port, the difficulty of access. They also praised the perseverance of the citizens who had been beset by such an extremity of hunger and struggled with such starvation, and yet had put off the time of surrender for so long: when our men took the city only five measures of corn were found in it.

And although at first the common people took it hard that the city should come under our authority on these terms, yet in due course they began to be pleased: their costly effort was praised and they believed their achievement worthy of permanent remembrance, which was the result of their own labour and expense.

The city was therefore divided into three parts: two were assigned to the kings of Jerusalem, the third to the Venetians, following the agreement they had made.

Then with great happiness and joy, they all returned home.

The siege of Tyre by the forces of the Latin kingdom of Jerusalem and their allies in 1124.

—3—
THE SECOND CRUSADE
1147–1149

On Christmas Eve 1144, Imad ad-Din Zanghi, the Turkish atabeg of Mosul, broke into the city of Edessa and massacred its Frankish inhabitants. The city had always been strategically vulnerable and, since 1131, incompetently governed by its irresponsible count, Joscelin II of Courtenay. An embassy was dispatched to the papal curia and reached Eugenius III in autumn 1145. The pope issued the great crusading bull, *Quantum praedecessors*, dated 1 December, and addressed to the king of France, Louis VII.

Yet the Second Crusade was not a simple response to the loss of Edessa. Neither Louis nor Conrad III of Germany, who arrived separately at Constantinople in October 1147, preparatory to their journeys to the Holy Land, took the vow with Edessa in mind. Louis had been planning a pilgrimage to the holy places since at least early 1145. He had consulted the Cistercian abbot, Bernard of Clairvaux, who in turn, had advised the king to seek papal backing. Louis explained his intentions to a baronial assembly at Bourges at Christmas 1145, but there is no evidence that *Quantum praedecessores* had reached France by then. The loss of Edessa, therefore, increased the military character of his expedition, but was not in itself its chief stimulus. Moreover, the barons were not enthusiastic, even after the papal bull had been received, and their lacklustre response may have persuaded Bernard that the appeal should be broadened. Following the reissue of the bull on 1 March 1146, the abbot preached to a great gathering at Vézelay at Easter. Letters were then sent to the English

---

The Byzantine Emperor and
Empress with the Virgin
Mary, symbolizing
Byzantine grandeur.

---

and the Spanish. Conrad had not intended to go on crusade, nor had the pope expected him to, but this situation was transformed by Bernard's arrival in Germany, drawn there by the need to counter the anti-Semitic rabble-rousing of an errant Cistercian monk, Radulf. Once there he preached before Conrad at Frankfurt in November 1146, and again at Speyer at Christmas. In the face of Bernard's eloquence the king agreed to take the cross.

At Constantinople and during their hazardous journey across Asia Minor many crusaders experienced deep feelings of antipathy towards their supposed Byzantine allies. Moreover, those who reached Syria and Palestine attacked not Edessa or even Aleppo, which might have sapped Zanghid strength, but Damascus, seat of a hitherto friendly Muslim power. Most strikingly, however, probably the majority of those who took vows never reached the east. Two separate expeditions were diverted to Iberia, a region occupied by Islam since the early eighth century, to which Urban II had given high priority. In October 1147, Alfonso VII of Castile and Count Raymond-Beregar of Aragon mounted a combined land and sea operation with the Genoese, and captured Almeria from the Almoravids. Crusaders from north-west Europe, sailing to the east from the Channel ports, were persuaded instead to help in the conquest of the Tagus Valley, a campaign which led to the capture of Lisbon in October 1147.

Six months earlier, at Frankfurt, on Germany's eastern frontiers, German lords gained official sanction to crusade against the allegedly pagan Slavs (or Wends). These proved to less easy victims than had been imagined and little religious or territorial gain was achieved. Meanwhile, as the papacy allowed the main military forces of crusading Europe to divide their strength in at least three different theatres of war, other groups in northern France and the Rhineland mounted unofficial crusades against the Jews.

While the campaigns in Spain, Portugal and Germany were all but over, crusaders in the east were still struggling to reach their destination. In the absence of mass sea transport, which came only in the late 12th century, large armies going to the Holy Land had to travel across Asia Minor – a logistical nightmare. In the face of Turkish attacks and the ambigous attitudes of the Byzantines, by February 1148, the splendid French and German armies were in tatters.

Crusaders who could afford it sailed to Syria; the remaining survivors left for home. Louis VII of France took ship from Attlaia to Antioch, which he reached in March; Conrad III of Germany, forced by illness to return to Constantinople, arrived at Acre in April.

In some aspects the world which they entered was familiar, especially in the composition of its ruling classes. In Jerusalem, the monarchy was well established on the basis of hereditary right under Queen Melisende, who governed in the name of her young son, Baldwin III, since the death of her husband, King Fulk, in 1143. Antioch was ruled by Raymond of Poitiers, uncle of Louis's wife, Eleanor of Aquitaine. The county of Tripoli, between the two, was held by Raymond II, great-grandson of Raymond of Toulouse. As in the west, the barons were granted fiefs by the ruler and in return were expected to provide military support, although a limited number of families had started to concentrate power in their own hands – to the long-term detriment of the monarchy. The hierarchy of secular (non-monastic) clergy paralleled that of the west.

There were also evident differences. Urban living and commerce were more prominent than anywhere in the west, except for limited parts of Italy. Towns were larger and more numerous, their economies based more obviously on money. Many knights held little or no land, and the market for mercenaries was one of the most active in the Christian world. The ruling classes obtained a high proportion of their incomes from urban taxation, while in many towns the representatives of the maritime cities of Italy, especially Venice, Genoa and Pisa, lived in privileged enclaves, distinct from the rest of the population both territorially and juridically. Non-noble Franks, many descended from the foot-soldiers of the First Crusade, formed a burgess class, whose members included craftsmen, administrative officials and soldiers. Intermarriage with local Christians and, occasionally, converted Muslims was not uncommon, and many Franks lived in Muslim dwellings and sometimes adopted Muslim dress and diet. Beneath the Frankish hierarchy the subject population was relatively undisturbed: Greeks and Syrian and Armenian Christians predominated in the north, Muslims in the south.

It was a society dominated by the quest for security. With the exception of Edessa, the Frankish states clung to the seaboard, which extended from the Cilician borders to the Sinai Desert. Important Muslim cities menaced their eastern flank, in particular Aleppo, which Baldwin II of Jerusalem tried unsuccessfully to capture in 1124. Zanghi's second son, Nur ad-Din, who had taken over the Syrian territories after his father's death in 1146, had continued to build up his power in the north. Only the potential threat posed by the Byzantine Empire, which might support Antioch, made him cautious. Egypt, as always, was less formidable; the Fatimid caliphate was ineffective, and Egyptian methods of fighting were more vulnerable to Frankish cavalry charge than were the hit-and-run tactics of the Turks. Nevertheless, the Egyptians clung stubbornly to the key port of Ascalon in the south and effectively prevented further Frankish expansion, until the city fell in 1153.

The crusader states were defended by castles and fortresses, the largest of which were more grandiose than anything in the west. Most of the important strongholds had been taken over from previous occupants, Byzantine or Muslim, and had not been built to any grand strategic plan. Defence relied upon holding strongpoints until an attacker was forced to retreat. For this reason, the Franks fortified manor houses and colonized villages for the few who ventured to live outside the towns. Many castles were held by the two great military orders, the Templars and the Hospitallers.

Communications with the west remained the Frankish lifeline, enabling crusaders to be mobilized in exceptionally large numbers when the occasion arose. However, such crusades were a mixed blessing. Although they opened up the possibility of making war on the enemy, high-born westerners were not always amenable to the plans of the local Franks. Moreover, when the crusaders returned to the west they left the permanent settlers with the same problems as before, possibly exacerbated by their activities.

Certainly, the relative ease with which Nur ad-Din was able to take over Damascus (hitherto unfriendly towards the Zanghids) in 1154 seems to have been a direct consequence of the estrangement between the Franks and the Damascenes brought about by the Second Crusade.

The Second Crusade ended with the Franks' failure to capture Damascus in 1148. The decision to attack was taken at a meeting of the High Court at Acre on 24 June 1148. The objective had been the matter of some debate, but it is likely that Louis, whose strongest desire had been to visit the holy places, was reluctant to return north to Antioch: he did not trust Raymond, its ruler. Rumours circulating about an alleged affair between Queen Eleanor and Raymond can only have hardened his view. King Conrad, already established in the kingdom of Jerusalem, did not have any strong reason for taking his army to Nur ad-Din's capital at Aleppo. Even if the local powers had argued against the Damascene

plan they would have found it difficult to sustain their view against those of two such important kings. The attack itself was mismanaged. When the crusaders heard that Nur ad-Din's forces had reached Homs they abandoned a well-supplied position on the western side of the city in the hope of achieving a quick victory on the poorly defended eastern section. The gamble failed and, on 28 July, they had no alternative but to withdraw. Conrad left the east on 8 September, but Louis continued his pilgrimage until the early summer of 1149 in order to take a full part in the Christmas and Easter ceremonies.

The failure of the Second Crusade provoked a series of strong reactions. For some the expedition had been the devil's work from the beginning, while others detected the treachery of human agencies, including the Byzantines, the local Frankish baronage and the Templars. But the most evident target was Bernard of Clairvaux – who chose to present himself as God's servant, indifferent to human calumnies.

The First Crusade achieved the glorious capture of Jerusalem, the Second ended ignominiously with the retreat from Damascus. Not surprisingly, the sources reflect this contrast. While many chroniclers hastened to write up the triumph of 1099, few found inspiration in the events of 1148. Indeed, except for those who captured Lisbon, the participants were so disheartened that they were reluctant to record the crusade in any detail, and consequently the historian is much more dependent upon armchair critics than previously. Those who did comment were concerned to justify, to blame, or to admonish, and the structure of their work is as much conditioned by their knowledge of failure as that of their predecessors had been by success. But this very difference in tone makes these authors valuable, for their reactions illustrate a range of attitudes towards crusading which had hitherto been largely submerged. Moreover, much more than the chroniclers of the First Crusade, they bring out the growing diversity of objectives; Helmold of Bosau, for instance, distinguishes clearly between the different elements fighting in Germany, Iberia and the east, an analysis which prefigures the great variety of late medieval crusading in eastern Europe and the Mediterranean. Such perceptions were possible because papal bulls and St Bernard's letters provided between them a more systematic exposition of the nature of the crusade than had in the past been offered. From now on both the potentialities and the problems were exposed with much greater clarity.

We who had been occidentals have become orientals; a man once Italian or French has here become Galilean or Palestinian; and the man who once lived in Reims or Chartres now finds he is a citizen of Tyre or Acre. We have already forgotten the places of our birth.

Some of us already own houses and servants in this country. Some have married women who are Syrian or Armenian perhaps, or even Saracens who have received the grace of baptism. He who was once a stranger here is now a native, and every day, our dependants and relatives follow us here. For he who was poor there finds now that God has made him rich here. He who had little money now has countless gold coins. He who did not hold even a village there now enjoys a whole town which God has granted him.

Why should anyone return to the west who has found an east like this?

With the capture of Tyre in 1124 the crusader states had reached their greatest extent. Crusaders who settled in the east adopted many of its customs, as recorded by Fulcher of Chartres in 1127.

Edessa falls to Zanghi, 1144

The crusader states needed all the help they could get to defend themselves against Imad ad-Din Zanghi, Turkish emir of Mosul and Aleppo since 1128. His aim was to rule in Damascus, and in the 1130s he expanded his power against Christians and Muslims alike. In 1144 Zanghi seized the opportunity to attack Edessa, while its ruler, Joscelin, was campaigning on the Euphrates. This account of its fall was written by Michael the Syrian.

The initial capture of Edessa, which the Turks took from the Franks, happened as follows: this city had for a considerable time been surrounded by Turkish territory, and was therefore in a weak position from the outset. Just then, Joscelin, the Frankish count of Edessa, decided to declare war on Zanghi, emir of Mosul.

As soon as Joscelin had left Edessa [to go to the aid of a Muslim ally, threatened by Zanghi], the people of Harran sent word to Zanghi that Edessa was unprotected. So Zanghi gathered an army together and on Tuesday 24 November 1144 he besieged Edessa with a force of innumerable soldiers.

They camped in front of the Gate of Hours next to the

Revanda, one of the castles of the county of Edessa. The fortifications of Edessa were swiftly overrun by Zanghi's attacking forces.

church of the Confessors. Zanghi sent a request to the people of the city: 'Surrender if you do not wish to die, for there can be no survival for anyone otherwise!'

Hugh, Latin archbishop of the Franks, who had been left in charge of the city, refused this request; 'We shall not surrender,' he declared, trusting the messengers he had sent to Antioch and Jerusalem urging a swift deliverance of this excellent city.

On 21 December 1144, Zanghi ordered an assault on the city by all available means. Seven petraries began stoning the people who had gathered on the walls to defend it: old and young, men and women, priests from the mountain monasteries, standing together beneath a hail of arrows. When Zanghi saw these unfortunate people fighting so heroically, he ordered his soldiers to dig a tunnel under the wall. From the inside, the people had also dug a tunnel under the wall and were advancing against the invaders. But Zanghi's ploy failed, as the people built an inner wall facing the entrance to the enemy's tunnel.

Zanghi's soldiers then dug tunnels under both towers and the section of wall joining them, placing wooden beams all along the tunnels. Zanghi tried once more to persuade the people to surrender: 'We shall send two of our men inside the wall. Send two of your men also, that they may see with their own eyes the tunnels we have dug under the wall. Surrender before you all die by the sword, for I do not wish you to perish.' But the people, trusting in the strength of the inner wall they had built, and expecting the imminent arrival of help from the Franks, refused to surrender; instead they treated him with contempt and ridicule.

So the besiegers set the wooden beams alight, and by dawn the battle raged furiously. The atmosphere was thick with smoke; knees and hearts flinched at the sounds of trumpets and charging troops mingling with the cries of the people. When the wood was consumed, the walls and the two towers collapsed, leaving the newly built wall inside visible to the Turks, who stared at it in amazement until they noticed that there was a gap between the old wall and the new. The soldiers prepared to charge through this gap, and the people, with the archbishop and bishops, stood ready to defend it.

Soon the breach was filled with corpses from both sides. Meanwhile the walls had been left deserted, and the Turks, seeing this, put ladders against them to climb up. The first to reach the top was a Kurd, who began shouting and stoning the people. When they saw him, they took fright and, turning away, fled to the citadel.

From then on, no one could recount without trembling the dreadful events which followed in the early hours of that Saturday 24 December 1144.

The Turkish armies

The Muslim armies of the 12th century contained all manner of troops, from untrained peasants to well-armed, professional soldiers. However, Turks were generally their principal element, and the greatest threat to the crusaders.

The cavalry was the most important part of the Turkish army. In comparison to the heavily armed crusader knights, Turkish horsemen were lightly equipped, with coats of mail and conical helmets, often bearing inscriptions from the Koran. Their small round shields were so different from the long, kite-shaped crusader type that they became a standard feature of western images of Muslim soldiers. In attack, the Turks used lances, swords and clubs, but their main weapon was the lightweight bow. A knowledge of the theories of horsemanship and archery, combined with regular training, enabled the Turks to develop such dexterity that they could shoot from horseback without slowing, and turn in the saddle to fire when in retreat.

A volley of Turkish arrows did not have great penetrative force but they were fired in such quantities – 'like locusts', or 'like rain' so that 'the sun was almost hidden' – that they caused confusion among enemy troops, and a disastrous breakdown in the crusaders' formation.

Contemporaries considered the Turks' horses to be faster and more agile than the crusaders' mounts, and Turkish horsemen used their mobility to attack the crusader army in the flanks and rear, as well as in front, and to avoid the impact of the knights' charge, the most potent weapon available to a feudal army in the west during the 12th century. When used against the Turks the collective charge could leave the crusaders in disarray and vulnerable to a counter-attack. Moreover, the Turks frequently used a feigned retreat, often in conjunction with an ambush: the prelude to disaster for the crusaders.

Because close combat was usually necessary, the Turks were unlikely, however, to defeat a Christian army simply through mobility and sustained firepower, and because the crusaders had the advantage of heavy armour, the Turks approached only if they could be reasonably confident of victory. To this end they repeated the pattern of weakening the crusaders and disrupting their formation, before moving in to achieve final success in close combat, throughout the 12th century. The crusader knights had to be disciplined, even under severe pressure, if Turkish tactics were to be overcome.

Zanghi shows mercy

The Turks entered Edessa with staves and swords drawn, indiscriminately slaughtering the old and the young, men and women, priests, deacons, monks, nuns, virgins, infants at the breast, and those promised to each other in marriage! The Syrian boar was victorious and devoured the sweetest fruit.

What a bitter tale! The city of Abgar, beloved of Christ, Edessa was trampled underfoot because of our wickedness: the priests massacred, the deacons sacrificed and their assistants beaten to death, the churches ransacked and the altars thrown to the ground. Alas, what a calamity! Fathers denied their sons, mothers forgot the love they bore their children! As the swords cut them down many fled to the mountain-top, some gathered their children around them as a hen gathers her chicks, and waited huddled together to die by the sword or be taken into captivity.

At the sight of such violence, aged priests carrying the relics of martyrs made no attempt to escape; nor did they cease chanting their prayers, until the sword silenced them for ever. Later they were found where they had fallen, their blood spilt all around them, still clutching their relics, which miraculously the Turks had not seized.

Those who fled to the citadel found the gate barred against them, the Franks inside having been ordered to keep it so until the archbishop appeared in person. Since he did not escape until later, thousands of people suffocated there and the mound of their bodies rose higher than the gate. When the archbishop did arrive, the gate was opened for him but he

Eastern war machines from a 12th-century manuscript. A crossbow mounted in a shield (top left); a device for loading a catapult (bottom left); a trebuchet (above).

was unable to enter, and as he attempted to do so he fell among the dead and was killed by a Turkish soldier.

When Zanghi saw this carnage he forbade any further killing. Soon after this, he saw Bishop Basil [of the Jacobite Church] being dragged naked at the end of a rope. Noticing that he was old and had his head shaven, Zanghi asked who he was and, on being told that this was the Syrian [i.e. native Christian] bishop, began to reproach him for having refused to surrender the city. Basil answered bravely: 'What has happened is for the best.' 'How so?' demanded the emir, and the bishop continued: 'For you, since you have won a great victory because of our resistance. For us, because we have deserved your respect. As we kept faith with the Franks, so

we shall with you, since God has allowed us to become your slaves.'

Seeing that Basil was brave and spoke Arabic fluently, Zanghi ordered him to be given a robe and invited him into his tent to discuss the reconstruction of the city. A herald was then despatched to announce that all survivors could return home safely.

Two days later, those inside the citadel were given a promise that their lives would be spared, and they surrendered. The Turks spared the lives of the Armenians and the Greeks who had survived, but they killed the Franks wherever they found them.

It is not up to us to describe this calamity any further, it belongs to the prophet Jeremiah and his like, to call upon the keeners and the women mourners to compose elegies in verse for this unfortunate people.

The pope calls for a new crusade

Zanghi was to die only two years later, in 1146, but before that, the Franks in the east had decided to appeal for help. In 1145 an embassy from Outremer, headed by Hugh, bishop of Jebail, arrived at the papal curia at Viterbo, and Pope Eugenius III decided to call for a new crusade. On 1 December 1145, he issued the bull *Quantum praedecessores*, addressed to Louis VII, king of France, and the French nobility.

We have learned from the accounts of the ancients how much our predecessors the pontiffs of Rome worked for the liberation of the Church in the east. Our predecessor, Pope Urban II of blessed memory, spoke forth like a trumpet, and took care to solicit the sons of the Holy Roman Church from all parts of the world to discuss this very matter. At his voice, the peoples beyond the Alps – particularly the courageous and energetic warriors of the French kingdom – and also those from Italy, came together inflamed with the ardour of charity to liberate our Saviour's glorious Sepulchre from the filth of the pagans, by a huge joint expedition. Through the grace of God and the efforts of your fathers, who were energetic in spreading the Christian name by force in that part of the world, the Holy City and many more cities have been held until our own time by Christians.

But now, for our sins and those of the people themselves, has arisen something that we are unable to mention without profound grief and sadness: the city of Edessa, which, it is said, was alone in serving the Lord under the authority of the

Christians at a time when the whole land in the east was held by pagans, has now been captured by the enemies of the cross of Christ.

The archbishop of that city and all his clergy, along with many other Christians, have been killed there; and the relics of the saints have been scattered and trampled by the infidels. We ourselves know, and we cannot believe it can have escaped your notice, how much danger there is in this for the Church of God and for the whole of Christendom.

So in the Lord's name we advise, we request, we command all of you, and enjoin you for the remission of your sins, to do the following: those who are men of God, the potentates and nobles, should gird themselves for battle like men and strongly attack the hordes of infidels, who glory in the fact that they almost always triumph over us; and so defend the Eastern Church which was freed from their tyranny by the shedding of your fathers' blood.

We, therefore, taking measures with paternal care against the apathy of your people and the destitution of the Church, by the authority granted to us by God, do grant and confirm that remission of sins which our predecessor Pope Urban II established, for all those who decide in a spirit of devotion to undertake and perform this work. And we decree that their wives and children, and their goods and possessions too, will remain under the protection of the holy Church, of ourselves and our archbishops, bishops and other prelates of the Church of God.

Also, by our apostolic authority we forbid that there should be any litigation concerning those possessions they had in time of peace, when they first agreed to wear the cross, until it is clearly known that they have returned home or are dead.

Furthermore, since those who fight for the Lord should not turn their attention to costly clothes, or to the cultivation of their appearance, or to dogs or hawks or anything else which might imply wantonness, our admonishment to you in the Lord's name is that anyone who has decided to undertake this holy work should be utterly uninterested in clothes made of spotted or grey fur, or in gold or silver armour, but should apply all their effort and care to such arms, horses and so forth as will help them conquer the infidels.

Whoever is oppressed by debt, and undertakes this holy journey with purity of heart, shall not pay interest on the money he has not repaid; and if they, or others on their behalf, have been imprisoned because of interest, by our apostolic authority we absolve them from their obligation and their pledge.

By the authority of Almighty God and of Peter the first among the apostles, granted to us by God, and in accordance with the institution of our predecessor, we grant remission and absolution from sins, such that whoever devotedly undertakes and performs this most holy journey, even if he is killed there, shall obtain absolution for all those sins of which he makes confession with a contrite and humble heart, and shall have the enjoyment of eternal reward from the repayer of all men.

Vetralla, 1 December 1145.

Louis VII was, it seems, already making plans for an armed pilgrimage, and he responded to the pope's call with enthusiasm. Odo of Deuil, who later became abbot of Saint-Denis, was Louis's chaplain on the Second Crusade, and he describes the king's attempts to gather support. Louis and Pope Eugenius had the backing of the most influential ecclesiastic of their day, Bernard, Cistercian abbot of Clairvaux.

On 31 March 1146 the glorious king of France and duke of Aquitaine, Louis VII, being twenty-five years old, in order to be worthy of Christ undertook to follow him by taking the cross. This happened at Vézelay, at Easter.

On the previous Christmas, this same pious king had held court at Bourges. Having invited in his concern more of the bishops and nobles of the realm to his crown-wearing than is usual, he first made known to them his secret desire. Then that devout man, Godfrey, bishop of Langres, spoke authoritatively about the devastation of Edessa, the oppression of the Christians and the arrogance of the pagans, and advised all to take up arms with the king to aid the Christians, for the sake of the King of all. Zeal for the faith burned and shone in the king, together with contempt for worldly pleasure and temporal glory: he was in himself an example more persuasive than any speech. But Louis did not immediately harvest that which the bishop then sowed with his words.

Another appointment was made: everyone was to assemble on Good Friday, at Vézelay, and then on Easter Day those who were inspired by heaven would take up the cross. Meanwhile the king sent messages to Rome to Pope Eugenius III with regard to this matter. Those who joyfully took the messages brought back letters sweeter than the honeycomb, which decreed obedience to King Louis, and promised to those who took up the sweet yoke of Christ remission of all their sins, and protection for their children and wives. The supreme pontiff wished he could be present to give his blessing to the holy task; but he delegated this office to Bernard, the holy abbot of Clairvaux.

The interior of Vézelay Abbey, looking east towards the Holy Land. Louis VII of France took the cross at Vézelay before setting out on the Second Crusade.

Bernard of Clairvaux

Bernard of Clairvaux was born into a noble family at Fontaines near Dijon in 1090. He joined the Order of Cîteaux in 1112 and, three years later, became abbot of Clairvaux. He taught Suger, abbot of Saint-Denis, and Pope Eugenius III, and was also close to Louis VI of France and his son, Louis VII.

Following Pope Eugenius's request that he preach the Second Crusade, to recover Edessa, Bernard made his first appearance at Vézelay on 31 March 1146, where he recruited Louis VII and a large number of French noblemen. In the winter of 1146–7, he preached the crusade in the Low Countries and in Germany, whose king, Conrad III, eventually took the cross together with many of his followers.

The success of the 'honey-tongued preacher' was interpreted in terms of a 'miracle': according to one contemporary, his view of the crusade was received as a 'divine augury'. Bernard's popularity in Germany was indeed remarkable; he preached in Latin and French, while German was the only language understood by large sectors of the population. Bernard also sent messengers to remote places in the Low Countries and the Rhine Valley, while his letters were read throughout Europe to crowds anxious to share in his aura of holiness.

His success in enlisting nobles and knights, peasants and elderly people, women and children, eventually ran counter to the plans of Pope Eugenius, who regarded the crusade as a military expedition whose main participants would be French and Italian knights. To Bernard, it was primarily a unique opportunity given by a forgiving God for the salvation of mankind, and the individual act of repentance each Christian should perform before his Redeemer. The cross worn by the crusaders attested to their readiness to share Christ's agony on the cross for the salvation of mankind. Repentance and penitence were at the very heart of their journey, while the hardships they suffered during the pilgrimage to Jerusalem served to advance the salvation of their souls.

Bernard's success was related to the power of preaching in the Middle Ages, a reflection of the oral culture of the times. In addition, his charismatic character, formally recognized in his canonization in 1174 some 20 years after his death in 1153, gave the Second Crusade the impetus it needed.

At last, 31 March, that day which the king desired, came; the abbot arrived, armed with apostolic authority and his own holiness; and a great crowd of those who had been summoned also arrived at the same time and place. The king took up the sign of the cross sent to him by Eugenius III and many of the nobles joined him. Since there was nowhere in the town which could accommodate such a crowd, a wooden platform was constructed for Bernard of Clairvaux outside the town, so that he could address his audience from a raised position. He mounted the platform, accompanied by the king, with a decorated cross.

When he had spoken, everyone around began shouting for crosses. When he had given out, we might even say had sown, the bundle of crosses which he had prepared, he was forced to tear up his clothes and sow them. It was decreed at last that they would set out at the end of the year.

An idea of both the power and the content of Bernard's preaching can be gained from his letters. This one was addressed to the people of eastern France and Bavaria in 1146.

My address to you concerns Christ's business, in which lies our salvation. I say this, so that the authority of the Lord might excuse the unworthiness of the speaker. I am no great man, but my love for you in Christ Jesus is very great. This is the reason I am writing to you; I would approach you more willingly in the flesh, but my desire to come to you is not matched by an opportunity. See, now is the acceptable time, now is the day of full salvation. 'The earth shook and trembled' [Psalm 18.7], because the God of heaven begins to destroy his land. His, I say, for there he was seen, and for more than thirty years he lived as a man among men. And now, because of our sins, the enemy of the cross has raised up its sacrilegious head, devastated with the sword the blessed land, the promised land, has almost reached the point of invading the very city of the Living God and, were there none to resist, is about to pollute the holy places dyed purple by the blood of the spotless Lamb.

What are you doing, brave men? What are you doing, servants of the cross? Will you thus give holy things to dogs and pearls to swine? How many sinners have confessed their sins there with tears and have obtained forgiveness, once the filth of the pagans had been eliminated by the swords of your fathers! The wicked sees this and is envious; he gnashes his teeth and wastes away. If ever the enemy is by chance able to occupy Jerusalem – may God prevent it – he will stir up the vessels of his iniquity, leaving no sign or trace of such piety.

What are we to think, brothers? Has the hand of the Lord

THE SECOND CRUSADE 1147–1149

grown shorter or become powerless to bring salvation? Could he not send twelve legions of angels, or even just speak the word, and his land would be freed? He is all-powerful according to his wishes. But, I tell you, 'the Lord thy God is testing thee' [Deut. 13.3].

Therefore, since your land flourishes with brave men and is famous for the strength of its youth, gird yourselves manfully and take up joyful arms for the name of Christ.

Conrad III takes the cross

The pope had not originally envisaged German participation in the expedition, but at Christmas 1146, the power of St Bernard's preaching persuaded Conrad III, king of Germany and Holy Roman Emperor-elect, and the German nobility, that they too should take the cross.

Otto, bishop of Freisingen, was Conrad's half-brother, and himself a participant in the expedition. In this account he tells of the enthusiasm of the Germans for the crusade.

When countless people in France had been roused to undertake the expedition across the sea, Bernard of Clairvaux decided to go to Germany in order to convince that kingdom with his preaching, for he hoped by his sacred exhortation to persuade the Holy Roman Emperor-elect, Conrad III, to take up the cross. When Conrad heard of this, he declared that a general council should be held at Christmas 1146 at Speyer. Bernard attended the council and persuaded Conrad to take up the cross, together with his nephew Frederick of Swabia and other nobles and leading figures; both in public and in private he performed many miracles.

After this Conrad travelled to Bavaria, and there held another general council in February. In the place of Bernard of Clairvaux he took with him Adam, abbot of Ebrach, a devout and learned man. Having duly celebrated Mass, the abbot ascended the pulpit. When the letters from Pope Eugenius and the abbot of Clairvaux had been read, he gave a brief homily, through which he persuaded nearly all those present to profess for the expedition. Having been roused already by rumours they had heard, all those present ran of their own accord to take up the cross.

At that time three bishops took up the cross, that is, Henry of Regensburg, Otto of Freisingen and Reginbert of Passau; also Henry, duke of Bavaria, the king's brother, and countless men from the ranks of counts, nobles and knights.

Even, strange to say, a crowd of brigands and thieves arrived, so great that no sane person could doubt that a change, as sudden as it was unexpected, had happened by the hand of God.

Welf also, the brother of the previous Duke Henry and one of the most noble princes of the realm, professed for the expedition with many followers on Christmas Eve at his own estate at Peiting.

Vladislav, duke of the Bohemians, Ottokar, margrave of Styria, and the illustrious Count Bernard of Carinthia took up their crosses not much later, together with a large retinue. But the Saxons refused to set out for the east, since they had as neighbours [the Slavs and Wends] people given over to the filth of idols.

They, therefore, took up crosses to declare war on these peoples, differing from us only in that they did not merely sew their crosses into their clothes but held them aloft mounted on a wheel.

Attacks on the Jews, 1146–7

As in the early stages of the First Crusade, there were a number of attacks on Jewish communities in the Rhineland. Otto of Freisingen describes the origins of these pogroms.

In 1146, a certain Cistercian monk called Radulf, a man of the most devout appearance carefully counterfeiting pious severity, but of only mediocre education, entered the regions bordering on the Rhine and inflamed many thousands of people to take up the cross: people from Cologne, Mainz, Worms, Speyer, Strasburg and other neighbouring cities, towns and villages. But he carelessly sowed this idea into his teaching, that the Jews who lived in all these cities and towns should be slaughtered as if they were the enemies of the Christian religion. The seed of this doctrine germinated in many cities and towns of France and Germany, and took root so firmly that many Jews were killed in violent uprisings. Many others fled for protection under the wings of Conrad III. So it came about that a fair number of Jews who were fleeing for their lives found sanctuary in a town called Nuremburg, belonging to the emperor.

But the abbot of Clairvaux sent letters or messengers to the peoples of France and Germany, in which he clearly showed that the Jews were not to be killed because of their wickedness, but scattered. As witness to this he quoted the psalmist, who says in Psalm 59: 'God shall let me see my desire upon mine enemies. Slay them not', and also 'Scatter them by thy power' [Psalm 59.10–11].

St Bernard saves the Jews

We have heard with joy that zeal for God burns in you, but wisdom must not be lacking from this zeal. The Jews are not to be persecuted, nor killed, nor even forced to flee. 'God,' says the Church, 'says "Slay not my enemies, lest my people forget"' [Psalm 59.11]. Alive, the Jews are signs to us, a continual reminder of the Lord's passion. Because of this they were scattered into every nation, so that while they are paying the just penalty of such a crime they may be witnesses to our redemption. Therefore the Church, speaking in that psalm, added: 'Scatter them by thy power; and bring them down, O Lord our shield' [Psalm 59.11]. So it happened: they were scattered and brought low everywhere, enduring harsh captivity under Christian princes. But 'at evening let them return' [Psalm 59.14] and in time there shall be respite for them.

From St Bernard, *Epistolae*

St Bernard of Clairvaux, abbot of the Cistercian Abbey at Clairvaux, wearing the white habit of the Cistercian order.

The anonymous Würzburg annalist describes the slaughter which took place in his own city.

I shall relate just one example from many of the slaughter of the Jews, which took place at Würzburg. In the month of February 1147, the pilgrims, as has been mentioned, were gathering in the city. On 24 February an amazing thing happened: the body of a man was found chopped up into many pieces. Two large pieces were found in the river Main, that is, one among the mills towards the suburb called Bleicha, another towards the town of Thunegersheim, while the remaining pieces were found in a ditch opposite the tower which is generally called Katzinwichus. When all the scattered parts of the body had been gathered together, the body was taken to an inn inside the city, and there was buried in a churchyard.

As if this gave them a just cause against the Jews, both the citizens and the pilgrims were seized by a sudden frenzy, and broke into the homes of the Jews, killing old men and young, women and little children, without discrimination, without delay and without mercy. Furthermore, signs were said to occur at the grave of the body which started the trouble: the dumb spoke, the blind could see, the lame walked and other signs of this kind happened. For this reason the pilgrims began to honour the man as if he were a martyr, and carried round relics of the body. When they demanded that he should

be canonized, Siegfried, the bishop of Würzburg, who was a true man of religion, resisted their importunity. This aroused such enmity against the bishop that he was forced to take refuge in a tower to avoid being stoned and the canons were in such fear of their persecutors that even on the most holy night of Maundy Thursday, they did not dare to ascend to the choir and sing Matins. At last Easter Week came and the pilgrims began their journey; so finally the riots ceased and peace returned to the city.

This is indeed what happened at Würzburg. You may infer without my mentioning it how they behaved in other cities.

The Jewish rabbi Ephraim of Bonn, who was 13 at the time of these events, tells of the fear engendered by Radulf, but explains how St Bernard rescued the Jews from their persecutors.

In the year 1146 the ungodly Radulf, who was a monk, persecuted Israel treacherously. He rose up against the people of God like the wicked Haman to destroy them, to murder them and to annihilate them. He came from the land of France and travelled all over Germany – may the Lord preserve it, amen – to assemble and to mark out and to sully Christians with the horizontal and vertical sign [i.e. to sign potential crusaders with the cross]. He went and barked (he was called 'the barker') in the name of Christ to go to Jerusalem to fight the Muslims. Everywhere he went he spoke ill of all the Jews of every land, and he incited the serpent and the dogs against us saying: 'First avenge Christ, the crucified one, upon his enemies who stand before you; and then only, go to fight against the Muslims.'

We, the Jews, heard this and we were frightened, losing our courage in the face of the rage of the oppressor who was organizing our destruction. We cried out unto our God saying: 'Alas, fifty years have not yet passed, since our blood was shed for the sake of the unity of your holy name [1096]. "Wilt thou draw out thine anger to all generations?"' [Psalm 85.5].

God heard our cries and had mercy upon us. He sent after this ungodly monk another, who was a respectable priest, one of the greatest and most honoured. He knew their laws and was a person of understanding. His name was Bernard, abbot of Clairvaux in France. He also barked, as is their custom, saying, 'It is good that you march against the Muslims, but anyone who touches a Jew to take his life, is as touching Jesus himself. Radulf, my pupil, who said that the Jews should be destroyed, did not speak correctly. For it is written about them in the book of Psalms: "Slay them not, lest my people forget"' [Psalm 59.11].

The Christians honoured this priest as one of their saints; we have not investigated whether he received a bribe to speak well of Israel.

When they had heard this, many desisted from their evil plan to annihilate us. In his mercy, God let us stay alive. We also gave our wealth as a ransom for our lives and did not refuse them any of the silver or gold which they asked from us. For if our Creator in his mercy had not sent us this Abbot Bernard and his subsequent letters, then no remnant or vestige would have been left of Israel. Blessed be our redeemer and saviour, blessed be his name.

Crusade against the Wends, 1147

As the French and German kings gathered their armies ready to set out for the east, in the spring of 1147 several German princes obtained approval for crusades against the Slavs or Wends instead. St Bernard's letter encouraged this expedition.

I have no doubt that it will have been heard in your land, how God has aroused the spirit of kings and princes to root up from the earth the enemies of the Christian name. Great blessing, great richness of divine mercy!
Those who seemed utterly lost have been converted, turning from their evil ways and ready to do good. But the devil fears another loss even more from the conversion of the nations, since he has heard that they will all enter into the Kingdom and that all Israel will be saved. He thinks that the time for this is imminent, and now his skilful wickedness is busying itself with the full force of its deceit to try to obstruct this great blessing. Therefore he has aroused his depraved offspring, his wicked children, the pagans whom the fortitude of the Christians has endured for far too long, disregarding to its own peril the pagan traps and treachery, rather than grinding down under its heel their poisonous heads. But as Scripture says, 'Pride comes before a fall' [Proverbs 16.18]: it will happen, God willing, that their arrogance will be humbled and the route to Jerusalem will not be impeded.

Since the Lord has committed the preaching of this word of the cross to my weakness, on the advice of the lord king Conrad III, the bishops and leaders, who have come together at Frankfurt, we announce that [another] Christian force should be armed against the pagans in order to destroy them utterly, or at least to convert the nations to take up the standard of salvation, promising to them and to those who have set out for Jerusalem the same indulgence for their sins.

This army will observe the same practices in clothes, arms, trappings and everything else as did the other one, and the same reward.

It was agreed by everyone in the council at Frankfurt that copies of this letter should be sent everywhere, and that the bishops and priests should read it out to the people of God, and that they should sign themselves with the sign of the holy cross and arm against the enemies of the cross of Christ who are beyond the Elbe. Everyone should gather at Magdeburg on 29 June 1147.

Helmold of Bosau was a priest, possibly of peasant background, who was a contemporary of the Wendish Crusade. In an account written in 1167–8, he describes the fruitless attempts of the Wendish prince, Niclot, to avert the crusade, and how, when these failed, Niclot attacked his Christian neighbours first.

When Prince Niclot, leader of the Wends, heard that an army would be gathered to destroy him, he called together all of his people and began to fortify the castle of Dubin, to be a refuge for the people in time of need. He sent messengers to Count Adolf [Christian ruler] of Holstein, reminding him of the alliance they had made, and at the same time asking him to make himself available for discussion with him and for taking part in counsel. But the count refused, saying that this would

The Wends

Helmold of Bosau, writing in the late 1160s, considered that the Slavs had remained the most obdurate of all the peoples of the north in the face of attempts to spread Christianity. He was referring to the Wends, a branch of the Slavs who lived in the lands between the rivers Elbe and Saale and the Oder, and who, since as early as the eighth century, had been subject to the pressure of missionaries, churchmen and warriors trying to persuade or force them into the Christian and Germanic orbit. Although the process was near completion by the late 12th century, traces of Wendish culture and traditions survived four centuries later.

The Slavs had spread slowly from the region of the middle Dnieper over several centuries, some into the areas vacated by Germanic tribes migrating into the Roman Empire. The Wends, distinct from their neighbours in Poland to the east and Bohemia to the south, were subdivided among the Abodrites, the Wilzi, the Pomeranians and the Sorben. The most crucial element in the maintenance of their identity appears to have been adherence to their religion, which was centred upon elaborate wooden temples, often richly carved and furnished. The temples contained effigies of their gods and were enclosed within a palisade in which grew sacred groves of oaks. The Wends seem to have practised ritual sacrifices, including that of humans; Helmold claims that on one occasion visiting merchants were offered 100 marks if they would provide a priest for this purpose. A strong sense of community expressed itself in respect for parents, care of the sick and the elderly, and hospitality to visitors.

The Wends' economic organization was determined by their environment — forest, marsh, lakes, coast and islands — in which they cultivated rye, raised cattle, fished and hunted. They traded in fish, furs, wax and honey, and slaves captured during their frequent raids on neighbouring tribes.

German expansionism, particularly ferocious during the tenth century, continually threatened this culture and eventually provoked rebellions in 983, 1018 and 1066. The subjugation of the Wends was a long and bloody process to which the Wendish Crusade contributed little. More important were the campaigns of Henry the Lion, duke of Saxony, during the 1160s and 1170s, although he made no effort to convert his new subjects, thinking more of material than of spiritual gains.

be a rash step for him to take because it would offend the other Christian princes.

When Niclot realized that it was not possible to prevent the expedition from setting off, in secret he prepared a naval force, and having crossed the sea his fleet put in at the mouth of the Trave, from which he intended to overrun the whole province of the Wagrians before the Saxon army could pour over his own frontiers.

In the evening he sent a messenger to warn Count Adolf, as he had promised, but this was entirely useless, for the count was away. At dawn on 26 June 1147 the Slav fleet came into the mouth of the Trave. Then the citizens of the city of Lübeck, hearing the distant roar of the army, called to the men of the city, saying, 'We have heard the sound of great shouting, like the sound of an invading horde, and we do not know what it is.' They sent messengers around the city and to the market-place to tell them of the imminent danger. But the people were all drunk, and they could not be moved from their beds.

The enemy surrounded them and set fire to their ships, loaded with merchandise. On that day three hundred or more men were killed. Next, those in the citadel suffered a terrible siege for two days. The barbarians ranged around the whole of the Wagrian territory, and demolished whatever they found. The region called Dargune was consumed by voracious flames, courageous men who happened to have made an attempt at armed resistance were slaughtered and their wives and children made captives.

When the Slavs had violated at their pleasure the land of the Wagrians, they came to the district of Süssel to destroy the colony of Frisians there. But no greater battle was fought than by the priest Gerlav and that small band of men in the fortress of Süssel, and they defended the fortifications against the hands of the destroyers. When Count Adolf of Holstein heard of this he assembled an army to fight the Slavs and throw them out of his land. Learning this news the Slavs went back to their ships and sailed away, loaded with captives and with various possessions which they had stolen in the land of Wagria.

Meanwhile the news spread over the whole of Saxony and Westphalia that the Slavs had broken out and had started the war first; the whole of that expedition which had the cross as its sign hurried to go down into the land of the Slavs and to punish their wickedness. The army was split in half, and made many siege-engines and besieged two different fortresses. [At Demmin the siege was unsuccessful.] At Dobin, the army of the Danes came too, and joined with those who were besieging the town, so the siege increased in interest.

One day, those who were shut up inside came to the conclusion that the Danes were fighting rather sluggishly (for they are very warlike at home, but less so when abroad), and so they burst out suddenly, killed many men, and left them lying thickly on the ground. No help could be brought to the Danes because there was a stretch of water in the way. The army was moved to anger by this, and worked with a firmer purpose towards taking the city. But the vassals of Duke Henry of Saxony and of Albert the Bear, margrave of Brandenburg, said to each other: 'Is not this land which we are devastating our own land, and is not this people which we are fighting our own people? Why therefore do we find ourselves to be our own enemies, and destroyers of our own incomes? Will not their loss rebound upon our lords?'

So from that day they began to induce a feeling of reluctance in the army, and to lighten the siege by frequent truces. For as often as the Slavs were beaten in combat, the army was restrained from following them as they fled and from capturing the citadel. In the end, when our men were weary of this, an agreement was made that the Slavs should accept the Christian faith, and that the Danes should release their captives. So many of the Slavs were falsely baptized, and the Danes released from captivity all the old and useless men, but kept the others, whose youth made them fitter for service. Thus it was that the great expedition was disbanded with moderate gain. Immediately after this the Slavs became worse, for they did not live up to their baptism, nor did they restrain their hands from pillaging the Danes.

The Baltic crusade

While Helmold's account is concerned with Saxony, Vincent of Prague, writing at about the same time, describes how the Bohemian princes also decided to crusade against the Slavs.

When Bernard's preaching, in the form of a letter, reached the ears of Vladislav, duke of the Bohemians, his bishop, his clergy and all his people, the duke was pricked deep in the recesses of his heart, and for love of the Lord and for the sake of the remission of his sins, he, together with his twin brother, Lord Henry, his younger brother, Lord Theobald, and other nobles left off governing their duchies, and wore the cross with the intention of crossing the sea and fighting the pagans.

Henry, bishop of Moravia, took on the cross in the name of Christ and, together with many of the bishops of Saxony and the Saxon militia, went to Pomerania to convert the Pomeranians to the Christian faith. When they reached the capital of that country, a city by the name of Stettin, they besieged it by armed force as strongly as they could. But the Pomeranians displayed crosses over their citadel, and sent messengers together with their bishop, called Albert, who had been given to them by the late Lord Otto, bishop of the church at Bamberg, who had first converted them to the Christian faith, and they asked why the Saxons had come and attacked them. If they had come to confirm them in the Christian faith, they said, this should be achieved not by war but by the preaching of bishops. The Saxons had set this great expedition in motion more with a view to conquering territory than to confirm anyone in the Christian faith, but the bishops of Saxony, on hearing [that Stettin was a Christian city], held a council with Prince Ratibor of Pomerania and Albert, bishop of Pomerania. Then, despite having lost many knights and princes, they went home; for when they were not fighting on God's behalf, a happy result would be no easy thing to achieve.

Crusade in Portugal, 1147

Crusaders from England, Normandy, the Low Countries and the Rhineland sailed for the east from the ports of north-west Europe but were persuaded to take part in the siege of Lisbon, which fell in October 1147. The anonymous Magdeburg annalist reflects on the role of the German contingent.

They sailed along the river Tagus, and on the second day they came to Lisbon, on 28 June 1147. This city, according to the histories of the Saracens, was founded by Ulysses after the fall of Troy, and was built with a marvellous construction of walls and turrets on top of a mountain that is invincible by human strength; around it the whole army pitched their tents, and on 1 July, with the help of divine virtue, they captured the suburbs.

After this they made various assaults on the walls, with great numbers of casualties on both sides, and took their time, up to 1 August, in making siege-engines. At great expense they constructed two towers by the shore, one on the eastern side where the Flemish were established, and the other on the western side where the English had pitched their camp. They put together four bridges on the ships, so as to open up access over the walls of the city.

The army put all these measures in motion on 3 August 1147, but its men were pushed back by a contrary wind and were somewhat damaged by catapults, and withdrew their ships. Then, while the men of Cologne were fighting on their side of the city against the Moors, the English took too little care of their turret, and a fire suddenly took hold, which they were unable to extinguish. The men of Cologne began to undermine the walls with one of their machines. When the Saracens saw this, they poured a mixture of oil and fire on to the machine and reduced it to ashes, and they hurled stones at the soldier in charge of the machine as he was trying to break the wall. The Saracens caused innumerable deaths by catapults and by arrows, but they in turn were killed in even greater numbers by similar means.

Meanwhile the Saracens in the city, who had plenty of food, were stealing food from their fellow citizens to such an extent that a large number died from starvation, and some did not shrink from eating dogs and cats. A good number of these gave themselves up to the Christians and undertook the sacrament of baptism. Some of them had their hands cut off and were sent back to the walls by our men, where they were stoned by their fellow citizens. Many things happened both good and bad (such are the vicissitudes of war) which it would take too long to enumerate.

At last, around the time of the Nativity of St Mary [8 September 1147], a certain man of Pisa who was very industrious fitted together a wooden tower of astonishing height in that part where the English tower had previously been destroyed, and this admirable work was finished by about the middle of October, at vast expense and by the exertions of the whole army.

Another man dug out a huge hole underneath the wall with his engine and with the help of many men, and on 29

The miracle of the clouds

We were near the mouth of the river Tagus in Portugal when a wind came down from the mountains of Cintra and shook the ships with a storm of such astonishing violence that some of the boats sank with all hands. The storm lasted until we reached the entrance of Oporto, on the river Tagus.

As we were entering the port, a miraculous sign appeared to us in the air.

For behold, great white clouds which were coming along with us from the direction of the Kingdom of France were seen to run into some large clouds flecked with black coming from the Portuguese mainland; and like ordered lines of battle, with their left wings conjoined, they conflicted with an amazing impact: some were making their attack on the right and the left, some were circling the rest as if looking for access, and some pushed through the others so that they vanished like vapour.

At last the great cloud which was coming from our direction and which was taking with it all the impurity of the air, so that on the near side the sky appeared the purest azure, pushed back with its force all the clouds coming from the mainland, and alone was in possession of the air while all the other clouds appeared to be fleeing to the city.

Seeing this, we cried out: 'See how our cloud has won! See, God is with us!'

So at last the tossing of the storm ceased. After a short time, around the tenth hour of the day, we reached Lisbon, which was not far from the mouth of the river Tagus.

Anonymous, 1147–8

September 1147 the Saracens fought with the men of Cologne over it until evening. Our men blocked off the path by which the enemy were hoping to return so that few could get back without receiving a blow. Then they worked day and night and finished the hole, filled with smooth planks. Fire was applied and the wood burned, and there was a collapse in the wall over a length of two hundred feet. The men of Cologne attacked with a great shout, hoping that the guards had fled. But when they reached the place of the collapse, they found a mound of ruins and Saracens ready to defend it. They attacked none the less, and the battle which started at midnight did not finish until daylight. Beaten back by a multitude of blows, our men withdrew from battle until the English tower was moved up by orders from command.

The Saracens were heavily afflicted on all sides by the battle. Now the tower filled with warlike men loomed over the walls. In the same hour the army on our side of the city tried to break through the wall, while the men of Lorraine were apparently carrying on the fight, and they made an astonishing assault on the Saracens.

Meanwhile the king's knights, who were fighting from the

The sea front at Lisbon; Christian besiegers in the 12th century saw similar clouds as portents of victory.

top of the tower, were terrified by the Saracens' catapults, and fought weakly, until a point was reached at which the Saracens would have come out and burned the tower if one of our men, who chanced to come into their way, had not prevented them. When the rumour of this danger reached our ears, we sent the best men in the army on our side to defend the tower, so that our hope in it should not come to nothing.

When the Saracens saw the men of Lorraine ascending the tower with such fervour and valour, they were so terrified that they laid down their weapons and asked to shake hands as a sign of peace. And so it came about that their prince Aichada made an agreement with us on these terms: that our army should take all their belongings, and their gold and silver, and the king should have the city and all the land around it, with the Saracens stripped of all they had. This divine – not human – victory was won over two hundred thousand and five hundred Saracen men on the feast of the Eleven Thousand Virgins, 24 October 1147.

Louis VII departs for the east

Some crusaders stayed on in Portugal, in order to colonize the captured cities, others continued by sea to Outremer.

Meanwhile the main French and German armies had decided to take the land route to the east. On 8 June 1147, Louis VII and his army set off from Saint-Denis, the great royal abbey just north of Paris. Its celebrated abbot, Suger, was Louis's principal adviser, and St Denis his patron saint. Odo of Deuil recounts the scene of Louis's departure.

On his way to Saint-Denis, Louis VII performed a laudable act, which few and perhaps none of his high station would imitate. At the end of a visit to some monks in Paris, he went outside and entered a leper colony. I saw him go in with only two companions. He stayed inside for a long time; the rest of his huge retinue remained outside.

Meanwhile his mother, Queen Adela, his wife, Eleanor, duchess of Aquitaine, and countless others, had gone on ahead to Saint-Denis. When he himself arrived there, the king found the pope, Eugenius III, Abbot Suger and the monks gathered together. Then he humbly prostrated himself on the ground and adored his patron saint, Denis. The pope and the abbot undid a small gold door and brought out a silver reliquary, so that the king might be rendered even more eager by seeing and kissing the relic which his soul loved. Then, having taken up the oriflamme, the royal standard, from above the altar and having received the pilgrim's wallet and a blessing from the pope, Louis withdrew from the crowd to the monks' dormitory [to prepare for his departure].

The delay [before he went] was unendurable to the crowds, to the king's mother and to the queen, who were almost fainting from emotion and the heat. It is impossible to attempt to describe the grief and lamentation which took place there. Meanwhile, the king, with a few of his companions, dined in the refectory with the monks, and, having received the kiss of peace from everyone, left amid the prayers and tears of all.

Conrad III departs for the east

Otto of Freisingen gave a brief description of the progress of the German and French armies towards Constantinople, but could not bring himself to provide any further details.

When the bitter winter cold was over, when the earth gave birth in the kindly warm showers of spring, flowers and grasses were growing, and the green fields smiled to the world, showing the happy face of the earth, King Conrad III started out for the Holy Land.

He moved his troops from Nuremburg, and travelled along the Danube having boarded ship at Regensburg. He led so great a multitude that the river seemed hardly wide enough for those who were sailing and the fields hardly wide enough for those on foot.

Louis VII, king of France, followed with his men not far behind Conrad. With him travelled, from our people, the people of Lorraine, Stephen, bishop of Metz, Henry, bishop of Toul, and many nobles from Germany and Italy. Indeed, since the result of this expedition, brought on by our sins, is well known, I shall leave the description of it to another time or another writer.

A quite different perspective, and a fuller account of the crusaders' progress through imperial territory, is provided by the Byzantine writer John Kinnamos. An imperial secretary, he compiled his narrative probably in the 1180s, on the basis of eye-witness reports.

And now, quite simply, the whole of the west set its forces in motion. The convenient pretext was that these people would cross from Europe to Asia to fight the Turks, recapture the church of the Holy Sepulchre in Palestine and explore the holy places.

In actual fact they intended to take the land of the Byzantine Empire by assault and overthrow everything in their way. Their army was countless. When the Emperor Manuel I Comnenus learned that they were very close to the boundaries of Hungary, he sent ambassadors to sound out the westerners' intentions and, if they had come intending no harm to the Byzantines, to make them confirm this on oath.

When the ambassadors had accomplished their mission to the barbarians, they returned to Constantinople, and the western kings continued on their journey. Their armies were not mixed with each other, but the Germans advanced first with the French considerably behind them. I do not know why they did this, whether it was because each nation considered itself a worthy match in battle, or whether they were concerned that supplies should not run out. They advanced, as innumerable as the sand on the sea-shore. Not even Xerxes could boast as many myriads, when he bridged the

Hellespont with boats, as were in the advancing armies.

When they arrived at the Danube, at the point where the Emperor Manuel had made arrangements for their crossing, he ordered most of the secretaries, who were sitting on either bank of the river, to record the cargo of each ship. When they had counted up to ninety myriads, they could not count any further, so great was this multitude.

When they approached Nish, metropolis of the cities in Dacia, Michael Branas, who had been entrusted by the emperor with governing that area, provided them with necessities, as he had been instructed. Then they came near to Sofia, and two men of the nobility went up to them to give them a fitting welcome. Up until now the barbarians [the western armies] had been in difficult terrain (for from the river Danube as far as Sardika there are many high and terribly inaccessible mountains), and they had advanced quietly, without doing anything contrary to the wishes of the Byzantines. But when they reached the plains, which follow on from the difficult areas of Dacia, they started to reveal their hostile intentions. They treated unjustly those who were offering them items for sale in the market, and if anyone resisted their plundering, they put him to the sword. Conrad of Germany turned a blind eye to all that was going on: he either paid little attention to those who complained, or, if he listened at all, he put it down to the folly of the crowd.

When the Emperor Manuel heard this, he sent an army against them immediately, under the command of Prosuch, a man experienced in battle. When Prosuch met them near Edirne, for a while he followed them at a distance, restraining the disorderly ravages of the crowd. But when he saw them acting even more violently, he then openly engaged them in battle, for the following reasons.

One of the more distinguished Germans, who was weak in body, had retired into a monastery near Edirne, taking with him his money and all his possessions. Some Byzantines from the infantry divisions plundered this monastery and set fire to his lodging; when they had thus destroyed the man, they seized his money.

When this incident came to the ears of Frederick, duke of Swabia, nephew of Conrad III, a man of unbelievable ferocity, unrestrained in attacking and unyielding in temperament, he returned in haste to Edirne, although he had followed Conrad's route for two days. He set fire to the monastery, where the German had died, and thus gave a reason for war between the Byzantines and themselves.

Prosuch joined battle with Frederick for this reason, routed him and made a great slaughter of barbarians. It was this Frederick who ruled the Germans after Conrad, but thereafter the Germans gave up their former boasting, since they had learned the might of the Byzantines in action.

Odo of Deuil's chronicle was intended to warn future crusaders of the problems they would encounter, both environmental and human. Here he gives the events of the journey from a French perspective.

At Regensburg we all crossed the Danube over a fine bridge, and found a large fleet of ships which carried our baggage and a great many people to Bulgaria. Some people loaded two- and four-horse carts into the ships, in order to hold supplies ready for the wastes of Bulgaria. But both before and afterwards there was more hope than real use in these carts. I am saying this as a caution to later travellers. Although they had a great many four-horse carts, if one had an accident they were all equally delayed, and the pack-animals, in avoiding the hindrance they caused, often met with disaster. Therefore there were many deaths among the horses, and many complaints at the shortness of the day's travel.

Louis VII at Regensburg

The people of Regensburg received the king of France, Louis VII, in majestic style. But since I cannot narrate every story of how people showed their devotion to the king, I shall say once and for all that all the towns, forts and cities as far as Constantinople showed him kingly honour.

When the tents had been pitched and quarters had been provided for the king, the messengers from the Byzantine emperor, Manuel I Comnenus, were summoned. When they had greeted the king and delivered the messages entrusted to them, they stood by awaiting an answer, for they would not sit down uninvited. When they were instructed to do so, they positioned the chairs which they had brought with them and sat down. We saw there what afterwards we learned to be the Byzantine custom, that the whole retinue stands while the lords sit. You could see young men standing immobile, with bowed heads and looking silently and intently at their lords, ready to obey them at a single nod. They do not wear cloaks, but the rich are dressed in short, close-fitting silk clothes with narrow sleeves, which allow them to move unimpeded like athletes. The poor dress in a similar fashion but using cheaper material.

The first and longest section of the letters brought by these Byzantines attempted to win our goodwill in an excessively and insincerely emotive language which would shame a buffoon, never mind an emperor. But I should not waste time talking about such things when there are other matters to treat. I could not manage it in any case, since Frankish flatterers, even if they try, cannot match the Byzantines.

The common market of Islam

The civilization of medieval Islam stretched from the Atlantic to India along the northern, and frequently mountainous, border of the African and Arabian deserts. Its cities, some the greatest in the world, were rich and could afford to buy goods from Europe, tropical Africa and the Far East. In addition to importing basics, such as food, they provided markets for necessities, like timber and metals from Europe, and luxuries, such as porcelain and spices from China and the Indies; gold – both a luxury and an essential to a currency which included the gold dinar – came from West and East Africa. There were also slaves, both white and black.

The establishment of the Fatimid caliphate in Egypt in the tenth century helped to link Mediterranean trade with the Indian Ocean via the Red Sea, and encouraged trading across the Sahara. Cairo became the greatest of all Islamic cities, with a population of 250,000. Syria, with Damascus and Aleppo, and Iraq at the head of the Gulf, attracted Asia's overland trade. In the Muslim west, Tunis replaced Kairouan, ruined by invaders in 1057, and Seville, Cordoba, famous for gold, silver, silk and leather.

The priceless asset of this intercontinental commercial network was the universality of Islam. A body of shared urban cultural and moral ideals, the Arabic language as a lingua franca besides being the language of learning, and the standard set by the gold dinar, all ensured that the Muslim and Jewish merchants who conducted Islamic commerce were everywhere at home and could correspond over thousands of miles, exchanging favours and trading through the medium of international letters of credit. This mutual trust was supplemented by both Muslim and Jewish law, both of which were applicable throughout the Islamic world. Contracts made in Spain could be enforced in Egypt and money and goods were pooled in lucrative ventures. Disputes could be brought before the qadi, or Muslim judge, or the official supervisor of a group of merchants.

However, there was no uniformity of taxation in accordance with the law of Islam. Trade was subject to non-Islamic taxes, which could be high in themselves, and exorbitant at the hands of tax-collectors. Although payment inferred that merchants received state protection there were vast tracts where state authority could not reach, and travel was slow and often dangerous.

At first the king allowed all this nonsense to be set forth, although he blushed and did not know where it all came from. In the end, however, he could hardly bear any more flattery of this kind. Godfrey, bishop of Langres, a devout and spirited man, spoke up out of pity for the king and annoyance at the delay caused by the need to use interpreters. 'Brothers,' he said, 'do not keep on repeating words like "glory", "majesty", "wisdom" and "piety" with regard to the king. He knows himself and we know him well, just say what you want freely and quickly.' But the proverb has always been well known which says, 'I fear the Greeks, even when they bear gifts.'

The last section of the letters, however, the part that was actually pertinent to the matter, contained these two requests: that the king should not take from the emperor any city or fort in his land; moreover, the king should restore to the emperor any place which had previously been under the latter's jurisdiction, if the king should succeed in driving the Turks out; and that this should be ratified by an oath on the part of the nobles. The first request seemed quite reasonable to our council. As regards the second, many days were spent debating the matter, while the Byzantines complained about the delay, fearing, so they said, that the emperor would take steps to protect himself by burning the pasture lands and destroying supplies. 'He said he would do this,' they said, 'if we were delayed, taking our delay as a sign that you do not come in peace. If he were to do this, you would not afterwards find sufficient supplies on your road, even if the emperor were supporting you.'

At last, however, certain men made an oath on Louis's part for the security of the emperor's lands, while the Byzantines made a similar oath on behalf of Emperor Manuel to provide convenient markets, suitable exchange and other things as seemed useful to us. The second matter, since they could not resolve it, was deferred until such time as both monarchs might be present.

Up to this point we had incurred no loss from any man's ill will and feared no traps from the cunning of the crafty. From the moment we entered Byzantine Bulgaria, however, our valour bore labour and our senses were exercised. Just before we entered the wilderness, at a poor city called Branitchevo, we went back across the river Danube to buy provisions in a certain Hungarian town which was not far away.

Here we first came up against the copper money called 'staminae', and we sadly gave five pennies for one of them, like losing a mark for twelve sous. So it was that, at the very entrance to their domains, the Byzantines were stained by perjury, for you should remember what was mentioned above, that they had sworn on their emperor's behalf to provide convenient markets and suitable exchange for us.

We then crossed the wilderness and entered a rich and beautiful land which stretches out without interruption right up to Constantinople. Here we first encountered difficulties. All the other regions, which sold us provisions properly, found us completely peaceful; but the Byzantines locked up their cities and towns, and sent down items for sale on ropes from the walls. Victuals provided in this manner were not sufficient for our vast army, so the pilgrims, who could not bear to suffer privation in the midst of plenty, obtained necessities for themselves by plunder and pillage.

A boat loaded with stores and provisions. The primitive logistics which supported the crusading armies often broke down and the crusaders were reduced to scavenging or looting to supply their most basic needs, or to starvation.

Conrad arrives at Constantinople

The Würzburg annalist describes Conrad's arrival at Constantinople about a month ahead of Louis, and his journey into Anatolia.

Meanwhile Conrad III was received in magnificent style by the emperor of Constantinople, Manuel I Comnenus. During their conversations together, King Conrad indicated that he had come to fight the Saracens, and asked Manuel I Comnenus to show him and his army the best route to the Saracen lands. The emperor of Constantinople replied:

'Great prince, I do not oppose your desire, but since I see that what you propose cannot be of advantage to you or your great army, I must give you advice. The road to the Saracen lands is very isolated, and is rendered excessively perilous by its remoteness; but it is even more difficult and burdensome to lead such a huge army through the dry wilderness. The closest Saracen land to you is the sultanate of Rum [in Anatolia]. Both I myself and my father of divine memory have often led campaigns against that country, and as often returned unsuccessful, for never could the necessary supplies hold out because of the excessive length of the journey. Therefore, glorious king, I consider it better to give up your warlike intentions rather than, by proceeding ill-advisedly, to succumb on the road to hunger, thirst and need, or even – perish the thought – to suffer the final punishment of losing your life.

But if you still want to persist in your plan, I suggest that you choose a few thousand men from your army, and hurry with them to fight for Jerusalem against those who daily plunder the Christians. For it is more glorious to place your hope in God and gain victory over your enemies with only a small force, than to trust in your great multitude, and yet lose the uncertain glory of victory.'

Conrad considered what had been said in his heart and held careful discussions with his generals and other knowledgeable men. Finally, although he judged Manuel's counsel altogether sensible and healthy, he still suspected some problem, and replied:

'Even if the road we must take is steep and difficult, yet for God for whom all things are possible, we will fight the barbarians. Your task is to show us the way to Rum, and to appoint some guide for us from among your people, who will lead us through the pathless places which are little known to us, and bring us to the lands of the barbarians.'

When Manuel heard Conrad's determination, he gave orders for a fleet to be prepared, and for his servants to distribute among the pilgrims eleven thousand bows and more spears and other kinds of weaponry that can be counted. Therefore Conrad and his host crossed the Bosporus, and came to Nicaea, where they rested for three days.

On the fourth day, [one part of the crusading force, consisting of] all the non-combatants took the coast road under the leadership of the bishop of Freisingen, one Otto, who was the brother of Conrad. The whole strength of this army directed its course towards a Saracen city called Laodicea. Soon, shrivelling up from hunger and thirst, they were reduced to such misery that they slaughtered the horses, camels and asses which were surplus to requirements for transport, but the flesh of the pack-animals was not enough to relieve their hunger, nor the blood enough to relieve their burning thirst.

Many succumbed, so that when the Saracens, having discovered their weakness, made a sudden and unforeseen attack and tore them apart, no one offered any resistance. They killed the older people, and led the younger ones in captivity to undergo miserable slavery. Meanwhile Louis VII, the king of France, came to their aid, and, being unaware of what had transpired, fell upon the barbarian hordes with his men, but almost all those with him were destroyed, while he himself just managed to escape with only a few companions. What voice, what tongue could tell how much Christian blood the bestial frenzy of the barbarians poured out, and how many ways they found to torture them? This is what happened at Laodicea to those who followed the king of France and the bishop of Freisingen.

We still can see to this day, to our grief, Christian men of all ages returning from that barbarous captivity, some blinded, others – I cannot say it without groaning – with their arms and hands cut off, others with the soles of their feet burnt and rubbed in salt, others with their eyes torn out, or with ears, nose or lips cut off: they were sent back once they had been thus handicapped.

Meanwhile, [the rest of the crusade] all the knights and armed men had set out from Nicaea over the Anatolian plateau in company with the king and headed for the sultanate of Rum. They were led by Focas, whom the Emperor Manuel had appointed as their guide. Once they had entered the great wilderness and could find nothing which seemed suitable to eat, and when the food which they had brought with them began to fail, their souls, as is written, gradually failed in the midst of their troubles. They kept going more in the hope of help than in the strength of their powers. One by one, a steady stream of men and horses died from hunger.

Disaster overtook Conrad's army when the Saracens seized his camp. The Emperor Manuel persuaded him to return to Constantinople.

What more? Forty days after they had set out from Nicaea, they entered the wilderness on the borders of Rum. It was not enough that they had not been able to find food for so many days; still more, they now lacked water, which up to this point they had been able to find, as the one solace of life. Grief was added to grief, and with this tribulation they continued their slow progress for four days.

Meanwhile, the Saracen rulers, who had been terrified by the rumour of the approaching army, came together to support the sultan of Rum, and made plans to plunder the Christian forces.

The sun was setting at the end of the fourth day, when some men came to Conrad and the leaders claiming to have found drinkable water [at the river Bathys, near Dorylaeum] at the foot of a certain mountain. The king was excited by this news, and straightaway hurried from the camp with his companions to the mountain to see for himself whether it was true. The mountain was about four miles from the camp. When he had been gone a little while, gradually all the leaders and most of the nobles left the camp during the night and followed him.

Meanwhile, in the silence at the dead of night, a sudden noise broke out in the camp, and, quite unforeseen, the presence of a wicked band of Saracens was revealed by flying arrows. Suddenly the barbarian hordes poured into the Christian camp and slaughtered the miserable pilgrims who were barely still alive after all their toil. Nothing could be heard except the depths of grief and the groans and crashes of the dying; on the other side nothing except the awful shout: 'Death to the pilgrims!' as the Saracens urged each other on with mouths contorted like dogs'.

All that night, up to the dawn of the fifth day, the Christians were struck down and captured as they wandered like sheep among the pathless places. Around ten thousand Christians,

The king of France asks for money

Your love for us has incited us to write to you as quickly as we can, from these eastern lands, about our circumstances. For we know that you long to hear about this and that nothing can be more welcome to you than to receive good news about us.

From the time when we left the frontiers of France [in the summer of 1147], the Lord made our journey prosperous, and divine mercy has brought us safe and sound as far as Constantinople, with our army very happy and safe. There, we were received with joy and honour by the Emperor Manuel, and when we had spent some time there to prepare what we thought necessary for the journey, we made our way through Anatolia. There, however, partly through the deceit of the emperor, and partly through our own fault, we sustained heavy losses, and we were much distressed by many dangers.

There were constant ambushes from bandits, grave difficulties of travel, daily battles with the Turks who had come by permission of the emperor into his own territory to hunt down the army of Christ, and who obstructed us with all their force, to our detriment. Since food could not be found in many places, the army was for a time badly afflicted by famine; and on one day, so far as divine judgement for our sins allowed, many of our barons died.

It will be better for you to hear of them from the messengers who bring news, since our grief does not allow us to speak further. We ourself were frequently in danger of our life; but thanks to God's grace were freed from all these dangers and escaped the attacks of the Turks. We reached Attalia with our army intact, by God's protection. There, we held a long and involved debate about what road to follow next, and it was decided that we should go quickly to Antioch by ship.

We followed this advice, and with most of our commanders reached that city, after a good voyage, on 19 March [1148]; and it is from there that we are sending this letter.

Be assured that either we will never return, or we will come back with the glory of God and the French. It remains only to ask that you remember us often, and that you always and everywhere recommend us to men of religion for their prayers.

Since our money is not a little depleted because of many expenses of various kinds, it is a matter of the utmost urgency that you strive to collect more, and whatever money you have amassed you should send to us as quickly as possible by reliable messengers. For save by great expense and great effort, we cannot prosecute the business of Christ.

Farewell.

From letter of Louis VII to Abbot Suger, 1148

'We who had been occidentals have become orientals'

So wrote Fulcher of Chartres, chronicler and veteran of the First Crusade, around the year 1120. Although the Frankish settlers and their descendants controlled the political and military power in the crusader states, they were always in a minority. Most of them congregated in the towns and cities of Outremer where they came into close contact with eastern Christians, and, particularly after 1110 when they stopped killing or expelling non-Christians from captured cities, with Muslims and Jews.

The sophisticated and cosmopolitan urban culture in which they found themselves exercised a significant influence on the Frankish residents, many of whom adopted eastern fashions in food, dress and other aspects of their daily lives. Thus, the 12th-century warrior and author, Usama Ibn Munqidh, described the experience of a fellow Muslim who was invited to dine at the home of an elderly knight, an early settler in the east. The Frank assured his guest that all his meals were prepared by Egyptian women and that pork never entered his house.

The Frankish inhabitants of the Latin east learned to coexist not only with the Muslims who lived under their rule, but also with those in the surrounding Islamic states. For political, military, or economic reasons, Christian leaders and their Muslim counterparts often entered into alliances or truces that temporarily suspended hostilities between them, during which the erstwhile enemies enjoyed relatively cordial relations.

This attitude of tolerance often puzzled newly arrived crusaders who had come to the east eager to fight the infidel. Usama Ibn Munqidh observed that Christians fresh from Europe were always ruder than Franks who, through long contact, had become familiar with Muslim ways.

However, even though the Franks of Outremer had adopted eastern ways of life and come to understand, and even to respect, the Muslims, they could never forget that the very existence of the Latin principalities in Syria and Palestine depended ultimately on their continued ability to wage war successfully against their Muslim adversaries. The Templars, who treated Usama with grace and courtesy, were regarded by Saladin as Islam's most implacable foes.

who were arriving by a different route, saw the situation of their brothers and manfully flew to arms to avenge their deaths and to seize back their own. Immediately the hordes of the infidel engaged, trusting in their numbers and strength. The battle raged fiercely and continued until noon without a clear victory.

The glorious Conrad III was ignorant of the seizure of his camp and the disaster which had occurred. Suddenly he looked up and saw the battle from afar, and immediately he snatched up his standard, for he was a most energetic soldier, and shouted out to the listening people: 'Great warriors, I see men valiantly resisting our enemies and, if I am not mistaken, the flash of their arms suggests that the resisters are allies, since the Saracens do not use breastplates in battle. Let anyone who has zeal for God come with me! Let us fight for our brothers! Let heaven's will be done!'

With these words he rushed off and threw himself and his forces into the battle. At last, with the Saracen forces struck down in untold slaughter and even put to flight, with the help of God he freed his companions from their desperate situation. And so with the whole army united he returned to Nicaea, where he remained for a few days.

Then Conrad divided his army into two sections. One section was ordered to return home, while the other was to go with him to Jerusalem. So it was that on 27 November 1147 he set out, accompanied by a host which was still great, and came to Ephesus, the place of St John the Evangelist which is called 'the Hall of the Sun', from where he intended to sail should appropriate conditions arise. Meanwhile the pilgrims who had been dismissed had returned to Constantinople, where the emperor, Manuel Comnenus, out of love for his wife the Empress Irene [formerly Bertha of Sulzbach] who was Conrad III's sister-in-law, helped them to an easy passage; and so they all gradually returned home.

Then Manuel sent very friendly letters to Conrad, in which he offered every sort of encouragement to persuade him to deign to come back with his army to Constantinople, from where to sail to Palestine at a more suitable season. He even sent him a large fleet, including three ships adorned in kingly magnificence with gold and silver and various brightly coloured decorations.

In accordance with this sensible plan Conrad, together with his following, put to sea and, after an easy voyage to Constantinople, was received with the greatest honours by the emperor, who had come down to meet him with all his leaders. At the harbour of the Hellespont, Emperor Manuel offered to King Conrad two cavalry detachments of almost two thousand horses, adorned with trappings. These were distributed among the army. In this fashion Conrad entered the royal city with the Byzantine emperor in all honour.

Early in 1148 Conrad himself wrote to his regent, Abbot Wibald of Stavelot, from Constantinople, where he was recovering from illness.

The Byzantine emperor, Manuel I Comnenus, receiving a Frankish king. Conrad III found Manuel, who was married to his sister-in-law, a generous ally during the Second Crusade.

When we reached Nicaea with the army intact and unified, wishing to complete the expedition in good time, we began to advance against Rum, taking a short cut which was shown to us by trusted guides, and carried with us what provisions we could. But after ten days of journeying, with ten days still to come, nearly all the army (and especially the knights) ran out of food; and at this point the hordes of Turkish foot-soldiers attacked and killed ceaselessly. We, in turn, aggrieved at the flight of our men who were being destroyed as much by the crush of soldiers dying around them as by the arrows of the enemy, had all the leaders and barons call to their men, and led the army back to the sea from the land they had deserted. We preferred to keep them safe for a greater conflict.

But when we had reached the sea at Ephesus and pitched camp, Louis VII, the king of France, happy at this unexpected moment of quiet, came without our knowing to our tent, dis-

tressed, it is true, at the hunger and weariness of the army but not a little pleased to have us as an ally. He and all his commanders faithfully and devotedly offered their services to us, and further put at our disposal their money and whatever else they had. So they joined up with our forces and commanders, of whom some remained with me, while some were too sick or did not have enough money to follow us.

In spite of all our difficulties we reached Ephesus in time to celebrate Christmas, and there we rested for a few days, because we and many of our men were suffering from sickness; we were all for moving on as soon as we had recuperated, but our sickness worsened, and we were not strong enough to travel. So the king of France and his army went on, unhappily, but our illness held us back for a long time.

When our kinsman by marriage, the Emperor Manuel Comnenus, heard of this, he was extremely upset, and came to see us at the utmost speed, bringing our kinswoman, the

Eleanor of Aquitaine

Eleanor of Aquitaine has become celebrated more through legend than through historical fact. According to the only account to be written before the failure of the Second Crusade and the break-up of her marriage to Louis VII of France, there was great rejoicing at Vézelay when she took the cross with her husband. She was praised for the good example she set to the other nobles, and for the vast resources her inheritance from her father William X, the great duchy of Aquitaine, made available to the crusaders. Modern historians have suggested that this was why she was 'allowed' or 'encouraged' to go to the Holy Land. The reasons given by medieval writers varied from her excessive love for Louis, which made her unwilling to be away from him, to his exceptional love for her – or even his jealousy, which made it impossible for him to trust her alone in France.

Odo of Deuil, the 'official' historian of the Second Crusade, has virtually nothing to say about Eleanor, but later historians, particularly English and northern French writers, have blamed the failure of the expedition on her presence and that of other noble women, many of whom were encouraged by her example to accompany their husbands to the east. The result, according to William of Newburgh, was that the Christian camp was no longer chaste – an important issue for a pilgrim army. In spite of the regular prohibitions of any kind of luxury on the crusades, the women were accused of taking lavish supplies, and even of slowing down the army with the weight of their baggage. It was said that because the wives of knights and nobles could not bear to be without their chambermaids, the crusader force became simply a rabble of women; and, above all, that the temptations offered to men by their presence made adultery open, causing God to turn from the army and scorn the crusaders' efforts to aid the Holy Land.

The story of her adultery with her uncle, Raymond of Antioch, in 1148, was first hinted at by John of Salisbury, a contemporary, and revived earlier accusations that they had had an affair when Eleanor, aged about 13, had been left under his protection while her father was on pilgrimage to Compostella. An anonymous 13th-century minstrel of Reims is probably responsible for exaggerating this rumour into a fully fledged romance between Eleanor and Saladin, who in fact was only about 11 years old in 1148.

beloved Empress Irene, his wife. He generously gave to us and our commanders his own money and the necessaries for the journey, saw to it that we were cured quickly by his own doctors, and practically forced us to come back with him to his palace in Constantinople; there he treated us with as much honour as he ever, to our knowledge, showed to any of our predecessors.

From there we have decided to set out for Jerusalem on Sunday. God willing, we will get together a new army there over Easter, and move on to Edessa. We ask you to pray that God may deign to make our journey successful.

Favourable winds finally arose, as the Würzburg annalist recalls, and Conrad was able to set sail for Jerusalem.

At last, a season suitable for sailing called him to the sea with its soft-breathing zephyrs, and Conrad resumed his journey and his toil.

The emperor of Constantinople generously supplied him with whatever seemed necessary, behaving in accordance with kingly practice.

So it was that as Conrad and his army were on their way to sail to Jerusalem in all honour, they were accompanied to the shore by Manuel Comnenus and his empress, Irene, together with a large retinue. When farewells and good wishes had been expressed on both sides, the whole fleet unfurled its sails and cast off.

An eclipse of the sun happened in that year also, that is on Sunday 26 October 1147, being the feast of St Amand the Confessor, at the sixth hour, on the twenty-eighth day of the moon.

Louis and Eleanor at Antioch

In March 1148, Louis VII and his wife, Eleanor of Aquitaine, landed at St Symeon on the coast of northern Syria, and were greeted with enthusiasm by Prince Raymond of Antioch, uncle of the French queen.

The following view of events is provided by William, archbishop of Tyre, who wrote the most important account of the kingdom of Jerusalem between the death of Fulcher of Chartres in c. 1127 and his own death, which was probably early in 1185. However, his information here was obtained second-hand, as he was studying in France at this time.

When Prince Raymond of Antioch heard that Louis VII, the king of France, whose arrival he had been awaiting with the utmost eagerness for many days, had reached his land, he summoned the nobles and the principal people of the whole region and, with this chosen train, went out to meet the king. He brought Louis in state into the city of Antioch, showing him every respect, with all the clergy and the entire people coming out to meet him.

Raymond had realized earlier, when he heard of the king's arrival, that he would be able to increase the principality of Antioch with his help. With this in mind, even before the king had begun his journey, Raymond had sent to him in France fine gifts, and had bestowed on him presents of great value in the hopes of winning his favour. Nevertheless he was also counting on Queen Eleanor's intervention with her lord the king. Eleanor was the king's inseparable companion on his journey, and was also Prince Raymond's niece, being the daughter of the prince's eldest brother, Duke William X of Aquitaine.

Rumours of philandering between Raymond of Antioch and his niece Eleanor, Louis VII of France's wife, set a bad example to other noble ladies on the Second Crusade.

Women crusaders

The Byzantine historian, Nicetas Choniates, records that the armies of the Second Crusade had, in their ranks, women riding astride horses in what he regarded as a shameless manner. Their military appearance, he says, made them more masculine than the Amazons. This impression is reinforced by Ambroise, who wrote about the Third Crusade (1189–90) and describes how many of the women who took part in the crusaders' siege of Acre attacked the Turks with huge knives, bringing back severed heads in triumph.

Crusaders such as these were not part of Urban II's original plan. He had hoped to assemble an army of fighting men and had forbidden women to take part unless they were accompanied by male relatives. As canon law was developed in a more systematic fashion during the 12th century, attempts were made to regularize their position: they could take crusading vows, but it was expected that they would redeem them for money. Only women of such status and wealth that they could provide a large retinue of fighting men were regarded as suitable participants. In practice, women went on crusade from the beginning, and although their role in battle was normally less dramatic than at Acre, they performed vital services such as keeping the tired and thirsty troops supplied with water. Their fate, if the army was defeated, was likely to be slavery, if not death.

Many women crusaders conformed to papal injunction and travelled with male relatives, at least until their protectors died or were killed. Others, however, earned their living in occupations which included washerwomen, flea-pickers and prostitutes.

Wives left behind while their husbands were on crusade also suffered. In the 12th century, marriage vows were considered important enough to override a man's promise to crusade if his wife did not wish him to go, but in his desperate efforts to recruit crusaders, early in the 13th century, Innocent III abrogated this right. Moreover, women were given little help in solving the acute personal and legal problems which arose when a husband did not return. A wife often had no means of knowing her husband's fate, but remarriage ran the risk of committing bigamy. The 13th-century canon lawyers set the length of time for which wives were required to wait before marrying again at periods which ranged from five to 100 years. The crusades offered two main roles to such women: chaste wife or scapegoat for disaster.

Therefore, as I said, Raymond showed King Louis every kindness on his arrival, and he treated the nobles and leaders who came in the king's entourage with the same attention and great liberality; in all he outdid everyone in showing honour to each, and acted with the greatest munificence. Raymond's greatest hope was that, with the king's help, he would be able to subjugate the neighbouring cities, that is, Aleppo, Shaizar, and some others, provided he could induce the king and his leading men to accept the plan. Such despair had fallen on our enemies at the king's arrival, that not only did they lack confidence in their powers, but even seemed to despair of their very lives. Therefore in solemn council and in the presence of the lord king's leaders and his own, Prince Raymond made plain to the lord king the idea he had conceived, stressing that his suggestion could be performed without difficulty and would bring honour and utility equally.

When he saw that he was making no progress, the king being set on going to Jerusalem in fulfilment of his ardent vows, Raymond, being frustrated in his designs, changed his attitude. He began to hate the ways of the king and openly to plot against him.

Queen Eleanor, who was a foolish woman, sided with him, and he planned to take her from the king, either by violence or by secret designs. As I said, she was a highly imprudent woman. In defiance of her royal dignity, and neglectful of the laws of marriage, she was unfaithful to her husband's bed.

When the king discovered this, he forestalled the prince's attempts: on the advice of his nobles he brought forward the time of his departure and left Antioch in secret with his people. He, who had been received with such honour on his arrival, left ignominiously.

Another account of the troubles between Louis and Eleanor is given by John of Salisbury, a well-informed observer at the papal court between 1148 and 1152. His connections there gave him material not found in other chronicles.

In March 1148, the most Christian king of the French, Louis VII, came to Antioch, and there he was nobly received by Prince Raymond. The prince was uncle to the queen, Eleanor of Aquitaine, and owed the king loyalty, love and respect for many reasons. But while they were staying there to console, nurse and refresh the survivors from the wreck of the army in Anatolia, the prince's familiarity with Queen Eleanor and his almost uninterrupted series of meetings with her made the king suspicious.

Louis's suspicions became much stronger because the queen decided to remain in Antioch, while he was getting ready to leave; and the prince was very keen to keep her there, if this could come about without the king objecting. When the king hurried to take her away, she mentioned their kinship, and said that it was illegal for them to stay married together any longer, since they were related to the fourth and fifth degrees. People had talked about this fact in France before they left, when the late Bartholomew, bishop of Laon, had calculated the degree of their kinship; but it was not certain that this supposition was reliable.

The king was very disturbed at this; and although he loved the queen with an almost excessive passion, he agreed to divorce her if his own councillors and the French nobles would permit. There was, among the king's secretaries, a knight by the name of Terricus Gualerancius, a eunuch whom the queen had always hated and mocked; he was devoted to the king and on very close terms with him, as he had been with the king's father. He boldly persuaded Louis not to allow the queen to stay any longer in Antioch, both because 'guilt could hide under the name of kinship' and because there was a danger of long-lasting disgrace if, in addition to all his other misfortunes, the king could be said to have been robbed of his wife or to have been abandoned by her. He said this either because he hated the queen, or because he really believed it, perhaps influenced by some general rumour.

So she was torn away, and forced to set out for Jerusalem with the king. Resentment rose in their hearts and, much as they might try to pretend otherwise, it did not recede.

The attack on Damascus, 1148

On his arrival in the kingdom of Jerusalem Louis, together with Conrad and the other leaders, attended a great council at Acre on 24 June 1148, hosted by Baldwin III, king of Jerusalem, and his mother and regent, Queen Melisende. As William of Tyre shows, the assembly made the controversial decision to attack Damascus, whose emir was their only effective ally against the growing power of Nur ad-Din, Zanghi's son and successor.

The princes who attended the council at Acre came from lands that were of great importance, and it therefore seems worthwhile, and fitting, to record [some of] their names here. The most notable was Conrad, king of the Germans, Holy Roman Emperor-elect; in his train were the following ecclesiastical members of his court: his brother Otto, bishop of Freisingen and a man of letters; Stephen, bishop of Metz; and Henry, bishop of Toul, brother of Count Thierry of Flanders. The papal legate Theotwin, bishop of Porto, who had been born in Germany, also accompanied the emperor by order of Pope Eugenius.

The Christian princes at the council of Acre on 24 June 1148, prior to the attack on Damascus; an illustration to William of Tyre's account of the Second Crusade.

Louis, that most saintly king of France, whose memory is for ever sacred, was there, and with him were Thierry, the great and splendid count of Flanders, brother-in-law of the king of Jerusalem; and other high-ranking nobles. All are exemplary men, whose names are worth recording, but because it would take too long to write them here they have been omitted on purpose.

Baldwin III, king of Jerusalem, a most promising young man, was there from our own lands, and his mother Melisende, a woman of wisdom and circumspection, courageous and as wise as any prince in the world. Patriarch Fulcher, Robert, master of the Knights Templar, Raymond, master of the Hospitallers, and other ecclesiastical and lay nobles accompanied them. It would take too long to name each one. All these important nobles had come together, as we have said, at the city of Acre in order to consider, first of all, when would be the best time, and where the best place, to try, by God's will, to extend the boundaries of the kingdom and bring additional glory to the Christian name.

The subject was discussed in detail and, as is the custom with matters as important as this, different factions gave diverse opinions, whose advantages and disadvantages were argued. Finally, everyone agreed that, under the circumstances, the best course would be to besiege Damascus, a city which presented a great threat to us. When this decision was made, the herald was ordered to make it known that on the appointed day everyone must be ready to lead their troops to the region.

All the military strength of the realm was therefore assembled, both horsemen and foot-soldiers, natives and pilgrims. The two great monarchs, Conrad and Louis, both beloved of God, also came with their armies. Then, on 25 May 1148, the combined forces, with the cross of salvation at their head, marched to the city of Tiberias. From there they were taken along the shortest route, by the Sea of Galilee, to Caesarea Philippi, where their leaders talked with people who were familiar with Damascus and its surroundings. Then, after discussions among themselves, they decided that the best way to lay siege to the city was to start by seizing the orchards which surrounded most of Damascus and gave it a great deal of protection. Once these had been captured there was no doubt that Damascus itself could be seized with ease.

The Damascene chronicler, Ibn al-Qalanisi, was in Damascus when the Franks attacked it.

The [Hijra] year [of the Muslim calendar] began on Friday 21 May with the sun in Gemini. Early in the year news began coming in from various sources that the Franks' ships had

Damascus, the city 'full of blood'

Damascus, which is also called Phoenicia of Lebanon, is the greatest city of Lesser Syria. The city derives its name from a certain slave of Abraham's, who is believed to have founded it. This is interpreted as 'bloody' or 'full of blood'. It is situated in the countryside, in a land which would be sterile and dry, were it not irrigated by ancient water-courses which bring the water down from a higher level. The river, which flows down from a neighbouring promontory, enters canals in the higher parts of the region and from there can be brought down into the plain quite freely, where it is directed through all the different parts of the lower region to render fertile the sterile fields. The remaining water, for there is an abundant supply, feeds orchards along the banks, which are planted with fruit-trees. It then turns along to the eastern wall of the city and so flows on.

On its western side, from which our army was approaching, and on its northern side, Damascus is surrounded far and wide by orchards like thick groves and dark woods, which stretch out for five miles or more towards Lebanon. In order to avoid uncertainty over ownership and to stop people entering at will, the orchards are shut in by walls, albeit of mud, since stone is scarce in that region. The enclosure is done in such a way that each person's possession is clearly marked and protected by the wall, but the paths and public highways are left open, although they are narrow, so that the people of the suburbs and those who tend the orchards can reach the city with their pack-animals laden with fruit. But these orchards also provide a valuable defence for the city, for because of the density and frequency of the trees and the narrowness of the roads it seemed difficult, or even impossible, to approach the city from that side.

It was in this place, however, that our princes had initially decided to introduce the army and open a way to the city.

From William of Tyre, *Historia*

arrived along the coast and that they had landed on the shores of Tyre and Acre and joined those Franks who were already there. It was said that even after killing, disease and hunger had taken their toll there was still an estimated hundred thousand men. They made their pilgrimage to Jerusalem and then some of them returned to their countries by sea. A great many of them had perished by disease, including some of their kings; but Conrad III, their greatest king, and others of lesser rank had survived.

There was, however, disagreement among them as to which of the Islamic lands and Syrian cities they should attack. Eventually they decided to move against Damascus. In fact, they were so confident of taking it that they had already planned how to share out its districts and estates. Several reports to this effect arrived and the governor of the city, Emir Mu'in ad-Din, began making preparations to engage the Franks and thwart their evil intentions. The places he feared would be attacked were fortified and men were posted along the roads and passes. Supply routes to the Franks' positions were cut, wells were filled in and watering-places were poisoned.

Meanwhile, the Franks had begun their march on Damascus, their huge well-equipped army, estimated at fifty thousand horsemen and foot-soldiers, greatly swelled by their baggage train and a large number of camels and cattle. As they neared the city they made for a place known as Manazil al-Asakir ('the camps of the armies'), but they found that the water supply there had been cut off. They then headed for al-Mizza [a village to the west of the city], where there was water nearby, and there they set up camp. They marched towards the water with their cavalry and foot-soldiers and on Saturday 24 July 1148 they engaged in battle with the Muslim forces who had drawn up against them, having been joined by a number of regular soldiers and Turkish fighters as well as volunteers, irregulars and young men from the town.

After fierce fighting the infidels [i.e. the Franks] gained the upper hand over the Muslims owing to their superiority in numbers and equipment and they took control of the water. Their forces spread throughout the orchards and camped in them. They even moved up to the town and occupied a section of it which no troops, either previously or since, have ever been able to defend. It was on this day that the imam and jurist Yusuf al-Findalawi was killed by the water near al-Rabwa [a village near al-Mizza]. Refusing to retreat, he had stood firm against the Franks, in accordance with God's commands in the Koran. The same fate befell the ascetic Abd ar Rahman al-Halhuli.

The Franks now began cutting down trees and building defences with them. They also pulled down a number of enclosures. The night passed with the townspeople deeply shocked and demoralized by the horror of the scenes they had witnessed. However, early the next morning, which was Sunday 25 July, the Muslim forces made a sortie against the Franks and after repeated charges by each side against the other the Muslims gained the upper hand and inflicted heavy casualties on the Franks. Emir Mu'in ad-Din in particular distinguished himself in the battle, displaying such gallantry and endurance the like of which had never been seen. The fighting went on for many hours with the infidel horsemen unable to find an opportunity to make one of their infamous charges.

Eventually the sun sank low in the sky and as night fell the weary combatants withdrew to take rest. The soldiers spent the night in the field across from the Franks and the townspeople stood guard on the walls watching the enemy, who were now so close. Meanwhile letters had been sent to the governors of neighbouring districts asking for assistance and reinforcements. Turkish cavalry and foot-soldiers had been arriving and early the next morning the Muslims, their confidence restored and their fears dispelled, made another attack. They held their ground against the Franks and poured such a rain of arrows on their camp that large numbers of men, horses and camels were killed. That same day saw the arrival of a sizeable contingent of bowmen from the Beqaa and other areas, whereby the numerical strength of the Muslims was increased and their fighting power effectively doubled.

That night both sides withdrew to the positions they had established during the day. Early on the morning of Tuesday 27 July the Muslims mounted a lightning attack, swooping down on the Franks and surrounding their camp while many of them were still asleep. They broke down the barricades the Franks had constructed with the trees from the orchards with a hail of arrows and rocks. The Franks, out of fear and cowardice, were reluctant to come out and not one of them made a stand. It was thought they were effecting some kind of false appearance to deceive the Muslims. Later a small group of horsemen and foot-soldiers appeared and started skirmishing in order to prevent a full assault by the Muslims, hoping perhaps that they would find the chance to launch their own attack or secure for themselves some way of escaping.

Anyone who came close to the Muslim army was killed, either shot by one of the archers or run through with a lance. A large number of the young men from the area became more audacious and they started lying in wait for those Franks who were already making their way back along the roads. They killed all those they captured and brought their heads in to claim rewards for them. A large number of heads were brought in.

Nur ad-Din

After the death of Malik Shah in 1092, the cohesive empire of the Seldjuk Turks disintegrated as contending atabegs (regents) and governors seized the opportunity to establish their own kingdoms. After nearly four decades of anarchy, Imad ad-Din Zanghi emerged as ruler of Mosul (1127) and as the sultan's governor at Aleppo (1128). From this powerful state, he waged war against the crusader state of Edessa, which he seized in 1144 and where he met a violent death two years later, in 1146. But his principal goal remained Damascus, held by the Burid dynasty, which was only to be captured by his son and successor in Aleppo, Nur ad-Din, in 1154.

Nur ad-Din, the Nureddin of western chroniclers, was tall and dark, learned, just and of unimpeachable piety. He enjoyed polo and hunting. Personally abstemious, he spent all his wealth upon building mosques, colleges and public amenities. Highly effective in war, his policy of continuing harassment of the crusader states was so successful that the powerful Byzantine emperor, Manuel I Comnenus, marched into Antioch in 1158–9 and brought it under an imperial protectorate.

Meanwhile, Nur ad-Din and the Franks had turned their attentions towards Egypt, the allegiance of which was vital but suspect to both sides. Self-sufficient and immensely wealthy, in the early 1160s it lay at the mercy of rival viziers. During the struggle of two viziers, Shawar and Dirgham, Nur ad-Din was asked to intervene but demurred. However, when Egypt was invaded by Amalric I of Jerusalem, at the head of a crusading army in 1163, he despatched his atabeg Shirkuh and Shirkuh's nephew Saladin, who, after six years, finally expelled the crusaders in 1169.

In 1172, Nur ad-Din, who had assumed control of Mosul on the death of his brother in 1170, requested Saladin to join him in an attack on Karak. Saladin, sensing danger, failed to do so and in a fury Nur ad-Din considered invading Egypt. It took all the subtlety of Saladin's father Ayub to calm the sultan. While Nur ad-Din campaigned in Anatolia against the Seldjuk Kilij Arslan in 1173, Saladin seized the opportunity to strengthen his control of Nubia and southern Arabia. These conquests were undertaken in the name of Nur ad-Din who, in 1174, was acknowledged as sultan of al-Jazirah, Syria, Egypt and Konya. He died in the same year and was buried in Damascus.

News was also reaching the Franks of the rapid approach of the Muslim armies who were ready to wage a holy war against them, and were eager to annihilate them. The Franks realized then that they faced certain destruction and after discussing the situation it became clear that if they were to extricate themselves from their hopeless predicament then they had no alternative but to retreat and by dawn of the following day, Wednesday 28 July, they were fleeing in disarray. The Muslim forces followed in swift pursuit, and throughout the morning many men and animals in the rearguard fell victim to their arrows. The Franks left behind them an enormous number of dead, both men and many of their magnificent horses. The stench from their corpses was so foul that it almost overcame the birds in the air. They had also burned down al-Rabwa and al-Qubba al-Mamduda (the Long Pavilion) during the night.

The people were overjoyed that God had brought about their deliverance and they gave him thanks and praise that he had answered the prayers they had offered to him so often during the days of their ordeal.

Failure of the Second Crusade

William of Tyre attributes the Christian failure to take Damascus to cupidity.

At the height of the fighting, the citizens, amazed at the number and the valour of our army, began to lose faith in their own power to resist. They barricaded with huge beams all the suburbs of the city in the area where our men were encamped, their only hope being that while the Christians were engaged in breaking down these barriers, they themselves would be able to flee with their wives and children through the opposite area of the city. It seemed reasonable to suppose that the Christian people would soon hold the city, had divine favour been with us. But He who is terrible in his plans for the sons of men had decided otherwise. For while the citizens had packed their bags and decided to leave the place, they began to presume on our cupidity and came up with the intention of storming with money the souls of those whose bodies they could not overcome by fighting. They used various arguments, even bringing a countless quantity of money, to persuade some of our leaders to play the part of the traitor Judas.

These men, corrupted by gifts and promises, persuaded the kings and the pilgrim leaders, who trusted completely in their loyalty and industry, to transfer the army to the opposite side of the city. They claimed that on that side, looking south and east, there were no orchards to defend the city, nor was the access to the wall impeded by any moat or river.

The kings and the leaders of the whole army believed them, and deserted the place which they had previously occupied with great effort and loss of men. They transferred their whole force and under the traitors' direction set up camp on the opposite side of the city. When they realized that their new position was a long way from the water and lacked the abundance of fruit of the previous one, and that their supplies had now almost failed, they complained too late that there had been treachery.

Now a severe shortage of food was beginning to hit the camp, for the soldiers had been led to believe before they set out that the city would be taken very quickly, and so had brought only a few days' supplies with them. This was especially the case with those new to the Holy Land. They became doubtful and wondered both in private and openly what they should do: it seemed hard, if not impossible, to return to the position they had deserted. Therefore the pilgrim leaders held counsel together, and they decided to return home. The kings and leaders were covered in confusion and fear and, their business unaccomplished because of our sins, were forced to leave.

The men returned to their own kingdoms by the same route as they had come, and held in suspicion all the ways of our princes, rightly declining to take any part in their plans. This was the case, not only while they remained in the east: even after they returned to their own lands they remained mindful of the wrongs they had suffered.

The result of this was that thereafter pilgrims coming this way were neither so many nor so ardent, and even today those who do come do not want to fall into the net of treachery and so seek to return home quickly.

The Würzburg annalist by contrast ascribes the débâcle to the treachery of the Templars.

King Baldwin would have fulfilled his desire at Damascus, had not the greed, trickery and envy of the Templars got in his way. For they accepted a huge bribe from the Philistines [the enemy] to give secret aid to the besieged inhabitants. When they could not free the city by this means, they deserted the camp, the king and their companions, at night. Conrad III was enraged by this and, in hatred of the Templars' deceit, relinquished the siege and left the city, saying that he would never again come to the aid of Jerusalem, neither himself nor any of his people. The king of Jerusalem, who also detested the arrogance of the Knights Templar, was deeply embarrassed and much grieved by this.

Otto of Freisingen tried to derive a lesson from the failure of the Second Crusade, and to excuse St Bernard, but could find no very convincing arguments.

Even though our expedition was not good for the increase of our holdings or for the comfort of our bodies, it nevertheless

The right way to pray

This is an example of Frankish barbarism, God damn them! When I was in Jerusalem I used to go to the al-Aqsa mosque, beside which is a small oratory which the Franks have made into a church. Whenever I went into the mosque, which was in the hands of Templars who were friends of mine, they would put the little oratory at my disposal, so that I could say my prayers there. One day I had gone in, said the *Allah akhbar* and risen to begin my prayers, when a Frank threw himself on me from behind, lifted me up and turned me so that I was facing east. 'That is the way to pray!' he said. Some Templars at once intervened, seized the man and took him out of my way, while I resumed my prayer. But the moment they stopped watching him he seized me again and forced me to face east, repeating that this was the way to pray. Again the Templars intervened and took him away. They apologized to me and said: 'He is a foreigner who has just arrived today from his homeland in the north and he has never seen anyone pray facing any other direction than east.' 'I have finished my prayers,' I said, and left, stupefied by the fanatic who had been so perturbed and upset to see someone praying facing towards Mecca.

I was present myself when a Frank came up to Emir Mu'in ad-Din – God have mercy on him – in the Dome of the Rock, and said to him: 'Would you like to see God as a baby?' The emir said that he would, and the fellow proceeded to show us a picture of Mary with the infant Messiah on her lap. 'This', he said, 'is God as a baby.' Almighty God is greater than the infidels' concept of him!

From Usama Ibn Munqidh, *Autobiography*

was good for the salvation of many souls, as long as you understand 'good' not as a gift of nature but as 'utility'. It is from the usage of the word 'good' as 'utility' that the division which we mentioned above emerges, that is, that something can be called 'good' either simply or in a secondary sense, and when this secondary sense is used the word is equivocated because of the diversity of utility. And so something can be called 'good', that is, 'useful', either simply or in this secondary sense.

However, if we were to say that the holy abbot Bernard was inspired by the Spirit of God to preach the crusade to us, but that we, not observing his salvation-bringing instructions because of our arrogance and licentiousness, rightly brought home only loss of wealth and persons, this line of argument would not be out of harmony with reason or with ancient examples.

Bernard himself declared that it was better for opprobrium to be heaped upon him than upon God.

Do they not say among the heathens: 'Where is their God?' [Psalm 79.10]. No wonder. The sons of the Church, and those who are counted among the Christians, are prostrate in the desert, or killed by the sword, or devoured by hunger. Strife is widespread among princes, and God has made them err in the pathless places and not on the path. Contrition and unhappiness lie on their paths; fear, grief and confusion are in the inner chambers even of the kings. How confused are the feet of those coming to announce peace, to announce good news! We have said 'Peace', and there is no peace; we have promised good things to come, and behold, chaos – as if we had performed our task rashly or irresponsibly. We have run our course wholeheartedly, not as though we were running into uncertainty, but following your [the pope's] bidding, or rather God's bidding through you.

It means nothing to me to be judged by those who say the good is bad and the bad is good, making light of darkness and darkness of light. And if it is necessary that I choose one out of two things, I would prefer that the mutterings of men were directed against us than against God. For me it is a good thing, if he deigns to use me as a shield. Gladly do I take upon me the malicious tongues of detractors and the poisoned arrows of blasphemers, so that they do not reach him. I do not refuse to be inglorious, so long as there is no attack upon God's glory. Who would grant me to glory in these words: 'For thy sake I have borne reproach; shame hath covered my face' [Psalm 69.7]? My glory is to become a consort of Christ, who said: 'The reproaches of them that reproached thee fell on me' [Rom. 15.3].

The triumph of Nur ad-Din, 1154

The Second Crusade did nothing to protect the Latin states of Outremer from Nur ad-Din, son of Zanghi. In 1150, Turbessel, the last outpost of the former county of Edessa, was ceded to the Byzantine Empire. In 1153 Baldwin III of Jerusalem captured the great city of Ascalon from the Fatimid caliphs of Egypt, but in 1154 Nur ad-Din captured Damascus. Ibn al-Qalanisi traces his triumph.

The [Muslim calendar] year began on the first Wednesday in Muharram [18 March 1154], with Gemini in the ascendant. In the second week of that month Emir Asad ad-Din Shirkuh [Saladin's uncle] reached the outskirts of Damascus in his capacity as envoy from Nur ad-Din, lord of Aleppo. He set up camp at a place called al-Qasab. He had about a thousand troops with him. This move caused some hostile resentment in Damascus and Mujir ad-Din, prince of Damascus, declined to go out to meet Asad ad-Din Shirkuh or to deal with him in any way.

Supply routes had been cut and prices were already beginning to rise when Nur ad-Din and his army arrived to join Asad ad-Din Shirkuh on Sunday 18 April. They camped at Ayun al Fasariya not far from Duma. The next day they moved on and halted on the lands of an estate known as Bayt al-Abar in the Ghuta. They marched on the city from the east and were met by a large number of soldiers and townsmen. There was some fighting and then both sides withdrew.

These attacks continued on a daily basis until early on the morning of Sunday 25 April, by virtue of God's divine ordinance and to the great good fortune of King Nur ad-Din, the people of Damascus and all men. Nur ad-Din mustered his troops, who were now ready for some serious fighting, and mounted a major assault on the city. As usual, soldiers came out to meet them and some fighting took place. Nur ad-Din's troops then attacked at a number of points from the east and the Damascenes were pushed back to the wall near the Kaisan Gate and the tannery on the south side of the city.

Owing to a combination of the divine will and incompetence by the authorities there was not a single person manning the walls save for a small group of Turkish reservists in one of the towers, and it was unlikely they would put up any resistance. Some foot-soldiers ran over to the bottom of the wall, and a Jewish woman standing above let down a rope. One of the soldiers reached the top of the wall without anyone inside realizing, and the others followed him up. They hoisted Nur ad-Din's standard and put it up on the wall.

Their cries of victory echoed round the city and the citizens and soldiers ceased to put up further resistance, for they had harboured an affection for Nur ad-Din and were aware of his justice and good reputation. A woodcutter rushed over to the East Gate and broke off its locks with his axe. It was opened and the troops entered with ease and moved quickly through the streets. There were no shows of resistance. The Thomas Gate was also opened and more troops entered the city. After them came Nur ad-Din himself and his officers.

Mujir ad-Din, realizing he had been defeated, fled with his entourage to the citadel. A message was sent to him guaranteeing his safety and the security of his property. He then came out to meet Nur ad-Din, who gave him a reassurance that he would be well treated.

Nur ad-Din himself entered the citadel the same Sunday. He immediately issued a proclamation guaranteeing the safety of all citizens and forbidding the looting of houses.

Mujir ad-Din removed from his rooms in the citadel all his furnishings and personal belongings and, despite their great quantity, took them over to the residence of the Atabek [the Turkish commander], which had been his grandfather's home, and stayed there for a few days. Nur ad-Din then

The south wall of the citadel of Damascus which Nur ad-Din took in 1154. His triumph contrasted with the failure of the Second Crusade.

instructed him to move up to Homs, with those of his followers and associates who wished to remain with him. A document had already been prepared giving Mujir ad-Din and his troops charge over a number of districts there and off they set, in accordance with God's preordained decision.

Two days later Nur ad-Din summoned the jurists and merchants who represented the citizens, and addressed them in terms which greatly added to their joy and peace of mind. Nur ad-Din was keen to promote measures which would improve the lot of the people and restore prosperity. The citizens showered praise upon Nur ad-Din.

It was announced after this that the duties levied on the melon market and the vegetable market would be abolished and that rights to the irrigation channels would be guaranteed for all. A decree to this effect was drawn up.

People rejoiced at the prospect of good times ahead, and rich and poor, peasants and artisans, offered prayers to God to grant the emir a long life and give him victory.

4

THE THIRD CRUSADE

1189–1192

The failure of the Second Crusade created widespread disillusionment in the west. Some contemporaries questioned the value of such expeditions and it was no coincidence that there was an interval of over 40 years between the reversal of Christian fortunes at Damascus and the launch of the Third Crusade. In the 1150s, 1160s and 1170s the beleaguered Latin kingdom of Jerusalem sent a series of embassies to the west, telling of Muslim successes against the Franks and appealing for aid. In 1165 Pope Alexander III reissued Eugenius III's crusading bull *Quantum praedecessores* and in the following year an income tax was levied in support of the Holy Land. However, in spite of repeated promises and even some financial assistance, no western king was prepared to lead a new crusade. Instead Henry II of England and Louis VII of France waged war over the English king's French possessions, and their mutual suspicion and rivalry meant that one was not prepared to leave for the east without the other. By the 1170s it had become clear that an essential preliminary to a new crusade was peace between the two kings, and between Henry II and his four sons.

At that time the Latin kingdom faced both a political crisis over the succession to the throne of Jerusalem and its most formidable foe, Saladin. On his death in 1174, Amalric I was succeeded by his son, Baldwin IV, a minor who suffered from leprosy. In spite of his disabilities, Baldwin proved to be an able military commander, but it was clear that he would leave no direct heir and the regencies necessitated by his bouts of illness

---

Saladin orders prisoners
chained. He is shown as a
European king, usual in
Western manuscripts.

151

exacerbated tensions within the kingdom and contributed towards the establishment, in the early 1180s, of two rival factions: the court party – Baldwin's eldest sister Sibylla and her husband, Guy of Lusignan – and the native barons, led by Raymond of Tripoli, who favoured the king's second sister Isabella, married to a local noble, Humphrey of Toron. Baldwin died in 1185 and was succeeded by his nephew Baldwin V, son of Sibylla by her first husband, William of Montferrat. However, he ruled for only 17 months and on his death his mother Sibylla and his aunt Isabella disputed the succession. Sibylla, who had the support of the master of the Temple and the patriarch of Jerusalem, won. She was crowned queen of Jerusalem in the church of the Holy Sepulchre, and crowned her husband Guy as king. The barons, including Isabella's husband, but with the exception of Raymond of Tripoli, who remained obdurate and retired to Tiberias, made their peace with the new king.

Such was the state of the Latin kingdom as Saladin gradually consolidated his Muslim power base. Within less than a year of succeeding his uncle Shirkuh as vizier of Egypt in May 1174, he was invested by the caliph with the government of Egypt and parts of Syria. During the next decade his central aim seems to have been the reunification of Nur ad-Din's territories, and by the end of 1183 he had encircled the crusader states along the coast. Saladin bided his time, taking advantage of a period of truce with the Christians in 1185, but in May 1187 Reynald of Châtillon, lord of Transjordan, gave him an excuse to resume the offensive when he attacked a Muslim caravan travelling from Cairo to Damascus. In May and June 1187 Saladin gathered his forces and on 2 July attacked the town of Tiberias. Simultaneously, the Christians under the leadership of Guy of Jerusalem had been assembling a large army at Saffuriyah from all parts of the Latin kingdom. Raymond of Tripoli, whose own wife was in Tiberias, advised the king against risking an open battle, but Guy decided to confront the Muslim force.

On 3 July the Christian army left Saffuriyah and advanced across the barren and waterless terrain to Tiberias. After a night without food or water, they took up position south of a hill crowned with two peaks – the Horns of Hattin. There the famous battle much lamented by western chroniclers and praised by their Muslim counterparts took place. The Christians were decisively defeated. Guy and many of his nobles were taken prisoner and the kingdom's holiest relic, a fragment of the True Cross discovered in Jerusalem in 1099 by the first crusaders, was seized by the Muslims and paraded through Damascus. Saladin followed up this victory by attacking the principal towns and ports of the Latin kingdom. By September the only important port south of Tripoli not in Muslim hands was Tyre, which had been saved by the intervention of Conrad of Montferrat, brother of Sibylla's first husband. The final act in this story was the surrender of the Holy City, Jerusalem, to Saladin on 2 October after a short siege.

The news of the disaster at Hattin reached the west in the autumn of 1187. The old pope Urban III is reported to have died of grief, but his successor Gregory VIII issued a moving appeal for aid, the encyclical *Audita tremendi*. In November, the archbishop of Tyre called Western rulers to the aid of the Latin kingdom. By the end of March 1188, Henry II of England, his eldest son Richard, Philip II of France and the Holy Roman Emperor Frederick I Barbarossa had taken the cross. The Third Crusade was born. Councils were held at Le Mans and Geddington; ordinances regulating aspects of the crusade were promulgated, as was the unpopular Saladin tithe, a tax of a tenth on incomes. Archbishop Baldwin of Canterbury and the historian Gerald of Wales were among those who preached the cross.

Once again, however, the French and English kings were deflected from the task in hand by their mutual suspicion and rivalry. The German army set out on schedule, but also failed to fulfil its early promise. *En route* to the Holy Land it was harassed by supposedly friendly Byzantine forces and in June 1190 the elderly Frederick I drowned while crossing the Goksu, a shallow river in Asia Minor.

On his release from captivity in the spring of 1188, Guy had promised not to bear arms against Saladin. In August 1189, however, he resumed the offensive. Refused entry into Tyre by Conrad of Montferrat, who had ambitions for the crown of Jerusalem, Guy marched south to Acre and took up position outside the city walls. In the following months his small force was augmented by advance contingents from England, France and Flanders, including Baldwin, archbishop of Canterbury, and the remnants of the German crusade. The French and English kings eventually arrived in the spring and summer of 1191, Richard I of England, who had succeeded Henry II in 1189, having paused in Sicily and Cyprus on the way. Acre surrendered after a long, hard siege in July 1191.

After dividing up the city, the most pressing task for Richard and Philip was to settle the complex and long-standing dispute over who should rule the kingdom of

Jerusalem. A compromise was reached: Sibylla's husband Guy, a widower since 1190 and without direct heirs, would retain the kingdom of Jerusalem – which despite its title was now based at Acre – for the rest of his life; after his death Isabella and her latest husband, Conrad of Montferrat, the hero of Tyre, would succeed him. Philip then set sail for the west. His early departure was criticized and chroniclers lamented the rivalry between the French and English kings which had, in their view, limited the expedition's achievements. Philip left a sizeable French force under the command of the duke of Burgundy, and the scene was now set for the final stages of the Third Crusade.

Under the terms of the agreement for the Muslim surrender of Acre, Saladin was to return the relic of the True Cross and Christian prisoners were to be exchanged for Muslim hostages. However, progress was slow and Richard finally lost patience and massacred some 2,700 Muslims in sight of Saladin's army; a deed which later chroniclers contrasted with Saladin's more chivalrous treatment of Frankish prisoners. On 22 August 1191, Richard led the Christian army south from Acre and on 7 September achieved a victory over the Muslims at Arsuf. On 19 September the Franks reached Jaffa, the most practicable base for a march on Jerusalem.

Richard could have advanced immediately to the Holy City, but instead proceeded to Ascalon to refortify its walls, limiting Saladin's ability to bring up reinforcements from Egypt.

In spring 1192, disturbing news reached Richard that his younger brother John was negotiating with his old rival Philip. This persuaded him to step up truce negotiations with Saladin. On 26 July he returned to Acre. On 2 September a three-year truce was signed with Saladin and on 9 October Richard set sail for the west. He left the Latin kingdom more secure than it had been, and in the charge of Henry of Champagne. Conrad of Montferrat, by now the new king of Jerusalem, was murdered by the Assassins, for reasons which are unclear, and his widow Isabella married Henry of Champagne.

Until his death in 1199 the English king continued to express a desire to resume the campaign against the Muslims in the east, and Philip II Augustus similarly showed interest in another expedition. However, the Christian banner was next raised by the Holy Roman Emperor Henry VI. In the spring of 1197 an impressive German army assembled in the ports of southern Italy. It reached Acre in September, and quickly captured Beirut and Sidon, which had been abandoned by the Muslims. Once again fate intervened. On 28 September 1197 Henry VI died of a recurrent fever at Messina, leaving baby son, the future Emperor Frederick II. On 1 July 1198 a truce was agreed with the Muslims and the German nobles returned home.

Events before and during the Third Crusade were recorded by a number of western historians, some of whom were participants in the expedition. Valuable texts of contemporary letters, such as the colourful exchange of correspondence between Emperor Frederick I and Saladin, are preserved within the framework of their narratives. The best such source for the crusade of Richard I and Philip II Augustus is the *Itinerarium regis Ricardi*, compiled in the early 13th century by Richard, a canon of the Augustinian priory of Holy Trinity in London. His first book describes events in the Latin kingdom between 1187 and 1190, and was probably based on an eyewitness account written by a Templar chaplain in 1191–2; the remaining five derive from an old French rhyming chronicle composed between 1195 and 1196 by Ambroise, possibly a Norman clerk, who gives first-hand accounts of difficulties facing the Christian army. Roger of Howden's *Chronica* supplements the *Itinerarium*, and provides details available only to a member of Richard's entourage – as with the king's encounter with Joachim of Fiore at Christmas 1190. Roger, parson of Howden in Yorkshire, is known to have been present at the siege of Acre, and may well be the same man as Roger, the royal courtier and chronicler.

On the summoning and preaching of the crusade the noted crusading bull of Pope Gregory VIII, *Audita tremendi*, is supplemented by the crusading *excitatoria* of Peter of Blois and by Gerald of Wales's account of his preaching tour of Wales with Archbishop Baldwin of Canterbury.

The *Historia de Expeditione Frederici* is an apparently eyewitness account of the ill-fated German crusade, and a counterbalance to German views of the Byzantines is provided by the 13th-century Greek historian Nicetas Choniates.

On the Muslim side, Imad ad-Din al-Isfahani was secretary to Nur ad-Din and then to Saladin, and chronicled the latter's life and death. In 1188 Baha ad-Din Ibn Shaddad joined the sultan's household where he remained, a faithful member, until Saladin's death in 1193. Their accounts of Saladin's character, of the battle of Hattin and of the fall of Jerusalem contrast with the Christian sources.

86

Salading rex Ægypti.   Raꝺ

By way of introduction, and so that the eager curiosity of future generations may be more fully informed about Saladin, this great persecutor of Christianity, I will say something here about his origins. He was of Kurdish stock, and his parents were not noble. However, in spite of this lowly beginning, his life did not follow the pattern of common folk.

His father's name was Job, and he himself was known as Joseph. Following the teaching of Mohammed, it is the practice among many of these pagans to bestow a prophetic name on those to be circumcised, along with the mark of circumcision. However, their rulers, anxious to derive incentive from their very names to be staunch defenders of the law of Mohammed, take names connected with the word 'law' itself. 'Al-Din' means 'religion', which is why he was called Saladin, meaning 'upholder of the law', or 'peacemaker'. Our rulers are known as emperors or kings, theirs as 'soldani' (sultans), as it were 'sole dominators'.

The first indications of Saladin's taste for power appeared under Nur ad-Din, sultan of Damascus. Saladin made a disgraceful income out of the prostitutes of that city, none of whom could ply her filthy trade without first buying a licence from him. The money he thus obtained by pimping he lavished on entertainers, purchasing the people's indulgence for all his whims by displays of generosity.

He was inspired with hopes of the kingdom by the prophecy of a certain Syrian, who foretold that he would hold sway over Damascus and Cairo. So he began to aspire to greater things than the kingdom beyond whose narrow limits and boundaries he had never gone. As time went on and he became older and stronger, he hankered after a soldier's life. He offered himself for military service to Humphrey of Toron, a distinguished Frankish ruler in Palestine, and received from him the girdle of knighthood after the French manner.

At that time, a certain pagan [the vizier] called Shawar was administering the whole of Egypt under [the Fatimid caliph, probably al-Adid] Molanus ('Lord' in their language), who had been forced to pay an annual tribute to the victorious king of Jerusalem, Amalric I, who died on 11 July 1174. Molanus, considered by his subjects to be so powerful that the Nile rose at his command, showed himself to the Egyptians, to be seen and worshipped, only three times a year. Moreover, punctiliously fulfilling the requirements of his pagan religion, he kept the same number of concubines as the days of the year. Growing old and feeble among all these young women, he left the government of the country to Shawar. Saladin, who at that time happened to be on military service there, in Egypt with his uncle Shirkuh, treacherously murdered both the unsuspecting Shawar and Molanus and obtained power over all Egypt. Not long after Nur ad-Din died, 15 May 1174, Saladin married his widow, put the heirs to flight and ruled the country with her.

Such was the power of playful Fortune, changing the course of events at will. That pimp, king of the brothels, who campaigned in the taverns, and devoted his time to gaming and the like, was suddenly elevated to sit among the rulers. The possessor of a glorious throne, he ruled the Egyptians, held sway over the Damascenes, controlled Edessa and Mesopotamia and conquered the recesses of India.

Overcoming the surrounding countries, either by guile or by force, he welded many sovereign nations into a single monarchy, holding supreme power over all their kings. But the greedy tyrant, not satisfied with these possessions, concentrated all his efforts on an attempt to seize the inheritance of the Lord, Palestine. And when the opportunity arose, he had hopes of gaining something beyond his wildest dreams.

The Latin *Itinerarium regis Ricardi* was compiled in the early 13th century by a canon of the priory of Holy Trinity in London, who wrote this account of Saladin's parentage and early career.

Saladin, ruler of the Levant

Saladin's Muslim biographer, Baha ad-Din Ibn Shaddad, who was a member of his entourage, writes an adulatory pen portrait.

God – may he be exalted – has said, 'And as for those who fight for us, we guide them along our path. Indeed, God is on the side of those who do good.' There are many texts on jihad in the Koran. Saladin was extremely diligent in waging this holy war, and it was constantly on his mind. One could swear by one's right hand without fear of contradiction that, from the time he first set out, intent on jihad, until he died, he did not spend a single gold or silver coin except on jihad and pious works. His heart and mind were so taken over by this burning zeal for jihad that he could speak of nothing else. Out of his desire to fight for God's cause, he left behind him his family, children, country, home and all the towns under his control.

Saladin was sociable, well mannered and entertaining. He could recite by heart the genealogies and battles of the Arab tribes, and knew all their exploits. He could even recall

A portrait of 'Saladin, rex Aegypt', from a 14th-century manuscript showing great personages of world history.

Saladin

Born in 1138 into a Kurdish military family at Takrit in present-day Iraq, Saladin entered the service of Nur ad-Din at Damascus in c. 1155, and accompanied his uncle, Shirkuh, on three campaigns to Egypt between 1164 and 1168. Exploiting the vulnerability of the moribund Fatimid caliphate, Shirkuh became vizier in January 1169, but died soon afterwards. Saladin seized power and, in 1171, abolished the Fatimid caliphate and brought Egypt under the sway of the powerful sultan, Nur ad-Din.

When Nur ad-Din died in 1174, Saladin married his widow and cautiously began to assume his mantle and to seize his territories. His victory at Hama (1175) secured central Syria, and after Nur ad-Din's son and successor al-Malik al-Salih died in 1181, Saladin made himself uncontested ruler of a unified Muslim Levant, with vast forces at his disposal. On 4 July 1187 he defeated the crusaders at Hattin, and on 2 October, after capturing the major coastal towns, apart from Tyre, made a triumphant but peaceful entry into Jerusalem.

Saladin lost Acre in 1191, and signed a truce with Richard I of England in September 1192. He died six months later in March 1193. The unity of his empire was soon broken with the division of his territories among his brothers and sons.

Between 1175 and 1185 Saladin had maintained generally peaceful relations with the crusaders and strengthened the Egyptian army and fleet. Building on the Sunnite religious revival which had gained momentum under Nur ad-Din, Saladin thereafter used the concept of holy war (*jihad*) to unite the Muslims and imbue them with a common religious ideal. His popularity with the masses was enhanced when he survived several Assassin attacks. Although fired by personal and family ambition, he was actuated by genuine religious fervour and personal piety.

Friend and foe alike viewed Saladin as an honourable man in dishonourable times, and crusader chroniclers – even in the bitterest hour of defeat in Jerusalem – praised his magnanimity. However, he was criticized in Muslim sources, even during his lifetime, for nepotism, extravagance, taking up arms against his fellow Muslims and failing to capture Tyre, so allowing the crusaders to remain in Outremer. Nevertheless, despite recent attempts to demythologize him, Saladin continues to excite admiration today.

the genealogies of their horses. In addition he had studied the curiosities and wonders of the world. As a result, those who sat with him learned from him things they would never have heard elsewhere. He would put his friends at ease and raise their spirits. If anyone was sick he would ask about his illness, his treatment, his food and drink and whether there was any change in his condition.

The purity of Saladin's character was always evident: when in company, he would allow no one to be spoken ill of in his presence, preferring to hear only of their good traits; when he himself spoke, I never saw him disposed to insult anyone; when he took up his pen to write, he would never use words to harm another Muslim.

He always stuck to his promise and was loyal. No orphan ever came before him without Saladin's praying for God's mercy on the child's parents and offering to help him maintain the same level of livelihood as his father had afforded him. If an older member of the orphan's family was still alive and capable of accepting the responsibility, Saladin would hand the child over to him; and if the child had no relatives, Saladin would set aside enough for him to live on, and send him to someone to take care of him and his upbringing. Similarly with the aged, he always treated them kindly and generously. He continued to behave in this way until the day that God called him to the seat of his grace and mercy.

Battle of Hattin, 1187

Saladin gradually consolidated his position, gaining control of Egypt, Damascus, Aleppo and Mosul. He also made periodic invasions of the Latin kingdom of Jerusalem. Then, on 4 July 1187, he decisively defeated the Christian forces at the Horns of Hattin. The disastrous battle and its aftermath were bewailed by the author of the *Itinerarium*.

The opposing lines were drawn up at a place called Hattin, in the hills behind Tiberias on the Sea of Galilee. At the precise instant that the fighting began, Raymond III, count of Tripoli, left the spot, feigning flight. The story is that he did this by prearrangement, so that our troops should scatter, apparently stricken by terror at the desertion of the one who should have been their support, while the spirits of the enemy were raised. So the Lord 'gave his people over also unto the sword' [Psalm 78.62], embroiled in conflict, consigning his inheritance to slaughter and pillage, as the sins of mankind demanded. What more is there to say?

The tears of Saladin

Once during the siege, when I was riding at the sultan's side against the Franks, an army scout came to us with a sobbing woman beating her breast. 'She came from the Frankish garrison', the scout explained, 'and wants to see the master. We brought her here.' Saladin asked his interpreter to question her. She said: 'Yesterday some Muslim thieves entered my tent and stole my little girl. I cried all night, and our commanders told me: the king of the Muslims is merciful; we will let you go to him and you can ask for your daughter back. Thus have I come, and I place all my hopes in you.' Saladin was touched, and tears came to his eyes. He sent someone to the slave market to look for the girl, and less than an hour later a horseman arrived bearing the child on his shoulders. As soon as she saw them, the girl's mother threw herself to the ground and smeared her face with sand. All those present wept with emotion. She looked heavenward and began to mutter incomprehensible words. Thus was her daughter returned to her, and she was escorted back to the camp of the Franks.

From Baha ad-Din Ibn Shaddad, *Sultanly Anecdotes*

To cut a long story short, so many were slain, so many wounded and so many thrown into chains that our people, completely destroyed, were a pitiable sight even to the enemy. Worse still, the Cross of our salvation, that life-giving wood, was taken into the hands of the enemy and along with it fell its bearers, the bishop of Acre and the preceptor of the Holy Sepulchre; one killed, the other captured.

When Guy of Lusignan, king of Jerusalem, saw the Cross fall, he was overcome with pity. He rushed forward and flung his arms around the Cross, hoping to snatch it back, if God so willed, or at least to die beside it. So the Holy Cross suffered yet another insult because of our wickedness. Not the Ark of the Lord, not Jewish kings led away captive can compare with this disaster of our time, when King Guy had as fellow-prisoner the glorious Cross. Some of the captives – and their numbers were as amazing as they were pitiable – were kept unharmed to await the victor's will. The rest were despatched to heaven in a swift and merciful death by the murderous sword.

Among others, Reynald of Châtillon, lord of Oultrejourdain, was brought before Sultan Saladin. The tyrant, driven by rage, or possibly out of respect for such a great man, struck off that proud and venerable head with his own hand. All the Templars, with the exception of their master, he ordered to be beheaded, determined to wipe them out completely, for he knew their reputation for superiority in battle.

Then what a passionate rivalry of faith and courage ensued! Many of the captives, claiming to be Templars, vied together in a rush towards the butchers. Gladly they offered their necks to the swordsmen, under a holy pretence. Among these soldiers of Christ was a certain Templar called Nicholas. He was so successful in urging others to their death that, in the rush to get ahead, he himself only just managed to be the first to win the glorious martyrdom he so earnestly desired.

Evidence of the miraculous power of God's mercy was not lacking: throughout the three following nights, while the bodies of the holy martyrs still lay unburied, rays of divine light shone clearly above them.

When the noise of battle had ceased, and Saladin beheld the captives being dragged away and the dead strewn about, he raised his eyes to heaven and thanked God for the victory, as he always did when things went well for him. One of his most frequent remarks was that our wickedness, not his power, gave him this victory, and the turn of events bore him out. For our army, however small, generally prevailed, with God's help. On this occasion, however, we were not with the Lord, nor he with us, and our troops were utterly worsted, even before the fight, although there were reckoned to be more than twenty thousand of them. In fact the might of the entire kingdom had gathered there by royal decree for that disastrous conflict. Only those who, by reason of age or sex, were exempt from bearing arms, remained in the protection of the castles or cities. This fateful battle was fought on 4 July 1187. In that short space of time, all the glory of the kingdom of Jerusalem was shattered and destroyed.

The account of the battle given by Saladin's own secretary and chronicler of his military campaigns, Imad ad-Din al-Isfahani, gives a quite different perspective.

The sultan, Saladin, stayed up that night of 2 July 1187 until he had positioned each company's detachments of front-rank archers and had filled their wooden and leather quivers with arrows. The number of arrows he distributed amounted to four hundred loads, not counting the supply carried by seventy dromedaries he brought on to the battlefield, from which anyone could take a supply of arrows.

As the day of 3 July dawned, our archers emerged, setting alight the people of hell-fire with a blaze of arrows. There was a creaking of bows and a plucking of strings on that day. And the army poured down on the Franks their scorching rays. As the heat flared up the forces of evil began to fade. A searing thirst descended: the air burned as passions turned to fear. Those dogs, panting, their tongues lolling, plagued by a havoc of their own making, turned their minds to thoughts of water only to be met by the flames of hell and to be overcome by the fire of the midday sun.

That took place on the Friday, the day of congregation in the mosques. Behind our army at no great distance was Lake Tiberias. The road to it had been barred from the Franks. Devastated by a thirst fed by fiery fuel, they stood patiently, steadfastly, obstinately; then struggling, rabid with greed, they drank what water their flasks contained. They lapped up whatever was held in the surrounding man-made wells, exhausting even the source of their tears as they teetered on the brink of calamity. Night came and the storm of battle subsided. They camped bewildered, drunk with thirst, yearning for the lake.

O God! What a night guarded by the angels, and what a dawn, its breezes a succession of God's mercies. The Sultan Saladin, trusting in God's victory, passed among the ranks, encouraging them and promising them the victory they expected from God, and urging them to jihad. They were strengthened by the sight of him, renewing their efforts, blocking the enemy's attack and repelling them. The sultan had a slave named Mankurus, fighting at the very front. His horse, being rather headstrong, dashed off with him far away from his companions. As his friends were unable to keep up, he found himself isolated among the Franks. His feet caught fast in this mire of death, he fought until they finally overwhelmed him. On capturing his head, they imagined they had taken one of the sultan's sons. As for him, he took his martyr's place by the All-Merciful.

The Muslims, on witnessing his martyrdom and the cruel treatment he had received, felt their zeal well up, their hearts intent on God alone. The army appeared as though at full strength, and victory within reach. Victory occurred on that day, Saturday 4 July 1187. Tormented by thirst, the Franks succumbed to defeat, impotent to recover from their fall. The breeze was in their direction, and beneath their feet was grass. Some of our holy warriors set fire to the grass. Its flame bore down on them, and its heat became intense. They, the people of the Trinity, were consumed by a worldly fire of three types, each invincible and obliterating: the fire of flames, the fire of thirst, and the fire of arrows. The Franks longed for release, and attempted a sortie, but in vain.

No matter how hard they fought they were repulsed; no matter how often they rallied, each time they were encircled. Not even an ant crawled out from among them, nor could they defend themselves against the onslaught. They retreated to Mount Hattin to escape the storm of destruction; but on Hattin itself they found themselves encompassed by

Saladin shown defeating the Franks at Hattin, and seizing the relic of the True Cross from its defenders. His victory opened the way to Jerusalem, which he took soon after.

fatal thunderbolts. Arrowheads transfixed them; the peaks laid them low; bows pinned them down; fate tore at them; calamity chewed them up; and disaster tainted them.

Not since the Frankish occupation of the Syrian coast had the Muslims' thirst for victory been quenched to the extent it was on the day of Hattin, 4 July 1187. God – may he be honoured and glorified – gave the upper hand to the Sultan Saladin and enabled him to perform that in which kings had proved themselves deficient. By his grace, God guided him to obey His command and, by performing his duty, to attain the goal set before him; the road leading to his enemies' destruction and his followers' conquest God made straight for the sultan. He reserved for him this most illustrious of days, this most righteous of victories, this happiest of joys and this most abundant of successes. Were no other merit his than that of this day, in majesty and valour Saladin would still stand out above all the kings of former times let alone those of this age. Yet this propitious attack was but a prelude to the conquest of Jerusalem, a tightening of the knot on his way to an inescapable and ultimate triumph.

Saladin takes Jerusalem, 1187

In the following weeks Saladin captured Acre, Beirut, Sidon and other Christian strongholds; and on 2 October 1187 his army took Jerusalem itself. The author of the *Itinerarium* described the brave efforts of the citizens to defend the Holy City.

With the omens prophesying success, the victorious Saladin made for Jerusalem full of haste, and hate. He set up his engines, laid siege to the city, and, with his usual unholy insolence, broke into the holy places. Long ago, when our troops took Jerusalem after their victory at Antioch in 1099, they had raised a stone cross above the wall to commemorate the event. This the savage horde demolished with a heavy missile, bringing down a great part of the wall with it. The citizens put up what barriers they could, but everything our people tried was fruitless and unsuccessful. In vain they wielded bows, catapults and slings. It was as though both weapons and engines were clearly proclaiming the wrath of the Lord and foretelling the doom of the city.

People from surrounding fortresses flocked into Jerusalem from every side, putting their trust in the holiness of the place rather than in its defences. But in that great multitude of men scarcely a dozen soldiers were to be found. Priests and clerics, though fighting was forbidden to their Orders, became warriors, battling for the home of the Lord.

The terrified and craven mob kept running to the patriarch Heraclius and the queen Sibylla, who were at that time in charge of Jerusalem. They complained tearfully and urged that negotiations be started with Saladin immediately about handing over the city. The pact which followed was more to be deplored than commended. For each person a ransom was paid: twelve sovereigns for a man, five for a woman, one for a child. Anyone who could not pay was taken captive. So it happened that while a good many people were able to find the payment for their safety, fourteen thousand who could not pay went under the yoke of perpetual slavery.

Those who could buy their freedom had a choice: they could either make the journey to Antioch, or sail under safe-conduct to Alexandria. A bitter day it was indeed, the day on which the people left their holy place and went their different ways into exile. On that day, 2 October 1187, the queen of all the world's cities was taken into bondage, and the inheritance of her sons brought under the yoke of strangers.

This holiest of cities had been held for about eighty-nine years by our people, from the time when the Christians took it, along with Antioch, in a mighty victory. But Saladin drove the Christians out and re-took it, in 1187.

After Jerusalem had been handed over, a muezzin climbed the high mount of Calvary and there, where Christ on his cross put an end to the law of death, the proclamation of a bastard law rang out.

A contemporary Arab portrait of Saladin.

Lament on the fall of Jerusalem

Neither counts, dukes nor crowned kings can escape from death: when they have amassed a great treasure, great the grief when they have to abandon it.

Alas, unfortunates, we have laboured so hard to satisfy the pleasures of the flesh which are so soon lost and past. That is why it is better to gain paradise where all services are doubly repaid.

We have too long delayed going to God's assistance to win back the land from which he was chased and exiled because of our sins. There each one will accomplish his desire, because he who sets aside his riches for God will in truth win paradise.

Those whom God permits to return will be greatly honoured in this world. He who has a loyal love in his country will keep the memory wherever he goes. My God, let me enjoy the best of ladies, so that I can find her again alive and well, when God has accomplished his task.

No man can stand against death, not count, duke or crowned king. For whoever has amassed a huge earthly treasure shall lose far more, and reap misery.

Far better to set out in a good cause. For when they've been shoved underground, what price then towns and castles?

Alas, prisoners! How we suffer for the fleshly pleasures we have enjoyed. Therefore alert our noble youth to the dangers. Good deeds deserve a place in heaven. They are doubly recompensed, while evildoers lose all.

As I love God, we have delayed too long to travel in his service and seize that land from which the Turks have ejected us and exiled us. There, may everyone achieve all he desires, in recompense for sins which we must hate so much. Because anyone who expends his wealth for the Lord shall achieve a heavenly crown.

A man whom God allows to return safely home will be greatly honoured in the world. He who loved well in his own country, must take his memories and souvenirs everywhere he goes. May God allow me to enjoy the best lady once more, and find her in full health and beauty, when his great cause is finished. And may he extend his mercy to those brave lords whom I loved so much, that I nearly forgot God above!

Anonymous, *Parti de mal et a ben aturné*

Another shocking deed of this cruel foe was as follows: they pulled down with ropes the cross surmounting the church of the Hospitallers, smashed it and spat upon it, then dragged it through the city dungheap as an insult to our faith.

As Imad ad-Din shows, Christian sorrow at the loss of Jerusalem was equalled by Muslim rejoicing.

The Muslims took possession of the city on the Friday, 2 October 1187, at precisely the time when the noon Friday prayer was due. Sultan Saladin's standard was hoisted up on the battlements, and the gates of the city were closed to keep the people in until ransom could be demanded of them and collected. The period for the obligatory prayer was almost over, making its performance impossible since they were unable to comply with certain of the Friday prayer's preliminaries and stipulations. The al-Aqsa mosque, and the mihrab in particular, was a den of pigs and filth, crammed full with new buildings of theirs, occupied by all manner of infidels, evildoers, oppressors and criminals. It would have been a crime to delay in purifying it, awash as it was in impurities. Work was directed at what was most important and useful, namely keeping guard over the people until they had complied with the stipulations upon them and paid their share of their ransom. The taking of Jerusalem coincided with the night blessed by the Prophet's ascent to heaven, thus completing what has already been described by victories and rejoicing.

The Sultan Saladin held court in the camp outside Jerusalem so that the nobles, commanders, dervishes and religious leaders could meet and congratulate him. His bearing was one of humility and sombre dignity, surrounded by pious scholars and jurists. His face was bright with joy and his hopes were crowned with the glory of success. He had opened his doors, bestowing gifts, no longer hidden but speaking freely. He was quick to welcome the guests, who covered his carpet with kisses. His expression shone, while giving off a sweet perfume. The sense of triumph descended on him, garlanding him in a moonlike halo. The Koran reciters sat reading and repeating sections of the Book, poets stood reciting their verses. Pennants were raised and unfurled, as pens inscribing the news. Out of joyous emotion tears welled up in eyes, and hearts were overcome by the rapture of victory; and lips invoked God in prayer.

Conrad arrives at Acre, 1187

After the fall of Jerusalem, only two coastal towns, Tyre and Tripoli, remained in Christian hands. Tyre was saved by the prompt and courageous action of Conrad, marquis of Montferrat, whose father William had been captured at Hattin. Conrad set out for Jerusalem in 1185, but delayed in Constantinople. When he heard of Saladin's invasion, he set sail for Acre. As the *Itinerarium* shows, on arriving there he realized that it had just been captured by Saladin's forces, and proceeded to Tyre.

One of those who came by way of Constantinople was Conrad, marquis of Montferrat, who on 14 July 1187 dropped sail and anchored one day at sunset outside the port of Acre. Conrad's suspicion was aroused by the silence of the city, for on other occasions the arrival of ships always produced loud rejoicing; fear increased when Saladin's standards were spotted about the place. His companions' courage failed when they saw pagan galleys approaching, but he told them to be quiet and put himself forward as spokesman for all. When messengers were sent to ask who, pray, were they, he stated boldly that this was a cargo ship and he was the master. He knew, he said, what was going on, but he was a good friend of the sultan, and he promised faithfully that at dawn the next day he would come into the city with his merchandise.

That night, with the wind behind him, he made for Tyre, of which he took command, and prepared its defences. His coming was a good thing for Christians arriving there, and would have enhanced his personal reputation if he had carried on as he started. The marquis of Montferrat, an Italian, was a man of outstanding energy, willing to try anything. But a beginning, however splendid, deserves censure rather than praise if the end is shameful.

Appeals for a crusade, 1187

News of the disaster at Hattin and the loss of Jerusalem reached the west in the autumn of 1187. On 29 October, Pope Gregory VIII issued his celebrated crusading encyclical *Audita tremendi* for circulation among the Churches of the west.

Bishop Gregory, servant of the servants of God, sends greetings and an apostolic benediction to every one of Christ's faithful that this letter might reach.

After hearing of the severity of the dreadful judgement which the Lord has inflicted on the land of Jerusalem, we and our brothers were thrown into confusion and buffeted by such a depth of horror and grief that it was not clear what we ought to do.

In order to take advantage of the discord which has recently grown in the Holy Land through the malice of devil-driven men, Saladin arrived in those regions with a host of armed men. He was met by King Guy of Jerusalem and the

---

A rich Frankish wedding

An alluring worldly spectacle deserving of record was a nuptial procession which we witnessed one day near the port of Tyre. All the Christians, men and women, had assembled, and were formed in two lines at the bride's door. Trumpets, flutes and all the musical instruments were played until she proudly emerged between two men who held her right and left as though they were her kindred. She was most elegantly garbed in a beautiful dress from which trailed, according to their traditional style, a long train of golden silk. On her head she wore a golden diadem covered by a net of woven gold, and on her breast was a like arrangement. Proud she was in her ornaments and dress, walking with little steps of half a span like a dove, or in the manner of a wisp of cloud. God protect us from the seduction of the sight.

Before her went Christian notables in their finest and most splendid clothing, their trains falling behind them. Behind her were her peers and equals of the Christian women, parading in the richest apparel and proud of bearing in their superb ornaments. Leading them all were the musical instruments. The Muslims and other Christian onlookers formed two ranks along the route, and gazed on them without reproof. So they passed along until they brought her to the house of the groom; and all that day they feasted. We thus were given the chance of seeing this alluring sight, from the seducement of which God preserve us.

From Ibn Jubayr, *The Travels of Ibn Jubayr*

The Damascus Gate in the old walls of Jerusalem. The city surrendered to Saladin after a two-week siege.

bishops, the Templars and Hospitallers, the barons and knights, along with the people of that land and a relic, the Cross of our Lord, through which, in remembrance of and faith in the passion of Christ, who hung upon it and redeemed mankind, there was hope of certain protection. They met in battle and after many of our people had been slain, the Lord's Cross was taken, the bishops butchered, the king captured, and almost all either cut down by the sword or imprisoned in enemy hands; so much so that only very few managed to run off or escape. Still worse, the Templars and Hospitallers were beheaded before Saladin's own eyes. We need not detail here how, when our army was annihilated, Saladin's army later attacked and plundered everywhere, so that only a few places remained which did not fall into their hands.

But we ought not to become so utterly dejected that we lose faith, nor believe that God, when he has been soothed by our repentance, will not bring us gladness after our grief.

We, who despite the deep distress of that land, have to take account not only of the sin of the inhabitants of that land, but also of our own sin and that of all Christian folk, must be careful in case what is left of that land is lost, and the might of the Saracens is turned against other places. For we hear everywhere of scandals and arguments between kings and princes. So it is vital that everyone thinks on this, and acts, and takes care of the wildness and wickedness of our enemies; and because they are not afraid to plot against God, we should in no way hesitate to act on God's behalf. Accept

with thanks, in so far as you can, this opportunity for repenting and doing good, and offer your possessions, and then offer yourselves, and work for the recovery of that land in which the Truth was born from the earth for our salvation; and do not pay attention to profit or worldly glory, but to the will of God, who in his own person has shown us to lay down our lives for our brothers, and give him your wealth which, like it or not, you will at last have to leave to heirs you know nothing about.

Therefore to those who undertake this journey with a humble and contrite heart, and who die in repentance for their sins and in the true faith, we promise a plenary indulgence for their misdeeds, and eternal life. Whether they survive or perish, they should know they are to have remission of penance imposed for all sins for which they make due confession, by the mercy of Almighty God and on the authority of the apostles Peter and Paul, and our own.

Furthermore the property and family of all such men, from the time they take up the cross, are to be under the protection of the Holy Roman Church, and of the archbishops, bishops, and other prelates of the Church of God, and there is to be no claim made against the property which, on taking up the cross, they peacefully owned, until there is definite news about their return or death, but their property is to remain

Financing the crusades

The main source of finance for participants in the First Crusade was mortgaging or selling property. Each knight had to equip himself with a horse and armour and enough money to buy provisions *en route* to the east, while nobles had to provide for combatant and non-combatant members of their households. No less important was the need to pay for prayers for their salvation. Many crusaders mortgaged their lands, buildings, pasturage rights and other revenues such as tolls. The agreements usually provided for a property to be returned to its original owner if he survived the crusade, or to his heirs after a specified period.

Although this practice continued, the main source of revenue in the 12th and 13th centuries was papal and royal taxation. Little is known about the crusading tax levied by Louis VII in 1146, but in 1166 both he and Henry II of England raised a tax on incomes for the defence of Christianity. There was a similar levy in 1185.

The Saladin tithe of 1188, levied by Henry II and Philip II Augustus of France in support of the Third Crusade, aroused bitter resentment and was regarded as a heavy burden by both laity and ecclesiastics. There were also fears that it would lay the foundations of a system of national taxation. These were justified when, in 1201, Philip Augustus and King John of England agreed to raise a tax of one 40th of the proceeds from lands and rents to help finance the Fourth Crusade.

In the 13th century the greatest contribution came from papal taxes on ecclesiastical revenues. The first, a 40th, was levied in 1199 by Pope Innocent III, who experienced great difficulty and delays in collecting the proceeds; some receipts from the Italian church were still due in 1208. It was 1215 before Innocent levied another clerical income tax, a 20th for three years, but over the next few decades an elaborate system of ecclesiastical taxation evolved, with collectors appointed by the pope for the different regions.

Payment for the commutation, redemption and deferment of crusading vows was another source of revenue. Originally conceived to allow everyone to contribute towards the crusade, while restricting participation to those able to fight, the system was subject to abuse by the mid-13th century, with redemptions sold to anyone prepared to pay: the sale of indulgences.

intact and undisturbed; they ought not to be compelled to pay interest, if they are indebted to anyone.

Moreover, they ought not to go off in expensive clothes, or with dogs or hawks or anything else which might seem intended for ostentation and luxury rather than necessity, but instead take plain clothes and equipment, to show they are acting in penitence rather than affecting idle vanity.

Ferrara, 29 October 1187.

The sense of grief was echoed in a poem by Berter of Orleans, quoted in the chronicle of Roger of Howden.

All brave men should now shoulder the burden of Tyre, make trial of their strength, and battle every day; they must be graciously distinguished by the glories of combat. As those about to go to war, the need is for hard battlers, not for molly-coddled pleasure-seekers. For it is not those that pamper the flesh with endless delight who reach God with their prayers.

It is the wood of the Cross, the sign of the Lord, that the soldiers follow for it has not failed, but has gone ahead in the might of the Holy Spirit.

Once more fresh Philistines have captured the Cross, his Cross, who was condemned. They have taken the ark of God, the ark of the New Covenant. But since it is clear that these are the forerunners of the Antichrist, against whom Christ wishes us to stand, what can they say, when Christ returns, those who have not stood firm?

It is the wood of the Cross, the sign of the Lord, that the soldiers follow for it has not failed, but has gone ahead in the might of the Holy Spirit.

The cross-despisers trample on the Cross, whereat the oppressed faith grieves. Who does not burn for revenge? As he values the faith, let him buy back the Cross, whomsoever the cross has redeemed.

It is the wood of the Cross, the sign of the Lord, that the soldiers follow for it has not failed, but has gone ahead in the might of the Holy Spirit.

As you listen to what I offer, take up your cross, and make this pledge: 'I give up myself to him, who as a victim surrendered his body and soul, by dying for my sake.'

It is the wood of the Cross, the sign of the Lord, that the soldiers follow for it has not failed, but has gone ahead in the might of the Holy Spirit.

In September 1187 Amalric, patriarch of Antioch, wrote to Henry II of England, recounting the sufferings of the Latin kingdom and the conquests made by Saladin, and pleading for help from the old king and his people.

Amalric, patriarch of Antioch, by the grace of Holy God and of the Apostolic See, sends greetings to Henry II, king of England by the same grace, and his lord and friend. May he rule in the name of Him through whom kings rule.

It is with tears and sobbing that we report to your excellency the dreadful and inexpressible anguish that we feel for the unexpected and grievous misfortune which has lately befallen us, or rather all of Christendom.

On 4 July 1187 Saladin, having mustered a great force of foreign enemies, fought a battle against the Christians in the land of Jerusalem, and destroyed their forces. He lorded over them at will, and the life-giving Cross was exposed to the ridicule of the Turks. The king and the master of the Temple were captured, as was Prince Reynald, who was murdered by the wicked Saladin with his own hands. A vast body of men were killed or captured later in the cities which he took. As for the remaining towns, I am dreadfully worried, not knowing when they too might fall into Saladin's hands, and their inhabitants be captured or killed, particularly as it is common knowledge that they are short of provisions, horses, weapons and defenders.

Therefore, since you surpass the other western kings in prudence, wealth and wisdom, it is your help which we have always looked towards. We pray that you will hurry to bring your powerful aid to the Holy Land.

Henry promises help

In reply Henry II promised to lead a new crusade to assist the beleaguered Christians in the Latin east.

To the venerable fathers in Christ and to his friends Amalric and Heraclius, the patriarchs of Antioch and Jerusalem, to Bohemund III, prince of Antioch, and to all the Christian people of the Eastern Church, Henry, king of England by the same grace, duke of Normandy and Aquitaine, and count of Anjou, sends health and consolation in Christ.

According to what our sins have deserved, the Lord, in his divine judgement, has allowed the land which was redeemed by his own blood to be defiled by the hands of unbelievers. So it is proper for us and for all who belong to the Christian faith to provide help and advice with all our might.

So then stand firm and you will soon see the Lord's help which has been prepared for you. For sooner than you believe such numbers of the faithful will come to help you by land and sea as no eye has seen, no ear has heard, no human heart conceived. These are the ones the Lord has prepared to help your land.

I and my son Richard, among other princes, rejecting the trappings of this world and scorning all its pleasures, putting aside everything which is of the world will shortly, with the help of the Lord, visit you in person with all our power.

Farewell.

In January 1188, Henry met with Philip II of France at Gisors in northern France. They agreed a truce in their latest war, and took the cross.

Shortly afterwards a council was held at Le Mans, at which the so-called Saladin tithe, a general tax upon incomes to finance the crusade, was promulgated. Its terms were quoted by the English chronicler, Roger of Howden, who went on the Third Crusade.

Everyone is to give a tenth of his income and property in the present year in the form of alms as a subsidy for the land of Jerusalem, with the exception of the weapons, horses and equipment of the military, and of the horses, books, clothes, vestments and all kinds of sacred vessels of the clergy, together with the precious stones belonging to either the clergy or the lay-folk. Excommunication has already been pronounced by the archbishops, bishops and rural deans in every single parish against anyone who does not legitimately pay this tithe in the presence and at the assessment of those whose duty it is to collect it.

This money is to be collected in each parish in the presence of the parish priest, the rural dean, one Templar, one Hospitaller, a member of the household of our lord King Henry II, a yeoman from the baron's household and his clerk, together with the bishop's clerk. If anyone gives less than he ought, according to assessment of these men, four or six true men from the parish should be chosen to state under oath the amount he should have declared, and then he will be bound to pay the extra which has been omitted.

Clerics, however, and knights who have taken up the cross will not pay this tithe. Instead the revenues from their property, and whatever is their due from their dependants, are to be collected by the aforementioned body of men, and returned to them intact.

Holy relics

Relics which the crusaders brought back from the east to northern Europe provided a focus for the new and more intimate devotion to Christ and his mother which had been increasing in fervour since the mid–11th century. They included the apostles' bones, and stones and dust from places mentioned in the Old and New Testaments, but the most popular were relics associated with the passion of Christ. In 1238, Baldwin II of Jerusalem sold the Crown of Thorns to Louis IX of France, who built for it the Sainte-Chapelle in Paris.

The relic of the Cross of Christ was central to this devotion. Its cross-beam, traditionally supposed to have been discovered by the Empress Helena, mother of Constantine I, in 326, had been kept in the church of the Holy Sepulchre in Jerusalem for the veneration of pilgrims, particularly on Good Friday, a custom copied in the ceremonies of the Veneration of the Cross in the west. In 614, Chrosroes II of Persia removed it to his capital when he captured Jerusalem, but 13 years later, when the Emperor Heraclius defeated the Persians, he took it to Constantinople and then restored it to Jerusalem.

The Christians claimed to have hidden the relic when al-Hakim took the city in 1009, producing it with great effect some 90 years later when the crusaders arrived in 1099. In 1187, however, it fell into the hands of the Muslims, and Richard I failed, in spite of lavish offers, to recover it from Saladin.

The beam itself disappeared, but fragments that had been detached were collected by crusaders and brought back to Europe, where they became the cherished possessions of churches and monasteries and a focus for pilgrims. Richard himself brought back two fragments of the Cross.

Other relics connected with the passion, such as the nails that held Christ to the cross, thorns from the Crown of Thorns, pieces of Christ's seamless robe and bottles containing his tears, were bought or stolen and brought home to be enshrined in reliquaries of great beauty.

The 'hairs of the Virgin' combined devotion to Mary with the passion: it was said that when Christ's mother stood at the foot of the cross, she tore out her hair in grief. John the Apostle collected the hairs, which he kept as a relic. Ilger Bigod, a French crusader, brought back with him a collection of these hairs, which he claimed to have obtained in the Holy Sepulchre, and distributed them to churches and monasteries in France and England.

Moreover, the bishops are to write to every parish in their dioceses on 25–7 December, to announce that everyone should collect the aforementioned tithe due from him by 2 February and that each should pay it the following day to whomever is present of those specified above, at the appointed place.

Like most subsequent taxes, this levy was unpopular with those who had to pay it and Gerald of Wales, one of the most colourful figures in the 12th-century Church and a prolific writer and historian, recounted criticism levelled at Henry II when he visited Portsmouth.

On King Henry II's arrival at Portsmouth in July 1188 he was approached by a certain noblewoman called Margaret of Bohun. She had come from a distant part of the realm.

She spoke to him about a number of matters and finally addressed him thus:

'My lord, I have never felt such fear about your position as I do now. Whenever some setback has befallen you in the past, the goodwill of your people has always brought events to a fortunate issue. But now, I am sad to say, things will turn out to the contrary.'

The king questioned her and learned that the reason for her protest was the exaction of the Saladin tithe. He was stirred to anger and replied:

'It is a worthless people that speaks ill without cause. Hereafter, if I live and am able to return, they will have good reason to curse me.'

But the Lord not only looks into words, but also into hearts since 'what is evilly gained has no good outcome'. Soon afterwards [6 July 1189], Henry II met an unexpected death, which not only proved that the tax was unjust, but also cancelled his cruel threat.

In France opposition to the tax was such that in the summer of 1189, Philip Augustus was forced to issue an ordinance abolishing it in future.

Philip by the grace of God king of France. Eternal salvation to his revered and beloved uncle William, count of Champagne, and with like goodwill to the archbishop of Reims and to all people of the same province, ecclesiastical and lay.

In order to win back the Holy Land, a single tithe will be levied on the moveable property of prominent people in our kingdom, both ecclesiastical and lay. But we do not wish the extraordinary nature of this measure to be perpetuated.

The miracle of the Cross

At the meeting at Gisors, Josias, archbishop of Tyre, was present. He was filled with the spirit of wisdom and understanding, and preached the word of God to the kings and princes in a wonderful way, and so turned their hearts to taking up the cross. Those who had been enemies before were made friends that very day, what with his preaching and God's help. From his hands the kings of France and England, Philip II and Henry II, received the cross, and at the same time the sign of the cross appeared above them in the sky. When they saw this miracle, many rushed together to take up the cross. When the kings whom I have mentioned above took up the cross, each adopted tokens for themselves and their men, to help distinguish between the nations. The king of France, Philip Augustus, and his men wore red crosses, the king of England, Henry II, and his men wore white crosses, and Philip, count of Flanders, and his men wore green crosses. Then they returned to their own lands, to raise what was required for their expedition.

From Roger of Howden, *Chronica*

Thus, on receiving a joint appeal from churchmen and nobles we have decided to pass a law, valid in perpetuity, that no further tax will be levied for the same or for a similar reason. Such an offering should be made for the salvation of souls of the faithful.

It seems to us that God is offended rather than pleased if, from the tears of the poor and widows, a sacrifice is demanded that is neither pleasing nor acceptable to God. It is just that none be exempted from this ordinance to whom our royal majesty has been extended. We have also decreed that immoveable property and lands and the rights of ownership, whether feudal by grant or custom, remain inviolate and unchanged. It is not our wish that the incidence of this tax should cause a limitation on anyone or act to his detriment, nor that anyone should feel that he is experiencing gain or loss or suffering excessive inconvenience.

Therefore it is our wish that everything should remain in the same condition that it was for forty days before we assumed the sign of the cross. So that this document may retain its validity we declare that it be confirmed by the authority of our seal and by our royal signature.

Given at Paris in 1189, in the tenth year of our reign.

At the council of Le Mans in 1188, the kings also made provisions regulating the behaviour of those who took the cross, and the privileges accorded to them by their crusading status. They were recorded by Roger of Howden.

It has been decreed by our lord the pope, Clement III, that whatever clerk or layman has taken up the cross should be freed and absolved of all sins of which he has repented and confessed, by the authority of God and the blessed apostles Peter and Paul.

It has also been enacted that all clerics, knights and yeomen who undertake this trip are to have the tithes of their lands and bondmen, and are to pay nothing themselves.

It has also been enacted that no one is to swear profanely, that no one is to play games of chance or dice, that no one after next Easter is to wear beaver, or gris, or sable, or scarlet, and that everyone should be content with but two dishes. No one should bring any woman with him on the pilgrimage, except perhaps a washerwoman on foot, to be above suspicion. No one is to have torn or tatty clothes.

It has also been decided that all clerics and laymen, who are to set out on this pilgrimage, can legally mortgage their revenues, whether church or lay or otherwise, from the Easter when they set out, for up to three years.

It has also been enacted that whoever should die on the pilgrimage, is to leave the money he has brought with him on the pilgrimage to be divided to maintain his bondmen, to assist the land of Jerusalem, and to feed the poor, according to the advice of sensible men appointed for the purpose.

Philip II Augustus, king of France.

The archbishop of Canterbury preaches crusade in Wales

One of those who preached the Third Crusade was Archbishop Baldwin of Canterbury. His preaching tour of Wales in 1188 formed the subject of Gerald of Wales's *Itinerarium Kambriae*, which includes a number of telling anecdotes about those who took the cross. In this work, Gerald, who accompanied the archbishop on his travels, also recorded his own successes as a crusading preacher and the healing powers of the archbishop.

At Radnor in Wales, the archbishop of Canterbury, Baldwin, met Rhys the son of Griffith, prince of South Wales [on about 5 March]. Rhys had in his company a number of noblemen from his part of the country. A sermon was thereupon delivered by the archbishop on the subject of the crusade and translated into Welsh by an interpreter. A powerful exhortation was delivered by the archbishop and the justiciar who wrote it on the instructions of the king, which contained many promises.

Gerald of Wales was the first to set an example to the rest by stepping forward. There followed a vigorous argument among all those present, and this was assisted by the words that had already been spoken. Gerald carried on numerous and anxious arguments with himself. Eventually he was persuaded by the wrongs being committed at the time, by the insults to the cross of Christ and by his own reasoning, and, falling down at the feet of the holy man, he reverently put on the sign of the cross. Peter, bishop of St Davids, and a monk of Cluny followed him. As for Rhys, his mind was fully made up to go on crusade, and he spent the next fifteen days conscientiously providing himself with equipment, pack-animals, followers, money and other things necessary for a major expedition.

However, Rhys had a wife, Gwendolyn, the daughter of Madoc of Powys, who, by the vice common to that country, Wales, was a blood relation in the fourth degree. She, as women do when driven by sinfulness, turned him completely away from his noble intent.

At Haverfordwest [which they reached on 22–3 March], the first speech was delivered by the archdeacon of St Davids, Gerald of Wales. The word of the Lord was graciously expounded and a huge crowd was drawn to him, consisting of men-at-arms as well as common folk.

Although the word of the Lord was delivered in Latin and

The birdlime of the devil

Having to do with women is the birdlime of the devil. Therefore I do not agree with female participation in a major campaign to be carried out by men. However, a territory stripped of its population cannot be restored without the presence of women; therefore including women in a crusade can be considered useful in order to resettle conquered land with a new population. Nevertheless, it is more prudent to await the outcome of the war resulting from the coming expedition, since only after victory has been secured shall we be able to settle a pacified territory.

And since the issue of war is doubtful, because it can be affected by numerous circumstances unless God brings success, it is preferable for women to stay at home where they cannot be a hindrance or a danger to the common enterprise.

What is one to think about a crusade by the poor which depends on beggary alone? Certainly, people of that kind who lack arms and food will scarcely be able to cope with the rigours of a long campaign. Hunger brings on helplessness and they end up at last as objects of derision to the enemy. Of course lightly armed men, even if they are poor, can in my opinion be of value. Through their submissiveness and the grace of God, they can assist the wealthy, who in turn relieve them with their charity. For the most part they can be very useful because, being lightly laden, quick moving and daring, they can carry loads, perform watch duties, bring kindling and water, run errands, look after things and do other essential jobs.

There is some point and occasionally advantage in including old men and veterans in a crusade, but it is seldom that they serve any purpose. On the whole, I think they would be a burden to an army. They would consume supplies without exerting themselves when it comes to the fighting. For their efforts in battle are no more valuable than those of children, unless they are confined to looking after armour and in the handling of weapons. But for this, younger men can better show others what to do, owing to their superior agility.

From Ralph Niger, *De re militari*

French, many were in wonderment and it was regarded as a marvel even by those who knew neither tongue, so that they were moved to tears and they rushed in crowds to put on the sign of the cross.

It happened that there lived in that area an old woman who had been blind for years. On learning of the arrival of the archbishop of Canterbury, she arranged for her young son to stand at the spot where the sermon was to be delivered, so that he should bring back to her even a small piece from the fringe of the archbishop's vestment. However, her son was unable to get near the archbishop because of the dense crowd, so he marked out a piece of earth beneath the feet of the preacher. When the crowd broke up he carried the lump of soil back to his mother who received the gift with delight. She went down on her knees, facing the east, and as she earnestly prayed she applied the earth to her face and eyes. All at once she recovered the blessing of sight which she had almost lost, thanks to the goodness of this saintly man and to her own faith and devotion.

Despite all the efforts of Baldwin, archbishop of Canterbury, and the other preachers of the crusade, the dissensions between Henry II and his sons, including Richard, count of Poitou (later King Richard I and known as the Lionheart), and the rivalry between England and France continued to dominate events and delayed the departure of the crusading army. Frederick I Barbarossa, the Holy Roman Emperor, who had taken the cross in March 1188, by contrast set out as planned in May 1189.

In England one of the main advocates of the crusade was Peter of Blois, the archbishop of Canterbury's secretary, who had been at Rome when news of the fall of Jerusalem reached the pope. In 1188 or 1189 Peter wrote an impassioned exhortation to Christians to assist the beleaguered Latin kingdom, entitled *De Hierosolymitana peregrinatione acceleranda*, in which he was highly critical of the kings' failure to depart for the east. Even the emperor was not absolved from blame.

It now appears likely that the Lord has rejected the great lords of the land to whom he had offered the leadership of the crusade, and has chosen men of lesser reputation. It was for these that he reserved the victorious issues of this life and the glory of the entire undertaking.

The Holy Roman Emperor, Frederick Barbarossa, and the king of France, Philip Augustus, swore their devotion to this course of action. Had they set out relying on a chosen few and on the devotion of men of lower rank, and not on a burdensome and undisciplined multitude, they would have removed the yoke of the extortioner and brought permanent peace to the earth. But if our lords, perhaps using a counsel of higher wisdom, decided to defer this course for so long, why, I ask, did they not choose men of foresight and vigour; men who could pile up supplies, gauge the dangers, prepare the crossings and scout out the strength of the enemy.

Frederick takes the cross

The setting for the Emperor Frederick I to take the cross was a special court, summoned by the pope's representative, Cardinal Henry of Albano, at Mainz in March 1188. The anonymous author of the *Historia de Expeditione Frederici*, a contemporary or near contemporary ecclesiastic, describes the assembly.

On 27 March 1188 a court of Christ was convened at Mainz consisting of princes, bishops, dukes, margraves, counts, nobles and the cream of the knights available to fight. Here, and not without the copious tears of many men, the Holy Roman Emperor Frederick I took up the sign of Christ's cross and declared that he was preparing himself for the memorable journey of Christ with a stout heart, putting himself forward as a celebrated leader for the faithful members of the crusade and as their proud standard-bearer. Quick to follow his example were the most noble princes, bishops, dukes, margraves, counts, nobles and brave knights, as well as many priestly clerics who, in a like manner, signed themselves with the mark of the Holy Cross.

No one at that time in the whole of Germany was thought to be of manly standing who was seen without the sign of the life-giving cross and was not going to join the fraternity of those assigned to Christ. In these boldest of combatants there burned the glorious passion for fighting against those who had invaded the Holy City and the Holy Sepulchre of our Lord, reckoning the whole and almost innumerable multitude of enemies as nothing. For them, indeed, life was Christ, death was a prize to be won.

Overleaf: Saladin's castle at Sahyun in Syria. Originally a Byzantine castle, it was taken over by the Franks early in the 12th century and captured by Saladin in 1188, after his victory at Hattin. He kept the castle almost unaltered, and it was never retaken. An immense ditch, 130 metres long by 25 metres deep, defends its main approach.

The emperor sent an envoy to Saladin, threatening war if the holy places were not surrendered, and the text of his letter of defiance is given in the *Itinerarium*.

Frederick, by the grace of God ever-august ruler of the Holy Roman Empire, and mighty conqueror of its enemies, to Saladin, protector of the Saracens. I bid you quit Jerusalem as the pharaohs of old fled before the Jews. As befits our majesty, we acknowledge the receipt of many letters sent to us in the past by your highness concerning this difficult business, letters which would have served your purpose better if there had been any sincere intention behind the words. We have now decided to address your majesty by letter in return.

You have profaned that holy land over which we rule by command of the Eternal King, as guardian of Judaea, Samaria and Palestine. Concern for our imperial office demands that we look with serious attention upon a crime of such bold and heinous presumptuousness. Wherefore we require you to give back the land, and everything that you have taken, and, in addition, to pay a fine commensurate with such dreadful crimes, as laid down by divine law.

Otherwise, lest we appear to be initiating an unjust war, we now fix a date a year from 1 November 1188, for a trial by battle, by the merit of the life-giving Cross and in the name of the true Joseph.

With God's help you will find out by experience what our conquering eagles can do, our battalions of many races, the wild German flying to arms even in time of peace, the untamed folk from the source of the Rhine, the young men of the Danube who do not know the meaning of flight, tall Bavarians and crafty Swabians. Then there are the wary Franconians, the sword-players of Saxony, the restless Burgundians and lecherous Alpine tribes; Bohemians eager for death, Bolognians wilder than their own wild beasts, pilots from Venice, sea-captains from Pisa.

In the end, on the day I have named, a day of joy, gladness and reverence for Christ, you will also find out that my own right hand, which you accuse of being feeble with age, has not forgotten how to wield a sword.

The same chronicle gives Saladin's reply, which expressed equal confidence in a Muslim victory.

We have decided to include also in this work the sultan's letter of reply. The tyrant's overweening confidence in his power to resist shines clearly out therein. We shall set it out in its original frank and direct wording.

To that true king and our friend, the great and noble Frederick, ruler of Germany, in the name of God the compassion-ate, by the grace of the one God, the powerful and all-surpassing victor, the everlasting, of whose reign there is no end.

We would beg to inform that true, great and mighty king, our good friend the ruler of Germany, that a certain man called Henry of Dietz has arrived here saying he is your messenger, bringing us a certain document which he says is from you. We have caused this document to be read and, after hearing what he had to say, given him a spoken answer. This is our written reply to the document.

If you are going to reckon up those who share your intention of coming against us, naming them and saying 'the king of this or that country, such-and-such a count, archbishop, marquis, or warrior', and if we wanted to specify those who are in our service, those who obey our command, ready at our word, those who would fight in our forces – all this could not be contained in writing.

If you are counting up numbers of Christians, there are more, many more, Saracens than they. Moreover, there is an ocean between you and your counted Christians, while there is none between the countless Saracens and ourselves, nothing to hinder their coming to our aid. The Bedouins are with us – who would be enough by themselves to deal with our enemies – and the Turks; if we set them loose on our foes they would annihilate them. At our bidding the peasants would fight vigorously against anyone invading their land, plundering them and wiping them out.

What else? On our side we have warlike emirs, who have opened up the land for us, subduing our foes. They will not tarry, these rulers of paganism, when we call upon them. And when, as your letter says, you are all gathered together, with the enormous multitude your messenger talks of, it is in God's might that we shall come out against you. The coastal lands will not be enough for us. God willing, we will sail across, and, with his strength, take possession of all your territories. For, if you come, you will bring every resource with you, you will be over here with all your people. We are well aware that no one will be left in your country able to defend himself, let alone safeguard the land. When God, in his strength, has granted us victory over you, all that remains will be the unopposed capture, by that same strength and will, of all your possessions.

The combined forces of Christendom have twice come against us in Egypt, once at Damietta and once at Alexandria; the coastal lands of Jerusalem were in Christian hands. In the area around Damascus, and even in Saracen country, there were individual lords, fighting successfully from their separate strongholds. But you know how on both occasions the Christians returned, and the end to which they came.

Our people are well endowed with lands. God has richly

added unto us territories far and wide, held in our power. Egypt with its dependencies, the land of Damascus, coastal Jerusalem, Mesopotamia with its castles, Edessa and India with their adjuncts. By God's grace all these are in our hands and all the rest of the Saracen realm bows to our rule. If we gave orders to the great Saracen emirs, they would not say us nay. Were we to summon Nasr, caliph of Baghdad, God bless him, he would arise from the high throne of his kingdom and come to our majesty's aid. By God's power and might we have captured Jerusalem with its land; only three cities remain in Christian hands, Tyre, Tripoli and Antioch, and these will inevitably be taken.

If you want war, and God wills it that we take possession of all Christendom, we will meet you, as you have suggested in your letter, by his strength. But if you are prepared to discuss the advantages of peace, we shall require the commanders of those three cities to hand them over to us. We will return your holy Cross and free all Christian captives throughout our land. We will keep peace with you and allow you a single priest at the Holy Sepulchre. We will give back the abbeys which existed at the time of pagan rule, and treat them well. We will permit pilgrims to visit and maintain peaceable relations with you throughout our lifetime.

This document we have written by way of answer to the one which came to us through the man called Henry, if that document does come from the king. May the Lord raise us up by his will to fulfil his purpose. It was written in the year 1188, by grace of the one God. God save our prophet Mohammed and his offspring, and God preserve the safety of the sultan of the Saracens, lord high king and victor, defender of the world, keeper of the banner of truth, reformer of the world and the law, custodian of the two sacred places and of holy Jerusalem, father of conquerors, Joseph son of Job.

Frederick's crusade, 1189

Frederick set out for Jerusalem, accompanied by a large German army, in May 1189. En route, as he told his son Henry (the future Emperor Henry VI) in a letter of 16 November 1189, the Germans were harassed and provoked by the Byzantines, who proved so obstructive that Frederick contemplated besieging Constantinople itself.

Frederick, by the grace of God, Holy Roman Emperor and ever august, sends greetings and the sincere affection of a father to his beloved son Henry, the great and august king of Rome.

Since you expressed a wish to be further informed con-

cerning the state of our own personage and the progress of the glorious army of the life-giving cross, it seems worth reporting first that as soon as we reached the borders of the empire of our brother emperor of Constantinople, Isaac II Angelus, we sustained no little loss in the plundering of our property and in the massacre of our men, a loss reckoned to have been clearly instigated by the emperor himself. For some bandit archers, lurking in dense thorn bushes by the public highway, never ceased ambushing with their poisoned arrows several of our men who were unarmed and walking somewhat carelessly, until the bandits were completely surrounded by crossbows and by our knights; being caught red-handed they paid the price and met their just deserts. On one single day, thirty-two were strung up like outlaws and ended their lives miserably on a gibbet.

None the less, the remaining bandits harassed us from the mountain slopes throughout the whole wooded expanse of Bulgaria and molested us in night attacks even though a vast number of them were dreadfully tortured in turn by all kinds of devices by our army.

Moreover, the emperor of Constantinople infringed every single agreement, sworn in his name and on his behalf by his chancellor at Nuremberg at Christmas 1187, and almost withdrew from us the right to exchange and trade by his threats. Also, he had the narrow paths blocked by felled trees and great rocks rolled in the way, and gave orders that every ancient fortification that had collapsed through age, which is to say the defence and fortification of the whole of Bulgaria, be reinforced with movable siege-towers and battlements against ourselves and all Christianity. But we Germans, supported by heavenly aid, used Greek fire and reduced the defences and stonework to embers and ashes.

In this way we successfully negotiated every single barrier by the grace of God, and reached the plain of Circuwicz in Bulgaria, which is filled with all kinds of good things, and so spent six long weeks struggling through Bulgaria. After that, on 24 August we reached Philippopolis, a city of Bulgaria most secure and rich, and we occupied the place as if it had been derelict.

What then? The next day, 25 August, we received a most conceited letter from Isaac II Angelus, full of threats and fawning and cunning in equal measure. That was the first time that we were completely certain of the capture of our envoys. Taking little thought for his own reputation, the Emperor Isaac had them thrust shamefully naked into a prison, against the law of all nations and envoys.

When they heard this, the whole army of the cross was enraged and did not cease from devastating and seizing cities, towns and castles, until the emperor of Constantinople indicated to us in a letter that our envoys would be returning

Frederick Barbarossa

When he took the cross in 1188, the Holy Roman Emperor Frederick Barbarossa was nearly 70 years old. In 1147–8, as duke of Swabia, he had accompanied his uncle Conrad III, king of Germany and Holy Roman Emperor-elect, on the disastrous Second Crusade. After succeeding Conrad in 1152, Frederick received many pleas for help from the barons of Outremer, but events nearer home absorbed all his energies for more than three decades.

Once he had brought some degree of order to his German kingdom, Frederick deployed its resources in five major campaigns in Italy, in an attempt to realize the authority implicit in his coronation as Holy Roman Emperor in 1153. However, the papacy and substantial sections of the Italian nobility and townspeople resisted him, and in 1176 he suffered a major defeat by the league of Lombard towns at Legnano. At Venice, in 1177, he accepted disadvantageous peace terms from the league and the papacy. Disturbances in Germany preoccupied him for the next decade, but in 1188 Frederick pledged himself to return to the east.

Frederick's years had not diminished his vigour, gallantry and charm – his nickname, Barbarossa, came from his flowing red beard. Nor had his long and arduous struggles with the papacy undermined his belief in the importance of the Holy Land. But although his many setbacks had taught him prudence, he could still be quixotic: having gathered the largest army ever yet to set off for a crusade (contemporary figures put it at 100,000 or even 150,000) at Ratisbon, he led it along the difficult land route used by the First Crusade instead of taking the easier way by sea. The Byzantines and the Seldjuk Turks were hostile; his troops were short of water and food and many men died. Nevertheless, Frederick had almost broken through to Antioch, when, on 10 June 1190, he was drowned trying to cross the shallow river Goksu.

Saladin, who had regarded Frederick and his great army as a dangerous threat, rejoiced on hearing of his drowning. 'God', commented the Muslim chronicler Ibn al-Athir, 'thus liberated us from the evil of such a man.' For the Germans he became the focus of legend. To the beleaguered crusaders of Outremer, however, his death was a major setback in their struggle against Saladin.

with great honour. In the end, after many delegations and rovings of envoys, he implemented a cunning plan. He sent back our envoys to our majesty as though everything had been fully settled and took more than two thousand marks of their money, promising secure passage, an abundance of ships, good trading and the usual exchange. But since we had absolutely no faith in the pledges and pretences of the Byzantines, we decided to winter at Philippopolis in Bulgaria.

Our son, Philip, duke of Swabia, the brother of your own sublime personage, is going to stay with a great part of the army in the city of Stara Zagora, which is ten miles distant from Philippopolis, until the warmth of spring dispels the chill of winter's blast.

Since the crossing of the Hellespont is impossible unless we obtain from the emperor of Constantinople the most important hostages and subject the whole of Romania to our rule, we urge that you send envoys to Genoa, Venice, Ancona, Pisa, and elsewhere to get the help of knights and vassals to come by sea and meet us at Constantinople around the middle of March 1190 when we can ourselves attack the city from the landward side.

Furthermore, we should urge your discreet and regal presence that you have the money still owed us immediately collected and have it sent on to Tyre [to await us], since you know that we will incur great costs as a result of the unexpected delay. And although we have a wealth of the finest knights in the service of the life-giving cross, we must have recourse to divine help through prayer. So we earnestly beseech your regal benevolence that by the zeal of the extreme devotion of the religious people in our empire you have prayers offered on our behalf to God in the vigilance of their duty.

We have lost more than a hundred pilgrims who by dying have gone to the Lord. We have sustained the greatest loss in horses. Many of our pilgrims from our empire are held captive in Constantinople, and we have now spent twelve weeks at Philippopolis.

The early 13th-century Greek historian Nicetas Choniates shows that the Byzantine reaction to the crusading army was rather different.

Not a single year passed without a public disaster. It was as if God had decreed that no day would be quiet and peaceful. For, as if barbarians hanging round our necks were not enough to punish us, an even worse evil befell us: Frederick, the king of the Germans, sent ambassadors to the Emperor Isaac II Angelus to seek permission for all his forces to travel through the provinces of Byzantium, just as though these ter-

Frederick I Barbarossa, shown above taking leave of his sons, and below, in the woods of Hungary with his army.

ritories were friendly towards the Germans. He sought provisions to be bought for them as they marched, and wanted his ambassadors to bring him an answer by return.

John Ducas, the Byzantine chancellor, was sent back to Barbarossa as a messenger. Pledges were exchanged that the German king would be able to traverse the territories without injury and, in turn, Barbarossa undertook that no city, village, castle or town would suffer at the hands of his army. Indeed, the Byzantines promised to provision them abundantly, so the army would lack for nothing; on the contrary, everything would be available so that pack-animals and men would have all they wanted supplied to them at their leisure, and almost pressed right into their mouths. Then the legate John Ducas returned to his people and announced to the Emperor Isaac the conditions that had been agreed.

175

Expectations of Frederick were great, but the army was broken by his death, in southern Turkey, in June 1190. Only a few Germans managed to reach the Holy Land and take part in the siege of Acre.

At this time the whole army of the Holy Cross, both rich and poor, both sick and those who seemed well, were still equally struggling against both the heat of the sun and the warmth of the season, on a difficult route over boulder-strewn rocks which were scarcely accessible to birds and the occasional ibex. Frederick Barbarossa, utterly unswayed by any danger, wanted to avoid the mountain-tops and temper the excessive heat, and so he attempted to swim across the fast-flowing river Goksu, although everyone tried to stop him. He entered the water and plunged into the stream. Then he, who had often escaped massive dangers, wretchedly perished. When the other nobles rushed to him, they were too late to give help and could only pull him out and bring him at last to shore.

As a result of his death, everyone was greatly distressed, and shaken by such dreadful grief that some, poised between hope and fear, ended their lives with him. Still others despaired and, as if considering that God did not care for them, they renounced the Christian faith.

Sorrow and unrestrained grief not unreasonably filled everyone's heart over the death of so great a prince. They had good cause to grieve, like the prophet saying: 'Alas! We are sinners; the wreath has faded from our brows; there are sad hearts everywhere.'

Richard I and Philip II at Messina, 1190

The kings of England and France eventually set out from Vézelay in July 1190 and arrived at Messina in Sicily in September of that year. Here Richard, who had a family dispute to settle with the ruler of Sicily, Tancred, count of Lecce, sacked Messina on 4 October 1190. As the *Itinerarium*'s author explains, his success only exacerbated the tensions between himself and the French king, Philip Augustus.

On 4 October 1190 Richard I of England captured Messina with a single onslaught, in less time than a priest would have taken to sing matins. Many more citizens would have perished had not the king in his mercy given orders to spare them. But who can estimate the quantity of wealth they lost? The victors seized for their own use all the gold, silver and valuables they could find. They also fired the galleys, reducing them to ashes, to prevent the citizens from escaping to fight again; they even seized some of the noblewomen for themselves.

Suddenly, after all this, the French noticed Richard's flags and standards flying above the walls and ramparts of the city. At this the king of France, Philip II, was outraged, conceiving feelings of jealousy which were to endure all his life.

Jealous of Richard's successes, Philip found his arrogant attitude hard to bear, and was resentful at receiving no credit for what he considered he had achieved by his own personal merit and efforts. Even when his men were in terrible danger, and he could see with his own eyes that heavy losses were being sustained, not only did he fail to keep his word and go to Richard's help against a determined foe (which he was bound by their treaty to do), he even vigorously fended Richard off from the very gate of the city they were trying to capture, Messina, because that was where he and his men had their headquarters and he scented trouble.

When, as we have described, the city had been taken and Richard's banners flew from the walls, the king of France's counsellors advised him to make Richard remove his flags from their superior position, replacing them with Philip's, thus acknowledging his superiority. Richard was furious, seeing what had happened, and considering the demands of their treaty; he did not even take the trouble to reply.

In the end, with the help of intermediaries, Richard's rage cooled off and the angry exchanges ceased. The man who appeared obdurate in face of hostile attacks yielded to the soothing words of his friends and agreed to Philip's demand. He handed over to him the oversight of the ramparts he had taken, with guardians from both sides, pending a decision from King Tancred of Lecce about recent events. Richard was very forceful, and remained inflexible when met with threats and boastful language, but he could be moved by soft words and prayers. So the standards of both kings were raised above the walls, until the faith and friendship of the king of France should be proved firm.

Four days later the kings patched up their disagreements. Richard and Philip laid down regulations for the conduct of the two armies, which reflected the difficulty of maintaining discipline in such a diverse force, and the importance of regulating trading during the journey.

On 8 October 1190 at Messina, in front of their earls and barons and the clergy and the people, the king of France,

Richard I and Philip II allowed dicing in their armies – but only if a nobleman or cleric was present.

Philip Augustus, and Richard I of England swore upon the relics of the saints that each would defend the other and their army in good faith, on that pilgrimage, both in going and returning, and the earls and the barons swore that they would strictly and securely keep the same pledge.

Then the said kings, with the advice and consent of the whole crusading army, decided that:

All pilgrims who die on the way in this pilgrimage should, according to their own wishes, dispose of all the armour, horses and clothing which they had used, and they should act likewise according to their own judgement with respect to half the property which they have with them on the journey, provided that they send nothing back to their own country.

Clerics will give whatever orders they wish about their chapels and all utensils belonging to those chapels, as well as about all their books.

The other half of the property is to be handed over to the discretion of the bishops, the masters of the Temple and the Hospital, the earls and barons, who are to use this money for the relief of the land of Jerusalem as they see fit.

This is what the kings have sworn in person strictly and faithfully to observe throughout the whole journey and either side of the sea, and with regard to all the pilgrims of both kingdoms, both those who are to come as well as those who have already come.

The archbishops and bishops have promised on their word of honour to observe the same pledge. The masters of the Temple and the Hospital have agreed that the same pledge should be observed by their respective Orders, and the earls and barons have sworn in person that the same pledge should be observed.

In addition no one in the whole army is to play at any kind of game for money except for knights and clerics, and they are not to lose more than twenty shillings in the course of a day and a night. If, however, any knight or cleric should lose more than twenty shillings in the course of a full day, they should for every time that they have exceeded twenty shillings pay one hundred shillings to the aforementioned archbishops, bishops, earls and barons, who should keep this money and add it to the funds mentioned above.

The kings, however, can gamble at their own pleasure, and in the lodgings of the two kings their men-at-arms might gamble, with the permission of the kings, up to twenty shillings. Also, in the presence of archbishops, bishops, earls and barons, and with their permission, men-at-arms can gamble up to twenty shillings.

But if men-at-arms or sailors or any other servants are found to have been gambling of their own accord, they are to be whipped naked through the army for three days unless they are prepared to ransom themselves on the judgement of the aforementioned men; the same thing applies to other servants.

If it is sailors who have gambled they are to be drenched in the sea, as sailors do, in the early morning for three days once a day, unless they are prepared to ransom themselves on the judgement of the aforementioned men.

Again, if any pilgrim borrows anything from someone else on the way, he is to pay back what he has borrowed; but as to what has been borrowed before the trip, there is no need to make repayment on the way.

Furthermore, if any hired sailor or any man-at-arms or anyone else except for clerics and knights should leave their master while on this pilgrimage, no one else is to accept them unless it has been done with the consent of his master.

If anyone foolishly attempts anything contravening these solemnly enacted decrees, he should know that he is subject to the excommunication of the archbishops and bishops of the whole army.

Richard I and Philip II

The leaders of the Third Crusade, Richard I the Lionheart, king of England, and Philip II Augustus of France, were divided by an old, bitter rivalry. In 1189 Richard had inherited the French fiefs of Normandy, Aquitaine, Poitou, Anjou and Maine from his father, Henry II of England, as well as the wealthy and prestigious English kingdom. Philip Augustus, who as king of France was Richard's overlord for his French lands, had fewer resources under his direct control – his royal domain was confined to the areas around Paris and Orleans – and, since his accession to the French throne in 1180, had plotted and campaigned to reduce the Plantagenet menace. Richard, who before 1189 had been party to Philip's plans to dismember Henry's empire, was, by 1190, the Plantagenet champion. He was diverted from his struggle against Philip into the fulfilment of his crusading vows only by pressure of public opinion and his own love of adventure.

The kings' political rivalry was echoed and increased by a mismatch in their personalities and temperaments. Philip was sickly and nervous, cunning and cruel, relying on duplicity rather than force to achieve his ends. Richard was far more exciting and charismatic, as cruel as Philip, and a rash and dashing man of action. A fearsome warrior, his fiery temper was legendary.

By the time the two kings reached Sicily, disagreements began to surface over Richard's sack of Messina and the division of the spoils. Other bones of contention emerged later: for example, at Acre, Philip supported the claim of his cousin, Conrad of Montferrat, to the throne of Jerusalem, whereas Richard gave his backing to a rival, Guy of Lusignan. The problem was settled by a compromise and Philip departed for France, in July 1191, but started to plot against Richard again, with his younger brother, John. When news of this reached Richard, in April 1192, he made a truce with Saladin and set off for home.

Many contemporaries believed that the bitter rivalry between the two kings undermined the success of the crusade, which was in many ways merely an interlude in their wars. Despite repeated promises, neither king ever returned to Palestine: Richard was killed in a minor skirmish, in 1199, while Philip died peacefully and piously in 1223, having captured almost all the Plantagenet lands in France, save Aquitaine, from Richard's successor John.

It has also been decreed by the kings that a trader, whatever the merchandise in which he trades, cannot buy bread in the army for resale, nor flour, unless a stranger has brought it and made bread from it. The same applies to corn unless, in the same way, he has made bread from it or has kept it back to take with him across the sea. It is altogether forbidden to buy dough, and it is forbidden to buy any of these things in a town or within one league from a town. But if anyone has bought corn and has made bread from it he is allowed to make a profit of only one farthing per measure, not including the bran.

As for other traders, in whatever merchandise they deal, they are restricted to making a profit of one penny in ten. No one is to test by sounding it the money of our lord the king, on which the stamp can be seen unless it has been damaged inside the rim. No one is to buy dead meat for resale, nor any living animal unless he kills it inside the camp. No one is to

Philip II and Richard I at Messina. Philip's attempt to share the credit for Richard's triumphant conquest of the town kindled a feud between the two kings that dogged the rest of the Third Crusade; though Messina was a Christian city seized by Richard in the course of a private dispute.

Joachim of Fiore's prophecy

While in Messina, Richard I, king of England, heard that there was a certain religious man in Calabria called Joachim, the Cistercian abbot of Corazzo, who possessed prophetic powers.

Richard sent for him and freely listened to the words of his prophecy. For Joachim was learned in divine scripture and used to interpret the visions of St John the Evangelist which John tells of in Revelation.

This was one of the visions of St John the Evangelist: 'A woman that wore the sun for her mantle, with the moon under her feet, and a crown of twelve stars about her head. She had a child in her womb, and was crying out as she travailed, in great pain of her delivery. Then a second portent appeared in heaven; a great dragon was there, fiery-red, with seven heads and ten horns, and on each of the seven heads a royal diadem; his tail dragged down a third part of the stars in heaven, and flung them to earth. And he stood facing the woman who was in childbirth, ready to swallow up the child as soon as she bore it. She bore a son, the son who is to herd the nations like sheep with a crook of iron; and this child of hers was caught right up to God's throne, while the mother fled into the wilderness, where God had laid a place of refuge for her, and there, for twelve hundred and sixty days, she is to be kept safe' [Rev. 12.1–6].

Here is Joachim's interpretation. A woman that wore the sun for her mantle, with the moon under her feet, signifies the Holy Church overshadowed and enveloped with the sun of Justice which is Christ our God and under his feet is the world with its vices and wickedness which should always be trampled. And a crown of twelve stars about her head: the head of the Church is Christ whose crown is the Catholic faith which the twelve apostles preached. She had a child in her womb, and was crying out as she travailed, in great pain of her delivery, like the Holy Church which always delights in newcomers to its family, and is at pains from day to day to gain for God those souls which the devil tries to snatch away and drag off with him to hell.

The dragon signifies the devil who has seven heads. The devil's head is wholly evil; St John cites the number seven, giving a finite number for what is infinite, since the devil's heads are infinite in number, namely the persecutors of the Church and the wicked.

St John also says in Revelation: 'There are also seven kings; five have fallen already, one is reigning now; the last has not come yet', and the aforementioned Joachim explains that in this way. The seven kings are the seven chief persecutors of the church whose names are Herod, Nero, Constantius, Mohammed, Melsermut, Saladin and Antichrist. Five of these have fallen already, namely Herod, Nero, Constantius, Mohammed and Melsermut; one is reigning now, namely Saladin, who is oppressing the Church of God. He holds it in his power, along with our Lord's Sepulchre, Jerusalem, and the Holy Land. But he will soon lose them.

Then the king of England asked him: 'When will this be?' Joachim answered him: 'When seven years have passed since the capture of Jerusalem.' Then the king of England said: 'So why have we come here so swiftly?' Joachim answered him: 'Your arrival is necessary, for the Lord will give you a victory over his enemies and will exalt your name above all princes of the earth.'

From Roger of Howden, *Chronica*

Food in the Holy Land

In 1120, Baldwin II of Jerusalem abolished duties paid on essential foodstuffs being brought into the city: wheat, barley, beans, lentils and chick peas.

In addition to these staples, there was an impressive range of culinary raw materials. The olive oil of Palestine had been prized since Roman times, while vegetables included globe artichokes, asparagus, cabbage, lettuce and truffles. Spices, such as pepper, cumin, coriander, cinnamon and ginger, and mastic, are common in medieval recipes, and were among commodities exported from Acre to Europe in the late 13th century.

At this time the Dominican friar Burchard of Mount Zion recalled seeing fennel, sage and rue growing wild in the fields, and parsley, mint and other herbs also flourished, as today. Hare, quail, partridge, deer and wild boar might have fallen to hawk or bow, and archaeological excavation has shown evidence of sheep and goats as well as cattle.

Dairy products, including yoghurts and cheeses, were an important part of a meal, and fish was readily available on the coast and around the Sea of Galilee.

The variety and the novelty of fruits were a source of amazement to westerners: dates, bananas, melons, water melons, gourds and grapes, which came in hugh bunches. Lemons, oranges and pomolos were used for sauces to eat with chicken or fish. Pears, apples, cherries and nuts were imported from Damascus. Grapes, figs and apricots were often dried, and some were made into conserves or syrups, which were diluted with water to make refreshing drinks, or with snow from Mount Hermon or Lebanon to make sorbets.

Wine, although forbidden by Muslim dietary law, was produced by Christians in Bethlehem, the Rafaim Valley, Nazareth and Sidon.

The best honey came from Jerusalem, where bees could feed on wild thyme in the Judaean hills; and sugar cane was grown and refined as sugar in the Jordan Valley and around Tyre and Acre for export to Europe.

Despite this array of foodstuffs, at least two religious houses in Jerusalem imported sides of bacon, barrels of tunny fish, cheeses and wine from Sicily for their own use in the 12th century. And the raising and consumption of pork (also forbidden to Muslims) increased dramatically in areas where Christian Franks settled.

sell his wine too dearly after the first proclamation for price regulation. No one is to make bread for sale except for a penny a loaf and all traders should know that the proclamation is to apply to all land within three miles of the lighthouse of Messina.

In all transactions an English penny is to be given for four pence in the money of Anjou. Furthermore it should be known that all the above has been decreed with the advice and the consent of the king of France, Philip Augustus, the king of England, Richard I, and the new king of Sicily, Tancred of Lecce.

The siege of Acre, 1189–91

In August 1189, Guy of Lusignan, king of Jerusalem, laid siege to the Muslim forces in Acre. Saladin came to relieve the city, but despite skirmishes, a long-term stalemate was reached, as the two armies began to fraternize between battles.

In October 1190, the chaplain of Baldwin, archbishop of Canterbury, who had arrived by sea from Marseilles with an advance contingent, wrote to the monks of his cathedral priory, reflecting Baldwin's complaints about the behaviour of the Christian army besieging Acre.

I know that you are deeply anxious to receive definite and reliable information about how things stand with the lord archbishop Baldwin and our army.

On 14 September 1190 the lord archbishop, with his entire staff, landed safely and in good health at Tyre. He waited for some while for the kings of England and France, who had not yet arrived, and then he travelled to our army at Acre.

I weep and am deeply grieved to report that our army has given itself over to disgraceful pursuits and indulges in idleness and lust instead of the practice of virtue. The Lord is not present in the camp; there is no one who does good. The commanders envy each other and one strives to outdo the other in rank and status. The lower ranks are in want and find none to relieve them. Purity, sobriety, faith, love and charity are missing from the camp. As God is my witness, I should hardly believe it had I not seen it with my own eyes.

The Turks besiege us, and every day we are exposed to harassment and violent attacks. Meanwhile, our soldiers skulk in their tents, and those who promised them a speedy victory, like convicts tamely suffer the enemy's contumely. Saladin's strength continually increases while our army daily falls off in numbers and strength. On 25 July 1190 more than four thousand foot-soldiers were slain by the Turks. More-over many of our leaders have met their end – the queen of Jerusalem, Sybilla, Count Stephen, brother of the archbishop of Reims, and countless others.

At the time that the bearer of this letter left us, that is, on 21 October 1190, Kings Richard and Philip still have not arrived, nor has the town of Acre been captured.

Once more, farewell.

King Guy's army had endured much suffering and privation during the lengthy siege. The *Itinerarium*, which was probably an eyewitness account of events, gives graphic details, and also commends individual acts of bravery.

Meanwhile the food shortage came to a crisis; the middle-rank troops as well as the lower were tormented by hunger, which, as it grew, became not just severe but unremitting. The situation was aggravated by worsening feelings about the provocative behaviour of the marquis, Conrad of Mont-ferrat, who was secretly passing food supplies only to those who were allies and accomplices of his wicked designs [on the throne of Jerusalem].

Winter was not far off. It used to be a time of plenty and easy living, overflowing with a variety of delicacies, but times had changed, and they were now paying for all this with stark shortages. Stomachs once belching from over-indulgence were now rumbling with emptiness which they tried to assuage with a voracity made indiscriminate by weakness. All supplies had been used up, and the hunger of the troops was still unsatisfied, exacerbated by the absence of bare necessities, and made even more irritating by the lack of their accustomed luxuries. Hot weather added no little peril to the prospect of famine.

What more can be said? A measure of wheat small enough to tuck under your arm was selling for a hundred pieces of gold, a fowl for twelve shillings and an egg for sixpence. The price of other foods can be assessed from such examples.

> How they loathed the marquis,
> All their comfort gone!
> Cheated them of food, he did,
> Starving every one.

The story goes that starvation then drove them to a crime which may perhaps be regarded as forgivable on the grounds that God created all things for mankind, giving them into his hand for his aid. Priceless chargers were slaughtered so that men should not perish while horses survived. They devoured the horseflesh as a great treat, sometimes without even skinning them. Horses' guts were sold for ten shillings. Even noblemen and the delicately nurtured sons of magnates would fall upon and devour any plants they saw growing, grazing like beasts of the field.

Wherever it became known that a batch of bread was in the oven, a large mob would gather, clamouring and shout-ing: 'Here's the money! Take as much as you like as long as you give us plenty of bread.' They each wanted to be served first, holding out the money for bread they never laid their hands on, and probably never would, as others violently seized it before them.

Some were to be seen running about like mad dogs, des-perate with hunger. If they found bones thrown out and gnawed by dogs three days ago, they would seize them, gnawing where there was nothing left to gnaw at, suck them and lick them. Not that they got anything, except the pleasure, as it were, of gnawing at the memory of the meat.

One of our men happened to be in the trench outside the city wall. He may have been trying to find a weak spot there, or perhaps was hoping to pick off one of the enemy with the crossbow he was carrying. After wandering about a bit, he halted. He was well protected with armour, as a foot-soldier usually is, his head and throat covered by iron mail, with body armour consisting of a thickly padded linen cuirass, commonly called a 'pourpoint', with an almost impenetrable lining of needlework quilting. As he looked up he was struck in the throat by a crossbow dart, aimed with great force by a Turk on the top of the wall. It penetrated all the armour we have mentioned, his iron neckpiece, and even the padded 'pourpoint', when it was stopped by an amulet he had round his neck, hanging down on to his chest.

One of our fellows was spreading a net outside the camp, to keep off the Turks or catch them if they attacked, when one of them rode rapidly towards him. Our man saw him coming, left what he was doing and fled. He reached the camp, and the Turk, failing to catch him, gave up the chase, turned back, and angrily began to tear up the net. He had pulled out some of the pegs and the ropes which held it down, and was quickly and carelessly rolling it together, when it became caught around his horse's head. The beauti-ful beast, outraged and maddened, charged round in circles, trying to free itself, and becoming more and more entangled. Some of our men saw what was happening and rushed towards him. The Turk, realizing that his horse was snared, leapt off and fled on foot.

The fine animal was carefully and with some difficulty freed from the net, part of which was broken. The onlookers agreed among themselves that the owner of the net should have the horse, in recompense for his damaged property.

Richard I sacks Cyprus

Finally, in March 1191, the kings of France and of England sailed from Messina. Philip went direct to Acre, but Richard, blown by a storm, had to take a longer route by way of Crete and Rhodes to Cyprus whose Greek ruler, Isaac Comnenus, had imprisoned some English crusaders. In retaliation Richard invaded the island. The *Itinerarium* describes the riches which the crusaders found there.

During May 1191, King Richard I took Cyprus in fifteen days, and gave it to his people to occupy. He found all the keeps well provisioned and the castles crammed with treasures and wealth of every kind, gold vessels, cups and dishes, silver jars, great pots and casks, gilded saddles, bridles and spurs, as well as precious stones of great value. There were also robes of scarlet, and priceless silken fabrics in marvellous designs. What more can be said? King Richard found that the pretender king, Isaac Comnenus, had collected examples of every kind of wealth that Croesus is said to have possessed; he took everything, regarding it as a trust to finance his expedition.

When all this had been accomplished, Richard sent the army with the baggage to the city of Limassol, ordering that every attention be given to the repair of the fleet for transit.

Richard now sailed from Cyprus for Palestine and arrived outside Acre on 8 June 1191.

During the week of Pentecost, Richard landed with his company at Acre. The earth shook with the joy of the Christians, as everyone rejoiced greatly and the happy events were greeted with a fanfare of trumpets. The occasion turned into a day of jubilee, and there was exceeding gladness among the people.

But the Turks, in the besieged city, were thrown into terror and despair at his coming; they realized that the size of the king's fleet completely dispelled any hopes they might have had of getting away and returning home.

The two kings, Philip and Richard, escorted each other politely from the harbour with exaggerated courtesies. Then Richard retired into the tent which had been prepared for him to make his dispositions. He gave careful consideration to the quickest way of taking the city and the best use to make of surprise attack, trickery and engines.

Pen cannot fully describe nor tongue tell the people's rapture at his arrival. A calm, unusually clear night was, they

Woman crusader's heroic death

Among those carrying soil to the city ditch to build an earthwork for the assault, was a certain woman who was working hard and diligently to further the task. Without stopping she went tirelessly to and fro, encouraging the others, until finally her zeal brought an end to life and work simultaneously. A great crowd of all ages and both sexes was bustling about trying to complete the task as soon as possible; this woman was hurrying to deposit her load when a Turk, lying in ambush, struck her a fatal blow with a javelin. She fell to the ground and lay writhing in agony. With what breath she had left she spoke to her husband and others who had hastened over when they heard her groans.

'My love,' she said, tearfully but urgently, 'my dear lord, I beg and beseech you by our sacred marriage vows and by the love we have shared, don't let my body – for I shall soon be dead – be moved from this spot. I can do no more for the work alive, but if my corpse has a share in it I shall feel I have made some contribution. Let it lie in the ditch in place of a load of earth – it will soon turn to earth, anyway.' She earnestly begged the crowd around her to make sure that this was done, and not long afterwards breathed her last.

From Itinerarium regis Ricardi

The siege of Acre

The siege of Acre was one of the longest of the Middle Ages. It began in the summer of 1189 when Guy of Lusignan, king of Jerusalem, marched from Tyre to Acre with a small band of supporters. They had no chance, at this stage, of capturing the city from the Muslims, and their position was made even more difficult when a relieving army led by Saladin arrived: the Christians were not only besiegers, but were themselves besieged.

Two years later, in July 1191, the siege was successfully concluded when the Muslim garrison surrendered to the crusader army led by Richard I of England and Philip II Augustus of France. Until the arrival of Philip and Richard in 1191, a stalemate had persisted.

Richard's appearance, in particular, had a dramatic impact. His fleet intercepted and sank a Muslim vessel from Beirut, carrying supplies and reinforcements for Acre's garrison. From then on the crusaders were able to maintain a blockade of the city by both land and sea.

Richard and Philip's armies brought a massive increase in the Christians' firepower. Philip's most effective stone-throwing machine was called 'God's Own Catapult'. As well as making efforts to knock down the walls, the crusaders tried to undermine them. A tunnel, supported by wooden beams, was dug under a tower or a stretch of wall. A fire was started in the tunnel and, when the wooden beams were burned through, the masonry collapsed. When the combined effects of artillery and mining were judged to have sufficiently weakened an area of the walls, the order would be given to mount a frontal assault. Although none of these was completely successful, they weakened the Muslim defenders. By July 1191, with disease rife in the city, the walls in a state of collapse and no prospect of relief from Saladin's army, the garrison was forced to surrender.

Jerusalem was not recaptured by the crusaders and Acre became the capital of the Latin kingdom. In many respects it was an obvious choice. The principal port of the Palestinian coast, at the end of a major trade route from Asia to the Mediterranean, it provided a ready market for much of the produce from the fertile plain that surrounded it. Acre became overcrowded, with large numbers of drug sellers and prostitutes, and a high murder rate. The Christians finally lost the city to the Muslims in 1291.

reckoned, smiling upon him. Horns resounded, trumpets rang out, while pipers added their shrill notes. Drums were beaten and the deep booming of the war trumpets could be heard. Yet it was as though all these discordant sounds joined together to create a harmony pleasant to the ear. Hardly anyone refrained from making some sort of contribution to the general hubbub of praise and jubilation. To show the gladness of their hearts they burst into popular songs, or, as encouragement for the present generation, told forth the 'glorious deeds of old antiquity'.

Some toasted the singers with wine in precious cups, others drank indiscriminately to high and low alike, passing the night in a frenzy of dancing.

Jubilation was heightened by the fact that Richard had subdued the island of Cyprus, which would form a convenient and essential base for his huge army.

To demonstrate the delight they were all feeling they banished darkness with flaming torches and twinkling tapers. This multitude of lights seemed to turn night into day, so that the Turks thought the whole valley was on fire.

The fall of Acre, 1191

The Muslims within the besieged city had suffered as much as their Christian besiegers, and on 12 July 1191 Saladin was persuaded to withdraw and Acre capitulated.

On 12 July 1191 Saladin finally decided to give in to the prayers of the besieged, especially as many of them were parents, friends and relations of emirs, provincial governors and powerful allies who were pressing this course of action upon him. They represented to Saladin that, in accordance with his promise made under the law of Mohammed's followers, he was bound to provide those under siege with a safe and honourable deliverance in their hour of need. If, made captive by the fortune of war, they met death in disgrace and mockery, the Mohammedan law faithfully observed by his forebears would be violated as far as he was concerned. If Mohammed's worshippers were taken by the Christians, his own good name and reputation would be greatly diminished.

They begged Saladin to be swayed by the consideration that an élite section of the Turks, in accordance with his wishes, had for so long suffered under siege, defending the city for him. Let him be mindful of the misery of the wives and families of the besieged, who had not seen them since the siege began three years ago. Better to surrender the city than to lose such brave and noble folk. Saladin yielded to these arguments, and agreed that they should try to make as favourable a peace as possible. Steps were taken to discuss the negotiation of a fitting formula. When messengers brought news to the besieged of the decision of Saladin and the provincial governors, great was their joy.

Straightaway their leaders came out to our kings and, through an interpreter, offered to surrender the city of Acre, hand back the holy Cross and free two hundred and fifty noble Christian captives. When our men dismissed this as inadequate they offered two thousand noble Christians and five hundred humbler prisoners whom Saladin ordered to be sought throughout the land. It was also stipulated that the Turks leaving Acre should take nothing but the clothes they stood up in, leaving their armour and all their possessions and food. Moreover they were to pay a ransom of two hundred thousand Saracen talents (equalling two hundred thousand sovereigns) to our two kings. As surety, they were to give hostages.

When Richard and Philip and their chief advisers had held a conference as to whether to settle on these terms, they finally decided to accept what was offered, and agreed to the conditions, namely that when guarantees of security had been given, documents drawn up and hostages taken, the Turks should leave the city empty-handed.

The crusaders entered the city with mixed feelings, conscious of the price of their victory.

The army had maintained the siege of Acre throughout two winters and a summer, from 28 August 1189 to 12 July 1191, up to the middle of the autumn in which, as we have related, the Turks were defeated; a fate which they richly deserved.

In addition to enormous outlay and expenses, countless Christians met their death. Someone has put it on record that, not counting the great majority too numerous to mention, the tally of distinguished victims was as follows: in the army six

Overleaf: Acre, captured by the Christians in 1191.

Acre, city of Christian pigs

On arriving at the city of Acre – may God destroy it – we were taken to the custom-house, which is a khan prepared to accommodate the caravan. Before the door are stone benches, spread with carpets, where sit the Christian clerks of the Customs with their ebony inkstands ornamented with gold. They write in Arabic, which they also speak. Their chief is the Sahib al-Diwan (chief of the Customs), who holds the contract to farm the customs. He is known as al-Sahib (the director or master), a title bestowed on him by reason of his office, and which they apply to all respected persons, save the soldiery, who hold office with them. All the dues collected go to the contractor for the customs, who pays a vast sum [to the government].

The merchants deposited their baggage there and lodged in the upper storey. The baggage of any who had no merchandise was also examined in case it contained concealed and dutiable merchandise, after which the owner was permitted to go his way and seek lodging where he would. All this was done with civility and respect and without harshness and unfairness. We lodged beside the sea in a house which we rented from a Christian woman, and prayed God Most High to save us from all dangers and help us to security.

May God exterminate [the Christians in] it and restore it to the Muslims. Acre is the capital of the Frankish cities in Syria, the unloading place of ships 'sailing smoothly through the seas, lofty as mountains' (Koran lv.24) and a port of call for all ships. In its greatness it resembles Constantinople. It is the focus of ships and caravans, and the meeting-place of Muslim and Christian merchants from all regions. Its road and streets are choked by the press of men, so that it is hard to put foot to ground. Unbelief and impiousness there burn fiercely, and pigs [Christians] and crosses abound. It stinks and is filthy, being full of refuse and excrement.

The Franks ravished it from Muslim hands in 1104 and the eyes of Islam were swollen with weeping for it; its loss was one of Islam's griefs. Mosques became churches and minarets bell-towers, but God kept undefiled one part of the principal mosque, which remained in the hands of the Muslims as a small mosque where strangers could congregate to offer the obligatory prayers. Near its mihrab is the tomb of the prophet Salih – God bless and preserve him and all the prophets. God protected this part [of the mosque] from desecration by the unbelievers for the benign influence of this holy tomb.

From Ibn Jubayr, *The Travels of Ibn Jubayr*

archbishops, one patriarch and twelve bishops died; in addition forty counts and five hundred great nobles met their end, with priests, clergy and a host of common folk whose number cannot be counted.

Philip and Richard divided the city between them and reached a compromise about competing claims for the throne of the Latin kingdom from Guy of Lusignan and Conrad of Montferrat. During the crusade the French and English armies reflected the tensions between their kings; their behaviour was much lamented, as in the *Itinerarium*, and it was contrasted with that of the force led by the legendary emperor Charlemagne in his campaigns against the Muslims.

The mighty king Charlemagne, famous in name and deed, who conquered so many lands and subdued so many realms, is never reported to have encountered strife in his army – not when he set out against Spain, nor when he led his expedition to gain possession of Saxony, annihilated the notorious Widukind, and performed many other famous exploits. Nor was there any unrest among his allies when he marched through Rome to meet the powerful Aguland – Aguland who came ashore at Rossano in Calabria with a strong band of Saracens, invincible save with God's help.

Never, in all the campaigns in the war-torn land of Jerusalem, where so many infidels were slain, so many victories won, nor anywhere else on earth where tales are told of famous battles fought under leaders of olden days, never was an army fighting under one commander riven by dissension; never did discordant feuds split asunder allies from different countries. Diverse races fighting under a single general were not divided by envy, nor were insults and reproaches heard among them. On the contrary, they all treated each other with honour and courtesy, and for the sake of unity were known as one race, where no quarrel could last long. This is how the French once vanquished all comers, and our armies today could well follow the example of those men of old.

Philip returns to France, 1191

On 31 July 1191, Philip II set sail for the west. Ambroise, in his old French rhyming chronicle, a possible source for the later books of the *Itinerarium*, portrayed Richard as the hero of the expedition, and strongly criticized the French king's departure.

At that time, as I understand it, after Acre was surrendered to us and when the Turks were to give back the True Cross, the news spread through all the army that the king of France, Philip Augustus, whom the people trusted, wished to return home and was making preparations to do so.

God's mercy, what a time to run! Everything was turning for the worse when he, who should have maintained many men, instead wished to leave. The king said he was departing because he was sick. Well, say what you like – that's what he said – but no one can persuade me that illness is an excuse for deserting the army of that great King who leads and directs all kings. Now I'm not saying he didn't turn up, nor that he didn't bring plenty of iron and wood, lead and tin, gold and silver with him, nor that he failed to look after many people, like the greatest king on earth, as all the Christians readily admit.

All the more reason for him to have remained and done his best, without slacking, in the poor devastated land which had been so dearly bought.

The information was uncovered, confirmed and broadcast throughout the army, that the king intended to return and was getting ready day by day. All the French nobles were filled with rage and despair that their head (of which they were just the limbs) should be evidently keen to leave. He would not stay for their sakes – no matter how much they wept and implored him!

And when they saw they could not make him change his mind nor divert him from his purpose – I tell you truly – they blamed him most fearfully, and almost disavowed him, their own king and lord.

The French king continued his preparations, paying heed to no one who urged him to stay and not return to France. He made his escape with a great following of nobles and soldiers. Leaving behind him the duke of Burgundy in charge of his people, he demanded that King Richard provide him with two galleys.

You should have seen his men rush to the port and take charge of two fine ships, strong and swift. This gift was freely given and evilly returned.

King Richard, who was staying in Syria in service of the Lord God, not trusting the French king – just as their fathers had not trusted one another and had done each other harm on many occasions – made him swear an oath on holy relics that he would not invade Richard's lands nor attack him while he was on God's journey and pilgrimage. When he got back to France, Philip should give him forty days' warning before he made trouble or war or harmed Richard by any hostile act. The king of France gave his word and gave pledges of his good faith through his great nobles, such as

Turkish tricks

The Turks, unlike our men, are not weighed down with armour, so they are able to advance more rapidly, and often inflict serious damage on our forces. They are almost unarmed, as they carry only a bow, a spiked club, a sword, a reed lance tipped with iron and a loose-slung knife. When forcibly driven off they flee on very swift horses, the fastest in the world, like swallows for speed. Also they have this trick of halting their flight when they see that their pursuers have given up the chase. An irritating fly, if you drive it off, will leave you, but when you desist, it returns. As long as you go on swatting it, it keeps off, once you stop, back it comes. This is just like the Turk – when you give up the pursuit and turn back, then he comes after you, but if you drive him off again, he will take flight. So while King Richard kept up the chase they fled, but when he turned back they threatened his rear, not always with impunity, but often inflicting severe losses on our men.

From *Itinerarium regis Ricardi*

Hugh, duke of Burgundy, and Henry of Champagne, count of Troyes, and five or more others, so I'm told, though I can't name them.

In August 1191, Richard the Lionheart wrote to his justiciar in England to announce the fall of Acre and his intention to return home in a few months.

Richard the king of England, to the justiciar of England, greetings.

You should know that we suffered much from sickness since the start of our expedition, but by God's mercy we recovered fully. You know well enough how much honour was vouchsafed us through divine compassion at Messina.

Thereafter, while continuing our journey, we turned aside to Cyprus, where our people who had suffered shipwreck hoped to find shelter. But a tyrant there, Isaac Comnenus, had usurped to himself the title of emperor. Fearing neither God nor man, he advanced with a strongly armed force to prevent us from landing. He inflicted additional suffering on men whose ships had been wrecked, by plundering and imprisoning them with the intention of letting them perish from starvation.

It is easy to understand to what anger we were aroused to punish such villainy. Supported by divine aid we engaged this enemy in battle and gained a quick victory. We now have the enemy leader beaten and bound as our prisoner as well as his only daughter and we have taken control of Cyprus with all its fortifications.

Then in a cheerful and confident mood we entered the harbour of Acre. Within a short period of our arrival and that of the French king we regained Acre and the Holy Cross, taking seventeen hundred prisoners. However, the French king left us after fifteen days to return to his own country.

We, on the other hand, are more concerned with the love and honour due to God than an audacious interest in the acquisition even of many territories. Nevertheless, as soon as we have restored the territory of Syria to its original status we shall return home. So you can assume that we will enter home waters next Lent. We are also instructing you to pay special attention to the furtherance of our interests.

Witnessed by me at Acre, 6 August 1191.

The battle of Arsuf, 1191

The crusading army next set out from Acre on 22 August and met Saladin's forces in battle just north of Arsuf – not far from Jaffa, which Richard considered of great strategic importance – on 7 September 1191. The crusaders eventually won the day, although the scale of their victory was probably exaggerated by the author of the *Itinerarium*.

As the Christians kept up the slaughter, hammering away with their swords, the Turks began to panic and weaken. For some while the battle swayed to and fro, each side returning blow for blow and striving for victory. Some retreated, covered in blood, others, though wounded, rushed on to their death. Many flags could be seen fallen to earth, with banners of all shapes and sizes and countless pennants and standards. Trusty swords lay scattered around, metal-tipped darts, Turkish bows and clubs bristling with sharp teeth. Over the battlefield more than twenty cartloads of bolts, javelins, arrows and other missiles could have been collected.

Great numbers of bearded Turks lay dead and mutilated. With a courage born of despair others kept fighting, but, as

Muslim fortifications

Muslim rulers in the Near East depended on fortifications. Before the Mamluk seizure of power in the mid-13th century, the Muslim world was fragmented, apart from short periods such as the last ten years of Saladin's life (1183–93). Each ruler needed to secure his position by building or rebuilding city fortifications and, in particular, citadels; and at the same time citadels and city walls were a symbol and expression of the local ruler's power. The towers and walls were built to a great scale, and the large blocks of masonry, often bossed, harked back to Syrian masonry of classical times.

There was no lack of building skill. Shortly before the arrival of the crusaders certain rulers had built effective and elegant fortifications, as when in 1087–91 the walls of Cairo were reconstructed by a Fatimid caliph, or when in 1089 a tower was added to the theatre, converted to a citadel, at Bosra in Syria for the Seldjuk prince of Damascus.

The citadel of Cairo was constructed between 1170 and 1208 by Saladin and al-Adil; in its first form it was defended by semicircular towers of limited diameter. A city wall enclosing a wider area than the one constructed in the late 11th century was built by Saladin from 1176. Some of the towers in this wall are four storeys high. A circular central chamber rises to a dome at first-floor level; the dome is surrounded by a corridor giving access to arrow-slits. The platform above is the third level, and the raised wall-walk at the edge of the platform is the fourth. The towers could be held independently of the wall, and were intended partly as a store for materials and a residence for troops.

The norm in Syria was square or rectangular towers, on three storeys, and simple open-backed bastions. In citadels such as those of Aleppo and Damascus, the towers were close-set. Mamluk builders continued earlier Ayubid designs and masonry with little change, whereas Turkish princes in northern Mesopotamia, Anatolia and parts of Armenia seem generally to have rebuilt Byzantine fortifications without change of design but in superior masonry.

Apart from the concept of the donjon or keep, there is nothing in crusader fortification (as opposed to decoration and interior vaulting) that cannot be found in Muslim building, generally prior to the crusader examples.

our forces gained ground, some were knocked from their horses and hid in the undergrowth, while others swarmed up trees, only to be pierced by arrows, falling to earth with dreadful screams. Yet others left their horses of their own will and slipped away in flight by hazardous byways to the sea, where they hurled themselves into the deep from cliffs as much as thirty metres high.

Thus the enemy army was gloriously routed, so that for two miles nothing could be seen but a fleeing mob. They who had been so steadfast, so fierce and so swollen with pride, by God's help fell in their arrogance.

In October 1191 Richard himself described the campaign in a letter to the abbot of Clairvaux.

Richard, by the grace of God, king of England, duke of Normandy and Aquitaine, and count of Anjou, sends greetings and the hope of continuing happiness to a venerable man and his best loved friend in Christ, the abbot of Clairvaux.

[After our victory at Arsuf], with God's guidance, we reached Jaffa on 29 September 1191 and fortified the city with ditches and a wall with the intention of protecting the interests of Christianity to the best of our ability. After his defeat Saladin has not dared to face the Christians, but like a lion in his den has been secretly lying in hiding and plotting to kill the friends of the Cross like sheep for slaughter.

So when he heard that we were swiftly heading for Ascalon, he overthrew it and levelled it to the ground. Likewise, he has laid waste and trampled on the land of Syria.

13th-century tiles from Chertsey Abbey, Surrey, showing symbolically Richard I's triumph over Saladin.

The Assassins

Because of the hostility of Sunnite Muslims to the doctrine of the extremist Shi'ite groups, much Shi'ite activity during the ninth and tenth centuries was conducted in secret by emissaries (dais) dedicated to subverting the Sunnites to their ideals. In this way an Ismaili dynasty, the Fatimids, established itself in Tunis and conquered Egypt in 969, creating a caliphate intended to rival and eventually supplant that of Baghdad. They held undisputed leadership of the Ismailis for over 100 years until well into the 11th century, during which the Nizari faction achieved supremacy. In Islamic literature they were called Hashishiyun, from which the name 'Assassins' was coined by western writers, because of the belief that their obsessive dedication, most manifest in outrageous murders, was the result of taking hashish.

In 1090 the Persian Hasan-i Sabah seized the mountain fortress of the Alamut, though still deferring to the Fatimid caliph, al-Mustansir. After the caliph's death Hasan claimed leadership of the Assassins. A puritanical man, who executed two sons for misdemeanours, he reorganized the group. He promoted the dogma of the absolute authority of religious faith manifest through the divinely inspired and infallible leader, and emphasized the futility of life in pursuit of political goals. The agents (fidawis) in the field were veteran initiates. In Syria in 1113, the Aleppo community, some 200 strong, was arrested en masse for murder and its leaders were executed. There was a similar purge in Damascus in 1129. But in 1140, a colony was established in the cliffs of Masyaf, its leaders sent from the Alamut. Rashid ad-Din Sinan, who came in 1169, survived several assassination attempts from the Alamut and became known as the Old Man of the Mountain. He directed the Syrian Assassins for 30 years.

The objects of the Assassins' aggression were not the Christians, with whom their relations were relatively amicable, but the Sunnite Muslims. However, they were not averse to hiring their services to the highest bidder, and their most famous victims include the vizier al-Afdal and Caliph al-Adil in Egypt, Raymond II of Tripoli, Conrad of Montferrat, Albert, patriarch of Jerusalem, and Philip of Montfort. Others who survived attacks were the sultans Nur ad-Din and Saladin. Masyaf was besieged many times but never taken until Sultan Baybars' sustained attack in 1273, after which the faithful dispersed.

Therefore we consider it grounds for good hope that soon, God willing, the inheritance of the Lord will be fully regained. Since in its recovery we have exhausted not only our money but our strength and body as well, we bring it to the attention of your fraternal personage that we certainly cannot remain in the country of Syria after Easter.

Duke Hugh of Burgundy, together with the French in his command, Count Henry of Troyes with his men, and the other earls, counts, barons and knights who in God's service have already spent themselves on God's behalf will return home unless, through the skill of your preaching, time and provision is made for them both in troops by which the land may be peopled and protected, and in money which they may more liberally spend in the service of God.

Therefore, it is with many tears and falling at the feet of your holy personage that we offer our humble prayers, earnestly asking you that as befits your office and honour you make it your business to induce the princes and nobles throughout Christendom together with the rest of God's people and prompt them to serve the living God, so that after the aforementioned festival of Easter they might guard and defend the inheritance of God which we ourselves will, God willing, more fully possess by that Easter time.

Therefore, just as you encouraged us and the rest of God's people before the beginning of this expedition to serve God, and to restore his inheritance to him, now too there is a great need to firmly incite God's people to carry out the same plan.

Witnessed by myself at Jaffa on the first day of October 1191.

Richard in Palestine, 1192

As the *Itinerarium* relates, the decision now facing the army was whether to march to Jerusalem, or refortify Ascalon whose walls were being dismantled by the Muslims.

In the year of our Lord 1192, on 13 January, a council was called of the wiser among the leaders of Richard's crusader army. They decided to discuss whether, after making enquiries from the natives, it would be better to press on with the capture of Jerusalem or to turn elsewhere. The Hospitallers, Templars and others, brought strong arguments to bear in favour of abandoning further progress altogether. Every effort, they said, should be concentrated on rebuilding the city of Ascalon. From there a watch could be kept on the supply routes of the Turks from Cairo to Jerusalem. The leaders agreed with this policy, namely that Ascalon, just taken from the Turks, should be strengthened, and a watch kept there to cut off their supply route.

But when the decision to hold back became known to the army, the people were terribly cast down. They had had high hopes of visiting the Lord's Sepulchre, and to see them suddenly dashed caused many sighs and groans. Their previous excitement at the thought of pressing on was completely dispelled by the disappointing prospect, and the announcement brought depression in place of anticipation.

In fact Richard never reached the Holy City, although on 12 June 1192 he saw it from a distance.

On Friday 12 June 1192 a spy informed King Richard that some Turks were ambushing travellers in the hills. Early in the morning he set out from Beit Nuba [12 miles from Jerusalem] to find them, and surprised them at dawn by the spring of Emmaeus. In the attack twenty Turks were taken and the rest scattered. The only prisoner to be spared was Saladin's personal herald, whose duty it was to announce his decrees. Three camels, horses, mules and some fine Turkomans were captured. The king also obtained two good mules laden with precious silk garments, as well as many kinds of spices, including aloes.

Richard hunted the Saracens closely as they fled through the hills, killing as he went. Pursuing one of them into a valley, he had just unhorsed him, pierced and dying, and was crushing him underfoot when he looked up. There, afar off, the city of Jerusalem appeared before his eyes.

Meanwhile, on 28 April 1192, Conrad of Montferrat, who was to succeed Guy as ruler of the Latin kingdom, had been murdered by the Assassins.

When the legation had done its work, Henry of Champagne with the rest of the envoys and their companions had made a detour to Acre where they organized themselves better. When they were about to rejoin the army at Ascalon, Conrad, marquis of Montferrat, was detained at Tyre by his unexpected death.

He was peacefully making his way home, very happy and joking, from a dinner engagement with the bishop of Beauvais. He had just reached the city toll-booth when two youths, Assassins, made a sudden attack on him. They were unencumbered by cloaks and thrust at the marquis with the daggers they held in their hands. They penetrated his chest with these, lethally wounding him, and were ready to make a swift getaway.

The marquis immediately fell from his horse and was rolling on the ground, fatally wounded. One of the murderers was immediately cut down while the other ran straight into the nearest church. In spite of this he was snatched from it and dragged as a condemned man through the middle of the town until his last treacherous breath.

Masyaf castle, one of the principal bases of the Assassins, from which agents were sent out to slay enemies of the 'Old Man of the Mountain', whether Christian or Muslim. Often the Assassins allied with the Franks against Muslim rulers.

Before he died he was closely questioned as to whether they had acted at someone else's instigation and why they acted as they did. He confessed that they had been sent to kill Conrad a long time ago and that they had undertaken the task on account of the authority of the one who had sent them and because it was wisest to obey him. It was soon clear that he spoke the truth. The two youths had been in the service of the marquis himself for some time, waiting for a suitable opportunity to do the deed. The young man said that they had been sent by the Old Man of the Mountain [Rashid ad-Din Sinan, sheikh of the Assassins], and it was he who had judged the marquis worthy of death and ordered him to be killed within a certain fixed period. For the Old Man of the Mountain took care to kill in the same way all those he thought unfit to live.

Indeed the Old Man of the Mountain, according to the custom of his ancestors, brought up for his service a great many noble boys in his own palace. These he taught every kind of worldly wisdom, knowledge and language so that wherever in the world they were, among whatever race, they would know how to conduct themselves with easy familiarity without an interpreter.

Those whom the Old Man considers to have reached adulthood are admitted to his presence and, to free them from their sins, he indicates a certain powerful and tyrannical man whom they are to kill. For performing this task he presents each with his own dagger, which is very sharp and has a horrifyingly long blade. They immediately and obediently set out on the task ahead until they meet whichever tyrant has been indicated to them. They then work in his service until the time is right to finish their task, a task which will, they hope, fit them for heaven.

This was the background to the murder of Conrad, marquis of Montferrat. He was now breathing his last and his men, protecting him on all sides, carried him gently to his palace. They were inconsolable in their weeping and grief because so short a time before he had been with them enjoying the evening.

When Conrad had received the saving sacraments of the faithful he firmly enjoined his wife to be vigilant in taking care of Tyre and told her not to yield it up to any man except King Richard, or to any man to whom the kingdom belonged by hereditary right.

At that moment he died and was buried at the Hospital amid great lamentation. Thus the earlier exultant happiness was cut short and the peak of lordship, which had been long desired but not experienced, had completely disappeared. Now, as you can see, the relief that was to come to that deserted land had been snatched away and much sadness had replaced the earlier joy.

Conrad's widow, Isabella, queen of Jerusalem, married Henry of Champagne, who took over the kingdom though not the crown. Richard was both ill and worried by news from home and in September he agreed a truce with Saladin.

Safa al-Din, Saladin's brother and governor of the coastal area, negotiated peace on these terms, namely that Ascalon (a threat to Saladin's empire) should be razed, not to be rebuilt for the three years beginning the following Easter 1193.

After that, irrespective of who was the more powerful, the place called Ascalon was to go to whomsoever happened to be holding it.

Saladin also conceded that Jaffa should be given back to the Christians, to be held freely and peacefully with all its surrounding hill and coastal region. He confirmed a permanent peace between Christians and Saracens, reserving the rights of both to free passage and access to all places, including the Holy Sepulchre, without payment of toll. Merchandise should be conveyed without hindrance throughout the land and trade was to be carried on freely.

When these terms had been put into writing and read to Richard, he gave his consent. He could not hope for more, sick as he was, with little prospect of help, and not more than a couple of miles from the enemy lines. Anyone who maintains that any other reaction was possible in the matter of this treaty must incur the charge of dishonest thinking.

When all these things had been done, Richard, whose pride, even at crisis point, always strove desperately to rise to the heights, sent messengers who announced to Saladin, in the hearing of many princes, that he was only asking for a temporary, three-year truce.

Indeed he just wanted to see his own land again, and re-equip himself with men and money. Then he would return and wrench Jerusalem from Saladin's grasp if, indeed, Saladin had the confidence to resist.

Saladin sent back messengers swearing that, by Almighty God and the holy law, he held Richard's integrity, pride and excellence in such high esteem that, if he had to lose his land in his lifetime, he would rather it were taken by one of such power and courage than by any other prince he had ever seen.

How blind and darkened are the eyes of men! They plan out what they will do in the far future, totally ignorant of what the morrow may bring forth. So the king of England projected his anxious thoughts a long way ahead, and hoped one day to recover the Holy Sepulchre. He did not consider how all human life hangs on a slender thread.

Richard's capture, 1192

Richard set sail from Acre in October 1192, but did not reach England until 1194, for en route he was captured by Leopold, duke of Austria, a dangerous enemy who handed him over to the Emperor Henry VI. Both were cousins of the murdered Conrad of Montferrat, and their actions show they believed Richard to be responsible for his death. Richard was eventually released on payment of a large ransom.

All night they sailed by the stars, and as the next day dawned, King Richard gazed back devoutly at the land he was leaving, lost in thought for a long time. Many heard him as he uttered this prayer: 'Oh Holy Land, I leave you in God's keeping. May he in his grace grant me length of days that at his good pleasure I may sometime bring unto you the succour that is in my heart.' Then he urged the crew to raise all sails to the wind to cross the stormy seas as quickly as possible.

Little did Richard suspect the trials and tribulations which lay ahead, and the afflictions he would endure in the hands of wicked conspirators, as he continued in the service of God on his weary pilgrimage.

On 11 November 1192 King Richard, exhausted by the long, rough sea-voyage, landed at the earliest opportunity on the first land that came into sight, which was a place called Corfu, ruled by Constantinople. Rightly suspicious, in the light of past events, of the wiles of the Emperor Isaac II Angelus and his Byzantines, he did not wish to be seen. So, happening to fall in with some pirates, he wisely agreed to pay whatever they asked to transfer him quickly to some safer shore.

Leaving the royal fleet he put off his kingly garments and boldly entrusted his life to savage pirates. He changed his clothes, but not his spirit – for what would he not dare, great-hearted King Richard?

With four companions he sailed across to Slavonia, and thence to Aquileia, entering the territory of Duke Leopold of Austria. There, in Vienna, on 20 December 1192, he was taken prisoner.

The death of Saladin, 1193

Richard never returned to Outremer. On 4 March 1193 another figure departed from the stage, with the death of Saladin. Roger of Howden quotes a letter from the doge of Venice to Richard I announcing this event.

To the most serene Lord Richard, by the grace of God king of England, duke of Normandy and Aquitaine and count of Anjou: Henry, by that same grace doge of Venice, ruler of Dalmatia and Croatia, sends greetings and sincere regards. You will know from the certain news given to us that Saladin, that enemy of the Christian faith, has died. One of his sons, al-Afdal Nureddin, has turned his forces against Damascus. A second son, al-Aziz Uthman, is lord of Cairo and Alexandria. Saladin's brother, al-Adil [Safa al-Din], has surrounded Cairo with a large army. This shows that there is the greatest disagreement between them. Farewell.

Baha ad-Din Ibn Shaddad gives a fuller and moving account of Saladin's death.

The Sultan Saladin died at Damascus after morning prayers on Wednesday 4 March 1193. On that day, at dawn, the Kadi El-Fadel and I had hastened to the sultan's palace only to find that the sultan's soul had already ascended to stand before God's merciful justice.

Since Islam and the Muslims lost their four caliphs, never had our faith and its true believers suffered such a loss as befell them when the sultan died. The whole world was filled with a grief so profound, that only God could realize its true depth. I had often heard people say that they would be prepared to sacrifice their life for that of someone dear to them, and I had always thought that if they were to be confronted with such a choice, they would soon recant these words.

But on that day, if I and others had been asked 'Who will lay his life down in exchange for the sultan's?', I am convinced that each of us would willingly have done so.

The pope calls for a crusade

Efforts to persuade western princes and nobles to go to the aid of the Latin kingdom continued after Richard's return to England. In 1195, Pope Celestine III urged Christians to take the cross. Ralph of Diceto includes parts of his letters in his chronicle.

Bishop Celestine, servant of the servants of God, sends greetings and an apostolic benediction to his venerable brothers the archbishop of Canterbury, Hubert Walter, envoy of the Apostolic See, and his suffragan bishops appointed in the province of Canterbury.

The merciful and compassionate Lord God, in order to

restore the fall of mankind did not hesitate in his mercy from assuming the flesh from a virgin's womb nor yet from undergoing the trial of death. He did not want us to fall again into the hands of the devil through our lack of merits.

But in our times we are affected neither by the warnings of holy scripture nor by the punishments of our own weakness. For this reason the Lord has been willing to lay his hand heavily upon us to such an extent, and to convey the land of his own birth into the hands of pagans, a thing that we cannot describe without bitterness in our hearts. Moreover, grieving as we must with the prophet, we have heard with our own ears that the corpses of saints have been given to the birds of the sky to eat, and their blood to the beasts of the earth to drink. We have likewise heard of the abominable destruction wrought in that holy place where, so it is said, a whore's brothel has been set up where there was once a table of bread and holy preaching, and where there is to this day stabling for pack-animals in the place where the corpse and tomb of Christ stood and was visited by the faithful.

Furthermore, Jerusalem, once the vision of peace, the land promised to the ancient fathers, where our Lord chose to suffer for us and to make plain the clear signs of his divinity, is now trampled under the feet of wicked men and defiled by the filth of those for whom we once felt only fear and horror. The city, then, is despoiled of its wealth and accustomed glory, bereft of men of religion and deserted by men of faith.

What Christian, aware of such desolation, can hold back his tears? Let those who can, try cold steel against the persecutors of their faith to bring swift vengeance for the wrong done to the Cross. Let them please the Lord with continual prayer. For behold! Satan has fallen upon us to sift us like wheat in this disaster.

We should not be amazed at those, including several of the world's princes, who have so far set out to fight the Saracen heathen with spear and sword, even though they have accomplished nothing wholly successfully. The Lord in his mercy does not save those who exult in spear and sword, but will save them in the multitude of their miseries. For this reason, then, dearest friends, keep faith deep in your hearts that the Lord may exalt in his miracles.

Let those who have carried military arms among Christian folk take up now the sign of the cross and let them neither despair for their small numbers nor glory in their multitude. If they are willing, with due humility, to rush to the defence of the land of Christ's birth, passion, resurrection and ascension, then the Lord who brings an end to all, who hurled Pharaoh's chariots and armies into the sea will teach their hands to battle and their fingers to war. He will soon puff away the mass of pagans like chaff before the wind and grind them down like the dust on the streets.

As for you, my brothers, bishops and archbishop, you should labour with constant and unceasing prayers to the Lord and with continual preaching to persuade the people subject to you to take up the sign of the cross and strive to rebut and confound the persecutors of the Christian faith.

Moreover, to those who for love of God undertake the labour of this trip, we grant remission of penance imposed in priestly ministry, just as our predecessors are known to have granted in their own times. For they who have undertaken the labour of this journey with contrite heart and humble spirit are to obtain a plenary indulgence for their sins, and eternal life thereafter.

Finally, Hubert Walter, brother archbishop, to whom the care of the mission to the kingdom of England has been entrusted by the Apostolic See, we ask that you put your efforts into continuous encouragement in the kingdom of the illustrious King Richard of England, our dearest son in Christ, to send well-trained knights and foot-soldiers to the defence of the land of Jerusalem.

Given in the Lateran on 25 July 1195, in the fifth year of our pontificate.

The German crusade, 1195–8

The crusading initiative was taken up by the Emperor Henry VI, son of the crusader Emperor Frederick I Barbarossa, who hoped that leadership of an expedition to the east would consolidate his position in Germany. At a series of assemblies between October 1195 and March 1196 [Gelthausen and Worms], a number of Germans took the cross; the following Christmas they set out for the Holy Land.

A great throng of high-ranking nobles and men of war, in the hope of winning remission of their sins, donned the sign of our Lord's passion. Many letters containing exhortations from Pope Celestine III were read out in the cities and parishes of Germany.

When the contents of these became known, people were inspired by heaven also to take up the cross, the victorious emblem of our Lord's passion. Among these there were four hundred doughty warriors from the city of Lübeck. Thus afire with the burning zeal of dedication to the Christian cause, all, whether rich or poor, prepared to set out in the coming summer. The Emperor Henry VI himself hastened to Apulia, to facilitate the progress of the crusade. For he wanted his ardour to reflect in the preparations he would make for the crusaders as they arrived.

The main German fleet reached Acre on 22 September 1197. Its leader, Henry, duke of Brabant, did not wait to discuss tactics with the nobility of Outremer. Instead the Germans occupied Sidon and Beirut; then, after reaching a truce with the Muslims in July 1198, most of the leading crusaders returned home. Henry VI himself never reached the Holy Land, for he had died at Messina on 28 September 1197, as Arnold of Lübeck relates.

While the army was staying at Beirut and destroying its walls, an ill-omened report reached them of the death of the Emperor Henry VI. He had died at Messina, in Sicily, on 28 September 1197. This report caused great sadness among the people of God, and the news weakened the efforts of brave men, because, as usually happens at times of such changes, one thought he had lost his rank, another his estate, another his inheritance.

Thoughts like this came flooding into the minds of almost everyone. One brave man's conscience told him that, if he were at home, the empire might be his. Another feared that the new emperor would be against him. Yet in the middle of all these changing notions a spirit of prudence prevailed. For the leaders held a council and decided this: that all the German nobility present there should swear an oath to the last emperor's son, Frederick [II].

This decision brought an end to the disturbance.

The tomb of Saladin in Damascus, where he died on 4 March 1193, not long after his respected adversary Richard I had left the Holy Land.

5

THE FOURTH CRUSADE
1202–1204

In 1204 the army of the Fourth Crusade attacked and sacked Constantinople, capital of the Byzantine Empire, seat of the patriarch of the eastern church, and treasure-house of a magnificent heritage, cultural, artistic and intellectual, that stretched back to the heyday of the Roman Empire. In calling for a crusade, in 1198, the pope, Innocent III (1198–1216), had hoped to send a force to Palestine to build on the small gains made by the Germans in 1197–8. But the expedition slipped beyond his control and ended in tragedy.

Its beginnings had been promising. In an attempt to attract large numbers of crusaders, Innocent, in an encyclical of August 1198 issued to all the Christian faithful, redefined – and improved – the nature of the indulgence offered to sinners who took the cross: instead of declaring that such an act of penance would be satisfactory to God, he promised on God's behalf that a full remission of sins would stem from fulfilling the crusading vow, and 'a greater share of eternal salvation'. Geoffrey of Villehardouin, a leading figure in the crusade , wrote in his description of the expedition that 'because the indulgence was so great, the hearts of men were moved, and many therefore took the cross'.

However, it was mainly the common people who responded to the pope, galvanized by the popular preacher Fulk of Neuilly; knights and nobles were lukewarm and kings showed no interest. With no great lay ruler to bear the costs of the expedition, Innocent, in 1199, imposed a tax of a 40th of annual income on the Church. Resistance was considerable:

Venice, with the four bronze horses stolen from Constantinople visible on the façade of St Mark's.

some revenues were still being collected in 1217, and papal plans looked set to founder. But in November 1199, a group of French nobles led by Theobald, count of Champagne, and Louis, count of Blois, took the cross at a tournament at Ecry. During the next three months many other knights joined them.

The leaders of the crusade decided to take the sea route to the east, and sent six delegates to negotiate transport with Venice, a major maritime power in the Mediterranean. In February 1201 they concluded a treaty with the doge, Henry Dandolo, and his council. A price for the transport and supply of the army was fixed, and a Venetian offer to provide an extra 50 armed galleys in return for half the profits of the crusade was accepted. The treaty, ratified by the pope, contained a secret clause, which agreed that Egypt would be the initial destination.

Theobald died in 1201 and a new leader for the crusade was found: the valorous Boniface, marquis of Montferrat, a close friend and leading vassal of Philip of Swabia, king of Germany, who had been elected as Holy Roman Emperor in 1198 in succession to his late brother Henry VI, but whose claims were opposed by Innocent. Boniface was therefore unlikely to pay much heed to papal instructions. Philip of Swabia was married to a Byzantine princess, Irene Angelus, whose father, the Emperor Isaac II Angelus, had been blinded, deposed and imprisoned by his brother Alexius III in 1195. Alexius, Isaac's son and Irene's brother, had also been imprisoned, but had escaped from Constantinople, and at Christmas 1201 arrived at a great court at Hagenau atttended by both Philip and Boniface.

It is unlikely that at this stage any serious plans were made to restore him and his father to power in Constantinople, but viewed in retrospect his presence was ominous. So too was the violent hostility felt towards the Byzantines by Dandolo, who in 1182 had been semiblinded in an anti-Latin pogrom in Constantinople.

When the crusaders began to gather at Venice in the summer of 1202, it was clear that their numbers fell vastly short of the delegates' estimates, and the leaders of the crusade faced a debt of 34,000 silver marks for ships they did not need – money they had no way of finding. The doge therefore proposed that the crusaders should assist Venice in its maritime wars by helping it to capture the port of Zara from Emeric, king of Hungary – even though the Hungarian king had taken crusading vows – and repay their debt from the booty. Although many crusaders defected, and although Innocent expressly forbade the attack on Zara, the

enterprise was carried through in November 1202. Agreement was then reached with the young Alexius to restore him and his father Isaac to the Byzantine throne in return for further financial help that would enable the crusade to go to the east. Innocent excommunicated the Venetians, and forbade any attack on the eastern empire; but the letters containing his prohibitions failed to arrive in time; had they done so, they would almost certainly have gone unheeded.

In July 1203 the crusaders besieged and took Constantinople, released Isaac and crowned Alexius, his son, as Emperor Alexius IV. The new ruler was slow to fulfil his promises to his Frankish allies, who became increasingly angry. Then in February 1204 Alexius IV and Isaac II were murdered by a rival, Murzuphlus, who seized power and was crowned Emperor Alexius V. Murzuphlus ordered the Franks to leave Constantinople but the crusaders, short of food and money, could afford neither to go on to the east nor to return home, and decided to attack Constantinople once more, to share out the booty, and to found a Latin empire.

In April 1204 the crusaders captured and looted Constantinople; and in May, Baldwin, count of Flanders, was elected and crowned Byzantine emperor, holding a quarter of the captured lands: Thrace and northwestern Asia Minor, Lesbos, Chios and Samos. Boniface of Montferrat founded a new kingdom of Thessalonica, including Macedonia and Thessaly, and the Venetians took large tracts of the Adriatic coast, the Ionian islands and Crete. (The Byzantine Greeks established three small states in exile, centred on Epirus, Trehizond and Nicaea.) The Frankish conquerors settled down to subjugate their new lands, and no thought was given to continuing with the crusade. At first delighted by news of the capture of Constantinople, Innocent was later horrified when news of the atrocities committed by the Frankish forces reached him.

Despite the débâcle of the Fourth Crusade, Innocent showed a continuing commitment to the crusading ideal. His pontificate marked important developments in the theory and practice of crusading which, in the long term changed the whole organization and scope of the movement.

An early example is the crusade he proclaimed against Markward of Anweiler, a renegade German follower of the late Holy Roman Emperor Henry VI. Markward was trying to carve out a principality for himself in southern Italy and Sicily, against the interests of Innocent himself and those of the pope's ward, the young

Frederick II, Henry VI's son and heir. Since the 11th century the papacy had used traditional methods, such as excommunication, against its secular opponents; but now, in 1199, Innocent III wrote of Markward as 'another Saladin', who was allied to the Muslims living in Sicily and was working to overthrow the recently proclaimed Fourth Crusade. Anyone who resisted him would receive the same indulgences as those who went to the east. This was a clear development of the idea of the political crusade.

Also in 1199 Innocent stated his responsibility, as vicar of Christ and head of the Church, to protect it from its enemies within. The Albigensians, a sect of Cathar heretics, had grown in strength in the French Languedoc over the previous half-century and had failed to respond to concerted preaching campaigns. From the early 11th century, secular powers had increasingly acted for the Church to crush heretics by force. After the murder of the papal legate in the Languedoc, Peter of Castelnau, in 1208, Innocent called for war against the Albigensians, and, by promising an indulgence to those who fought, transformed a campaign into a crusade.

The indulgence could be gained by just 40 days of military service, a provision which weakened the impetus of the crusading army; and despite twenty years of violent and brutal warfare, from 1209 to 1229, little impact was made on the heretics. It took the repressive powers of the Inquisition, established in 1233, almost a century to wipe out Catharism in the region.

Innocent's attempts to bring about the conversion of pagans in the Baltic region also widened the scope of crusading. In 1204, in a letter to the archbishop of Bremen, Innocent offered the crusading indulgence to anyone who fought the heathen along the Baltic as a priest or a member of the military Orders. The offer had no time limits, and established the Baltic Crusade on a permanent footing.

From 1210, Innocent allowed Alfonso VIII of Castile, who was engaged in a major struggle with the Almohad caliphs, certain crusading privileges, and in 1212 proclaimed a new crusade in the region. With the support of knights and foot-soldiers from Spain and the Languedoc, Alfonso and his allies Sancho VII of Navarre and Peter II of Aragon won a major victory over the Almohads at Las Navas de Tolosa. In 1213 Innocent set aside the crusading privileges in the Iberian peninsula, but this check on Almohad power eventually proved to be a turning-point in the Spanish *Reconquista*.

In the same year the ferment of popular enthusiasm for crusading produced a spontaneous movement of children in France and Germany, known as the Children's Crusade. Although it collapsed, it was symptomatic of a continuing popular interest in crusading, which Innocent had every intention of canalizing.

In 1213 he began planning what was to be the Fifth Crusade. The financial provisions he incorporated were of considerable importance: he enacted that anyone was to be allowed to take the cross, but those unable to fight were permitted to redeem their vows by making money payments. In 1216, the Fourth Lateran Council approved a papal decree allowing a three-year tax of a 20th of all church income, and papal commissioners were appointed to organize its collection. Crusading finances were established on a firm footing.

Innocent's contribution in developing and extending the whole framework of crusading ranks with that of Urban II (1088–99) in its significance. But his ambitions outstripped his authority, and the achievements of his crusades were often less than he had hoped. His principal weakness was his lack of direct control over the secular magnates who fought God's wars for him, and that, seen most starkly in the Fourth Crusade, is why many of his crusading plans foundered.

Papal letters, the official records of Innocent's crusades, are supplemented by the evidence of participants or close observers. The chronicles of Geoffrey of Villehardouin and Robert of Clari give differing accounts of the Fourth Crusade: Villehardouin's is the work of one of the leaders while Robert of Clari's viewpoint is that of the 'humble knight'.

Other observers range from the author of the *Deeds of Innocent III*, who is determined to represent Innocent in the most favourable light, to the distinctively Byzantine view of the imperial civil servant Nicetas Choniates. The late medieval Russian Chronicle of Novgorod puts the events of 1204 in the wider context of the Russian world.

The major sources for the Albigensian Crusade are all by men with detailed knowledge of events: Peter des Vaux's uncle became bishop of Carcassonne in 1212; William of Tudela's *Chanson de la Croisade contre les Albigeois* has the vivid observation of an eyewitness. Two English writers are represented here: the St Albans historian Matthew Paris, always hostile to the papacy and the French; and John of Garland, who became professor of grammar at Toulouse in the 1240s.

Jerusalem has been unhappily wasted and its Christian population woefully slaughtered. There has followed the deplorable invasion of that land where the feet of Christ stood and in whose midst God our king, in earlier times, saw fit to accomplish our salvation. There has befallen the loss – most humiliating to us – of the life-giving cross on which the salvation of the world depends and through which the fear of death is removed. Wherefore the Apostolic See is stricken with anguish and weeping over so great a disaster. Its throat has grown hoarse with endless cries and its eyes have almost exhausted their tears of bitter lamentation.

Therefore, my sons, take up as your shield the spirit of fortitude, relying not on bodily or on numerical strength but on the power of God; and, according to your means, stand by

him through whom you have your being, your life and your possessions.

Let all, collectively and individually, prepare themselves by next March, 1199, to defend the land where our Lord was born. According to their means, let cities, counts and barons arrange in their budgets for the sustenance of a predetermined number of fighting men, to serve there for at least two years. Our everyday concern with the welfare of our churches presses on us all the time, but our desire to relieve the eastern land of all its sufferings is first and foremost in our minds.

For if rescue is too late in coming, the locust's caterpillar will devour what remains and new disasters will be worse than earlier ones.

But we do not wish to lay unbearably heavy burdens on

Tourneying knights at the time of the Fourth Crusade. Such tournaments were important social events for the feudal aristocracy, and fit occasions for taking the cross.

sons in Christ, the illustrious kings of France and England, to restore peace or at least to arrange a five-year truce, as well as to urge their peoples to follow the cross. Meanwhile, we order Soffredo of Pisa to obtain the assistance of the Venetians for the Holy Land.

Rieti, 15 August 1198.

In the letter above, Pope Innocent III calls upon the rulers of France and England (and also the contenders for the Holy Roman Empire, Otto of Brunswick and Philip of Swabia), to abandon their quarrels and, with the rest of Christendom, go to the aid of the Holy Land.

French nobles take the cross

The papal legate Peter of Capuano persuaded the English and French kings to arrange a truce and, late in 1199, at a tournament at Ecry, the French nobility took matters into their own hands. Among those who took the cross at the tournament was Geoffrey of Villehardouin, who describes here the early stages of the Fourth Crusade.

On 28 November 1199, a tournament was held at the castle of Ecry in Champagne. There by the grace of God, Count Theobald of Champagne and Count Louis of Blois both took the cross. Theobald was then only twenty-two years old and Louis twenty-seven.

Early in 1200 the barons of France held a council at Soissons, to decide when to leave for the crusade, and which route to take. They were unable to do so on that occasion, feeling that as yet too few had taken the cross. However, two months later, they reconvened at Compiègne. All the counts and barons who had taken the cross were gathered there. After much discussion, it was finally decided to send out the most trustworthy envoys that could be found [to make travel arrangements for the crusaders], with full power to negotiate on behalf of their lords.

Count Theobald of Champagne, Count Baldwin of Flanders and Hainault, and Count Louis of Blois each sent two envoys. To these six they entrusted the entire conduct of the matter,

others while we appear unwilling to stir a finger, indulging in talk but doing nothing, or very little. Let us who, though unworthy, serve as his deputy on earth, present a good example to others by coming to the help of the Holy Land, as we have resolved to do, by offering persons as well as property.

We have chosen as legates our sons, Soffredo of Pisa and Peter of Capuano, both cardinals, devout men, renowned in learning and honour, strong in word and deed. With our own hand, we place upon them the sign of the cross, so that they may lead humbly and religiously the army of the Lord. Let them not be supplied with mendicant charity but maintained at the expense of ourselves and our brothers. Moreover, through them we are arranging to supply other adequate assistance to that same land. In the mean time we command Peter of Capuano to come into the presence of our beloved confirming this by properly sealed charters, in which they committed themselves to take full responsibility for any treaty entered into on their behalf, at whatever port or city the envoys went to.

Treaty with Venice

The six envoys, having agreed that the port of Venice could best provide them with the large number of ships necessary, left France and rode in such rapid stages that they arrived at Venice in the third week of February 1201.

The doge of Venice, Henry Dandolo, a wise and noble man, received them with great honour, and both he and his people greeted them warmly. When the envoys delivered their letters of introduction, the Venetians were most curious to know what manner of business had brought them to Venice, since all the letters said was that the envoys should be trusted in all respects and that any decision taken by the envoys in their name would be honoured.

The envoys said: 'Your grace, if it would please you to call a meeting of your council tomorrow, we will then inform you of our lords' requirements.' The doge asked them to wait four days, by which time his council would be ready to assemble and they could make their wishes known.

So they waited for the day he had appointed and entered the palace, which was extremely luxurious and beautiful. The doge and his council were assembled in one of the halls, where the envoys delivered the message from their lords: 'Your grace, we have been sent to you by the highest-ranking barons of France who have taken the cross. They wish to avenge the honour of Jesus Christ and, by the grace of God, reconquer Jerusalem. Knowing that there is none so powerful as you and your people, they beg you in the name of God to take pity on the Holy Land and the shame inflicted on Jesus Christ, and consider how you might provide them with a fleet.'

'How is this to be achieved?' asked the doge. The envoys replied: 'In any way you see fit to recommend or advise, provided our lords can fulfil your conditions.' The doge said: 'Truly, this is a momentous request they are making of us, their aims are high. We will answer you a week from today. Do not wonder at the delay, a request of such magnitude requires careful consideration.'

On the day agreed, the envoys once again returned to the palace. I cannot report everything that was said, but the doge closed the meeting with these words: 'My lords, this is what we have decided, subject to the approval of the full council and the people; it is for you to decide whether you are able to fulfil our conditions. We shall build transports to

---

In praise of Boniface of Montferrat

My lord marquis. Every young nobleman's highest concern is whether to choose the path of glory or let it be – just as you chose, my lord. From the beginning you sought glory, so as to make you, as the lord, and me, a young knight, honoured everywhere.

If I attempted to sing of all the honourable deeds I have seen you perform, my lord, it might well tire both of us – me in the telling and you in the listening. But I have seen you give in marriage to counts, marquises and powerful barons, a hundred maidens who were vulnerable, and without expectations. Yet youth did not lead you astray with any of them.

I have seen you enfief a hundred knights; destroy and ruin a hundred others; raise up good men and bring treacherous and wicked ones low. No flatterer ever found favour with you! I have seen you protect so many widows and orphans, and rescue so many unfortunates, that surely they should lead you to heaven, if a man may enter there through the quality of

his mercy. For any man worthy of your compassion need only ask you in order to receive help. It is always your wish to rule with mercy. In your court all noble customs rule: generosity and courtly love, fine clothes, elegant armour, games, the music of trumpets and viols, and song. You keep open house at mealtimes.

For my own part, I may boast that I have always known how to behave in a chivalrous manner; to give and serve, and to be patient and discreet. I have never done any man wrong. Nor can anyone reproach me that I left your side in battle. Nor that I feared death, if by risking it I could increase your glory. Nor that I ever tried to dissuade you from a chivalrous act.

Since I know you so well, my lord, you must reward me as much as three other men. This is only just, my lord marquis, for in me you may find witness, knight and poet.

From Raimbaut de Vaqueiras, *Epic Letter*

carry four thousand five hundred horses and nine thousand squires, provide ships for four thousand five hundred knights and twenty thousand foot-soldiers, and supply provisions for men and horses for nine months. This, at least, we are willing to provide. It will cost you four marks per horse, and two marks per man. We will hold to these agreements for one year, from the day we set sail from Venice in the service of God and Christendom, wherever that may lead us. The total cost so far is ninety-four thousand marks.

'But we shall go further: for the love of God, we shall also provide fifty armed galleys, on condition that so long as our joint venture lasts, we are entitled to half of all the conquests made by sea or on land. You must decide whether these terms are feasible and acceptable to you.'

The Deeds of Innocent III, written by an anonymous Roman cleric between 1203 and 1208, after the diversion of the crusade, first to Zara in Yugoslavia and then to Constantinople, reveals the existence of a secret clause in the treaty with the Venetians. This proposed an attack on the centre of Ayubid power in Egypt, which was strategically sensible, but may have put off those crusaders who wanted to go to the Holy Land.

The crusader counts of France sent their envoys to Venice to arrange for the provision by hire of an adequate number of suitable ships. They also negotiated a treaty in which it was laid down that both parties would carry out joint operations, some going to Syria and the rest to Egypt, to seize Alexandria and neighbouring areas.

The treaty was duly ratified by both parties. Both sides then sent a joint embassy to the Apostolic See with a request that the pope should give his apostolic sanction to this agreement that had been entered into for the liberation of the Holy Land. The pope had a foreboding of what these activities portended.

Therefore he returned a careful reply, stating that the agreement was in order as long as the signatories avoided harming other Christians, unless the latter wrongfully interfered with their progress, or if there was some other just cause for such an action, or if they were obliged to resort to such measures through necessity. Under those circumstances they would have to consult the legate of the Holy See. The Venetians refused to accept the papal endorsement under these conditions. As it happens, the accuracy of the pope's conjecture about their intentions was confirmed by later developments.

Boniface, leader of the crusade

Villehardouin returned to Champagne about the beginning of June to find the count of Champagne terminally ill. He describes attempts to find a new leader for the crusade and the final selection of Boniface, marquis of Montferrat.

One of the envoys, Geoffrey of Villehardouin, returned to Troyes in Champagne. There, he found his lord, Count Theobald, laid up with an illness but very glad to see him nevertheless. When Count Theobald learned the results of their negotiations, he was so delighted that he decided to go for a ride immediately. It was a long time since he had ridden. Alas that he should have taken that decision then, for it was the last time he ever mounted a horse.

He became so ill that he made his last will and testament, dividing all the money he was to have taken on the crusade between his men and his companions. No other man at that time had so many devoted followers. He charged each man on receipt of his portion, to swear by the holy scriptures to join the army leaving from Venice, as he himself had sworn to do. Many did not keep faith and were severely blamed later. The count also requested that a part of the money be set aside for the army to use as they saw fit.

Count Theobald died, and made the finest ending of any man in the world. He left behind his wife, Countess Blanche, who was both beautiful and good, and daughter to the king of Navarre; she had a young daughter by him, and was pregnant with their son at the time.

The death of Count Theobald was a great loss to the crusaders and all those who were to set forth in God's service. At the end of June 1201, they met once more in council at Soissons to decide what to do. This was attended by Baldwin, count of Flanders, Louis, count of Blois, Hugh, count of Saint-Pol and many other honourable knights.

[After much discussion about the leader for the crusade] Geoffrey of Villehardouin made a proposal: 'My lords, if you will allow me, I have a suggestion to make. Marquis Boniface of Montferrat is an honourable knight, and one of the most respected men of our time. If you ask him to join us here and take the cross in place of Theobald, count of Champagne, and you put him in command of the army, I am sure he will accept immediately.'

In June 1201 the marquis of Montferrat arrived to attend the council which had once again met in Soissons. A great many counts, barons and other crusaders were gathered there. When they heard that he was coming, they went to meet him and paid him great honour. The next morning the

Venice and the Venetians

To the Byzantines, the leader of the Fourth Crusade was the doge of Venice, Henry Dandolo. Although he was over 80 in 1201 and blind, Dandolo was still vigorous and harboured a strong hatred of the Greeks, reflecting the extent to which the once cordial relationship between Byzantium and Venice had deteriorated.

As early as the eighth century, when Byzantium had recognized the first *dux* or *doge* as independent ruler of Venice, the city had looked towards the empire as an ally and protector, and by the end of the tenth there were many Venetian merchants in Constantinople. In 992 they were granted privileges by Emperor Basil II, allowing them reduced customs dues and preferential treatment from Byzantine officials. In return the Venetians assisted the emperor whenever he fought in Italy, particularly by providing ships for the imperial fleet. This association of trading and military interests was extremely successful in the 11th century when, as a reward for naval assistance against the Norman invasions of southern Italy by Robert Guiscard and Bohemund, the Venetians were granted warehouses and wharves by Alexius Comnenus, in about 1082, and permitted to trade freely throughout most of the empire. Artistic links between the two cities were at their closest at this time.

A century later, however, Venice had become Byzantium's mortal enemy. During the 12th century the Byzantines gave trading privileges to other Italian cities such as Genoa and Pisa; and the Venetians, for their part, began to form alliances with the crusader states which occupied lands, such as the region of Antioch, which the Byzantines still considered theirs. Serious trouble broke out in 1171 when Manuel Comnenus ordered the arrest of all the Venetians in the empire and the confiscation of their property. When, in 1182, many western merchants were massacred or fled from Constantinople, Henry Dandolo swore to revenge the attack.

Venice wished to expand its trading activities in the empire with complete legal and fiscal freedom to achieve maximum profit. Byzantium could not stand by and watch the Venetians usurp imperial rights and antagonize imperial subjects. When Byzantium tried to reimpose its authority, Venice countered by seizing it after diverting the Fourth Crusade to Constantinople.

council assembled in a meadow at the abbey of Notre-Dame de Soissons. They urged him, in the name of God, to take the cross and accept command of the army in place of Count Theobald of Champagne, so that he could receive the money and lead his men. They fell at his feet in tears and he in turn knelt at theirs and agreed heartily.

At once Nivelon, bishop of Soissons, together with two Cistercian monks the marquis had brought with him from his own domain, accompanied him to the church of Notre-Dame and attached the cross to his shoulder. The council at Soissons ended and the marquis returned home to make preparations, advising the others to do the same, until they should all meet again in Venice.

News now reached the barons that many of their fellows were travelling by various routes to ports other than Venice [from which they intended to sail direct to the Holy Land]. This seriously worried them, as it meant that they could not pay the money due to the Venetians, nor fulfil their promises to them. They therefore decided to send reliable envoys to meet Louis, count of Blois, and other crusaders who had not yet arrived at Venice, to persuade them that Venice was the best point of departure for the crusade. Count Hugh of Saint-Pol and Geoffrey of Villehardouin were chosen for this mission. They rode to Pavia, in Lombardy, where they met Count Louis with many valiant knights and other good people. So persuasive were they, that many who might otherwise have left from other ports, agreed to go from Venice.

Unfortunately, many other brave knights and squires decided to travel by land to Apulia. This was a great loss for the crusading army. What a tragedy that so many chose not to leave from Venice! How Christendom would have gained and the land of the Turks lost, had it been otherwise.

Crusaders fail to honour treaty

The Venetians had been generous, and more than fulfilled their obligations. They were ready to set sail, and demanded that the counts and the barons honour their promises and make the agreed payment.

The barons held a meeting to assess the situation: 'My lords, the Venetians have more than honoured their obligations, but since so many have decided to leave from other ports, there are now too few of us paying our passage to cover the sum we agreed to pay. In the name of God, let every man give as much as he can, so that we can discharge our debt. It would be better to give everything we have left now, than to lose what we have already paid and fail to honour our own obligations. Furthermore, if this crusade does not take place, the Holy Land is lost.'

Dandolo: Ioanne   Dandolo: Franc̄   Dandolo: Andrea   Dandolo

Andoli, quisti venrro parte d'Altin, e' parti' da Torcello

The Dandolo line, with their arms. Henry Dandolo, doge of Venice at the time of the Fourth Crusade, is on the left.

This proposal provoked serious disagreement. The majority of the barons and the men objected: 'But we have all paid our passage. If they want to take us, we will go willingly, if not, then we shall find an alternative.' Clearly they were in favour of disbanding the army. Others – a minority – refused to give up: 'We would rather go penniless than see the army disbanded and ruined: God will repay us when he pleases.'

Immediately after this meeting, Count Baldwin of Flanders gave all he owned and had borrowed; so did Louis, count of Blois, Boniface, marquis of Montferrat, Hugh, count of Saint-Pol and all those who belonged to their parties. What beautiful gold and silver plate was carried into the doge's palace! But when they had all given everything they possessed, they were still thirty-four thousand marks short of the sum agreed upon. And those who had been unwilling to give any more than their passage, remained obdurate and rejoiced, thinking that now, surely, the army would be ruined and have to disband. But God, who gives back hope to the despairing, did not suffer this to happen.

The doge offers a compromise

The doge spoke to the Venetians: 'My lords, these people are unable to repay us the sum agreed upon; by right what they have already paid belongs to us; however, we should be severely criticized if we were to exercise that right. So let us offer them a compromise: the king of Hungary captured Zara from us. This city is one of the strongest cities in the world and, however powerful we are, we shall never recapture it without help. If the crusaders are willing to help us recapture it, we will defer payment of the remaining thirty-four thousand marks they owe us until such time as, God willing, we reconquer it together.' This compromise was bitterly contested by those who wished the army to be disbanded, but in the end, it was agreed upon.

The following Sunday, a joyful gathering of Venetians, most of the barons and the crusaders, assembled in the church of St Mark. Before High Mass began, Henry Dandolo, doge of Venice, climbed up to the lectern and spoke to his people: 'My lords, you are sharing the greatest enterprise ever undertaken, with the most valiant people in the world. I am old and weak, I need rest, my health is failing. Even so, I believe no one can lead and advise you as I could, who am your lord. If you would allow me to take the cross, and be your guardian and protector, and let my sons safeguard the state of Venice, I shall go and live or die with you and the crusaders.'

When his people heard this, they cried out with a single voice, 'In the name of God, take the cross and come with us!' A great wave of emotion swept over everyone. Many people wept. This gallant man had good reason to remain at home, he was old, and though his eyes shone so beautifully he was quite blind, having lost his eyesight after a head injury. He had a great heart. How unlike he was to those who had sought to avoid danger by leaving from other ports.

The doge came down from the lectern and knelt in front of the altar, weeping copiously; they sewed the cross on to his tall cotton hat because he wished everyone to see it. That day many of the Venetians took the cross, although up to then few had chosen to do so. The crusaders were also filled with great joy and emotion when he took the cross, because of his wisdom and courage.

Soon after, the warships, galleys and transports were delivered to the barons, ready at last to set sail. But by then so much time had passed that September was approaching.

The time had now come for the barons to assign the warships and transports to their various commanders. Heavens! What fine, strong war-horses were then put below deck! As soon as all the ships had been fully loaded with arms and provisions, and the knights and sergeants had come aboard, the shields were hung round the bulwarks and round the castles fore and aft, while banners, many and beautiful, were quickly hoisted aloft.

The warships, I can assure you, carried more than three hundred petraries and mangonels, as well as a plentiful supply of all such mechanical devices as are of use in taking a city. No finer fleet of ships ever set sail from any port. They departed from Venice on 8 November 1202.

Zara surrenders to the crusaders

Our army arrived before Zara on 10 November and saw the city enclosed by high walls and lofty towers. You would have sought in vain for a more beautiful place, or one more strongly defended, or more prosperous. As soon as the crusaders caught sight of it they were filled with amazement, and said to each other: 'How could such a city be taken by force, except by the help of God himself?'

On 12 November, certain citizens of Zara came out of the town and went to speak with the doge of Venice in his pavilion. They told him they were ready to place the city and all their possessions at his discretion, provided their lives were spared. The doge replied that he could not agree to such terms, nor indeed to any others, without first consulting the barons, with whom he would talk the matter over at once.

The doge of Venice then addressed the counts and barons. 'My lords, the people of Zara wish to surrender, at my discretion, on condition that their lives are spared, but I would not make any agreement without consulting you.' To which

they answered: 'We not only advise you to agree, we beg you to do so.' Then they proceeded to the doge's pavilion to ratify a treaty. On arrival they learned that the delegation from Zara had already left, on the false advice of those who wished the army disbanded. [An agreement could therefore not be concluded.]

Guy, Cistercian abbot of Vaux-de-Cernay, then stood up and said: 'My lords, in the name of the pope I forbid you to attack this city, because it is a Christian city and you are crusaders.' On hearing this, the doge, angry and frustrated, replied: 'My lords, this city agreed that I should negotiate at my discretion. Your people have now prevented me from doing so. Furthermore, you had promised to help me recapture Zara, and I order you to do so.'

The counts, barons and their supporters conferred together: 'Those who hindered the signing of this agreement have been extremely presumptuous: not a day has passed without some attempt on their part to have the army disbanded. We shall be disgraced if we do not help recapture this city.' After which, they went to the doge and said, 'Your grace, we shall help you recapture this city, in spite of those who oppose it.'

So the decision was taken. The next morning, they camped in front of the city gates, setting up their petraries, mangonels and other engines of war, of which they had plenty. On the seaward side they hoisted scaling ladders from the warships. The petraries began stoning the walls and towers. The battle lasted five days, when the sappers were ordered to dismantle the walls. The inhabitants finally gave way, and decided to accept the terms they had previously refused.

The city of Zara was surrendered to the mercy of the doge; all lives were spared. Afterwards, the doge addressed the counts and barons. 'My lords, we have recaptured Zara by the grace of God and your assistance. Winter is coming, we cannot leave here before Easter, as we could not so easily provision the army elsewhere. This city is very rich and well supplied: we shall divide it equally between us.' This was carried out as agreed. The Venetians occupied the harbour side of the city, where their ships lay anchored, and the French, the other side. The best houses were suitably allocated; the army broke camp and moved to lodgings within the city walls.

Shortly after this a most unfortunate conflict exploded between French and Venetian soldiers. Scuffles broke out and soon spread, everyone rushed for their arms, battles raged in every street with swords, lances, crossbows and spears. There were many wounded and killed. After a while the Venetians, unable to sustain the fighting, began to lose heavily. Armed men of goodwill attempted to restore the peace, but as soon as they stopped the fighting in one quarter,

Betrayal of Isaac II Angelus

Now listen to one of the strangest tales and most wonderful adventures you have ever heard. The emperor of Constantinople, whose name was Isaac II Angelus, had been taken prisoner by his brother Alexius in 1195. Alexius gouged his eyes out and kept him imprisoned for several years, together with his young son, also named Alexius. After this act of treachery he proclaimed himself Emperor Alexius III. The young prince, later Alexius IV, escaped from prison [in 1201] and boarded a ship bound for the port of Ancona in Italy. From there he set off to visit Philip of Swabia, king of Germany, who was married to his sister, Irene. On his way, he stayed in the town of Verona in Lombardy and met many crusaders going to join the army.

The companions who had helped him escape had given him this advice: 'Nearby, in Venice, there is an army of the best people in the world and the bravest knights, preparing to sail for the Holy Land. Tell them how you and your father came to be so unjustly dispossessed. They are bound to take pity on your plight. Beg them to help you, and follow their advice if they agree to do so.' Prince Alexius saw the wisdom of this and acted accordingly. He sent messengers to the marquis, Boniface of Montferrat, and to the barons. They were all very shocked on hearing this tale and answered: 'Since Prince Alexius is on his way to see King Philip, we will send envoys with him. If he agrees to help us reconquer the Holy Land, we in our turn will help his father Isaac II Angelus, and him, to recover the kingdom they lost so unjustly.'

From Geoffrey of Villehardouin, La Conquête de Constantinople

it broke out in another. The battles continued most of the night until finally, after much effort and great difficulties, the leaders succeeded in stopping them.

This was the greatest disaster that could befall an army, and the crusade was very nearly destroyed. But God did not suffer this to happen, and eventually peace was restored.

Agreement to attack Constantinople

While the army stayed at Zara an agreement was made with Alexius, the son of the blinded and deposed Byzantine emperor, Isaac II Angelus: his father was to be restored to the Byzantine throne in return for considerable financial help for the crusade to Egypt. This provoked further division in the army about whether to help Alexius and still more men left the army and went their own way.

In late October 1202, Boniface, marquis of Montferrat [who had not yet joined the army] arrived at last at Zara with many other important men. Two weeks later the envoys of King Philip and of Prince Alexius also arrived from Germany. The barons and the doge of Venice met in conference in a palace where the doge was staying and the envoys delivered their message. 'My lords,' they said, 'these are Philip's words: "I am going to send you my wife's brother Alexius. I place his life in God's hand – may He save it! – and in yours. It is for God, for right and for justice that you fight; therefore you must if you can restore to their inheritance those who have been wrongly dispossessed. And he will give you the best agreement any nation has ever had, and the most generous help in conquering the lands beyond the sea.

' "First of all, if God lets you restore him to his inheritance, he will bring the whole Byzantine Empire back under the jurisdiction of Rome, which it left long ago. Next, he knows that you have spent your own money and that you are poor; he will therefore give you two hundred thousand marks of silver, and food for all members of the army, both great and small. Also he will himself accompany you to the land of Egypt with ten thousand men, or if you prefer will send them, at his own cost; he will do you this service for one year. And all the days of his life he will maintain five hundred knights in the land beyond the sea and will support them from his own resources." My lords,' said the envoys, 'we have full authority to confirm this agreement, if you are ready to do so.'

A meeting was called for next day to discuss it. Many points of view were put forward. There were speeches from Guy, Cistercian abbot of Vaux-de-Cernay, and from the party who wanted to split up the army; they said that they would never agree to these proposals because it was making war on Christians, and they had not left home to do that.

But the other party replied, 'Fair sirs, in Syria you can do nothing, as you can see very well from those who have left us and gone to other ports.'

Innocent III

Lothar dei Conti di Segni, later Pope Innocent III (1198–1216), was born in about 1160 into an influential Roman clan. Educated first in Rome, he became a canon of St Peter's before studying at the University of Paris, under the great master, Peter of Corbeil. Before returning to Rome, he went briefly to Bologna, which was renowned as a centre of canon law, and studied with Huguccio of Pisa. In 1190, at the early age of 29, he was created cardinal.

Elected pope at the age of 37, Innocent's fervent ambition was to recover the Holy Land for Christ. He tried to prevent war in Europe, not only because it was a human tragedy but also because it diverted rulers from their crusading obligations; but he never claimed direct secular authority, believing, rather, that it was essential to bring rulers to agree for spiritual reasons, and lest they be regarded as 'worse than the Saracens'. Through reforming the Church, Innocent hoped to make it worthy to convert pagan and infidel alike before the advent of the end of the world, which his understanding of the apocalyptic vision suggested was imminent. The Greek Church, separated from Rome since 1054, could help in this, and within eight months of becoming pope, in August 1198, Innocent had started negotiations for its return to Rome. His hopes for that were destroyed by the disastrous events of the Fourth Crusade. Almost equally disastrous in the long term was his promulgation, in 1208, of the Albigensian Crusade against Cathar heretics in the south of France.

The process of Christianization was slow and uncertain in the Baltic and in 1199 Innocent proclaimed a crusade in defence of the Church of Livonia. To avoid confusion among new converts, Innocent proposed in 1201 that all missionaries, whether white Cistercian monks or black Augustinian canons, should wear the same habit and follow the same rule, united into one uniform religious community as the outward and visible sign of their apostolic life-style. The institution in 1202 of the Sword Brothers, crusaders in Livonia, and the Knights of Dobryzn in Prussia, was parallel to this mission. In 1210 Innocent supported yet another military Order, the Teutonic Knights, extending the concept of the crusading vow to cover military action in defence of missions. Innocent died in July 1216, preaching the Fifth Crusade in Perugia.

Now Boniface of Montferrat intervened, along with Baldwin of Flanders, Louis of Blois, Hugh of Saint-Pol and their adherents, and declared that they intended to make this agreement because they would be disgraced if they rejected it. And so they went to the doge's lodging; the envoys were sent for and the agreement was confirmed, as you heard above, upon oath and in letters with seals affixed. There were only twelve men willing to make these oaths on behalf of the French; no more could be found to do it.

The French army spent the whole of that winter at Zara, in danger from the king of Hungary. Men's hearts were not at ease, for one party was working to break the army up and the other to keep it together. Many of the lesser men stole away aboard merchant ships. Some five hundred took refuge in one such vessel, and they were every one of them drowned. Another group fled overland, meaning to go through Slovenia, but the local inhabitants attacked and killed many of them; those that were left fled back again to the army. Very many slipped away like this, and the army grew less daily.

Indeed, you can see that if God had not loved this army it could never have held together, when there were so many people wishing it ill.

The barons now held discussions and announced that they were going to send word to the pope at Rome, Innocent III, because they knew that he was displeased with them for having taken Zara. Chosen envoys delivered the message just as the barons had given it to them, saying to the pope: 'The nobles ask you to forgive them for taking Zara for they did this because they had no other way of keeping the army together; they ask you as their good father to send them your orders, which they are ready to obey.'

Pope threatens excommunication

In response to the embassy, Pope Innocent III wrote to the leaders of the expedition. He firmly forbade any attack on the eastern empire – but his letter arrived too late to stop the expedition continuing towards Constantinople.

We have wept for all Christian people because they are being brought down where it was thought that they were being uplifted. Many who had come before you to save the Holy Land heard that you had not gone there after them, and so returned to their own countries, losing heart because of your recent expedition to Zara. Still, we rejoice because, on receiving our letters, you followed the apostolic command. By conforming to your oath you have perceived the blessing of absolution, in respect of the sentence of excommunication you incurred over the matter of Zara. I hope that your penitence is genuine so that in showing a manifest regret over past sins you will take care not to do anything similar hereafter.

Therefore none of you should rashly flatter yourself that it is acceptable for you to seize or plunder Byzantine lands on the grounds that it has a lesser allegiance to the Apostolic See, or that Emperor Alexius of Constantinople has deposed his brother Isaac, even blinding him, and has usurped the throne. It is not for you to sit in judgement on their offences; nor have you put on the sign of the cross for the purpose of punishing this offence, but in order to avenge the insults to the crucifix, in obedience to which you specifically bound yourselves.

Instead, give up these pointless diversions and feigned commitments: cross over to save the Holy Land; punish the wrongs committed against the cross; you will take from an enemy spoils which, if you dally in Byzantine territory, you would perhaps have to extort from brothers. Otherwise, since it is neither possible nor incumbent upon us to do it, we cannot promise you the remission of sins.

Pope Innocent III. He was one of the great medieval popes, but was unable to alter the course of the Fourth Crusade after the Venetians diverted it to Zara and Constantinople.

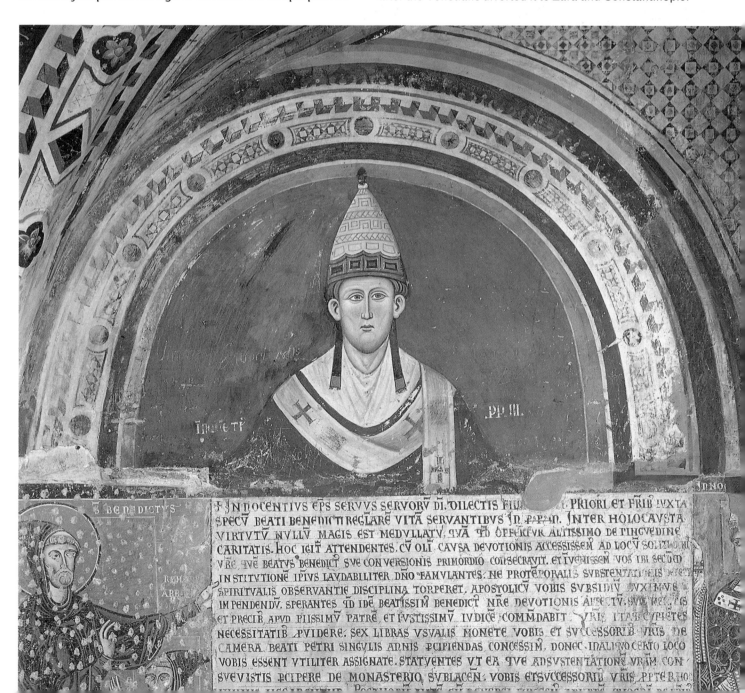

Use and abuse of excommunication

Excommunication was the Church's equivalent of outlawry. The offender was placed outside the Christian community and was denied the sacraments and Christian burial; he was shunned by fellow Christians, his oaths were worthless, his contracts were of dubious validity and he was prevented from pleading in ecclesiastical courts. However, the family and servants of, for example, an excommunicated head of a household were allowed to have continued contact with him to bring him back to a proper sense of duty. If the excommunicate confessed his sins and underwent sincere penance, his absolution was obligatory and the ban was lifted, either by the pope or by the bishop who had first imposed the sentence.

Imposed upon a king, excommunication became a political as well as a spiritual weapon. To place a ruler outside the Christian community could undermine his relations with his subjects, encouraging them to withdraw their fealty and acting as a pretext for rebellion. Innocent III excommunicated Philip II of France, the candidates for the Holy Roman Empire, and John of England.

In the case of Zara, Innocent specifically threatened an automatic sentence of excommunication against the crusading army should they attack the city. His letter, intended to be read out to the host gathered in Venice, was not made known to them until they stood before the walls of Zara – too late to have any effect. The crusaders were contrite after the attack and begged absolution from the pope. Innocent allowed it to all who promised obedience to the papacy and begged forgiveness from the king of Hungary.

The Venetians, agents for the crusading army, were the exception. Unwilling to give up Zara, to beg papal forgiveness, or to promise future obedience, they remained excommunicate. Their obstinacy raised a problem which Innocent had to resolve or face the certain disintegration of the crusade: could a Christian army continue to travel with those whom it was bound to shun? The pope's ruling was based on the leniency allowable to a family in regard to its members or servants. The crusaders would not be affected by the doge's sin but, instead, were to work to bring him to his senses. This plan did not succeed: the Fourth Crusade culminated in the sack of Constantinople.

When he heard from Alexius III that the crusading army was on its way to invade Byzantine territory, Innocent in reply expressed his hostility to Philip of Swabia – whose imperial and royal claims he opposed – and distanced himself by implication from the activities of the crusaders.

We have received the letters and messengers from your imperial dignity with that benevolence which is fitting. We have carefully studied what your envoys proposed, as well as the contents of the letters. These envoys and the letters state categorically that the Christian army which is on its way to rescue the Holy Land intends to invade your highness's territory, and to make war on Christians. Thus it accords with our dignity to recall them from such a venture, lest they defile their hands with Christian blood and thereby incur the anger of God.

Touching your highness, your envoys asked that we should refrain from giving the slightest support to Alexius, the son of Isaac II Angelus, who has turned to Philip of Swabia [king of Germany] in order to gain power at your expense with his help. However, Alexius was in no position whatever to justify his right to the throne.

On the other hand, we feel that we must answer your imperial prudence in this wise. Alexius appeared before us and our brothers. Also present were many Roman nobles. He submitted to us a serious matter, saying that you had unjustly arrested his father Isaac Angelus and caused him to be cruelly blinded. Then you kept both father and son imprisoned for a long time. He submitted to us that, because he had been unable previously [while in prison] to have recourse to us, we were bound to secure justice for him, since like the apostle we were obligated equally to the wise and to the unwise.

We replied to him as we saw fit. He left us and hastened to his sister's husband, Philip of Swabia. These men wasted no time in despatching envoys to the commanders of the Christian host, to say that they should join with him in invading the realm of Constantinople, and help him with moral and political support to regain it. He made liberal promises to aid the Holy Land with expenses and grants of money. He was also ready in every way and under all circumstances to submit to our rule and honour the holy Roman Church as much as his own kingdom. It was their wish that we discuss the matter while they waited on us to make our decision. To this end, they asked our dear son Peter of Capuano to return to our presence and to enquire our will on the matter. When your envoys enter our presence we shall deal with them in a way that should be deservedly satisfactory.

Crusaders convene at Corfu

By early April 1203, and after yet more desertions, most of the army had embarked for Corfu. Doge Henry Dandolo and Boniface of Montferrat waited at Zara for young Alexius to join them. As Villehardouin relates, they met the rest of the army at Corfu.

At Corfu, they found the army encamped before the town in tents and pavilions, and the horses unloaded from the transports for rest and refreshment. When the army heard that Alexius had reached harbour, many good knights welcomed him with all joy and humour. He had his tent pitched in the midst of the army and the marquis of Montferrat had his own put next to it, for the young man's sister's husband King Philip had put him under the marquis's protection.

They stayed three weeks in this island, which was very rich and fertile. During their stay a large section of the army declared that this operation seemed to them very long and very dangerous, and that they would stay in the island and let the army depart; with the help of the inhabitants of Corfu, they would go by ship to Brindisi. Some of the principal leaders were involved in this.

When this news reached Boniface of Montferrat, Baldwin of Flanders and the barons of their party they were very much dismayed and said, 'My lords, we are in great trouble. If all these men leave us, our army will be reduced to nothing and we shall win no victories anywhere. But let us go to them and beg them not to hinder the liberation of the Holy Land.'

So they all went in a body into a valley where the others were holding discussions. The barons fell at their feet weeping bitterly and said that they would not budge until the dissidents had promised not to desert them. When they saw this the dissidents were much moved. Then they went aside and talked privately together. The upshot was that they agreed to stay until 29 September 1203 on the understanding that after that date they would, at a fortnight's notice, in good faith and without trickery, be supplied vessels in which they could leave Constantinople and sail to the Holy Land.

This was agreed and sworn.

The crusading flotilla rounded Greece, crossed the Aegean Sea, and prepared for the next stage of its journey at Abydos.

The ships that had not taken a southerly course had entered the channel of Abydos, where the Hellespont meets the open sea. The troops stayed at Abydos for a week while waiting for those warships, galleys and transports that had not as yet come up to join them. During that time they took possession of the corn as it was reaped, for it was the harvest season; and they had great need of such supplies, having little of their own stores left. By the end of the week, since God had granted them fair weather, all the remaining ships and the rest of the barons had reached Abydos.

The whole fleet then set sail together from the port. At the moment of departure, the Hellespont to eastward, with the full array of warships, galleys and transports, seemed as it were in flower. It was, indeed, a marvellous experience to see so lovely a sight. The ships sailed onwards up the straits, until, on 23 June 1203, they came alongside St Stephen's, an abbey some four or five miles distant from Constantinople, and from which point all those on board the ships had a full view of the city. Here the fleet came into port and the ships cast anchor.

I can assure you that all those who had never seen Constantinople before gazed very intently at the city, having never imagined there could be so fine a place in the world. They noted the high walls and lofty towers encircling it, and its rich palaces and tall churches, of which there were so many that no one would have believed it to be true if he had not seen it with his own eyes, and viewed the length and breadth of that city which reigns supreme over all others. There was indeed no man so brave and daring that his flesh did not shudder at the sight. Nor was this to be wondered at, for never before had so grand an enterprise been carried out by any people since the creation of the world.

The early 13th-century Greek chronicler Nicetas Choniates gives a jaundiced account of Alexius III, the Byzantine emperor.

Emperor Alexius III had heard about the movement of the Latins a long time ago, but he was in no way better disposed towards the people of Constantinople. Extravagance somehow tends towards slackness with regard to common utility and necessities. Some tried to induce him to replenish his armouries, to make the necessary preparations for war and to undertake the construction of a fleet: it was as though they were talking to a corpse. He made a laughing matter of the reports about the Latins, playing the coward.

He was very enthusiastic about the construction of bath houses, the levelling of hills for threshing-floors and the filling-in of ravines: he purposelessly devoted his time to such and similar activities. There were eunuch guards over the thickly planted hills reserved for the kings for hunting purposes; these guards protected the hills as though they were

The Comnenus dynasty

The Comnenus family came to prominence when Alexius I Comnenus seized power in 1081 and established a dynasty which ruled until 1185. In the late 12th century, however, the disreputable Andronicus I Comnenus gained the imperial throne, at first, in 1183, as joint emperor with the young Alexius II, son of Andronicus's cousin, Manuel I Comnenus. Andronicus forced the young emperor to sign his mother's death warrant, then murdered him and married his child-bride, Agnes of France. Although he worked hard to root out corruption at court and improve the administration of the empire, his harsh and vengeful policies antagonized most of the aristocracy, including other members of the Comnenus family who had in the past provided the holders of important offices. One of them, Isaac Comnenus, set himself up as rival emperor on Cyprus. In 1185, Andronicus was ousted by an aristocratic revolt, and killed by the mob. His successor, Isaac II Angelus, was descended from Alexius I's daughter, Theodora.

The chaos in the empire went from bad to worse. In the provinces, local magnates appropriated property and defied imperial justice with impunity. Taxation was heavy and unfairly applied. Isaac was overthrown by his brother Alexius III Angelus, who had him blinded and imprisoned together with his son, also called Alexius. The young man escaped in 1201 (probably with Italian help) and fled first to Italy and then to his brother-in-law, Philip of Swabia. He succeeded in persuading the army of the Fourth Crusade to campaign to reinstate him as the rightful emperor in Constantinople. When the crusading fleet arrived off the city, Alexius III Angelus fled; the old emperor, Isaac, was restored and his son was crowned with him as Alexius IV, in August 1203. However, the new emperor was unable to tread the delicate line between not offending his crusader supporters and placating Byzantine public opinion, which was increasingly outraged by the behaviour of the westerners camped outside the walls of the city. The crusaders, who had formally sworn to serve Alexius IV for a year, renounced their oath. Alexius, without their support, was overthrown by a faction led by Alexius V Ducas (Murzuphlus) and the rule of the Comneni and their kinsmen came to an end in Constantinople. The dynasty survived only in the far-off Black Sea enclave of Trebizond.

divinely planted paradises, threatening anyone who tried to cut any timber from them for shipbuilding. The emperor was guilty of regarding as stupid anyone he did not respect, and of favouring those who babbled.

The Franks had known for a long while that the Roman empire in the east had become nothing more than a drunken orgy of intoxication, and that Byzantium was celebrated as simply Sybaris for its luxury. They had an incredibly good journey, the sea breezes throughout being gentle, filling their sails and blowing the ships along; they reached the city of Constantinople virtually unnoticed. Their ships rode at anchor sufficiently far away from the shore to be out of missile range. The light vessels put in to Scutari.

Arrival at Constantinople, 1203

On 24 June 1203, St John the Baptist's day, the fleet passed in front of the walls of Constantinople. The barons were billeted in the palace at Chalcedon – on the other side of the Bosporus from Constantinople. The Emperor Alexius III drew up his forces in tents on the opposing shore and, as Villehardouin relates, sent a messenger with a letter.

The envoy stood before the barons and said, 'My lords, Emperor Alexius III sends to tell you that, after crowned heads, you are the noblest men in the world and belong to the noblest land. He wonders very much why or for what purpose you have entered his land and realm. You are Christians and so is he. He knows that you set off to go to the Holy Land beyond the sea for the sake of the True Cross and to save the Sepulchre. If you are poor or in want, he will be glad to supply you from his own wealth and provisions, as long as you leave his lands. He would not wish to do you any other harm, and yet he is well able to do so, for if you were twenty times as many as you are, you could not leave without death and defeat.'

By the advice and agreement of the doge of Venice and the other great lords, Conon of Béthune stood up, a good and wise knight and very eloquent, and answered the envoy.

'Fair sir,' he said, 'you have told us that your lord wonders very much why we have entered his land and his realm. Neither land nor realm of his have we entered, for he holds it wrongly and sinfully against God and against reason; on the contrary, it belongs to his nephew Alexius, here enthroned among us, who is the son of his brother, Emperor Isaac. But if the emperor were willing to place himself in his nephew's mercy and yield crown and empire to him, we would beg

Alexius to forgive him and to grant him enough to live on richly and well. If you do not return to us with this message, do not dare return to us at all.' With this reply the envoy left and went back to Emperor Alexius in Constantinople.

First siege of Constantinople

Robert of Clari, writing from the viewpoint of the humble knight, goes on to tell the story of the first siege of Constantinople, 5–17 July 1203. The reported arguments are less subtle than those of Villehardouin and the descriptions more impressionistic.

After the envoys had left the crusaders at Chalcedon, Henry Dandolo, the doge of Venice, spoke to the barons and said, 'My lords, I strongly recommend that we send ten galleys, with the youth Alexius and his followers in one of them, under the flag of truce, to the shores of Constantinople to ask the inhabitants of the city whether they recognize the young man as their lord.' The

The skyline of Constantinople, as magnificent as the view the crusaders must have seen in 1203.

barons replied that this was an excellent suggestion, so they made ready these ten galleys and sent the youth, with many armed men to accompany him, up to the walls of the city. They rowed back and forth in front of the walls and showed the people the young man, asking them if they recognized him as their lord. The inhabitants said that they did not, and that they did not know who he was. The men in the ships told them that this was the son of Isaac II Angelus, the former emperor, but the people of the city replied that they knew nothing about him. So they returned to the army and reported what had been said.

Then the order went out for every man to arm himself. When everyone was ready, they all made their confessions and took communion, for they were all very afraid of landing at Constantinople. They deployed their troops and ships, their transports and galleys; the knights boarded the transports with their horses and they got under way. Their brass and silver trumpets were sounded – more than two hundred of them – and many tabors and kettledrums.

The naval power of the city of Venice

In 1201 representatives of the crusading army which Pope Innocent III had convoked in France made a far-reaching agreement with the Venetians. Venice would supply them with ships for their journey and its citizens would themselves participate in the crusade.

Venetian maritime development had been well advanced by the late 11th century and throughout the 12th the city's overseas commerce with Egypt, the crusader states and the Byzantine Empire had continued to expand. Towards the end of the century, Venice was sending two seasonal caravans to Constantinople every year, each consisting of 10–12 transport galleys, one or two large sailing ships, and a few escorting war galleys. By the 1170s there may have been more than 1,700 Venetians living in the Byzantine Empire at any one time.

During the early crusades, the city in the lagoons sent a number of fleets to the Holy Land. In 1123 it provided a transport fleet for northern crusaders as well as a battle fleet – a total of up to 120 ships. The expedition won a major victory over the Egyptians off Ascalon and was instrumental in the success of the siege of Tyre. In 1148 a large Venetian fleet aided Byzantine resistance to a Sicilian attack on Corfu. By 1171 Venice could send 100 war galleys and 20 sailing ships to the Aegean in response to Byzantine hostilities. The galleys were built new at Venice in four months.

Although at the time of the Third Crusade, the doge recalled some Venetian ships from abroad, Venice did not participate in the crusade on a large scale. In 1191, however, Venetian ships did sail to assist Richard I of England's siege of Acre with a combined Italian fleet whose passengers included the archbishop of Ravenna.

Venice was the only Italian city with the necessary political organization, maritime infrastructure and experience to meet the requirements. As well as sailing ships and war galleys, the fleet included transport galleys for horses with stern ports in the hull for embarkation and disembarkation: medieval landing assault craft.

Ten years later, however, the size of the Venetian commitment to the Fourth Crusade was immense, unparalleled in the history of the Italian maritime republics, a fact that explains much of the subsequent course of the crusade.

When the inhabitants saw this great fleet and heard the sound of the trumpets and the drums' great din, they all rushed to arm themselves and climbed on to the houses and towers of the city. It really seemed to them that sea and land were shaking and that the sea was completely covered with ships. In the mean time, the emperor had summoned his men, all armed, to defend the shore.

When the crusaders and the Venetians saw the Greeks who had come armed against them on the shore, they held a council of war, and finally the doge of Venice said that he would go in advance with all his men and, with God's help, he would take the shore. So, with his ships, his galleys and his transports, he placed himself in front at the head of the army, and they positioned their crossbowmen and archers in the front rank in barges, in order to clear the Greeks from the shore. Once they were all drawn up in this way, the fleet advanced towards the shore. When the Greeks saw that the pilgrims were not deterred from advancing for fear of them, they fell back, not daring to wait for the fleet to land.

When they reached the shore, the knights rode out already mounted from the transports, for these were constructed so that the doors could be opened and a gangplank pushed out which allowed the knights to ride out on to land on horseback. When the knights emerged from the transports, they gave chase to the Greeks, pursuing them as far as a bridge near the furthest point of the city; on this bridge there was a gate through which the Greeks escaped into Constantinople. The knights having returned from the pursuit, they all discussed the situation.

The Venetians pointed out that their ships would not be safe until they were in the harbour, so they decided to bring the ships in. Now Constantinople's harbour was securely closed with a great iron chain fastened at one end in the city and, on the other side, at the Galata tower, which was extremely strong and very well manned by defenders. They laid siege to this tower and took it by force. With the chain broken, their vessels were brought into the safety of the harbour; they also seized some of the Greek galleys and ships which were in there.

Then all the pilgrims and Venetians met to plan their attack on the city. It was agreed that the Franks would attack from the land and the Venetians by sea. The doge of Venice said that he would have siege-engines and scaling-ladders made in his ships to enable them to mount an assault on the high walls. The knights and all the other pilgrims set out to cross over a bridge some six miles away, for there was no closer way of crossing to Constantinople. When they reached the bridge, the Greeks held the passage but the pilgrims drove them back by force. When they came to the city, the great lords set up camp opposite the Blachernae palace, which belonged to the emperor and which was situated at the furthest point of the city.

Once they had drawn up the three divisions which were to fight the emperor, they organized the other four, which were to guard the camp, under the command of the marquis of Montferrat.

Then they took all the boys who looked after the horses and all the kitchen-lads who could bear arms, and they equipped every single one of them with rolling-pins, copper pots and pans, and padded jerkins. They looked so hideously ugly that the emperor's common foot-soldiers, who were outside the walls, were so terrified at the very sight of them that they did not dare budge nor advance towards them, and the camp was never threatened from that direction.

Alexius crowned emperor, 1203

On the night of 16–17 July 1203, Emperor Alexius III collected as much money as he could carry and fled, leaving his wife Euphrosyne and daughter Eudoxia. The people of Constantinople went to the prison where his blinded brother, the deposed emperor, Isaac II Angelus – father of young Alexius – was held and proclaimed him to be restored to his throne. Next, when Emperor Isaac II Angelus had fulfilled the terms of the agreement made at Zara, the barons brought his son the young Alexius into the city to an enthusiastic welcome from the people.

He was crowned as Alexius IV on 1 August 1203 and began to make payments to the army, but not quickly enough to satisfy the soldiers. Tensions mounted and, on 14 November, there was a final breach between Alexius IV and the doge, as Robert of Clari recounts.

The doge of Venice, Henry Dandolo, sent word to Alexius IV, asking him to come to the harbour to speak with him. The doge gave orders for four galleys to be made ready; he boarded one and ordered the other three to accompany him for his protection. When he approached the shores of the harbour, he met Emperor Alexius IV, who had come there on horseback. The doge spoke to him and said, 'Alexius, what are you doing? Remember that we rescued you from great misery; we made you lord and crowned you emperor of Constantinople. Will you not keep your agreement with us? Won't you carry things through?' 'No,' said the emperor: 'I will do no more than I have already done.' 'No?' said the doge. 'You wicked scoun-

drel! We raised you from the dungheap and we will plunge you back in it! You are now our enemy, and I give you warning that from now on I will do everything that I can to destroy you!'

With these words the doge left and went back to the army.

Murzuphlus crowned emperor

A conspiracy was now set in train against Alexius IV. Its leader was Alexius III's son-in-law, the perfidious Murzuphlus, 'bushy eyebrows', who had become a close adviser of Alexius IV. Robert of Clari gives a graphic description of his coup.

Meanwhile, a faction among the Greeks gathered together and plotted high treason. They wanted another emperor, one who would deliver them from the Franks, for they did not think Alexius IV was capable of this. Finally, Murzuphlus said, 'If you will trust me and make me emperor, I will rid you of the Franks and of Emperor Alexius IV so completely that you will never have to be afraid of them again.' He undertook to do this within the week and they promised him that they would put him on the throne.

So on 1 February 1204 Murzuphlus set off purposefully. He took some soldiers with him and, under cover of darkness, he slipped into the chamber where his lord the emperor, who had once freed him from prison, was sleeping. A cord was put around the emperor's neck and Murzuphlus had him strangled, him and his father Isaac II Angelus also. Then he went back to the others who had promised to put him on the throne and told them what he had done. They crowned him and made him emperor.

Then the cry went up throughout the city: 'Can this be true? By my faith, Murzuphlus is emperor – he has murdered his lord!' People in the city threw written messages into the pilgrims' camp to inform them of what Murzuphlus had done; and when the barons heard the news, some said that they did not give a fig for the death of Alexius IV, since he had not kept his bargain with the pilgrims. Others said that they were sorry he had been killed in that way.

It was not long before Murzuphlus sent word to Louis of Blois, Baldwin of Flanders, Boniface of Montferrat and all the other great lords, ordering them to leave his lands, for they

Overleaf: A Venetian view of the siege of Constantinople. The crusaders breached the city's walls by leaping on to its towers from bridges in their ships' masts.

Byzantine politics

In its heyday, about the year 1000, the Byzantine Empire had extended from southern Italy in the west to the foothills of the Caucasus in the east and from the river Danube in the north to Syria in the south. But by 1204, large tracts of Asia Minor had come under Turkish control. In the early 12th century Byzantium had been able to use the victories of the First Crusade as a springboard for renewed campaigning against the Seldjuk Turks in Anatolia, but many of these reconquests were short-lived. In the 1140s and 1150s, Emperor Manuel Comnenus was able to consolidate his gains only on the western coastlands of Asia Minor. In 1176 his defeat by the Turks at Myriocephalum in eastern Anatolia reflected Byzantine inability to control land routes to the Holy Land and so link with the crusader states.

Elsewhere, too, Byzantine ambitions came to grief. In 1158, the Byzantines finally made a treaty which recognized Norman possession of southern Italy and Sicily; and their power was also on the wane in the Balkans, where Hungary had gained control in the north. Although Manuel's armies defeated the Hungarians in 1151 and 1156, Hungary and other Balkan regions such as Serbia and Bulgaria were increasingly independent and, when weaker Byzantine emperors came to power at the end of the century, these kingdoms harried their old ally.

Local Balkan rulers had always looked westwards for support against Byzantium, and, partly to counter this, Manuel made alliances with western powers (some western customs, such as jousting, became increasingly popular at the Byzantine court). However, the division between the eastern and western Churches always stood between Byzantium and the states of the west. The Byzantines were not prepared to accept papal primacy, or such Latin practices as a celibate priesthood and the use of unleavened bread for communion, and had been appalled to see western clergymen active in crusading warfare. And although they supported the papacy against the Holy Roman Emperors, the fundamental doctrinal differences remained.

The Third Lateran Council of 1179 reiterated papal claims to supremacy over the Byzantine Church and even though Innocent III disapproved of the actions of the Fourth Crusade, he capitalized on the capture of Constantinople in 1204 by setting up a Latin patriarchate and proclaiming the union of the Churches.

were well aware that he was emperor now, and if he found them still there a week later, he would kill all of them. When the barons heard Murzuphlus's message, they said, 'What! A man who murdered his lord treacherously and by night dares to send us this message?' And they sent word back to say that he was their enemy and he should be on his guard against them: they declared that they would not raise the siege before they had avenged the man he had murdered, recaptured Constantinople, and taken in full the payment which Alexius IV had promised them.

Second siege of Constantinople

Then the bishops of Soissons, Troyes and Halberstadt, all preached sermons throughout the camp. They proved to the pilgrims that this was a holy war, since the Greeks were treacherous murderers, they had assassinated their rightful lord Alexius IV and were in fact worse than the Jews. The bishops said that they granted absolution, in God's name and by the authority of the pope, to everyone who fought the Greeks. They commanded all the pilgrims to confess their sins and to take communion with sincere piety, and told them that they should not be afraid of attacking the Greeks because these were God's enemies.

Orders were given to seek out and expel all loose women from the company, so all these women were put on board a ship and sent far away from the camp.

On Monday 12 April 1204, in the morning, all the pilgrims and Venetians equipped and armed themselves fully. The Venetians repaired the assault bridges high in the masts of their ships; then they lined up ships, galleys and transports side by side and set off to the attack. The line of the fleet stretched out over more than three miles. When they neared the shore and were as close as they could get to the city walls, they dropped anchor. Then they mounted a furious artillery attack, bombarding the walls and hurling missiles and Greek fire at the towers, but these were all covered by leather hides and the fire did not take hold. The city's defenders fought fiercely. They had more than sixty stone-throwing siege-engines and every time these were fired, missiles hit the ships, but the vessels were so well protected by timber planking and interwoven springy vines that the rocks did not do much damage, although each one was so big that one man could not have picked it up on his own.

Emperor Murzuphlus occupied a high vantage point. He ordered his silver trumpets and war-drums to be sounded, and there was a great row. He was shouting encouragements to his men, yelling 'Come here! Go there!', and sending them where he could see they were most needed.

The city's towers were so high that in all the Latin fleet there were only four or five ships tall enough to be able to attack them.

On top of the stone towers the Greeks had built wooden towers – up to five, six or sometimes seven storeys high – and these were manned by soldiers who defended them.

The pilgrims kept up the attack until, by God's miracle, the sea, which is never calm there, carried the bishop of Soissons' ship forward against one of these towers. A Venetian and two armed knights were perched high on the assault bridge of this ship. In the swell the ship swayed against the tower; the Venetian grabbed hold of the tower, clinging on with fingers and toes, and scrambled inside. The soldiers – English and Danes (the Varangian guard) and Greeks – who were on that storey looked around, then they fell on him with axes and swords and hacked him to pieces.

When the swell carried the swaying ship forward against the tower once more, Andrew of Oreboise, one of the two knights, did not hesitate: he seized hold of the wooden super-structure, clung on with all his might and main and struggled inside, landing on his knees. The defenders rushed at him with axes and swords and rained blows on him, but, by God's grace, he was wearing armour and they did not wound him. He was protected by God, and it was not His will that the rule of the Greeks should endure, nor that this knight should die there. On the contrary, because of their treachery, their disloyalty and the murder that Murzuphlus had committed, it was His will that the city should be taken and all its people dishonoured. The knight got to his feet and drew his sword. When the Greeks saw him standing there, they were dumbfounded and so afraid that they fled to the storey below. When the men there saw that their fellows above were fleeing, they did not dare stay any longer either, and they too abandoned their positions.

The second knight entered the tower, followed by many others. They took stout ropes and lashed the ship securely to the tower so that more could climb in, but when the swell carried the ship away again, the tower shook so violently that it

Christians loot Constantinople's treasure

Emperor Murzuphlus strengthened the nobles and all the people, as he wanted to start a fight with the Franks, and they did not obey him, and all of them ran away from him. And the emperor ran off after them, and caught up with them at the horse-market and made many complaints against his boyars and all the people. Then the emperor, the patriarch and all the boyars fled from the town; all the Franks entered the town on Monday 12 April, and stopped at the place where the Greek emperor had stood, by St Saviour's, and stayed there for the night. Next morning at sunrise they went into the church of Hagia Sophia and tore down the doors, and cut them to pieces, and the pulpit cased in silver, and twelve silver pillars, and four pillars of the icon case. They cut up the icon bracket and twelve crosses which hung over the altar with bosses between them, like trees taller than a man, and the altar rails between the pillars, which was all silver. They tore the precious stone and the great pearl from the marvellous altar, and where they put the altar itself is not known.

They took forty large cups which were in front of the altar, and the censers and the silver lamps, whose number we cannot tell, with priceless feast-day dishes.

Mosaic of the fall of Constantinople, from Ravenna, made soon after the event. The Venetians wanted to crush their Byzantine trading rivals.

The gospels for the services and the holy crosses, priceless icons, all this they stripped. Under the altar roof they found forty barrels of pure gold, in shelves in the walls and in the places where dishes are kept, an unheard-of quantity of gold and silver, so great as to be uncountable, and of priceless vessels. All this was in Hagia Sophia alone; but they also stripped the Holy Mother of God in Blachernae, where the Holy Spirit comes down every Friday. About the other churches man cannot tell, as they were countless.

From *The Chronicle of Novgorod*

seemed the ship would surely pull it down, so fear and necessity made them untie the ropes. When the defenders below saw that the Franks were occupying the tower, they abandoned the tower altogether.

Murzuphlus saw all this. He was shouting encouragements to his men and deploying his forces where he saw the attack was fiercest. While this tower was being so miraculously taken, the lord Peter of Bracieux's ship was swept against another tower. The men on the assault bridge attacked until, by God's miracle, this tower was also taken.

Murzuphlus takes flight

When the traitor, Emperor Murzuphlus, saw that the Franks, all on horseback, were inside, he was so afraid that he abandoned his tents and his treasure and fled back into the city, which was very big indeed, for people there say that the distance around the city walls is more than twenty-seven miles, while inside the city measures a good six miles in length and another six across. So it happened that my lord Peter of Bracieux had Murzuphlus's tents, his coffers and the jewels which he had left behind. When the men defending the walls and the towers saw that the Franks had entered the city and that their emperor had fled, none dared to stay there and they took to their heels. In this way the city was taken.

Towards midnight on 12 April 1204 Emperor Murzuphlus the traitor learned that all the Frankish troops had entered the city. This struck such fear into him that he dared not stay there any longer, so he crept away in the middle of the night and no one knew anything about it. When the Greeks realized that their emperor had fled, they sought out a leading figure in the city, named Theodore Lascaris, and right there and then they made him emperor. But Lascaris did not dare stay in the city either; before it was light he boarded a galley and crossed over the Bosporus to Nicaea, a very fine city. There he stayed and became its lord and emperor.

The next morning the clergy and priests in all their vestments, the Varangian guard and men of other nations, came in procession to the Frankish camp to beg for mercy; they told the Franks what the Greeks had done, and said that all the Greeks had fled and that no one was left in the city except the poor people. When the Franks heard this they were very glad. Then it was proclaimed throughout the camp that no one should take possession of a house before it had been decided how houses and booty were to be divided. Thereupon all the great and powerful men met in assembly. They decided that they would divide the best houses in the city among themselves, and neither the ordinary soldiers nor the poor knights in the host ever knew anything about this.

The sack of Constantinople, 1204

From that moment on the great lords began to betray the trust of the common people and deceive their companions-in-arms, and they paid dearly for it later, as I will tell you. So they sent men to seize possession of all the best and richest houses in the city, before the poor knights and soldiers of the host realized what was going on. When the common people

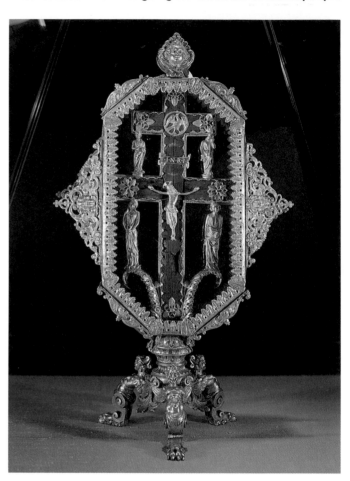

woke up to what was happening, each one rushed in to grab whatever he could find. They seized a great quantity of booty, but still more was left, for the city was very large and populous. So Boniface of Montferrat took over the palace of Boukoleon, the church of Hagia Sophia and the patriarch's houses, and the other great lords and counts seized the richest palaces and abbeys that they could find. From the time the city was taken, no harm was done to the inhabitants, either rich or poor; those who wanted to leave were allowed to go, and those who wanted to stay stayed, but it was the most important men who left the city.

Then orders were given for all the booty that had been taken to be brought to an abbey in the city. Ten leading knights were chosen from among the pilgrims and ten Vene-

Above: The bronze horses of St Mark's in Venice; perhaps the most famous items the Venetians looted from Constantinople.
Left: A piece of the True Cross in a gold reliquary; one of the countless treasures taken from Constantinople to Venice.

tians who were thought to be trustworthy, and they were set to guard the booty. There was so much treasure heaped up there, so many precious gold and silver vessels, cloth of gold and rich jewels, that it was a wonder to behold. Never since the beginning of the world has such wealth been seen or been won – not in Charlemagne's day, nor even in Alexander's. I do not think that in the forty richest cities in the world you could find such treasure as we found in Constantinople.

The Greeks used to say that two-thirds of the world's wealth was concentrated in Constantinople and the other third scattered throughout the rest of the world.

But those very men who were supposed to guard the booty stole it. Each of the powerful men took gold objects, or silken cloth embroidered with gold thread, or whatever else he wanted and stole away with it. So it happened that these men began to steal the treasure, and the booty was never shared out among the common soldiers and poor knights who had helped to capture it. All they ever received was some of the plain silver, such as the silver jugs which the women of the city used to carry to the baths. The rest of the treasure which should have been shared out was wickedly hidden, as I have described. All the same, the Venetians

Constantinople. The depredations of 1204 left the city too weak to resist the advance of the Ottoman Turks, who finally overwhelmed the city in 1453.

received their half-share; the precious stones and the huge treasure which was left to be distributed disappeared as the result of greed and disloyalty.

When the city was taken, the palaces were occupied and the pilgrims quartered, as I have said, and they found enormous wealth in the palaces. The palace of Boukoleon was very rich and built as I will describe to you. Inside this palace, which was held by the marquis of Montferrat, there were at least five hundred interconnecting halls, all decorated with gold mosaic. This palace also contained thirty chapels, both big and small. There was one called the Holy Chapel, so rich and fine that all its hinges, locks and other similar parts which are usually made of iron were of silver; every column was either of jasper or porphyry or some other precious stone. Its floor was of white marble so smooth and clear that it looked like crystal; this chapel was so rich and magnificent that it would be impossible to describe to you how very beautiful it was. Inside, there were many precious relics: two pieces of the True Cross as thick as a man's leg and about one metre long; the tip of the lance which pierced our Lord's side; and two of the nails which were driven through his hands and feet. There also was a crystal phial which contained a good quantity of his blood, the tunic which he had worn and which they stripped from him when he was taken to Calvary, and the blessed crown which was placed on his head and which was made of reeds as sharp as daggers. This chapel also contained pieces of our Lady's robe and the head of John the Baptist and so many other relics that I could not truthfully describe them all to you.

Baldwin elected emperor

Villehardouin gives more details about the sharing-out of the booty, and describes the election of Baldwin of Flanders as emperor of Constantinople.

Great was the joy of the Franks at the glory and the victory God had given them, for those who had been poor were now raised to riches and delight. Rightly did they praise our Lord for it, for they were no more than twenty thousand armed men altogether and yet with God's help they had captured four hundred thousand men or more, and that in the strongest city in all the world, a great city and the most strongly fortified.

It was then proclaimed throughout the army in the name of its commander, Boniface, marquis of Montferrat, and of the barons and the doge of Venice, that all goods should be brought together as had been agreed and sworn on pain of excommunication. Three churches were chosen as collection points and French and Venetian guards posted, the most reliable that could be found. Then everyone began to bring his plunder and put it with the rest.

Some brought their goods honestly, others did not, for greed, root of all evils, was not idle: from now on the covetous began to hold items back and our Lord began to love them less.

The goods and booty were collected; and you must know that it was by no means all brought forward, for there were many who kept items back in spite of [threats of] the pope's excommunication. What was brought to the churches was put together and divided half and half between the Franks and the Venetians, as had been sworn to in the agreement. And when they had divided it, they then also paid fifty thousand marks of silver to the Venetians, and shared out a good hundred thousand among their own men.

As for stealing, much justice was done on those who were caught and many were hanged. The count of Saint-Pol hanged one of his own knights, shield on neck, who had kept plunder back. Many were those, both great and small, who kept goods back but were never discovered. You can tell how enormous the wealth was, for even without what was stolen and without the Venetians' share, the total came to more than four hundred thousand marks of silver and at least ten thousand horses of various breeds. Thus was the plunder of Constantinople shared out, as you have heard.

Then the leaders met in conference and the commons of the army declared that they wished to appoint an emperor, as had been agreed.

On 9 May 1204, the meeting continued until they were all in agreement. Then they came out to the doge of Venice and the assembled barons. You may be sure that everyone looked at them, anxious to know their choice. Nivelon, bishop of Soissons, spoke to them and said, 'My lords, we are agreed, thanks be to God, in our choice of emperor; and you have all given your word to accept as emperor the man whom we shall choose and to come to his aid if any oppose him. Now we will tell you his name: it is Baldwin, count of Flanders and Hainault.'

The date of the coronation, 16 May 1204, arrived and with great joy and great honour Baldwin, count of Flanders, was crowned emperor in the church of Hagia Sophia. The festivities and joy were beyond description, for the knights and the barons did all they could in celebration.

Boniface, marquis of Montferrat, and Louis, count of Blois, did him honour as their lord. After all the joy of the coronation, he was led in a great and triumphant procession to the rich palace of Boukoleon, richer than any ever seen.

When the celebrations were over, the emperor discussed his affairs. Boniface of Montferrat required him to keep the promises he had made, which bound him to give the marquis the land beyond the straits, near Turkey, and the islands of Greece. The emperor acknowledged that he did indeed owe him these lands and would be very glad to grant them to him.

Seeing that the emperor meant to keep his word to him so handsomely, the marquis asked him to give him instead the land of Salonika, because it was near the realm of the king of Hungary, whose sister he had married.

There was considerable discussion about this, but eventually matters were so managed that the emperor did grant it him and he did homage for it.

The whole army was delighted, for the marquis was one of the most highly regarded knights in the world and much beloved by all the knights, for no one gave to them with greater generosity. And that is how the marquis of Montferrat was kept in this land, as you have heard.

The outcome of the Fourth Crusade did nothing to discourage the crusading spirit of the Roman Church. On the contrary, after the loss of Constantinople considerable activity followed within Europe itself, directed against what Pope Innocent III described as the internal enemies of Christendom.

The Baltic Crusade, 1204

In 1199 Pope Innocent III appointed Albert of Buxtehude, as archbishop of Riga and leader of the Baltic Crusade, which lasted until the mid-13th century. In his letter to Albert of 1204, Innocent in effect set up a permanent crusade in the region, by permitting priests and laymen in northern Germany, who were unable to get to the Holy Land, to commute their vows by fighting the pagans of Livonia instead.

Since up to this time the race of Livonia, on the shores of the Baltic Sea, has been enveloped in the darkness of unbelief and has not come to the knowledge of truth, so recently the Lord has sent into that land a tide of holy preaching ... Our venerable brother Albert, the archbishop of Riga, has made arrangements for its conversion. He has recruited those religious orders which are as firm in discipline as they are in doctrine, namely the Cistercians and the Augustinian canons, to fight with spiritual weapons against the beasts of the land, and an order of laymen wearing the habit of the Templars, who shall manfully and powerfully fight against those barbarians who are injuring the newest plantation of the Christian faith. Archbishop Albert has been anxious to bring back those who have wandered from their Christian faith to a renewed acceptance of it. But since there is much to be harvested – and workers in the field are few – the archbishop has humbly asked us that priests and other clerics of areas adjacent to the Baltic who have affixed the sign of the cross to their shoulders and have vowed to go to Jerusalem, should be thought worthy of sending to preach Jesus Christ to the Gentiles. Also, laymen who on account of poverty or bodily weakness cannot make the journey to Jerusalem we should allow to set out to Livonia against the barbarians thereby commuting their vows in the manner which we allow.

Given at the Lateran, 10 October 1204

The Reconquista, 1212

Meanwhile, in Spain the Almohad caliphs were regaining power at the expense of the kingdom of Castile. In the spring of 1212, Innocent III proclaimed a new crusade against them in Spain. Alfonso VIII of Castile's army was joined by those of Peter II, king of Aragon, Sancho VII, king of Navarre, and by crusaders from France, León and Portugal.

On 17 July 1212 the Christians won a resounding victory against the Almohads at Las Navas de Tolosa. This letter from Innocent III congratulates Alfonso on his triumph, which was a turning-point in the Reconquista.

God the protector of those who hope in him, without whom nothing is strong, nothing firm, has multiplied the mercy which he has showered on you and all Christian people. He has poured out his wrath on the heathen and upon those 'Which have not called upon his holy name' [Psalm 79.6].

We have learned more fully from your serenity's letters how he, who shows hands how to fight and prepares fingers for war, has renewed the miracles of the Old Testament and in a great and terrible battle has saved his people who had been cast down ... We have called together the clergy and people of the city of Rome and have given thanks to him who alone accomplishes great miracles ... Moreover, beloved son, we advise you in your prudence to ascribe the victory given to you and all Christian people to the mercy of God. Do not say in your heart: 'My own strength and the might of my hand has given me this great victory.' Rather remember God,

for it is he who gives you power and might ... Give the glory and honour to God, saying with the prophet: 'The zeal of the lord of Hosts has done this thing' [Isaiah 9.7]. As the enemy exults in chariots and cavalry, so you exult and glory in the Lord your God.

Given at the Lateran, 26 October 1212

Albigensian Crusade, 1209–29

Innocent III's pontificate also saw a crusade directed against heretics, the internal enemies of Christendom: the Cathars, also known as the Albigensians, who were by the second half of the 12th century widespread in southern France. This letter written in 1170 by Raymond V of St Gilles, count of Toulouse, to the Cistercian General Chapter, describes the menace of the Cathars, and their beliefs.

To his lordship and reverend Cistercian abbot, Alexander, and to all the convention appointed in General Chapter.

I, Raymond, count of Toulouse, duke of Narbonne and marquis of Provence, facing ruin in matters spiritual, am strengthened in hope of salvation by their blessings and supported by their prayers.

Seeing that in the treasure-house of your learning and wisdom it becomes clear that in our part of the country little foxes are tearing down the vines which have been planted by the hand of the Highest One; springs are waterless and clouds are rent by whirlwinds; men toil to empty the fountain which lies open in the house of David for the washing away of filth and impurity; streams spread their poisonous slime to uproot the trees which have been planted alongside the river courses; I beg and implore you to rise up against them.

So much has this foul disease of heresy taken hold, that almost all its acolytes believe that they are demonstrating their loyalty to God. And the wicked one who administers the mystery of evil takes on the appearance of an angel of light to the sons of disobedience, so that wife is sundered from husband, son from father and married woman from her husband's mother.

Alas and woe! Even those who perform priestly duties are corrupted by the evil of heresy. The ancient places of religious worship, formerly venerated, lie neglected and derelict; baptism is rejected; the eucharist is despised; repentance is held to be of small worth; the doctrine of the creation of man and the resurrection of the flesh is denied and cast out; all the sacraments of the Church are annulled.

The Albigensian Crusade in Southern France, 1209–29

The Albigensian heresy – so-named after Albi, one of its main centres – took root in the French Midi in the 12th century. The Albigensian Crusade (1209–29) was launched by Pope Innocent III only after preaching campaigns had failed, but it devastated the area and failed to crush the heretics. Only the French Crown, which gained control of the region in 1229, profited from it.

I strive to place bounds on and bring an end to this kind of disbelief. Yet I realize that my strength is lacking to bring a matter of such enormity to a conclusion. My better lands have had a foretaste of the corruption of heresy and have fallen away. With them the greatest part of the population has rushed to abandon the faith, so that I neither am able nor dare to accomplish what I intend. And so with feelings of humility in my heart I turn to you, in the hope that you will extend to me the hand of your counsel and help, as well as your skill in speech, to uproot this evil of apostasy.

Let it be known that the poison of heresy remains so ingrained that it cannot be cut out except by the strong hand and far-reaching arm of God. For the head of such power stays unmoved like a rock so that the stones of a sling are turned to straw. Since, therefore, we have to accept that spiritual powers are unable to amputate the viciousness of heresy, it is necessary to impose punishment with the power of material weapons.

To this end I am urging you to call on the king of France, Louis VII. It seems to me that if he were here in person this wickedness would be terminated. Indeed, in his presence I will open the gates of towns, villages and castles and submit them to his judgement. I will point out to him the heretics and will help him for whatever action he has need of me, even to the shedding of blood, in order to obliterate all the foes of Christ. Farewell.

The *Histoire Albigeoise* was written by Peter of Vaux, between 1212, when he accompanied his uncle, Guy, bishop of Carcassonne, to the court of Raymond VI, count of Toulouse (1194–1222), and his death in 1218 or 1219. Here he describes how Raymond VI tolerated heretics.

One day Count Raymond of Toulouse told the heretics that he wanted to have his son Raymond brought up at Toulouse among heretics to learn their faith (or rather lack of it).

Again one day he said that he wanted to donate one hundred marks of silver so that one of his knights could assume the heretics' faith, into which he had often invited him, and which he had caused to be preached to him on a number of occasions. Furthermore, whenever the heretics gave him any food-gifts or offerings, he accepted them most gratefully; he would not allow anyone to eat any of them except for himself and some of his close circle.

Still further, as we have learned for certain, he often venerated the heretics by kneeling on the ground, asking for their blessing, and kissing them.

One day, Count Raymond was expecting some men who should have called on him. But when they did not come, he said: 'It is quite clear that the devil has made this world, because nothing works out the way we want it.'

In 1199, Pope Innocent III wrote to Philip II of France and the French nobility, urging them to take up arms to eradicate heresy in the Midi, hinting at confiscation of the heretics' land and promising the same indulgence offered to those who went to the Holy Land – a measure of Innocent III's concern for heresy.

The ingrained corruption of abominable heresy grows persistently in areas of Toulouse and does not cease to breed monstrous offsprings. Through these it infects others with the filth of its particular madness. It revives incessantly and the hateful succession of the cursed flourishes as they vaunt themselves in their empty imaginings while spurning the doctrines of the true faith. The more they hear the preaching of the truth the more freely they pile up their falsehoods for others and believe, in their lying statements, that they are special people.

Under the guise of religion which they maintain they alone possess, they take many people off their guard and make them copies of their own malice. They are like that woman who beautifies herself like a harlot and proclaims: 'I have decked my bed with coverings of tapestry, with carved works, with fine linen of Egypt' [Proverbs 7.16].

In fact the heretics, under the cover of heavenly speech, and with bright colours of eloquence, promise to set aside for those who heed them a goodly bed in which to rest with hearts free from the troubles of evildoing. It is rather the case that they are weaving with cords of sin a place of destruction.

In the words of the prophet: 'The inhabitants of Samaria shall fear the calves of Bethlehem' [Hosea 10]. For the heretics lie when they say that they live in Samaria, that is, under the protection of the Lord's commandments, seeing that they have no understanding of God's law.

Let us apply ourselves without cease, and with the help of many, to enforce correction on this vile breed of people who are active in your realm, and who vaingloriously congregate for the express purpose of undermining Christian faith. Let us thwart their manifold and guileful delusions. Having surrendered themselves to heresy, they are neither impressed by the force of reason nor intimidated by threats, nor can they be won over by kindness. Hence ulcers which do not

The flying crosses

It happened, as God ordained, that the chaplain of the church at Minerve could not see the crosses. Then one night he entered the church and gave himself to prayer, asking the Lord to deign to show him what almost everyone had seen. Suddenly he saw countless crosses, not on the walls, but scattered in the air, and among them was one which seemed larger and more eminent than the others. Soon the larger cross went out of the church, and all the crosses went out after it and began to head straight to the city gates. The priest was utterly stunned, and followed the crosses until they were on the point of leaving the town. Then the priest thought he saw someone heading for the town, with a venerable and decorous appearance, and holding an unsheathed sword. With the help of the crosses he killed another huge man who was leaving the town right on the threshold. So the priest, now almost out of his mind with amazement, ran to the lord bishop of Utica, fell at his feet and told him the whole story in detail.

From Peter of Vaux, *Histoire Albigeoise*

respond to treatment with dressings must be cut out with the knife. Those who hold cheap the correction of the Church must be crushed by the arm of secular power.

We believe that your aid must be invoked, dearest son, to avenge the wrong done to Jesus Christ, to trap the foxes which cease not to ravage the vineyard of the God of Sabaoth. We counsel and urgently exhort your royal highness, for the remission of sins, to rise up in your strength and to uproot those degenerate sprigs which put down deep roots but bring forth not fruit, only worthless tendrils.

Let the followers of treacherous heresy learn to be contrite by virtue of your power, and be brought at least to an acquaintance of the truth through the afflictions of war. So that you may apply yourself with greater confidence to this task we are placing your land, your subjects and their property under the protection of St Peter. If anyone, which is something we cannot believe, should presume to commit a crime against you and yours we will weigh that offence when it has been reported to the Apostolic See and see that it is punished with canonic censure.

Furthermore, it is our wish that the property of the heretics be confiscated by the state. Let there be granted to you whether you act personally, or through the agency of others, as well as to those of your people who have taken up arms for the suppression of these traitors, a remission of sins. For we feel that indulgence must be extended to participants in this action no less than for those who toil to save the Holy Land. The need for this we want you as well as them to keep before their eyes.

Call for a punitive crusade, 1208

Frequent preaching expeditions had been sent to the Midi under the leadership of papal legates but had made little impact. On 14 January 1208 the legate Peter of Castelnau was murdered and the pope believed that Count Raymond was involved. On 10 March Innocent wrote angrily to the king and people of France, recounting the event and demanding vengeance.

We have been informed of an atrocious incident that is a matter of universal grief for all the Church. Brother Peter of Castelnau, of sacred memory, was a man renowned among pious men for the goodness of his life and famed for his learning. He was sent by us along with others as a missionary into the particular province of Toulouse to bring the peace of God and to spread the faith. In the ministry entrusted to him he enjoyed marked success; and he continued to make progress as you would expect of someone who had studied in the school of Christ what he taught others. So the devil raised up against him his servant Raymond, count of Toulouse, who, for the enormity and number of transgressions he had committed against God and the Church, had often incurred ecclesiastical censure. A turncoat, both cunning and fickle, he often feigned penitence and received absolution. Finally, he could no longer suppress the hatred he felt for Peter of Castelnau, not because the word of God that Peter preached was intended to stir up wrath among nations and reproach among peoples but because in the case of the count his greater offences earned the sterner rebuke.

The count, Raymond VI, invited him and his colleagues, who were acting as legates of the Apostolic See, to the town of Saint-Gilles, promising to render full satisfaction on all charges which were being brought against him. At the meeting the count at one moment promised truthfully and willingly to carry out the wholesome admonitions given him, at another, like someone false and obdurate, he rejected the advice utterly. When at last the legates indicated their intention to leave the town, he openly threatened them with death, saying that he would keep a watchful eye on their journey, whether by land or water. Matching words to deeds he despatched accomplices to a chosen place of ambush. In spite of the prayers of my dear son, the abbot of Saint-Gilles, and the protests of the town councillors and citizens, the count's insane fury remained unassuaged.

The townsfolk escorted the legates to the Rhône under the protection of an armed escort, notwithstanding the angry objections of the count. When they retired for the night, they little knew that several of the count's cronies were quartered with them. These same men, as became evident in the outcome, were after their blood.

The following morning at daybreak, on 14 January, Mass was celebrated as usual. These harmless soldiers of Christ were preparing to cross the river when one of these attendants of Satan, brandishing his lance, struck at Peter. Taken off guard by this treacherous attack, Peter received a thrust from behind that passed through his ribs. He, a man of God, looked back at this villain and emulating the example of his master and of St Stephen said to him: 'May God forgive you as I forgive you.' He kept repeating those words, redolent of holiness and fortitude. Ignoring the bitter agony of his wound in his hope of heavenly bliss and though at the point of death, he, together with the companions of his ministry, went on making plans for the strengthening of peace and the faith.

At last after many words of exhortation he joyfully slept in Christ.

The Albigensian Crusade

The spread of heretical sects in western Europe from the late 11th century posed the challenge to the Church of defending its position at home while it was committed to do battle against the infidel in the Holy Land.

A particularly powerful group, the Albigensians, emerged in the mid-12th century as a coherent sect from a ferment of heretical groups. A branch of the Cathars, it was based in the triangle defined by Agen, the Pyrenees and Béziers, an urban area in which the clergy had minimal influence. Basing their beliefs on dualist doctrines which affirmed the existence of two eternal principles of good and evil, its members rejected the flesh and all material creation as evil, did not acknowledge the sacraments, the doctrines of hell and purgatory, or the resurrection of the body, and developed their own Church and ritual. In the 1160s the town of Albi became the see of the first Cathar bishop in the Midi, and large numbers joined the sect, which was also viewed favourably by nobles.

In 1179 the third Lateran Council encouraged Christian princes to reduce the Albigensians to servitude while it conferred two years of indulgences and crusader privileges on those who committed themselves to the sacred enterprise. Pope Innocent III also commissioned Cistercian monks to preach in the area and in 1206 they were joined by Dominic Guzman, later St Dominic, founder of the Dominican Order. It was the murder of the papal legate Peter of Castelnau in 1208, probably by one of the aides of Raymond VI, count of Toulouse, that brought about the Albigensian Crusade, proclaimed by Innocent in 1208: now the crusading ideal was used against Christians, in Europe, to foster political interests, relegating the Holy Land and the struggle against the infidel to second place.

Although the war against the Albigensians ended officially in 1229, with the Peace of Paris, the systematic persecution of the heretics continued. In 1223, Pope Gregory IX charged the Dominican Inquisition to undertake the final extirpation of the Albigensians, all trace of whom disappeared by the end of the 14th century. In addition, each inhabitant of the centres of the heresy had to swear every two years that they would support the Church and combat heresy. Laymen were forbidden to possess a Bible or any book of religious ritual in the vernacular, and every parish had a team of heretic hunters.

Crusaders march into Languedoc

The French responded to Innocent's call. The *Chanson de la Croisade contre les Albigeois*, written *c.* 1213 by William of Tudela, gives a vivid description of the armies from the north entering the Languedoc in the spring of 1209.

The host that gathered was huge – a fine sight! I reckon there were twenty thousand knights, fully armed, and more than two hundred thousand foot-soldiers from the towns and villages, not counting the clerics and traders. Everyone came here, from near and far and from the Auvergne, Burgundy, the Ile de France and the Limousin. There were people from all over the world:

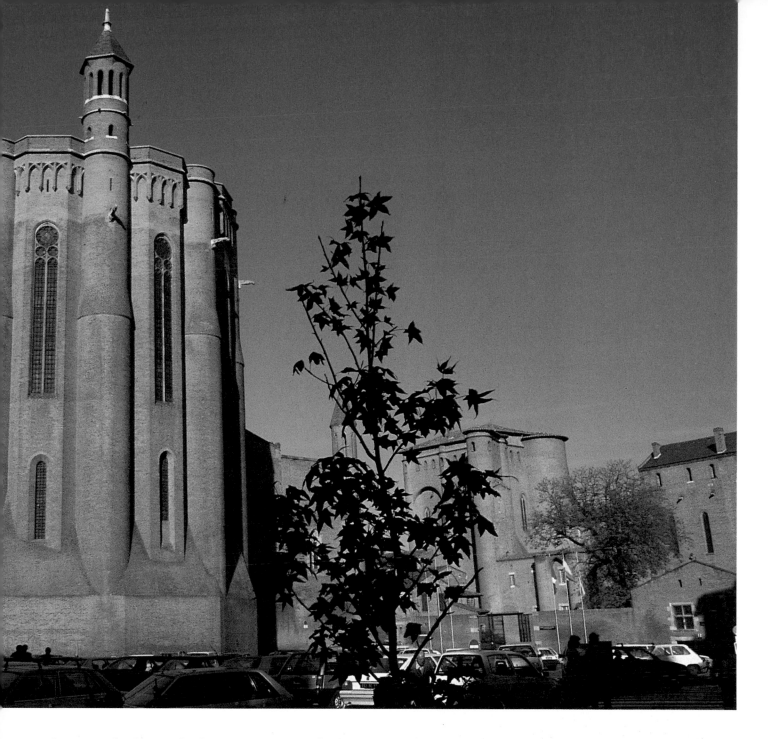

Germans, Flemings, Poitevins, Gascons, men of Rouergue and Saintonge.

Another host of crusaders came to the Agenais, but not as numerous as that of the French. They took Puylaroque without meeting any resistance. They razed Gontaud and ravaged Tonneins. But Casseneuil is strong. What's more it was well defended by its garrison of nimble Gascon foot-soldiers, all expert missile-men.

The host besieged Casseneuil, defended as it was by Seguin of Balencs, his knights and archers. They would have taken it and the crusaders could have won much booty, had it not been for the interference of Guy, count of Auvergne (who did very well financially out of this), who quarrelled with the archbishop of Bordeaux. I do not know how they divided the spoil, nor the form of their agreement. The host

The east end of Albi Cathedral; built as a fortress of the Catholic faith in the town which had given its name to the Albigensian heresy because of the many Cathars in the area.

condemned many heretics to be burned and many of their fair women were cast into the flames. For they would not convert, no matter how much we implored them to do so.

The bishop of Le Puy went toward Les Casses; he levied many a penny from Caussade and Bourg Saint-Antonin. From the latter place he went back to Casseneuil, for it seemed to him that the divided host was too weak and he wished to reunite both parts. The inhabitants of Villemur suffered a cruel misfortune at the hands of his troops. A lad told them that the main host wished to set out from Casseneuil and that the crusaders had already raised the siege of that place. At this news the bishop's men set fire to the town, which burnt all Monday until evening, when they fled by the light of the moon. I shall tell you no more about this for the moment.

The Béziers massacre

On 18 June 1209 Count Raymond of Toulouse was reconciled to the Church in front of the passion of Christ at Saint-Gilles. The armies from the north then invaded the lands of Raymond Roger, viscount of Béziers and Carcassonne, and a vassal of both Raymond of Toulouse and Peter II, king of Aragon. One result of this was the massacre of Béziers reported here, by Arnold, abbot of Cîteaux, in a letter to the pope.

In July 1209 the army advanced on the city of Béziers. Commanders of a number of fortresses in the neighbourhood, afflicted by a sense of guilt, fled from the sight of the crusaders. The garrisons and others who had remained true to the faith stayed behind and surrendered to the crusader army, which was now approaching in a mood of high confidence. They placed themselves, their property and the fortress under its protection and expressed loyalty and submission.

On 22 July Béziers was brought under siege. It was evident that the city was strongly defended by its natural position, the size of its garrison and its stock of provisions. Therefore it seemed that it could hold out against any army, no matter how formidable. But determination and strategy are of no avail against God.

While negotiations were being carried on with the barons, with the object of freeing those people in the city who were believed to be Christians, some menials and other common fellows who were not bearing arms, without waiting for orders from the leaders, launched an assault. Our men were taken by surprise as the cry went up, 'To arms, to arms!'

Within a space of two or three hours the moat and wall were crossed; and thus fell the city of Béziers.

Our forces spared neither rank nor sex nor age. About twenty thousand people lost their lives at the point of the sword. The destruction of the enemy was on an enormous scale. The entire city was plundered and put to the torch. Thus did divine vengeance vent its wondrous rage.

Carvings of the flagellation of Christ from the west front of the abbey church at Saint-Gilles, where Raymond of Toulouse was reconciled to the Catholic Church.

As the word got round of this miraculous event all hearts were struck with fear. People fled into the hills and pathless places between Béziers and Carcassonne, abandoning more than one hundred forts. These were crammed with food, supplies and equipment, which the refugees had been unable to carry with them. Numerous castles were so strong because of their position, the size of their garrisons and the abundance of their resources, that it seemed they could withstand a very long siege by our army. Then, with the Lord God as our guide by whose love we are led, the army of Christ reached Carcassonne in force on 1 August.

So that the land which God gave into the hands of his servants should be preserved for the honour of himself, for the honour of the Roman Church and of all Christendom, a noble gentleman, Simon of Montfort, was chosen by general agreement to be viscount of Béziers and Carcassonne, and overlord and ruler of the territory.

We understand that he is well known to your holiness; a man formidable in war, deeply religious and determined with all his strength to combat the evil of heresy. His eagerness to restore the authority of the Church in those territories can be clearly gauged from the following facts: he decreed that in the entire area which God had entrusted to his administration, tithes and first fruits should be paid with full immunity to the churches; if anyone should oppose this decree such a person would be regarded as his own and the Church's enemy.

Therefore on his behalf and with him we present to your beatitude humble and sincere prayers so that you may deign to listen with your wonted goodwill to the petitions which he will submit to you through solemn emissaries who are on their way to the apostolic seat. We pray that he may receive the blessing of the Roman Church in his efforts to cleanse the land completely of the evil of heresy. It is a fact that the bulk of the army has returned home because a campaign which it seemed would drag on for two or three years was completed in two months.

Nevertheless, many soldiers and other reliable people have remained with him.

Provided he receives subventions from the Church in whose interest he is acting, he should have no difficulty, not only in retaining the territory he has already won, but, with the exception of Toulouse, also completing the elimination of the heretics and occupying all the remaining territory. Apart from cities, he has under his control more than two hundred excellent castles. Moreover, he has in chains the former viscount of Béziers who had been the protector of the worst of the heretics. It is clear that he requires a considerable reinforcement in men and other resources to guard the present area under occupation and to extend his control over additional territory.

Burning of the heretics

The *Histoire Albigeoise* describes Simon's firm treatment of the heretics of Carcassonne and Montpellier in 1210–11. The perfecti, a small élite, at the core of the Cathar sect, which followed a rigidly austere and disciplined way of life, received particularly harsh treatment.

Gilbert, abbot of Vaux-de-Cernay, decreed that the lord of the castle of Carcassonne and everyone inside, including those attesting the heretics' creed, as long as they were willing to be restored and subject to the authority of the Church, would escape with their lives, and the count would retain the castle. Even the perfecti among the heretics would none the less escape, if they were willing to convert to the Catholic faith.

When a noble and devoted Catholic man who was there, Robert Mauvoisin, heard that the heretics whom the crusaders had come to destroy were to be freed, he was worried that they would be prompted by terror, since they had been captured, to promise whatever our men wanted. He opposed the abbot to his face, and said that our men would not accept this in any way. Then the abbot told him: 'Don't worry. I believe very few will convert.'

After discussion, our men entered the town of Carcassonne with the cross in front and the count's banner following, and approached the church singing the Te Deum. When the church had been restored, they placed the Lord's cross on top of the tower, and pitched Simon of Montfort's banner elsewhere. For it was Christ that had captured the town and it was right that his banner should take precedence, be placed in a pre-eminent position, and bear witness to the Christian victory. In any case the count had not yet entered the town.

When this had been done, the venerable abbot of Vaux-de-Cernay, who had been with the count in the siege, heard that a great number of heretics had gathered in one of the houses. He went to them and offered words of peace and promises of salvation, wishing to convert them to better things. But they interrupted him, and all said with one voice: 'Why are you preaching to us? We don't want your faith. We deny the Church of Rome. You're wasting your time. Neither life nor death can turn us from the beliefs we hold.' When he heard this the venerable abbot soon left the house and went to see the women, who were gathered in another building,

The expulsion of Cathar heretics from Carcassonne. Many fled to northern Italy to escape persecution, others preferred to be burned at the stake rather than desert their faith.

Simon of Montfort and the Albigensians

After Innocent III's crusading forces had massacred Albigensian heretics in Béziers and Carcassonne in the summer of 1209, the Church needed a secular leader to consolidate the gains of orthodoxy in the Languedoc. Its choice fell upon Simon IV of Montfort, modest, prudent, pious and above all , a gifted military commander.

In his late forties, Simon had amassed considerable power and wealth in France and England. Born at Montfort-l'Amaury near Paris in about 1160, he had inherited its lordship in 1181, and, on the death of a maternal uncle in 1204, had added the important earldom of Leicester in England to his lands (his son, also named Simon of Montfort, played a momentous role in Henry III's reign).

A participant in the Fourth Crusade, he had opposed its diversion to Zara and Constantinople, believing that its proper goal was to fight the infidel. In 1209, in answer to the Church's call, Simon IV, now viscount of Béziers and Carcassonne, took up the leadership of a force against the Albigensians, Christendom's internal enemies, whom he regarded as an even greater threat. Almost ten years of unremitting war with the heretics and their supporters – who resented the extension of northern French power in the region – was conducted against all the odds. Simon had only a small core of winter stalwarts on whom he could depend: summer parties of crusaders from northern France and Germany came south for the 40 days needed to earn a special indulgence from the Church and then departed.

Simon's reprisals against heretic forces were savage even by contemporary standards: in 1210, 100 men from the captured garrison at Bram had their eyes gouged out and their noses and upper lips cut off. But such horrific methods were effective, and Simon used them to offset the precariousness of his power and to further what he saw as God's cause.

He was killed in 1218 while besieging Toulouse. William of Tudela, the author of the *Chanson de la Croisade*, reported that the epitaph on his tomb at Carcassonne portrayed him as a saint and a martyr; but only, he commented, 'if one may seek Christ by killing men and shedding blood, by winning lands by violence, by fostering evil and snuffing out good, and by slaughtering women and children, then must Simon surely shine resplendent in heaven'.

intending to offer them some words of preaching. But if he found the male heretics difficult and obstinate, he found that the female heretics were more obstinate and more difficult in every way.

Soon Simon of Montfort entered the castle and came to the house where the heretics were gathered together. Since he was a Catholic man and wished them all to be saved and to come to recognize the truth, he first urged them to convert to the Catholic faith. But having no success, he had them dragged out of the castle. There were one hundred and forty or more perfecti. A huge fire was kindled and they were all thrown into it. It was not hard for our men to throw them in, because they were so obstinate in their wickedness that they all threw themselves in. Only three women escaped, whom a noble lady snatched from the flames and had restored to the Holy Church. When the heretics were burned, all the others who were in the castle renounced the heresy and were restored to the Holy Church.

Raymond of Toulouse sentenced, 1211

Attempts were now made to persuade Raymond of Toulouse to confirm earlier promises of orthodoxy made between 1209 and 1211. He wanted to be absolved from complicity in the murder of the legate Peter of Castelnau and from the charges that he had allowed heresy to flourish in his lands. But the Church struck a hard bargain. The *Chanson de la Croisade* describes attempts to force his capitulation in February 1211, its humiliating terms being tantamount to abdication.

At a council at Arles, the leading churchmen of the Languedoc reaffirmed in writing all the judgements which had been laid upon the count of Toulouse who awaited them outside, exposed to wind and rain, along with the king of Aragon, Peter II. Abbot Gilbert of Vaux-de-Cernay presented the document to the count, in the sight of all present, assisted by Master Thedisius, the best and wisest cleric in the world [notary of the legate Milo], Raymond, bishop of Uzès and a hundred other clerics. When the count received the document, he secretly instructed a scribe to read it to him. When he heard the scribe calmly read the contents to him, he called out in sorrow and indignation to the king of Aragon: 'Come here, lord king,' he said, with a bitter laugh, 'and listen to this document and the strange commands which the legates instruct me to obey.' The king had it read a second time and, after he had heard it, calmly spoke these simple words: 'There's much in need of improvement here, by the all-powerful Father!'

The count, so preoccupied that he did not beg leave, without replying a word and with the document in his hand, rushed off to Toulouse; then to Montauban, to Moissac and Agen, all in one journey.

The count of Toulouse had the document read out everywhere so that all should understand its contents: knights, townsmen and priests who chant the Mass. The first words of the document read as follows: 'That the count shall keep the peace, as shall all those with him, and that he shall give up maintaining bands of marauding soldiers immediately. He shall give the clergy all their rights; they shall receive everything they ask of him. He shall expel from his protection all the perfidious Jews and all followers of the heretics – whoever the clergy shall denounce to him. He shall give the clergy everything, and present himself at their mercy in a year's time, to do their pleasure and follow their wishes. Further, he shall eat no more than two sorts of meat, nor wear rich clothes, but only plain brown cloth, which he shall endure for a long time.

'All his castles and fortresses shall be destroyed, and no knight is to reside in the town square, but only outside in the countryside, like the peasants.

'Count Raymond must cross the sea and travel to the Holy Land on pilgrimage, and remain there for as long as the monks and Roman cardinals, in whose power he has been placed, shall wish. Finally, he shall enter a military Order, either the Templars or Hospitallers. And when he has done this he shall give up to the monks and cardinals all his castles. If he does not do this he shall be hunted ruthlessly until he is destitute.'

Battle of Muret, 1213

Count Raymond's refusal to agree to the terms led to his excommunication by Pope Innocent III in April 1211, and to an open breach with the Church. With his support the people of Toulouse appealed to Peter II, king of Aragon, whom they saw as a valuable ally against Simon of Montfort and the greedy northern crusaders.

A confrontation took place between Peter II and the Toulousains, and the northern French forces at the battle of Muret on 12 September 1213. The *Chanson de la Croisade* describes Simon of Montfort's victory.

The good king of Aragon, Peter II, mounted on his war-horse, came to Muret and raised his fleur-de-lis war standard before the place. He besieged it with the many brave followers he brought with him outside their own lands. He led the flower of his Catalonians and from Aragon many brave fighters. He believed that he would find no opposition worthy of him.

The men of Toulouse set out immediately with all their military equipment, to Muret, to join him. Knights, aldermen and townspeople left by the bridges, hastening to Muret where they left their harness, fine armour and many gentlemen. Raymond VI of Toulouse and all his forces, the townsmen of Toulouse and all the common people assembled there. This was a great sin – God and the faith guide me – for which everyone condemned them! They set up petraries and bombarded the walls, attacking Muret on every side. The attackers broke into the new town altogether, so pressing the French who were there, that they were forced to take refuge in the castle keep.

But then the king of Aragon heard that Simon of Montfort was coming to Muret that evening. He very much wished to take him there. So he commanded the host to stop tearing down the barricades and palisades, but to leave them in one piece, and that everyone should return to his quarters. The barons all left at once and made their way through the tents, each to his own hearth. High and low alike began to eat and drink. When they had eaten, they saw, arriving on the low ground, Simon, bearing his banner and followed by numerous Frenchmen, all of them on horseback. The water-meadows shone like crystal, reflecting their helmets and swords. I swear, by St Martial, that never, among so few men, were so many brave vassals to be seen. They entered Muret through the market-place and went, like high-born men, to their lodgings where they found plenty of bread, wine and meat. The next day, at dawn, the good king of Aragon and all his commanders went to hold council outside, in a meadow, with Raymond, count of Toulouse, Raymond Roger, count of Foix, and the loyal and brave Bernard IV, count of Comminges, and many others. The king spoke first.

'To arms!' went up the cry, and everyone went to arm themselves. They spurred their horses right up to the gates, so that the French were forced to lock themselves within. They hurled their lances at the door. The attackers and defenders fought on the threshold, throwing spears and javelins and giving great blows. Both sides shed their blood, so that the door was reddened with it. The attackers were not able to break in and returned to their tents straightaway; all could be seen sitting together for dinner. But Simon of Montfort had given his troops in Muret the order to saddle up, to see if it was possible to take those outside by surprise.

Bishop Folquet blessed them all. William de la Barre deployed them. He formed them into three divisions, with all the banners in the front rank, and then they charged straight at the tents.

Everyone charged towards the tents, across the marshland, banners flying and pennants streaming. The plain shone with shields, helmets studded with beaten gold, mail and swords. The good king of Aragon, when he espied the attackers, gathered a small band of vassals and companions to stand against them. The men of Toulouse took to their heels, paying no heed to count or king. They suspected nothing until the French arrived, hurling themselves towards the place where the king had been recognized. He cried out: 'I am the king!'; but no one heard him. He was struck and badly wounded, so that his blood flowed on to the ground. Then he fell dead, stretched out. When the others saw this they knew all was lost. Of these unfortunate fighting men, it was miraculous if anyone escaped alive: the massacre among them lasted until they reached Rivel. All the people of Toulouse, high and low, ran together to the river Garonne. Those who were able to do so swam across it, but many did not make it. All their gear was left behind in the camp. For the current, which is rapid, carried them off and drowned them. So the news of this terrible event was spread, that so many men were dead and laid low. It was a most fearful massacre.

Siege of Toulouse, 1218

Simon of Montfort's successes increased tension in the Languedoc; and an attempt by Count Raymond and his supporters to reassert themselves in their territories resulted in Simon of Montfort laying siege to Toulouse. Here he was killed on 25 June 1218. An English poet, John of Garland, describes the battle.

Both sides attacked at once, blood-steeped weapons flew, and men fell, cut down by them. Stones were loosed from slings and arrows from bows. And the many wounds drove out men's souls like leaves. The men inside threw down hot lead and melted glass, striving to hurt by any means. Those outside were protected by every kind of device: shields, mantlets, battering rams and unconquerable siege-engines. As they came to the ditches, fighting

A siege in progress. The attackers mine the walls, using a wheeled mantlet to protect them from a rain of rocks and fiery substances thrown down by the defenders. Simon of Montfort was killed before Toulouse by just such a missile.

became fiercer, blood-drenched were the swords. Yet by the strength of Christ a way through was opened. Our men quickly threw their torches on the houses of Toulouse and retreated.

The women of the city ran out to douse the flames while the men dashed out against the enemy throng. Those Amazons, armed with shields against the flames, snatched at the fires with hooks and quenched them with water. Jabbing at the helmets with rods, they sliced through our men's breastplates with their tridents so the entrails ran freely out.

The cavalry cleared the plain, filling it with the bodies of those they felled: so the enemy fled. Those who had gone out earlier lay dead in the ditches or in the middle of the tracks. This river flowed with blood, red with slaughter on account of the Cross.

When Simon of Montfort pinned down the enemy to the walls, the battle grew fiercer. Simon had sent away his horse and stood puzzling out a way to enter the city with his forces, by a trick, perhaps. By chance, there was in the city a little petrary, one of many there. It was causing much trouble and women took turns to feed it stones, so that they might play a part in the fight. All women are like Eve in that they are eager to deal out harm: but the first Eve was more wicked! These machines pitched stones and rocks into the ditched area before the walls.

Ill fate guided the course of a rock which fell on Simon's helmet; and so there fell the Church's strongest champion. No lament followed, neither did the enemy rejoice at his end. His body was taken away by night, and thus God's soldier departed the scene.

The new Dominican Order

While the battles against the heretics raged, attempts to convert them by preaching continued, most notably by St Dominic and his new order of friars. The chronicler Jordan of Saxony traces the genesis of the Dominican Order.

In 1206 Pope Innocent III sent twelve Cistercian abbots to preach the true faith against the Albigensians. The archbishops, bishops and abbots held a council to find out the best way of accomplishing their mission. While the council was taking place, Diego, bishop of Osma in Castile, was journeying through Montpellier where the council was taking place. The prelates received him with honour and asked him to advise them since he was known to be holy, wise, prudent, just and eager to preserve the true faith. He began to enquire into the customs of the Albigensians and studied the methods by which they persuaded people to join their wicked religion by their preaching and the way they pretended to be holy. He compared how the heretics seemed with the grandeur of those whom the pope had sent, with their money, expensive horses and fine clothes ... The bishops asked Diego what he advised them to do. He told them to do as they saw him do and he straightaway sent his followers back to Osma with all his fine trappings and kept with him just a few clerks, including [his subprior] Dominic.

[Diego returned to Spain in 1207 leaving Dominic behind in the Languedoc.] Brother Dominic had only a church at Fanjeaux and a few other possessions. The revenue from these was all there was to support Dominic and his companions. Anything to spare they gave to the sisters at the convent of Prouille [which Dominic founded in 1207 for women converted from Catharism]. The Order of Preachers [the Dominicans] had not yet been constituted, though there had been some discussions about this. But Dominic was busy in his preaching and not concerned about details. Nor had the rule that Dominic and his brethren might not own any possessions been made.

When the time drew near for the bishops to journey to Rome for the Lateran Council of 1215, two men from Toulouse, well suited by character and intellect, offered themselves to Dominic. The first of these, Peter Seila, gave to Dominic and his companions the fine houses which he had formerly owned in Toulouse and from that time the brethren began to live in those houses at Toulouse. From this time onwards, all the brothers who were with him began to live the humble, ordered life of the religious.

Until the death of Simon of Montfort on 25 June 1218, Brother Dominic remained an industrious preacher of God's word. What great injuries he suffered from the heretics! Yet he despised their traps. When, once, they threatened him with death, he said: 'I am not worthy of the glory of martyrdom; I have not yet earned this death.' Those enemies of truth were astounded to hear him speak like this and laid no more snares to entrap him.

Simon of Montfort's son and successor, Amalric, was unable to make much headway against the heretics after 1218, particularly once Raymond VII of Toulouse, who was popular in the Midi, had succeeded his father as count of Toulouse in 1222. Eventually, in 1226, Louis VIII, king of France, swept down to the Languedoc at the head of a crusading army and took Avignon after a three-month siege, effectively reducing the east of the duchy of Toulouse. The campaign, here described by the noted 13th-century English historian Matthew Paris, ultimately ended with the Peace of Paris, sealed on 12 April 1229.

Late in 1225 and early in 1226, there was a general preaching in France by the papal legate, Romanus, cardinal deacon of St Angelo. Its intention was that all who could bear arms should take the cross against Raymond VII, count of Toulouse, and his people, all of whom were alleged to be infected with the contagion of heresy.

In June the crusaders reached Avignon, the first place in the count's territories. They proposed first to attack this town and then destroy all his lands along with the inhabitants. King Louis VIII and the legate asked for a passage through Avignon as a trick, saying that they came peacefully and asked only to march through the town to shorten the journey. But after discussion, the citizens refused to believe what the king and the legate said and replied that the demand to enter the city was a stratagem rather than to cut short the journey.

This reply made the king furious and he swore that he would not leave until he had taken the city. Siege-engines were suitably placed and King Louis gave the order for a fierce attack to be launched on the city. This therefore began. The king's forces used petraries, mining and slings, and tried whatever weapons they had to hand. The citizens of Avignon had never faced a siege before and they used everything in their power to resist the enemy which was unexpectedly attacking them. When the siege had been going on for a very long time, a great number of men had died from lack of food.

Before the French had arrived, Raymond VII of Toulouse, a man most experienced in battle, had moved all the elderly and the women and children quite a distance away, as well as the horses and pack-animals. To all these he had given a supply of food. The famine to which the besiegers were subjected not only destroyed men, it also affected the horses and baggage animals. The count we have often mentioned had had the meadows throughout the whole area ploughed up so there was no fodder for the baggage animals except what the French had brought with them.

The French were therefore compelled by need to leave their camps in search of victuals for themselves and fodder for the animals. As they went near the city walls, they were picked off in large numbers by the count and his men, who were hiding ready to ambush them. Indeed, during the siege the French were often in danger of death, both they and their animals, from the lethal missiles and the damaging stones from the citizens who were so earnestly defending themselves. Hunger affected them all but the poor were especially badly off without money to buy food.

In addition to the other hazards which ceaselessly assailed the besiegers, there arose from the corpses of the men and animals which lay scattered around, great clouds of fat, black flies. They got into the tents, pavilions and shelters, generating a horrible noise and infecting the food and drink. As the men were unable to drive the flies from the pots and cups, the flies inflicted sudden death on the French.

The king and especially the legate were overcome with confusion. If so great an expedition had to retreat without achieving its objective, the French and the Romans would be full of reproaches. The leaders of the army were worried because they thought that a longer delay would result in a proportionate number of deaths, so they urged everyone in the camp to renew their efforts to take the city. A large group of soldiers pressed over a bridge which crossed the Rhône and, either because of their weight or because the citizens had sabotaged it, the bridge collapsed and pitched about three thousand men into the swiftly flowing river. At this the citizens shouted exultantly and the French groaned in their increased confusion.

It was at this point that the citizens saw an opportunity: while the French were sitting at table eating and drinking, the citizens charged out in a mass and attacked an enemy which was not expecting such a thing. They killed up to two thousand Frenchmen and then retreated into the city unharmed. This upset King Louis VIII very much and he ordered that the corpses be thrown into the Rhône because they were starting to decompose and there was no cemetery near big enough to take them all. The people of Avignon also increased the fortifications between them and the French camp. With no other sort of punishment at their disposal, all that the legate and the choir of prelates could do was bind the count in anathemas, and the citizens and all the people of the region too.

Then Louis VIII, to escape the pestilence which raged fiercely in the camp, took himself off to a certain abbey which lay not far from the siege to wait until the city could be captured. There, Theobald, count of Champagne, came to see him, demanding that he should be allowed to go home according to the French custom, seeing that the siege had lasted longer than forty days. When the king refused him the leave he sought, the count answered that [according to his feudal rights] he was not bound to be on guard for more than forty days and did not wish to be there any longer. The king was enraged at this and said that if he went away, he would lay waste his land by fire. At this, the count, so rumour has it, procured some poison for the king to drink on account of his love for the queen with whom he was conducting a secret affair. The count did go away and the king became very ill. The poison worked its way into his vitals and brought him to

his last breath. There are those who say that it was not the poison which killed the king but dysentery. Louis VIII died on 8 November 1226.

Start of the Inquisition

The Albigensian Crusade did little to extirpate Catharism from the Midi. Far more effective was the Inquisition, set up by this letter of Gregory IX in 1233.

To Brother Robert of the Order of Preachers. We rejoice in the Lord for, a little while ago, we gave instructions to our brethren the prior of Besançon and Brother William and in our letters to you that you should take great care in finding out the true extent of that wicked heresy established in Burgundy. You are to perform the functions of prior over these men and are to go to La Charité in the diocese of Autun. It has a very bad reputation for that vice about which I have written. There propounding and preaching the teachings of Catholic and evangelical truth to the inhabitants of the town, you are to take care to warn them that they can return to Catholic unity only when vice of this sort is utterly abandoned.

When you have preached to them in this way many of them will take pains to tell you of the many different sorts of wickedness and error in which they have been deeply involved. Father will not spare son or wife, son father, wife children or husband, or any of their partners in this crime.

The wicked ministers of Satan have scattered their evil through the province of Bourges ... they have done their work by deceiving the shrewd and seducing the simple-minded. They seem to be pious but they completely deny all virtue. Their sermons are smoother than olive oil; but they are as sharp as javelins because their tails sting like the scorpion. They bite like the asp, like a snake, scattering their venom like a hornet.

So do not delay over these dangerous matters we have committed to your wise action ... to root out with the assistance of the local bishop the wickedness of heresy from the aforementioned town and its surrounding regions.

Continue to work assiduously against those who receive, support or defend those who are excommunicated. Lay sentences of interdict upon their lands and do whatever else you think is necessary ... If there are some who have forsworn their damnable heresy and desire to return to the unity of the Church, you may give them the benefit of absolution.

So that you can more freely carry out the office entrusted to you and your colleagues, we grant to all those

The Children's Crusade

Penitential movements of children were not unprecedented in the Middle Ages and, by the 13th century, the cult of the Innocents, the children of Bethlehem murdered on Herod's orders, was widespread. It brought a recognition that the youngest members of the Church, the children, personified the first martyrs of the faith.

Yet the Children's Crusade is in a category of its own, a protest against the institutionalization of the crusade which was blamed for the Christian downfall on the battlefield of Hattin (1187). The innocent children, ready to fulfil the challenge which God had hitherto denied to sinful knights, represented the sacrifices of a penitent society. It was believed they would be able, unarmed, to recapture Jerusalem from the hands of the infidel. Although the children's expedition never enjoyed the official blessing of the Church and was therefore technically not defined as a crusade, it is closely connected with the religious zeal of the times.

In the summer of 1212, groups of children, originally from France and Germany, took the initiative to liberate the holy places. Headed by Stephen of Cloues, one contingent departed from Vendôme and eventually reached Marseilles. Neither ecclesiastical nor secular authorities were concerned enough to disband them. The German group, led by Nicholas of Cologne, travelled along the Rhine, crossed the Alps and reached Genoa. Thousands of ten- to 18-year-old children were joined by other crusaders, notably members of the low clergy. 'Miracles', such as Stephen's vision of Christ who, disguised as a poor pilgrim, requested him to recover his sepulchre, encouraged the children's leaders to assume the functions of the clergy and to administer sacraments, which strengthened the Church's already hostile attitude towards them. However, large sectors of the population regarded the children as orphans, all of whose needs should be supplied.

Weakened by hunger, and suffering from their long journey, some of the German boys sailed from Pisa, to an unknown fate. A small group settled in Brindisi, but the majority, hopeless and frustrated, tried to make their way home. Worse still was the fate of the French children who were shipped by Marseilles merchants to Bougie in Algeria and Alexandria in Egypt. Two of the ships were lost, while the survivors were sold in the slave markets of North Africa.

who come to your preaching and that of your colleagues, freedom from twenty days' penance imposed on them.

Given at the Lateran, 19 April 1233

The Inquisition, operated by Dominican friars, tortured, interrogated and burned many heretics in the Midi, including, in 1234, 210 at Moissac. Gradually, the Cathar leaders fled to northern Italy, but rank and file communities continued to live in some isolated strongholds in the foothills of the Pyrenees. The most powerful was Montségur, which was besieged by a crusading army from 13 May 1243 until 14 March 1244. On its capitulation, several hundred heretics were massacred, only three escaping, as an eyewitness, Peter-Roger of Mirepoix, later testified.

When the heretics came out from the fortress of Montségur, which was handed over to the Church and the French Crown by force, Peter-Roger of Mirepoix held back within the fortress Amiel Aicart and his friend Hugh, they being heretics; and the night on which the other heretics were burnt, he concealed these heretics, and allowed them to escape. This was done so that the Church of the heretics might not lose its treasure, which was hidden in the forest; and the fugitives knew the place where it lay . . .

The Children's Crusade

In 1212 a gathering of children marched from France and Germany into Lombardy with the aim of going to Palestine. As the Annals of Marbach show, their journey ended tragically.

At that time there took place a pointless adventure involving children and stupid people who donned the sign of the cross without any idea of its significance. This they did, more because they had nothing better to do, than because they had any concern for the good of their souls. Youngsters of both sexes joined in, and not only the under-aged, but even adults, among whom

Soldiers besiege a town and massacre the inhabitants. The crusaders in the Languedoc often slaughtered both Cathars and Catholics, claiming that 'God would know his own' and preserve the innocent while leaving the guilty to be slain.

R.P.
MANVSCRIT

Explano sup̄ sept̄e hystorie. . . . .

Et corpora eorum in platea ciuita
ris magne proicientur. . . . . .

Et uicer eos ⁊ ocid; eos. ⁊ in
cet antxp̄e eos quos sedu
xit ⁊ ut ei credant. Occid;
at sc̄os qui confessi d̄m fuint. Sp̄u
lir̄ uero nunc in ecc̄lia uincit ⁊ q̄
euglio ⁊ legi credunt. Occidet aut̄e
eos qui xp̄o credunt ⁊ in peniten
tia uiuunt ⁊ sicut d̄ns in euangl̄io
air. Tradet uos in p̄ssura ⁊ occide
rir uos. Om̄nis enim qui ecc̄lie nō
sentir ⁊ duo testamenta occidit.

Duo
rum dixit unum corp9. aliquāto
corpora ut legis ⁊ euangl̄ij nume
rum seruaret ⁊ ecc̄lie unum cor
pus ostender. Corp9 non solum de
occisis ⁊ set ⁊ de uiuis dixit. Et d̄
at dixit p̄licetur ⁊ s̄pnetur ⁊ si
cut scp̄tum e. Tu uero odisti disci
plinam ⁊ pieasti sermones mōs
post te. In platers ciuitatis mag
ne pieentur ⁊ in medio ecc̄lie q̄

were unmarried girls and married women. Off they went with empty purses.

The whole of Germany was affected by this movement as well as parts of France and Burgundy. Their parents and friends were unable to restrain them from taking part in this march, so great was their determination. Things reached such a pitch that everywhere in towns and in the countryside people dropped their tools and gear and joined those who were passing by. It often happens that in the face of unusual events we are apt to be credulous. Thus many thought that this movement sprang not from foolishness but from piety and divine inspiration. Consequently they assisted them with funds and supplied them with food and other necessities.

Clerics and people of sense spoke out against what they judged was a useless and senseless action. In turn they were bitterly opposed by members of the laity who described the churchmen as unbelievers whose envy and avarice were a stronger motive for their hostility than a concern for truth and justice. But like all ventures which are undertaken without proper and prudent deliberation this one too ended in sorry failure. When this agglomeration of people reached parts of Italy they broke up and were scattered about towns and cities where many were abducted by the local populace and held as servants or slaves. Others are said to have reached the coast where they were tricked by seamen and ships' masters and then carried off to far-distant places.

Those that were left did in fact reach Rome and then learned that they could not make any further progress because they had no backing from any authority. Now at last it dawned on them that all their toil had been to no avail. For all that, they were not released from their vow of the cross, except children under the age of discretion and others who were nearly senile. Thus confused and deceived, they began their return home. Whereas, previously, they had been wont to pass from place to place in droves or in organized groups, always with exhortatory hymns, now they made their way back singly, in silence and hungry, objects of derision to everybody. Many maidens were raped, losing the flower of their virginity.

Another contemporary, the monk Aubrey of Trois-Fontaines, gives an account from a French standpoint and provides more details as to the fate which befell the children.

In 1212 a rather remarkable expedition took place: children from many different areas took part. The first to reach Paris came from the region around Vendôme. Then about thirty thousand of them journeyed to Marseilles to take ship for Saracen lands. But vagrants and other wicked men who had joined them so damaged the whole venture that only a very few of such a great crowd came home: some perished at sea and others were sold as slaves. Of those who did manage to escape, some promised Pope Innocent III that they would cross the sea as crusaders when they came of age.

The men who betrayed the children are said to have been Hugh Ferreus and William Porcus, merchants of Marseilles. As captains of the ships they ought to have conveyed the children across the sea at no cost as they had promised before God. They had filled seven large ships with them and when they were two days out – at the island of St Peter [off Sardinia] at the Rock called Recluse – a storm blew up and two ships were lost. All the children from those two ships were drowned and, so it is said, several years later Pope Gregory IX had a church built on the island, called it the New Innocents and endowed it with twelve prebends. In the church are the bodies of the children which the sea had cast up there and they are displayed incorrupt to pilgrims.

Those double-crossing sea-captains sailed the five remaining ships to Bougie and Alexandria and there sold all the children to Saracen noblemen and merchants. Caliph an-Nasir of Egypt bought four hundred captives for his own use, all of them clerics whom he wanted to keep separate from the others. Among them were eighty priests and he treated them more honourably than he usually did. This was the same caliph who had once studied at Paris disguised in clerical garb. While there he had learned many of our customs and had recently given up sacrificing camels' flesh.

In that same year in which the children were sold, at a gathering of Saracen chieftains at Baldach, eighteen children were slain in various ways, martyred because they were completely unwilling to give up the Christian faith. But the rest the Saracens carefully brought up as slaves.

One of the clerics we have mentioned who was a witness of all these events has reliably reported that, of those whom the caliph bought for his own use, not a single one apostasized from Christianity.

The final destination of many of the children who went on the Children's Crusade: an Arab slave market.

6

THE 13TH-CENTURY CRUSADES

The diversion of the Fourth Crusade to Constantinople in 1203–4 meant that very little help from the west reached the crusading settlements in the Holy Land during the early years of the 13th century.

At first sight the situation of the refounded kingdom of Jersualem appeared little short of desperate. Its Frankish inhabitants controlled only a narrow coastal strip of territory centred on the great port of Acre, its capital, with far fewer inland castles and estates than their 12th-century predecessors had held. Strategically they hardly seemed able to resist renewed Muslim attacks which threatened to drive them into the sea. They also lacked strong and effective leaders.

Since 1186 the royal family had produced no male heirs, and a succession of kings – Guy of Lusignan, Conrad of Montferrat, Henry of Champagne and Amalric of Lusignan – had ruled through their marriages to the royal princesses Sibylla and Isabella, sisters of Baldwin IV of Jerusalem. Amalric's death in 1205 was followed by an interregnum, until the crown passed in 1210 to John of Brienne, a new arrival from the west nominated by Philip II of France to marry Maria, Isabella's eldest surviving daughter. John in his turn left only a daughter, Isabella, who brought the kingdom to the Holy Roman Emperor Frederick II, ruler of Germany and Sicily, through a marriage contracted in 1225.

During this period, and especially during the rule of a baronial regent, John of Ibelin, between 1205 and 1210, the kingdom became steadily more oligarchic. The local aristocracy, under the leadership of the powerful

Louis IX of France
leaving Aigues-Mortes
and taking ship for
the Holy Land.

Ibelin family, worked through the royal court to limit royal power and impose collective decision-making. Although John of Brienne tolerated this, Frederick II found himself in open conflict with the baronial leaders when he came east to assert his authority in 1228–9. His Italian, German and local agents and their forces carried on the struggle, which escalated at times into civil war, until they were ejected from the kingdom by the native barons in 1243. The kingdom of Cyprus remained closely linked to the mainland and was inevitably drawn into the conflict. The northern territories of Tripoli and Antioch, under the single rule of Prince Bohemund IV after the death in 1201 of his father Bohumund III, were in dispute with the Cilician Armenian princes, and in no better condition. Further complications arose because of the continuing mutual rivalries of the Italian city states – Venice, Genoa and Pisa – and the great military Orders – the Templars, the Hospitallers and the Teutonic Knights – on which they depended for the ships and manpower no one else could provide. Although crusaders' strategic position was not inherently indefensible, it seemed their own internal divisions doomed them to disaster. The shocked reactions of a number of contemporaries, especially western crusaders, to the disagreements in the Holy Land show that they came close to sharing this bleak view. Internal divisions not only imperilled the practical success of the Christian forces, but also the supply of divine aid on which the whole crusading enterprise was thought ultimately to depend. This emerged all too clearly in the recriminations which followed final defeat in 1291.

Nevertheless, in the first half of the century, the crusaders retained nearly all the coastal cities and therefore, with the exception of Jerusalem itself, almost every major centre of Frankish settlement from the 12th century. Although they lacked the strategic buffer of inland estates stretching as far as the Jordan Valley, they were supplied from the fertile coastal plain and had the revenues generated by its exportable products, notably sugar. The transit trade passing through the crusader settlements in the early 13th century was probably greater and more valuable even than it had been in the 12th. Spices, dyestuffs and other luxuries of the east were increasingly sent overland to Muslim centres like Damascus, and then to Christian ports for shipment to western Europe, despite the costs involved. There were greater problems with the main alternative routes: the southern one through Egypt and Alexandria or the northern one through the Black Sea and Constantinople. The great lords of the Frankish east were able to sustain their military establishments from the revenues of trade, and frequently paid their knights in money rather than by granting them landed estates.

Furthermore, there was little sign of a determined Muslim offensive. One reason was that the Muslim rulers, like the Franks, profited from good mutual trade relations. A second lay in the antagonisms between Saladin's relatives and descendants, the members of the Ayubbid family, who took over different parts of his empire after his death in 1193. Although they maintained the rhetoric of holy war, none of them was secure enough to commit his forces to a prolonged campaign against the Franks, with the extra hazard of provoking a new crusade from the west. And although Muslim princes sometimes combined to ward off a common threat, as when Syrian troops went to the aid of Egypt after the fall of Damietta during the Fifth Crusade in 1219, these pacts never lasted long. The crusaders in the east were therefore involved in prolonged periods of phoney war, making truces with at least some of their Muslim neighbours in 1204 (for six years), 1212 (for five years) and 1221 (for eight years).

The Holy Roman Emperor, Frederick II's 10-year truce with Sultan al-Kamil, concluded in 1229, fended off the Muslim threat while the kingdom of Jerusalem, riven by the internal divisions he had helped to create, was at its most vulnerable.

The fragile balance of power in the Muslim world also explains al-Kamil's willingness to return Jerusalem to Christian hands in 1229, just as he had previously offered great concessions to save Damietta in 1218–20.

This period bred a false complacency among Franks in the Holy Land: a sense that the Muslim threat was never as serious as it seemed and that some kind of diplomatic deal could always be arranged with them. That attitude persisted , in some ways, until the end of the century, even though the Mongol invasions of the 1250s disrupted the profitable trade routes, destroyed the balance of power in the Muslim world and led to the rise of the militant Mamluk sultans in Egypt.

Western crusaders had no real role to play during this period. Small groups came and went, like pilgrims, without changing the political situation. The large armies, in 1218 and 1248, made Egypt their objective in the hope of conquering new territory or extorting major concessions by posing a threat to the centre of Ayubbid power. Small or medium-sized forces, like those of Frederick II in 1228–9, Theobald of Champagne and Richard of Cornwall in 1239–41, or Edward of England in 1271–2, disrupted truces and initiated conflicts, but with little chance of success except in making small, local gains. It was generally hoped that they would undertake limited campaigns, usually as a prologue to another round of diplomacy, and employ their resources on useful works like strengthening fortifications. These tactics provided ample scope for disagreement, and for disillusion to set in among idealistic crusaders newly arrived from the west. Such tensions were not new in the 13th century, but they were getting more serious.

The whole aspect of crusading was different when seen from the west. Although the Holy Land was unique in its prestige and drawing power, it was not the only goal. The Fourth Crusade had opened up new prospects of conquest and settlement in the Latin empire of Constantinople, even though the Byzantines had established a government in exile, took back all of Asia Minor by 1235, and captured Constantinople itself in 1261. In southern Greece the principality of Achaea was a flourishing and prosperous state with a strong chivalrous tradition, and drew many knights from the west. Spain and the Baltic were other major theatres.

At the centre of Christendom, popes supervised the whole range of crusading enterprises, with enhanced powers to initiate or validate expeditions by granting a widening range of spiritual benefits to participants, and by protecting the crusaders' property and interests while they were away. They could tax, or attempt to tax, clergy throughout Europe, to subsidize expeditions.

Nevertheless, there is little sign of overall planning: in the late 1230s the papal court was apparently undecided over whether Jerusalem or Constantinople had most need of the forces mustering for a new crusade.

Since Spanish crusades now appealed predominantly to Spaniards, and Baltic crusades to Germans and Scandinavians, they were not usually thought of as endangering support for the Holy Land. Successive popes allowed them to be preached repeatedly, even continuously.

'Political' crusades were launched by popes from the 1240s onwards to secure their power in Italy and set up a client kingdom in Sicily, but diverted resources away from the east and weakened papal prestige because of the unpopular crusading taxes that were imposed to finance them. In the 1270s, grandiose schemes to put Charles of Anjou, king of Sicily, at the head of a Medi-terranean empire including Frankish Greece and the kingdom of Jerusalem came to nothing.

In practice, little was done to strengthen the Holy Land to resist the encroaching power of Baybars, sultan of Egypt from 1261, and his successors.

A wealth and variety of crusading chronicles were produced during these troubles, even if by no single writer of the stature of William of Tyre in the 12th century. An important development, from the Fourth Crusade onwards, was the appearance of histories and memoirs in French, the language of the secular aristocracy, rather than in Latin. These accounts are closer to the lifestyle and attitudes of the knights who actually fought in the crusades.

Good examples include John of Joinville's praise for King Louis IX's knightly qualities during his Egyptian campaign in 1249–50, and Philip of Novara's defence of the courtesy and chivalry shown by his lord John of Ibelin in his dealings with the Holy Roman Emperor Frederick II in 1228–9.

However, chroniclers were also also influenced by theorists and preachers, from popes downwards. Louis IX's attempt to negotiate with the Mongols, and Joinville's interest in them, reflected contemporary debates about whether it was better to convert infidels or to attack them.

The Muslim chroniclers frequently copied material from one another, but also incorporated eyewitness accounts. Like their rulers and patrons, they had to balance the celebration of holy war, *jihad*, against the realities of local and regional interests. Ibn al-Athir (d. 1233) and Abu Shama (d. 1268) saw events from the perspective of Northern Syria. In the next generation, Ibn Wasil and Ibn Abd al-Zahir, who both died in the 1290s, served the Mamluk sultan Baybars and his descendants. Abu al-Fide (d. 1331) wrote in the next century, but had witnessed the fall of Tripoli and Acre, in 1289 and 1291, as a young man.

The most comprehensive crusading chronicles of the 13th century, in relation to the Holy Land, were the continuations of William of Tyre, written in French and covering the period to 1277. Compiled by a number of mostly anonymous authors, some in the east and some in the west, they describe the whole sweep of crusading to the Holy Land from the reconquest of Jerusalem by the Byzantine Emperor Heracles in AD 629 to their own day, and are known as the *Estoire d'Eracles*.

When the great men of Acre heard that John of Brienne was on his way from France, they armed three galleys and sent them to bring him in. John and the great men who were with him went aboard the galleys, made the journey and disembarked on the sea front at Acre, where everyone went out to meet him, mounted and on foot, all the clergy in procession, both Latin and Greek, and even the Jews with the Torah. They brought him into the town with great rejoicing and a loud noise of trumpets, pipes and drums. This was on a Wednesday, 13 September in the year 1210.

As soon as John of Brienne had landed and taken up residence in Acre Castle, he summoned all the knights and required them to agree to his marrying their lady, Queen Maria, heiress of the kingdom of Jerusalem. He married her next morning on 14 September in the church.

Leaving behind other knights to defend Acre, John of Brienne and Queen Maria went to Tyre. Their coronation took place there on a Sunday, 3 October 1210.

While King John and Queen Maria were at Tyre for their coronation, one of the sons of Melec el Adel known as Coradin – this was because his mother was a Kurd – arrived in force at Acre and found the troops outside the town. He harried them so that the Christians trembled; but they stood firm and suffered no loss. Coradin withdrew his men and went back to his own country.

On the third day after the coronation the king and queen and all the others left Tyre and returned to Acre.

The *Estoire d'Eracles*, an Old French continuation of William of Tyre's history, describes, above, how John of Brienne became king of Jerusalem. He now had to face the involved internal politics of the Latin kingdom, conducted against a background of successive conflicts and truces with Muslim neighbours.

The siege of Damietta, 1218

At the Lateran Council of 1215, Pope Innocent III stressed the urgent necessity of bringing help to the Holy Land. Egypt was then the key to the power of the Ayubid sultan, al-Adil, Saladin's brother and successor, who died that same year. This letter from James of Vitry, bishop of Acre, to Pope Honorius III, Innocent III's successor, describes the mustering of the army in Outremer in 1217, and its siege of the Egyptian port of Damietta on the Nile delta.

James, by divine mercy humble minister of the church of Acre, to Honorius, reverend lord and father in Christ, high pontiff by the grace of God – I kiss your feet in due and pious reverence.

You will know that in the year of our Lord 1217 the commanders were here at Acre; that is, Andrew II, king of Hungary, Hugh of Lusignan, king of Cyprus, Leopold VI, duke of Austria, John of Brienne, king of Jerusalem, the Templars and Hospitallers, the generals and their retinues, cavalry and infantry. Their multitude was beyond count, and, as those who were captives in the city of Acre tell us, there was no comparison between the Frankish and Egyptian armies either in arms or horse, or even in soldiery. Therefore, the crusaders laid their plans, and after a few days came almost to Damascus, laying waste to many farms and houses and destroying orchards and olive trees and all the fruit trees, and doing whatever harm they could to the Saracens, some of whom they led away captive as they withdrew. But, as you will know, we lost more of our own men in that same foray than we captured from the enemy.

When several days had passed, however, our leaders took counsel and went to Mount Tabor, whence, after making an assault without using any engines, they immediately withdrew. Indeed, it was said that if they had pressed their attack strongly they would easily have taken the fortress; but the cry of the whole populace is that a few men's bad faith was the obstacle to success, as much in this case as in what I have already related.

Then they marched a third time, against a fortress which is called Belfort and against Belinas, which is also known as Caesarea Philippi, where they suffered considerable loss of horses, cattle and men.

Fighting between the attacking Frankish army and defending Egyptian forces at Damietta in 1218.

The Kurds

The Kurds appear in the history of the crusades as warriors in the service of the princes of Syria, out of whose ranks came Saladin and the Ayubid dynasty, which he founded and which ruled Egypt and Syria from 1171 to 1250.

They were a people of the mountains north and north-east of Iraq, migrant shepherds and villagers, who controlled the routes from the winter-grazing on the plains of northern Iraq to the summer pastures on the plateaux of Anatolia and Iran. With the coming of Islam from the seventh century, they had been attracted into the service of Muslim rulers as cavalrymen, and when the 'Abbasid empire, centred in Baghdad, disintegrated in the tenth century, had begun to establish warrior principalities that reached their peak in the early 11th century. In mid-century, however, all of these succumbed to the Seldjuk invasion, and Kurdish dominions were considerably reduced.

The Kurds themselves came under Seldjuk overlords based in western Iran but especially at Mosul, the capital of northern Iraq. Imad ad-Din Zanghi, atabeg of Mosul (1127–46), invaded Kurdish territory in the course of his empire-building. Kurds in their familiar role as soldiers of fortune took service with him, and entered Syria in his armies. Among those who made their fortune were the brothers Ayub and Shirkuh, whose father Shadhi had emigrated from the city of Dwin on the Araxes north of Mount Ararat.

Under Zanghi's son Nur ad-Din (1146–74), Ayub became governor of Damascus, while Shirkuh conquered Egypt, where Ayub's son Saladin established the Ayubid dynasty. The Ayubids annexed the Syrian wing of the Zanghid empire; but although their dominions stretched to include some western Kurdish territory in the mountains of Anatolia, and Kurds were a prominent minority in their armies, their regime was neither national nor nationalist. It belonged rather to the Seldjuk pattern of government based on the military supremacy of the Turks, the ethics of honour, and the championship of Islam.

The situation was changed yet again by the Mongol invasions of the 13th century. Mosul was incorporated into the Iranian empire of the (initially pagan) Mongol Ilkhans, and the Kurds, with so many other peoples, were relegated to provincial subjects.

All this took place between 1 November 1217 and 1 January 1218.

After the feast of the Epiphany, 6 January 1218, Andrew, king of Hungary, seized his opportunity and made his way home by land from Acre to Tripoli, from Tripoli to Antioch, and so at last to Constantinople, and thence finally to his own country. At the same time and in similar fashion, Hugh, king of Cyprus, withdrew, taking Bohemund IV, count of Tripoli, in order to give him his sister Melisende's hand in marriage; but not long afterwards, the king of Cyprus died at Tripoli, and the Saracens defeated the count of Tripoli, who was forced to make a truce with them. Thus the Christian army was diminished, and, immediately after the departure of the kings, it was decided to send a company to strengthen the fortifications of the city which is called Caesarea.

John of Brienne, king of Jerusalem, Leopold VI, duke of Austria, Ralph, patriarch of Jerusalem, the bishop of Acre and the Hospitallers made their way to Caesarea, along with all the rest of the army, except for the Templars, and stayed there until the fortress was strengthened and well fortified. But the Templars, who were unwilling to shroud themselves in a cloak of deception in order to avoid putting both themselves and their property entirely at the service of God and the Holy Land, did a noble thing on their own account, freely expending wealth so great [on building a new castle, Atlit], that it is a wonder whence they obtained it: for their fortress at Atlit now gave more trouble to the Saracens than the whole Christian army had done previously. And so in the course of time the whole army returned to Acre, except for that pious company which remained to help the Templars in their work; and from the middle of Lent, King John and Duke Leopold and the other nobles began to debate more and more often how they should proceed.

At this point, a certain schoolmaster named Oliver arrived; he was a cleric of the church of Cologne, who had preached the crusade on its behalf by the mandate of the pope, and had commissioned many boats and innumerable men for the crusade. These same boats had passed the winter in Spain, and now arrived at Acre.

One day, then, when all the commanders were in council, this schoolmaster urged them to do something on behalf of his followers, and, inspired by the Holy Spirit, they decided unanimously to go to Cairo.

So it came about that on 24 May 1218 they set out by sea from Acre, whence, by the favour of God, they arrived, after a fair passage, at Damietta, a very great city of the Egyptians which stands on the bank of the river Nile. There the whole Christian army immediately occupied an island in this same river, laying siege both to the city itself on the opposite bank and to a very strong and extremely well-fortified tower which stands in the middle of the Nile – which would have prevented our progress up the river completely, and more-over effectively obstructed our siege of the city – and with God's help, after much labour and toil and not without the loss of good men, we miraculously captured it. It was taken, with divine assistance, on 24 August 1218, and a hundred and thirteen men were slain, besides those who were drowned in the river attempting to escape. Therefore, the object and desire of all our army is, first, to cross the river and attack the sultan of Cairo, who has drawn up his vast army not far away on the opposite bank; secondly, to lay siege to the city itself with vigorous assaults; and thirdly, to attack forcefully their galleys and ships.

And so may the righteous hand of God cast down the enemies of the cross of Christ and inspire the faithful to his praises for ever. Amen.

The hardships of both sides during the siege are told by the German chronicler Oliver of Paderborn, the 'schoolmaster' from Cologne, secretary to Cardinal Pelagius, papal legate of Honorius III.

The suffering in Damietta from the long siege, from the sword, starvation and pestilence, was grievous beyond description, and the people's only hope lay in the truce which Sultan al-Kamil [who had succeeded al-Adil in August 1218] had promised to the townsmen. Famine was great and there was a lack of wholesome food, although there was an abundance of mouldy bread. The grain grown in this part of Egypt does not keep, because of the softness of the soil in which it is cultivated, whereas further inland, in the region of Cairo, it is preserved artificially for years. I have heard that one fig was sold in Damietta for eleven gold pieces. The people's sufferings from hunger made them susceptible to various kinds of diseases: among the other illnesses which afflicted them, it is said that at night they were struck by a kind of blindness, so that they could see nothing even with their eyes open.

Al-Kamil offers peace terms

Sultan al-Kamil deceived the poor wretches from day to day with empty promises, and persuaded them not to surrender. In the end they blockaded the gates on the inside, in case one of the townsmen should come to us and tell us how these days of suffering were afflicting them. But any who were able to escape through a postern-gate or by ropes suspended from the walls were swollen and starved, and provided clear

proof of the plight of their fellow townsmen. Supplies of bread and fodder were also diminishing in the Saracen army, which was drawn up against us outside the city.

Moreover, the Nile, which usually floods after the feast of St John the Baptist on 24 June right up to Holy Cross Day on 14 September, and waters the plain of Egypt, failed in this year to rise as far as the marker which the Egyptians are accustomed to set, but, as I understand, left a large area of the land dry, so that they could not plough or sow it at the proper time. So Sultan al-Kamil, fearing dearth and famine, but still desirous of retaining Damietta, offered, together with his brother al-Mu'azzam 'Isa, prince of Damascus, the fol-lowing terms to the Christians: he would return the Holy Cross, which had been captured in one of Saladin's victories, as well as the Holy City, and all the captives who could be found alive in the kingdoms of Cairo and Damascus; he would also pay for the repair of the walls of Jerusalem and, moreover, would restore the whole kingdom of Jerusalem except for Kerak in Transjordan and Montreal in the Idu-maean hills, for the retention of which he undertook to pay tribute as long as the treaty should last. These two places are in Arabia and contain seven very strong fortresses, through which Saracen merchants and pilgrims bound for or return-ing from Mecca are accustomed to pass; and whoever has firm control of them could, if he so desired, do grave damage to Jerusalem with its farmlands and vineyards.

John of Brienne, king of Jerusalem, Ranulf, earl of Chester, and the German captains persistently advised that these terms were to the advantage of Christendom and should be accepted; nor was this surprising, for they would have been content with the much less favourable terms which had been offered before, if they had not been opposed by sounder counsel.

But the papal legate Cardinal Pelagius, with Ralph, patri-arch of Jerusalem, the archbishops and bishops, the Tem-plars and Hospitallers, all the Italian captains and many other prudent men, effectively opposed the treaty, arguing reasonably that Damietta must be captured above all. The difference of opinion led to a quarrel, but this was soon set-tled for the sake of the common good.

Damietta fell in November 1219. After a long delay, and urged on by the papal legate, the army advanced up the Nile in the summer of 1221, but soon got into difficulties.

While this was taking place in Egypt, al-Ashraf, king of the Persian city of Jazira, al-Mu'azzam 'Isa, prince of Damascus, and the rulers of Hamah and Homs, met together

Templars and Hospitallers

The military Orders combined the two dearest ideals of medieval Christendom: chivalry and monasticism.

Born amidst the struggle for survival of the young crusader kingdom of Jerusalem, the Templars (1118) defended Christian pilgrims across the Holy Land. In its early stages the new Order was modest: knights lived on alms and shared their few horses. Baldwin II of Jerusalem allowed them to use a wing of his former palace in the Dome of the Rock. Known to the crusaders as the Temple of Solomon, it gave its name to the Order, which came to be known as the Poor Knights of Christ and the Temple of Solomon. Its monastic code, although rejecting immoderate abstinence, called for moral strength, chastity and integrity, and made the Templars the most reliable knights of Christ, ready to offer their lives in the holiest of wars: the crusade.

These aims were also shared by the Hospitallers or the Knights of St John in Jerusalem. Founded in the mid-11th century, they originally devoted themselves to the care of pilgrims and the sick who reached the Holy Land. Only later did they follow the example of the Templars and take on a military role, combining their previous commitment to welfare with fighting for the faith.

The Templars and Hospitallers became the Holy Land's only regular army and its most experienced fighting force. In the battle of Hattin (1187), both Orders recruited some 600 knights, about half of the Christian forces on the battlefield. Their military importance was acknowledged when they received special treatment from Saladin after the battle.

The papacy rewarded them generously for their commitment to defending pilgrims and Christian citadels: they were placed under papal protection, accorded property rights over any booty they won from the Muslims, and exempted from paying tithes on all territories taken from the infidel.

Templars and Hospitallers were eminently suitable for pious laymen, whose aggressive instincts they used against the infidel. Nobles and knights who were not ready to relinquish all material goods joined for specific periods or with a particular status which did not impose all monastic duties on them. Both Orders rapidly amassed great wealth – the Templars acted as bankers to both the French and English crowns – and built up large territories along the Christian frontier.

at Homs with a great multitude of cavalry which they had gathered in the east, so that the inhabitants of Antioch and Acre and the other coastal cities, whose fighting men were away on campaign, were struck with fear. The Muslim rulers debated at length whether they should go in person to reinforce the army in Egypt, or whether they should divide the Christian army by besieging one of their garrisons. They were afraid to go too far from their own borders; on the other hand, they were of the opinion that they could not easily capture a fortress of the Hospitallers or Templars in a short time.

At length, the advice of those who urged that they should go to Egypt prevailed, particularly as their brother Sultan al-Kamil frequently sent them messengers on swift camels begging them to come, adding that the Christians had taken up a position which could not be abandoned without danger.

Treaty forbidden by the pope

Alice, queen of Cyprus, wrote to the legate Cardinal Pelagius (who was at Damietta) about these forces and their plans, as did the Templars and Hospitallers to the heads of their Orders, urging them not to leave Damietta, or, if they had already left, to make sure that they were in a very secure position. But now, for our sins, all sound judgement departed from our leaders. John of Brienne, king of Jerusalem, considered the situation more deeply, and decided that it would be better to accept the terms which had been offered several times by the enemy, than to expose loyal troops, who had come such a long way, to the hazards of fortune. But Pope Honorius III prohibited us from making any treaty without the special mandate of the Church of Rome, and Emperor Frederick II forbade us by letters sealed with gold from making peace or truce with the Saracens.

Meanwhile, we strengthened the fort with a deep ditch. But the strength of our adversaries grew every day, while our company diminished and trickled away. The way lay open for those who, in growing cowardice, went out openly or secretly into the plain and deserted us.

Moreover, many ships which had sailed back to Damietta to bring supplies were not able to return: for on 18 August 1221, four of our galleys were captured or sunk in the river, adding to the enemy's boldness.

Unknown to us, Sultan al-Kamil had sailed some of his ships down the channel into the main stream of the river below our camp, closing the river to our ships so that they could sail neither up nor downstream. On either bank as far as Damietta he wisely placed a continuous series of watchmen with a host of armed men to watch day and night, with the result that our people were able neither to send messages nor to receive them.

From the day on which we lost control of the river, our counsellors met frequently to discuss whether it would be more expedient to stay in the camp and await the galleys which had been promised by the emperor, Frederick II, or to make a sortie at whatever cost, in view of the shortage of supplies. The majority was in favour of a sortie, which was rather dangerous because of the approach of the enemy and because the flood-waters would certainly constitute an obstruction. But one from among the humbler ranks, who saw and heard these events and recorded them with unskilled but truthful pen [i.e. the author himself], gave it as his opinion that we should await reinforcements within our fortifications, with the sick and infirm whom neither ships nor animals would suffice to carry, since our supplies would still last, if carefully rationed, for twenty days. This advice was not, however, accepted, and it was decided instead to make a sortie by night. In this, the opinion of the bishop of Passau and of the Bavarians prevailed.

The Franks' disastrous sortie, 1221

So, on 26 August 1221 in the first watch of the night, while the tents were being pulled down, the men, wilfully ignoring the dictates of reason, first set fire to the shelters, while others, almost eagerly, betrayed our flight to the enemy and invited the Egyptians, who had just now composed themselves for sleep, to pursue us. At the same time, the Nile was in full flood and had filled the plain with more turbulent water than usual. Moreover, the kings, who were approaching through the desert, had made camp for the night beside the river Tanis at Symonis, where a bridge had been built.

The Nile at Damietta; a strategic port at the head of the Nile delta and a goal for 13th-century crusaders.

Our disastrous situation was exacerbated by the fact that the men were mostly drunk that night with wine which could not be taken away on account of its quantity, and had therefore been offered free of charge and guzzled heedlessly; they were now left behind asleep in the camp or lay in the road and could not be roused, and were for the most part slaughtered or captured and so lost to us. Others plunged into the flood-waters in the darkness of the night and were left struggling helplessly in the deep mud. Still others fell upon the boats, and weighed them down so much that they sank. On the same night we lost the camels and mules bearing burdens of silver vessels, clothes and tents and, more injuriously, arrows for our defence. The Templars led the rearguard, in the greatest peril, keeping well together with their weapons held in readiness to protect those who were marching ahead of them. But the men in front headed off in different directions and wandered through the dark night like stray sheep.

The Egyptians had become aware of our flight on seeing the fire and smoke, and swiftly pursued us, soon overtaking us and inflicting more injury on the Christians than I am able to relate.

Nor had those who sailed down the channel in the boats avoided peril and injury. Cardinal Pelagius's ship, carrying many of the sick and the food supplies, was as well equipped as a fortress with armed men and archers, and manfully protected the galleys which naturally kept close to it. But speeding on too rapidly, perhaps because of the strength of the current, it dangerously outdistanced the land army and could not provide food for us when we required it. Moreover, one of our boats, full of German soldiers under Louis, duke of Bavaria, became separated from the legate's ship, and was surrounded on all sides by enemy galleys: despite sinking one of them in the deep water and defending herself for a long time, she was fired and perished with all her crew. A boat of Pelagius's, carrying many material goods, was taken, and a small galley of the Templars', in which were fifty crossbows and other arms, was also lost to us.

Why do I waste time enumerating all the losses which we sustained? 'As for that night, let darkness seize upon it; let it not be joined unto the days of the year; let it not come into the number of the months. Lo, let that night be solitary, let no joyful voice come therein' [Job 3.6–7]. At the beginning of that night, Sultan al-Kamil had sent messengers in haste to order the cutting of the dike which that race calls '*calig*', and over which we would have to pass. That was a memorable night for the Egyptians – and for us.

And so, on 30 August 1221, the adversity of our circumstances forced us to make a lamentable peace, and so that we might have our fill of bread we surrendered to the Egyptians, we who had been so humiliated in this hostile land not by the bow or the sword but by flood and famine.

Muslims recover Damietta, 1221

The contemporary historian Ibn al-Athir of Mosul gives a Muslim view of the rescue of Damietta from the crusaders.

When it became obvious to the crusaders in the citadel and in their camp outside the walls of Damietta that they had been surrounded on all sides, that their supplies might be cut off at any time, and that fate was staring at them with bared teeth, their hearts became humbled, their cross-shaped standards began to droop and the devil, who had been spurring them on, abandoned them. They started to parley with Sultan al-Kamil and his brother al-Ashraf, seeking a truce by which they could hand over Damietta without compensation.

As messages were being exchanged, there approached on 30 August 1221 a great army from the direction of Damietta, accompanied by a thick cloud of dust and an almighty uproar. At first the Muslims thought that reinforcements had arrived for the Franks, and feelings of fear arose among them. However, it was al-Mu'azzam 'Isa, governor of Damascus, who had finally reached them. This strengthened the hearts of the Muslims while increasing the discouragement and despair of the Franks.

Peace was concluded on condition that Damietta be surrendered, and the terms came into effect on 6 September 1221. The Frankish kings, their counts and bishops were transferred to the camp of al-Kamil and al-Ashraf as hostages, to guarantee the surrender of Damietta. Their number included John of Brienne, king of Jerusalem, Cardinal Pelagius, the legate of the pope of Rome, and others, twenty in all. They sent an order to their priests and monks in Damietta to surrender the place to the Muslims on 8 September 1221. It was a memorable day.

It seems strange to relate that no sooner had the Muslims taken possession of the town than reinforcements arrived by sea for the Franks. Had they preceded the Muslims' entry into Damietta, the Christians would certainly have refused to surrender it. However, the Muslims preceded their arrival so that God might accomplish that which had been decreed. Only a few of its population remained there. They were scattered as if by the east wind, some of them leaving of their own choice, some dying, and some being taken by the Franks.

When at last the Muslims entered the town, they saw that the Franks had greatly strengthened its fortifications, making it virtually impregnable. But God – may he be praised and exalted – restored justice, returning it to its rightful guardians, and he gave the Muslims a victory they had not expected. The height of their hopes had been to regain Damietta by handing back to the Franks the towns which had been captured from them in Syria; but God granted them the return of Damietta, while those towns which were now under their control remained as before. God be praised and thanked for having bestowed on Islam and on the Muslims the defeat of this enemy.

Frederick II and his crusade, 1228

In 1222 John of Brienne, king of Jerusalem, travelled to the west to negotiate the marriage of his daughter and heiress Isabella to the Holy Roman Emperor Frederick II. The *Estoire d'Eracles* describes the momentous wedding and its outcome.

In 1222, John of Brienne, king of Jerusalem, made the kingdom as secure as he could, considering its poverty, and appointed the constable, Odo of Montbéliard, as regent in his place. Then he went aboard the galleys together with the legate Cardinal Pelagius and the master of the Hospital, Brother Guerin Montaigu. Brother Peter Montaigu, master of the Templars, refused to go, but sent an excellent man in his place, a brother called William Cadel.

They reached Apulia and landed at the port of Brindisi. The

Emperor Frederick II sent to meet them and did them much honour, supplied them more than adequately with horses, and paid their expenses lavishly as far as Rome, where he himself went, taking them with him. Once in Rome, they discussed the question of the land of Syria from many points of view. Among other matters it was agreed that the emperor should marry Isabella, daughter of King John, who was heiress and lady of the kingdom of Jerusalem. John of Brienne

The wedding of Holy Roman Emperor Frederick II to Isabella, daughter of the king of Jerusalem, in 1225. Frederick neglected his wife in favour of his harem at Palermo.

promised on oath to give her to Frederick in four years' time, when she would be old enough, and the emperor promised that he would take her, and that within two years of his marrying her he would cross the sea and go on crusade to Syria; if he did not, let him be excommunicated.

When these matters were thus settled, King John crossed the mountains and went into France, where he was greeted with honour and joy. And when he reached King Philip II, at Paris, he was given a most honourable reception. King Philip was delighted to see him, but he blamed and rebuked John severely for arranging his daughter's marriage without informing or consulting him.

In November 1225 Emperor Frederick II and John of Brienne, king of Jerusalem went to the neighbourhood of

Brindisi to await Isabella's arrival and stayed at a castle called Oria. As soon as they heard that Queen Isabella had come, they went to Brindisi. The emperor lost no time; on 9 November he married the queen in the archiepiscopal church, and they received the blessing. But the very day of the wedding the emperor spoke his mind to King John and demanded that he invest him with the kingdom of Jerusalem and with all the rights belonging to his wife. When King John heard that, he was astonished, for Hermann of Salza, master of the Teutonic Knights, who had been anxious to arrange this marriage, had given him to understand that the emperor would let him hold the kingdom of Jerusalem during his lifetime. But when King John saw how matters stood, there was nothing else he could do, and he invested the emperor with the kingdom of Jerusalem and with all his daughter's rights.

Next morning, 10 November, the emperor took his wife and went as far as Foggia, without letting King John know that he was going. The king felt utterly let down at this, but he hid his feelings and followed them, staying at St Laurence, a town near Foggia. From here he went to see his daughter the empress, and his son-in-law the emperor, who gave him an extremely cold welcome and at once began to utter threats. Frederick also spoke to the lord of Sidon and the other Syrian knights with King John, insisting that they do him homage, and so they did.

Frederick lands in Cyprus, 1228

Frederick had promised Pope Honorius that he would set out for the Holy Land in 1227, but political problems delayed his departure. Honorius's successor, Pope Gregory IX, excommunicated him; and it was while under the ban of the Church that Frederick arrived in the east. He landed first in Cyprus; his entanglements in its politics are explained by Philip of Novara, who supported the group which opposed the emperor.

On 28 June 1228 Emperor Frederick crossed the sea to go to Syria at the command of Pope Gregory IX, and landed first at the city of Limassol in the island of Cyprus. He brought with him seventy galleys, transports and other vessels, but a large part of his army and household and his master of horse and the horses were already at Acre. Amalric Barvais, a leading baron of Outremer, and his supporter Gavin of Chenichy, and a great number of their friends and followers, went aboard

Frederick II

Known as 'the wonder of the world' by his admirers and 'Antichrist' by his enemies, the Holy Roman Emperor Frederick II dominated and shocked his age. Thanks to his upbringing in Sicily and his enquiring mind, he had a greater knowledge of Islam (even to the point of speaking Arabic and keeping a harem) than any previous crusader; and he regained Jerusalem for the west – while excommunicate – and without bloodshed.

King of Sicily since 1198, Frederick took the cross in 1215 at his coronation as king of Germany. For the next 13 years he was too busy establishing his rule in Germany, Sicily and Lombardy – he had been crowned Holy Roman Emperor in 1220 – to go east. However, in 1225 when he married Isabella, daughter and heiress of John of Brienne, king of Jerusalem, he stepped up his preparations for a crusade, and left from Brindisi in September 1227, but was forced to return because of sickness. Pope Gregory IX, since the early stages of his pontificate Frederick's bitter enemy, excommunicated and denounced him, but in 1228, still under the ban, the emperor left for Palestine.

In Cyprus, *en route* to the east, and in Palestine, Frederick quarrelled with the leading baronial family, the Ibelins, who had been embezzling revenues on Cyprus. However, even they hoped he would restore the kingdom of Jerusalem to the Franks – although Frederick's way of doing so surprised Christian and Muslim alike.

The sultan of Egypt, al-Kamil, had intended to use Frederick as a counterweight to his brother and rival, al-Mu'azzam 'Isa, king of Damascus, and was prepared to cede him Jerusalem in return, but when Frederick reached Palestine, al-Mu'azzam was dead and so the sultan had little need of him. None the less, Frederick deftly forced al-Kamil to surrender Jerusalem (except for the mosques of the Temple Mount), Bethlehem and Nazareth, and to agree to a 10-year truce.

On 17 March 1229 Frederick reached Jerusalem where, disregarding his excommunication, he entered the Holy Sepulchre and announced that he had come to fulfil his coronation vows; contrary to common opinion, he did not crown himself king of Jerusalem. He pleaded publicly for reconciliation with the pope, but that same year Gregory IX launched a holy war against the kingdom of Sicily, and Frederick was forced to hurry back home.

armed ships and set sail to meet the emperor off shore; as soon as they saw him they made accusations against John of Ibelin, lord of Beirut, *bailli* of the kingdom of Cyprus, who had not deserved this from them. They did the worst they could for him and his heirs and his whole kin, and gave the emperor to understand, according to what is reported, that if he were himself to take Cyprus, then all his household's needs in Syria could be supplied from Cyprus, and in addition Cyprus could provide him with and maintain a thousand knights.

The emperor gave them a hearty welcome and made liberal promises, saying he would certainly put his trust in them; they were delighted, and came ashore with him in Cyprus. None the less the emperor sent a very courteous letter to John of Ibelin, lord of Beirut, who was in Nicosia, requesting and begging his beloved uncle to come and talk to him and to bring him the young king of Cyprus, Henry I of Lusignan, and his three children and all his friends.

The emperor's envoy was received with great honour at Nicosia and his arrival splendidly celebrated. John of Ibelin summoned his friends and asked their advice both for Henry the young king and for himself, and with one voice they all cried out that neither he nor his children should put themselves in the emperor's reach, nor take their lord the king to him, for the emperor's evil deeds were too well known; many a time he had said and sent fair words but his actions had been foul and terrible. They advised him therefore to find some way to protect himself.

John of Ibelin replied to this counsel saying that they were advising him in loyalty and love, but that he would rather be captured or killed and suffer what God had ordained than to allow anyone to say that he or his kinsmen or any of the men this side of the sea had checked or turned aside the service of God or the conquest of the kingdom of Jerusalem and Cyprus; for he did not wish to do wrong to our Lord.

Winter was approaching and Emperor Frederick II had had news from his own country that Pope Gregory IX and John of Brienne were making war on him in Apulia. This made him very anxious, and he hurried to get to Syria and arrange some kind of truce with the Saracens, so as to return to his own land quickly. For this reason he made peace proposals to John of Ibelin, and discussions were held by clergy and others until agreement was reached.

In the end, the emperor and all his barons promised John of Ibelin on oath that they would keep peace with him and would in no way reduce his or his supporters' strength, except by the decision of the courts of Jerusalem and Cyprus.

A portrait of Holy Roman Emperor Frederick II from his treatise on falconry, *De arte venandi cum avibus*, which typified his many-sided talents.

John of Ibelin and his men gave their word on oath to return the castle of St Hilarion [Dieu d'Amour] to the control of Henry I, the young king of Cyprus; to accompany the emperor and serve him at their own expense as long as he was in Syria; and not to retaliate against him or his party because of any past events.

Emperor Frederick and his forces went immediately to Famagusta; his fleet came there from Limassol and they took ship, leaving Famagusta on 2 September 1228 at nightfall. That same night, the old prince of Antioch, Bohemund IV, left there and fled in a galley and landed at one of his own castles, called Nephin. There he thanked God that he had escaped from the emperor, for he had arrived in Cyprus after the lord of Beirut had made his peace, and the emperor had commanded the prince to order all his vassals of Antioch and Tripoli to do him homage as the Cypriots had done. The prince then counted himself dead and disinherited, so he pretended to be ill and unable to speak, only shrieking terribly, 'Ah, ah, ah!' He kept this up until the emperor went away, as you have heard, but as soon as he reached Nephin he regained his health.

Frederick recovers Jerusalem, 1229

Ibn al-Athir describes Frederick's negotiations with the sultan of Egypt, al-Kamil, and his recovery of Jerusalem by treaty – an event which shocked both sides equally.

On 18 February 1229 the Franks – may God curse them – under the terms of a treaty [made at Jaffa] took control of Jerusalem – may God return it swiftly to Islam. The reason for that was that Emperor Frederick, king of the Franks, had departed by sea from the Frankish lands and headed for the coast of Syria. His soldiers had preceded him, landing on the coast and laying waste the Muslim towns which surrounded them. At Tyre they were approached by a group of Muslims from the mountainous region surrounding the city, who submitted to them and joined forces with them.

The greed of the Franks had been strengthened by the death of al-Mu'azzam 'Isa, ruler of Damascus – may God have mercy on him. His successors, al-Ashraf and al-Kamil, arranged to meet; they exchanged numerous messages with Emperor Frederick II, king of the Franks – may God humiliate them. As a result of this exchange it was established that they would surrender to him Jerusalem and its dependencies but that the other towns like Hebron and Nablus, the Jordan Val-

ley and Malatiyah [a city in Mesopotamia], would remain within the hands of the Muslims. Thus only Jerusalem and its environs were to be handed over to the Franks. The walls of Jerusalem were in ruins, having been destroyed by al-Mu'azzam 'Isa. The Franks took possession of Jerusalem and, on 17 March 1229, Frederick II entered the city. The despair and pain the Muslims felt at this defied description. But neither force nor power exist except with God, the Most High, the Omnipotent. May God, the Most Generous, facilitate its conquest and its return to the Muslims. Amen!

Once in Jerusalem the emperor, although still excommunicate, wore his imperial crown, as the *Estoire d'Eracles* relates.

When the truce with al-Ashraf and al-Kamil had been made and sworn to, the emperor left the Cypriots at Jaffa but took all the others away with him to Jerusalem. Here, on 18 March 1229, he went into the church of the Holy Sepulchre and had a golden crown placed on the high altar of the choir; he went to it, picked it up and put it on his head. No priest or prelate or any cleric said or sang anything whatever; and that day he held high court in the house of the Hospital of St John.

After that Frederick pretended he was going to fortify the city, but he suddenly left the town without letting anyone know he was going except that at midnight he sent for the constable of the kingdom, Odo of Montbéliard, and ordered him to stay there, he and all the men of the kingdom, to defend the city. From there he went away to Acre. Then he sent orders to Odo to put a deputy in charge of the town and join him in Acre.

Frederick arrived back at Acre on 23 March; the city was seething with discontent as Philip of Novara recalls.

Emperor Frederick II was now at odds with all parties in Acre, and especially with the Templars. There were then some very valiant brothers of the Temple. Brother Peter Montaigu was very noble and brave. Brave too, and wise, was Hermann of Salza, the master of the Teutonic Knights. None of the men belonging to the kingdom were on good terms with the emperor. His behaviour was menacing in the extreme, and he kept his galleys armed, the oars rigged and ready, even though it was winter. Many people said that he meant to apprehend John of Ibelin, lord of Beirut, and his sons, and some of his friends, the master of the Templars and others as well, and send them away to Italy. Others said he was going to kill them at a conference he had had them summoned to, but that they were aware of this and went to it in such strength he did not dare to do it. However, he made his truce with the Saracens, such as they wanted it, and went to Jerusalem and then to Acre. John of Ibelin, lord of Beirut, never left him.

At Acre, the emperor gathered his forces and called together all the townspeople; there were many on his side. He addressed the people and told them what he wanted, uttering many complaints about the Templars. Then he laid siege to the Templars' headquarters at Acre.

I do not know how many days the siege lasted, but the emperor left it in a shameful way. He had his journey secretly prepared for, and at daybreak, on 1 May 1229, he went aboard a galley near the butchers' street. Thus it happened that the butchers and the very troublesome old women living in that street sped him and his party on their way and pelted them very unpleasantly with guts and offal. When John of Ibelin and Odo of Montbéliard heard what was happening, they ran there, and drove off and scolded the men and women who had been pelting him; then from dry land they called out to him on the galley, and commended him to God. The emperor replied almost inaudibly, whether well or ill I do not know, and said that he left as his deputies John, lord of Sidon, and Garnier l'Aleman. Thus the emperor left Acre, cursed, hated and reviled, and returned to Cyprus.

The crusade of Richard, earl of Cornwall, 1240

In 1239 Frederick II's treaty with al-Kamil expired, and in response to the preaching of a crusade by Pope Gregory IX, an army under Theobald IV, king of Navarre and count of Champagne, set out for the east. Theobald recovered Beaufort, Safed and Ascalon for the kingdom of Jerusalem. However, he treacherously broke a pact made with as-Salil Ismail, ruler of Damascus, and he retired home in 1240 under a cloud.

Shortly after Theobald's departure, Richard, earl of Cornwall, brother of King Henry III of England, arrived at Acre. His successes are recounted by the *Estoire d'Eracles*.

On 11 October 1240 there arrived at Acre Richard, earl of Cornwall, brother of King Henry III of England, bringing with him a fine company of knights and also great wealth. When he reached Acre, Richard stayed in the house of the Hospital of St John.

After he had been some time in Acre, and had armed and equipped himself and his men, he went to Jaffa; there he

The Emperor is a materialist

When the time came for the midday prayer and the muezzins' cry rang out, all his pages and valets rose, as well as his tutor, a Sicilian with whom he was reading [Aristotle's] *Logic* in all its chapters, and offered the canonic prayer, for they were all Muslims. The emperor Frederick, as these same custodians recall, had a red skin, and was bald and short-sighted. Had he been a slave he would not have been worth two hundred *dirham*. It was clear from what he said that he was a materialist and that his Christianity was simply a game to him. Al-Kamil had ordered the qadi of Nablus, Shams ad-Din, to tell the muezzins that during the emperor's stay in Jerusalem they were not to go up into their minarets and give the call to prayer in the sacred precinct. The qadi forgot to tell the muezzins, and so the muezzin 'Abd al-Karim mounted his minaret at dawn and began to recite the Koranic verses about the Christians, such as 'No son did God beget', referring to Jesus, son of Mary, and other such texts. In the morning

the qadi called 'Abd al-Karim to him and said: 'What have you done? The sultan's command was thus and thus.' He replied: 'You did not tell me; I am sorry.' The second night he did not give the call. The next morning the emperor summoned the qadi, who had come to Jerusalem as his personal adviser and had been responsible for handing the city over to him, and said: 'Qadi, where is the man who yesterday climbed the minaret and spoke these words?' The qadi told him of the sultan's orders. 'You did wrong, qadi; would you alter your rites and law and faith for my sake? If you were staying in my country, would I order the bells to be silenced for your sake? By God, do not do this; this is the first time that we have found fault in you!' Then he distributed a sum of money among the custodians and muezzins and pious men in the sanctuary; ten *dinar* to each. He spent only two nights in Jerusalem and then returned to Jaffa, for fear of the Templars, who wanted to kill him.

From Sibt Ibn al-Jawzi, *Mirat al Zaman*

stayed with the other Christians in that place. While he was there, the Templars put great pressure on him to return to the truce and agreements made with as-Salil Ismail, ruler of Damascus, and to confirm it on oath.

But the Hospitallers sent messages urging him, as they had done already at Acre, to uphold the truce made with the sultan of Egypt, al-Kamil, in 1229. Earl Richard refused to do either, but said that if the Christians in Jaffa wanted to go and take up quarters in Ascalon, he was prepared to fortify the castle there. The barons of the army, the Templars, the Hospitallers and the Teutonic Knights discussed this, and decided that it was consistent with the treaty they had with the sultan of Damascus, and with the well-being of Christendom. So they agreed to it, and when they had collected enough workmen and materials they left Jaffa and went to Ascalon. Once there, they settled in and began the work.

The castle was fortified in the same way as had been done by Richard I, king of England, the uncle of this Earl Richard who was now fortifying it. When this was done, Richard garrisoned the castle as well as he could, and then sent to Jerusalem for a knight called Walter Pennenpié, who was castellan of Jerusalem for the emperor, and held the city of Jerusalem in accordance with the 1229 truce made with the sultan of Egypt. As soon as Walter reached Ascalon, Earl Richard delivered the castle over to him, to be held for the emperor. He then returned to Acre on 3 May 1241, hired a ship and went home to his own country; the army went back to Jaffa. Wherever the Christian army went, the sultan of Damascus and his whole host were not far behind. After they had remained a considerable time at Jaffa, the pilgrims who had stayed behind wanted to return home; so they went to Acre and there hired their ships and went home to their own countries; all the other Christians then went back to Acre.

In his *Chronica Maiora*, Matthew Paris, the great English historian of the 13th century, gives an extract from a letter by Richard of Cornwall describing the problems he faced in the Holy Land.

'In the Holy Land, justice was banished; strife reigned in place of peace, division in place of unity and hatred in place of love. Truly there were many in the land who sowed the seeds of such strife and more who gathered the fruits which grew from them. I took some care to heal these dissensions; but the ways of peace have as yet made no impression, since the devotees of discord will not listen to her voice.

'For they win support with money, so long as it lasts; but when the time comes to avenge insults, their friends soon desert them, inventing specious excuses, since they care not at all for their comfort.

'Taking the opportunity afforded by this state of affairs, and by the fact that the enormous Frankish force, almost double the size of the Saracen army, was laid low by its own perverse behaviour, the enemies of the cross grew so impassioned that a few of them thought little or nothing of facing much greater numbers of our men. When we first arrived, and the noblemen who were expected to aid us had left, the task of restoring order to the country seemed a serious and difficult one. We hoped on our arrival to join with the other Christians in avenging the dishonour of the cross on its enemies with all our might, as was incumbent upon us because of our vow, by attacking their lands and strengthening them when occupied; but, hearing of our arrival fifteen days before we reached Acre, my lord the king of Navarre, Theobald IV, who was then the general and commander of the army, and Peter Mauclerc, count of Brittany, departed with a vast number of men. Before they left, in order to appear to have achieved something, they had made a treaty with an-Nasir, ruler of Transjordan; the terms were that he would return the prisoners captured at Gaza, whom he had in his custody or under his control, together with some lands as specified in the treaty. As security for these arrangements, he handed over his son and his brothers as hostages, fixing a time-limit of forty days for their completion. But before the terms were fulfilled, the king and the count departed, paying no heed to treaty or time-limit.'

When Earl Richard heard that the precious bones of the French nobles who were, as I said before, defeated and wretchedly slaughtered at Gaza through the wrath of God, were exposed unburied to the air (for beasts and birds had completely consumed the flesh), he was deeply moved to pity. Preparing carts and pack-horses, he hastened thither and had all the bones of those martyrs carefully collected and brought back to be buried with honour in the cemetery at Ascalon; and he provided for the maintenance of a priest to celebrate daily masses for the souls of the dead in perpetuity. When the people throughout the whole kingdom of France heard that the earl had performed such a pious task, among other charitable offices, he earned their undying gratitude and praise. For he had ransomed alive and liberated thirty-three imprisoned nobles, fifty knights and pilgrims of lower rank and many knights and servants of the Templars and Hospitallers, and afterwards had the bones of the dead honourably buried.

A 13th-century street in Acre, once occupied by crusaders. Acre was one of the last Christian strongholds in the Holy Land, finally falling to the Muslims in 1291.

Saint Louis, king of France

Louis IX's departure for the east in 1248 was the fulfilment of a personal vow, to serve the Christian faith; although Blanche of Castile, the king's mother and queen regent, would have preferred that he devote himself to his kingdom. Louis took every precaution to ensure peace in France while he was away on crusade, but his six-year absence and Blanche's death led to popular unrest and political upheavals.

Already a seasoned campaigner in wars against his vassals earlier in his reign, Louis prepared the expedition with great care, particularly the financing and provisioning of his army. His campaign followed the itinerary of the Fifth Crusade (1217–19), whose forces had captured Damietta and then marched unsuccessfully on Cairo. But he underestimated the difficulties of the terrain – each of the innumerable canals leading into the Nile delta had to be taken – and although he demanded a high level of discipline within the army, his campaign failed because of disobedience among the leaders of the attack on Mansourah. It would have been wiser to organize a retreat immediately; but Louis maintained his position, while the army weakened and the Egyptians cut off its supply routes.

Louis showed great courage and genuine concern for the welfare of his men, maintaining the medieval tradition of a leader consulting his chiefs of staff before each major engagement; but his refusal to be evacuated because he did not wish to abandon his men, in spite of ill health and the advice of Charles of Anjou, contributed to the final disaster.

His ascetic life-style gained him the respect of fighting men on both sides. The Franks of Outremer valued the fact that he did not abandon them after leaving Egypt, and his good humour and magnanimity also earned him the esteem of his Muslim foes. His prestige remained unaffected by the disastrous end of his campaign and his capture by the enemy.

John, lord of Joinville, one of his biographers, claimed that this crusade, which taught him the meaning of failure, gave a greater depth to his spiritual existence. After his return to France in 1254, he continued to lead the life-style of a penitent (mandatory for crusaders during a crusade) right up until his death in Tunis in 1270, on his second crusade. Louis was canonized by Pope Boniface VIII in 1297.

The Turks capture Jerusalem, 1244

The order reimposed by Richard did not long outlast his departure. The Frankish leaders' rapprochement with Damascus prompted as-Salih Ayub of Egypt to make an alliance with the violent nomadic Khwarazmian Turks, freebooting Kipchak tribesmen driven to Mesopotamia from central Asia by the Mongol conquests; it was they who in 1244 swept down on Jerusalem, leaving desolation in their wake, and finally ejected the crusaders. A letter from Robert, patriarch of Jerusalem, and other eastern leaders, quoted by Matthew Paris, describes these events.

Trusting in the help of as-Salih Ayub, sultan of Cairo, the Khwarazmians marched with their wives and families and many thousands of armed horsemen into the Holy Land, the Lord's inheritance, which the sultan had, it is said, bestowed upon them. Their arrival was so sudden that neither we nor our neighbours could have foreseen it, and so they met with no resistance as they were entering the province of Jerusalem, from the direction of Safed and Tiberias. But although we took care and trouble to restore the Holy Land, perturbed as it was by these new enemies, to its former peace and tranquillity, the Christian forces were not strong enough to expel these Khwarazmians, and they occupied the whole land from Latrun, which is near Jerusalem, as far as Gaza.

By common consent, together with the masters of the religious houses, that is the Orders of the Temple and the Hospital of St John, the master of the Teutonic Knights and the nobles of the kingdom, we summoned to the aid of the Christians as-Salil Ismail and al-Mansur Ibrahim, the sultans of Damascus and Homs, who were allied to the Christians by treaty and had special grievances against the Khwarazmians. As-Salil Ismail and al-Mansur Ibrahim were bound by treaty to defend the territory of the Christians against all other Saracens. They had promised and sworn faithfully to come to our aid, but their help was very long delayed, and while the Christians, who were very few in number, hesitated to stand alone against the heathen, these same Khwarazmians began to make frequent incursions into the city of Jerusalem, which was practically unfortified.

The Christians who were in the city feared the invaders' brutality, and more than six thousand of them assembled together to flee to the lands of the Christians. Leaving a few people behind in the city, they began their journey through the mountains with all their families and goods, relying on the treaty which they had made with an-Nasir, ruler of Trans-

The defenders of Jerusalem: crusading knights going out to defend the Holy City against the Muslims.

jordan, and with the Saracens of those mountains. But the Saracens set upon them and slew some of them cruelly with the sword, making pitiful captives of others and offering Christians of both sexes, and even nuns, for sale to the other Saracens. Some of them who escaped and made their way down to the plain of Ramleh were attacked and massacred by the Khwarazmians, so that of all that great host, scarcely three hundred survivors were left more or less alive.

At last, these heathens entered Jerusalem on 11 July 1244 and brutally disembowelled, before the Sepulchre itself, all the Christians who had stayed behind and withdrawn to the church of the Holy Sepulchre. And, decapitating the priests who were celebrating Mass at the altars, they proclaimed together: 'Here we pour out the blood of the Christian people, where they poured out wine in honour of their God, who they say was hanged here.'

Moreover, I have to relate with sorrow and sighing how they laid sacrilegious hands on the Sepulchre and defiled it in many ways, completely destroying the marble wall which surrounded it, and desecrated the mount of Calvary, where Christ was crucified, and the whole church, with all the foulness that was in them. They carried off the sculpted columns which were placed before the Lord's Sepulchre, taking them as a symbol of victory and an insult to the Christians, to the tomb of the wicked Mohammed. And violating the tombs of the blessed kings who were buried in the same church, they scattered their bones as an affront to the Christians. In their wickedness they exceeded all the Saracens, who, despite frequent occupations of the Christian lands, always maintained the holy places to the best of their ability.

Louis IX takes the cross, 1244

In the same year that Jerusalem fell, Louis IX, king of France, dedicated his life to the service of the cross. The story is told by his faithful friend and retainer, John, lord of Joinville, who in the early 14th century wrote a life of the saint-king.

In 1244 it happened by God's will that King Louis, who was then in Paris, was taken very seriously ill, and came at last so near to dying that one of the two ladies who were tending him wanted to draw the sheet over his face, maintaining that he was dead. But another lady, who was on the opposite side of his bed, would not allow it, and said she was sure his soul was still in his body.

As the king lay listening to the dispute between the two ladies our Lord worked within him, and quickly brought him back to such a state of health that although up till then he had not been able to utter a word he now recovered his speech. As soon as he was able to speak he asked for the cross to be given him; and this was promptly done. When the queen mother, Blanche of Castile, heard that the power of speech had come back to him she was as full of joy as it is possible to be. But on learning that he had taken the cross – which she heard from his own lips – she mourned as much as if she had seen him lying dead.

After the king had taken the cross his example was followed by his three brothers and many others.

Louis spent four years preparing for his crusade, which did not leave France until 1248. Joinville vividly describes his own arrangements.

During Easter, in the year of our Lord 1248, I summoned my men and vassals to Joinville. On that Easter Eve, while they were present, my first wife gave birth to our son John, lord of Ancerville. My brother, the lord of Vaucouleurs, and other rich nobles, took it in turn to organize banquets on the Monday, Tuesday, Wednesday and Thursday, so we spent the whole week feasting and dancing. On the Friday I spoke to them: 'My lords, I am leaving for the Holy Land, and know not whether I shall return, therefore if any of you bears a grievance towards me, let him speak, and I shall make reparation to him who asks anything from me or my people, as is my custom.' Then I left the meeting in order not to influence the proceedings and afterwards I agreed to their decisions without demur.

As I wished to leave without taking anything which did not belong to me, I mortgaged most of my lands and since my lady mother was still alive, I left for the Holy Land with less than a thousand pounds in rents to my own name. I departed with ten of my knights and was one of the three standard-bearers. I tell you this so you will understand that without the help of God, who never deserted me, it would have been very hard for me to withstand the hardships of the six long years I spent in the Holy Land.

As I was preparing to leave, John, lord of Apremont, sent a messenger to let me know that he was taking nine knights with him, and proposing that we should hire a ship together. So our people were sent ahead to hire a ship for us in Marseilles.

The abbot of Cheminon gave me my wallet and pilgrim's staff, and I also went to visit Blécourt and Saint-Urbain and other places where there were relics. Finally, I left Joinville on foot, bare-legged, wearing only a shirt, and did not dare turn back for a last look at my castle, lest my heart fail me at the thought of the two children I was leaving behind.

In August 1248, we boarded our ship at Marseilles. That day, the doors of the hold were wide open and all the horses we were taking to Outremer were led inside. Then the doors of the hold were securely closed, much as one caulks a barrel, because once out to sea the doors are below the waterline.

When the horses were all aboard the captain shouted to his men, 'Are you ready?' 'Yes, captain,' they replied. 'Then let the clerics and the priests come on board.' When they were on board the captain called out to them: 'Sing in God's name' and together they raised their voices and sang 'Veni Creator Spiritus'. Then the captain ordered the sailors to unfurl the sails, which they did.

Louis IX lands in Egypt, 1249

Arriving in Cyprus in September 1248, Louis made further preparations, and in May 1249 set off with his army for Damietta, where the now sick and aged Sultan as-Salih Ayub awaited them. Joinville describes how the French force landed in Egypt and fought its way ashore.

When I returned to my ship, I put the small boat in charge of one of my squires, Hugh of Vaucouleurs, whom I knighted there and then. We began to row towards the shore, until we came alongside a boat moored next to the great ship aboard which King Louis was. His people, realizing that we moved faster than they did, shouted for us to join the standard of Saint-Denis which was carried aboard another ship further up. I did not believe them, so I ordered a landing opposite a large Turkish force of at least six thousand mounted men. When they saw us land, they spurred their horses in our direction. Seeing this, we planted the points of our shields and the shafts of our lances firmly in the sand, so that the spear ends faced the enemy. When they realized they were in danger of being impaled, they turned tail and ran.

Baldwin of Reims came with a thousand mounted knights, and I, who had neither squire, knight or groom from my own country, was grateful to God who never ceased to come to my aid.

To our left, John of Ibelin, count of Jaffa, made a most impressive landing. His galley glided towards us resplendently decorated with his coat of arms, which are *or* with a

Louis IX of France taking the cross prior to his departure for the east as a crusader.

cross of *gules patée.* There were at least three hundred rowers; each of them carried a shield, also decorated with his coat of arms embossed in gold. They seemed to fly towards us, so fast did they row. At the same time the heavens thundered with the noise of shields clanging, the clash of cymbals, the booming of drums and the sound of the Saracen horns. As soon as the ship beached on to the sand, the count and his men leapt ashore, fully armed and gorgeously attired, and formed up alongside of us. I forgot to mention that when the count alighted he had his pavilion set up. Immediately the Saracens regrouped in front of us, spurring their horses, ready to charge, but when they saw us standing fast, they retreated.

To our right, roughly at the distance of a great crossbow shot, the ship carrying the standard of Saint-Denis also

The doves of war

Carrier pigeons were unknown in the crusaders' homelands but they learned of them from the Turks, who attached messages to the birds' tails – a method which may explain why birds were often brought down by falcons. In one such incident in 1099, a pigeon carrying a letter from Tripoli to Jerusalem fell prey to a falcon: the chronicler who describes the event quotes a weighty message, 164 words of extravagant invective.

Another bird used by the Muslims, this time during the siege of Tyre in 1111, carried a message under its wing, equally unsuccessfully. It crash-landed on a Turkish ship and its message allowed Baldwin I of Jerusalem to kidnap a shipload of enemy warriors.

In 1124 the inhabitants of Tyre, again under siege, were once more let down by a pigeon, bringing news of reinforcements, which fell into the Franks' camp. The crusaders substituted a note saying that the city should surrender as no help was forthcoming and sent the bird on its way. The disheartened citizens opened their gates.

By now, the Christians were also using pigeons. At about the same time, when they were besieged in Azaz, a pigeon smuggled out through enemy lines was sent back to the city with a promise of relief. It came down in the Turks' camp; they substituted a message recommending surrender but the garrison spotted the forgery.

In 1171 Nur ad-Din set up a pigeon post throughout Syria to provide the swiftest possible warning of attacks on the long frontier with the Franks. Officials guarded and maintained the birds and watchmen were posted on the borders, each with a pigeon from the next city to release when trouble flared. The message was passed from city to city until the news reached Nur ad-Din.

In 1190, during the crusaders' siege of Acre, the city was completely cut off except for pigeons and swimmers. The Arab historian Imad ad-Din al-Isfahani waxes lyrical about the birds' loyalty, courage and reliability. The swimmers who brought them out of the city seem to have been equally courageous, but more expendable.

The use of pigeons was commonplace during the next half-century. When Louis IX of France landed in Egypt in 1249, three messages were sent by pigeon post to the sultan, as-Salih Ayub of Egypt, but received no reply because he was ill.

landed. When King Louis learned that the standard had landed, he strode along the ship's deck and, ignoring the papal legate, jumped into the sea. In water up to his armpits, with his shield around his neck, his helmet on his head and holding his sword, he waded towards his people standing on the beach. When he reached dry land and saw the Saracens, he enquired who they were. On being told, he grasped his sword and, brandishing his shield, would have charged into them had his nobles not restrained him.

Three times the Saracens sent messages to Sultan as-Salih Ayub at Cairo by carrier pigeons, warning him that the king of France had landed. They never received an answer because the sultan was ill; so, thinking he was dead, they abandoned Damietta. King Louis then sent a knight to find out what was happening; when he returned, having visited all the sultan's palaces, the knight confirmed that Damietta had indeed been abandoned. So everyone sang 'Te Deum Laudamus' with ringing voices; after which we mounted our horses and rode to set up camp outside Damietta. The retreat of the Turks from Damietta had been accomplished very inefficiently: they had not cut down the bridge of boats, which would have been a severe setback for us; they did, however, burn down the storehouses where all the provisions and spices were kept, and thereby did us a great disservice. The consequences of this were similar to what would have ensued if (God forbid!) someone had set fire to the Petit-Pont in Paris.

The battle of Mansourah, 1250

In November 1249 the crusaders advanced on Mansourah, the town built by al-Kamil to celebrate his victory over the Fifth Crusade in 1221. The dénouement in 1250 was equally disastrous for both sides, one problem being in crossing the many branches of the river Nile. The French king nevertheless achieved some initial success, as Joinville relates.

In February 1250 King Louis IX sent for his barons and pleaded with them to give up some timber from their ships in order to build a causeway to lay across the river. He convinced them that there was no source of timber other than the boats used to ferry our luggage up the river. Each one gave what he could spare, and when the wooden causeway was completed it was estimated that at least ten thousand pounds' worth of wood had been used. But it was impossible to use the causeway to reach the Saracens because our men could not dam one side of the river up as fast as the enemy could set it free on their side.

Constable Imbert of Beaujeu informed the king that there was a Bedouin willing to show us a fording-place which could be crossed easily, in return for five hundred Byzantine gold bezants. The king agreed to pay the Bedouin, provided that he showed us the place first. This he refused to do, so he was paid immediately. The king decided that the duke of Burgundy and the nobles of Outremer should guard the camp, while he and his three brothers led an expedition to cross the ford the Bedouin had spoken of. This expedition was to take place on 8 February 1250.

On that day, as dawn was breaking, we all gathered at the ford, ready for the crossing. The horses began swimming until they found their footing in midstream; on the other side three hundred Saracens were waiting for us. There were a few men drowned during the crossing. We decided to go up-stream and found a dry spot to land without losing anyone else, thank God! When we reached the opposite bank the Turks fled.

After initial successes, part of the French army, led by the king's brother, Robert, count of Artois, was cut off and annihilated. Joinville himself spent most of the battle defending a strategic bridge, which spanned a stream near its junction with the river; this Louis had decided to hold.

Everyone said afterwards that all would have been lost on that day if the king had not been present. Two barons described to me how six Turks had seized the bridle of the king's horse and were about to take him prisoner, but he saved himself with great sweeps of his sword.

When our men saw how bravely Louis defended himself, they took heart, and several of them left the river-crossing and came to his aid.

A Muslim releasing caged pigeons. Carrier pigeons allowed the Saracens to communicate rapidly over long distances.

The battle of Mansourah in February 1250; a victory for Louis IX of France (wearing a crown in the picture). However, he was captured by the Saracens in April 1250, during the retreat from Mansourah. He was ransomed early in May, in return for 800,000 gold bezants and the port of Damietta. Despite this debacle, he returned to Europe with his prestige enormously enhanced by the Fifth Crusade.

Louis IX's expenditure for 1252 in the Holy Land

HOUSEHOLD	£	s	d
Costs of food	31,595	11	10
Clothes and furs for the king	104	12	9
Mantles for knights and clerics	312	10	0
Armour and clothes for the same	12,910	8	11
Gifts of robes and silver	771	10	0
Alms	1,515	3	9
Crossbowmen and sergeants-at-arms of the household	4,494	6	6
For 115 war-horses, pack-horses and mules bought for the household	1,916	18	11
TOTAL household costs of the king and queen	53,621	2	8

WAR AND SHIPPING	£	s	d
Pay of knights serving for wages	57,093	17	10
Gifts and subsidies promised to knights serving without wages	23,253	18	4
Mounted crossbowmen and sergeants	22,242	13	6
Replacements for 264 war-horses	6,789	17	0
Crossbowmen and sergeants on foot	29,575	0	6
Carpenters, war-engineers and other labourers	689	12	3
Common expenditure (including £41,366 14s 9d for labourers in several towns overseas and £967 13s 9d for the ransoming of captives)	66,793	19	6
Spent on shipping	5,725	15	0
TOTAL for war and shipping	212,164	13	11

Extracts from the royal accounts of Louis IX, king of France

When the Turks realized that we would not abandon the bridge, they positioned themselves between the stream and the river, as we had done coming downstream. We advanced on them, ready to charge if they attempted to rush the bridge and reach the king. In front of us stood two of the king's sergeants. The Turks ordered a large group of peasants to pelt these sergeants with clods of earth, but they were not able to reach us; however, we were covered with arrows meant for the sergeants.

Luckily I had found a tunic padded with tow belonging to a Saracen and, turning the split side towards me, used it as a shield to great effect. I received only five javelin wounds, but my horse was wounded in fifteen places.

The good count of Soissons, John, hard pressed as we were, managed to be humorous even then: 'Seneschal, let these dogs howl! By God's hat (this was his favourite oath) we shall remember this day when we are safely home in our ladies' company!'

Towards nightfall, as the sun was going down, the constable returned with the king's archers. They assembled in front of us and when the Saracens saw the crossbows being drawn, they fled.

Seeing this, the constable said: 'Seneschal, all is well. Go to the king and do not leave him until he has dismounted outside his pavilion.'

As we rode back I made Louis take his helmet off and lent him my steel cap, so that he could breathe the fresh air. Just then, Brother Henry of the Hospitallers came up to us, having crossed the river. He kissed the king's mailed hand, and the king asked for news of his brother, Robert, count of Artois. Brother Henry answered that he did indeed have news, and was certain that the count of Artois was in paradise at that very moment. 'Sire, be of good cheer, never before has it

Eunuchs

Eunuchs, called *khadim*, *khasi* or *tawashi* during the 11th to 13th centuries, and given pleasant names like Murjan (coral), Fayruz (turquoise), Kafur (camphor) and Mithqal (sequin), came from the same regions as other slaves – Ethiopia, Transoxania (modern Uzbekistan), eastern Europe, the western Sahara and elsewhere – and therefore from both black and white ethnic groups.

Since castration, as deforming a creation of Allah, was criticized within Muslim territory, the necessary operations on the boys were usually performed in their countries of origin. The Byzantines, who also made extensive use of eunuchs, were severely castigated for emasculating their own kind. Many died during the process, but the survivors' prices were much higher than those of normal slaves and they remained an extremely valuable commodity. Long term side-effects of the operation included emaciation, loose limbs, added height and often a distinct timbre of voice.

Their religious and military education differed little from that of other slaves, and they joined households as servants or guardians in the harems. Others were drafted into military regiments, often as special corps, as under the Fatimid caliphs and the sultans Nur ad-Din and Saladin.

Eunuchs were by no means necessarily effete: until the 13th century, as 'men of the sword' they could aspire to the highest military honours. Intensely loyal to their masters, and unlikely to found dynasties for obvious reasons, they were often appointed governors of provinces. Great generals and ministers among their ranks included Qaraqush (blackbird), the Turkish atabeg of Saladin.

With the rise of the Mamluk state after 1260, their status declined. Although Turkish-speaking eunuchs were still drafted into the army, there were restrictions on their military rank and they were more often entrusted with protecting young Mamluks or given administrative positions. African eunuchs were usually employed in royal harems, where they held positions of great influence. After retirement, eunuchs were given sinecures as guardians at Mecca and Medina or other revered sites. Some eunuchs were freed from slavery by their masters – considered one of the most pious of acts – after which some became extremely rich, running their own households and occasionally even marrying; many built magnificent mosques and tombs.

been given to a king of France to earn such honour as you have won this day. To do battle, you have swum across a river, you have dismayed and routed your enemies from the battlefield, captured their war-engines and tents, and there, victorious, you will rest tonight.' As the king answered that God should indeed be praised for the gifts he had bestowed on him that day, great tears fell down his face.

Louis's defeat and capture, 1250

In the end, however, the crusaders were defeated by the Mamluk Rukn ad-Din Baybars, who took over command of the Egyptian army on the death of the vizier Fakhr ad-Din. Abu al-Fida gives an Arab view of these events.

At dawn on 9 February 1250, they approached the Muslim lines, and launched a surprise attack on the Muslim camp outside Mansourah. Fakhr ad-Din had been taking a bath in Mansourah. Quickly he mounted his horse. A group of Franks came across him and killed him. Always happy in this world, he died a martyr. The Muslims together with the Turks then attacked the Franks, forcing them back on their tracks, the rout continuing for some time. As for Turan Shah, the new sultan of Egypt, he had left the castle of Kayfa, arriving in Damascus during Ramadan of that year. There he celebrated the 'Id al-Fitr feast [7 January 1250] before reaching Mansourah on Thursday 24 February.

The fighting grew more intense between the Muslims and the Franks, both on land and water, the Muslim ships descending on the Franks and capturing thirty-two of them, of which nine were galleys. Weakened by this engagement, the Franks sent word, asking for Jerusalem and part of the coast in return for their surrender of Damietta to the Muslims; but they received no answer.

As the Frankish forces continued to oppose the Muslims at Mansourah, their rations began to dwindle, all supplies from Damietta having ceased to arrive since the Muslims had cut off the route between their camp and Damietta. Unable therefore to maintain their position, the Franks decamped on the night of 7 April 1250, making for Damietta. The Muslims followed in hot pursuit. As dawn came, the Muslims had caught up the Franks, thrashing at them with their swords; only a few survived. Reports suggested that among the Franks the number of dead reached thirty thousand.

The French king, Louis IX, and his party of nobles, withdrew to a village and asked for mercy. They were granted safety by Muhsin, eunuch of the former Sultan as-

Salih Ayub, until they were arrested and taken to Mansourah. The king of France was put in irons and left in the house occupied by the chief secretary, Fakhr ad-Din ibn Luqman, under the charge of Sabih, eunuch of Sultan Turan Shah.

The historian Abu Shama, living in Damascus, describes how the news of the victory spread through the Muslim world.

On 20 April 1250 the cloak of the French king arrived in Damascus, having been sent by Sultan Turan Shah to his representative there, Emir Jamal al-Din Musa ibn Yaghmur, who wore it himself. I saw it on him. It was a deep scarlet lined with the fur of ermine, and on it was a gold buckle.

Our eminent and pious friend Najm al-Din Mohammed ibn Isra'il composed three short poems, each in praise of the sultan and the emir. The first one reads:

And as for France's mantle which
Came as a gift for the emirs' Lord,
[Once] white as paper in colour, it has
Been dyed with the blood from our swords.

The second is addressed to the emir:

Unique of this never-ending age,
Praise is permitted once excellence is attained.
May you ever, in glory and grandeur,
Wear the spoils of enemy kings.

The third was included by the emir at the head of a letter to Sultan Turan Shah:

Lord of all the kings of this age,
By God's victory you have realized his promise.
May our sovereign ever conquer the enemy's strongholds
And clothe his servants in the spoils of kings.

Louis IX, the wise king

While in captivity, Louis IX made arrangements for the surrender of Damietta. The Arab historian Ibn Wasil, who was in the service of Sultan Baybars, reveals that his captors were impressed with the king's wisdom.

Emir Husam ad-Din described a conversation he had had with King Louis IX. 'The king of France,' he said, 'was an unusually wise and intelligent man. During one of our conversations I asked him: "How did a man of your majesty's character, wisdom and good sense ever conceive the idea of embarking on a ship, riding the waves of this sea and journeying to a land so full of Muslims and warriors, assuming that you could conquer it and become its king?" Louis laughed, but said nothing. "In our land," I continued, "when a man voyages on the sea, exposing himself and his worldly goods to such risks, his witness is not accepted as evidence in any court of law." "Why not?" asked King Louis. "Because such behaviour implies to us that he is lacking in sense, and such a man is unfit to give evidence." Louis laughed and declared: "By God, whoever said that was right; whoever ruled thus was not in error."'

Louis IX's embassy to the Mongols

Louis was set free in exchange for the surrender of Damietta and a great ransom, paid by France. En route to the Holy Land, he had sent an embassy to the Mongols, as Joinville relates.

While Louis IX was in Cyprus, the king of the Mongols had sent envoys to him, with messages intimating that he would assist the king in reconquering the kingdom of Jerusalem. The king sent his own envoys, bearing gifts. One of his gifts was a tent of scarlet cloth, as a chapel, embroidered with motifs of the annunciation, the nativity, the baptism of Christ and the story of the passion; with the ascension and the coming of the Holy Spirit. He hoped that this gift would encourage the Mongols to join our faith. He also sent all that was necessary to celebrate Mass: chalices, books and two friars to chant the service.

Once they had arrived in Antioch, the envoys still had a year's journey on horseback, riding thirty miles a day, before reaching the great king of the Mongols, Goyuk Khan. The land they travelled through during this long journey was subject to the Mongols. They came across many cities which had been destroyed, and huge mounds of human bones.

When the great king of the Mongols received the messages and gifts from our king, he summoned several of the kings who were not under his domination, promising them safe conduct. The scarlet cloth chapel was pitched before their eyes, and he said to them: 'Sires, the king of France has bowed down to us, if you do not behave likewise, we will send him against you, that he may force you to do so.' Quite a few of them submitted to him, from fear of the king of France.

When our envoys returned, they were accompanied by envoys from the king of the Mongols carrying the following message: 'Peace is beneficial, because those who walk on four legs can graze in tranquillity, and those who labour on

The practice of ransom

Louis IX's captivity was surprisingly brief. Taken on 8 April 1250, apparently dying, he was released a month later on 6 May – and this despite being considered a formidable foe by the Muslims. Sultan Turan Shah and contemporary historians expressed great pride at his capture.

The ransom demanded by the sultan was an exorbitant one million bezants and, rather than buying his freedom with money – the proposed sum was enough to buy the release of all his companions as well as crusaders taken in previous battles – Louis proposed instead the surrender of Damietta. The sultan therefore reduced his demand to 800,000 bezants. The war treasure taken by Louis's army and stored in the nearby royal fleet was used to pay part of the ransom, and the king and his high-ranking companions were freed. Louis's brother, Alfonso, count of Poitiers, was held in captivity as surety for the remaining sum. The Muslims were slow to release the other men captured at Mansourah and Louis deferred his departure from the east for four years, until they were liberated in 1254.

The payment of ransoms had long been acceptable between the crusaders and their enemies. In 1119, when crusader prisoners taken at the Field of Blood were put to death by the victor, Il-Ghazi, in an excess of zeal, fellow-Muslim voices were raised in protest at the loss of the ransom money that might have been paid in exchange for their freedom. Normally negotiations started immediately. Bohemund, prince of Antioch, was released after three years in captivity (1100–3); and Baldwin II of Jerusalem and Jocelin of Courtenay were set free one year after their capture in 1123 on condition that they left hostages as surety for the unpaid portion of their ransom.

After the battle of Marj Ayun in 1179, Saladin released Baldwin of Râmes on the promise of a ransom of 10,000 bezants and the release of 1,000 Muslim prisoners, while the body of Odo of Saint-Amand, grand master of the Templars, was only returned to the knights after they had agreed to free one of their Muslim captives. Custom required that a vassal should sell his fief in order to pay his lord's ransom, and the religious Order of the Trinitarians, founded at the end of the 12th century in France, made its principal aim the collection from the Christian nations of the west of the ransoms required to free crusaders captured in Outremer.

The court of a Mongol king. Louis IX's attempts to woo the Mongols with gifts were replied to with polite threats.

two legs can till the ground which yields the harvest in tranquillity. We have sent to tell you this, because you will only have peace under our terms. Witness the example of those kings who rebelled against us (and he cited quite a few); in the end we forced them all to submit by the sword. We command you to send a yearly tribute of gold and silver if you wish to retain our goodwill. Otherwise we will destroy you and your people as we destroyed those we mentioned above.' As you can imagine, our king rued the day when he had sent his envoys to the great king of the Mongols.

The rise of Baybars, 1261–3

Meanwhile in the Holy Land, Baybars, sultan of Egypt from 1261, had won a great victory against the invading Tartars at the battle of Ain Jalud in 1260, and occupied most of Muslim Syria. This contemporary account by Ibn Abd al-Zahir describes his dealings with the declining crusader states, whose rulers he found perfidious and disunited.

In 1261, while Rukn ad-Din Baybars, Mamluk sultan of Egypt, was on his way to Syria, the count of Jaffa, John of Ibelin, sent him a messenger offering submission and carrying provisions. The sultan treated him with respect, issued him with a decree guaranteeing him authority over his territory and sent him back to Jaffa safely. When the news of

Mongols' way of life

The Tartars ate no bread, but only meat and milk. Their favourite meat was horseflesh which they first marinated in yeast and then let dry until it could be sliced like black bread. Their favourite and strongest beverage was mare's milk, to which they added herbs, and which they then left to ferment. The great king of the Tartars was also presented with the gift of a horse laden with flour. This horse had travelled for three months, and on his arrival the king of the Tartars gave the flour to the King's friars!

Many Christians follow the Greek Orthodox Church. When the Tartars want to wage war on the Saracens, they send these Christians against them; and when they have a grievance against the Christians, they send the Saracens. Many childless women go into battle with the men, and are paid according to their strength. The envoys also related that these men and women warriors ate together in the households of the rich men they serve, but that the men never dared to touch the women, because of the law laid down by their first king. The women who have children look after them, and prepare food for those going into battle.

The men carry raw meat placed between the saddle and the horse blanket. When the blood has been thoroughly drained from the meat, they eat it raw. What they cannot eat they keep in a leather bag, and when they are hungry they always choose the oldest meat first. I saw one of our prison guards doing this, he was one of the Khwarazmians who are the sultan of Persia's men. When he opened the bag, we would hold our noses, the stench was so unendurable.

From Joinville, *Histoire de Saint Louis*

Sultan Baybars of Egypt

Born in about 1228 into a nomadic Turkish tribe on the south Russian steppes, Baybars was captured by slavers in the Crimea and taken to Syria, where he was sold and trained as a mamluk, or slave soldier. Eventually, probably in 1247, he came into the possession of the Ayubid sultan of Egypt, as-Salih Ayub. In 1249, as deputy commander of the Mamluk regiment, he played a leading part in the Muslim defeat of the crusaders at Mansourah. In the turbulent decade that followed the death of as-Salih Ayub and the murder of as-Salih's son, Turan Shah, Baybars was prominent in the intrigues and civil strife that plagued Egypt and Syria. The Mamluk sultan Qutuz made him one of the commanders of the army which defeated the Mongols at Ain Jalut in Palestine on 3 September 1260, but in October Baybars assisted in the murder of Qutuz and replaced him as sultan of Egypt and Syria. The true founder of the Mamluk state, he relied on military victories to impress his subjects and political purges to intimidate them.

Baybars was stockily built, loud-mouthed and ferociously energetic. The Dominican friar William of Tripoli described him as austere, ruthless and secretive, and said he despised the Christians of his time for their weakness, and believed that they were failing to live up to the heroic standards of their ancestors.

In Syria, Baybars and the Mamluk army fought on two fronts. The main threat came from the Mongols, who launched repeated attacks on northern Syria from Iraq or from their vassal state, Cilician Armenia. But the crusader fortresses and ports on the narrow coastal strip extending from Jaffa in southern Palestine to Antioch in northern Syria also challenged Mamluk control of the hinterland. The storming of Antioch in 1268 was Baybars's greatest and most profitable triumph. He had planned to attack Tripoli in 1271, but the arrival of a small contingent of crusaders under Prince Edward of England (later Edward I) persuaded him to conclude a truce with its count.

Baybars died in 1277, probably from food poisoning, although there were rumours that he had inadvertently drunk poison he intended for someone else. One of Islam's greatest soldiers, and an able administrator, he never fully adapted to the ways of his subjects, remaining to the last a Turkish warrior.

the sultan's arrival in their lands had been definitely confirmed, the Franks sent large quantities of provisions and messengers to greet him.

When Baybars reached Damascus, a messenger arrived from Acre, requesting safe conduct for other messengers who were on their way from the various provinces. The sultan wrote to the governor of Banyas to give them permission. The leaders of the Franks came and sued for peace. But the sultan was not easily moved, and set down many conditions. When they refused he reprimanded them, treating them with contempt. His army had already set off to raid their territory towards Baalbek, and the Franks implored him to call it back.

A peace was agreed, allowing the Franks to hold the coastal strip from Tyre to Jaffa and to have free passage throughout Palestine. But the Franks soon broke their oath.

At the same time there was mounting inflation in Syria, owing to the large amount of goods imported from the Franks' territory. So a peace was agreed on the same terms that had existed up to the end of the reign of al-Nasir Saladin, ruler of Aleppo and Damascus, together with the release of all the prisoners taken since that time until the time of the truce. Messengers were then sent out to inform them of the terms of the treaty. John of Ibelin, count of Jaffa, and John of Ibelin, count of Beirut, also agreed to the terms of the truce as they had existed in al-Nasir Saladin's time. The roads became safe once again and imports increased.

The sultan began to gather the prisoners and send them to Nablus as laid down in the treaty. The Franks, on the other hand, were slow to reciprocate; when this had gone on for some time, the sultan decreed that his prisoners be moved to Damascus and put to work on constructions there. When the Franks complained, he replied: 'If you are willing to comply with the conditions of the treaty, then all well and good, but if not then we will have no alternative but to declare a state of jihad.'

In April 1263 Sultan Baybars summoned messengers from the various parties among the Franks and asked them, 'What do you intend to do now?' They replied, 'We shall adhere to the truce between us.' The sultan's answer was this: 'Why, then, did you not do this before we came here and spent sums so vast that had they flowed, they would have formed seas. We have not damaged your crops or anything else, yet you have prevented food and provisions reaching our troops. When we were in Damascus you sent us a copy of the oath which we swore, but when we sent you a copy you did not swear to it.

'We sent our ambassador to inform you of the prisoners' arrival but still you sent no one. Nor did you show any pity for those prisoners of your own faith who turned up at the doors of your houses, just so you would not be deprived of the labour of the Muslim prisoners you have. You also agreed to return the money you had taken from the merchants but then you changed your minds. We then sent ambassadors to Constantinople, and we wrote to you asking you to allow them to set sail, and you advised them to go to Cyprus. But there they were taken, put in chains and confined. It is reported now that one of them died.

'We, on the other hand, have always treated your ambassadors well. It has become customary that messengers and ambassadors should not be harmed, and that even in time of war they should be allowed to move around freely. If this happened against your wishes then it is a blemish on your honour. The ruler of Cyprus is of the same faith as yourselves, yet he besmirches your honour.'

The sultan went on, 'In the time of as-Salil Ismail, you received the towns of Safed and Shaqif, in return for which you agreed to help him against the late Sultan al-Malik as-Salih [ruler of Damascus, 1237]. The government you helped ended up in ruin, yet the sultan did not retaliate against you when he conquered their ·territory; on the contrary, he treated you well.

'In return for this you went and joined forces with the king of France, Louis IX, and came with him to Egypt.

'When have you ever kept any of your promises to Egypt, and when have you ever been successful in your attempts to help her? The kingdom of Syria and other places now belong to me, and I do not need your help. You will therefore return to the people of Islam all you have taken by these methods, and you will release all Muslim prisoners. I shall accept no other solution.'

When they heard this the Franks were greatly perturbed and said, 'We shall not break the truce and we beg the mercy of the sultan to continue the friendly relations it lays down. We shall also refrain from causing your deputies to complain and we shall release the prisoners.' Then the sultan said, 'You should have done all this before I set out in these wintry rains, and before the army arrived here.' At this the messengers departed.

The sultan gave orders that the Franks should not spend the night in the camp. He then ordered the demolition of the church of the Virgin in Nazareth, which is the most important place of worship for them. It is said that Christianity originated there. The sultan sent Emir Izz ad-Din Amir-Jamadar to Nazareth and he razed the church to the ground. Not one of the Franks dared to put a foot outside the gates of Acre, or to utter a single word.

The crusade of Edward of England, 1271–2

In 1271–2 Edward, eldest son of King Henry III of England, and the future Edward I, came to the Holy Land on crusade. Like Richard of Cornwall before him, he was astonished at the divisions between the various factions in the remaining Frankish lands. This account by a Templar of Tyre describes his visit.

On 9 May 1271, Prince Edward, son of Henry III, king of England, landed in Acre, after a stormy crossing in which his ship had been struck and almost sunk by a storm. He brought his wife, Eleanor of Castile, with him. Later in September, Edmund, brother of Edward, also landed in Acre.

In the same year, Sultan Baybars besieged Montfort Castle, very near Acre, belonging to the Teutonic Knights, and took it on 12 June by agreement that the defenders' lives be spared; on 16 June he led them before Acre and let them go. The men in Acre were all up in arms, that day, to defend the land. But when Edward saw the sultan's mighty forces, he saw very well that he had not got enough men to fight him. So none of the Christians dared go out against him; and the next day the sultan left and went away to Egypt.

After that, Edward led a raid against a rich settlement called St George, nine miles from Acre, taking Templars and Hospitallers and others from Acre with him. This was at the end of June, when it was very hot. They destroyed the settlement, killed many Saracens and took a lot of plunder; but a good many of our men died from eating honey and other things, as foot-soldiers so often do; they died by the wayside, both from heat and exhaustion, and from the hot foods they had eaten.

Hugh of Lusignan, king of Jerusalem and Cyprus, crossed from Cyprus to Acre and did great honour to Prince Edward and there was great friendship between them. They were joined by Bohemund VI, prince of Antioch, but the prince did not stay long in Acre and went away to his own land of Tripoli.

Now I will tell you what happened to Edward. A Saracen man-at-arms came to Acre to be baptized. Edward had him christened, and took him into his household. This man established himself as a servant to Prince Edward, one who would go and spy out the Saracens and discover where they were vulnerable. He performed this service several times; it was through him that our troops went to St George; so Edward came to trust him so well, that he gave orders that the man should never be refused access to him night or day.

One night, the Saracen went to the bedroom where Edward and his wife were sleeping; he took the interpreter with him, and made out that he had just come back from a spying trip and wanted to speak to Edward. The prince opened the door himself, wearing only his shirt and drawers. The Saracen went up to him and struck a knife into his hip, making a deep and dangerous wound. Edward felt the blow and hit the man full on the temple with his fist, which knocked him senseless to the floor for the moment; then the prince picked up a table knife which was in the room and struck the man on the head and killed him.

The alarm was raised among his attendants, who saw their lord was hurt and roused the whole of Acre. The lords came to the wounded prince and sent for all the physicians and slaves, who sucked the wound and drew out the poison, so that he made a good recovery, thanks be to God. Edward left the Holy Land on 22 September 1272, and crossed the sea to return to England.

The fall of Tripoli, 1289

The death of Baybars in July 1277 gave a temporary respite to the remaining Frankish settlements, but in 1289 Tripoli fell to his successor, al-Mansur Qalawun. The Templar of Tyre continues the story.

Sultan al-Mansur Qalawun laid siege to the city of Tripoli on Thursday 17 March of the same year, and all the Christians living nearby went there for safety. The sultan set up his siege-engines both great and small, he placed his wooden tower and his catapults opposite the town, then he set his sappers to mining underground and advanced past the outer fosses.

The city of Tripoli had strong stone walls, but the sultan attacked it at its weakest point: this was the Bishop's Tower, which was very old. The siege-engines battered it till it broke to pieces; so too with the Hospitallers' Tower, which was new and strong, but which they cracked apart till a horse could have gone through the gap.

The sultan had so many men that every embrasure had twenty Saracen archers shooting at it, so that none of our crossbowmen dared show an eye to take aim; any who tried to shoot was struck at once; and so the town was in a very bad state. The Venetian merchants, who had two galleys there, went aboard them, so as to escape to Armenia, for they saw that the land was almost lost.

Then the Saracens saw that there were very few defenders and pressed home their attack until at last the town was so weakened that the Saracens took it by assault on 26 April of that year. This was for lack of defenders; one after the other they abandoned the defence.

Many great lords escaped; many others died, who had been left behind; and many brothers of the Hospital of St John too were killed or taken. And that is how the disastrous loss of Tripoli occurred, as I have told you. The sultan had it completely razed to the ground, so that you will not find one house standing. He did this because the Saracens had built a town in a place less than three miles from the sea above Tripoli, called New Tripoli.

Abu al-Fida presents a different perspective of the fall of Tripoli.

In the year 1289, Sultan al-Mansur Qalawun left Egypt for Syria with his Egyptian troops, during the months of January and February. He set off, pitching camp by the city of Tripoli on Friday 18 March 1289. The sea surrounds the major part of this city, no land-based attack being possible except from the east, that side affording only the narrowest of fronts. On arrival, the sultan aimed a great number of catapults, both large and small, at the city, placing it under a state of siege and attacking it so fiercely that he conquered it by the sword on Tuesday 26 April 1289.

The sultan's army entered the city by force, its population fleeing towards the harbour. A few of them escaped by boat, though the majority of the male population were killed while their children were led away into captivity. The Muslims took with them a huge amount of booty. When the Muslims had ceased killing and plundering the people of Tripoli, the sultan ordered that it be razed to the ground. In the sea near Tripoli there was an island, on which stood a church named the church of St Thomas. Between the island and Tripoli lay the harbour. When the Muslims took Tripoli, many of the women fled to the church there.

The Muslim army, defying the sea, made the crossing to the island, swimming with their horses. They killed the menfolk who were there and claimed as booty the women, children and property. After this island had been cleared of all people and plunder, I crossed over in a boat. I found it covered in corpses which were putrefied to such an extent that the stench made it impossible for one to remain there.

Having conquered and destroyed Tripoli, the sultan returned to Egypt. This city had been held by the Franks for one hundred and eighty-five years and a few months.

The fall of Tripoli, one of the last Christian cities left in Outremer, in 1289. The Venetians and others who fled the city by sea can be seen escaping at the bottom.

The fall of Acre, 1291

The Templar of Tyre gives an eyewitness account of the fall of Acre in May 1291. Its capture began the final wreck of Frankish power in the Holy Land.

Sultan al-Ashraf Khalil had his tents and pavilions set up very close together; they stretched from Toron towards Samaria so that the whole plain was covered with them. The sultan's tent was high up on a hillock, where there were a fine tower and gardens and vines belonging to the Templars. This tent was bright vermilion all over, and had one door open towards Acre.

It is the custom of the sultans that in whatever direction the sultan's tent door is open, then all men know that the sultan must go that way. He remained inactive for a week, except that now and then our men skirmished with theirs and a few died on both sides.

Then at the end of the week, they got their siege-engines set up and ready. One of these weapons was called *Haveben*, which means 'Furious', and was aimed at the Templars' quarter of the city, and another, called *Mansur*, 'Victorious', was directed against the Pisans' quarter. The other big one attacked the Hospitallers' quarter and the machine on wheels shot at a tall tower called the Accursed Tower, which is at a salient point on the walls.

Henry II of Lusignan, king of Jerusalem and Cyprus, had summoned his forces in Cyprus; he collected them, left Famagusta, and arrived in Acre on 4 May 1291.

A few days after King Henry arrived, envoys were sent to the sultan. The sultan left his tent and went to the gate in the town called the Legate's Gate; all shooting was forbidden.

The envoys came unarmed into the sultan's presence. He asked, 'Have you brought me the keys of the town?' But the envoys replied that this was not a city to be surrendered so easily and they had come to ask him to show some sort of mercy to the poor people. To this Sultan al-Ashraf Khalil answered, 'I will do you this much grace: give me nothing but the stones; take everything else and go out and go away. I do this for the sake of your king who is young, as I am myself.'

The envoys told him that this was not possible and he said, 'Then go away, for I will not do anything else for you.' And as he was saying this, by some unknown chance one of the crusaders' weapons at the Legate's Gate loosed off its stone, and it fell so near the tent where the sultan and the envoys were that the sultan – out of youth, not meaning to do wrong – stood up and put his hand to his sword, drew it at least a hand's breadth and said, 'Ah, you flea-ridden swine, what is to stop me cutting your heads off?' But Emir Shujai said to him, 'My lord, God forbid we should soil the iron of your sword with the blood of swine! The men who shot behaved like traitors, but you will let these go, as men who are in your power.' The envoys went back into Acre and both sides resumed shooting at each other with mangonels, and behaving like enemies. When the new tower, known as the King's Tower, was taken, most men sent their wives and children out to sea in ships. In the morning of Thursday 17 May, the weather was so bad and the sea so rough that the women and children could not bear it and went back to their homes.

Then on Friday 18 May 1291, before daybreak, there came the loud and terrible sound of a kettledrum, and as the

Franks' heads sent to the sultan

During the course of the siege, the Franks launched a sortie by night, taking the army by surprise. They routed the sentinels, reaching as far as the tents, where they got entangled in the ropes. One of their horsemen fell into the cesspit used by some of the officers, and there he was killed.

Seeing that our troops had begun to outnumber them, the Franks fled back to the town. The Hamah troops managed to kill some of them. As dawn broke al-Malik al-Muzaffar, ruler of Hamah, had a number of Franks' heads fixed to the necks of the horses which the Hamah troops had captured that night, and sent them to Sultan al-Ashraf Khalil.

The army's stranglehold on Acre tightened, until eventually God afforded them its conquest by sword on Friday 17 June 1291. During the Muslim onslaught, one group of its population managed to flee in ships. Within the city were a number of fortified towers, like citadels, in each of which a vast company of Franks had barricaded itself. When the Muslims had killed and sacked so vast a part of Acre as to defy calculation, the sultan commanded those still putting up a resistance from within the towers to come out and to leave no one inside. He then ordered that they be decapitated outside Acre, right up to the last one. Finally he ordered that Acre be razed to the ground.

From Abu al-Fida, Historical Compendium

وكـاد يزعـج الجمـال الشـير والنشـد
مـا الحـج سـير كتأونيـا واذلاجـا ولا اعتـام لجـنا لجـنا واحـلا جـا

Saracen forces in the field. Atop the camels ride kettledrummers, beating the drums which signalled the final assault on the city of Acre.

drum sounded, the Saracens assaulted the city of Acre on every side. The place where they first got in was through this damned tower which they had taken.

They came in countless numbers, all on foot; in front came men with great tall shields, after them men throwing Greek fire, and then men who shot bolts and feathered arrows so thickly that they seemed like rain falling from the sky.

When Henry of Lusignan, king of Jerusalem and Cyprus, witnessed this disaster, he went to the master of the Hospitallers; they saw clearly that no advice or help could do any good, so they fled and went aboard the galleys.

That day was appalling, for nobles and citizens, women and girls were frantic with terror; they went running through the streets, their children in their arms, weeping and desperate; they fled to the sea shore to escape death, and when the Saracens caught them one would take the mother and the other the child, they would drag them from place to place and pull them apart; and sometimes two Saracens would quarrel over a woman and she would be killed; or a woman was taken and her sucking child flung to the ground where it died under the horses' hooves.

The fall of Sidon and Beirut, 1291

Tyre, too, was abandoned by the Franks in May 1291, and, despite brave resistance, Sidon and Beirut fell to the Mamluks soon afterwards.

Now I will tell you about the town of Sidon, which belonged to the Templars. The grand commander, and some other Templars who had escaped in the boats, made straight for Sidon and went into the castle on the sea [at the edge of the city], where they found that the garrison had gone to an island where there was a mill. Then Sultan al-Ashraf Khalil sent an emir of his, Shujai, who attacked the castle on the sea with siege-engines, did all the harm he could, and took the town of Sidon, which its inhabitants had abandoned.

The new master of the Templars was called Theobald Gaudin. Finding himself under attack, he took counsel with his brothers. On their advice and promising that he would send them help to rescue the castle, he went away to Cyprus. But once in Cyprus, he did not trouble to send them reinforcements. Then the Templars in Cyprus who were friends of those in Sidon sent word to them, to advise them to consider giving up, as the master showed no sign of sending them any sort of help. When the brothers in the castle heard that, they were thoroughly disheartened. So they agreed to surrender and go to Cyprus. On the night of 14 July therefore they went away. Once the castle of Sidon was abandoned, the Saracens marched in and immediately pulled it down.

Emir Shujai then left Sidon and passed near Beirut. On 31 July its garrison came out of the castle and went to meet him to do him honour and because of a message he had sent them [promising safe conduct]. But he, the devil, had them all taken, took the town and the castle, and had the walls of the town torn down and the whole castle razed to the ground.

Now you must know that when the men in Atlit saw that all was lost, they saw very well that they could not defend the castle, so they abandoned it and went to the island of Cyprus and afterwards the Saracens had it all pulled down.

And so, as you can see, the whole of Syria was lost, and the Saracens took and destroyed it. Now everything was gone, and no Christian held an inch of land anywhere in Syria.

7

THE LAST CRUSADES

When Acre fell to the Mamluks in 1291 Christendom had been bombarded with too many crusading appeals, and had witnessed too many disappointments, to respond with a simple outpouring of religious enthusiasm and military energy. Suspicion of the motives of the papacy and of Christendom's kings and princes went deep, and the reaction to the terrible events of 1291 was characterized as much by recrimination and bitterness, as by fervour for reconquest.

The Knights Hospitaller and Knights Templar, robbed of their role as defenders of the Holy Land, were criticized on the grounds that their quarrels, and lack of firm commitment, had been responsible for the loss of the holy places. Philip IV of France capitalized on this in 1307 by ordering the arrest of all the Templars in his kingdom on the charge of heresy. A protracted, brutal trial of the Order ended in its suppression in 1312. The Hospitallers and the Teutonic Knights, the third military Order dedicated to the defence of the holy places, found new roles associated with the crusading movement. The Hospitallers conquered the island of Rhodes by 1310, which placed them in the front line in the struggle against the Turks of Anatolia. The Teutonic Knights already possessed lands stretching along the eastern Baltic littoral and moved their headquarters to Marienburg, in Prussia, in 1310; their future lay in the conflict against the pagan Lithuanians and schismatic Russians in the east.

These developments were pointers towards two of the most important crusading arenas of the 14th and 15th centuries. But in the 50 years

Constantinople, the ancient capital of the Byzantine Empire, which fell to the Ottoman Turks in 1453.

following 1291 the recovery of the Holy Land remained the most important consideration and the period witnessed an outpouring of detailed plans and projects unprecedented in crusading history. The reasons are clear: without a foothold on the mainland of Syria, the danger of an invasion becoming a débâcle was heightened; while the escalating cost of all forms of warfare meant that painstaking strategy and strict budgeting were essential. Crusade planning, diplomatic negotiations and military preparations were engaged in at the court of Edward I of England, and at those of the French kings between 1300 and 1336. Although this activity proved sterile, and was brought to an end by the outbreak of the Hundred Years War between England and France in 1337, it testified to the fact that the crusading ideal remained deeply embedded in the religious and social values of the period.

Unable to express its crusading zeal in recapturing the Holy Land, Christendom's nobility found other areas in which to display its chivalric prowess by fighting the infidels. Alfonso XI of Castile, with the aid of foreign volunteers, defeated an army of Muslims from Granada and North Africa in 1340 at the battle of Salado, and in 1344 took the great port of Algeciras. Throughout the century the Teutonic Order conducted a series of inconclusive wars against the pagan Lithuanians; the campaigns were dubbed *reysen* (journeys) because armies had first to cross an extensive no man's land (the 'wilderness') before they reached the enemy's forts. Operations were carried out with brutal destructiveness. None the less, because the Teutonic Order honoured its foreign guests with hunts, feasts and prizes for the best fighters, the *reysen* were immensely popular with crusaders from all over Europe.

The fiction was maintained for some decades that the *reysen* constituted crusades against a pagan people. For example in 1390 Henry Bolingbroke, earl of Derby and later Henry IV of England, arrived in Prussia, and took part in a *reysa* which besieged the Lithuanian capital, Vilnius. Later he looked back with affection on his expedition, which he obviously enjoyed.

Two of the most important crusades of the century were directed against Egypt and Tunisia. Viewed by contemporaries as great chivalric enterprises, they were also inspired by economic motives. The Egyptian campaign, led by Peter I of Lusignan, king of Cyprus and titular king of Jerusalem, was portrayed as a crusade to retake the Holy City, but mounted primarily because the king was concerned about the Mamluk port of Alexandria undercutting the western trade that passed through the Cypriot port of Famagusta. Peter's army took and sacked Alexandria in 1365, but the crusaders were forced to abandon it to a Mamluk relief army within six days. In 1389–90 a Genoese delegation to the French court proposed a crusade to take the Hafsid port of Mahdia in Tunisia, probably because they too feared that their Mediterranean trade was imperilled. A truce with England was in operation and a French crusading army was assembled and transported to Tunisia in the summer of 1390. After a siege of nine or ten weeks a Muslim relief army arrived, the Genoese negotiated a favourable trade treaty, and the crusaders withdrew.

Both these expeditions were signs that the crusading movement lacked overall strategic purpose. However, by the 1360s the phenomenal rise of the Ottoman Turks had given a new focus to western crusading zeal. Originally one of the emirates which took power in Anatolia when the Seldjuk sultanate disintegrated in the last decades of the 13th century, their territory bordered on the decaying Byzantine Empire, and in their campaigns against Byzantium, Ottoman leaders were able to portray themselves as *ghazi* warriors, engaged in wars for booty and for the glory of God. Having built up their base in Anatolia, they crossed into Europe and by 1355 they had virtually cut Constantinople off from the west. The first crusading response was in 1366, when Count Amadeus of Savoy led a successful expedition to assist the Byzantine Emperor John V, his cousin.

A series of devastating Turkish victories followed, however, demonstrating the sophistication and superiority of the Ottoman forces. In 1371 the Serbs were crushed at Crnomen. Sofia fell in 1385, and Thessalonica two years later. In 1389 a coalition of Christian princes in the Balkans was defeated at Kossovo, and Sultan Bayezid I began the task of organizing direct Ottoman rule over most the Balkan peninsula. These successes were paralleled in Asia Minor where the sultan earned the title Thunderbolt (*Yildirim*) because of the speed with which he moved across his empire.

After Kossovo, Christendom's leaders realized that a full-scale effort had to be made to counter Bayezid's advance. Throughout the early 1390s England and France drew up plans for a crusade against the Turks, and by the end of 1394 it appeared that England, France and Hungary could jointly field an army in the following spring, with Venetian naval help. However, the crusaders who travelled east in the summer of 1395 were mainly French, under the aegis of Philip the Bold, duke of Burgundy, and of his son John of Nevers.

Although King Sigismund of Hungary advised them to take up a defensive position, they preferred to strike deep into occupied Bulgaria and besieged the Danubian fortress of Nicopolis. Bayezid's army met them there on 25 September and inflicted a crushing defeat on the Christians. Hungary, the beleaguered city of Constantinople and the petty Latin states in Greece – notably the duchy of Athens, under Catalan rule, and the principality of Achaea, controlled from Naples – now seemed doomed.

But an extraordinary and unlikely ally for the Christians appeared in the east: Tamerlane, a Mongol warlord, whose successful onslaught on Bayezid's territories in the early years of the 15th century resulted in a long period of civil war and rebellion in the Ottoman Empire: it took almost 40 years to regain the position of strength it had attained before his arrival.

The Christian west failed to attack the Turks during this period of setback. Instead the most important crusades of the early 15th century were waged against the Hussites of Bohemia. John Hus was a university lecturer and popular preacher at Prague, whose extreme religious views, which in many ways foreshadowed Protestant doctrines, were condemned by the Church. Hus was burned as a heretic at the Council of Constance in 1415, but, the Bohemian revolt which followed was not purely religious in origin; it also incorporated a rebellion against the political rule of the Holy Roman Emperor Sigismund and a Czech nationalist uprising against German influence and power. Sigismund persuaded Pope Martin V to launch an expedition against the Hussites in 1420, the first of a series of crusades all of which failed to subjugate Bohemia. The collapse of the last great expedition, in 1431, compelled Sigismund to seek a peaceful solution to the crisis.

By now, the west's attention was once more fixed on the Ottomans, who had retaken Thessalonica in 1430. They annexed the despotate of Serbia in 1439 and Pope Eugenius IV resolved to help the Hungarian forces on land by sending galleys to the Hellespont, hoping to prevent the Turks from ferrying troops across the straits from Anatolia. An attempt to implement this strategy in 1443 failed, but the Hungarians, led by John Hunyadi, inflicted a number of resounding defeats on the Turks, which encouraged the pope to make another attempt in 1444. The crusading flotilla reached the Hellespont in good time, while Ladislas of Hungary's army marched towards Varna, on the Black Sea coast. But the galleys failed to stop Turkish troops crossing from Asia; nor did they sail to the assistance of the Hungarians at Varna. When Sultan Murad met Ladislas in battle at Varna in November, the Christians were outnumbered and defeated.

The fall of Constantinople was now only a question of time. In 1448 Hunyadi fought and lost a three-day battle against the Turks at Kossovo, where the Serbs had suffered defeat 59 years earlier. The Albanian chieftain Skanderbeg waged a bitter guerrilla struggle against the Turks, and Philip the Good of Burgundy sent naval help to the Byzantines. But such resistance was inadequate. Mehmed II succeeded Murad II as sultan of the Ottoman Empire and in the spring of 1452, determined to establish his reputation, started preparations for the siege of Constantinople. Troops and artillery were positioned a year later. The Byzantine Emperor Constantine XI had hardly enough soldiers to man the walls, and in the early hours of 29 May 1453 the Turks launched a decisive attack and took the city.

So it was that a period in crusading history which began with the final expulsion of the Christians from the Holy Land, ended with the extinction of the East Roman Empire, whose proud successor the Ottoman state now became. In both cases common factors lay behind the disasters: on the one hand, powerful, centralized, and militaristic Islamic states; on the other, a hopelessly divided and militarily weak, Christendom.

The chroniclers Philip of Mézières, William of Machaut, Jean Cabaret d'Orville and the biographer of Boucicaut illustrate the chivalric nature of much 14th-century crusading. They capture the *élan* and gallantry which characterized the crusades to Alexandria, Magdia and Nicopolis, and vividly express the excitement generated by early success or the harassed tone of the debates in which the crusaders confronted intractable strategic situations.

The pilgrim Ludolph of Sudheim, the spy Gilbert of Lannoy, the ship's doctor Niccolo Barbaro, and the diplomatic envoy Ruy Gonzalez de Clavijo, represent the rich tradition of travellers who described to their co-religionists in the west the extraordinary sights and events they had witnessed. The Muslim Badr al-Din al-Aini provides a flavour of Mamluk historiography in his account of the terrible Mamluk invasion of Cyprus in 1426, while the eulogistic biography of Mehmed the Conqueror by the Greek Kritovoulos documents the greatest sultan of the early Ottoman period.

On Friday 13 October 1307, at precisely the same time, the first glimmer of dawn, all the Templars throughout the kingdom of France were arrested and delivered to various prisons at the command of the king, Philip IV. Among those detained was the master of the whole Order, Jacques of Molay, who was seized at the Templars' Paris house. The reason for all this was that it had long since come to the king's attention from many different sources and on the evidence of many men – some of whom were professed members of the Order itself – that the Order and its leaders had been entangled in and infected by abominable crimes. Although the members of the Order denied the crimes, the accusations could be proved to the satisfaction of the law . . . And all these crimes they were suspected of, the French king, Philip IV, caused to be publicly proclaimed in the hall of the royal palace in the presence of representatives of the clergy and people on the following Sunday.

In October 1307, Philip IV of France suddenly ordered that the Templars in his kingdom be seized and imprisoned, events commented on above by the contemporary continuator of William of Nangis's chronicle.

The suppression of the Templars

A letter sent by Philip to provincial administrators in Normandy – one among the many – written on 14 September 1307, explains his motives for the arrest.

There has sounded in our ears a report of a matter exciting bitterness and grief, whose very thought arouses horror and terror on hearing it. It is a hateful crime, a damnable sin, an abominable deed, an abhorrent disgrace, deeply inhuman – or rather, completely lacking in all human feeling. And we can now believe the report owing to its substantiation from many sources. It cannot be doubted that such great sins in their enormity have burst their banks, to become an offence to the Divine Majesty and the whole of Christendom, a shame on mankind, a pernicious demonstration of evil and a scandal of universal proportions.

By the testimony of a great number of reliable witnesses, the brothers of the Order of Knights Templar have been behaving as though they were wolves under sheep's clothing, and villainously trampling on the religion of our faith under the dress of religion.

They are again crucifying in these days our Lord Jesus Christ, by bringing to him wounds more grievous than those he bore on the cross. For on initiation into their Order, his image is presented to them, and they deny him three times with wretched and miserable blows, and with horrific cruelty spit three times into his face.

Then, taking off their everyday clothes, they line up in the presence of the Visitor or the deputy who is receiving them for initiation. Next he kisses them; first at the bottom of the spine, secondly on the navel, and finally on the mouth, in accordance with the profane rite of their Order – but for shame on human dignity. Not fearing to break human law, they bind themselves with a vow of initiation to give themselves over, one to another, to that disgusting and terrifying vice of sexual intercourse – when asked and without excuse.

That treacherous, mad race, given over as it is to the worship of idols, does not fear to commit these and other sins. It is not just their deeds and detestable acts but also their terrifying words that taint the earth with their repulsiveness.

We were hardly able to give the matter our attention earlier, since we were well aware of the sort of informers who would broadcast so awful a rumour. However, the number of them multiplied and the rumour grew stronger.

Accordingly, we established an investigation designed to uncover the truth. We then held conference on the matter with our most holy father in the Lord, Pope Clement V, and a fuller council with our prelates and barons, in which we dealt carefully with the charges; and the more fully we investigated the matter, the graver were the abominations that we found.

You know that to defend the freedom of the Church's faith the Lord has set kings apart, as observers from our royal heights, and that before all the desires of our heart we strive for the advancement of the Catholic faith. Accordingly, we held a thorough enquiry through the offices of our beloved brother in Christ, William of Paris, an inquisitor into heretical perversion authorized by papal authority. Here, at least, the Templars gave in to the just entreaties of the aforesaid inquisitor, who later called in the help of our strong arm. We acknowledged it was possible that some were guilty and some innocent, but it was expedient to try them, and, if necessary, to acquit them after the correct judicial examination.

Thus we decreed that every single member of the aforesaid Order in our kingdom be, without exception, taken into custody to await trial in the ecclesiastical court, and that all their goods, both moveable and immoveable, be seized by our hand and be faithfully kept.

Philip IV's men arrest and imprison the Knights Templar after the revelations of their supposed crimes.

The end of the Templars

Jacques of Molay, the last grand master of the Temple, was burnt at the stake on the Ile-des-Javiaux, an island in the Seine in the centre of Paris, on 18 March 1314. He had been hastily condemned as a relapsed heretic after retracting his confessions that the Templars had denied Christ and spat on the cross, heretical crimes allegedly forced upon new entrants during obscene reception ceremonies.

The execution ended his long and terrible ordeal. With other Templars in France, he had been arrested seven years previously in a series of simultaneous operations early on 13 October 1307.

Although these were the work of agents of the French king, Philip IV the Fair, they had ostensibly been carried out on the orders of the papal inquisitor in France, William of Paris, and the proceeedings which followed were technically those of the Inquisition.

Confessions were obtained, many by torture, and Pope Clement V was presented with a *fait accompli*. The pope clearly doubted that an Order which had shed so much blood in the cause of the Church militant could be so riddled with heresy and corruption, but the French king's arbitrary action raised the wider question of papal authority. Clement therefore ordered the arrest of the Templars in other countries and took control of the proceedings. From 1308 to 1312 he blocked Philip by legal obstacles, but finally had to agree to the Order's suppression. Its property was granted to the Hospitallers.

Philip IV's motives are a matter of controversy. His devotion to the monarchical cult and his morbid religiosity could have been exploited by counsellors with more mundane and material motives in mind. The Templars were wealthy in money and lands, especially in France, and their goods were a temptation to a government which often had to grapple with financial crises. Moreover, the loss of Acre in 1291 had left the Order vulnerable to attack on the grounds of its failure to protect the Holy Land. Few would argue today that the Templars were guilty, yet the grand master, elderly, confused and frightened, provided little leadership during the trial.

Clement died a month after Molay's execution and seven months later Philip followed. Before the flames consumed him, it was claimed, Molay called both his persecutors to answer for their crimes before God within the year.

Therefore we command that you, singly or together, personally see to the matter as far as concerns the district of Rouen [the archbishopric], and take every single brother of that Order, without exception, into custody to await trial at the ecclesiastical court. We command, through the content of this present document, all our judges and faithful subjects to obey you promptly and strenuously in all the above.

Written in the royal abbey of St Mary, near Pontoise, on 14 September 1307.

The deposition of Jacques of Molay

The pope appointed commissioners, mainly bishops whose sympathies lay with Philip IV, to examine leading Templars in France. On 28 November 1309 they heard the evidence of Jacques of Molay, grand master of the Templars, in Paris.

On Friday 28 November 1309, the lords commissioners congregated. Brother Jacques of Molay, grand master of the Order of the Temple, had, on the preceding Wednesday, requested the lords commissioners' permission to take counsel.

When asked by the lords commissioners if he was willing to defend the Templars, Jacques of Molay replied that he would defend himself only to Pope Clement V, who had reserved judgement on the most important members of the Order. He said that meanwhile, for the exoneration of his conscience, he wanted to set forth three things about the Order.

The first was that he did not know of any other Order in which the chapels and churches of the Order had better and more beautiful adornments and reliquaries pertaining to the worship of the Divine, and in which there was better observance of the Divine through the priests and clerics, with the exception of cathedral churches.

The second was that he did not know of any other Order in which more alms were given than by the Templars; for, in accordance with their rules, they gave alms three times a week to all who wanted them.

The third was that he did not know of any Order, nor of any nation, who more readily exposed their persons or shed so much blood in the defence of the Christian faith against its enemies.

When the reply came that dying in battle was no advantage for the salvation of souls when the basics of the Catholic faith were missing,

Jacques said that this was true, and that he himself truly believed in one God and the three persons of the Trinity and in all other things pertaining to one Catholic faith.

And finally Jacques, master of the Order of the Temple, humbly asked the lords commissioners and the royal chancellor to see to it that he might be able to hear Mass and they, praising the piety he displayed, said they would comply with his request.

Philip IV oversees the burning of heretics. When Jacques of Molay, master of the Templars, was burned in 1314, he was said to have cursed Philip and Pope Clement V, calling them to join him before God's tribunal. Both died soon after.

Hospitallers capture Rhodes

In 1306, members of the Order of the Hospital of St John of Jerusalem (the Hospitallers), dissatisfied with their cramped position on Cyprus, began the conquest of Rhodes from the Greeks and Turks; by 1310 they had transferred their headquarters to the island, over which they exercised a virtually independent rule, and which they colonized and fortified against the Turkish emirates of the nearby Anatolian coastlands. Their men and money continued to come from their western possessions – augmented by the Templars' estates from 1312 – which were organized in priories and commanderies occupied by priests, sergeants and a minority of knight-brethren, most of whom were recruited from the lesser nobility and the gentry. Two or three hundred knights and a few sergeants and priests garrisoned Rhodes, governing the Greek inhabitants, maintaining a small naval force and encouraging the commerce and pilgrim traffic of its harbour.

Although during the 14th century the Order became increasingly impoverished, its numbers reduced by plague after 1348 and its lands a prey to endless European wars, it still made an important contribution to crusading against Islam. It was successful in containing the naval aggression of the Anatolian emirates on the Aegean and participated in the capture of Smyrna in 1344. It fought in the Hellespont with the papal legate Peter Thomas in 1359, and went with Peter I of Cyprus to Antalya, in Turkey, in 1361. In 1365 it provided men and shipping for the fleet which sailed, under Peter's leadership, from Rhodes, to sack Alexandria. But a Hospitaller force sent by Pope Gregory XI to Epirus in northern Greece was ignominiously defeated by the Christian Albanians near Arta in 1378, and the defence of Smyrna, given to the Order in 1374, became increasingly difficult with Ottoman power growing.

Present at the disastrous crusade of Nicopolis in 1396, a year later the Order occupied Corinth and defended the Peloponnese against the Turks for several years. Smyrna was lost to the great Mongol conqueror Tamerlane in 1402, but replaced about five years later when the Order constructed a new castle at Bodrun, the ancient Halikarnassos, on the mainland opposite Kos. In 1440 and 1444 Rhodes survived attacks by Mamluk fleets from Egypt, while Ottoman advances, which culminated in the capture of Constantinople by Mehmed II in 1453, forced the Hospitallers into an ever more defensive posture.

Eventually, in 1312, Pope Clement V suppressed the Order. In 1314 the grand master, Jacques of Molay, was burned at the stake, and legend related that as he died he cursed the king and the pope.

The greatest beneficiaries of the suppression of the Templars were the Hospitallers, who took over most of their lands, a large and valuable patrimony scattered throughout western Europe. The Hospitallers had in the mean time allied with certain Genoese in conquering Rhodes from the Byzantines; the Order's headquarters were moved there in 1309 and the whole island was subjugated the next year. A contemporary chronicler describes the invasion.

The Grand Master Fulk of Villaret, and the valiant Brothers of the Hospital gave thanks to God and to the Virgin Mary for the wealth and abundance which had come to them. They built a great castle and conquered all around, collecting many fine men who wished to come to Rhodes to reconnoitre and to colonize the island. Then they had many places in Anatolia submit to their authority, which gave them tribute. They did not allow the passage of evil traders, nor might any such load up in Anatolia with passengers, or goods, or anything else for transportation to Egypt. And if any should set sail, the Hospitallers had galleys to seize and despoil them.

In this way God ordained divine aid for the noble master and the valiant knights of the Hospital. They freely held a great franchise, and combined mastery of the seas with independence of any other authority.

Schemes to recover the Holy Land

The fall of Acre in 1291 inspired many treatises over the next century on how the recovery of the Holy Land might best be achieved. One theme – here expressed by Marino Sanudo Torsello – is in favour of an economic blockade of Egypt.

To complete the most holy work of the recovery of the Holy Land – bedewed as it is with the most precious blood of our dear Lord Jesus Christ – it is absolutely necessary that a solemn prohibition of trading with Egypt be proclaimed throughout the world, namely, that Christians and even Saracens could not sail in

The Hospitallers in Rhodes. They held the island until 1522, when they were finally forced to yield it to the Ottomans.

their ships to Egypt with their cargoes of timber and iron and pitch and little children, nor could they pick up spices, sugar, cotton and other goods there, and carry them back.

When Acre and Syria were lost [in 1187], a solemn prohibition was made against entering the lands ruled by Saladin, or returning from there with merchandise. Among other things it contained a command that anyone who broke the prohibition should be 'for ever disgraced and held to be intestate'.

Let this now be done again, but in such a way that the offenders are neither able to make a will, nor able to take possession of anything bequeathed or left to them. Similarly, they should not be admitted to public office, all legal acts should be forbidden them and their goods should be confiscated for the public treasury.

At the time such a prohibition was made, it was enforced on the sea only; that is to say, those who transgressed the prohibition by sea were prosecuted, but not those who transgressed it on land. But now is the right time for establishing the prohibition – throughout the whole world – on land too, so as to allow its enforcement to proceed with more vigour. If we guard the sea alone, and not the ports as well, we cannot be sure of stopping everyone travelling by sea to the lands ruled by Muslims.

The reasoning behind the above is this: our armed galleys cannot stay at sea during a storm, and even when it is calm the crews are most unwilling to stay outside port on winter nights. Similarly during summer the galleys cannot stay for long at sea because of the need to put in to land to pick up supplies of drinking water.

There are a number of other reasons why we cannot satisfactorily patrol the sea with great ships containing armed crews. First the Mediterranean is too large an area to patrol; secondly the Muslim coastline is extensive; and thirdly those transgressors who, putting aside the fear of God, want to go down to the lands ruled by Muslims, can, choosing the time that suits them, sail on the high seas far from land and put in to shore at any point. Furthermore, they would be warmly welcomed in those lands and be treated humanely and with kindness, because the inhabitants depend on them.

Those accursed and wicked Christians who, around the time of the first promulgation of the edicts on this subject, travelled by sea to those regions, were the very image of the devil as they crossed between those parts and their countries for the sake of gain. The result of this bad example was that many more began a traffic which was to bring damnation on themselves.

So, if today's transgressors were, like heretics, to suffer persecution on land and sea, and if they were punished, they would be an example to everybody.

The same author provides Pope John XXII, to whom his treatise is addressed, with precise if daunting figures on the expense of launching a new crusade.

I can give an exact reply if your holiness would like to know the required annual expenditure on the said fifteen thousand foot-soldiers, three hundred cavalry and their ship-transports, plus food and other necessities, as well as the money needed for suitable negotiations with the Tartars. It would be two hundred and ten thousand florins by instalments over three years, reckoning a florin to be two shillings of Venetian groats. That is to say, sixty thousand gold florins annually to pay the said cavalry and infantry, and for suitable food and for such expenses as occur.

In the same way, we would need thirty thousand gold florins over the whole three-year period for ships, timber, iron and such materials as are necessary for the building of living quarters, as well as for sundry military matters and the replacement of such horses as might be destroyed or lost in the aforesaid service. In this way our expenses would reach the sum total of two hundred and ten thousand florins to be paid in instalments over three years. That is to say, seventy thousand florins in any one year – although your holiness could derive great benefit from the land of Egypt and its waters from the start of the first year until the Christians have started on living quarters at some coastal site, as I said, or even a hospital.

As regards the other necessities of food and ship-transports for the army which will come from the west, your holiness shall see to it that ordinances are formulated on this matter. Perhaps your holiness would like to know if the task in hand could be accomplished with fewer men and less expenditure. My reverent reply is that it could be done in such a way. I can say, without qualification, that control of the pure water supply to a point where one can move up and down the country from one's base with a few men will inevitably ensure mastery of the land. And the reason for this, as I said, is that Egypt being a very long and narrow land, much of it is spread out along the river Nile, in such a way that the inhabitants could not gather a force to guard it all. All they can do is catch the water, hold it and consume it.

In 1389 Philip of Mézières, formerly chancellor of the kingdom of Cyprus and one of the leading figures in the crusading movement in the 14th century, composed an allegorical and chivalrous treatise for Charles VI, king of France, in which he imagined four great armies from Europe travelling to the east.

Fair son, it would be advisable to come to an agreement with the other kings of Christendom that its holy forces should be divided into different groups to make the journey to the Holy Land.

That is to say, the kings of Hungary and of Bohemia and the Holy Roman Emperor, if he is there, and the German troops, should make their way straight to Constantinople by land, reclaiming the kingdoms of Thrace and Bulgaria and the empire of Constantinople and restoring them to the Catholic faith and to obedience to the Church of Rome, in addition to holding the Turks back and casting them out of Europe.

The lords of Prussia, together with the king of Lithuania, at the head of all their forces, should travel towards Constantinople through the kingdom of Russia and the surrounding countries and should liaise with the Germans to crush the power of the Turks.

On the other hand, the kings of Aragon, Spain, Portugal and Navarre should set off to conquer the kingdom of Granada, Tlemcen, Morocco and Tunis.

You yourself, fair son, accompanied by Richard II, your brother-in-law of England, by the Scots, the Irish, the men of Hainault, Holland and Zealand, the men of Liège and of Lorraine, the Savoyards, the Barrois, the men from beyond the Rhine and the knights from the kingdom of France, the forces of Lombardy, Tuscany, Apulia and Italy, you should take the sea route to Egypt, Syria, Armenia and Turkey.

Next, fair son, it is advisable that the crossing be extremely well organized and that everything be prepared on time so that you can set out to sea in the month of June, or July at the very latest; thus you will arrive in the eastern lands, which are hot, at the beginning of winter, in other words, during September or October at the latest. For if God's knights from the western lands, which are cold, were to find themselves in Egypt or Syria at the beginning of summer, they would die in great numbers, especially the ladies, from the unaccustomed heat. But if the Christians arrive in winter they will have time to get used to the climate of the east and to the gradual build-up of heat and will not be so badly affected in the summer.

The Latin kingdom of Cyprus

In about 1340 the pilgrim Ludolph of Sudheim visited the island of Cyprus, a focus for crusading expeditions in the 14th century.

The island of Cyprus is the noblest of all islands, and is very fertile in vines, corn, meat and fish. It is exceedingly well supplied with cities, castles and villages and is, in all, seventy miles in circumference. The island of Cyprus is a day's sail from the nearest parts of Egypt, Syria, Greece, Turkey and lesser Armenia. All of these places lie almost in a circle around Cyprus. This famous island once had a Byzantine king, Isaac Comnenus, but Richard I, king of England, acquired it by war in 1191, and kept that king bound in silver chains for the rest of his life.

The king of Cyprus had taken Richard of England's wife, Berengaria, prisoner, and it was for that reason that Richard, king of England, took Cyprus from him by the sword. He later sold the island to the Templars in 1192 for two thousand gold sovereigns. But soon afterwards the Templars sold it to Guy of Lusignan, king of Jerusalem; so when the Holy Land was lost, the noble Christian barons took themselves to Cyprus, where the seat of the kingdom of Jerusalem had been transferred.

Cyprus, land of plenty

You should know that in Cyprus all sorts of fruits and vegetables grow, the same as in Syria, though I do not believe that date palms and balsam trees grow there. The nobles, barons, knights and citizens who live there have large incomes so that a simple knight would have a yearly income of three thousand florins. The nobles also have dogs and falcons which consume those incomes. They even keep leopards for the chase; it is a characteristic of leopards that they take three leaps and if they do not catch their prey on the third leap, on that day they are dishonoured and neither eat nor drink. Nor do they acknowledge their master. Cyprus also has roe deer in the woods, goats and many other sorts of wild animal.

The merchants wear cloth of gold, rich silk, gold and gems and pearls and other costly finery. Once the author saw there four gemstones – a carbuncle, a sapphire, a pearl and an emerald – all sold to the sultan for sixty thousand florins. The island's apothecaries have every species of herb, including the precious aromatic ones, wood of aloes, and others which are difficult to find elsewhere in the world, but are plentiful enough in Cyprus.

From Ludolph of Sudheim, *De insula Cypro.*

The archbishop of Nicosia resides in the middle of the island and has three suffragans under him: the bishops of Paphos, Limassol and Famagusta, although the map of the province has it otherwise!

St Paul himself converted Paphos, a town which seems to have been destroyed in an earthquake. Near it is the place where St Hilarion lived and also a promontory two miles long and wide, surrounded by steep cliffs which no one can climb, unless by one particular staircase cut into the rocks.

There is no nobler wine in the world than from this place, for there are so many different sorts of grape which grow deep red, and various other colours, that it is scarcely possible to imagine. The same may be said of the flavours. Vines are to be found there which a man could scarcely encircle with both arms, bearing grapes in volume the equivalent of four men's heads. Although those vines are bigger than any others, there are none the less fine wines found in other places which are celebrated in song as 'the bunches of Cyprus'.

In the city of Limassol are found all the military Orders: that of the Hospital of St John, that of the Teutonic Knights, and that of St Thomas of Canterbury, an English Order. Nearby, up a high mountain, are monks of the Order of St Benedict. From that mountain, at sunrise, they can contemplate the heights of Lebanon.

The other city, called Famagusta, has the best port on the island; here all the merchandise of the Greeks, Armenians, Turks, Syrians and Egyptians is to be found in abundance. Cyprus is a central point to all these people for, with a favourable wind, they are able to travel there in a day's journey. Famagusta is the richest of cities, and that is why the present writer says that one day he saw a bride there who was more richly decked out than all the brides of France, should they have all been together in one place. That is what the French soldiers who were there used to think too.

Not far from Famagusta is a city called Salamis, once famous and now deserted, where St Barnabas suffered martyrdom and where St Epiphanius, most famous for his miracles, was archbishop. In the middle of Cyprus is the capital, Nicosia, where on account of the mildness of the climate there are always meetings of nobles and bishops, watching festival tournaments.

Many places and cities pay tribute to the king of the island, especially on the Turkish seaboard. One, the city of Satalia, holds public holidays on Sunday, on Saturday – the Jewish sabbath, and on Friday – the Muslim festival, and they keep August in honour of the creation of Adam. Men of all these faiths are tributaries of the kingdom of Cyprus. About the other noble features of the island it would take too long to tell. The few I have told here are sufficient.

The vision of Peter of Cyprus

Peter I of Lusignan, king of Cyprus and titular king of Jerusalem from 1359 to 1369, was a remarkable man who, during his short reign, gave his realm a leading role on the international stage. In 1347, when still a young man, Peter founded the Order of the Sword. The French poet and musician, William of Machaut, describes the vision which came to Peter.

At Famagusta, there is a cross which, if you are in your right mind, you must believe to be the cross of the Good Thief: for it stands on no stone or plinth, but floating unsupported in the air. A hundred thousand people have seen, venerated and believed in it. On Good Friday 1347, Peter, then a young man, went there in true contrition and deep devotion to pray. And at once a voice came to him and said, four or five times over: 'Son, wage this holy war and win your inheritance, the land God promised to the blessed patriarchs and to which he came for your sake in flesh and blood.' When he heard these words, so clear and unmistakable, four or five times repeated, he lodged them so firmly in his heart that never afterwards did he let them go.

Long and hard did Peter reflect upon this message. How should he accomplish so great a task? Indeed it is no wonder if he wakes and watches, deep in thought, for never in a thousand years has anyone engaged in such an undertaking. Now you shall hear what he decided: firmly and after long and careful thought he resolved to launch this campaign.

And so Peter founded an Order, the Order of the Sword, to attract good knights who had a devotion to the promised land; and it was also open to all men-at-arms who wanted to save their souls. This was the Order and its emblem: a sword of fine silver which stood hilt uppermost, like the holy cross we venerate, upon a blue ground, without other colours. Around it in gold was written, as I so well recall, 'With this keep loyalty'. Wherever he was, the king would wear this device. A thousand times I have seen and read these words.

Peter I calls for a crusade

In 1362 King Peter left Cyprus for western Europe, intent on raising the support of its rulers for a grand crusade to recover Jerusalem. With him went Philip of Mézières, his chancellor, who laments the failure of the western kings to keep their promises of support for Peter I's crusade.

Peter I, king of Cyprus, visited the Holy Roman Emperor, Charles IV, and the other western kings, for nearly a year and a half, at great expense and danger to himself, increasingly seeking their help for the sea-crossing. But alas, the sins of the world overhung them and the envy of princes remained steadfast, with the result that he found no man to give praise to God or care about the crusade, except in boasting and useless words.

There was none to take pity on the Holy Land, none to have compassion on his reproach – the shame of it! They all excused themselves, and sent the king of Cyprus away, empty-handed and in tears.

Then Peter, despairing of the Christian princes, and with no ally who trusted in God, returned in stages to Venice, and was there received magnificently by the Venetians.

Nevertheless, a substantial force, largely from Italy, had gathered at Venice, and on 27 June 1365 Peter sailed with them to Rhodes.

There, Peter revealed his plan: the crusade would attack and capture the Egyptian port of Alexandria, in order to compel the Mamluks to exchange Jerusalem for the captured port.

The fleet was ready to depart. The papal legate, Peter Thomas, accompanied by all the army's ecclesiastical figures, boarded the king's galley on 4 October 1365 to pronounce a general blessing on the army of God. Climbing into a conspicuous place in the galley so as to be seen by the whole army, King Peter I stood next to him, while everyone else stood and watched the legate; the standards and banners of the galleys and other ships were lowered. The legate blessed first the ships, then the arms, then the leading men and the sea and the whole army, calling on God's help for the honouring of the cross and the destruction of the Saracens.

King Peter of Cyprus and the whole army made their responses to the legate in an extremely pious fashion. When the benediction was over, on the king's galley there was suddenly raised on high the royal standard – a great red lion. All the army's trumpets sounded on an instant and numberless standards were lifted upon the air as the crusaders shouted with one terrible voice, giving thanks to God and saying: 'Long live Peter, long live our king of Jerusalem and Cyprus! Death to the Saracen infidels!' Then the legate, after saying farewell to the king and blessing him personally, returned to his own galley.

As always, I, Philip of Mézières, accompanied him in all these things.

The attack on Alexandria, 1365

At a blast from King Peter's horn, the galleys and other ships began to row slowly and gradually away from Rhodes and headed towards Alexandria, in Egypt, keeping to their given order. As our ships approached land, the Saracens, vigorously defending the harbour, covered them in arrows. The multitude of arrows then falling on the Christians was as great as raindrops upon the earth. But God defended us in a miraculous fashion, since they wounded but few or nearly no men.

As the galleys approached land, our men threw down ladders into the sea next to the shore, with the intention of disembarking this way. The Saracens, however, showed no fear of our crossbows, but entered the sea right up to their breasts and, covered with their shields, they continually beat off the attempts of our men to descend from their ships.

At last, after a battle lasting nearly an hour, with God's blessing a few of our men got down on to land and, gaining some ground after a hard-fought struggle, they began to take the upper hand. Then we Christians poured on to the land, since we were now able to disembark with more speed; the Saracens turned their backs and fled towards the city. Our men pursued them, and kept on pursuing them right up to the city gates. The Saracens, with some difficulty, closed the city gates against us and then climbed the walls to defend the city. Great is the glory and mercy of the Lord and his victory to all eternity!

Why say more? For King Peter I, surrounded by Christian soldiers, approached the city wall and placed a little fire in front of the iron gates. Within the hour, the Saracens abandoned the battlements; their spirits failed them, and, leaving the city, they fled towards Cairo.

The capture and sack of Alexandria are graphically described by William of Machaut, who also explains the city's subsequent abandonment.

When the gate had burned away to ashes, the king of Cyprus, the knights and the whole army joyfully entered the city of Alexandria. Once in, no Saracen was spared who could be caught and killed. Our men ran from street to street wounding, killing, or slaying each one. More than twenty thousand Saracens did they put to death. And they ransacked the whole town, for all the Saracens ran away because our men were hunting them. But God who knows and sees all, who directs and provides for all things, who does not forget his friends but always is on their side; God came running from his paradise to help the noble king; He gave him strength and

Peter of Cyprus the crusading king

'It has been said that he is tall (God break his back and make all his affairs go awry), blue-eyed (God raise him up blind at the resurrection of the dead and make him one over whom misery hangs), and blond (God impoverish him) . . .' So runs an Arab citizen of Alexandria's description of the crusading king of Cyprus, Peter I. Peter was born in 1329. In 1347, while still a prince, he had a vision, after which he founded the Order of the Sword, a lay brotherhood of knights dedicated to the recovery of the Holy Land. Two years later, he ran off to Europe, probably hoping to find support for a new crusade, but his father, Hugh IV, sent agents to capture him and Peter was briefly imprisoned.

In 1359 he became king and, in the early years of his reign, launched raids against Muslim emirates on the south coast of Turkey. But he had grander crusading ambitions and in 1362 set sail for the west. Peter spent the next three years wandering the courts of Europe, begging for men and money for a crusade. He was hospitably received and took part in many tournaments, but found little enthusiasm for his cause. Nevertheless, drawing on the support of Pope Urban V and on Cyprus's own resources, he had by 1365 recruited an army composed of Cypriot vassals and mercenaries and adventurers from western Europe. In October, a fleet of mostly Italian and Cypriot ships which had assembled in Rhodes was ready to set out; its secret destination, Alexandria, was at last made public.

Peter and his men took the city with ease but his triumph was short-lived. 'Honour, you are dead!' he lamented, but he was unable to persuade his booty-laden following to stay and hold Alexandria. After a week, he was forced to abandon the city. He continued to launch predatory raids against the coasts of Syria and Turkey, but in Cyprus the nobles were weary of his crusading obsession and his repeated demands for men and money. They resented the favoured treatment given to foreign mercenaries. In the eyes of many of his subjects, the king was capricious, cruel and only questionably sane. On 17 January 1369, just before dawn, two of his attending knights led a band of aristocratic conspirators into the royal palace in Nicosia. They found Peter in his bed and stabbed him to death.

power because He could see how he was striving to serve Him and to destroy his enemies. So did God ordain the outcome. The king's men were scattered throughout Alexandria, putting all to the sword. Those worthless Saracens – those of them who could – fled from the town. Never has there been such slaughter, not since the time of the Pharaohs.

The crusade comes to nothing

The crusaders then debated what they should do; a strong group, led by Turenne, argued the need for immediate withdrawal.

One of the knights, the viscount of Turenne, stood up and asked to be heard; he was listened to attentively.

'My lord,' he said to King Peter, 'if you want to put good, active men-at-arms to defend every wall, tower and turret, you have not got one-twentieth, no, God help me, not one-hundredth part of the men you would need, and so the Saracens could come in wherever they liked, through five hundred different places. Your artillery is exhausted and useless. There is another point: you have no food at all, and the people outside the town will keep it back, none will be brought in here, you will not be able to get provisions for money or for credit. Our horses have no hay or straw, and so they and we ourselves will die of hunger.

'Moreover, al-Ashraf Nasir, the sultan of Egypt, is close by. I tell you, he will bring five hundred times five hundred thousand men against the few of us, who will be fresh and well fed. You would be very greatly mistaken then, my lord, if you stayed here to have us all eaten up. For we are only a handful compared with the sultan's might; and we are in his country. He hates us all, and would never take ransom for any of us; nor are you expecting any help to arrive, I am sure of that, unless from heaven. Think what will happen when the sultan rides against us – we shall be caught like rats in a trap. Therefore, my lord, I do not advise that we stay here. Let us all go, for indeed it is time.'

It was the viscount of Turenne who made this speech and gave this answer. The king was astonished, for the viscount had promised that if King Peter could, by ruse or by courage, win any fortress in enemy country, he would serve him for a full year and would not leave him.

With this, all Peter's foreign allies set off without a blush and fled, telling the king there was no point in further discussion, for they wanted to leave; they would certainly not be able to hold the town and did not wish to do so.

The poet Petrarch was in Venice at the time of the capture. In a letter to the writer Giovanni Boccaccio, he gives an interesting commentary on the crusade and its tragic outcome.

The conquest of Alexandria by Peter I, king of Cyprus, was a great and memorable achievement, which would have created a powerful basis for the spread of our religion if only the valour demonstrated in its capture had been matched in its holding. Peter himself, it is said, was not found lacking, but his army, drawn together largely from northern peoples, who begin undertakings well but cannot sustain them, was to blame.

These northerners followed the pious king not from piety but from avarice. They deserted him at his moment of success, departing with their booty and frustrating his pious vow while satisfying their own greed.

The murder of Peter I, 1369

Peter now raided in Syria and visited Italy seeking support, but without success. Returning to Cyprus in 1368 he found his queen, Eleanor, had conducted an adulterous liaison with John of Morphou, titular count of Edessa, and had in addition cruelly mistreated Peter's favourite mistress, Joan l'Aleman.

Peter now became a tyrant. In January 1369, he was assassinated in his bed at dawn, as the Cypriot chronicler Diomede Strambaldi relates.

Very early on 17 January 1369, King Peter I of Cyprus was in bed, naked save for a shirt, and as he was unwilling to dress himself in the presence of his brother, who was with him, he said to him: 'Sir prince my brother, go outside for a moment while I dress.' So the prince went out.

Then Philip of Ibelin, lord of Arsuf, pushed into the room; in his hand he had a knife such as they used in those days, and after him came Henry of Jubail. When his brother had left the room, the king pushed back the sheets and rose to get dressed, but when he had put one arm into the sleeve of his jacket he saw the knights and shouted: 'Traitors, what do you want, coming against me at this hour in my chamber?' Each of them struck the king three or four blows.

The king cried, 'Help! Mercy! for the love of God!' but they had no mercy. John Gorap, the bailiff of the court, then rushed in and, finding the king still alive, took out his knife and cut off his head, saying, 'You meant to cut off my head, and now I have cut off yours, and all that you threatened has fallen upon you.'

All the knights went in and used their knives on him. They held his brothers captive until they had killed him, so that there would be no outcry.

Last of all came James of Nores the Turcopole who had not been party to the plot; yet, finding the king covered in his own blood and without his breeches, so as not to be left out he took his knife and cut off the king's testicles, saying: 'It is these which caused your death!' James felt compassion for the king, but he did this to be one of the knights' party.

The Genoese sack Nicosia, 1373

Francis Amadi, the author of a detailed chronicle about Cyprus's history, shows that in the confusion after Peter's death a feud between the Venetians and the Genoese over trading rights escalated and became uncontrollable.

The people of Famagusta sided with the Venetians, and in 1373 the Genoese attacked the port.

The Genoese sacked the rich city of Famagusta, in Cyprus, and took everything they could find; and then they tortured the soldiers in order to discover where they had hidden their possessions, and several died under torture. On 22 November 1373, to avenge Queen Eleanor for the death of her husband, the late King Peter I, they beheaded Philip of Ibelin, lord of Arsuf, even though he promised the admiral in command of the Genoese fleet much wealth if he were freed. But Philip's wife was in love with the admiral, who sent her word that Philip was to be killed and that he would not fail in what he had promised to do. The same befell the other knights, and the admiral had it proclaimed in the king's name that 'Whoever makes bold to lay hands on his lord will suffer this punishment, and this is the justice of God and of the king of Cyprus.' The Genoese killed many others, day and night.

When the Genoese saw that Nicosia was empty of lords, they sent part of their forces into the city and sacked it. They captured the walls, from the Market Gate as far as St Andrew's Gate, and held them: the tower above this gate was filled with earth and stones and above this gate they built a kind of fortress to protect themselves. Then they took Kyrenia, to enable them to hold Nicosia and the rest of the island.

Pilgrim traffic and maritime commerce

Pilgrim traffic and maritime commerce between the west and the Holy Land and the Levant were well organized by the 13th century. Pisa, Genoa, Venice, Marseilles, Montpellier and other cities had established trading factories in Acre and elsewhere, including Egypt where the Catalans joined them at Alexandria.

Ships followed well-defined sea lanes and sailed in caravans, as in the case of Venice, or independently. Pilgrim and commercial fleets left the west in early spring – in c. 1172 there were 80 ships at Acre at Easter – and either returned in the autumn or late summer, before the onset of bad weather, or prepared to winter in the east.

The traffic was regulated closely to protect pilgrims' interests and share of the vessels. Regulations governed the amount of deck space allocated for sleeping and stowing personal effects (1.5 x 0.6 metres), providing and cooking food, inspecting ships, captains' responsibilities, stops *en route*, and obligations to complete voyages.

Acre was the great seaport, the 'Constantinople of the Franks', and most traffic from the west passed through its custom-house: raw metals and metal goods, woollen cloth, timber, some herbs, furs and skins, cotton and linen, foodstuffs, a miscellany of manufactures, coinage and bullion. In return, the east offered spices, perfumes, dyes and chemicals, precious cloths, ceramics and even jewels. Trade routes moved further east from centres in the Byzantine Empire and Egypt, across the desert to Damascus and the coast of Palestine, and western merchants also captured much of the trade between the Levant and North-West Africa, and the Aegean and Black Seas. By the middle of the 13th century, the Mediterranean world was economically integrated.

The wealth of the east evoked rivalries, brawls, piracy and even trade wars. During the last decades of the 12th century Italian squabbling was a cause of weakness in the crusader states and in 1256 pent-up hostilities between Genoa and Venice erupted in a war which polarized the society of the Holy Land. Italians, Provençaux and Catalans continued to trade in Egypt; although there were ups and downs in relations with Egyptian sultans, mutual self-interest ensured that commerce continued.

The Mahdia crusade, 1390

North Africa, too, was a target area for medieval crusaders. In 1390 the two rival popes of the Great Schism, Benedict XIII (at Avignon) and Boniface IX (at Rome), sank their differences and supported a scheme proposed to Charles VI of France by the Genoese. This was for a crusade against the town of Mahdia in Tunisia, which was harbouring a highly effective corsair fleet, whose inroads into Italian trade in the Mediterranean had been so great during the previous decade that in 1388 Genoese, Pisan and Sicilian pirates had captured the island of Jerba. Now in 1390 a far larger force, including Spanish, Flemish and English troops, set off under the leadership of Louis II, duke of Bourbon. His biographer, Jean Cabaret d'Orville, gave a eulogistic account of his deeds.

I n 1390, the noble and valiant prince Louis, duke of Bourbon, set off from the city of Marseilles. With him went the lords who had come to join him, in accordance with the written instructions they had received. After the ships and galleys were fully laden at Port-Vendres with meat, wine, fresh water, armour and everything needed by the nobles of such an army, the duke of Bourbon and the other lords went aboard the upper decks and castles of the ships and galleys; the knights, men-at-arms and sergeants in great numbers, and the crossbowmen took up their allotted places. Then with the wind in their sails the vessels ran along the Genoese coastline.

Orders had been given that the troops should not disembark at Genoa, but should stay three miles off at sea, while the duke of Bourbon would land, for the Genoese had asked to see him. The duke went ashore and was made warmly welcome by the people, although he stayed there only a short time. They gave him a good supply of spices, syrups, Damascus plums and various drinks, which are good and strengthening for the sick, for which he expressed great gratitude. Then he left Genoa and rejoined his troops at sea.

The duke of Bourbon stood on deck on his galley, and rejoiced to see the ships lying close together, because the weather was kind and so calm that the sea hardly moved. He saw that his men were full of courage for the fight, and that he could achieve great things with their help; and he set off for Africa, for the wind had risen and they could now sail as they wished.

They sailed along the coast of Sardinia, where there were plenty of good towns where they could put in for food and avoid using up their supplies.

At Conigliera, in Sardinia (where they arrived in July), plans were made for the disembarkation before Mahdia. The lord of Coucy, a good captain and a very valiant knight, was to command the vanguard jointly with the count of Eu; they would land first, with six hundred men-at-arms given them by Louis, duke of Bourbon, and a thousand crossbowmen from Genoa and elsewhere to complete their force. Next would come the duke with the men of his own household and his own lands, bringing the main battalion. They would be followed by the rearguard under the lord of Castillon.

And so the lord of Coucy and the count of Eu disembarked near a Saracen mosque outside Mahdia and took up order of battle, expecting to be attacked. But no Saracen showed any sign of attacking them, and so Louis of Bourbon hurriedly disembarked from his galley and brought his whole battalion ashore, and all the rearguard as well. That night, the Christians slept in good battle array outside Mahdia, with all their ships at their back. Next morning the duke of Bourbon set siege to the city on land, while the Genoese besieged it by sea. The duke's siege lines stretched round all the land walls, and included the three gates into the city, but the siege by sea covered only one gate.

Typical medieval sailing vessels, with high sterncastles. One carries a compass, used in Europe as a navigational aid since the 12th century.

The Saracens, a full twelve thousand of them, seeing their town besieged by the Christians, decided to choose their own time to sally out all at once, through their three gates, upon the encampment of the duke of Bourbon and the others, so as to do the Christians great harm. And so they waited three days without coming out, in order to see what kind of watch was kept by the besiegers. After three days, at a time when the army was at dinner and the Saracens could see only a few men, they poured out of Mahdia by these three gates to attack the camp. But the Christians kept good watch – every man was always in arms; so they flung them back with such vehemence that the Saracens lost three hundred men killed. The men of the duke of Bourbon's camp pressed so far forward in this encounter, and they fought so well, that they killed many Saracens at the gate into Mahdia. The Saracens were so frightened that, for the next three weeks, they made no sallies but concentrated on fortifying their town.

Failure of the crusade

These initial successes did not, however, lead to ultimate victory. Jean Cabaret d'Orville relates the discussion which caused the crusaders to abandon the siege.

Louis of Bourbon sat outside Mahdia – he had set his heart on taking it. It would have been a great triumph if he could have done this in the face of the Moorish emirs, and he strove hard to achieve it, as did the lords and the men-at-arms of his company. He talked with some of the captains and commanders of the Genoese contingent, and they said to him, 'My lord, this town is exceptionally strong, you can see that for yourself, and very strongly garrisoned. And then there are those emirs over there with all their men; in our opinion they are not going to leave the field and nothing you can do will make them give battle; they are delaying us to make us use up our provisions. Moreover, we have no sows or bricoles in our ships nor any other siege weapons to bring up to the walls, our scaffold is burned and the falcon beaks destroyed. We really do not know what we can say.' 'There is nothing for it,' said the duke, 'but to make more.'

While the Genoese were discussing this with the other Genoese captains and commanders aboard the galleys, the Mahdians went to ask for a treaty. What they wanted was that the Genoese should make the duke of Bourbon raise the siege, and they on their side would get Ahmad, emir of Tunis, their lord, to promise that his army would do no harm to the Christians for ten years. The Genoese said they would be glad to report this offer to the duke of Bourbon. In reply, the duke told the Genoese that they were to tell the Mahdians boldly that the crusaders had not come there to make a bought peace but to conquer them. Further, they were to tell their lord that Christians had no truck with him and he was worth nothing. But at this the Genoese replied that they had not enough supplies left to maintain their ships, and that the mounted forces had almost nothing to eat.

Realizing that the Mahdians were negotiating in good faith, the Genoese proposed another treaty to them: for fifteen years they should pay the duke and the commune of Genoa the same sum of money which Ahmad, emir of Tunis, took every year from Africa – the emir was to get none of it – and in this present year they should pay twelve thousand gold sovereigns for the cost of the army; and they should give such good and reliable guarantors as should be required. The guarantors the Genoese asked for were Catalans, Neapolitans and men from Sardinia, rich merchants living in Mahdia; they were to see that the treaty was kept. The treaty took four whole days to agree, because these rich merchants did not at first wish to grant it; but after long discussion they saw that if the town was lost they would be ruined, as Ahmad their emir gave them so little help. So they agreed to the treaty and the Genoese reported this to the duke of Bourbon and his knights.

At this the duke called all the knights together, both French and English, to decide whether this treaty was honourable or not. The duke called on the lord of Castillon, one of the most senior men in the army and one of the most valiant knights to be found, and asked him his opinion. 'The treaty which the Africans are offering', said the lord of Castilon, 'is as honourable as if the town had fallen, for you are forcing them into subjection and tax-paying with or without their consent, and that in the face of their whole power. As for me,' he said, 'who am only a poor knight, I consider this as honourable as if I had been in three battles.'

The Nicopolis crusade, 1396

After concluding an agreement with the Mahdians, the crusaders returned home, having achieved almost nothing beyond furthering Genoese commercial interests in the Mediterranean. Meanwhile, the Ottoman Turks had during the course of the 14th century overrun large tracts of Asia Minor, and, under Bayezid I, 'the Thunderbolt', invaded the Peloponnese in 1394. Sigismund, king of Hungary (later Holy Roman Emperor), was as alarmed as the Byzantine emperor, Manuel II Paleologus, and in 1394 the Roman pope, Boniface IX, and the Avignon pope, Benedict XIII, proclaimed a crusade in response to Sigismund's diplomatic endeavours – and perhaps too in response to exhortations such as this one by the French poet Eustace Deschamps.

To all the princes of Christendom, kings, counts, dukes, knights and barons, who have spent so much time fighting against each other, burning, destroying and killing: we are brothers, one people and one law which Jesus Christ sought to buy with his blood; let us get together, let us organize ourselves to conquer the Holy Land with a true heart.

We have left it too long in the hands of God's enemies, and we should be ashamed. Alas! we are frightened; there are not many of us and we are so busy trampling on each other that soon we will have nothing left to live on; let us remember the good duke Godfrey of Bouillon, who crossed the sea at his own expense, I believe, to conquer the Holy Land with a true heart.

He conquered Jerusalem; let us be aroused to do the same. We call on the kings of France, of Spain, of Aragon and of England, on the agreement of the Genoese, the Venetians, the men of Cyprus and of Rhodes, and the king of Portugal; we shall call on Navarre. Pope, emperor, all of you, join forces to conquer the Holy Land with a true heart.

Most of these nations answered the appeal, and in late July or early August 1396 a vast army assembled at Buda, on the Danube, and met up with Sigismund's own forces. The crusaders swept down into Bulgaria, held by the Turks, massacring Muslims and Christians alike, until it met with its first serious resistance at the city of Nicopolis in Bulgaria, which it besieged. The Turkish sultan, Bayezid I, who had himself been besieging Constantinople when he heard about the advance, left the Byzantine capital and marched with an equally large army to relieve the city.

The anonymous *Life* of John of Boucicaut, marshal of France, who was regarded by contemporaries as the epitome of the chivalrous ideal, describes the battle of Nicopolis, where the flower of French chivalry fell on the field.

On 10 September 1396, Sigismund, king of Hungary, and his army arrived before the town of Nicopolis. He laid out his troops admirably and immediately had two good mines begun. These were dug under the ground as far as the walls of the town and were so broad that three men-at-arms could fight in them side by side. He remained a good fortnight at this siege. Meanwhile the Turks, I think, were not daydreaming but busy making great preparations to attack Sigismund. They did this so secretly, however, that the king knew nothing about it. Whether there was treachery among his spies or how it happened I do not know, for although he had set

Hungarian forces clashing with the Turks. The Hungarians wear full armour; the Turks are fancifully represented by the manuscript artist, as was often the case.

plenty of men to keep good watch on the Saracens' intentions, not a word was heard about it until the fifteenth day after he began the siege, and for this reason he was not on his guard against them.

On the sixteenth day, that is 24 September 1396, just at dinner time, messengers came hurrying to tell the king that the sultan, Bayezid I, and his Turks, with an enormous army, were so near that he would barely have time to get his men armed and into battle array. When King Sigismund, who was in his quarters, heard this news, he was horrified and sent word hastily throughout the camp that each man must arm and leave his quarters.

The Turks counter-attack

Sigismund was already in the field when John, count of Nevers, and the French, sitting at dinner, were told that the Turks were upon them and that the king was drawn out in full battle array upon the field. Hearing the news, John and his men leaped to their feet and swiftly put on their armour; then they mounted and in proper rank and order went to join the king, whom they found already in excellent battle formation; they could see their enemies' banners ahead of them.

Opposite them the Turks arrayed their battalions and put both horse and foot into good battle order. Then to deceive our forces they arranged this trap: a great mass of Turkish horsemen formed into one large battalion right in front of their infantry; behind the cavalry they set huge quantities of sharpened stakes, which they had brought with them on purpose. They set them at an angle, the points towards our men, and just at the height of the horses' bellies. By the time they had done this, which did not take them long, our troops had almost reached them.

When the Saracens saw that we were near enough, the whole cavalry battalion wheeled away in tight formation like a cloud and moved to the rear, behind the stakes and behind their infantry; in which there might be some thirty thousand bowmen. When our men had reached them, the Saracens began to shoot at them so thick and fast that never hail nor rain fell more heavily from the sky than the arrows now flew; in a few minutes they had killed great numbers of our horses and men. The Hungarians, who do not usually stand firm in battle and are not able to hurt their enemies except as they gallop away in flight, retreated and fell back for fear of the arrows, like cowards and cravens.

But John of Boucicaut, the good marshal of France, who was unable to see the sharp stakes so wickedly set just in front of them, began to speak like the valiant warrior he was and said, 'Hurry, let us attack them boldly, and in this way we shall avoid their arrows.' John, count of Nevers, and his Frenchmen supported this advice; at once they spurred on to charge the Saracens, and rode straight in among the stakes which were strong, rigid and sharp, so that they drove into the horses' bellies and killed many of them and injured the men who fell from the horses. Our men were very much hampered there, and yet they rode through.

Failure of the crusade

But now listen to the wicked, treacherous and cowardly behaviour of the Hungarians. As soon as they saw our men entangled in the stakes, the Hungarians turned their backs and ran. Of all the Hungarians not one stood by our men, except one great lord of that country, whom they call the great count of Hungary, and his men. But like the wild boar which thrusts ever more fiercely on the more it is attacked, just so did our brave Frenchmen overcome the strength of the stakes and all the rest and rode past them like good and courageous fighters.

The French nobles, frantic at the loss of their men both from the arrows and the stakes, charged the Saracens with such strength and courage that they terrified them all. Again and again, these lords and experienced knights, men of great might, and the noble sons of the fleur-de-lis, forced the Saracens back. So did the great count of Hungary and all his men, who were disgusted by the vile and shameful flight of the Hungarians. But alas, what good did it do them, a handful of men against so many thousands? For they were so few that there they were fighting three to one. And yet by their tremendous strength, daring and courage they defeated this first battalion and killed many.

When Sultan Bayezid saw this, he was so alarmed by the great valour of the French that neither he nor his huge battalion of cavalry dared attack our men but fled, he and his troops, as fast as he could. Then someone told him that the French were only a very few, for the king of Hungary and all his men had fled and abandoned them. When Sultan Bayezid heard that, he returned to the battle with a very large force of strong and rested men, and so they charged against ours, who were already battered, wounded and worn out.

When the good marshal Boucicaut saw this attack coming and that those who ought to have supported them had run away, he became like a madman. Into the heart of the fray he spurred his charger, which was a strong and heavy horse and well protected, at such a gallop that he overthrew all he encountered. And it is an amazing thing to tell and yet quite true, as those who saw it bear witness, that he rode right through all the Saracen battalions and then turned and rode back through them again to his comrades. Ah God, what a knight! God keep him in strength. And so our men fought as long as their strength held out. And how amazing it was, for the Saracens were more than twenty to one against the Christians and yet our men killed more than twenty thousand of them, but at last their strength gave out. Ah, how sad and how disastrous! On that field there fell, at the hands of the rabble, the greater part of the Christian forces.

A squadron of Turkish cavalry, whose disciplined manoeuvring at the battle of Nicopolis was instrumental in defeating the crusading forces of Sigismund, king of Hungary, and his French allies. The débâcle at Nicopolis ended crusading efforts to save Constantinople from encirclement by the Ottoman Turks; but that last remnant of the Byzantine Empire was preserved until 1453 by Tamerlane's incursions, which diverted Ottoman attention to the east.

Tamerlane

Born probably in 1336, Tamerlane's career began as a sheep-stealer and rustler in Transoxania (modern Uzbekistan, USSR) when he received the wound which made him limp ('Timur the lame') for the rest of his life.

His robber band gradually swelled to include enough Chaghatay Mongol tribesmen to take control of Samarkand, Transoxania's chief city, in 1366. Here Tamerlane governed in the name of a Chaghatid prince descended from Genghis Khan. Although Tamerlane could not claim the same descent, he strove to model himself on the great 13th-century warlord and empire builder, and was accused by some of his Muslim subjects of preferring the laws of Genghis Khan to the law of Allah.

From Samarkand, he led armies of Chaghatay Mongol horse-archers in pursuit of the traditional Mongol goal of world conquest. During the late 14th century, Tamerlane's armies campaigned successfully in Iran, Iraq, the Caucasus, southern Russia, Afghanistan and India, relying on mobility and on the terror induced in opponents by the atrocities committed by the Chaghatay.

Transoxania and Iran were the heartlands of his empire, and Samarkand was his capital. He despatched drafted craftsmen and the spoils of war to embellish the city, though in practice he governed from the saddle. Although his rule over these regions was despotic and brutal, he brought them security of a sort and one of his court historians claimed that 'one hundred years of tyranny and oppression are preferable to two days of trouble and popular tumult'.

In 1400 Tamerlane invaded Mamluk Syria, where Damascus was sacked by his warriors. In 1402 he turned his attention to Turkey and defeated and captured the Ottoman sultan, Bayezid I, at the battle of Ankara. Byzantine Constantinople, the imperial city which had been blockaded by Bayezid for the past six years, was reprieved for another inglorious half-century.

However, Tamerlane had no thought of aiding Christendom. Before leaving Turkey, he led his army to Smyrna on the southern coast, garrisoned by the Knights Hospitallers. The Mongol forces stormed the town and fired the heads of knights from mangonels at a rescue fleet. After returning to Samarkand, Tamerlane planned an invasion of China, but died on its frontiers in 1405.

Tamerlane, Mongol emperor

In 1402, however, Bayezid I, then at the height of his power, was defeated by the great Mongol warlord Tamerlane. This letter, written to the Avignon pope, Benedict XIII, by Martin I, king of Aragon, is a bitter attack on the Mongol emperor – although the same king was subsequently to write to Tamerlane himself, congratulating him on his victory.

Most holy and blessed father,
We are striving to bring to destruction that Belial Tamerlane, who came from the east with countless battalions of armed men, weighed down with the spoils of the riches of the east. We now know that he has turned to the west and will not cease from pressing onward with his mighty army by land and sea. He has reached Smyrna, in Anatolia, and has smashed it and some of the stronger castles under the command of the master of the Hospitallers at Rhodes. Into these he has broken by force of arms and has put to the sword whomsoever he has found inside in accordance with his usual practice so that nothing is left but smoke and ashes.

Just before this victory, in 1401, the Castilian nobleman and ambassador Ruy Gonzalez de Clavijo, representing King Henry III of Castile, had visited Tamerlane's court at Samarkand, of which he wrote this remarkable account.

On Monday 8 September 1401, the Castilian ambassadors left the house where they were staying and set off for the city of Samarkand to see the lord Tamerlane. The journey to the city crossed a plain where there were gardens, houses and squares in which many things were being sold. By mid-morning, they had come to a large garden and palace outside the city, where the lord was. When they arrived, the ambassadors were instructed to dismount; outside the gate two knights came up to them and told them to hand them the presents they were bringing to the lord, for they would arrange to place them before the lord; these were the orders of the lord's personal servants. So the ambassadors handed the presents to the two knights.

The gateway to the garden was very broad and high and beautifully decorated with blue and gold tiles. It was guarded by many gatekeepers holding maces. Even though there were many people there, none of them dared approach the gate. When the ambassadors entered, they encountered six elephants with wooden castles mounted on their backs, each of which had two banners and carried men who made the elephants perform tricks for people. The ambassadors were made to move forward and then to wait a while before moving on again, all the time being held under the arm by the two knights. The emissary whom Tamerlane had sent to the king of Castile was with them, wearing Castilian dress, and this caused those who saw him to laugh at his attire.

They were brought before an aged knight seated on a low platform. He was the son of one of Tamerlane's sisters, and they bowed before him. They were then taken before three boys seated on a platform; they were grandsons of the lord and the ambassadors bowed before them too. They handed over the letter that Henry III, king of Castile, had sent to Tamerlane. The three boys stood up and took the letter to the lord, whereupon the ambassadors were ordered to step forward.

Tamerlane was seated in the porch before the entrance to several fine residences. There was a platform on the floor, and in front of it a fountain which spurted water very high and in which there were some red apples. Tamerlane was resting on small round cushions embroidered with silk, and was dressed in a plain silk robe, while on his head he wore a tall white hat with a ruby, pearls and other precious stones on top.

When the ambassadors saw the lord, they bowed, placing their right knee on the ground and crossing their arms across their chest. They then moved forward and bowed a second time, and then a third time, and at the third bow remained still, each with his right knee on the ground. The lord bade them rise and approach him, while the knights who were holding them by the arm let go, for they dared not go further forward. The lord bade them come closer still. He asked this so that he might see them better; his sight was poor, for he was so old that his drooping eyelids covered his eyes. He asked after Henry III of Castile saying: 'How is my son the king? How are things with him? Is he in good health?' The ambassadors replied, and told him of the reason for their mission.

Tamerlane listened to what they had to say, and when they had finished he turned to several knights who were seated at his feet. 'Behold,' he said, 'here are the ambassadors who have been sent to me by my son, King Henry III, who is the greatest king of the Franks, who live at the end of the earth and are a great people. I shall give my blessing to my son, the king. It would have sufficed for him to have sent you with the letter and without the gifts, for I would have been just as content to hear of his health and his affairs, as I am to receive his gifts.'

As the ambassadors were taking their leave of the lord, he had brought before him the presents that the king had sent him; he took the presents and was greatly pleased with them. He divided the scarlet cloth among his wives, of whom the khanum, his principal wife, whom he had with him in the garden, received the largest portion.

A barbarian palace

At the centre of the garden, there is a splendid palace built in the shape of a cross, which is sumptuously decorated. In the middle of the house there are three alcoves, suitable for a bed or a dais, while the floors are of glazed tiles. The largest of these alcoves contains a silver-plated screen, as high as a man and three metres across, and in front of it there is a bed made up of silk sheets embroidered with gold placed one above the other on the floor; this is where the lord would sit. The walls are decorated with hangings of rose-pink silk, and these hangings are in turn ornamented with silver-gilt leaf, beautifully set with emeralds, pearls and other precious stones. Above these decorations, there hang down strips of silk, thirty centimetres wide, which have similar ornamentation to the hangings. From these strips of silk hang silk tassels in several colours and when the wind blows they look most pretty as they swing from side to side.

On the floor there are carpets and rush mats. In the middle of the house, before the door, there are two gold tables, each with four legs, and each is all of a piece. They are one and a half metres long and on them stand seven golden phials, two of which are set with large pearls, emeralds and turquoises, while each has a ruby near the mouth. In addition, there are six round gold cups, one of which has large round clear pearls set on the outside, and in the centre it has a ruby, two fingers' breadth across and of a fine natural colour.

From Ruy Gonzalez de Clavijo,
Embajada a Tamorlán

Mongol customs

When ambassadors and envoys came to Tamerlane, they would be much feasted. After they had been seated in their places, the servants brought quantities of mutton, boiled, dressed and roast, and of roast horse. The meat was placed on large round pieces of embossed leather. As soon as the lord called for meat, numerous men would bring it to him, dragging it along on the pieces of leather, for such great quantities were placed on each. When they were within twenty paces of the lord, carvers came to cut up the meat, kneeling down in front of the leather. They wore aprons and had leather over-sleeves so as not to get grease on themselves.

They took hold of the meat and cut it up, placing it in bowls, some of gold or silver, some even of glazed pottery and others of china, which are very valuable and expensive. The most prized cut was a haunch of the horse, with the loin but without the leg. They cut it into pieces, sufficient for ten gold and silver dishes; on them they also placed the loin of the sheep, with the leg but not the hock. On the dishes they also put pieces of horse's tripe, as large and round as a fist, and whole sheep's heads.

In this way they filled many dishes and they arranged them in rows. Men then came with bowls of broth and crumbled salt into them. They poured a little of the broth over each dish as sauce, and took some thin pieces of bread, which they folded four times and placed on the meat in the dishes.

When this was done, the courtiers of the lord, and the leading nobles present, took hold of the dishes, which needed two, or even three, men to lift them, for one man alone did not suffice. When the boiled and roast meat was removed, they brought mutton, meatballs and rice prepared in a variety of ways. These were followed by quantities of fruit: melons, grapes and peaches, and from gold and silver bowls and basins they were given mare's milk and sugar to drink, which is a pleasant beverage which they prepare in summer.

From Ruy Gonzalez de Clavijo,
Embajada a Tamorlán

Tamerlane enthroned in his splendid court at Samarkand, capital of an empire stretching from Delhi to the Black Sea.

The Hussites

When, from 1405, John Hus, rector of Prague University and leader of the movement against the worldliness and corruption of the Bohemian Church, called for reform, there was nothing heretical in his views. However, the Church was determined to maintain discipline by making an example of him. Summoned under safe conduct to the Council of Constance, he was condemned as a heretic and burned in 1415: the Holy Roman Emperor Sigismund, brother and heir of the Bohemian king Wenceslas IV, agreed to set the safe conduct aside on the grounds that no faith need be kept with heretics.

The news of Hus's death outraged Bohemia. The nobility assembled to lodge a formal protest, and Wenceslas could hardly retain control in Prague. When he died in 1419, the Czechs repudiated Sigismund's claim to the crown of Bohemia and installed an interim government of their own. This was the start of the Hussite Revolt, led by nobles, townsmen and reformist clergy. In 1420, they drew up the Four Articles of Prague, summarizing the main tenets of their faith, which could easily be comprehended by the whole population, and gave the movement unity of purpose.

There were also breakaway protests against the traditional authority of kings and churchmen among the poor of Prague and by the peasants, who set up armed camps, such as one named Mount Tabor, in expectation of the millennium, and radicalized the Hussite religious movement. When the Holy Roman Empire launched a series of crusades in 1420–32 against Bohemia to crush a threat to Catholic unity, Jan Žižka and his successors defeated them on a tide of religious fervour.

Although the crusades failed, disagreement between radicals and moderates, which had divided the Hussite movement since its inception in 1419, became increasingly prominent. In 1434, the radicals (Taborites) were crushed by the moderates at the battle of Lipany. Negotiations were opened with the Church's Council of Basle, Sigismund's title as king of Bohemia was recognized, and an agreement with the emperor and with representatives of the Church, legitimizing a moderate form of Hussitism, was reached in 1436.

However, the papacy never ratified these arrangements, the Czechs continued to be feared and hated as a nation of heretics, and the country was greatly impoverished by the wars.

The Hussite crusades, 1420–32

Between 1420 and 1432 five crusades were launched against the Hussites, a major heretical sect which threatened the political order of the kingdom of Bohemia. The founder of the movement, John Hus, had been burned for heresy in 1415, but his followers challenged the claims of Sigismund, king of Hungary and Holy Roman Emperor-elect, to the throne of Bohemia. Sigismund led a crusading army of some 20,000 men into Bohemia in 1420. He suffered defeat by the forces of the Hussite leader Jan Žižka – and the four subsequent Hussite crusades similarly foundered on the tide of Czech nationalism.

In this letter written to the people of Domažlice on 12 September 1421, Žižka describes the Catholic crusaders as the forces of Antichrist.

Dear brethren in God:
For the sake of the Lord God, I ask you to remain in the fear of God, as his most beloved sons, and not to complain when you are exposed to his chastisement. But remember him who wrought the strong foundations of our creed, the Lord Jesus Christ, defend yourself bravely against the misdeeds which those Germans commit against you, follow the example of the old Czechs who, their pikes firmly propped, defended not only God's cause but also their own. And we, dear brethren, seeking the law of God and the common good, will do the very best that is in our power so that anyone who can swing a club and hurl a stone should be up in arms.

And therefore, dear brethren, be it known to you that we are drafting men from all sides against such enemies and destroyers of the Czech land. Therefore you, too, order your priests to arouse the people to arms against such forces of Antichrist. Also call the people together in the market-place, so that all men, even the youngest and oldest, who are strong enough, may be up in arms at every hour of the day.

And we, God willing, will soon come to you. Hold ready bread, beer, fodder for the horses, and all weapons of war. For now is the time to fight against the foreign enemies at least as hard as against those inside our country. Remember your first fight when, little men against the great of the land, few against many, unarmoured against men in iron, you fought bravely and successfully. As yet the arm of God has not grown shorter. Therefore let your hope rest in God and be prepared. May the Lord God strengthen you!

Given at Orlik Castle on the Friday following the Nativity of the Virgin Mary.

The Catholic crusaders against the Hussites were equally critical of their opponents, as is clear from the letter written by Cardinal Henry Beaufort, a leading English ecclesiastic and politician, to the Hanse towns in 1427. Cardinal Beaufort asks this wealthy mercantile association for support for a proposed crusade against the Hussites, but when, in 1428–9, an army was gathered, it was diverted into the very English war with France which he here condemns.

My dear friends and illustrious colleagues:

Among the many disasters which Christendom has suffered in our times, we know of no other which has proved so great a hindrance to the faith and the Church as their internal divisions and factions. We cannot now understand the weakness, the inexperience of war, or the inconstancy of faith, that has changed the princes and the Catholic people into half-men, so that not just one man, but scarcely the whole lot of them in full array, would hardly have the strength to make threats or take their stand against the infidels.

By infidels, I mean especially the Bohemians, who are neither a noble people nor experienced in arms, and the sort of people whom neither nobility of birth nor intense effort in the exercise of arms could make better than anybody else.

We are weighed down with war between France and England, but when these two kingdoms have, God willing, made their peace, I shall diligently apply myself – as far as I am able and through the grace of God – to the gathering up of Catholic forces for the extermination of the Bohemian infidels. For the Most High knows of the excessively perverse types of torture which Christ's faithful have undergone at the hands of these incorrigible heretics.

Dear friends and illustrious colleagues, may the saviour in his prospering mercy deem it right long to preserve you.

The power of Mamluk sultans

In about 1421, Gilbert of Lannoy, a Burgundian nobleman, was despatched to the east on a reconnaissance mission by the duke of Burgundy and the English and French kings. As a result he wrote this vivid description of the style of Mamluk power.

It should be realized that Egypt, Upper Egypt and Syria are all controlled by one lord, namely a sultan of Cairo who rules over them all. The sultan never emerges in the normal way from among the native inhabitants of these countries, because it is said that the people are too wicked and too weak to be able to protect their country properly; so they choose as sultan some slave emir who, by his intelligence, courage and self-control, has got on so well in the world, and acquired so much power and so many friends, during the reign of the previous sultan, that, on the death of the sultan, he himself becomes lord. The same things, power and vested interests, keep him in authority; nevertheless, he cannot rest easy and is always in danger of being overthrown by some other emir who may usurp some of his power, by betraying him or conspiring with other people.

Even if a sultan has children, and gives orders during his lifetime that one of the said children should become lord after him, and even if the great emirs all agree to this, it rarely happens. Instead, the chosen heir is often taken prisoner and thrown into gaol for life or secretly strangled or poisoned by one of these same emirs. This lordship is very dangerous and power changes hands often.

It is said that a sultan of Cairo always has, both in Cairo and in the surrounding area, about ten thousand slaves pledged to him, some with two mounts, some with more, some with less, who make up his men-at-arms and who fight for him when necessary. And it should be known that these slaves are from foreign countries, both Christian and otherwise, such as Tartary, Turkey, Bulgaria, Hungary, Slavonia, Wallachia, Russia and Greece. They are not known as slaves unless the sultan bought them with his own money, or unless they were sent to him as gifts from foreign lands.

The sultan draws his bodyguard only from among these slaves, and gives them women and castles, horses and clothing. He takes them when they are young and gradually trains them, introducing them to warfare and rewarding each, according to his merits, with command over ten lances, or twenty, or fifty, or a hundred. In this way one may rise to become emir of Jerusalem, another to become emir of Damascus, another grand emir of Cairo and so on, filling the other important posts throughout the country.

It should be known that the true Saracens, whose country it is, do not have much to do with the ruling bodies of the large towns, especially in Egypt; instead the Mamluk slaves govern them. When the sultan wages war against some rebel emir or against one of his enemies, however, none of the common people of the large towns goes to fight, nor do the men from the fields; everybody goes on with his trade or his labour, leaving those who want to become lords to get on with it. When these slaves go to war, they are always on horseback, protected only by a rather basic breastplate, covered in silk, and a little round helmet; each is armed with a bow and arrows, a sword, a club and a drum which they use when they catch sight of their enemy in battle, at which point they all beat their drums to scare the enemy horses.

Rise of the Mamluks in Egypt

From the ninth century, Muslim rulers employed Turkish soldiers of servile origin, called *mamluks* (in Arabic meaning 'owned'), in their armies. Brought as youths from the Central Asian steppe, the young Turks were converted to Islam and given intensive military training. The harsh environment of the steppe made for hardy recruits, while the nomadic society into which they were born provided them with the rudiments of horsemanship and archery. After several years' training, the Mamluks were enrolled in the army as mounted archers. Muslim rulers had learned that exposure to civilization destroyed the unparalleled military prowess of 'barbarians', and only slaves fresh from the steppes were enrolled as Mamluks: their sons were normally not allowed to join what was a continually replicating, one-generation military caste.

The last important Ayubid sultan, as-Salih Ayub, sultan of Egypt from 1240 to 1249, significantly expanded the Mamluk element in his army, the mainstay of which was the Bahriyya, a unit of some 1,000 Mamluks, named after its barracks on an island in the Nile (in Arabic, *bahr al-nil*). Its two most famous veterans were Baybars and Qalawun, both future sultans.

The Bahriyya, led by Baybars, spearheaded the successful counter-attack against the crusaders during the battle of Mansourah (1250), and soon afterwards they murdered Turan Shah, as-Salih's son and successor, believing that he was discriminating against them. The throne of Egypt, after a short interregnum, was seized by a Mamluk officer, Aybeg. In 1260, after a decade of infighting, Mamluk troops under Sultan Qutuz and Baybars met a Mongol army at Ain Jalut in the Jezreel Valley in Palestine, and dealt them a decisive blow. In the aftermath of their victory, the Mamluks gained most of the Syrian possessions of the Ayubids, whose rule had been brought to an end by the Mongols.

Soon after the battle of Ain Jalut, Qutuz was murdered by Baybars, who was proclaimed sultan of Egypt, and who organized the centralized administration characteristic of the Mamluk state. He expanded and strengthened the army and waged relentless war against the Mongols, who controlled Persia, Iraq and Anatolia. In between, he turned his attention towards the Franks in Syria, beginning the steady conquest of crusader possessions that his successors completed by 1291.

The Saracens – the true natives, especially those in Egypt – are a wretched people, who just wear shirts, with no leggings or breeches, and with a band around their heads. As for the common people of the flat country, they have very few bows, arrows, swords or weapons of any sort.

There are large numbers of Christians throughout Egypt; I mention them only briefly here because they could only be of very limited help to western Christians in this respect.

The Mamluks invade Cyprus, 1426

The Genoese continued to dominate Cyprus after their raid on Nicosia in 1373. They used all means possible to maintain their commercial interests: in 1426 they sided with Barsbay, Mamluk sultan of Egypt and Syria, when he launched a major attack on the island. Strambaldi continues with the tale of Cyprus's humiliation.

In July 1426, news came to Janus, king of Cyprus, that the Mamluk army had arrived. Immediately the king commanded the army to assume battle order: sixteen hundred armed men on horseback, heavy and light, and four thousand foot-soldiers, arrayed inside and outside the city. These forces set out on the very same day, and arrived at Potamia. Word was sent to Rhodes and other places that they should send help, and it was expected at any time; and the king dined at Potamia.

The Saracens sent an old Mamluk, a renegade Christian, as ambassador to the king. But the knights did not allow the ambassador to appear before him; the king commanded that the Saracens' coming be hindered, so that they would not come upon him unprepared.

Turkish horsemen; an illustration from a Mamluk manual of cavalry tactics contemporary with the assault on Cyprus. The discipline and effectiveness of Turkish forces were partly a result of centuries of hard fighting against crusaders.

The desert people

There is a type of people, called Arabs, who live mostly in the deserts and several other places in Egypt. They have horses and camels and are very numerous. Sometimes some of them even wage war against the sultan, though they have little to eat, are poorly dressed and have no weapons other than a small lance, long and thin like a pliable javelin, and a shield rather like a large buckler. Nevertheless they are much more courageous than the Saracens, even though they all worship Mohammed, and they choose emirs and lords from among themselves.

The Arabs often wage huge wars against each other. They have neither towns nor houses and always sleep in the open, under shelters which they make to protect themselves from the sun.

From Gilbert of Lannoy, *Oeuvres*

On Friday 5 July 1426, the king with all his army came to Khirokitia; he dismounted in the village of Khirokitia with his cavalry and set up tents; these were so far apart that, because they had not brought a trumpeter, when they wanted to pass on a command it took the whole morning until midday.

The Mamluks wrote letters and sent them to King Janus by a peasant. These said: 'Most virtuous lord, we have come here and you, who are as the son of our sultan Barsbay, have sent none of your men to acknowledge us and ask us what we want and what we seek. Now we send to tell you to come out to us to make a new truce and to treat for peace; provided that you do not receive corsairs in your island to harm us, and that you hold our friends as your friends and our enemies as your enemies, like good friends and neighbours. Our lord sultan has given us his carpet that we may spread it out beneath you, so that you may sit down. When you come we will talk together and you will be satisfied, and we will go about our business; but if you will not come to us, we will come to you, and you may expect that Sunday will not pass before we meet together.'

When they had read the letter, the knights discussed it and the wording of the letter did not please them. Some said that the Mamluks were deceiving and flattering us, and they took the ambassador and tortured him so severely that they caused him to die a bad and unjust death. The same thing happened to another ambassador whom they put in the tower in Nicosia. There were many Mamluks who had been baptized, and they commanded these on pain of execution not to go out of the city, so that they would not go to join the Mamluk army. But when these Mamluks learned of the king's attitude they ran away into the mountains in fear so as not to be taken by the Mamluk army, and there were fifteen of these people, all of whom wished to die as Christians.

The Egyptian writer Badr al-Din al-Aini shows how the Mamluks overran the island, and rejoices at the defeat of the Franks.

With God's help, Mamluks landed in Cyprus on Thursday 4 July 1426, and immediately set up camp, some of them remaining on board ship, ready to do battle with the Franks should these appear. A mounted contingent was sent to Limassol Castle, which had been damaged by a previous Muslim expedition. When they reached it they found that the Franks had not only repaired it, but had also improved the fortifications by the addition of a deep moat. The Mamluks set their ladders against the castle walls, but these did not reach high enough. One of them, having divested himself of his armour, succeeded in climbing on to the top of the battlements. God gave him strength for the sake of the prophet Mohammed – may he be praised – and protected him from the sixty armed men and their war machines assembled inside the fortress. He was soon followed by the others; once inside, they killed the Franks who had gone into hiding and, having captured the castle, they raised the sultan's banner, sung God's praises and blessed the Prophet.

This news was conveyed to Sultan Barsbay on Saturday 13 July 1426. He was further informed that King Janus of Cyprus had reinforced the capital, Nicosia, and had at his disposal two thousand well-armed mounted men, and eight thousand brave foot-soldiers, and was therefore well prepared for battle; furthermore, that most of the inhabitants had fled into the rugged mountains of Cyprus.

The envoy had also brought five prisoners to the sultan's court; four of them became converted to Islam, but the fifth refused to do so and was beheaded at al-Rumayla to the accompaniment of shawms and drums. This was truly a day of celebration and there was rejoicing in heaven and on earth. The Nile rose, and the population took this as a good omen for future prosperity and a prompt victory.

Meanwhile, the soldiers captured Limassol Castle and razed it to the ground. And when on Saturday 6 July a Frankish ship sailed into Limassol harbour loaded with men and arms, the chief of the guard, Emir al-Mahmudi, sailed to confront it, accompanied by a second Mamluk ship. Defeated and disgraced, the Frankish ship attempted to escape by sailing close to the coast, followed on land by a troop of Muslim horsemen. Two of them, Arkmas al-Ala i and Iyas at-Tawil, discovered that the ship had anchored close to shore and that some of the soldiers had landed fully armed, so an attack was launched against them. They were routed, except for five of them who were put to the sword and beheaded; their heads were displayed on the ramparts of Limassol Castle.

Rise of the Ottoman Turks

On 7 July 1426, the Cypriot army was defeated in the battle of Khirokitia; the kingdom of Cyprus never recovered its full independence.

Ottoman power began to grow again: in 1444, a large Hungarian army, which had papal backing, laid siege to the port of Varna on the Black Sea. The Turkish sultan, Murad II, hastened to Varna's defence. This letter from Aeneas Sylvius Piccolomini, later Pope Pius II, to Filippo Maria Visconti, duke of Milan, tells of the disastrous defeat of the crusaders at Varna.

Then the Turkish emperor threw an army of forty thousand men across the sea. For the Christian fleet that had been sent the previous summer to guard the Hellespont had now retired home as spies had reported. Their leaders were said to have taken their money and the wealth of Asia but I cannot be persuaded, nor is it likely to be true, that they could have been so treacherous.

The sea lay open to the Turks. They crossed into Greece and joined their army which waited there and so were able to launch a massed attack on the Christians.

Our men did not shrink from joining battle, which began on the feast of St Martin itself, 11 November 1444. So fierce and savage was the fighting that rarely could such a battle have been fought between mortal men! For a long time its outcome was uncertain; it was contested with equal force by both sides. As long as our men fought for Christ and our opponents for Mohammed, enthusiasm for the battle was such that fifteen thousand were wounded on each side.

So long as the battle was equal, neither side wished to stop. The more blood was spilled, the keener the hand-to-hand fighting.

In the end both sides were drained of strength: limbs were so enfeebled that they had strength neither to wield swords nor to bend bows. Both sides were thus forced to be still for the best part of an hour until their strength was resumed and their spirits returned. Then the battle re-started. In the end the Turks won because they were more courageous, or because they were destined to win, or because they were greater in number.

Those who escaped from the field say that no battle as bloody has been fought anywhere in Europe within the memory of our fathers. They also say that no fewer Turks than Hungarians fell, and, if the rumour is correct, eighty thousand men died in this battle.

Soon afterwards, Murad II's successor, his son Mehmed II, made a serious effort to capture the greatest prize of all – Constantinople itself. In 1451–2 he built the great castle of Rumeli Hisar near the Bosporus, north of the city's walls, to menace shipping in the straits and as a base for his operations. Its construction is here described by Kritovoulos, a Greek who wrote a history of the deeds of Mehmed II which shows some sympathy for the Byzantines.

Sultan Mehmed, at the very first opening of spring 1451, prepared ships to carry equipment and sent them up from Gallipoli to the Bosporus.

He himself with a large army went by land. On arrival at the straits on the seventh day, he halted his army; and taking with him some of the strongest young men and also some of the older men whom he knew as having intimate knowledge of the surroundings, he himself reconnoitred on horseback to spy out the country and its topography, especially with the greatest care the narrow part at the crossing, exceedingly narrow, with its twisting curves, densely wooded promontories, retreating bays and bends.

At the swiftest point of the current, with its resulting whirlpools and eddies made by the promontories and everything else making the crossing most perplexing and difficult, he established his ferry. They said Hercules was the first man to pass here, and after him was Jason with his Argonauts.

On account of the great noise and swift current of these waters, borne down from the Euxine Sea, that very great and extensive sea to the north which comes down and ends in a very narrow part, great waves are raised by the rush and force of the current as it bubbles and swirls and drives boats along, dashing them against the rocks and sinking them unless indeed great care and skill are exercised by the sailors in them. On measuring the width of the strait to find the narrowest point, he found it to be about five hundred and fifty metres.

After examining and considering all these matters and deciding only after most careful thought, the sultan came to the conclusion that this was the most suitable place, and made up his mind to build the castle there. He marked out with stakes the location where he wished to build, planning the position and the size of the castle, the foundations, the distance between the main towers and the smaller turrets, also the bastions and breastworks and gates, and every other detail as he had carefully worked it out in his mind. He then portioned it out in detail, ordering his men to undertake the work with the utmost speed, and offering splendid prizes to those who should work best and most speedily.

The work of building began in the middle of the spring, and through the zeal and rivalry of all who were employed on the work, before the summer had entirely passed, he had walled the castle, the best fortified, safest, and most renowned of all castles ever built. He worked it out with very large stones, carefully selected and fitted together. The joints were strengthened with much iron and lead and many other things, and it was fortified and made secure by the great massive towers, solidly constructed and raised to a great

Overleaf: The castle of Rumeli Hisar near the Bosporus, built on Mehmed II's orders in less than a year to control shipping routes to Constantinople. The castle's construction was the prelude to Constantinople's fall in 1453.

height, and by the strength of the smaller towers and bastions plus the height and thickness of the wall.

He made the shape of the castle triangular. He planned this form and this place for the castle, in the first place so that he might control as much of the shore as possible, for the sake of the stone-hurling machines. The thicker parts of the wall were towards the sea, so that the machines might close the straits and sink the ships. And this by night as well as by day, unless a ship passed by the consent of the commander of the castle.

Thus the management of the castle was arranged for by him, and in this way he united the two continents and placed the crossing under his own control.

Mehmed the conqueror

Mehmed, in a rousing speech to his followers, now called for the capture of Constantinople, which was the last enemy stronghold within his extensive empire. The response was overwhelmingly in favour of war.

'My fathers and men of my empire! You all know very well that our forefathers secured this kingdom that we now hold at the cost of many struggles and very great dangers. Who does not know how, in the days of our forefather Bayezid, the whole west rose against us, from the ocean and Marseilles, and the inhabitants of the Pyrenees and of Spain, from the Rhine river and those of the extreme north, the Germans and Sigismund, king of Hungary. Nor did they have any less object in view than to destroy all our power and rule and to drive us out of both Europe and Asia, had it not been for the expedition of Bayezid at that time. His experience and daring prevented this, dispersed them, and completely conquered and annihilated them.

'And again, shortly after, when the city of Constantinople had stirred up Tamerlane the Great from Babylon against us, and urged him on, we suffered under him, as you know. And at that time we came within a very little of losing all our rule and power, that is, of losing one of the continents [i.e. Asia]. From that time up to the present, the city has unceasingly and constantly plotted against us, armed our own people against each other, created disorders, and disturbed and injured our realm.

'Nor will it give up warring against us and stirring up trouble, as long as we allow it to remain in their possession. We must destroy it, or else be enslaved under their hand.

'So then, my friends, since such a city as this has set itself against us and does all it can against us, should we hesitate

and do nothing? Shall we not hasten to destroy it before it does us great damage?

'My men, since I am of this opinion and have reasoned out the thing and have these motives, and since I am so stirred by these great crimes, I have gathered you together here, for I consider the situation no longer tolerable. I recognize the right of all who are so persuaded to make known their opinion to me. And I maintain that we must undertake this, and fight quickly, and must accept war and capture Constantinople with all determination and speed, or never lay claim to our realm any more, or to its possessions as our own, or think of anything as certain for the future. For our own realm cannot be free of fear, or our goods out of danger, unless this city be either captured or destroyed by us.'

So, when he had said this, he cast his vote for war. And practically all of those present applauded what was said by the sultan, praising him for his good will and knowledge, bravery and valour, and agreeing with him, and still further inciting each other to war – some of them because of their own ambition and hope of gain, hoping from that time on to make something out of it and secure more riches for themselves, others to please the sultan.

Those whose ideas were against the step, seeing the insistence and zeal of the sultan, were afraid, as it seems to me, and unwillingly yielded and were carried along with the majority. So the war was sanctioned by all.

Miraculous sign in the sky: omen of Constantinople's end

Although it was now clear that Constantinople's days were numbered, no substantial help came from the west, and on 6 April 1453 Mehmed laid siege to the city. Its defenders fought bravely but their situation was hopeless and was echoed in a miraculous portent seen on 22 May. This description is by Niccolo Barbaro, a Venetian ship's doctor who was at the siege and who kept a diary recording the events he witnessed.

On 22 May 1453, at the first hour of night, there appeared a miraculous sign in the sky which Constantine XI Paleologus, the noble emperor of Constantinople, took as a sign that his end was approaching, as indeed it was. This was the style and form of this sign: this evening, at the first hour of night, the moon rose, and it had lost its roundness; for the moon should have been full when it rose but this moon rose as if it were three days old, and there was very little of it to be seen, although the sky was cloudless and as clear as a pure crystal. The moon remained like this for about four hours and then grew rounder; it became full only at the sixth hour of night.

We all saw this sign, Christians and pagans alike, and the emperor of Constantinople was deeply afraid because of it, and so were all his nobles. This was because the Byzantines had a prophecy that said that Constantinople would never be lost until the full moon showed a sign in the sky, and this is what filled their people with fear. But the Turks in the field rejoiced greatly at this sign, because it seemed to them to mean that they would have the victory, which was indeed the truth.

The fall of Constantinople, 1453

Kritovoulos gives a detailed and graphic account of the last stages of the siege of Constantinople and the city's fall to the Turks.

On 28 May 1453, Mehmed began an inspection, on horseback, of his companies. He addressed them all, *en masse* and individually, with words of encouragement, and stirred them up for the fight, especially the captains of each company, all of whom he addressed by name. In this way he rode past the entire army, following the length of the land wall from sea to sea, and gave them the appropriate commands, exhorting them and rousing them all for the battle, and appealing to them to show their virtue. He then ordered them to rest after their meal, until the attack was sounded and they saw the signal. This done, he retired to his tent, ate and rested.

The people of Constantinople were struck by the unusual peace but they had been expecting this battle, and began spreading the rumour silently, one to another, as they returned to their own regiments to make preparations.

It was late afternoon, with the hour of sunset already approaching, so that the sun was upon the besiegers' backs and in the faces of the enemy defenders, as the sultan had planned. At this point, then, he gave orders, first for the trumpets to sound the attack, and then for the other instruments – flutes, pipes and cymbals – to join in, making the maximum possible noise. And so all the trumpets of the other companies sounded in alternation with the other instruments; the overall effect was a huge, terrifying sound, and everything shook and reverberated with the report. Then came the signals; and first of all the archers, the slingers and the operators of the cannons and guns advanced on the wall at a slow march, in accordance with the orders they had been given; when they

came within range, they took up their positions and fell to the battle. To begin with, each side attacked the other with powerful volleys: arrows from the archers, stones from the slingers, iron and lead shot from the cannons and guns; as they got nearer, they also pelted each other and were pelted, mercilessly and furiously, with axes and javelins. Great was the noise from both parties, with many oaths and insults; and many on each side were wounded; quite a number even died. This went on for about two or three hours, until dark.

Then Sultan Mehmed uttered a great cry, and called the shield-bearers, the heavy infantry and the rest of the soldiers to attack the outer wall. Fierce fighting ensued at close quarters with hand-weapons, the heavy infantry and shield-bearers struggling to force back the front line and to mount the stockade, and the Byzantines and Italians struggling to guard it and repel them. The battle continued in this way through most of the night, both sides putting up a strong, brave fight. Giustinianni, the famous Genoese soldier who was entrusted with the city's defence, and the Byzantines maintained a noticeable advantage, safeguarding the stockade and repelling the assault bravely. So this is what happened in that part.

The other generals and colonels, meanwhile, with their own regiments, and especially the commander of the fleet, also made an assault on the wall by land and, with their ships, by sea. They mounted a strong attack, the one group with bow and arrow and with cannon, the other with ladders, bridges, wooden towers and all kinds of engines, which they put up against the wall. Some even attempted to force their way over the wall, especially in the places where [the Turkish commanders] Zaganos and Karadja had their troops. But the Greeks strongly repelled them and pushed them off vigorously. It was a brave defence: they prevailed in the fight and showed true virtue; for nothing that happened – not the hunger that oppressed them, not their lack of sleep, not the continuous, unstinting battle, not the wounds, murders and deaths suffered by their dear ones before their very eyes – succeeded in turning them even slightly from their initial vigour and resolve.

When Sultan Mehmed saw that the companies he had sent in were getting much the worst of the battle and making no significant progress, he was furious. He decided the situation was to be endured no longer, and immediately sent in all the companies he had reserved for later, his best-armed, hardiest and bravest men, who were also greatly superior to the others in experience and strength. They were the thoroughbreds of his army: heavy infantry, archers, spear-throwers and the company that formed his personal entourage consisting of the so-called 'janissaries' and others. He cried out, exhorting them that now was the moment to show their virtue, and himself led the way to the wall as far as the fosse. At this point he ordered the archers, slingers and gunmen to stand some way off and shoot at the front line of men on the stockade and the broken wall. The other heavy infantry and shield-bearers he ordered to cross the fosse and mount a violent assault on the stockade. They went at it with a great, terrifying cry of rage and fury, like madmen; and, as they were young and strong and full of courage, and were fighting next to the sultan, they never let up but assaulted the stockade boldly, without any plan or forethought, breaking the barrels that had been placed in front, breaking off the beams and scattering the other material that had been amassed, and forcing the front line to turn and retreat inside the stockade.

Giustinianni and his entourage, and the Byzantines who were in that part outside the walls, inside the stockade, were putting up a manful fight, holding back the Turkish surge and preventing them from mounting the stockade. From both sides there was a great din and commotion, with people shouting oaths, insults and threats, pushing and being pushed, pelting and being pelted, killing and being killed; one side struggling with all its might to enter the city and reach the children, women and valuables; the other fighting nobly to repel them and to defend the goods they had, if not in the end to prevail beyond this too. But as they were fighting manfully, entering the fray with all courage and endurance, Giustinianni was fatally injured by a shot from a firearm, which pierced right through his armour to his chest. He fell on the spot and was carried to his tent, in a bad state.

All the men around him broke up in dismay at the event, and abandoned the stockade and the wall where they had been fighting.

Death of Emperor Constantine

Emperor Constantine XI had no possible course of action left to him: he had no other men at hand to fill the abandoned positions or to make up the battle line of the deserters; and the battle was very heavy now, so that each man had to look to the defence of his own line and position. Nevertheless, with the Greeks that remained there and with his own men, a very meagre number altogether, he stood before the stockade and defended it manfully.

Sultan Mehmed, who happened to be fighting nearby, noticed that [after Giustinianni had been wounded] the stockade and the place where the wall was broken were now unmanned and without a front line, and that some men were secretly making off, while those who remained were very few. From this he realized that there had been a desertion and that the wall had been abandoned, and he immediately cried out: 'The city is ours, my friends, it is ours already! The men are running from us; they cannot keep at their posts

The fall of Constantinople in 1453. Only 7000 men held the city in a last heroic effort, led by the last Byzantine emperor, Constantine XI, who died fighting to the last.

The last Byzantine emperor

Emperor Constantine XI died fighting in the way that I described. He had been a man of natural temperance and moderation in his private affairs, who had taken the greatest pains to attain to wisdom and virtue; he could also hold his own with the highly educated and was the equal of any of the foremost emperors before him, in the readiness with which he perceived the required course of action; more particularly, in his even greater readiness to follow it; in his great verbal and mental ability; and, most of all, in his ability to deal with practical affairs, which was characterized by remarkable accuracy in assessing the present – as was once said of Pericles – and exceptional reliability in anticipating the future.

He was prepared to do and suffer all things on behalf of his country and his subjects. Although he saw clearly with his own eyes the danger that threatened the city, and had the opportunity to save himself – as well as many people encouraging him to do so – he refused, preferring to die with his country and his subjects. Indeed, he chose to die first, so that he might avoid the sight of the city being taken and of its inhabitants being either savagely slaughtered or shamefully led away into slavery. When he saw that the enemy were forcing him back, and surging through the broken-down wall into the city, it is said that he uttered, in a great voice, these last words: 'The city is taken; and should I still live?' With that he thrust himself into the midst of the enemy and was cut down. Such was the virtue of the man and his care for the common weal; such also his ill fortune, throughout his life but especially at its end.

From Niccolo Barbaro,
Giornale dell'assedio di Costantinopoli

any longer. The wall is bare; it is a matter of little effort and the city shall be taken. So do not soften, go to it with all your hearts, and show yourselves true men, as I shall too beside you!' So saying he himself led the attack. A terrifying sound went up from their charge and their shouting. The Turkish troops overtook the sultan and proceeded to the stockade, and after some time spent in fierce battle, they turned back the Greeks and vigorously mounted the stockade. In the mêlée that followed there was much loss of life. And here it was that Emperor Constantine XI fell.

The Turks poured into the city through the gate; the rest of the army followed with a violent, powerful surge, then dispersed throughout the city. But the sultan stood before the great wall, surveying events: for day was already beginning to dawn.

The Turks enter Constantinople

Barbaro relates the horrors of the sack of Constantinople by the Turks.

The Turks were fighting on the St Romanus side, that is, on the land side, and with their pagan cannon, and the crossbows, and arrows without number, and the shouts of the pagans it seemed as though the air was splitting open. And they brought up the huge cannon which could throw a stone weighing five hundred and forty-five kilos, and sufficient arrows to fire against the whole length of the walls on that side, which is six miles. The arrows which fell inside the fortifications were enough to load eighty camels, and perhaps twenty camel-loads fell in the ditches.

This fierce battle went on until dawn the next day.

You must understand that an hour before daybreak the Turkish lord fired his great cannon, and the missile fell on the defences we had made and razed them to the ground, and because of the great smoke made by the cannon it was almost impossible to see anything. But the Turks began to come in behind the smoke, and about three hundred Turks entered the fortifications, and the Greeks and Venetians valiantly drove them out, and many of them, indeed almost all of them, were killed before they could enter the fortifications. At this time, because the Greeks had the best of this engagement and in truth believed themselves victorious over the pagans, we Christians were all greatly consoled. Having been driven back from the fortifications, the Turks fired their great cannon once more, and again those pagan dogs started to come in behind the smoke in a great rush, trampling on each other like wild pigs.

Having taken the inner barricade, the Turks and their auxiliaries held it in strength and so they came inside the fortifications, seventy thousand of them, and in such an onrush that they seemed truly to be sent from hell. The barbicans were soon full of Turks, from one end to another, which was six miles. But as I said before, those who were on the walls dropped rocks from above on the Turks below without ceasing and killed so many that forty carts would not have been enough to take away the dead Turks, and these were killed before they had entered the city. But now the Christians were full of fear, and the Most Serene Emperor ordered the tocsin to be sounded again throughout the city and also at the posts on the walls. Everyone was crying, 'Almighty God, have mercy!', men, women and nuns and young girls.

The sack of Constantinople

On 29 May 1453 the Turks entered Constantinople at daybreak. Before they entered the city, the confusion of those Turks and of the Christians was so great that they met face to face, and so many died that the dead bodies would have filled twenty carts. The Turks put the city to the sword as they came, and everyone they found in their way they slashed with their scimitars, women and men, old and young, of every condition, and this slaughter continued from dawn until midday. Those Italian merchants who escaped hid in caves under the ground, but they were found by the Turks, and all were taken captive and sold as slaves.

When those of the Turkish fleet saw with their own eyes that the Christians had lost Constantinople, that the flag of Sultan Mehmed the Turk had been hoisted over the highest tower in the city, and that the emperor's flags had been cut down and lowered, then all those in the seventy galleys went ashore, and so did those of the fleet who were on the Hellespont side.

They sought out the convents and all the nuns were taken to the ships and abused and dishonoured by the Turks, and then they were all sold at auction as slaves to be taken to Turkey, and similarly the young women were all dishonoured and sold at auction; some of them preferred to throw themselves into wells and drown.

These Turks loaded their ships with people and with great treasure. They had this custom: when they entered a house, they would at once raise a flag with their own device, and when other Turks saw such a flag raised, no other Turk would for the world enter that house but would go on looking for a house that had no flag; it was the same with all the convents and churches. As I understand it, it seems that there were some two hundred thousand of these flags on the houses of

Constantinople; some houses had ten of them, and this was because of the great joy of the Turks and by way of rejoicing in the victory they had won. These flags flew above the houses for the whole of that day, and for all that day the Turks made a great slaughter of the Christians in the city. Blood flowed on the ground as though it were raining.

The dead bodies both of Christians and of Turks were thrown into the Hellespont, and they were carried along on the current like melons in the canals. No news could ever be had of the emperor, Constantine XI, or his fate, whether he was alive or dead, but some said that he had been seen among the dead bodies, and that he killed himself when the Turks entered through the St Romanus Gate.

So the battle had lasted from dawn until the ninth hour. Until that hour, those who were taken were killed, and after that hour everyone was taken prisoner.

This was the end of the capture of Constantinople, which was on the twenty-ninth day of the month of May in the year 1453, which was a Tuesday.

Muslim soldiers sacking and pillaging. Constantinople had never fully recovered from its sack by the Franks in 1204. The Byzantine Emperor Michael VIII Paleologus took it back in 1261, but his descendants were unable to prevent the gradual conquest of their Empire by the Turks.

8

THE MEDITERRANEAN AFTER 1453

After the fall of Constantinople, the 'crusading agenda' continued to be set by the Turks under Mehmed II. The conquest of the city added enormously to the power and aggressive nature of the Ottoman Empire: it liberated the Turks from any fear of a crusading army using the city as the springboard for an assault on the heart of their territories, and provided them with an imperial capital from which they could more easily govern their lands in Europe and Asia. Its fall also enhanced their self-confidence, convincing them that they possessed a mandate to undertake ever greater conquests for Islam. One result of his increased confidence was the care with which Mehmed supervised the rebuilding, repopulation and provisioning of Constantinople, or Istanbul as it was now called. Another was the series of campaigns which the sultan launched against Christendom. These compelled the papal court to a flow of crusade preaching and taxation measures.

The pope who promoted the crusade with the greatest enthusiasm was Pius II (1458–64), the last great crusading pope and a worthy successor to Urban II and Innocent III. Like many of the humanists of the Renaissance, he had been appalled by the Turkish conquest of Constantinople and concerned for the fate of classical culture, lamenting that 'here is a second death for Homer and for Plato too'. Pius was encouraged by an extraordinary event in 1456, when Mehmed's siege of Belgrade, the key to Hungary, was repelled by an *ad hoc* crusading army recruited through the charismatic preaching of the Franciscan friar John of Capistrano. The

The battle of Lepanto, 1571, which ended Turkish naval dominance of the Mediterranean.

'miracle of Belgrade' seemed to show that ill-armed volunteers could succeed where professional fighters failed, because they enjoyed God's support. None the less, Pius was under no illusions about the importance of securing the commitment of Christendoms rulers. He summoned their delegates to a congress at Mantua in 1459, but the envoys arrived late and procrastinated on the crucial issues of manpower and money. Pius persuaded the congress to pass resolutions proclaiming a crusade, but when the time came for his expedition to cross the Adriatic, in the summer of 1464, the only powers which made significant contributions were Burgundy and Venice. Pius, who had intended to accompany the crusaders into the field, died of a fever in August, and the expedition collapsed.

Mehmed continued his conquests without encountering organized western opposition. Athens was taken in 1456, the Peloponnese in 1458–60 and Venice's great fortress at Negroponte in 1470. The death of Skanderbeg, the Albanian hero and commander-in-chief, in 1469 removed the chief obstacle to the Ottoman conquest of Albania.

In 1476 Mehmed defeated a coalition of Christian and Mongol powers in the eastern Balkans. Meanwhile Ottoman sea power had developed to such an extent that in 1479 he ended a long war with Venice by forcing the republic to accept unfacourable peace terms. In the following year he was confident enough of his naval capabilities to launch two simultaneous amphibious operations, an attack on the Knights Hospitaller at Rhodes and an invasion of southern Italy at Otranto. The siege of Rhodes failed, but the Turks seized Otranto and were preparing to follow up their success when Mehmed died in May 1481. The accession of Bayezid II threw the empire into chaos, diminishing the Ottoman threat to Christendom. One reason was that for much of Bayezid's reign the western powers played host to his brother Jem, a pretender to the Ottoman sultanate, who could not be allowed to return to the empire. Bayezid was therefore happy to pay a large sum for his brother to be kept in the west, and to refrain from hostilities.

Coincidentally, a year after Mehmed's death the conquest of Moorish Granada, one of the crusading movement's greatest successes, started. Since Alfonso XI's capture of Algeciras in 1344, the pursuit of the *Reconquista* had been handicapped by war between the Christian states in the peninsula, and political strife within Castile. But in 1469 the heiress to the throne of Castile, Isabella, married Ferdinand of Aragon, the eldest son of King John II.

Peace was reached between the two kingdoms in 1479, and was followed three years later by war against Granada. The dynastic union of Castile and Aragon made possible victory over Granada, and when, in the summer of 1483, the chance of exploiting internal divisions in the Moorish emirate presented itself, the 'Catholic Monarchs', as Isabella and Ferdinand became known, decided to attempt its total conquest.

Granada's mountainous terrain, well-fortified cities, and determined population gave it immense defensive strength, so that a prolonged and very expensive war was necessary. For the next ten years Castile's military and financial resources were concentrated on a series of arduous sieges, the most important of which were those of Ronda in 1485, Malaga in 1487, Baza in 1489, and Granada itself in 1491–2. The strain imposed by the war was immense: at Baza a Castilian army of 52,000 men had to be paid and fed for almost six months, an effort which brought Ferdinand's war administration to the brink of collapse. Because the war was regarded as a crusade, money to help pay the huge costs involved could be raised by crusade taxes and by selling crusade indulgences. The royal court was able to quell popular discontent with the argument that the war was being fought for the faith and that successes or failures were bestowed by God.

This was far from being a public relations exercise. The Catholic Monarchs themselves clearly believed that the final conquest of Moorish Spain was a grave responsibility: its achievement was a divine gift, which brought with it the twin duty of maintaining the purity of the faith within Spain.

The Granada war therefore promoted an atmosphere in Castile in which the establishment of the Inquisition became possible, and created a drive to expand its boundaries overseas which took the Castilians into North Africa, where they conquered Manilla in 1497, Oran in 1509 and Bougie and Tripoli in 1510.

These impressive Christian successes were more than offset by Ottoman advances. In 1515–17 Selim I won probably the greatest of all Ottoman victories when he destroyed the Mamluks and incorporated Egypt, Palestine and Syria within the empire. His successor, Suleyman 'the Magnificent', therefore drew on an unprecedented range of resources, which he used to foster a rich cultural life at his court, and also to renew the drive westwards: a land-based advance into central Europe, and naval expansion using bases along the North African coast. The threat this posed to Christendom was amply demonstrated when Suleyman captured Belgrade in 1521, and drove the Hospitallers from Rhodes in 1522. In 1526 Louis II of Hungary was defeated at the battle of Mohacs, and the ground was prepared for the first Ottoman siege of Vienna in 1529. However, Suleyman realized that campaigning in Austria stretched his lines of communications too far, and accordingly shifted hostilities to the Mediterranean. A massive naval conflict developed there, as Suleyman vied with Charles V, Holy Roman Emperor and king of Spain, for control of Algeria and Tunisia. The Turks took Tunis in 1534 but were driven out in 1535 by Charles, who led a crusading armada of more than 400 vessels. Three years later galleys supplied by Charles, Venice and Pope Paul III were resoundingly defeated by Suleyman's forces off Prevesa, in Greece.

With the rise of the movement for reform within the Church, the international unity and co-operation which had characterized the crusading movement at its height became a thing of the past. The Reformation permanently split Christendom and restricted crusade preaching to countries which remained Catholic. The crusade was one of the features of contemporary religious life which most aroused the anger of the reformers, because of the abuses associated with the sale of crusade indulgences, and also because Protestants believed the very principle of a war sponsored by the Church to be contrary to Christian doctrine. After 1529, each occasion on which the Protestant princes of Germany rendered assistance to Charles V cost the emperor concessions on the religious issue. Faced also with the hostility of the French, who forged an alliance with the Turks, he was unable to do more than contain the Ottoman pressure. Although Suleyman was diverted intermittently by warfare with Persia, as well as by internal reforms, Ottoman naval power remained in the ascendant throughout the middle decades of the 16th century. Spanish forts in North Africa were taken, the coasts of Italy and Spain were raided, and, in 1560, the troops of Philip II, Charles V's successor as king of Spain, suffered a humiliating reverse on the island of Jerba, off Tripoli.

The struggle for control of the Mediterranean reached its climax. The Turks failed to take Malta from the Hospitallers in 1565, but Selim II, who succeeded Suleyman in 1566, invaded Cyprus in 1570.

Pope Pius V organized a naval league in collaboration with Philip II and Venice, and in October 1571 the forces of the league defeated the Turks in the battle of Lepanto. Together the two fleets comprised about 500 vessels and 100,000 men. It was a great Christian victory: about 80 Turkish ships were destroyed or crippled, and 130 captured.

The ability of the Turks, soon after this defeat, to complete their conquest of Cyprus (1571) and expel the Spaniards from Tunisia (1574) proved that their losses were less damaging than they appear; while the fact that the struggle for naval control of the Mediterranean petered out after Lepanto shows that both sides had other priorities. Nevertheless, Lepanto's importance in raising the morale of Catholic Christendom is undeniable; as Cervantes put it in Don Quixote, the battle 'revealed to all the nations of the world the error under which they had been labouring in believing that the Turks were invincible at sea'. It was also the last major engagement in a series of wars stretching back to Mehmed II's conquest of Constantinople (1453), which were portrayed, preached and financed in the traditional manner as crusades.

The chroniclers for this chapter, like the events with which it deals, are unusually varied. Pius II's Commentaries, a unique source and an extraordinary combination of idealistic hopes and pessimistic expectations, records the pope's own version of his crusading plans and activity.

The Greek Kritovoulos and the Turk Asik-Pasa-Zade are the best historians of the achievements of Pius's formidable adversary, Sultan Mehmed II.

But perhaps the best indication of Mehmed's greatness is the jubilant celebrations which were held by the relieved Romans when they received news of his death in 1481; these were recorded by the diarist Jacobo Gherardi of Volterra.

Leading Castilian chroniclers, Diego of Valera and Ferdinand of Pulgar, have been chosen to describe key events in the war against Granada, alongside official pronouncements by Ferdinand and Isabella, whose justificatory tone is worth comparing with the attempt of Charles VIII of France to depict his expedition to conquer Naples as a crusade against the Turks.

The matter-of-fact style of Bernal Díaz's description of Cortés's dazzling victories in Mexico contrasts with the high rhetoric used by Christopher Columbus to relate his discoveries to traditional crusading ideas.

Hajii Khalifeh is one of the few accessible Muslim historians of the conquests and setbacks of Suleyman the Magnificent, which are also recorded by western historians like Francis Balbi of Correggio and Hubert Foglietta.

Sultan Mehmed II mustered the army of Islam, dedicated himself to the jihad and set off to besiege Belgrade. From the pillaged material which had been smashed on his orders in Constantinople, he had had cannons cast – from the copper horse, the strange cross and the bells. It was with these cannons that Mehmed began the battle when he arrived outside Belgrade.

The governors of Anatolia did not agree with this plan, and so they hatched a plot to thwart the conquest of Belgrade. They very much disliked the idea that Belgrade could be taken.

One day, there came a mighty army of Christian unbelievers into the region where Karadja had wanted to cross, which camped there, with the accursed John Hunyadi, ruler of Transylvania, at its head. At the same time, many ships arrived on the river, and the battle was joined.

While Karadja was bombarding the citadel of Belgrade from the moat, a mortar shell unexpectedly flew from the castle and hit the structure of the earthworks. The beams collapsed and fell on Karadja, and he died a martyr's death. Meanwhile a battle took place on the river and many of the ships were destroyed.

Sultan Mehmed commanded, 'Come, glorious soldiers, we must attack!' They charged, and the knights of the sultan ran full tilt towards the castle, but the Anatolians, all deceitful, did not charge. When the Christian unbelievers saw where the attack was being mounted, they hurled themselves as one against the Turkish knights. But the knights drove them to flight and killed many of them.

Then the sultan mounted his horse and said to his troops, 'Why do you hesitate?' and at once he stormed the Christian unbelievers and pushed ahead. Many of his knights who were standing ready at his side surged forward with him. They cast some of the unbelievers back into the castle, but killed most of them. There was a fierce battle, but then Mehmed discovered the treachery of the Anatolians, who did not want the citadel to be taken. So the sultan departed and returned triumphantly to his own land.

This campaign took place in the year 1456. In the same year there appeared two large comets, one in the west and one in the east.

The fall of Constantinople to the Turks had horrified contemporaries. In 1456, a substantial crusading army went to relieve Belgrade, under siege by the Turks, and won an unexpected victory. In the above account, the Turkish historian Asik-Pasa-Zade plays down the extent of the defeat of Mehmed II's army.

Mehmed II the Conqueror

Sultan Mehmed II, 'the Conqueror', went on to a remarkable career following his conquest of Constantinople.

His Greek biographer Kritovoulos extolls his virtues, including his toleration of Christians, his rebuilding of Constantinople, and his creation of a great Ottoman fleet.

After the capture of Constantinople, Mehmed sent for the Greek Christian Gennadios, a man of remarkable intellect. Many reports of his intelligence and wisdom had reached the sultan, and immediately after the conquest he sought him out, wanting to see him and hear his mind in action. So a painstaking search was carried out in Adrianople, at the end of which Gennadios was found in a village, sheltered by one of the Turkish potentates and being treated with great respect; for the man who held him appreciated his qualities, although he was an enemy.

When Sultan Mehmed met him, he was made quickly aware of the intellect, power of speech and personal magnetism of Gennadios. He was exceedingly impressed, and lavished on him great respect and honour, as well as the opportunity of access to his own person, and freedom of speech. He took great pleasure in the man's conversation and he honoured him with costly and valuable gifts.

Finally, the sultan made Gennadios patriarch of Constantinople, and high priest of the Christians: the leadership of the Church, and the attendant power and position (which were as great as had been the case under the emperors), were just some among many signs of esteem and many provisions with which the sultan gratified him.

Mehmed allowed Gennadios to hold many fine conversations on Christian faith and theology, freely and openly, in his own presence; he himself attended in the company of those of his own court who were particularly admired for their intellect; even among these he honoured Gennadios.

There were many more marks of respect besides; such was the reverence for a man's virtue of which not just Sultan Mehmed himself, but his whole entourage and that of his potentates too, were capable. Thus it was that, by the will of God and of his own free will, the sultan restored the Church to the Christians.

Sultan Mehmed II, painted at Constantinople by the Venetian artist Gentile Bellini shortly before his death in 1481.

Mehmed the Conqueror

Mehmed II inherited the Ottoman sultanate on the death of his father, Murad II, in 1451. After executing his younger brother, which shocked his court, he launched into an incredible series of military campaigns, the first of which, the taking of Constantinople, earned him the title of Abu I-Fath (conqueror). The fall of the city was greeted throughout the Islamic world, by allies and enemies alike, with jubilation and prodigious celebrations – the Muslims' most venerable opponent was finally vanquished and the threat of a resurgent Roman presence in the Middle East irrevocably laid to rest.

From 1454 to 1459 Mehmed campaigned in Greece and the Balkans and then in 1461 turned his attention to north-eastern Anatolia and took Trebizond; 1462 saw him back in Europe where he defeated the ruler of Wallachia, Vlad III Dracul the Impaler (inspiration of Bram Stoker's vampire), deposed him and installed his brother, Radu III, in his place. Cilicia fell to Mehmed in 1474, and in 1475 he took the Crimea from the Genoese. During these campaigns little new territory was added to his empire but he established total Ottoman domination over previously semi-autonomous principalities, a precursor to the vast Ottoman expansion of the 16th century.

Constantinople was now his capital, and he planned its expansion. He built a palace (now the Eski Saray) in the city centre and erected the two immense al-Fatih and Ayub mosques and, later, a magnificent palace, the Topkapi Sarayi, for the administration. He took his administrative duties seriously, and reorganized the Janissaries into a disciplined corps. But by far his most far-reaching decision was the publication of the Qanun-name, the code of law, which sanctioned the practice of fratricide by the sultan regnant 'for the order of the world'.

A competent lyric poet, and the first sultan to assume a pen name – Avni ('divinely guided') – he provided many poets with pensions. A craftsman in his leisure moments, he carved woods and ivory and worked in precious metals. But his overwhelming passion was gardening in the parks around the palaces. During his campaigns he must have collected many plants which he introduced into his gardens, lilies, crown imperials, narcissi, tulips and above all roses. It was a passion that was to occupy many a subsequent sultan.

Mehmed visits Athens

In 1459 Mehmed sailed from Corinth at the beginning of autumn, left the isthmus of Greece and, with his own household and some of the men of high rank, went via Megara to Athens. For he had conceived a powerful love for that city and its sights, from the many wonderful things he had heard about the intelligence and wisdom of its inhabitants in the past, about their virtue and courage and about the many remarkable deeds that, at their peak, they performed, in battle against other Greeks and against barbarians.

He longed to visit and explore the city, including the other quarters but especially the Acropolis and the places where those men had conducted their politics and performed those acts, as well as the general lie of the land, the neighbouring stretch of sea and the harbours – in a word, everything. He saw, admired and praised all this, but particularly the Acropolis, which he ascended and where – like the great, wise monarch and the philhellene that he was – he made conjectures from the evidence of the ruins and remains, about the ancient city and about more recent times. The present inhabitants he treated with generosity, out of reverence for their forebears; he presented them with many gifts and granted their every wish. After spending four days there he sailed on the fifth, and proceeded via Boeotia and Plataea, viewing all the Greek sites, enquiring closely about them and listening to the accounts of their history.

Rebuilding of Constantinople

The sultan spent the rest of the autumn of 1459 in Adrianople. At the start of winter he went to Constantinople.

On his arrival he was exercised by his usual concerns, and devoted himself entirely to the organization of the city, and its recolonization. First he selected from the Peloponnesians he had brought with him those whom he considered the best, and those with professional skills, and settled them inside the city. The rest he settled outside in the villages, providing them with corn and pairs of oxen, and every other requirement for immediate self-sufficiency, to enable them to till the land and be farmers. Next he brought from Amastris – a city in Paphlagonia on the coast of the Black Sea – and resettled in Constantinople, the larger and better part of its inhabitants, as he did also those of his Armenian subjects who were most powerful, well provided and wealthy, as well as those with professional skills or other accomplishments, and the entire merchant community. These people he transferred there from their homes; and not these only, but the similar classes among his other subject peoples.

The Acropolis, Athens, admired in 1459 by Mehmed II, who had conquered the city from its Italian rulers in 1456.

He then called together all the men of his rank, men who enjoyed considerable wealth and also considerable influence with him, and told them to build fine houses in the city, wherever they wanted, and to set up large numbers of excellent granaries, inns, markets and workshops, to raise temples and shrines, and to decorate the city with many other such things, sparing no expense, each according to his own resources of money and power. He himself chose the best place, in the middle of the city, and ordered its existing inhabitants to build there a temple that would rival the biggest and finest for height, beauty and size. For this purpose they were to collect and prepare the finest materials of all kinds: a quantity of marble and other kinds of precious stone, as well as columns, all of them of outstanding size and beauty, and a great deal of iron and bronze, lead and every other suitable material.

He also gave instructions for a palace to be built on the promontory where the ancient city of Constantinople juts into the sea, which was to be greater and more wonderful than any previous one in its grace, size, perfection and charm. In addition to this, many fine dockyards were to be built to receive ships and their accessories; and very large, strong buildings to store arms, cannon and other such equipment. He issued instructions for many other similar projects designed to improve the city and be of general utility, and to provide the necessary facilities for his own wars and battles; and he ordered that they be done quickly, appointing the most experienced and conscientious men as overseers of the works. For it was his purpose to make Constantinople the most powerful and self-sufficient city in all respects, enjoying its previous level of attainment in terms of power, wealth, reputation, sciences, arts and all other affairs and fine accomplishments, and in the quality of the buildings and monuments set up for the public good.

At the same time Mahmud, his general commander in Europe, who was his right-hand man and next to him in power, and who looked after all matters of state, built an enormous mosque of very great beauty in a prominent position in the city. It shone with bright stones and marble, and the stateliness of the huge columns was magnificent; moreover, it was graced with fine painting and sculpture, embellished with quantities of gold and silver and decorated with many other fine gifts, monuments and objects of wonder. Around it he set up poorhouses, inns and baths, showing great generosity in their construction, which was carried out with a view to providing the necessities while also making them great and beautiful.

In addition Mahmud built for himself splendid, well-appointed houses, and planted gardens around them, which were filled with plants in a way conducive to charm, pleasure and enjoyment. He channelled in an abundance of water and made many such additions. In all this he followed the will of the sultan to the letter, as well as using his private means and resources to embellish the city as much as possible with buildings and monuments of general utility.

Above: Among the many amenities installed in Constantinople by its new Turkish rulers were public baths, gracing the new Ottoman capital.

Right: Turkish builders at work. The rebuilding of Constantinople by Sultan Mehmed II after 1460 transformed the city after the depredations of the siege of 1453.

CHRONICLES OF THE CRUSADES

The Ottoman Empire

The Ottoman Turks first emerged in the late 13th century, under Osman I, as leaders of a band of Turkish *ghazis*, or warriors for the Faith, in north-west Asia Minor on the edge of the Byzantine frontier. Led by Osman and his successors, the *ghazis* fought to acquire plunder, as well as to extend Islam's boundaries and their rulers' domains.

In the 14th century, although *jihad* or holy war was a major theme in their propaganda, the Ottoman *beylicate*, or principality, expanded as much by conquering the territories of rival Turkish princes as by waging war on Christian powers. From the 1340s onwards, the Turks took advantage of civil strife within the Byzantine Empire.

In 1354 the Ottomans occupied Gallipoli, their first significant foothold in Europe, but their gains in the Balkans and Asia Minor were slow until the accession of Bayezid I, the Thunderbolt, in 1389. Bayezid annexed the few remaining Turkish lands in Asia Minor, and, in the Balkans, victory at Kossovo gave him mastery over Serbia. In 1392 he laid siege to Constantinople; but the siege was lifted in 1402 when the Mongol warlord Tamerlane led an army into Asia Minor and defeated the Ottoman sultan at the battle of Ankara.

Mehmed II captured Constantinople in 1453; he acquired an important dockyard and arsenal, and the Ottoman sultanate began to pose as much of a threat to Christendom on sea as on land. Mehmed's grandson, Selim I, 'the Grim' (1512–20), successfully invaded the Mamluk sultanate of Egypt and Syria. Cairo, Damascus and Jerusalem came under his rule in 1516–17. Turkish ships engaged the Portuguese in the Red Sea and Indian Ocean. His son Suleyman the Magnificent (1520–66) captured Rhodes from the Hospitallers in 1522 and occupied most of Hungary. But although he led the Turks to the gates of Vienna in 1529, he could not take the city, and an attempt to take Malta from the Hospitallers at the end of his reign also failed. Even so, the underlying strength of the regime was considerable, and the Ottomans continued to make gains at the expense of Christendom. Cyprus was conquered by Selim II, Suleyman's son, in 1570–1. Although the battle of Lepanto (1571) was a famous Christian victory, and led to renewed preaching of the crusade in Europe, the Turks rebuilt their fleet and the war between cross and crescent in the Mediterranean and in the Balkans continued into modern times.

Rise of Ottoman sea power

The sultan then gave orders for a considerable shipbuilding programme to add to the existing fleet, and for the maximum possible recruitment from among all his subjects for a force that would serve exclusively at sea. For he realized the importance of power over the sea, and realized, too, that the naval force of the Italians, and in particular of the Venetians, was very strong in numbers and controlled the sea at present: they ruled over all the Aegean islands, and even encroached on his coastline, both on the European and on the Asian side. He wanted to put a stop to this and, if possible, to gain firm control of the entire sea; if not, at least to diminish their control.

He also realized that the passage between the Thracian peninsula and the Hellespont was of exceptional strategic importance, and decided to line it on both sides with very strong watchposts and to join the mainlands of Asia and Europe, enclosing and firmly protecting the whole of the Black Sea and the Hellespont above that point by blocking this passage, so as to prevent enemy raids on his coastline there. It was the same procedure as he had previously followed with the Bosporus.

The last crusading pope: Pius II

Pius II, a renaissance humanist, became pope in 1458. The last great crusading pontiff, Pius, despite six years of strenuous efforts, failed to fire Christendom against Mehmed. Soon after his election to the pontificate, Pius – as he explained in his own *Commentaries* – summoned a congress at Mantua, in Italy, to promote his crusade. This speech made by the pope to the assembly on 1 June 1459, reflects his concern at the failure of western leaders to appreciate the gravity of the Turkish threat.

Brothers and sons. On approaching the city of Mantua, we hoped to find an assembly of royal ambassadors had preceded us. But we were deceived: there were only a few there. The concern of Christians for religion is not as great as we thought.

We set the date for the congress far in advance, so no one could plead that notice was too short. No one could blame the hazards of travel. Struggling under illness and old age, we overcame the Apennines and the winter weather. Gracious Rome did not delay us, even though, overrun with criminals, she needed our presence badly.

It was not without danger that we left the estate of the Church to bring help to the Catholic faith, which the Ottoman Turks are striving to destroy. Day by day, we saw their power increasing; we saw the soldiers who had already captured Greece and Illyricum invading Hungary, while the faithful Hungarians were beset with disasters. We were afraid of what would happen in the future if we did not act wisely now. We were afraid that with the Hungarians defeated, both the Germans and the Italians, and indeed all of Europe, would fall under Turkish control, which would certainly bring about the extinction of our faith. We made plans to avert this disaster: we called a meeting at Mantua; we called princes and peoples together so that we could construct a joint plan to protect the Christian faith. We came here full of hope, hope which we can now see was vain.

We are ashamed that Christians can display such apathy. Some devote themselves to lives of pleasure; others are held captive by greed. The Turks are willing to die for their own criminal faith, while we refuse to spend money or put up with any hardship for the sake of Christ. If we carry on like this, we are finished. Unless we can kindle a new spirit, we will soon be lost.

Therefore, men of faith, we urge you to ask God with never-ending prayers to give the Christian kings a different attitude; to stir up the spirit of his own peoples; to spark the hearts of the faithful so that now at last they may take up arms and take vengeance for the wrongs by which the Turks daily hurt our faith. Come, brothers, come, sons, with your whole hearts turn to God. Until we find out for sure what our princes intend, we will stay here. If they come, then we will make plans together for the safety of the state. If not, then we will have to go back home and bear with fortitude what God has given us. But as long as strength and life allow it, we will never relinquish the task of defending our faith, nor think it harsh, if circumstances demand it, to lay down our lives for our flock.

In January 1460 Pius dismissed the congress in a more heartened frame of mind, estimating in his closing address that the chances of raising a large army against the Turks were high.

In the presence of the senators and all the princes' ambassadors, Mass was celebrated in the cathedral church of St Peter. Asking for silence, the pope spoke from his throne: 'Brothers, we have now been waiting eight months for those who were called to the congress. You know who has come, and it is useless to hope that someone else who will be able to help our cause will arrive. At this point then, we may as well disperse. We have done what had to be done here: may God's cause have been well pleaded. Although we planned for a better outcome than this, yet we have not achieved nothing, nor lost all hope.

'We must explain the situation as it stands now, so that everyone can grasp what hope there is, and know which kings and peoples were enthusiastic and which indifferent towards the defence of the faith.

'The Hungarians, if they are given help, will use their best efforts to attack the Turks with all their combined strength. The Germans promise forty-two thousand and Burgundy six thousand men. The Italian clergy (with the exception of the Venetians and the Genoese) will give up a tenth of their income and the people a thirtieth. The Jews will give a twentieth of their property.

'The navy can be supported from all these resources. John, king of Aragon, promises the same aid. This is what has been solemnly promised in formal agreement by princes and ambassadors. Although the Venetians have made no public promises, when they see the expedition in preparation they will not fail us, nor be able to bear being thought inferior to their ancestors. Of the French, the Castilians and the Portuguese, we can say the same.

'In the throes of civil war [the Wars of the Roses], England can offer no hope, nor Scotland, hidden way off in the ocean. Denmark, Sweden and Norway are too far away to be able to send men and, since they are satisfied only with fish [so do not pay tithes on crops], they cannot send money either. The Poles, neighbours of the Turks in Moldavia, will not desert a cause which is their own. The Bohemians we will be able to hire with cash; they will not dare fight outside their country at their own expense.

'This is how the Christian situation stands. Italian money will provide the fleet, if not in Venice, then at least at Genoa or Aragon. And it will be as large as circumstances demand. The Hungarians will equip twenty thousand cavalry, and the same number of infantry who (along with the Germans and the Burgundians) will bring numbers in the camps up to eighty-eight thousand.

'Who can believe that the Turks will not be beaten by such forces? A large number of Albanians will join us, and there will also be many deserters from all over Greece. In Asia, the Armenians will mount an attack on the Turks from the rear.

'There is no reason for us to give up hope, if only God himself will bless our enterprise. Go and tell those at home what we have done here, go back and urge your masters to do what they have promised speedily. Do your utmost, through words and holy deeds, to make Divine Mercy favourable towards us.'

Pius II despairs of a crusade

By March 1462, Pius's hopes had turned to despair; it was evident that the rulers of the west were unwilling to give practical support for his enterprise.

Pius assembled six cardinals, whom he thought the most trustworthy and wise, and spoke to them: 'Brothers,' he said, 'perhaps you think (like practically everyone else) that we are neglecting the welfare of the commonwealth since, after returning from Mantua, we have made no efforts, through deed or word, to drive out the Turks and protect our religion, even though the enemy is pressing us more and more each day. We said nothing; that is true. We did nothing to fight against the enemies of the cross; that is clear. But the reason for our silence was lack of hope, not lack of energy. It is the means, not the will, which has been lacking. We have often debated whether we had the power to assemble the Christian force against the Turks by this or that means, and so act to stop the Christians falling prey to them. Many were the sleepless nights we spent in thought, tossing and turning from one side to another, bewailing the unhappy events of the present age. We wanted to declare war on the Turks and fight for our religion with all our force, but, comparing our strength with theirs, it was clear that the Roman Church cannot fight against the Turks with its own powers alone.

'We are investigating the ways to achieve it but no obvious solution presents itself. If we decide to call a meeting, the example of Mantua shows us that such action is ineffective. If we send ambassadors to ask the kings for their help, they are just ridiculed. If we impose taxes on the clergy, they simply make appeals to later councils. If we grant indulgences and invite them by means of spiritual gifts to give us money, then we are accused of greed. Our sole aim is thought to be the acquisition of gold. No one believes what we say; we are left without credit, like business men who let down their creditors.

'In such straits, what can we do? Shall we go out and face sure danger, and give ourselves up to the enemy of our own accord? Or shall we set off on an undertaking which is ludicrous? Yet, through those silent days and nights, one solution has come to mind – a very good one in our opinion, and perhaps even the only one. Listen; we will give a brief explanation and then you can judge the scheme.

'In 1453, the year of Constantinople's loss, Philip, duke of Burgundy, publicly made a vow to God that he would go out and fight the Turks, and challenge Mehmed to single combat, if either the Emperor Frederick, or Charles of France, or Ladislas of Hungary, or any other prince great enough for him to follow would also join the war. Not one of those named has yet been found girding himself for so great a contest. Because the terms of the vow have not been met, Philip thinks he has been excused. Yes, he has been excused but he is not yet released from his obligation.

'So, although we are old and ill, we have decided to take on the war against the Turks on behalf of the Christian faith, and to set out on that expedition; to order Burgundy to follow us who hold the position of both king and pontiff: thus we will demand the fulfilment of his oath and vow. If he agrees to our desires, he will come with a huge following of men; there will be many ready to follow so great a prince. After publicly promising seventy thousand, the king of France will be ashamed to send less than ten thousand men. Many will come of their own accord from Germany, England and Spain. The Hungarians will not fail to be there; it is their own cause which is at issue. The Venetians too will surely send a fleet when they see such great provisions being made.

'But before this, we need to be sure about the Venetians, and find out from them about the character of the Turks and how great their power is, for the Venetians know by what force and by what devices the Turks can be defeated. The seas lie open to the Venetians; if they do not join us then it will be pointless to persuade the Burgundians and the French to join the expedition. They must be first to hear our plans.

'When news of our plan has spread, it will shatter the

Pinturicchio's fresco from the Libreria Piccolomini at Siena, showing Pope Pius II at Ancona, where he died in 1464, endeavouring to lead a crusade.

deepest sleep like a thunderclap and fire the hearts of the faithful to protect their faith. Neither arms, nor horses, nor men will be lacking. We will easily dispose the war on land and on sea, after it is sure that the pope of Rome, with his holy senate, is going straight out to gain safety for all and he does not want any other man's silver since he is going to lay out his own gold, even his own body, for the sake of Christ. This is the plan which we have devised. You can judge whether it has its origins in our own mind or whether God inspired it.'

335

Hospitallers lose Rhodes

After the fall of Constantinople in 1453, Rhodes, Kos and the other outlying Hospitaller islands and the mainland castle at Bodrun were attacked or devastated by the Ottoman Turks. Thereafter, the Hospital maintained its position on Rhodes, negotiating a series of truces with the Ottomans while launching piratical naval attacks on Turkish shipping.

Under the Hospitallers, Rhodes enjoyed periods of comparative peace, especially after 1482 when Sultan Bayezid II's brother Jem was under Hospitaller protection in France, interspersed with moments of aggression, as when, in 1470, the Hospitallers collaborated in an attempt to save Negroponte, and when, in 1510, they sank the Egyptian fleet off Iskenderun.

Supplies and munitions continued to arrive from the west. The citizens of Rhodes, Latin merchants and settlers, were taxed to pay for their own defence. They lived alongside a Greek population led by its own clergy, which was mobilized to row the Order's galleys. The retention of the island depended on the capacity of the town of Rhodes to resist a major assault, and the refortification of the town was almost unceasing. After about 1490 enormously thick bastions and gun platforms transformed it into a powerful fortress.

The castle at Bodrun on the mainland was also greatly extended, using stone from the remains of the ancient mausoleum of Halikarnassos; classical slabs from its frieze were intermingled on its walls with the Hospitallers' own heraldic devices.

Supplies of food and ammunition were essential, as were determined leadership, the co-operation and collaboration of the Greek population and support from the Latin west.

In 1480 a few thousand defenders successfully fought off a Turkish attack on the town, inspired by the master, Peter of Aubusson, later made a cardinal, and encouraged by a vision of the Virgin.

In July 1522 a major Turkish army returned, with heavy artillery. The master, Philip of Isle Adam, organized another valiant defence but ran short of manpower and gunpowder. The Venetians on Crete insisted on a strict neutrality, no effective help arrived from the west, and the Greek population called for a surrender which the sultan, Suleyman the Magnificent, granted on terms. The Hospitallers left Rhodes on 1 January 1523.

Conquest of Moldavia, 1477

All Pius's subsequent diplomatic activity was in vain. At last, in June 1464, he took the cross at St Peter's in Rome and, determined to lead the crusade in person, set off for Ancona – where he died of the plague. Pius's fears for the future of Christendom were to be confirmed when, in 1476–7, Mehmed conquered Christian Moldavia. The Turkish campaign is described by Azik-Pasa-Zade.

Sultan Mehmed, who ruled all the lands of the infidel princes, and even the princes themselves, summoned Stephen IV, prince of Moldavia, with the command, 'Bring us your tribute, as, like the Wallachians, you are bound to us for your lands.'

But the infidel Stephen did not come and showed not the least respect. Then the sultan sent one of his commanders out with the instruction: 'Go there and invade the land of this infidel, so that I may see what the unbelievers do with you!'

The commander obeyed the sultan's orders and set off to invade Moldavia. He and his men were incautious; they did not know the land and in addition were few in number. One day the unbelievers came upon them; many of the Muslims were killed and some were taken prisoner. The sultan's commander escaped with those of his men who were left. He rode away, returned to the sultan and reported to him in detail what the accursed unbelievers had done. The sultan, seized by zeal for Islam, pondered deeply on possible action. He commanded his viziers: 'Go, arm yourselves, for we are setting off on a great campaign!'

Sultan Mehmed set off from Constantinople and came to the banks of the river Danube; crossed the Danube and for several days pushed on far into Moldavia. He was seeking the prince of Moldavia.

Finally Prince Stephen the infidel called his army together as well and went up into a steep mountain pass. He was ready for battle and had made all his knights dismount so that they should fight more fiercely.

Mehmed's army saw that these unbelievers had made excellent preparations to fight bravely against the army of Islam. They reported this to the sultan, who commanded: 'What are you waiting for? The honour of Islam is at stake! Gird your loins and close ranks!'

At once the Turks obeyed the orders of Mehmed their sultan. They charged forward and fell upon the army of the unbelievers. The unbelievers began to fire mortar shells, but the conquerors kept their zeal for Islam firm in their hearts.

They surged forwards, taking no heed of the cannons and guns, and won the upper hand over the unbelievers.

The Turks threw themselves on to the cannons the unbelievers were firing, and destroyed them in a trice. From early morning to late afternoon, the great battle raged. Then at last, Allah offered the fighters for Islam the opportunity for victory; they rushed the army of the unbelievers, and defeated it decisively.

They killed so many unbelievers that huge towers were made of their heads. They led away as slaves an immense number of unbelievers, and in the whole land, as far as the Ghazi Turks could go, they spared nothing, but burned and destroyed everything.

For two months the Turks roamed across Moldavia. They seized gold and food, goods and chattels, and took much booty. They led away whole packs of horses and flocks of sheep, and took in their arms the pretty girls of the land. And then under the triumphant leadership of Sultan Mehmed II they returned safe and in good shape to Constantinople.

This victory in the holy war was won in the year 1477 by Sultan Mehmed the Conqueror.

Ottoman Turks attack Rhodes, 1481

Following the failure of Pope Pius II to launch a crusade, Pope Sixtus IV, in alliance with the Venetians, raised a large fleet which in 1472 attacked Antalya and Smyrna.

Mehmed II did not retaliate until 1480, when he attacked Otranto in southern Italy and simultaneously besieged Rhodes. The Turkish historian Hajii Khalifeh, noted for his account of the rise of Ottoman sea power, gives an informed and detailed account of these offensives.

In 1480 Pasha Keduc Ahmed, a former grand vizier, came to Sultan Mehmed's court at Constantinople to persuade him to equip an expedition to Apulia, a district in Italy situated opposite Albania, which he was confident of capturing with ease. The sultan agreed to this proposition; so the pasha, having gathered the best warriors from Rum and

Vision of the shining virgin

Three thousand five hundred Turks died in the battle of Rhodes. Their bodies were found inside the city of Rhodes, on the walls, in the ditches, on their own defence works and by the sea. In order to prevent the spread of disease, the bodies were taken up from where they lay shattered and mutilated, and were immediately burned. According to those who later deserted, and who saw the army's numbers reckoned up by its leader at the time of the siege, nine thousand Turks were slain and fifteen thousand were injured. When the great calamities the army suffered are taken into account, the story and the numbers are fairly reliable, and the information was definitely passed on by the deserters.

The story went that the Turks were terrified by a marvellous vision, and in their fear retreated and left the battlefield. They say that in the midst of the battle the Rhodian prince ordered that banners of Jesus Christ and the Virgin Mary and St John the Baptist, protector of their faith, be erected on the walls. The enemy troops saw then a golden cross in the clear sky and above it a shining virgin brandishing a shield and a spear with, beside her, a man dressed in shabby clothes and

A Turk awestruck by an image of the Virgin.

surrounded by a bright host of soldiers. The vision induced in them so much panic that they were absolutely unable to go on.

The victory which resulted most certainly came from heaven: so small a force of Rhodian soldiers could not have resisted so powerful an enemy (who besides had control of the walls), had not divine protection been at work; so numerous an enemy could not have fallen in so short a time, had not God's angel awarded victory and cut down the enemy.

From Guillaume Caoursin,
Obsidionis Rhodiae urbis descriptio

Anatolia, together with thousands of janissaries and Arabs, set sail for Apulia.

During the initial battle, he captured the castle of Otranto as well as some of the surrounding fortresses, all of which he left well garrisoned.

The Christian governor of Apulia appealed for help to King Ferdinand I of Naples, who responded immediately. When he heard this the pasha, who knew that Sultan Mehmed II was dying, set sail for the court at Constantinople on the pretext of paying his respects to the new sultan.

In 1481 a fleet of forty ships carrying a Christian army arrived in Apulia and recaptured all the fortresses, putting most of the soldiers garrisoned in them to the sword. Encouraged by their success, they pursued the pasha – in vain, as he had already reached Constantinople in safety.

In 1480 the chief commander, Vizier Messih Pasha, was ordered to sail for Rhodes with three thousand janissaries and four thousand Arabs because the Muslim population there was being persecuted by the Christians. A fleet of ships from Constantinople, including sixty built in Gallipoli, sailed for Rhodes.

On their arrival they besieged the citadel from sea and land. First they attacked the west tower facing the sea, from which their troops were being harassed. They built a bridge to span the water in order to reach the tower, but this collapsed under the weight of so many soldiers, and at least a thousand of them were drowned. In spite of this they made another brave attempt and succeeded in raising their standard on the ramparts, which by now were covered by their troops.

Encouraged by the thought of the rich plunder inside the city of Rhodes, the soldiers were about to achieve a victory when the pasha, anxious that these riches should not fall into their hands, issued orders forbidding any plunder, saying that by right everything belonged to Sultan Mehmed. Hearing this the soldiers ceased fighting, and the besieged garrison, making a determined assault on them, put most of them to the sword. The resulting catastrophe and the martyrdom of so many men on that day was due both to the greed of Messih Pasha and to the selfishness of the troops.

In spite of fierce recrimination from his men, Messih Pasha decided to withdraw. He marched back towards Constantinople, attacking the fortress of Bodrun on the way, but on failing to capture it, he returned to the capital.

The Turks besiege Rhodes. Inside the walls stand the Knights Hospitaller, dressed in their Order's regalia. Forced to surrender Rhodes in 1522, the Hospitallers conducted a heroic defence of Malta against the Turks in 1565, and their navy helped win the battle of Lepanto in 1571.

Death of Mehmed II, 1481

Jacob Gherardi, a contemporary diarist who provides much valuable information about life in Rome during the late 15th century, records the jubilant celebrations held in the Holy City on the arrival of news of Mehmed's death in 1481.

The death of Mehmed II, the great sultan of the Turks, was reported in letters from the Venetian senate shortly before sunrise on the sabbath day, that is 2 June 1481.

The information can be summarized thus: Mehmed II died on 3 May, at about the second hour, before sunset, in his camp near Constantinople. On the following day, his body was carried secretly into the city; but there was a huge uproar once the news of his death became public. About sixty men of some standing were killed in the confusion, including the chief adviser, and the homes of many of the richest men were plundered. Some Jews, who were taking part in negotiations there at the time, had all their possessions taken from them in the chaos. Shortly afterwards, through the influence of one Isatius, even those who were set apart by their power and strength gave their support to Bayezid II, the older son of the dead sultan, Mehmed II. Isatius wanted these supporters to take over the father's guardianship of the younger son, Jem, in case he should in the meantime make an attempt on the throne, until the older son Bayezid could return to Constantinople. Messengers were sent off at once to fetch him.

The whole of the Roman senate and all the people were delighted at the news. The same news had resounded through the city three days before but no one believed what was heard until the lead-sealed letters of the Venetians arrived. On that same day, Pope Sixtus IV set off for the church of Santa Maria del Popolo, with the fathers and nobles, and solemnly celebrated Vespers there. The pope wanted to preside over the ceremony himself and gave the people his blessing as usual. A private ceremony of thanksgiving was held inside the Vatican in the presence of the fathers and bishops and the whole clergy of Rome.

On the same day, too, the orator was presented with one of the papal white horses in return for his news, with bridles and decorations with silks rich in silver and gold. From this type of horse come the ones which, riderless, and strikingly decorated, walk before the pope in procession. But in accordance with his country's laws, the orator offered the horse to the magistrate when he was about to take back news to the Venetians, as though offering it to a waiting treasurer.

Ceremonies were held for the three following days, in the basilica of St Peter, for the continuance of the joy produced by the death of a public enemy and to give thanks to God.

On each day the pope was present both at the thanksgiving and the rites which followed. When night fell over the city, fires were lit (especially on the higher parts of the temples) and bells were rung over and over in celebration. From Hadrian's monument, day and night without break or relief, was heard not just the sound of trumpets and pipes but the roar of carbine and cannon.

Charles VIII's 'holy war', 1494

In the same year that Mehmed died, 1481, Otranto returned to Christian rule. During the rest of the 1480s the papacy hatched further plans for a crusade, but nothing came of them. Such was the continuing strength of the ideals of crusading that when, in 1494, Charles VIII, king of France, invaded southern Italy, he proclaimed his campaign as a holy war, the prelude to an invasion of the Ottoman Empire. To add weight to his assertion, he was accompanied by the exiled Jem, brother of the sultan, Bayezid II.

Charles VIII, by the grace of God, king of France, to all Christian peoples who will read this letter, who have within them a love of the Catholic religion and who have faith in eternal salvation in Christ.

When we consider more closely than we would wish the innumerable losses and disasters, the slaughter and the carnage, the ravaging and the waste inflicted on noble countries and Christian peoples by the filthy and monstrous Turks, we desire, like our ancestors those most Christian kings of France, to range our armies against them and thus avenge those great crimes.

We have decided not to spare our own person, efforts or resources in pushing back the Turks' raging madness and recovering the Holy Land and the other territories, princes and peoples lost through the activities of the Turks. With the resources of our rich and peaceful kingdom, with the princes and nobles, helped by God whose cause we are embracing, with the help of the pope and the assistance of all princes and others faithful to Christ, we have decided to tackle this most holy task.

We intend, with God's support, to win back the kingdom of Sicily and Naples, because it was often restored to the Roman Church from the hands of various infidels by our ancestors; a further reason is that we are connected to the kingdom by hereditary right. Sicily would also afford us, in particular through the port of Valona, and through a few other places, the opportunity to gain access to those treacherous Turks. For these reasons, then, so that our armies may come and go easily, and that Sicily is itself a source of strength, we intend to recover it.

We have no designs on the kingly city of Rome; nor do we have any desire to inflict injustice or loss on any other land belonging to the Roman Church.

However, we need unhindered passage through several lands of the church to recover the kingdom of Sicily, and so fulfil our holy plan, and to ensure an easier and shorter route to Naples. For this reason, in the name of God we ask Pope Alexander VI, the college of cardinals and the officials, and the inhabitants of the Church's states, to help us against whatever obstacles the enemy puts in our way.

If there be no hindrance to our righteous mission, we think that we will have stormed the city of Naples and entered the enemy's territories, by the beginning of next spring [1495].

Those who think wrong-headedly and unjustly of our faith and stand in the way of our holy plan, we will pursue before the entire Church and all the princes of Christendom, whom we intend to call to a council about the successful outcome, with God's leadership.

Written at Florence, 22 November 1494, in the twelfth year of our reign.

Holy war in Spain

In 1495 Charles entered Naples and was crowned king in May, but his power collapsed within a year.

Meanwhile, in Spain, crusading fervour had lain dormant since the middle of the 14th century; but when in 1479 Ferdinand, husband of Isabella, queen of Castile, secured the throne of Aragon (thus uniting most of the Hispanic peninsula), the Catholic monarchs began to pursue a war against Granada, the last Muslim state in Spain. In a letter, Ferdinand and Isabella stress that their motives in this struggle were sacred rather than profane.

We, Ferdinand and Isabella, are especially grateful that Pope Sixtus IV has sent us confirmation of the crusade, because of the ever more pressing reason we have for requesting of his holiness every assistance that he can give us in this war. For his holiness will find that our motive for undertaking this war is not the wish to expand our realms or possessions, nor the wish to heap up treasures, for, if we wished to widen our dominion or increase our income, we could easily do so with considerably less risk, hardship and expense than is now the case.

The desire we have to serve God and our devotion to his holy Catholic faith cause us to subordinate all our own interests, in the hope that Christendom should be rid of a continual threat, which will be always at its doors if the infidels of the kingdom of Granada are not uprooted and driven out of Spain.

To this end, past pontiffs granted crusades at different times to our kings and ancestors; and never will it be found that the latter took or demanded any part of the money that was obtained on account of the said crusade. Even Nicholas IV [1288–92], who levied a tithe throughout Christendom in order to recover the Holy Land, did not consider any less just or less necessary the war against Granada than the war in the Holy Land.

Capture of Alhama: 1482

The war started with Spain's seizure of Alhama in 1482, a campaign here described by the Castilian chronicler Diego of Valera.

While Count Rodrigo Ponce of León, marquis of Cadiz, captain of the Castilian army, was in Marchena, several leaders came to him and they said that, if the marquis wanted, they could tell him of a way in which the city of Alhama could be taken without any risk. The marquis, knowing that the city was very large, very strong and very near to the city of Granada, was keen to learn more of what the leaders had to tell him. So he sent with them some of his own servants, men who could be trusted to verify what he had been told. These men pronounced true what the leaders had said, and reported that the city was not well guarded; they believed this was because the Moors took their safety for granted, as their city was so strong and situated so deep within their kingdom, on top of a high summit, completely surrounded by a river and accessible only by a single route up a very rough and steep hill. Therefore they all believed they had nothing to fear.

Before dawn, on Tuesday 10 February 1482, the marquis's troops arrived outside the city of Alhama. Those who carried the scaling equipment quietly set it up, and the first man to start the ascent was the mountaineer Ortega de Prado. They were not seen until they were well inside the city. As daylight was breaking, a commotion arose and the Christians who lived in the city, as well as all the other inhabitants, came running. When the Moors heard this, they thought that the fort was being invaded, and they decided to do the only thing they knew, to die fighting in defence of their city. So they gathered in the square and divided up the men among all the places from which they could best defend their walls.

The marquis of Cadiz and the other knights entered the city through the back gate in order to force the Moors to come out to fight. As the street was very narrow it did not allow for more than two men abreast to go through the gate, while the square where the Moors stood was very wide. So when the marquis's men entered the Moors killed them as they came in two by two, and began to shoot so many cannons and arrows and stones that no one else dared to enter through that narrow street.

Although the Christians received many blows in the narrow alleyways, they finally, by the grace of our Lord, drove the Moors fleeing from the square down towards the gates to Granada; there stood a mosque, very secure, where the Moors were surrounded; many were left dead or wounded.

Then the marquis of Cadiz ordered that the city gates be opened; his men entered, killing and taking prisoner any enemies they found. They took all the silver, gold and jewels and many more treasures too numerous to count. They took many Moors, men, women, boys, girls; one soldier took thirty heads large and small. After the city had been sacked, the Moors stayed in the mosque all day on Wednesday, defending it bravely. They were still there on Thursday, so the marquis ordered his men to set fire to it. So many Moors were hurt that finally out of fear they told the marquis that they would do as he wished; the marquis then divided them up among his knights.

On the morning of the following day, 13 February 1482, the Muslim king of Granada, Abul Hassan, arrived near Alhama with a powerful army, seven thousand on horseback and one hundred thousand on foot, and surrounded the city.

The siege lasted several days, and, since it took place during Lent, the Christians ate nothing but boiled wheat, chickpeas and beans. When the Moors saw that the Christians were not weakening, they worked to redirect the water supply away from the city; a few times the marquis waded into the water up to his knees to cut down and burn the barricades the Moors had set up. When the Moors saw the great effort of the Christians to defend the city, they decided to break camp [thus giving the marquis the city].

The Lion Court at the Alhambra in Granada; an example of the refined civilization of Muslim Spain which was to perish in the drive to create a unified Christian Spain.

Atlantic
Ocean

Trastamara

● Oviedo

A s t u r i a s

KINGDOM

● Pamplona

A l a v a

OF

● Santiago de Compostella

L e ó n

● León

Old Castile

NAVARRE

Ja

G a l i c i a

KINGDOM OF

● Burgos

Arag

Ebro

Braganza ●

Saragossa ●

T r a s o s   M o n t e s

● Valladolid

County of

LEÓN AND CASTILE

Oporto ●

Douro

Portugal

R i b a c o a

Salamanca ●

KINGDOM OF

B e i r a

● Avila

Coimbra ●

● Madrid

New Castile

PORTUGAL

N e w   C a s t i l e

B e l a t a

Alcantara ●

Tagus

● Toledo

M u r c i a

Cintra ●

Guadiana

● Lisbon

● Calatrava

● Ciudad Real

Jucar

A l e m t e j o

Mur

Cordova

A n d a l u s i a

● Baza

Guadalquivir

KINGDOM

● Seville

● Granada

OF

Setenil

A l g a r v e

Alhama ●

● Almeria

● Ronda

GRANADA

● Malaga

Atlantic Ocean

● Cadiz

Algeciras

● Ceuta

KINGDOM OF FRANCE

County of Barcelona

Gerona ●

KINGDOM OF ARAGON

Barcelona ●

Tarragona ●

Tortosa ●

Valencia

Balearic Islands

Menorca

Palma
Mallorca

Ibiza

Alicante

Mediterranean Sea

The Christian reconquest of Spain; 1037–1492

In 711 a Muslim army swept into Spain across the Straits of Gibraltar and by 718 had engulfed most of the Iberian peninsula. The Christians retained only a small coastal strip in the north – the kingdom of Asturias, later León – Castile. But Muslim expansion beyond southern France was checked, and the Emperor Charlemagne (768–814) pushed the frontier back to the river Ebro, allowing the subsequent emergence of the county of Catalonia and the kingdoms of Aragon and Navarre. In 1037 Ferdinand I of Castile resumed the struggle with the Moors, who, over the next 250 years, saw the gradual reconquest of their lands by Aragon, Castile and the kingdom of Portugal, founded in 1139. Crusading armies played a major role in the fighting. The last Moorish outpost, the kingdom of Granada, survived until 1492 largely because of the value of the tribute it paid to Castile.

Area reconquered from Moors, 1037–1100

Lands of El Cid, 1094–1102

Area reconquered from Moors, 1100–1200

Area reconquered from Moors, 1200–1270

Area reconquered from Moors, 1485–1492

⚔ Battles

0   100   200 km

Queen Isabella of Castile

The fall of Constantinople in 1453, and the resultant resurgence of the crusading spirit in Europe, prompted a determination in Spain finally to complete the Reconquest, by taking the Muslim kingdom of Granada, for more than a century the last area of unconquered Moorish territory in the peninsula. For the Catholic monarchs, Ferdinand and Isabella, who had had to fight for Isabella's Castilian throne, disputed by Juana and Alfonso V of Portugal, the campaign against Granada was an opportunity to confirm their authority by leading a national enterprise.

The war consisted of a series of sieges and was both protracted (1482–92) and costly. Spain was considerably helped by a dynastic split within the kingdom of Granada and by the willingness of the emir's son to negotiate with Ferdinand. The initial phase of the campaign relied heavily on the Andalusian nobles, who had had experience of skirmishes with the Moors and knew the terrain and weak points in city defences. As it wore on, the Catholic monarchs played a more active role, particularly in financing and supplying the besieging armies. They diverted money from taxes on ecclesiastical revenues levied for the war against the Turks, and raised further sums through obligatory loans. Ferdinand and Isabella also pledged the Crown's future revenues, property and, at times of greatest need, the queen's jewels. These pledges were redeemed during the 1490s.

Granada capitulated on 2 January 1492, when the keys of the Alhambra were handed over to the king. At first the defeated Muslims were generously treated, but the growing influence of the zealous Cardinal Cisneros, Isabella's confessor after 1492, gradually displaced that of the more tolerant Archbishop Talavera of Granada, her former confessor. There were mass conversions, more forced than voluntary, in 1499 and Cisneros's evangelization, impatience and lack of tolerance led to a revolt in the Albaicín in 1501. Uprisings followed in the Alpujarras and east and west of Granada.

The decision to impose on Muslims a choice between exile and conversion was taken in 1502 as an attempt to stop the uprisings. There is no doubting Isabella's personal piety; but her motives in waging war on Granada were as much a quest for political and religious unity in Spain as the desire to advance Christianity by crusading.

Capture of Setenil, 1484

Between 1483 and 1486 the Spanish overran the western half of the kingdom of Granada, including the important town and fortress of Setenil, which fell in 1484.

In September 1484, after the towns of Alora and Alozaina had been taken, Ferdinand the king asked the marquis of Cadiz where he thought they should go next. Cadiz replied that the Moors would receive no greater blow and the king no greater service than if they were to take Setenil. The king then ordered him to organize the siege, and, once this was done, the king would go there with his army.

The marquis arrived near Setenil on 6 September 1484, and on 10 September King Ferdinand arrived with all his army, and took great pleasure on seeing how the siege had been prepared. When the artillery had arrived he worked hard to set it up, working with such care that by Monday 13 September 1484 they had set up cannons in three camps near the weakest part of the town. When the Moors realized that they were being cornered by the encampment, they spoke to one of the marquis's men and told him to tell the marquis they would surrender the town if he guaranteed them the safety of their wives, children and possessions.

When King Ferdinand learned of this, he agreed that on the following Sunday he and his forces would be given the town, and that is what took place.

This was a great blow to the Moors, for Setenil was a well-protected town with fertile land that would be of great advantage to the Christians. Two days after the town had been captured, King Ferdinand set out with his remaining soldiers for Ronda [which he also took].

With the capture of Málaga in 1487, followed by Baza, Almeria and Guadix in 1488–9, the Spanish noose was tightening round Granada. The Castilian chronicler Ferdinand of Pulgar recounts the difficulties of provisioning and financing the Spanish armies.

We have recounted in this chronicle how no other conquest of lands nor kingdoms had required so many things, nor had run so many risks in bringing the necessary supplies to the armies, as this conquest of the kingdom of Granada which King Ferdinand and his wife Queen Isabella carried out. When other kings or emperors made war in foreign kingdoms

Queen Isabella of Castile, scourge of Spanish Muslims.

or provinces, they had supplies brought by sea, by river, or overland. However, in this war, it was necessary to bring supplies not only to the soldiers but to the people who resided in the land. There was no sea by which supplies could be brought, nor rivers that were navigable; the mountains were so high and the roads so rough that nothing could be brought by river or by land.

In addition to this, it was necessary that armed men escorted the mule train that brought supplies to the army camp, to protect it from enemies. And because no merchant would trouble to take supplies to sell even for his own profit, since it meant such a perilous journey, Queen Isabella, in order to fortify her army, hired at her own expense fourteen thousand mules and horses. In addition, she bought all the wheat and barley that could be found in the cities and villages of Andalusia, in the provinces of Santiago and Calatrava and in all the parishes from San Juan to Ciudad Real; she ordered some to collect it, others to bring it to the mill, others to work there, requesting the quantity to be milled and handing the wheat over to the supply train that carried it to the army camp; still others were responsible for collecting the barley and sending it on.

With every two hundred mules rode one man who was responsible for looking after the mule train, which rested only one day. Queen Isabella was continuously involved in this provision of supplies as were all those in her court. And officials, on her orders, were kept busy because it was necessary to send letters and messengers every day, as the fourteen-thousand-strong mule train that had been hired to bring wheat and barley did not stop. The supplies were received by the queen's officials and put in a warehouse. These officials then had to sell the supplies to the army at a fixed price.

The business of supplying the army was such that, counting the price of the wheat and the barley and the price at which it was sold and the costs that were incurred in the process, the Crown made a loss of four thousand marks.

The fall of Granada, 1492

In his chronicle Bernáldez, a country priest who was the chaplain of the archbishop of Seville, and contemporary to the events, gives a detailed account of the fall of Granada.

The months of July, August, September, October and November came and went and still the Moors refused to surrender. In December, however, when very little food was left, they sought an agreement with the king and queen. On 30 December it was agreed that the Alhambra and all the fortified places held by King Abu Abd-Allah and the Moors would be surrendered to King Ferdinand on condition that the Moors kept their laws and their property. All accepted these terms.

Isabella pawns her jewels

Because the campaign against Granada was prolonged and time had already consumed a great sum of the money from the crusades and from the taxes that had been gathered in order to wage this war, Queen Isabella had decided to borrow more money from all her lands. She then sent letters to all the cities and villages requesting a loan of a certain sum of money.

Moreover, Queen Isabella wrote to knights and ladies and merchants and to other important people asking them to lend what they could. And all of them, knowing that the queen always took care to repay such loans, gave what they could. And some knights and ladies, knowing the need that the queen was in and on what the money was to be spent, were moved to lend sums of gold and silver without being asked.

These loans, which in some cases amounted to tens of thousands of sovereigns, were not sufficient to cover the continuous expenses that occurred in the war, so the queen decided to sell a certain quantity of rights to collect taxes on estates and villages to however many people wanted to buy, receiving seven thousand sovereigns for the right to collect taxes on one estate. And those who had bought the rights could collect taxes from their cities and villages until the amount they had invested was repaid.

These pledges brought in a great sum of money. But even this was swallowed up in the continuous expenses incurred during the war, so Queen Isabella sent all her jewels, large and small, gold, silver, pearls and precious stones, to the cities of Valencia and Barcelona in order to pawn them; and they were pawned for a great many marks.

From Ferdinand of Pulgar, *Cronica de los reyes católicos*

The king and queen gave their assent, stipulating also that those who wished to leave should do so, that they should go when and whither they wished, and that they should be allowed to pass unhindered. The Moors were to hand over all the Christian captives and all those Christians who had up to that time become Muslims.

As a guarantee the people and the leaders of Granada, together with King Abu Abd-Allah, sent to the camp four hundred Moors, both adults and children, as valuable hostages to be held until such time as the city surrendered. But when the hostages had been handed over, many of the Moors, who are fickle, easily stirred up and susceptible to prophecies, heeded one of their number who was going about the city proclaiming that victory would be theirs, praising Mohammed and challenging the agreement. Some twenty thousand Moors rose up in the city.

When King Abu Abd-Allah saw this, he did not dare leave the Alhambra, but the next day, which was Saturday, he went into the Albaicín, where he summoned the local leaders. They arrived in a state of some confusion and he asked them what was going on. Abu Abd-Allah then expressed his own opinion and tried to calm them as best he could, saying that now was not the time to rebel, partly because of the shortages they were suffering and partly on account of the hostages. He urged them to bear in mind that they were staring death in the face and had no chance of help.

When he had finished, he returned to the Alhambra. The arrangement was that the strongpoints of the city would be surrendered at Epiphany, but Abu Abd-Allah, aware of the mood of the Moors, wrote to King Ferdinand informing him of the uprising and how the Moors had foolishly rebelled against the agreement. He did not intend to go back on the agreement, indeed he beseeched his royal highness to come immediately to accept the surrender of the Alhambra and not wait until 6 January. As he held the hostages, he should keep to the original agreement, in spite of the uprising.

When they received Abu Abd-Allah's embassy and the letter, the king and queen made ready to accept the surrender. On Monday 2 January, they left the camp with their army duly drawn up. As they came near to the Alhambra, King Abu Abd-Allah rode out, accompanied by many of his knights, with the keys of the city in his hand. He tried to dismount in order to kiss the king's hand, but the king would not allow it. The Moorish king kissed Ferdinand on the arm and gave him the keys, saying, 'Take the keys of your city, for I, and the men who are within, are your vassals.' King Ferdinand took the keys and gave them to the queen, who gave them to the prince, who in turn passed them to the count of Tendilla. The latter, the duke of Escalona and the marquis of Villena, with many other knights, three thousand cavalry and two thousand musketeers, were sent into the Alhambra. When they had taken possession of it, they hung Christ's standard, showing the Holy Cross, which the king always carried with him on crusade, from the highest tower.

The king and queen, the prince and the whole army knelt before the sign of the Holy Cross, giving thanks and praising the Lord. The archbishop and the clergy said the Te Deum. The soldiers inside then unfurled the standard of Santiago, which the master of Santiago kept with him, and the royal standard of King Ferdinand. The royal heralds proclaimed 'Castile, Castile!'

Present at this blessed victory, besides the king and queen, were the prince, Don John, and the infanta, Doña Joanna, their children, the cardinal of Spain and the archbishop of Seville, the master of Santiago, the duke of Cadiz and many other knights, counts, prelates, bishops and great lords, whom (for the sake of brevity) I shall not name.

On that same day, 2 January 1492, Ferdinand wrote exultantly to Pope Innocent VIII, announcing his victory.

Most holy Father: I Ferdinand, your most humble and devoted son, king of Castile, León, Aragon, Sicily, Granada, etc., kiss your feet and holy hands and most humbly commend myself to your holiness. May it please your holiness to know that it pleased God to give us total victory over the king and Moors of Granada, enemies of our holy Catholic faith, for today, the second of January of this year 1492, we have received the surrender of the city of Granada, together with the Alhambra and all the castles and fortifications of the kingdom that had still to be conquered and which are now under our command and authority.

I inform your holiness of this on account of the pleasure you will take in it, since our Lord has given to your holiness – after many hardships and expenses, much death and bloodshed among our native subjects incurred in the cause of the kingdom of Granada which, for seven hundred and eighty years, was held by the infidel – the result that past popes, your predecessors, so desired and worked for, achieved in your time and with your assistance, to the greater glory of our Lord God and of our holy Catholic faith, and the honour of your holiness and the holy Apostolic See.

Overleaf: The Alhambra in Granada, virtually the last Muslim outpost in Spain. Its surrender to Ferdinand of Aragon in 1492 put an end to Islamic presence in Spain.

Suleyman the Magnificent

When Suleyman I acceded to the Ottoman throne in 1520, almost 90 per cent of the empire was state property and at his disposal. By 1528 he enjoyed an annual revenue equivalent to 10 million ducats, more than twice that of the Holy Roman Emperor Charles V. He spent part of these resources on military campaigns to consolidate and extend the territorial gains of his predecessors, but much was also devoted to making his reign the most resplendent of any sultan. Lavish sums were expended on court entertainments, clothing and patronage of the arts, especially poetry, which flowered under the genius of Baki, 'king of poets'. However, Suleyman's greatest passion was building. All his cities were adorned with mosques, palaces, public baths, hospitals and fountains, and Istanbul, the capital, was provided with a system of aqueducts. The palace was extended and its interior richly decorated. Most splendid of all was the Sulaymaniyah; one of six mosques designed by the gifted architect Sinan, its scale and grandeur eclipsed both Hagia Sophia and Justinian's cathedral.

The splendour of his reign earned Suleyman the epithet 'the Magnificent' among contemporaries in the west. To his subjects he was known as the 'Lawgiver', because of the multiplicity of edicts he issued to crystallize the Ottoman state's system of justice and administration.

By temperament Suleyman was well fitted to rule his vast empire of some 14 million people. Tall and dark-eyed, with an aquiline nose, he was an imposing figure, noted for his self-control. He could act ruthlessly, but all paid tribute to his zeal for justice. He was not afraid to promote men of outstanding ability, such as his grand viziers Ibrahim and Rustem, but he may be criticized for the over-indulgence he displayed towards Khurrem, the Russian slave girl who became his favourite consort. As befitted the ruler of a military empire he was a courageous and able general who personally led his troops on 13 campaigns. His leisure pursuits were the study of the Islamic religion, poetry and history.

In 1553 Suleyman was forced to execute his eldest son, Mustafa, who threatened to lead a rebellion, and the death in 1558 of his beloved Khurrem provoked a civil war between her sons Selim and Bayezid. The reign of this 'Magnificent Sultan' came to an end with his death in September 1566.

Suleyman the Magnificent, new sultan of Turkey, 1520

In 1520, a new sultan, and the greatest of his line, Suleyman the Magnificent, succeeded in Turkey. During his long reign, which ended in 1566, the Turks under Suleyman seized places as far apart as Belgrade, Budapest, Baghdad, Algiers and Aden, and, in 1522, took Rhodes from the Hospitallers. This last triumph is described by Hajii Khalifeh.

In 1520 Sultan Suleyman, of blessed memory, became sultan of Turkey. After Belgrade's conquest [1521], the capture of Rhodes was considered to be the next vital step. Accordingly Suleyman gave instructions for the building of a great fleet. The second vizier, Mustafa Pasha, was appointed commander and a large number of Arabs and sailors were recruited.

In 1522, a day when the omens were good, about seven hundred ships set sail from Constantinople for the Mediterranean. The fleet anchored off Rhodes, and then the large ships were left to guard the channel while the pasha, with three hundred galleys, sailed into the bay where the fortress of Rhodes stood.

They placed their cannons in position and began the siege on the fifth of Ramadan. A week later, Bali Beg arrived from Egypt preceded by twenty-four galleys carrying more ammunition and provisions. Fierce battles raged until orders were given to capture the Arab tower from which enemy soldiers ceaselessly harassed the besieging army, but although the pasha's men crossed the moat and planted their standard on the rampart wall, they were eventually pushed back.

On the advice of the most experienced among the pasha's men and in spite of continuous fighting, an earth mound was built which, after five months' work, reached up to the rampart walls. Inside the fortress the besieged army, unable to protect itself from cannon and musket fire, surrendered on 5 Seffer 929 [20 December 1522]. The governor, Mighali Masturi [the grand master, Philippe de Villiers de l'Isle-Adam], was allowed to leave for Malta; when all the islands around Rhodes had been subjugated, on the fourteenth of that month the victorious Emperor Suleyman left in triumph and marched in rapid stages to Constantinople.

The Turkish sultan Suleyman the Magnificent, who led the Ottoman Empire to great power and prestige after his accession in 1520. His capital was Constantinople, once capital of the Byzantine Empire.

The sword of Sultan Suleyman the Magnificent, made soon
after the beginning of his reign in 1520. The blade is of steel,
the hilt of ivory, and the whole inlaid with gold and gems.
The motif on the blade (above) is of a fighting phoenix and
dragon. Such artefacts typify the splendour of Suleyman's
reign, the height of Ottoman splendour.

The Turks seize Tunis, 1535

In 1535 the Turks seized Tunis, but were driven out by a crusading force led by Charles V, Holy Roman Emperor and king of Spain.

Khair ad-Din Barbarossa, admiral of the Ottoman fleet.

At this time the kingdom of Tunis was held by Beni Hefsi under the sovereignty of Pasha Hassan. Khair ad-Din Barbarossa [a former Barbary corsair made grand admiral by Suleyman in 1530] wanted possession of the city of Tunis, in particular the port of Goletta which, due to its secure position, was a convenient port for a fleet to winter in. Having convinced Suleyman of this, he was given permission to capture it.

The Tunisians were discontented with the rule of Sultan Hassan, so Khair ad-Din Barbarossa was allowed to reach the castle of Halk-al-Vad, from which Sultan Hassan had already fled. Leaving the castle, Khair ad-Din entered the city of Tunis, nine miles away. Hefsi's supporters surrendered to him: he had them imprisoned and executed some of the sheikhs. Hassan and Khair ad-Din Barbarossa then fought a battle outside the city walls, in which three hundred Arabs were killed; Hassan, defeated, fled from Tunis.

Meanwhile, Charles V, king of Spain, encouraged by Pope Paul III, allied with John III of Portugal and prepared to sail with three hundred barges and galleys carrying twenty-four thousand men. At this point, the pope received a message from Hassan informing him that he had besieged Khair ad-Din Barbarossa with his Arab army in Tunis, and inviting them to come and capture him. So they decided to capture Tunis. On they sailed into Tunis harbour round the left tower and landed near the castle of Halk-al-Vad. Seeing this, the Tunisians lent their support to Khair ad-Din Barbarossa.

For thirty-two days and nights the Christians kept up a continuous barrage of artillery fire against the castle until their ammunition was exhausted. On three occasions the Muslims forced them off their mounds, killing many of them each time. But at last, unable to withstand the Christian onslaught any further, they evacuated the castle and retreated to Tunis. The Christians occupied the castle and were joined by Sultan Hassan with a small band of Arabs.

Khair ad-Din Barbarossa now assembled the Tunisians all together and urged them to fight for him. Nine thousand seven hundred men marched with him, including one reluctant faction who had seemed to favour the enemy. When the Christians arrived at the town of Tunis, Khair ad-Din Barbarossa and his army fought against them bravely, but before long the indecisive faction fled to the castle and would not return despite persuasion, so Khair ad Din retreated, removing his cannons into the castle. The next morning, Khair ad-Din Barbarossa attacked, and the Christians, distressed by the heat and lack of water, were about to retreat. But then the Algerians evacuated the city and fled, and the four thousand prisoners in the city freed themselves and closed the gates. The Christians having retreated, Khair ad-Din Barbarossa with two hundred loyal troops pursued the Tunisians, and the Christians entered Tunis and crowned Hassan king. They rebuilt the castle and left a garrison of four thousand soldiers to hold it. The traitors who had been responsible for the rebellion remained in the castle; most of them were executed.

The Hospitallers in Malta

After losing Rhodes in 1522, the Knights Hospitallers were based in Italy. Without land in the east, they still retained their western properties and manpower, their leaders, archives and traditions. Their corporate survival did not depend on retaining any one particular territorial base and they displayed an astonishing resilience.

Although French brethren preponderated the Order, it was the Holy Roman Emperor Charles V, ruler of Spain and of Habsburg Austria and Hungary, who enfeoffed Malta, and with it Tripoli, to the Hospital in 1530.

Malta depended on Sicily for its food supply and was small, arid and difficult to defend. Tripoli was even less attractive. The Hospitallers occupied the castle of Sant'Angelo in Malta's Grand Harbour and the adjacent buildings in Birgu, but they still hoped to recover Rhodes and made little attempt to fortify Malta.

Malta was a Christian outpost between the two great land empires of Spain and the Ottomans. In 1551, the Turks captured Tripoli and devastated the island of Gozo next to Malta. In 1565 they launched an attack on Malta itself, in an attempt to gain a naval base from which their galleys could threaten the whole western Mediterranean.

The logistics of galley warfare meant that the Turks were compelled to operate in the summer heat at the end of lengthy lines of communication. Although they could land large forces on Malta, they had also to supply them and to bring their artillery effectively into play. The Turkish troops landed on 18 May and at once met staunch, heroic resistance from the Hospitallers and the Maltese led by the grand master, Jean de la Valette, who was a veteran of the final siege of Rhodes.

The Turkish generals proved to be divided and indecisive. They failed to move quickly against Fort Sant'Elmo, which controlled the entrance to the Grand Harbour and was not overrun until 23 June; nor did they capture the inland fortress at Mdina (Notabile), from which a diversionary attack was launched against the Turkish camp at a critical moment, on 7 August.

Repeatedly repulsed in hand-to-hand fighting at Birgu, the Turks lost heart, fell sick, and then, faced by a substantial relief force sent from Spain and Italy, and led by the Spanish viceroy in Sicily, withdrew on 8 September.

Siege of Malta, 1565

Right at the end of Suleyman's reign, in May 1565, the Turks laid siege to Malta, the new headquarters of the Hospitallers. In June 1565, Pope Pius IV wrote to the princes of Catholic Europe – the Reformation had engendered hostility to crusading amongst protestant princes – appealing for help.

We have been made aware of the arrival of the Turkish fleet off the island of Malta through a messenger and through letters from the master of the Hospital of St John of Jerusalem.

This fleet (as no doubt you have heard) contained many more ships than a Turkish sultan had ever before sent against Christians, and, as well as large numbers of infantry, it brought with it siege equipment. The news gave us a great deal to worry about. For we can see in how much danger the safety of both Sicily and Italy will be, and how great are the perils which will hang over the Christian people if (may God prevent it!) an island so near to Sicily, and ringed with so many ports, should fall into the hands of an unholy enemy.

So, because we wish to go out to help that Order of soldiers which has always stood as a firm defender of the Christian faith, we have sent as much aid as we could to the master at Malta, and as soon as we could. Since at so crucial a time every Christian leader ought to help the Order, and each should beat back this common threat to the best of his ability, we have decided to write to you to rouse your sense of duty and urge you, for the sake of God and the safety of us all, that the Order may receive what it requires to resist the enemy. Without delay, it needs a subsidy of money, men and gunpowder, which should all be sent at once to Sicily, from where it will be transported direct to Malta.

The more promptly and the more generously you send these supplies, the more practical, praiseworthy and pleasing will your gesture be to both God and the Order.

Written at Rome, in St Peter's, on 7 June 1565.

A relief force of about 12,000 Spanish and Italians arrived on 8 September, and, as an eyewitness, Francis Balbi of Correggio, reports, drove the Turks away.

I do not believe that music ever so consoled the human senses as did the peal of our bells on 8 September 1565, which was the Nativity of our Lady. For the grand master of the Hospital ordered them all to be rung at the very time when the call to arms was usually sounded, and for three months we had heard them sounding only the call to arms.

That morning they called us to Mass, and a pontifical high mass was sung very early, thanking the Lord our God and his blessed mother for the mercies that they had bestowed upon us.

That same day a spy came to us, who reported that [the lull in the fighting had occurred because] a force had come to our aid; in his opinion it was very large, although in the enemy camp it was being said that there were no more than four thousand men.

Seeing that there was no longer any artillery to fear, the grand master ordered that his three galleys should leave the St Angelo channel and should then be armed.

During the whole day not a single Turk was seen in any of their trenches, although in the houses of Bormla [Cospicua] there were more than two thousand men hidden, guarding one of their guns which had been removed from its carriage. As it was uncommonly heavy, they could not remount it or remove it.

That same night Commander Antonio Maldonado, Brothers Juan Garcés and Miguel de Marzilla came from the city to Birgu [Vittoriosa], entering by the Castile Gate. They described to the grand master the relief force that had landed and how it had been led by Don García [de Toledo, Spanish viceroy of Sicily] in person and told him who were the other leaders, what their orders were and which famous knights had arrived and what the landing had been like.

They also described how his highness Don John of Austria, the half-brother of our lord, the most powerful and most Catholic king, Philip II of Spain, had left the court in great secrecy to take part in the enterprise. Although he was young in years, he had been nobly inspired. However, after his excellency had waited in Barcelona many days for a passage, and as no galleys came during that time, he returned to the court on the orders of his majesty.

From this brave action it is possible to judge the future spirit and courage of the prince, should the Lord preserve him.

Turks capture Nicosia, 1570

Five years later, in 1570, the Turks under Sultan Selim II attacked the kingdom of Cyprus, which had been held by the Venetians for the whole of the previous century. The fall of Nicosia is related by the Genoese writer Hubert Foglietta in a very literary account published in 1587.

Before dawn on 9 September 1570, the Turks were drawn up outside Nicosia, under their standards. With loud shouts and trumpeting they simultaneously charged the four towers: Podocataro; Costanza; Davila; and Tripoli. The defenders of the first tower were asleep, amid great general disorder. The Turks climbed unhindered over the wall and slew some of the defenders with their swords; the rest were woken by the noise and fled.

On hearing that the Turks had taken the tower of Podocataro, Nicolo Dandolo, the Venetian governor of Cyprus, whose sleeping quarters were by the Salines Gate, dashed from his house along with the bishop of Paphos. They mounted their horses and galloped round the other towers, gathering men to help those who were defending the Podocataro Tower. But they were too late, because the Turks were already in control of it.

In the other towers, however, the fortunes of war were more favourable to the Christians. They stoutly held their ground and three times the Turks were pushed back at great loss. But the Turks, now in the Podocataro, drove the Christians before them and made for the other towers. On the way there, they met no resistance and seized the redoubt. This was due to the fact that the besieged were already engaged in repelling an attack from outside, and were thus wholly concentrating on the enemy in front of them. So, when they found themselves attacked by the Turks on their flank, they were unable to cope with a double strain. They dashed for the gaps in the walls, desperately fought their way through the enemy and fled in various directions throughout Nicosia.

The natives of that city went back to their houses to try to save their wives and children, but the Venetians, who had no family ties to hold them back, faced the advancing Turks and engaged them. When they saw that the enemy was in control of the city, the Italians retreated to the main square where the governor, the other leading citizens and the Italians who had managed to escape were gathered.

The inhabitants saw that Nicosia had fallen to the Turks and they lost hope. They prostrated themselves with their wives and children and their dearest possessions before the Turks, and begged for mercy. But these cruel savages were unmoved by the tears of the miserable citizens and without regard for age or sex, put them to the sword.

The governor and the mass of people who had come to the main square held its entrances fiercely against the enemy. They would have been able to keep up their resistance for longer had not the pasha of Aleppo appeared in support of the Turks with six cannon: with these he fired on the crowd. Many were killed and those Christians who were left retreated into the palace and barred the gates. Then the pasha sent a prisoner he had taken, a monk, bearing a

The battle of Lepanto

The 16th-century Mediterranean world experienced a major conflict between Islam and Christendom; the Turks, continuing their advances into the Balkans and the Maghreb, confronted the might of Spain and Venice.

In 1571, six years after their defeat at Malta in 1565, the Ottoman Turks conquered Cyprus, and, joined by a North African contingent, their fleet gathered off the west coast of Greece. The Holy League, a Christian coalition of Venice, Spain and Pope Pius V, produced a truly crusading force, in the form of great fleets, financed, manned and equipped with the help of papal taxation and benefiting from formal crusading indulgences. The great expedition was commanded by Philip II of Spain's half-brother John of Austria, who arrived at the assembly port of Messina determined to give battle.

On 7 October 1571, some 200 Latin galleys met 210 Turkish galleys under Ali Pasha off Lepanto on the north shore of the Gulf of Corinth. All were heavily loaded with artillery, infantry and oarsmen, though the Turkish crews may have been weakened during their conquest of Cyprus. The main cannon, fixed at the bow of each galley, was aimed by steering the ship. Each fleet had one wing against the north shore, where the Venetians on the Latin left performed the extraordinary feat of pivoting their line, a manœuvre that involved back-paddling by the galleys closest to the land, so as to shut the opposing galleys against the shore, where some of their crews fled on foot. The Latins also secured the advantage in the centre where the rival flagships fought a bitter hand-to-hand battle, until Ali Pasha was killed by a musket shot. The battle was more even on the Latin right; the Turks found a gap between it and the centre only to be countered by the Latin reserves. The Turkish commander, Uluj Ali, escaped with about a dozen galleys but some 60 sank and 117 were captured: the Turks lost up to 30,000 men. Latin losses were also heavy; but victory was probably decided by the superior weight of the Latin galleys and by the Turkish failure to outflank them.

Lepanto brought the beleaguered Latins considerable psychological gains, but had no immediate territorial or decisive strategic consequences. Indeed, the Christians failed to follow up their triumph and the Holy League broke up. Within three years, in 1574, the Turks had rebuilt their fleets and captured Tunis.

message promising the governor that if they stopped resisting, everyone in the palace would be spared.

Dandolo and his men threw down their swords and sent one of their men back with the monk to arrange terms of surrender. But the Turks had already burst through the gates, and, without waiting for the monk to bring the governor's reply to the pasha, had dashed wildly into the palace and slaughtered all the men they found there, including the governor. The many noble ladies who had sought refuge there were taken prisoner.

Nicosia was given over to pillage; no sort of savage cruelty, insatiable greed and foul lust was omitted in the ill-treatment of the wretches who were captured by the Turks. Matrons, virgins – even children – all fell victim to their vilest passions. The bloodshed ended only when they were too tired or had had enough. The Turks respected neither age nor sex and they spared a life only in the hope of a huge ransom.

Battle of Lepanto, 1571

With the surrender of Famagusta, on 5 August 1571, the Turks had secured the whole island of Cyprus. Meanwhile in May 1570 a Holy League had been formed against the Turks. Its members were Spain, which paid half of the costs, Venice and the papacy, and its leader was Don John of Austria, half-brother of Philip II of Spain. An enormous fleet, which with its 209 galleys and many support ships was the largest armada assembled by the Christian powers in the 16th century, set sail in September 1571 from Messina. It came upon the Turkish fleet, of similar size, at Lepanto, and on 7 October engaged it in battle. The course of the struggle was outlined in a report issued in Venice on 19 October, the day the news arrived there.

This morning the galley of the magnificent Onfrè Giustiniano arrived with much firing of cannon, dragging the Turkish ensigns through the water and bringing the best possible news that this most serene republic of Venice, and indeed the whole of Christianity, could receive: the total rout and ruin of the whole Turkish fleet, which had taken place on Sunday 7 October, at about the third hour of the day.

The two fleets met near the place called Curzolari in the Gulf of Lepanto. The Turk was the first into the attack, to be met by the galleys of the noble captain Augustin Barbarigo,

The Turkish coastal fortress of Lepanto, off which the battle of Lepanto was fought in 1571. Within the harbour are galleons and galleys of the type which fought at Lepanto.

in a dead calm which lasted the whole day. These galleys caused great havoc among the enemy fleet: then the rest of the forces engaged, and both the naval battle and hand-to-hand fighting lasted continuously for five hours. The end of the battle came when Don John of Austria rammed the galley of Ali Pasha, the Turkish commander, in the poop while the most excellent general Veniero attacked it amidships with naked steel. The pasha was taken prisoner and, at once, Don John went aboard his galley and had him beheaded. The pasha's head was displayed, mounted on a frigate, and taken along to the furthest point of the Christian fleet to carry the news of the capture and death of the pasha and general of the Turks, and to hearten the Christians in their fight with the assurance of victory.

So it was that one hundred and eighty Turkish galleys were captured and towed by our fleet to Corfu. Of the rest of the Turkish force, some were sunk and some burned, upwards of fifteen thousand Turks were cut to pieces, seven

thousand were taken prisoner, and twenty thousand slaves were freed; and of the forty flagships in the Turkish fleet thirty-nine were captured. The survivor, that of Uluch Ali, had fled with five galleys but was followed by the same number of our ships. Of our fleet some ten galleys were destroyed with their men, the noble Signor Augustin Barbarigo was killed by an arrow in the face and also, it is said, about eighteen galley commanders, but that is not certain, and the magnificent Mark Querini was wounded.

There was much booty, and it is thought that every soldier has profited considerably. The city of Venice is rejoicing at this most glorious victory that God has given us, the like of which has perhaps never been seen in Christian times, and all is festivity and elation. His serene highness the doge, with the signoria and the foreign ambassadors, went at once to St Mark's, where Mass was sung with the 'Te Deum laudamus'.

All the people of the city are wild with delight, shutting up their shops, abandoning business and spending all their time in joy and celebration, thanking God who has given us such consolation. Those imprisoned for civil debts have been released and other celebratory measures will follow. May it please the Divine Majesty to grant that our captains who have won this victory may chase the dog from his throne in Constantinople itself, as there is reason to hope they may.

Philip II of Spain, too, rejoiced when news of the victory was given to him by the Venetian ambassador, Leonard Dona, as this letter by Dona to Alvise Mocenigo, doge of Venice, relates.

The news of the glorious victory at Lepanto granted to all Christendom and in particular to your serene highness by the benign hand of God, which you were good enough to send me by special courier, reached me on the last day of last month, two hours after midday.

The first sight of this not only filled me with overwhelming happiness but also made me realize that the abounding mercy of God towards us exceeds not only our deserts but even our own hopes. Having – and knowing no other way – to give some measure of thanks, I at once prostrated myself, my face and mouth to the ground, and praised, blessed and glorified with all humility his divine and infinite mercy.

Then I took your letter in my hand and, having at once devoured rather than read your words, I hastened immediately and without giving notice to his majesty King Philip II's palace, where I found that he was in his chapel attending Vespers for the eve of All Saints. I having informed his major-domo that I desired at all costs to speak to him on a matter of great cheer, King Philip was pleased to admit me within the curtains of his screen and to hear me. I entered his presence at the very moment when the choir was singing 'Magnificat anima mea Dominum et exultavit spiritus meus in Deo salutari meo', and with a loud cry of 'Victory, victory' and with praise to God, I explained to his majesty in ten words the gist of what your serene highness had written, adding that I had come to join with him in the 'Te Deum laudamus' before the Blessed Sacrament on the altar, and that in order to do so I would withdraw to my own place with the intention of telling his majesty the rest of the news at greater length in his chamber. But his majesty, with expressions of great joy, to the great honour of your serene highness, insisted that I should remain with him within the curtains, and when the

censing was over he made me tell him in detail everything you had written to me. And because I told him that I had also with me a sheaf of letters from his own ambassador, he expressed the desire to open and read his own letters then and there in my presence, which he did with great rejoicing, praising the goodness of God for such favour, and giving infinite thanks to your serene highness for this welcome news.

Then King Philip said that not only did he wish us to say the Te Deum together, but that it should be solemnly sung by the whole choir. So when Vespers were over, to the inestimable joy of all and with the sweetest harmony that I have ever heard, due thanks were given to the Almighty King of all Kings and of all armies, by the whole court on their knees. After this I accompanied the king to his apartments, still talking of the great event, and remained with him to his great pleasure until night had fallen. Then it seemed to me that I ought not to leave the palace without also giving an account to her majesty Queen Elizabeth of Valois, who, accompanied by two little princes, with a truly angelic modesty, was most glad to receive this service from your serene highness.

That night it was proclaimed through all the streets of Madrid, by command of his majesty, that on the following day, 1 November 1571, everyone should join the solemn procession ordered to give thanks to God for his favour. Along the way, which was very long, his majesty showed me extraordinary favour, desiring me to accompany him for a long while and saying many things about this glorious event with much delight.

I think that, quite apart from the great happiness that your news has given to the whole court, your serene highness has never spent money in sending couriers better than on this occasion, and by the same token it has also redounded much to the dignity and splendour of your embassy here. For although half an hour before my arrival at the palace his majesty had learned the plain news of this victory merely from the master of the Genoa post, which arrived by a courier at the same time as your own, his majesty had given little credit to the news seeing that it arrived in so trivial a fashion, and he had made no move to make any great demonstration until he had seen and heard me, your ambassador.

And now, rejoicing with your serene highness, I have nothing further to add save to remind myself and, in humble reverence, your excellencies and fathers, that God has given us this victory so that without fear, delivered from the hands of our enemy, we may serve him in holiness and righteousness all the days of our life.

Madrid, 2 November 1571

Philip II of Spain, whose navy helped crush the Turks at Lepanto in 1571.

Lepanto was the swan-song of the crusading movement, although western European writings occasionally echo crusading traditions into the 18th century, and crusading themes occur in accounts of European conquests in the New World.

Crusading and the New World

During the 15th century Europe's horizons began to expand as its explorers travelled down the coast of Africa and later across to the Americas. Prince Henry the Navigator (1394–1460), third son of John of Avis, king of Portugal, was a noted patron of voyages of discovery. Azurara's biography of the prince takes a manifestly uncritical view, but it gives an interesting account of the goals and motives for his explorations of Guinea on the west coast of Africa, which were heavily influenced by crusading ideals.

Prince Henry the Navigator was a man whose magnanimity was forever compelling him to begin and carry out great deeds. For this reason, he always kept his ships well armed and ready to set sail both as a defence against the infidel and because he wished to know the land that lay beyond the Canary Islands, for up to that time no one knew the nature of that land with any certainty, neither through writings nor through living memory. Some said that St Brendan had passed that way; others said that two galleys had made the voyage and never returned. But this appears unlikely to be true, for we cannot presume that if the galleys had gone there, some other ships would not have endeavoured to learn what voyage they had made. Prince Henry wished to know the truth of this, and, seeing that no other prince was interested in the matter, he sent out his own ships to those parts to survey them.

The second reason was that if they found by chance in those lands a population of Christians, or some harbours into which they could sail without danger, they could bring many kinds of merchandise to these kingdoms and establish a good trade, bringing great profit to Henry's countrymen.

The third reason was that the power of the Moors in the land of Africa was much greater than was commonly thought, and that among them there were no Christians nor any other kinds of men. And, because it is the natural prudence of every wise man to know the power of his enemy, Prince Henry undertook to discover the full extent of the power of the infidel.

The fourth reason was that during the thirty-one years that

Prince Henry had waged war against the Moors, he was unable to find a Christian king or lord who for the love of our Lord Jesus Christ would help him in that war. Therefore he wanted to find out if, in those parts, there were any Christian princes in whom the charity and love of Christ were so strong that they would aid him against the enemies of the faith.

The fifth reason was Prince Henry's great desire to spread the holy faith in our Lord Jesus Christ and to bring to our faith all the souls that wanted to be saved. I who write this story have seen many men and women of foreign lands turned towards the holy faith. And not only did I see these first captives made true Christians but their children and grandchildren as well, as if divine grace breathed in them.

But beyond these five reasons I have a sixth which would seem to be the root from which all the others have sprung, and this is the tendencies of the heavenly wheels. I wish to describe how this honourable prince was driven by the influence of nature to carry out these actions. It was because his ascendant was Aries, which is in the house of Mars and in the exaltation of the sun. And because Mars was in Aquarius, which is in the house of Saturn and in the house of hope, it signified that this lord would succeed in high and mighty conquests, especially in seeking out things that were hidden from other men, according to the nature of Saturn in whose house he is. And because he was accompanied by the sun, as I said, and because the sun was in the house of Jupiter, this signified that all his deeds and conquests would be loyally carried out to the pleasure of his king and lord.

Above: The arms of Prince Henry the Navigator in the sailing school he founded at Cape St Vincent in Portugal.

Right: A 16th-century map of the west coast of Africa, based on information gleaned by Prince Henry the Navigator and the explorers whose expeditions he sponsored.

MARE OCEANON

Henry the Navigator

Prince Henry the Navigator, the Portuguese Infante Dom Henrique, was the driving force behind Portugal's voyages of discovery in the Atlantic. His biographer described his motives as altruistic and inspired by the crusading ideal. Nevertheless, although Henry went on crusade to Morocco in 1415, 1437 and 1458, there were other motives for this expansion: to establish colonies, to exploit slavery and to aggrandize the Portuguese nation.

Overseas expansion was made possible by technological advance. The full-rigged carrack, a large ocean-going sailing ship, was adequate for transoceanic navigation. The caravel, developed by Prince Henry and his captains and first used on a voyage of discovery by Nuno Tristão in 1441, was small and shallow-drafted, with lateen sails and swivel-mounted cannon. It needed only a small crew, could carry ample supplies and was ideal for coastal work and beating against the wind.

Advances in navigational equipment were equally important. Refinement of the compass, development of the astrolabe and improvement of sea charts — techniques from Arab and Turkish seafaring — enabled navigators to fix their latitude at sea. Unravelling the mysteries of Atlantic currents and wind circulations permitted round voyages that avoided long hauls against winds and currents.

Henry's squire Gil Eannes made the first great leap forward in 1434 when he passed the medieval point of no return at Cape Bojador to the south of the Canary Islands. In 1462, Soeiro da Costa turned into the Gulf of Guinea past Cape Palmas (in modern Liberia) and in 1472 Fernão da Pó reached the turn of Africa to the south. Diogo Cão pressed south to Cape Cross (South-West Africa) in two brilliant voyages in 1482 and 1485, and Bartholomew Diaz, helped by an Arab navigator, rounded the Cape of Good Hope in 1487.

Portugal was not the first in these waters: as early as 1375, the atlas of Abraham Cresquas showed a Catalan *barca* off the African coast to the south of the Canary Islands, noting that it went there in 1346 looking for the *Rio de Oro*.

Isabella of Spain's sponsorship of Christopher Columbus's voyage in 1492 was therefore a natural extension of earlier Castilian activities in the Atlantic. Columbus wrote in his journal: 'I propose that all the profit from my enterprise should be used for the recovery of Jerusalem.' His royal masters and contemporaries had no such illusions.

Christopher Columbus, 1492–1504

In 1455, Pope Nicholas V was to provide formal legitimization of Portugal's overseas conquests in the bull *Romanus Pontifex*.

Between 1492 and 1504 the great Italian explorer Christopher Columbus went on four voyages and discovered the West Indies and the mainland coast of Central and southern America on behalf of his patrons, Ferdinand and Isabella of Spain. This letter, written to the Catholic monarchs in 1503, during his fourth voyage, exults at the discovery of the wealthy land of Veragua, in Central America, and envisages the possibility of Christendom liberating Jerusalem on the proceeds of the New World's gold.

When I, Christopher Columbus, discovered the West Indies, I said that they were the richest possession in all the world. I spoke of gold, pearls, precious stones, spices, and also of trade and markets in them, and, because all these things did not materialize at once, I became an object of criticism. This experience prompts me to speak now.

I dare speak of one thing, because there are so many witnesses to it, and this is that I saw in the region of Veragua [in Central America] greater evidence of gold on the first two days than in four years on Hispaniola, and that the lands of the area cannot be more beautiful, nor more extensively cultivated, nor the people more gentle, and there is a good harbour, a fine river, and it can be defended against the outside world. All this means safety for the Christians and a guarantee of their power, with great hope of honour and increase for the Christian religion.

The journey to Veragua will be as short as to Hispaniola, because it will be with the wind. Your highnesses, Ferdinand and Isabella, are as much lords of this region as of Jerez or Toledo; when they go there, your ships will be as if returning home. From there they will come away with gold. In other lands, they have to seize what is there in order to obtain it if they are not to return empty; and inland it is necessary for them to entrust themselves to a savage.

Genoese, Venetians and all those who have pearls, precious stones and other valuable objects, all take them to the ends of the earth to trade them or to convert them into gold. Gold is most excellent; gold means wealth and, with it, he who possesses it does what he wants in the world, even as far as bringing souls to paradise. When the lords of the lands in the region of Veragua die, their bodies are buried together with the gold they possess, so I am told.

Right: Prince Henry the Navigator. The items behind him, including a compass, a navigator's quadrant, a sextant and a pair of compasses, show his dual role as a patron of navigators and as a warrior.

PRINCE HENRY
OF
PORTUGALL

Below: Christopher Columbus shown in an allegorical style as the conqueror of the seas, holding in one hand the banner of Christ. Crusading ideals influenced his voyages, although they were not full-blown crusades.

The New World

There are key connections between crusading in the late 15th and early 16th centuries, and the great changes taking place in European life during that period: the Renaissance, the Reformation, and the discovery of the New World. Leading Renaissance humanists, horrified by the Turkish conquest of Constantinople and Greece, and alarmed at the prospect of an invasion of Italy, promoted the cause of the crusade by writing tracts, orations and didactic histories. The printing press also benefited crusading: appeals, and bulls of indulgence, could be disseminated and publicized rapidly.

The same cannot be said of the Reformation. In Germany in particular, the crusade was regarded as one means by which a corrupt and venal papacy exploited the faithful. Luther, for example, wrote that Jerusalem could be left in Muslim hands because it held only an empty tomb, while the war against the Turks should be conducted by secular rulers without any intervention by the Church. Although some Protestants later became more accommodating, Europe was largely divided along confessional lines in its attitude to crusading, and periodically riven by bitter religious wars.

Although the crusading movement died out in northern Europe, some of its ideas found fertile soil in the New World. Monarchs who financed the voyages of discovery, and the men who undertook them, were strongly influenced by the goals which had characterized the crusading movement. Among the reasons given for Henry the Navigator's exploration of the African coast were the hope of finding unknown Christian powers to help in the struggle against Islam, and the desire to convert the native population to Christianity. Christopher Columbus was convinced in later years that he had been chosen by God to recover Jerusalem. The *conquistadores* who conquered Mexico and Peru, eager for gold, were also the legatees of crusading. They were anxious to convert the natives against whom they fought, and their self-confidence, resilience and earnest piety were fed by an ethos created by generations of Iberian crusading.

If modern historians of the crusades find it increasingly difficult to say when the movement drew to a close, it is because its attributes and features can be detected in so many areas of activity and thought in the 16th century and later, in the Old World and the New.

Above: A sketch map drawn by Christopher Columbus on his first voyage in 1492–3, showing the coast of the island of Hispaniola (to the east of Cuba).

Right: The title page of Columbus' account of his voyage, showing the heathen Indians others set out to convert.

In the book of Chronicles and in Kings, Josephus claims that gold was obtained in the 'Aurea': if this were so, it is my assertion that those mines of the Aurea are one and the same as those of Veragua which stretch a twenty-day journey away to the west and are equidistant from the pole and from the equator. Solomon bought all that gold, precious stones and silver, but if your highnesses wish, you may simply order it to be collected there. In his will David left three thousand talents of gold from the Indies to Solomon to assist in the building of the Temple and, according to Josephus, it was gold from these lands.

Jerusalem and Mount Zion will be rebuilt by Christian hands: God has announced whose hands they will be, through the mouth of the prophet in Psalm 15. Abbot Joachim of Fiore said that he was to come from Spain. St Jerome indicated to the holy woman the way this would be done. A while ago the emperor of Cathay [China] sent for wise men to instruct him in the faith of Christ. Who will volunteer for this task?

If our Lord takes me to Spain, I pledge myself in God's name to take them there in safety. The people who came with me have suffered unbelievable dangers and hardships. Since they are poor, I beg your highnesses to instruct that they be paid immediately, and that you bestow honour upon each according to his rank, for I assure you that, in my opinion, they are bringing you the best news that ever reached Spain.

AMERICAE
PARS QVARTA.

Sive,
Insignis & Admiranda Historia de reperta
primùm Occidentali India à Christophoro
Columbo Anno M. CCCCXCII
Scripta ab Hieronymo Bezono Mediolanense,
qui istic ānis XIIII. versatus, diligēter omnia observa-
vit.
Addita ad singula ferè capita, non contemnenda scholia
in quibus agitur de earum etiam gentium idololatria.
Accessit præterea illarum Regionum Tabula
chorographica.
Omnia elegantibus figuris in aes incisis expres-
sa à Theodoro de Bry Leodiense, cive
Francofurtensi Anno ꝯ Ɔ Ⅼ XCIII.

Cùm prevelegio S. C. Maiestat.

Hernando Cortés, 1519–21

To the north of Veragua lay the equally wealthy land of Mexico, ruled by the Aztecs, and conquered by Hernando Cortés for Spain between 1519 and 1521. Among his small band of warriors was Bernal Diaz, who in his memoirs, completed by 1568, gave a vivid picture of the Spanish struggle to subdue the Emperor Montezuma. He also suggests that allied to the conquerors' greed for gold was a sense of mission: God and his saints were helping the conquistadors to take New Spain for the Holy Roman Emperor and king of Spain, Charles V. Thus crusading themes appear in his memoirs, as in this description of Cortés's two standards.

As soon as Hernando Cortés was appointed general, he began to collect arms of all kinds – guns, powder and crossbows – and all the munitions of war he could find, also articles for barter, and other material for the expedition.

Moreover, he began to adorn himself and to take much more care of his appearance than before. He wore a plume of feathers, with a medallion and a gold chain, and a velvet cloak trimmed with loops of gold. In fact he looked like a bold and gallant captain. But he had nothing with which to meet any expenses, for at that time he was very poor and in debt, despite the fact that he owned a large number of Indian slaves and was getting gold from the mines. But all this he spent on his person, on finery for his newly married wife, and on entertaining guests who had come to stay with him.

When some merchant friends of his heard that he had been made captain-general, they lent him four thousand pesos in coin, and another four thousand in goods, on the security of his Indians and his estate. Cortés had two standards and banners made, worked in gold with the royal arms and a cross on each side and a legend that read: 'Brothers and comrades, let us follow the sign of the holy cross in true faith, for under this sign we shall conquer.' Then he ordered a proclamation to be made to the sound of trumpets and drums, in the name of his majesty and of Diego Velazquez as his viceroy and of himself as his captain-general, that anyone who wished to accompany him to the newly discovered lands, to conquer and settle, would receive a share of the gold, silver and riches to be gained, and a large number of Indians once the country had been pacified.

On 25 March 1519 Cortés won his first victory against the Aztecs at Santa Maria de la Victoria.

The battle had lasted over an hour; it was now late, and we had eaten nothing. So we returned to camp, weary with fighting, took our supper, and rested.

It is here that Francisco de Morla arrived on a dapple-grey horse in advance of Cortés and the rest of the cavalry, and the blessed apostles St James and St Peter appeared. I say that all our deeds and victories were the work of our Lord Jesus Christ, and that in this battle there were so many Indians to every one of us that the dust they made would have blinded us, had not God of his unfailing mercy come to our aid. It may be that those glorious apostles did appear, and that I, a sinner, was unworthy to see them. However, I did see Francisco de Morla arrive on a chestnut horse at the same time as Cortés; and I seem to see that whole battle again with my sinful eyes, even as I write, with every detail as it took place. It may be I was not worthy to see either of the two apostles. But if so, since there were more than four hundred soldiers in our company, as well as Cortés himself and many other gentlemen, the miracle would have been discussed and evidence taken, and a church would have been built in their honour when the town was founded. Also the town would not have been called, as it was, Santa Maria de la Victoria, but Santiago or San Pedro instead.

Early next morning, 26 March 1519, many important persons came from Tabasco and the neighbouring towns, and paid us great respect. They brought a present of gold, consisting of four diadems, some ornaments in the form of lizards, two shaped like little dogs and five like ducks, also some earrings, two masks of Indian faces, two gold soles for sandals, and some other things of small value. I do not know how much all this was worth. They also brought some cloaks of the kind they weave and wear, which are very rough. For, as anyone who knows this province will tell you, there is nothing there of much value.

These gifts were nothing, however, compared to the twenty women whom they gave us, among them a most excellent person who when she became a Christian took the name of Doña Marina. I will say no more about them, but speak of the pleasure with which Cortés received these overtures. But there was one thing he must ask of them, he said, that they should bring all their men, women, and children back to the town, which he wished to see settled again within two days.

Cortés also asked of them that they should abandon their idols and sacrifices, which they promised to do. He expounded to them as best he could the principles of our holy faith, telling them that we were Christians and worshipped one true God. He then showed them a most sacred image of our Lady with her precious Son in her arms, and declared to them that we worshipped it because it was the image of the

Mother of our Lord God, who was in heaven. The Indians answered that they liked this great *tececiguata* – which is the name they give to great ladies in their country – and asked for it to be given them to keep in their town.

Cortés agreed to their request, and told them to build a fine altar for it, which they did. Next morning he ordered two of our carpenters to make a very tall cross.

Above: Hernando Cortés comes ashore on the coast of Mexico, and is greeted by Indians bearing gifts. Behind him, his men plant the cross, claiming the new land for the Catholic Church.

Overleaf: A Spanish galleon of the era of Cortés and his fellow conquistadors. The Spanish and Portuguese expeditions to the New World were undertaken to find gold and to spread the Catholic faith into a new hemisphere full of new infidels. Such motives were to drive a new generation of priests and soldiers to cross the Atlantic.

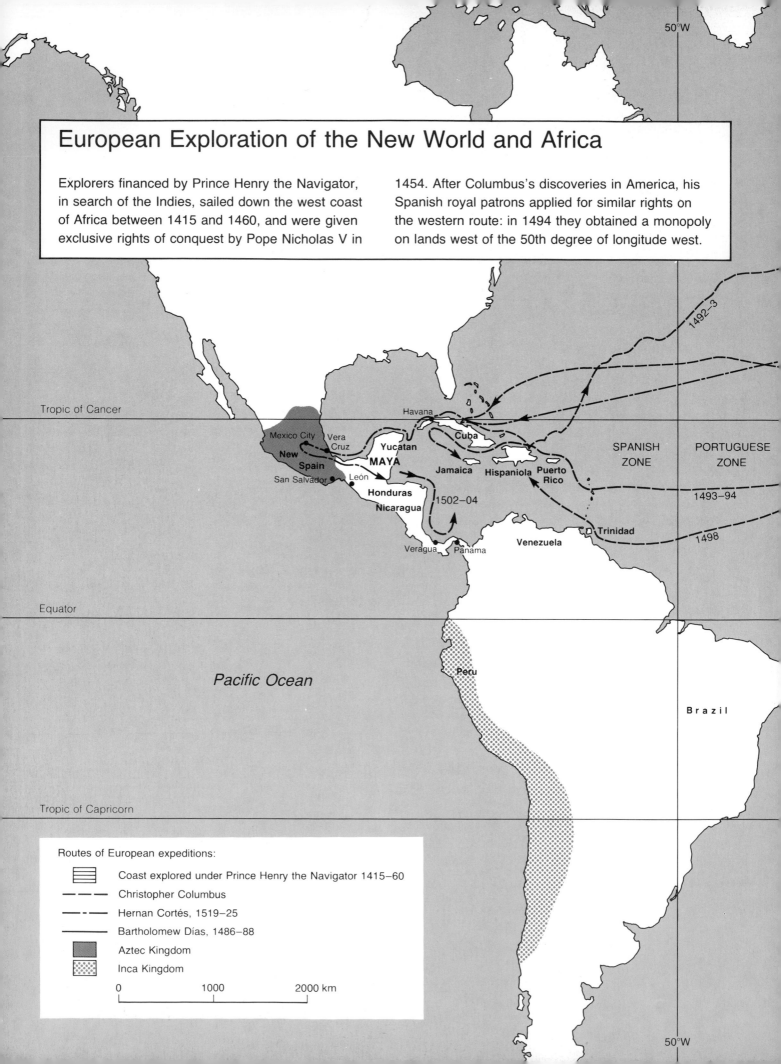

European Exploration of the New World and Africa

Explorers financed by Prince Henry the Navigator, in search of the Indies, sailed down the west coast of Africa between 1415 and 1460, and were given exclusive rights of conquest by Pope Nicholas V in 1454. After Columbus's discoveries in America, his Spanish royal patrons applied for similar rights on the western route: in 1494 they obtained a monopoly on lands west of the 50th degree of longitude west.

50°W

1492–3

SPANISH ZONE

PORTUGUESE ZONE

1493–94

1498

Tropic of Cancer

Havana

Mexico City   Vera Cruz
New Spain   Yucatan   Cuba
    MAYA
San Salvador   León   Jamaica   Hispaniola   Puerto Rico
        Honduras
        Nicaragua   1502–04   Trinidad
    Veragua   Panama   Venezuela

Equator

Pacific Ocean

Peru

Brazil

Tropic of Capricorn

50°W

Routes of European expeditions:

▦	Coast explored under Prince Henry the Navigator 1415–60
– – –	Christopher Columbus
–·–·–	Hernan Cortés, 1519–25
——	Bartholomew Días, 1486–88
▨	Aztec Kingdom
▦	Inca Kingdom

0   1000   2000 km

SCOTLAND

KINGDOM OF ENGLAND
AND IRELAND

London

Paris

FRANCE

SPAIN

Lisbon
Sagres
Madrid

Ceuta

Barbary

Azores

Madeira

Canaries

Arguin

Cape Verde
Islands

Guinea

Axim

Atlantic Ocean

Congo

Angola

Natal

HOLY ROMAN
EMPIRE

Venice

Rome

Vienna

HUNGARY

POLAND

Warsaw

Moscow

RUSSIA

Tartary

Black Sea

Constantinople

OTTOMAN

EMPIRE

Mediterranean Sea

Tripoli

Syria

Caspian
Sea

Persia

EGYPT

Nubia

Arabia

Mecca

Ormuz

Muscat

Aden

Indian Ocean

Madagascar

BIOGRAPHIES

ADHEMAR, bishop of Le Puy d. 1098
Close friend of Urban II, who at the Council of Clermont (1095) appointed him papal legate on the First Crusade. He played an important role in unifying and encouraging the crusading armies; died of disease after the capture of Antioch.

AL-AFDAL *c*. 1066–1121
As vizier to the Egyptian caliph, al-Afdal faced the crusader invasion of Palestine. He captured Jerusalem in 1098 but lost it to the crusaders in 1099.

ALEXIUS I COMNENUS Byzantine emperor 1081–1118
Alexius took over a weak government and an empire surrounded by enemies; he reigned for 37 years and established a dynasty. His appeal to Urban II for support against the Turks resulted – to his surprise – in the First Crusade.

ALEXIUS III ANGELUS Byzantine emperor 1195–1203
Alexius attained the throne by deposing his brother Isaac II. An inept ruler, his extravagance led to riots in the capital. His weakness attracted the attention of the Venetians, who persuaded the Fourth Crusade to direct its attack to Constantinople, and deposed him in 1203.

ALFONSO VI king of León 1065; Castile 1072; d. 1109
Reunited Castile, León and Galicia after a long civil war, and occupied Toledo in 1085. He was defeated by Yusuf Ibn Tashfin of Morocco at Zallaca in 1086.

ALP-ARSLAN Seldjuk Turkish sultan 1063–73
Alp-Arslan led a series of campaigns on the western front of his empire against the Byzantines, Armenians and Georgians. He won a resounding victory over the Byzantines at Manzikert in 1071, which opened up Asia Minor to Turkish conquest.

ANNA COMNENA
Favourite daughter of Alexius I Comnenus, who in old age (*c*.1140) wrote the *Alexiad* as a eulogistic memoir of her father. The work is a mine of information about imperial affairs, including the First Crusade.

ARNULF patriarch of Jerusalem 1099 and 1112–8
A controversial but eloquent figure, he went on the First Crusade as Robert of Normandy's chaplain. His election in 1099 was contested by the Provençal clergy and he was deposed within five months, becoming keeper of relics at the Holy Sepulchre. Re-elected without opposition in 1112, he was active in organizing the Latin Church in the east.

AL-ASHRAF KHALIL Mamluk sultan 1290–93
Skilled commander of the Egyptian and Syrian armies who captured Acre 1291, effectively ending the Latin presence in Palestine.

BALDWIN I king of Jerusalem 1100–18
Count of Boulogne, and youngest brother of Godfrey of Bouillon, he joined the First Crusade in 1096. Founded the county of Edessa – the first crusader state – in 1098. On the death of Godfrey (1100) he was elected king of Jerusalem. He repelled Egyptian attacks, enforced the authority of state over church and extended the boundaries of the kingdom.

BALDWIN II king of Jerusalem 1118–31
As Baldwin of Le Bourg, cousin of Baldwin I whom he succeeded as count of Edessa in 1100, and as king of Jerusalem in 1118. To secure the succession he married his daughter Melisende to Fulk of Anjou.

BALDWIN III king of Jerusalem 1143–62
Son and successor of Fulk of Anjou. His mother, Queen Melisende, ruled as regent until 1152. His reign saw a decline of Latin power in the east, exemplified by the fall of Edessa to the Muslims in 1144, the failure of the Second Crusade and the capture of Damascus and northern Syria by Nur ad-Din in 1154. Upon his death his brother Amalric succeeded him to the throne.

BALDWIN IV king of Jerusalem 1174–85
Suffered from severe leprosy which killed him at the age of 24, but put up a vigorous defence of his kingdom against Saladin. Appointed his five-year-old nephew, Baldwin V, his successor in the kingdom of Jerusalem in 1183.

BALDWIN count of Flanders and Hainaut; Latin emperor 1204–5
One of the leaders of the Fourth Crusade, elected emperor of the new Latin empire of Constantinople in 1204. Defeated at the battle of Adrianople 1205 by the people of Constantinople and Thrace with Bulgar support, he was captured and died soon afterwards.

BARSBAY Mamluk sultan 1422–38
Barsbay's rule of Egypt was oppressive and unpopular.

He led an expedition against Cyprus in 1427 and was captured by King Janus, who released him in return for an annual tribute.

BAYBARS, RUKN AD-DIN Mamluk sultan 1260–77
A Mamluk slave whose first military achievement was commanding the Egyptian army at Mansourah where Louis IX was captured. One of a group of officers who assassinated Qutuz, sultan of Egypt, in 1260. Between 1265 and 1271 he launched a great offensive against the Franks, taking and destroying one stronghold after another. Captured Antioch in 1268.

BAYEZID I Ottoman sultan 1389–1403
Founder of the first centralized Ottoman Empire, his nickname 'The Thunderbolt' is descriptive of his military qualities, which he demonstrated against the Byzantines and others. In 1396 he began a blockade of Constantinople which although ultimately unsuccessful, lasted seven years.

BERNARD OF CLAIRVAUX c.1090–1153
A Cistercian monk who became abbot of Clairvaux and transformed the Cistercian Order. Wrote the Rule for the Templars and gained papal recognition for them. In 1145 he undertook the preaching of the Second Crusade, inspiring many by his eloquence. Canonized in 1174.

BOHEMUND OF TARANTO prince of Antioch 1098–1111
As count of Apulia, campaigned against the Byzantines with his father Robert Guiscard, 1080–5. In 1096 he joined the First Crusade and became prince of Antioch in 1098. Imprisoned by Malik Ghazi of Aleppo from 1100 to 1103. His attack on Byzantine Durazzo in 1108 failed, and he was compelled to recognize Alexius I Comnenus, as suzerain.

BONIFACE OF MONTFERRAT king of Salonika 1204–7
Elected leader of the Fourth Crusade in 1201. He accepted the Venetian-led diversion to Constantinople and was among the conquerors of the city. Failing to secure election as emperor, he was made king of Salonika (Thessalonia) instead. He was killed in battle against the Bulgars in 1207.

COLUMBUS, CHRISTOPHER c.1451–1506
Born in Genoa, probably of Spanish-Jewish parentage. He made four transatlantic voyages with the backing of Ferdinand and Isabella of Spain. Inspired by biblical prophecy, in his later years he became obsessed with the idea of liberating Jerusalem, using gold from the New World to fund the campaign.

CONRAD III king of Germany 1138–52
Founder of the Hohenstaufen dynasty. Popular but ineffectual monarch whose contribution to the Second Crusade was insignificant.

CONRAD OF MONTFERRAT king of Jerusalem 1190–2
Uncle of the infant king, Baldwin V. He managed to avoid involvement in the Hattin disaster of 1187 and organized the defence of Tyre, the kingdom's last stronghold. In 1190 he married Isabel, heiress to the throne, and became king of Jerusalem. Died at the hands of an Assassin.

CONSTANTINE XI Byzantine emperor 1449–53
The last Byzantine emperor, a generous and brave man who was unable to defend Constantinople against the Ottoman Turks in 1453. Died in battle during the siege.

CORTÉS, HERNANDO 1485–1547
Cortés left Spain for the New World in 1504. Between 1519 and 1521 he subdued Mexico by a mixture of force and guile. In spite of a series of successful explorations in the American continent in the following 20 years he failed to retain Spanish backing and died in retirement.

DAIMBERT OF PISA patriarch of Jerusalem 1099–1102
Appointed by Pope Urban II as papal legate in 1098. As patriarch his intrigues brought him into conflict with Baldwin I, who had him deposed and banished from Jerusalem in 1102. Daimbert returned to Italy and won Pope Paschal II's support as patriarch, but he died on his way back to Jerusalem.

DANDOLO, HENRY doge of Venice 1193–1205
Dandolo was about 70 years old when elected but pursued a vigorous anti-Byzantine policy. Diverted the Fourth Crusade towards Constantinople in 1203 which resulted in the Latin capture of the city in 1204.

DOMINIC c.1170–1221
founder of the Order of Friars Preachers, also known as the Black Friars or Dominicans, mendicant communities dedicated to preaching and teaching. Tried to combat the Albigensian heresy by preaching and prayer, but did not share in the violence of the Albigensian Crusade. Canonized in 1234.

EDWARD OF ENGLAND 1239–1307
The future King Edward I, son of Henry III, who led a crusade to Palestine 1270–1.

EUGENIUS III pope 1145–53
A disciple of Bernard of Clairvaux, he was the first Cistercian pope. Eugenius proclaimed the Second Crusade in 1145, enlisting the support of Louis VII of France and of Bernard of Clairvaux. The failure of the crusade was a great disappointment to him.

FERDINAND II king of Aragon 1479–1516
Ferdinand married Isabella of Castile in 1469 and on her brother's death in 1474 they began their joint rule. They conquered Granada from the Moors in 1492. He was an impressive but not a popular king.

FREDERICK I BARBAROSSA Holy Roman Emperor 1155–90
A strong and charismatic ruler who imposed order in Germany, although he had limited success in restoring effective imperial control in Italy. In 1188 he decided to lead the Third Crusade, but was drowned in a river in Cilicia before reaching Palestine.

FREDERICK II Holy Roman Emperor 1211–50
Frederick was more interested in Sicily, where he was brought up, than in Germany. Took the crusading vow in 1215 but procrastinated to the point where the pope excommunicated him in 1227. Married Isabella of Brienne, heiress of Jerusalem, in 1225; undertook a crusade to the Holy Land in 1228 and regained Jerusalem by negotiation.

FULCHER OF CHARTRES 1058–1127
Educated at the cathedral school at Chartres. He took part in the First Crusade as chaplain to Baldwin of Boulogne, later king of Jerusalem. His chronicle is an important eye-witness account of the First Crusade and, especially, of the first 25 years of the Latin kingdom.

GEOFFREY OF VILLEHARDOUIN c. 1160–1213
Historian of the Fourth Crusade, who was also prominent in its organization and in the diplomacy and warfare following the capture of Constantinople. His Conquête de Constantinople was the first reliable record of these events to be written in French.

GIUSTINIANNI d. 1453
Admiral of the Genoese republic in 1450, commander of the fleet sent to help Constantinople in 1453. He distinguished himself in the defence of the city and was mortally wounded when the Turks conquered Constantinople.

GODFREY OF BOUILLON ruler of Jerusalem 1099–1100
Duke of Lower Lorraine since 1076, and a leader of the First Crusade. Commanded the troops which entered Jerusalem in 1099; offered the crown but chose to be 'advocate of the Holy Sepulchre'. Ruled for only one year.

GREGORY VII pope 1073–85
Great reforming pope who aroused much opposition as well as support in his lifetime. In the early years of his pontificate he planned to lead an expedition to free the Byzantine Empire from the Turks and liberate the Holy Sepulchre, an idea seen by some as a proto-crusade.

GREGORY VIII pope 1187
Gregory was about 77 years old when elected. His 57-day reign saw the proclamation of the Third Crusade. He died while trying to reconcile Pisa with Genoa so both cities would support the expedition.

GREGORY IX pope 1227–41
Started his reign by excommunicating Frederick II for failing to carry through his planned crusade. In 1228 Frederick led the expedition despite the ban and succeeded in securing Jerusalem.

GUNTHER bishop of Bamberg d. 1065
The effective leader of the 1064 pilgrimage to the Holy Land. Dealt well with harrassment by the Bedouin Arabs, but died on the return journey.

GUY OF LUSIGNAN king of Jerusalem 1186–92; king of Cyprus 1192–4
Arrived in the east as an adventurer from Poitou and married Baldwin IV's sister Sybilla. Crowned king – against some opposition – on Baldwin V's death in 1186. His military ineptitude led to his defeat by Saladin at Hattin in 1187, and his capture. He was forced to renounce his claim to Jerusalem in 1192 when Richard I gave him Cyprus.

AL-HAKIM caliph of Egypt 996–1021
Always unpredictable and ultimately insane, al-Hakim persecuted the Christians in particular. In 1009 he demolished the Church of the Holy Sepulchre in Jerusalem. He died at the hand of an unknown assassin.

HENRY VI Holy Roman Emperor 1191–7
Held Richard I of England hostage 1192–4, releasing him in return for a ransom and an oath of fealty. He had an interest in Norman Italy through his wife Constance, and hence in the Byzantine Empire. When he took the cross in 1195 he was probably planning to move against Constantinople. Set off in 1197 but died from malaria at Messina.

HONORIUS III pope 1216–27
Frail and elderly, he continued Innocent III's crusading activities, both in the east and against the Albigensians.

HUGH OF FLAVIGNY 1065–1115
In about 1090 Hugh began to write his chronicle, a 'universal history' from the birth of Christ to 1102. It is particularly important for the last years of the 11th century. Became abbot of Flavigny in 1096.

HUS, JOHN c.1372–1415
A lecturer at the University of Prague, then a founder of the university at Leipzig. He was condemned by the archbishop of Prague as a dangerous heretic, and in 1415

was burned at the stake. His ideas, which were influenced by the English reformer John Wycliffe, were less easily put down despite five crusades, and in 1436 the Hussite sect gained official recognition in Bohemia.

IBN AL-QALANISI c.1073–1160
Member of an important Damascus family and above all historian of the city. Used archives, his own observations and eyewitness accounts to write a vivid and reliable chronicle.

IL-GHAZI Seldjuk Turkish ruler d.1122
Joint ruler of Jerusalem when it was taken by the Egyptians in 1096. Governor of Baghdad 1100-5. In 1118 he was recognized as prince of Aleppo and prepared to attack the Franks. He won an overwhelming victory in 1119 at the Field of Blood; although he neglected to follow it up and take Antioch, he was one of the first emirs to check the crusaders' advance.

INNOCENT III pope 1198–1216
An exceptionally able pope who gave the crusades a high priority. Against his will the Fourth Crusade was diverted to Constantinople: he hoped it might lead to the reunion of the Churches. In 1208 he preached a crusade against the Albigensians in southern France, and in 1213 a new crusade against Islam.

ISAAC II ANGELUS Byzantine emperor 1185–95; 1203–4
An ineffective ruler, in 1195 he was deposed by his brother Alexius, blinded and imprisoned. His son Alexius escaped to the west and persuaded the crusaders to target Constantinople where they restored the old blind emperor in 1203. Deposed and killed during the riot of 1204.

ISABELLA queen of Castile 1474–1504
Isabella's marriage to Ferdinand of Aragon led to the unification of Spain; from 1481 they ruled jointly as 'the Catholic kings'. Isabella was known for her justice but also her intolerant orthodoxy, expelling Jews and Moors from her territories. She financed Columbus's expeditions.

DON JOHN OF AUSTRIA 1547–78
Illegitimate son of Emperor Charles V, half-brother of Philip II. In 1571 Philip gave him command of the naval forces of the Holy League which virtually annihilated the Turkish fleet at Lepanto, but Philip I's paranoid suspicions and John's early death prevented greater achievements.

JOHN OF BOUCICAUT marshal of France 1391; d.1421
In 1396 John took part in the crusade of Nicopolis but was taken captive. On regaining his freedom he organized an expedition to relieve Constantinople, which was under siege by Bayezid I. On his return to the west he was made governor of Genoa (1401–9). Taken prisoner by the English at Agincourt in 1415, he died in captivity in Yorkshire.

JOHN OF BRIENNE king of Jerusalem 1210–25; Latin emperor of Constantinople 1231–7
Accompanied Philip II of France on the Third Crusade and married Maria, queen of Jerusalem, in 1210. In 1225, arranged the marriage of his daughter Isabella to Frederick II, but failed to retain the regency of Jerusalem and went to Italy. Called to be regent for the child emperor, Baldwin II of Constantinople in 1228, he was elected Latin emperor at Baldwin's death.

JOHN OF IBELIN lord of Beirut 1197–1236
From 1225 leader of the crusader nobility of the kingdom of Jerusalem/Acre and of the opposition to Frederick II. Acted as regent for Henry I, king of Cyprus (1218–28) and established the Ibelin dynasty on the island.

JOHN OF IBELIN count of Jaffa 1247–66
Born on Cyprus. He was baili to the king of Jerusalem 1254–6. He compiled the Assizes of Jerusalem, a legal code reflecting ideal feudal law and designed to regulate the crusader kingdom.

JOHN OF JOINVILLE 1224–1319
John entered royal service as a knight in 1241 and followed Louis IX on crusade. He became a close friend of the king, who later made him seneschal of Champagne. In his last years (c.1309) Joinville wrote his Life of St Louis – a hagiographical but very human biography.

AL-KAMIL Ayubid sultan of Egypt 1218–38
The eldest son of al-Adil, al-Kamil was associated with his father in the conquest of Egypt in 1200. Shortly after the Franks' unexpected attack on Egypt in 1218 al-Adil died and his son became supreme head of the Ayubid realm. With his brothers' support he repulsed the Fifth Crusade by 1221. In 1227 there were rumours of a new crusade: al-Kamil made a treaty with Frederick II whereby Jerusalem was delivered to the crusaders.

LOUIS VII king of France 1137–80
A just and respected king, and leader of the Second Crusade (1147–9). In 1152 he divorced Eleanor, duchess of Aquitaine, who then married Henry of Anjou (later Henry II of England).

LOUIS VIII king of France 1223–6
Launched a crusade against the Albigensians in 1216, an initiative he resumed after his coronation, annexing Languedoc to the royal domain.

LOUIS IX king of France 1226–70
Launched a crusade in 1244 to save the Christian

kingdoms of the east. He met with initial successes in Egypt but was defeated and taken prisoner at Mansourah in 1249. After being ransomed, he went to Acre to oversee the fortification of the Christian cities (1250–4). Louis proclaimed a second crusade in 1270 against Tunis, where he died.

MALIK GHAZI d.1104
Also known as Danishmend, and a hero of Arabic legend, the founder of the Turkoman dynasty in the late 11th century. Harrassed the army of the First Crusade as it crossed Anatolia. Captured Bohemund near Melitene in 1100 but freed him in 1103 to secure an alliance against their common enemies, the Byzantines and the Seldjuk Turks.

MALIK SHAH Seldjuk sultan 1072–92
The last of the great Seldjuk rulers, he added to their conquests Syria and other territories. His death in 1092 was followed by quarrels among his sons from which the crusaders benefited.

AL-MANSUR QALAWUN Mamluk sultan 1279–90
Qalawun continued Baybars's policy of holy war against the crusaders. He besieged and captured Tripoli in 1289, and in 1290 set up the siege of Acre which his son, Sultan al-Ashraf, brought to a successful conclusion.

MANUEL I COMNENUS Byzantine emperor 1143–80
A brilliant ruler, soldier, diplomat and statesman, Manuel understood the western outlook, yet was fully conscious of dangers from the west. He tried and failed to reconquer Byzantine Italy.

MARIA queen of Jerusalem 1210–12
Daughter of Conrad of Montferrat and Isabel of Jerusalem, who married John of Brienne in 1210. Her death two years later deprived him of any title to the throne, although he ruled as regent for their daughter until 1225.

MARTIN V pope 1417–31
The pope whose election ended the Great Schism. Declared crusades against the followers of John Hus, but without significant success.

MATTHEW OF EDESSA d. before 1140
The writer of an Armenian chronicle covering the history of Syria 952–1136. His chronicle, though reflecting his violent prejudices, is invaluable, especially for his own lifetime.

MATTHEW PARIS c.1199–1259
Matthew joined the monastery of St Albans in 1217 and became annalist of the abbey in 1236. His *Chronica Maiora*,

a world history to 1259, is the most important western historical work of the 13th century.

MEHMED II Ottoman sultan 1451–81
His consolidation of Turkish rule laid the foundation for the enormous expansion of the Ottoman Empire in the 16th century. The conquest of Constantinople in 1453 was his most conspicuous achievement.

MURAD II Ottoman sultan 1421–51
Invaded Hungary in 1438 but met with little success. After making peace in 1444 he abdicated in favour of his son Mehmed II, but periodically emerged from retirement to deal with problems in Hungary and the Balkans.

NICEPHORUS BRYENNIUS d.1120
Grandson of the Byzantine general of the same name, Nicephorus married Emperor Alexius I Comnenus's daughter Anna Comnena. In c.1100, wrote the *Histories*, a comprehensive account of Byzantine disputes, politics and achievements. His attempt to gain the imperial throne failed, but his historical work is an important source for 11th-century Byzantium.

NICHOLAS OF COLOGNE
A leader of the Children's Crusade of 1212. An enormous army followed Nicholas but most dispersed in Italy when sea-transport was not forthcoming. One account says that Nicholas died there, another that he fought at Damietta on the Fifth Crusade and returned to Europe safely.

NUR AD-DIN ruler of Syria 1146–74
A just ruler and a talented general. Defeated in the army of the Second Crusade in 1148. Thereafter he captured Joscelin II of Edessa and gradually took all the Edessan fortresses. He defeated Baldwin III of Jerusalem in 1157, and from 1161 he was involved in Egypt where his career was closely bound up with Saladin's.

ODO OF DEUIL d.1162
A monk of Saint-Denis who attracted the attention of Abbot Suger. Appointed chaplain to Louis VII in 1147 and accompanied him on the Second Crusade. He kept notes on the crusade which were the basis of a comprehensive account of the expedition.

OLIVER OF PADERBORN
Bishop of Paderborn 1224–5 and cardinal-bishop of Sabina 1225–7. He preached the Fifth Crusade in Germany for Innocent III, with enormous success. Accompanied the crusade, became one of its leaders, and later wrote an important history of it.

OTTO bishop of Freisingen 1137–58
Half-brother of Conrad III and uncle of Frederick I Barbarossa, Otto was one of the best-informed and

reliable historians of medieval Europe. Studied at the University of Paris before joining the Cistercian Order in 1133. In 1146 he wrote his *Two Cities* and in 1169 his *Deeds of Frederick Barbarossa*.

PETER I OF LUSIGNAN king of Cyprus 1359–69
After his accession Peter travelled to France to recruit knights for a new crusade. On his return journey he captured two Seldjuk castles in Armenia. In 1365 he conquered and plundered Alexandria in Egypt, but was forced to retire by the Mamluks. In 1369 he was murdered by one of his knights.

PETER II king of Aragon 1196–1213
Inherited the rights of his father, Alfonso II, in southern France. Annexed Montpellier in 1204, and in 1212 he was on the victorious Christian side in the battle of Las Navas de Tolosa; this defeat of the Almohads was a decisive step in the decline of Muslim power in Spain.

PETER THE HERMIT c.1050–1115
Born in the region of Amiens in northern France. In 1096 he led the People's Crusade overland to Constantinople. He survived their massacre in Asia Minor and joined the main army. Tried to escape – unsuccessfully – during the siege of Antioch, but did complete the crusade and enter Jerusalem. In 1100 he returned to Europe and became prior of an Augustinian monastery in Belgium.

PHILIP II AUGUSTUS king of France 1180–1223
Participated in the Third Crusade in 1189, but immediately after the conquest of Acre in 1191 returned to France. He took advantage of Richard I's absence to seize his French lands but was defeated by Richard in 1194. He supported the crusade against the Albigensians but played no personal role in it.

PHILIP II king of Spain 1556–98
Under Philip, Spain and its empire reached their greatest power and extent. He waged a major naval war with the Ottoman Turks in the Mediterranean and inflicted a decisive defeat on them at Lepanto in 1571.

PHILIP OF MÉZIÈRES chancellor of Cyprus 1360–73
Went on crusade in 1345. He remained in the east, and in 1360 became chancellor to Peter I of Cyprus, whom he supported in this king's crusading projects. In 1373 he returned to France where he became counsellor to Charles V. After the king's death he retired to a monastery, wrote, and planned crusades until his death in 1405.

PIUS II pope 1458–64
Ordained in 1446 after a dissolute youth – which lasted 40 years. As pope, Pius summoned a congress to launch a crusade to halt the Turkish advance into Europe, but failed to gain support. He tried again in 1463 but the expedition, feeble from the start, came to nothing when he died.

QILIJ ARSLAN Seldjuk prince of Asia Minor 1086–1107
'Soliman', as the crusaders called him, ruled Nicaea from 1092. He crushed the followers of Peter the Hermit but the main crusading army forced him to give up Nicaea and defeated him at Dorylaeum in 1097. In temporary alliance with Malik Ghazi he annihilated the crusading armies of 1101. Killed in 1107.

RADULPH OF CAEN
Radulph travelled to the Holy Land in 1108 and joined Tancred. In c.1113 wrote his *Deeds of Tancred*, a work reflecting his violent prejudices.

RASHID AL-DIN SINAN leader of Ismailis 1163–93
The legendary 'Old Man of the Mountain' who headed the fanatical Syrian sect, the Assassins, in the second half of the 12th century. Played a prominent part in Syrian and Egyptian politics, successfully defending his people against the orthodox Muslim leaders, especially Saladin, and against the crusaders.

RAYMOND OF AGUILERS
Chronicler of the First Crusade: as a chaplain to Raymond of St Gilles, Raymond was well situated to write an account of events.

RAYMOND OF ST GILLES c.1041–1105
Count of Toulouse, who led the Provençal contingent on the First Crusade. Played a distinguished part but refused the crown of Jerusalem in 1099. In 1101 he founded the county of Tripoli.

RICHARD I king of England 1189–99
The rebellious son of Henry II. Ambitious to go on crusade, in 1190 sailed to Sicily, then on to Cyprus which he conquered from Byzantium. Played a leading part in the siege of Acre, but quarrelled with the other leaders and failed to recapture Jerusalem. Paid little attention to England, other than as a source of money.

RICHARD abbot of Saint-Vannes
Under three emperors in the first half of the 11th century Richard was a leader of the Cluniac reforming party. The Holy Roman Emperor, Henry III, found in him a zealous promoter of the Truce of God.

RICHARD earl of Cornwall 1209–72
Younger brother of Henry III of England who led a crusade 1240–1 which added territory between Ascalon and Jerusalem to the crusader kingdom. In 1254 he was a

candidate for the imperial throne but attempts to raise in England the money needed led to baronial revolts.

ROBERT GUISCARD duke of Apulia 1054–85
A member of the Hauteville family of Normandy who joined his brothers and other Norman adventurers in southern Italy. He and his brother – and vassal – Roger conquered Sicily from the Muslims. In 1071 he took the Byzantine possessions in Italy; spent his last years raiding the Byzantines in Albania and Epirus.

ROBERT OF CLARI d. c.1216
French knight and author of the Old French prose account of the Fourth Crusade, Robert was present at the siege and sack of Constantinople in 1204. He accompanied Emperor Baldwin's expedition to Salonika and then returned to France in 1205.

RODRIGO DIAZ DE VIVAR 1043–99
'El Cid' of Spanish epic. From the petty nobility, he entered the service of Alfonso VI but in 1081 was exiled by him. He then offered his services to the Muslim king of Saragossa and gained great fame in battles against the Christians. In 1093 he organized his own army and conquered Valencia; in 1099 he died as the respected head of a Christian state. 'Cid' derives from Arabic *sidi*, meaning 'lord'.

ROGER I count of Sicily 1062–1101
Youngest son of Tancred of Hauteville, who came to southern Italy in 1057 to help his brother Robert Guiscard. In 1062 he was made nominal count of Sicily under Muslim rule. In 1072 he conquered Palermo and began to organize the government of the island. After Robert's death Roger was recognized as his heir as duke of Apulia, making him overlord of Norman Italy.

ROGER OF HOWDEN d.1201
Studied at Durham and taught theology at Oxford. In 1175 he entered the service of Henry II of England. Accompanied Richard I on crusade. His chronicle of the two reigns represents an official view.

ROGER OF SALERNO prince of Antioch 1112–9
Roger succeeded his uncle Tancred at Antioch and established a strong government. In 1115 he won a victory over the Muslims of Aleppo at Danuth, but in 1119 an attempt to conquer Aleppo failed and he was killed at the battle of the Field of Blood.

ROMANUS IV DIOGENES Byzantine emperor 1067–71
Capable general, who gained the throne by marrying the widow of his predecessor, Constantine X Ducas. Initial campaigns against the Turks were successful but he was defeated at Manzikert in 1071 and captured by Alp-Arslan

who treated him honourably. On his release, his stepson Michael VI Ducas, who had usurped his throne, had him blinded and killed.

SALADIN ruler of Egypt 1169–93, Syria 1174–93
Set out to gain power, to put down the Shi'ites and to fight the crusaders. His opposition to the Franks culminated in victory at Hattin in 1187, to which the west responded with the Third Crusade. Saladin's empire fragmented after his death, but the chivalrous legend endured.

SHIRKUH Egyptian vizier d.1169
Saladin's uncle and patron, and one of Nur ad-Din's generals: his viziership lasted only two months before his sudden death.

STEPHEN OF CLOUES
A shepherd boy who saw a vision in 1212 and attracted a great following, associated with the Children's Crusade.

STEPHEN count of Blois d.1102
Married to the strong-minded Adela, daughter of William the Conqueror. In 1096, when he was about 50 years old, he took part in the First Crusade. Ran away during the siege of Antioch and returned to France. In 1101 he commanded a new crusade and was killed at the battle of Ramleh.

SULEYMAN IBN KUTULMISH d.1086
Ancestor of the Seldjuks in Asia Minor. Malik Shah entrusted to Suleyman the conduct of the war against the Byzantines, which he waged with great success in Asia Minor. He gained such a reputation that the crusaders called both his son and his grandson 'Soliman'.

SULEYMAN I Ottoman sultan 1520–66
Known as 'the Magnificent', a title reflecting his reputation as the greatest Ottoman sultan. Took part in person in 13 great campaigns, all of which extended his empire's power and territory. In 1522 he took Rhodes from the Knights of St John. His siege of Vienna in 1529 was unsuccessful, but in the same year he occupied Buda (Budapest). He was equally able in his domestic policies .

TAMERLANE Mongol khan 1370–1405
A powerful but destructive monarch. After seizing power in 1370, mobilized a powerful Mongol-Turkish army and conquered Persia. In 1385 he raided India. Invaded Anatolia in 1400 and at the battle of Ankara (1401), he destroyed the Ottoman army and captured the sultan Bayezid, whom he kept in a cage until his death.

TANCRED d.1112
Nephew of Bohemund whom he accompanied on the

First Crusade. Stayed in the east after the capture of Jerusalem; conquered Tiberias and became prince of Galilee. A contender for the throne of Jerusalem in 1100, supported by Daimbert of Pisa. From 1102 he was regent of Antioch for Bohemund and fought long and hard to consolidate the northern principality.

THEOBALD IV king of Navarre 1234–53
Practised poetry and the chivalrous arts, and made his court a brilliant centre of both. In 1239 he led a crusade in Palestine and conquered territory between Ascalon and Jerusalem for the crusader kingdom.

TOGHRUL BEG Seldjuk sultan 1038–63
The founder of his dynasty, Toghrul Beg compelled or persuaded most of the Muslim rulers of the eastern and central lands of the Baghdad caliphate to submit to him. He raided into Byzantine territory without much success.

TURAN SHAH Ayubid sultan of Egypt 1249–50
The last Ayubid sultan, he ruled for only a few months before being killed by his own troups.

TUTUSH Seldjuk ruler in Syria 1079–95
Awarded Syria by Malik Shah, his brother, though he had to conquer it himself. Died in the battles which followed Malik Shah's death and Syria was divided between Ridwan, prince of Aleppo, and Duqaq, prince of Damascus.

URBAN II pope 1088–99
Of noble birth, a monk of Cluny and protégé of Gregory VII, Urban supported his patron's reforming ideas but was above all a skilful diplomat. Encouraged the reconquest of Spain and maintained an alliance with the Normans in Italy. In 1095 he held synods in Piacenza and Clermont which gave rise to the First Crusade. He died a fortnight after the capture of Jerusalem, without knowing of the extraordinary success of the venture.

WALTER PENNENPIÉ castellan of Jerusalem d.1244
Frederick II's representative in Jerusalem, who was awarded Ascalon by Richard of Cornwall in 1240.

WILLIAM OF TYRE chancellor of Jerusalem d.1190
Born in the Holy Land, studied in Europe and returned home to be appointed archdeacon of Tyre in 1167. In 1170, appointed tutor to the future king Baldwin IV, who made him chancellor on his accession. Wrote his highly regarded history between 1169 and 1173, and became archbishop of Tyre in 1175.

YUSUF IBN TASHFIN Almoravid king 1061–1107
Yusuf unified Morocco and invaded Spain, winning a great victory at Zallaka in 1086 which enabled him to conquer all Muslim-held Spain with the exception of Saragossa. Bequeathed a vast empire to his son Ali.

ZANGHI emir of Mosul and Aleppo 1127–46
Waged unremitting war on the crusaders in the Holy Land, capturing Edessa in 1144. This provoked the ill-fated Second Crusade. Zanghi was murdered in 1146.

ŽIŽKA, JOHN 1376–1424
The skilled military leader who led the Bohemian Hussites against the invasion forces of Emperor Sigismund 1420–4. He was a member of the more extreme Taborite group who eventually triumphed and established the official Church of Bohemia.

GLOSSARY

Atabeg "Prince-father" or "regent"; originally a Turkish term for guardians or tutors of minor Seldjuk princes; eventually became actual rulers.

Bailli An administrator; in the Byzantine Empire, a regent exercising royal or princely powers in the absence of the ruler.

Bezant The western name for a Byzantine gold coin weighing 4.55 grammes.

Boyar A Russian term for a high-ranking nobleman, a courtier to the prince of Moscow.

Bricole A catapult for throwing stones or bolts.

Caliph "Successor" or "viceregent"; the title of the supreme head of a Muslim community, successor or viceregent of the Prophet.

Camlet A costly Eastern fabric made from angora goat's fleece.

Castellan The holder or governor of a castle.

Da'wa An accusation or arraignment in Muslim civil and criminal law.

Dinar A Muslim unit of gold currency, dating from the early days of Islam.

Dirham A unit of silver coinage in the Arab monetary system, worth about 4d English.

Diptych A devotional painting consisting of two tablets hinged together, used for liturgical purposes, particularly in the Byzantine Church. Names of bishops and saints were recorded on the diptych and recited during mass as a focus for liturgical prayers.

Emir A leader or commander; the shortened form of *Amir al-Mu'minin*, "commander of the faithful".

Eparch The title of the governor of a province of the Byzantine Empire.

Fascine A cylindrical bundle of wood for military use in siege warfare, filling ditches, etc.

Florin A Florentine gold coin of 3.54 grammes weight, struck from 1252 to 1533. The florin was famed for its unvarying weight and quality, and used as a standard for international trade.

Fosse A dry ditch, frequently used in defensive fortifications.

Franks A term used by Muslim chroniclers during the crusades to describe all Christian crusaders, irrespective of their nationality (see: Latins).

Greeks A term used by crusaders from western Europe to describe the inhabitants of the Byzantine Empire (see: Romans).

Greek fire A form of liquid fire based on naphtha, used by the Byzantine Empire's navy to ignite enemy ships. Greek fire was projected through bronze tubes carried on the prows of Byzantine galleys (similar tubes were mounted on the walls of Constantinople); or packed in cannisters to be hurled by catapult.

Id al-Fitr "Festival of the breaking of the Fast", a Muslim festival, also known as "the minor festival".

Imam Leader of a Muslim community or of public prayers.

Jacobite Church An independent Christian sect founded in the 6th century and abiding principally in Syria under its own patriarch. By the time of the crusades there were some 150 Jacobite bishops and archbishops in the Church.

Janissaries "New troops", the name given to the regular infantry created by the Ottoman Turks in the 14th century, which became the principal armed force of Ottoman expansion. The Janissaries were children of conquered Christian peoples, taken from their parents and converted to Islam when very young. They were educated in special schools and regarded as slaves of the sovereign; but the corps gained great power inside the Ottoman Empire.

Jihad A Muslim term for holy war; the spread of Islam by force of arms as a religious duty.

Khan A Turkish title, used a princely title in contrast to the supreme title (sultan), and for a ruler of a portion of the whole empire.

Latins Another term used by Muslim chroniclers to designate indiscriminately all Christian crusaders (see: Franks).

Mangonel A form of catapult often used in sieges. Early examples used a see-saw throwing arm, with a cup at one end for a missile, and men pulling ropes at the other end to launch the missile. Later examples used twisted skeins of hair or animal sinew to propel their shot.

Manicheans Followers of a religion founded in Persia in the third century ad by the prophet Mani. Manicheanism was a major inspiration for the Cathar heresy.

Margrave A German princely title.

Mark A weight of around 8 ounces, used from the 11th century as a unit of currency, equivalent in England to 13s 4d.

Mihrab A niche in a mosque indicating the mosque's orientation towards Mecca and the proper direction for Muslims to pray in. The mihrab was often the eastern door.

Miniver A kind of fur used to line and trim clothes.

Moor A name used by medieval Europeans to describe North African and Spanish Muslims.

Myriad A Greek numeral; ten thousand.

Oriflamme The banner of the abbey of St-Denis near Paris, used as a royal standard by French kings from 1124 to around 1415. The banner was red, and probably had three points holding green silk tassels.

Patriarch A bishop heading a province of the Eastern Churches. The Patriarch of Constantinople was the head of the Byzantine Church.

Perfecti The élite of the Cathar (Albigensian) heretics, who led highly austere lives and formed the core of the movement.

Petrary A form of stone-throwing catapult often used aboard ships.

Qadi A Muslim judge who administers religious law, the basis of civil law in Islam.

Ramadan The ninth month of the Muslim calendar, "the month in which the Koran was sent down", during which Muslims are required to fast.

Ratl A Muslim unit of weight dating from pre-Islamic times, varying with countries and periods. In medieval Damascus it equalled 600 dirhams, and in Aleppo 720 dirhams (see: dirham).

Romans The term by which the Byzantines referred to themselves (see: Greeks).

Seneschal A steward. The title covered those administering large royal estates in France, as well as other leading French royal officials in the 11th and 12th centuries.

Simoniac Any cleric guilty of buying and/or selling spiritualities (ecclesiastical benefices or offices).

Saracens A name derived from the Greek, *sara senis*, used by the Byzantines and subsequently by all Christians to describe all the Muslim peoples subject to the caliphs. The name originally referred to an Arab tribe of uncertain location.

Sow A movable structure with a reinforced roof used to protect besiegers from hurled or dropped missiles whilst they attacked the walls of a besieged castle.

Subvention A grant of money for support of a particular institution or project; also, an official levy.

Sultan A Muslim term for a powerful ruler; independent, supreme sovereign of a certain territory or empire.

Sumpter animals Pack animals or beasts of burden.

Trebuchet A catapult with a large counterweight at one end of a long beam, which was raised and dropped to launch a missile.

Vassal The tenant and follower of a feudal lord, who did military service for his lord in return for the lord's protection and a fief of land or money.

Vizier A Muslim state official or minister, often with vice-regal authority, sometimes chief minister of a sovereign.

BIBLIOGRAPHY

This is not intended as a comprehensive bibliography of all relevant works, but is a selection of books relating to the topics discussed in the chronicles and essays. Articles have not been included because they are more difficult for the general reader to obtain; most of the works cited here contain bibliographies which are a good starting point for more detailed reading on individual subjects.

Abulafia, D., *Frederick II: A Medieval Emperor*, Cambridge, 1983

Academy of Sciences of Armenia, *History of the Armenian People*, Yerevan, 1976

Alichan, L., *Sissouan ou l'Arméno-Cilicie*, Venice, 1899

al-Muqaddasi, *Description of Syria including Palestine*, trans. G. Le Strange, London, 1886

Ashton, E., *A Social and Economic History of the Near East in the Middle Ages*, London, 1976

Azcona, T. de, *Isabel la Católica*, Madrid, 1964

Babinger, F., *Mehmed the Conqueror*, Princeton, 1978

Barber, M., *The Trial of the Templars*, Cambridge, 1978

Bell, C., *Portugal and the Quest for the Indies*, New York, 1974

Benevisti, M., *The Crusaders in the Holy Land*, Jerusalem, 1970

Bentley, J., *Restless Bones: The Story of Relics*, London, 1985

Betts, R. R., *Essays in Czech History*, London, 1969

Boase, T. S. R., *Castles and Churches of the Crusading Kingdom*, London, 1967

Boase, T. S. R., ed., *The Cilician Kingdom of Armenia*, London, 1978

Bornazian, S., *Armenia and the Seldjuks in the 11th–12th Centuries*, Yerevan, 1980

Bradley, J. F. N., *Czechoslovakia; a Short History*, Edinburgh, 1971

Braudel, F., *The Mediterranean and the Mediterranean World in the Age of Philip II*, London, 1984

Burchard of Mount Sion, *Descriptio Terrae Sanctae*, trans. A Stewart, London, 1896

Cahen, C., *Pre-Ottoman Turkey*, London, 1968

Cahen, C., *Orient et Occident au Temps des Croisades*, Paris, 1983

Chaladon, F., *Histoire de la Domination Normande en Italie Méridionale et en Sicile*, Paris, 1907

Chandler, K. N., *Trade and Civilization in the Indian Ocean*, Cambridge, 1985

Chazan, R., *European Jewry and the First Crusade*, Berkeley, 1987

Christiansen, E., *The Northern Crusade: the Baltic and the Catholic Frontier, 1100–1525*, London, 1980

Cipolla, C. M., *Guns, Sails and Empires: Technological Innovation and the Early Phases of European Expansion, 1400–1700*, New York, 1965

Cresswell, K. A. C., *The Muslim Architecture of Egypt*, Oxford, 1952

Davis, E. J., *The Invasion of Egypt by Louis IX and a History of the Contemporary Sultanates of Egypt*, London, 1897

Dedayan, G., ed., *Histoire des Arméniens*, Toulouse, 1982

Delogu, P., *I Normanni in Italia: Cronache della conquista e del Regno*, Naples, 1984

Der Nersessian, S., *The Armenians*, London, 1969

Deschamps, P., *Les Châteaux des Croisés en Terre Sainte*, Paris, 1934

Ehrenkreutz, A., *Saladin*, Albany, 1972

Eidelberg, S., ed. and trans., *The Jews and the Crusaders: The Hebrew Chroniclers of the First and Second Crusades*, Wisconsin, 1977

Elisséeff, N., *Nur ad-Din: Un Grand Prince Musulman de Syrie au temps des Croisades*, Damascus, 1967

The Encyclopaedia of Islam, 2nd edition, London, 1955

Endress, G., *An Introduction to Islam*, Edinburgh, 1988

Erdmann, C., *The Origin of the Idea of Crusade*, Princeton, 1977

Fernández-Armesto, F., *Before Columbus: Exploration and Colonization from the Mediterranean to the Atlantic, 1229–1492*, Basingstoke, 1987

Finucane, R. C., *Soldiers of the Faith*, London, 1983

Gabrieli, F., *Arab Historians of the Crusades*, London, 1969

Gibb, H. A. R., *Studies of the Civilization of Islam*, Boston, 1962

Gillingham, J., *Richard the Lionheart*, London, 1976

Godfrey, J., *The Unholy Crusade*, Oxford, 1980

Guillou, A., Burgarella, F., Von Falkenhausen, V., Rizzitano, V., Fiorani Piacentini, V., and Tramontana, S., *Il Mezzogiorno dai Bizantini a Federico II*, Turin, 1983

Guilmartin, J., *Gunpowder and Galleys: Changing Technology and Mediterranean Warfare at Sea in the Sixteenth Century*, Cambridge, 1974

Hamilton, B., *The Albigensian Crusade*, London, 1972

Heath, I., *Armies and Enemies of the Crusades, 1096–1291*, London, 1978

Heath, I., *Byzantine Armies, 886–1118*, London, 1979

Heath, I., *A Wargamer's Guide to the Crusades*, Cambridge, 1980

Hellenkemper, H., *Burgen der Kreuzritterzeit in der Grafschaft Edessa und im Konigreich Kleinarmeniens*, Bonn, 1976

Hess, A. C., *The Forgotten Frontier: A History of the Sixteenth-Century Ibero-Pacific Frontier*, London, 1978

Heymann, F. G., *John Žižka and the Hussite Revolution*, Princeton, 1955

Hill, G. F., *A History of Cyprus*, Cambridge, 1940–52

Hillgarth, J. N., *The Spanish Kingdoms: 1250–1516*, Oxford, 1978

Holt, P. M., *The Age of the Crusades: The Near East from the Eleventh Century to 1517*, London, 1986

Holt, P. M., Lambton, A. K. S., and Lewis, B., eds. *The Cambridge History of Islam*, Cambridge, 1970.

Hookham, H., *Tamburlaine the Conqueror*, London, 1962

Housley, N., *The Italian Crusades: The Papal-Angevin Alliance and the Crusades against Lay Powers, 1254–1343*, Oxford, 1982

Housley, N., *The Avignon Papacy and the Crusades, 1305–1378*, Oxford, 1986

Humphreys, R. S., *From Saladin to the Mongols: The Ayubids of Damascus*, Albany, 1977

Ibn al-Furat, *Ayubids, Mamluks and Crusaders*, trans. V. and M. C. Lyons, Cambridge, 1971

Ibn Iyas, *Journal d'un Bourgeois du Caire*, 2 vols, trans. G. Wiet, Paris, 1955, 1960

Ibn al-Qalanisi, *The Damascene Chronicle of the Crusades*, trans. H. A. R. Gibb, London, 1932

Ibn Taghribirdi, *History of Egypt, 1382 to 1469*, trans. W. Popper, Berkeley/Los Angeles, 1960

Inalcik, H., *The Ottoman Empire: The Classical Age, 1300–1600*, London, 1973

Irwin, R., *The Middle East in the Middle Ages: The Early Mamluk Sultanate, 1250–1382*, London, 1986

James of Vitry, *Historia orientalis*, trans. A Stewart, London, 1896.

Jenner, M., *Syria in View*, Harlow, 1986

Jordan, W. C., *Louis IX and the Challenge of the Crusade*, Princeton, 1979

Kaminsky, H., *A History of the Hussite Revolution*, Berkeley and Los Angeles, 1967

Kedar, B. Z., ed., *Outremer: Studies in the History of the Crusading Kingdom of Jerusalem Presented to Joshua Prawer*, Jerusalem, 1982

Kedar, B. Z., *Crusade and Mission: European Approaches toward the Muslims*, Princeton, 1984

Kennedy, H., *The Prophet and the Age of the Caliphates*, London, 1986

Lare-Poole, S., *A History of Egypt in the Middle Ages*, London, 1901

Le Strange, G., *Palestine under the Moslems*, London, 1890

Lloyd, S., *English Society and the Crusade, 1216–1307*, London, 1988

Lloyd, S. and Rice, D. S., *Alanya*, London, 1958

Lomax, D. W., *The Reconquest of Spain*, London, 1978

Lombard, M., *The Golden Age of Islam*, Oxford, 1975

Luttrell, A., *The Hospitallers in Cyprus, Rhodes, Greece and the West*, London, 1978

Luttrell, A., *Latin Greece, the Hospitallers and the Crusades, 1291–1440*, London, 1982

Lyons, M. C., and Jackson, D. E. P., *Saladin: The Politics of the Holy War*, Cambridge, 1984

Maalouf, A., *The Crusades through Arab Eyes*, London, 1984

MacKay, A., *Spain in the Middle Ages*, London, 1977

Mantran, R., *La Vie Quotidienne à Constantinople au Temps de Soliman le Magnifique*, Paris, 1965

Mayer, H. E., *The Crusades*, Oxford, 1988

Menéndez Pidal, R., *La Espana del Cid*, 7th edition, Madrid, 1969

Mikaelian, G., *History of the Armenian State of Cilicia*, Yerevan, 1952

Möhring, H., *Saladin und der Dritter Kreutzug*, Wiesbaden, 1980

Morgan, D. O., *The Mongols*, Oxford, 1986

Muller-Wiener, W., *Castles of the Crusaders*, London, 1966

Murphy, T. P., ed., *The Holy War*, Ohio, 1976

Mutafian, C., *La Cilicie au Carrefour des Empires*, Paris, 1988

Nicolle, D. C., *The Armies of Islam, 7th–11th centuries*, London, 1982

Nicolle, D. C., *Saladin and the Saracens*, London, 1986

Nicolle, D. C., *Arms and Armour of the Crusading Era, 1050–1350*, New York, 1988

Norwich, J. J., *The Normans in the South, 1016–1130*, London, 1967

Norwich, J.J., *The Kingdom of the Sun, 1130–1194*, London, 1970

Peters, E.M., *The First Crusade*, Philadelphia, 1986

Powell, J.M., *Anatomy of a Crusade, 1213–1221*, Pennsylvania, 1986

Prawer, J., *The Crusaders' Kingdom: European Colonialism in the Middle Ages*, London, 1972

Prawer, J., *The Latin Kingdom of Jerusalem*, London, 1972

Prawer, J., *The World of the Crusaders*, London, 1972

Prawer, J., *Histoire du Royaume Latin de Jérusalem*, Paris, 1975

Prawer, J., *Crusader Institutions*, Oxford, 1980

Prawer, J., *The History of the Jews in the Latin Kingdom of Jerusalem*, Oxford, 1988

Pringle, D., *The Red Tower (al-Burj al-Ahmar): Settlement in the Plain of Sharon at the Time of the Crusaders and Mamluks, 1099–1516*, London, 1986

Pryor, J.H., *Geography, Technology and War: Studies in the Maritime History of the Mediterranean, 649–1571*, Cambridge, 1988

Queller, D.E., *The Fourth Crusade: the Conquest of Constantinople*, Leicester, 1978

Riant, P.E.D., le comte de, *Exuviae Sacrae Constantinopolitanae*, Geneva, 1878

Richard, J., *The Latin Kingdom of Jerusalem*, Amsterdam, 1979

Richard, J., *Saint Louis, Roi d'une France Féodale, Soutien de la Terre Sainte*, Paris, 1983

Riley-Smith, J.S.C., *The Feudal Nobility and the Kingdom of Jerusalem, 1174–1277*, London, 1973

Riley-Smith, J.S.C., *What Were the Crusades?*, London, 1977

Riley-Smith, J.S.C. and L., *The Crusades: Idea and Reality, 1095–1274*, London, 1981

Riley-Smith, J.S.C., *The First Crusade and the Idea of Crusading*, London, 1986

Riley-Smith, J.S.C., *The Crusades: A Short History*, London, 1987

Roden, C., *A Book of Middle Eastern Food*, London, 1968

Rodgers, W.L., *Naval Warfare under Oars, 4th to 16th Centuries*, Annapolis, 1967

Roscher, H., *Innocenz III und die Kreuzzuge*, Göttingen, 1969

Rudt-Collenberg, W.H., *The Rupenides, Hetumides and Lusignans*, Paris, 1963

Runciman, S., *A History of the Crusades*, Cambridge, 1951–4

Runciman, S., *The Sicilian Vespers*, Cambridge, 1958

Saunders, J.J., *A History of Medieval Islam*, London, 1965

Saunders, J.J., *The History of the Mongol Conquests*, London, 1973

Scammell, G.V., *The World Encompassed: The First European Maritime Empires, c.800–1650*, London, 1981

Schwoebel, R.S., *The Shadow of the Crescent: The Renaissance Image of the Turk, 1453–1517*, Nieuwkoop, 1967

Setton, K., ed., *A History of the Crusades*, Madison, 1975

Setton, K., *The Papacy and the Levant, 1204–1571*, Philadelphia, 1984

Siberry, E., *Criticism of Crusading, 1095–1274*, Oxford, 1985

Sinclair, T.A., *Eastern Turkey: An Architectural and Archaeological Survey*, London, 1987

Sivan, E., *L'Islam et la Croisade*, Paris, 1968

Smail, R.C., *Crusading Warfare, 1097–1193*, Cambridge, 1956

Somerville, R., *The Councils of Urban II*, Amsterdam, 1972

Sumption, J., *The Albigensian Crusade*, London, 1978

Throop, P.A., *Criticism of the Crusade*, Philadelphia, 1977

Turnbull, S.R., *The Mongols*, London, 1980

Usama Ibn Munqidh, *Autobiography: An Arab-Syrian Gentleman of the Crusades*, ed. and trans. P. Hitti, New York, 1929

Verbruggen, J.F., *The Art of Warfare in Western Europe during the Middle Ages*, London, 1977

Vyronis, S., *Byzantium and Europe*, London, 1967

Ward, B., *Miracles and the Medieval Mind*, London, 1982

Watson, A.M., *Agricultural Innovation in the Early Islamic World: the Diffusion of Crops and Farming Technique, 700–1100*, Cambridge, 1983

Wilkinson, J., *Jerusalem Pilgrimage*, London, 1988

Wise, T., *Armies of the Crusades*, London, 1978

Wise, T., *The Knights of Christ*, London, 1984

CHRONICLES

MGH   Monuments Germaniae Historica, Hanover, 1826–

MGH SS   MGH Scriptores

MGH SRG   MGH Sciptores Rerum Germanicarum

MPL   Migne, J.P., Patrologia Latina, Paris, 1844–55

MPG   Migne, J.P., Patrologia Graeco-Latina, Paris, 1857–66

RHC   Recueil des Historiens des Croisades, Paris, 1841–1906

RHC Occ.   RHC Historiens Occidentaux, 1844–95

RHC Or.   RHC Historiens Orientaux, 1872–1906

RHC Arm.   RHC Documents Arméniens, 1869–1906

RHC Grec.   RHC Historiens Grecs, 1875–81

1   The Muslim world before 1096

St Bernard, *De Laude Novae Militae*, from *S. Bernardi Opera*, ed, J. Leclerq and H.M. Rochais, Rome, 1963; vol. 3, Extracts.

Al-Maqrizi, *Khitat*, ed. B. Lewis in *Islam from the Prophet Muhammed to the Capture of Constantinople*, Oxford, 1987; I. Extracts.

Forged encyclical of 'Sergius IV', ed. A. Gieysztor, *Medievalia et Humanistica VI*, 1950.

Hugh of Flavigny, *Chronicon*, MGH SS VII, Extracts.

Nasir-i-Khosrau, *Journey through Syria and Palestine*, trans. G. Le Strange, Palestine Pilgrims' Text Society, London, 1893.

Albert of Aachen, *Historia Hierosolymitana*, in RCH Occ. IV.

Bishop Lietbert of Cambrai, *Chronicon S. Andrei Cameracensis*, MPL CXLIX.

Letter from Pope Victor III to Byzantine Empress Anna Dalassena, MPL CXLIX.

Letter from papal legation to Constantinople, headed by Cardinal Humbert of Silva Candida, MPL CXLIII.

Letter from Michael Cerularius to Peter, patriarch of Antioch, MPG CXX.

Annals of Niederaltaich, MGH SRG, 1891.

Lambert of Hersfeld, *Chronicon*, MGH SRG, 1895.

Life of Bishop Altmann of Passau, ch. 4, MGH SS, XII.

The Chronicle of Matthew of Edessa, trans. E. Dulaurier, Paris, 1858, Extracts.

Nicephorus Bryennius, *Histories*, trans. H, Grégoire in *Byzantion*, XXIII, 1953; I, Extracts.

Gesta Roderici Campi Doctoris, from R. Menedez Pidal, *L'España del Cid*, Madrid; 1929. Extracts.

Amatus of Montecassino, *History of the Normans*, ed. V. de Bartholomeis, Rome, 1935; book V Extracts.

Letter from Pope Urban II, MPL CLI.

Geoffrey of Malaterra, *Sicilian History*, ed. E. Pontieri, Bologna, 1927–8; II, IV. Extracts.

Anna Comnena, *Alexiad*, ed. B. Lieb, Paris, 1937–45.

William of Apulia, *Gesta Roberti Wiscardi*, ed. M. Mathiew, Palermo, 1961; book IV; book V. Extracts.

Letter from Pope Urban II, in *Byzantinische Zeitschrift* XXXVIII, 1928.

Bernold of Constance, *Chronicon*, MGH SS, V. 461

2   The First Crusade 1096–1099

Anonymous, *Gesta Francorum*, ed. R. Hill, London, 1962. Extracts.

Letters from Pope Urban II, ed. H. Hagenmeyer, *Die Kreuzzugsbriefe aus den Jahren 1088-1100*, Innsbruck, 1901. Extracts.

William of Malmesbury, *Gesta Regum*, ed. W. Stubbs, London, 1887–9. Extracts.

Fulcher of Chartres, *Historia Hierosolymitana*, ed. H. Hagenmeyer, Heidelberg, 1913. Extracts.

Guibert of Nogent, *Historia Hierosolymitana*, in RHC Occ. IV. Extracts.

Anna Comnena, *Alexiad*, ed. B. Leib, Paris, 1937–45. Extracts.

Albert of Aachen, *Historia Hierosolymitana*, in RHC Occ. IV. Extracts.

Salomon bar Simson, from A. Neubauer and M. Stern, *Quellen zur Geschichte der Juden in Deutscland*, Berlin, 1892. Extracts.

Letters from Stephen of Blois, ed. H. Hagenmeyer, *Die Kreuzzugsbriefe*, op. cit. Extracts.

Richard the Pilgrim, *La Chanson d'Antioche*, ed. S. Duparc-Quioc, Paris, 1977–8. Extracts.

Matthew of Edessa, *Chronicle*, in RHC Arm. I. Extracts.

Ibn al-Athir, *Sum of World History*, in RHC Or. II part 2. Extracts.

Raymond of Aguilers, *Liber*, ed. J.H. and L.L. Hill, Paris, 1969. Extracts.

Radulph of Caen, *Gesta Tancredi*, in RHC Occ. III. Extracts.

Letters from crusading princes to Pope Urban II, ed. H. Hagenmeyer, *Die Kreuzzugsbriefe*, op. cit. Extracts.

Caffaro, *De liberatione civitatum orientis*, ed. L.T. Belgrano, *Annali Genovensi*, Genoa, 1890. Extracts.

Orderic Vitalis, *Historia aecclesiastica*, ed. M. Chibnall, London, 1969–79. Extracts.

Sibt Ibn al-Jawzi, *Mirat al-Zaman*, in RHC OR. III. Extracts.

Snorri Sturluson, *Heimskringla*, ed. F. Jonsson, Oslo, 1966.

Walter the Chancellor, *Bella Antiochena*, ed. H. Hagenmeyer, Innsbruck, 1896. Extracts.

William of Tyre, *Chronique*, ed. R.B.C. Huygens, Turnhout, 1986. Extracts.

3 The Second Crusade 1147–1149

Fulcher of Chartres, *Historia Hierosolymitana*, ed. H. Hagenmeyer, Heidelberg, 1913. Extracts.

Michael the Syrian, *Chronicle*, ed. and trans. J.B. Chabot, Paris, 1899–1910; III. Extracts.

Papal bull of Pope Eugenius III, *Quantum praedecessores*, MPL CLXXX. Extracts.

Odo of Deuil, *De profectione Ludovici VII in Orientem*, ed. and trans. V.G. Berry, New York, 1948. Extracts.

St Bernard, *Epistolae* in *S. Bernardi Opera*, ed. J. Leclercq and H. Rochais, Rome, 1977; VIII. Extracts.

Otto of Freisingen, *Gesta Friderici primi imperatoris*, in MGH SS XX. Extracts.

Annales Herbipolenses (Würzburg annals), in MGH SS XVI. Extracts.

Rabbi Ephraim of Bonn, *Sefer Zekhirah*, in A. Neubauer and M. Stern, ed. *Quellen zur Geschichte der Juden in Deutschland*, Berlin, 1892. Extracts.

Helmold of Bosau, *Chronica Slavorum*, ed. B. Schmeidler and H. Stoob, Darmstadt, 1973. Extracts.

Vincent of Prague, *Annales*, in MGH SS XVII. Extracts.

Annales Magdeburgenses, in MGH SS XVI. Extracts.

Anonymous, *De exugnatione Lyxbonenesi*, ed. and trans. C.W. David, New York, 1936.

John Kinnamos, *Epitome Rerum ab Iohanne et Alexio Comnenis Gestarum*, Bonn, 1936. Extracts.

Letter of Louis VII to Abbot Suger, in *Recueil des Historiens des Gaules et de la France*, Paris, 1737–1904; XV.

Letter of Conrad III to Abbot Wibald, in MPL CLXXXIX.

William of Tyre, *Chronique*, ed. R.B.C. Huygens, Turnhout, 1986. Extracts.

John of Salisbury, *Historica Pontificalis*, ed. and trans. M. Chibnall, London, 1956. Extracts.

Ibn al-Qalanisi, *Chronicle*, ed. H.F. Amedroz, Leyden, 1908. Extracts.

Usama Ibn Munqidh, *Autobiography: An Arab Syrian Gentleman of the Crusades*. ed. and trans. P. Hitti, New York, 1929.

St Bernard, *De consideratione*, in *S. Bernardi Opera*, ed. J. Leclerq and H. Rochais, Rome, 1963; III. Extracts.

4 The Third Crusade 1189–1192

Itinerarium regis Ricardi, ed. W. Stubbs, Rolls Series, London, 1864. Extracts.

Baha ad-Din Ibn Shaddad, *Sultanly Anecdotes*, in RHC Or. III. Extracts.

Imad ad-Din al-Isfahani, from Abu Shama, *Book of Two Gardens*, in RHC Or. IV. Extracts.

Anonymous, *Parti de mal et a ben aturné*, in *Chansons de croisade*, ed. J. Bédier and P. Aubry, Paris, 1909. Extracts.

Ibn Jubayr, *The Travels of Ibn Jubayr*, trans. R.J.C. Broadhurst, London, 1952. Extracts.

Roger of Howden, *Chronica*, ed. W. Stubbs, Rolls Series, London 1868–71; II, III. Extracts.

Gerald of Wales, *De principis instructione liber*, from *Opera*, ed. J.S. Brewer, Rolls Series, London, 1861–91; VIII. Extracts.

Recueil des actes de Philippe Auguste, ed. H.F. Delaborde, Paris, 1916–43; I. Extracts.

Gerald of Wales, *Itinerarium Kambriae*, from Opera, op. cit.; VI. Extracts.

Ralph Niger, *De re militari*, ed. L. Schmugge, Berlin, 1977. Extracts.

Peter of Blois, *Opera*, in MPL CCVII, Extracts.

Anonymous, *Historia de Expeditione Frederici Imperatoris*, ed. A. Chroust, MGH SRG. Extracts.

Nicetas Choniates,*Chronica*, from RHC Grec. I. Extracts.

Epistolae Cantuarienses, ed. W. Stubbs, Rolls Series, London, 1876; II. Extracts.

Ambroise, *L'Estoire de la Guerre Sainte*, ed. G. Paris, Paris, 1897; II. Extracts.

Ralph of Diceto, *Opera Historica*, ed. W. Stubbs, Rolls Series, London, 1876. Extracts.

Arnold of Lubeck, *Chronica Slavorum*, MGH SS XXI. Extracts.

5 The Fourth Crusade 1202–1204

Die Register Innocenz III, ed. O. Hageneder and A. Haidacher, Graz/Köln, 1964; I. Extracts.

Geoffrey of Villehardouin, *La Conquête de Constantinople*, ed. E. Faral, Paris, 1938. Extracts.

Raimbaut de Vaqueiras, *Epic Letter*, from *The Poems of the Troubadour Raimbaut de Vaqueiras*, ed. J. Linskill, The Hague, 1964. Extracts.

Anonymous, *The Deeds of Innocent III*, MPL CCXIV; ch. 83. Extracts.

Pope Innocent III, *Letters*, MPL CCXV; V. Extracts.

Nicetas Choniates, *Historia*, ed. A. van Dieten, Berlin, 1975. Extracts.

Robert of Clari, *La Conquête de Constantinople*, ed. P. Lauer, Paris, 1939. Extracts.

The Chronicle of Novgorod, Camden Society 3rd series, London, 1914; vol. XXV. Extracts.

Letter of Count Raymond of Toulouse, from *Gervase of Canterbury*, vol. 1. Extracts.

Peter des Vaux, *Histoire Albigeoise*, ed. and trans, P. Guébin and E. Lyons, Paris, 1926–39; vol. I. Extracts.

William of Tudela, *Chanson de la Croisade contre les Albigeois*, Paris, 1960; vol. I. Extracts.

Letter of Arnold, abbot of Cîteaux, to Pope Innocent III, in MPL CCXV. Extracts.

John of Garland, *De Triumphis Ecclesiae*, ed. T. Wright. London, 1856; book 5. Extracts.

Jordan of Saxony, *Monumenta Ordinis Fratrum Praedicantium Historica*, ed. H. Scheeben, Rome, 1935; XVI. Extracts.

Matthew Paris, *Matthaei Parisiensis Chronica Maiora*, ed. H.R. Luard, Rolls Series, London, 1872–84. Extracts.

Letter of Pope Gregory IX, in MPL CCXVI. Extracts.

Peter-Roger of Mirepoix, *Les Registres de l'Inquisition*. Bibliothèque Nationale, Paris; vol. 22. Extracts.

Annals of Marbach, MGH; SS XVII. Extracts.

Alberic of Trois-Fontaines, *Chronicon*, RHF XVIII.

6 The 13th century Crusades

Estoire d'Eracles, from RHC Occ. II. Extracts.

Lettres de Jacques de Vitry, ed. R.B.C. Huygens, Leiden, 1960. Extracts.

Oliver of Paderborn, *Chronicle*, from *Die Schriften…Oliverus*, ed. Dr Hoogeweg, Stuttgart, 1894. Extracts.

Ibn al-Athir, from RHC Or. II. Extracts.

Philip of Novara, *Les Gestes des Chiprois*, ed. G. Raynaud, Geneva, 1887. Extracts.

Sibt Ibn al-Jawzi, *Mirat al Zaman*, from RHC Or. III. Extracts.

Matthew Paris, *Matthaei Parisiensis Chronica Maiora*, ed. H.R. Luard, Rolls Series, London, 1872–84; vol. IV. Extracts.

Jean de Joinville, *Histoire de Saint Louis*, ed. M. Natalis de Wailly, Paris, 1868. Extracts.

Abu al-Fida, from RHC Or. I. Extracts.

Ibn Wasil, *The Dissipator of Anxieties Concerning the History of the Ayubids*, Paris, 1702. Extracts.

Ibn Abd al-Zahir, in *Baybars I of Egypt*, ed. S.F. Sadeque, Pakistan, Extracts.

Chronicle of the Templar of Tyre, from Philip of Novara, *Les Gestes des Chiprois*, op.cit.

7 The last crusades

Continuation of William of Nangis, *Chronique latine…de 1300 à 1368*, ed. H. Géraud, Paris, 1843. Extracts.

Le Dossier de l'Affaire des Templiers, ed. G. Lizerand, Paris, repr. 1923. Extracts.

Marino Sanudo Torsello, from *Gesta dei per francos*, by J. Bongars, Hanover, 1611 (repr. 1972); II. Extracts.

Philip of Mézières, *Le Songe du vieil pélerin*, ed. G.W. Coopland, Cambridge, 1969; II. Extracts.

Ludolph of Sudheim, *De insula Cypro*, from *Archives de l'Orient Latin*, Paris, 1884; II. Extracts.

William of Machaut, from *La Prise d'Alexandrie*, ed. Mas Latrie, Geneca, 1877. Extracts.

Philip of Mézières, from *The Life of Peter Thomas*, ed. Smet, Rome, 1954. Extracts.

Diomede Strambaldi, from *Chroniques d'Amadi et de Strambaldi*, ed. Mas Latrie, 1891–3; vol. 2. Extracts.

Francesco Amadi, from *Chroniques d'Amadi*, op. cit.; I. Extracts.

Jean Cabaret d'Orville, *La Chronique du bon duc Loys de Bourbon*, ed. A.M. Chazaud, Paris, 1876. Extracts.

Eustace Deschamps, from *The Crusade of Nicopolis*, by A.S. Atiya, London, 1924. Extracts.

Anonymous, *Le Livre des Fais du bon Messire Jehan le Maingre. dit Bouciquaut*, ed. D. Lalande, Geneva, 1985. Extracts.

Letter of Martin I of Aragon to Pope Benedict XIII, from *Diplomatari de l'Orient Catalá*, ed. A. Rubió i Lluch, Barcelona, 1947.

Narrative of the Embassy of Ruy Gonzalez de Clavijo to the Court of Timour at Samarcand, ed. and trans. C.R. Markham, London, 1859. Extracts.

Letter of Jan Žižka to the people of Damazlive, from F.G. Heymann, *John Žižka and the Hussite Revolution*, Princeton, 1955.

Cardinal Henry Beaufort, from *Codex diplomaticus Lubecensis. Abteilung I. Urkundenbuch der Stadt Lübeck*, Lübeck, 1885; VII. Extracts.

Gilbert of Lannoy, from *Oeuvres de Ghillibert de Lannoy*, ed. C. Potvin, Louvain, 1878. Extracts.

Badr al-Din al-Aini, from *Annuaire de l'Institut de Philologie et d'Histoire Orientales et Slaves*, ed. and trans. J. La Monte and M.M. Ziada, 1939–44; VII. Extracts.

Der Briefweschel des Eneas Silvius Piccolomini from *Abteilung II, Fontes Rerum Austriacarum*, ed. R. Volkan, Vienna; vol. 61. Extracts.

Kritovoulos, *De rebus gestis Mechemetis II*, in *Fragmenta historicorum graecorum*, ed. K. Muller, Paris, 1870; vol. V-1. Extracts.

Niccolo Barbaro, *Giornale dell'assedio di Costantinopoli*, ed. E. Cornet, Vienna, 1856. Extracts.

8 The Mediterranean after 1453

Asik-Pasa-Zade, from *Vom Hirtenzelt zur Hohen Pforte*, ed. R.F. Kreutzel, Graz, 1959.

Kritovoulos, *De rebus gestis Mechemetis II*, in *Fragmenta historicorum graecorum*, ed. K. Muller, 1870; vol. V-1. Extracts.

Pope Pius II, *Commentarii*, Frankfurt, 1614. Extracts.

Hajii Khalifeh, *The History of the Maritime Wars of the Turks*, ed. and trans. J. Mitchell, London, 1831. Extracts.

Guillaume Caoursin, *Obsidionis Rhodiae urbis desriptio*, trans. J. Kay (1482), ed. H.W. Fincham, London, 1926, Extracts.

Jacopo Gherardi, *Diarium romanum*, in *Rerum italicarum scriptores*, Milan, 1723–51; XXIII. Extracts.

Charles VII of France, in *Ordonnances des Rois de France de la 3è Race*, Paris, 1723–1849; XX. Extracts.

Letter of Ferdinand of Aragon and Isabella of Castile, from *Hispania sacra*, 1951; IV. Extracts.

Diego de Valera, *Cronica de los reyes católicos*, ed. J. de M. Carriazo, Madrid, 1927. Extracts.

Fernando del Pulgar, *Cronica de los reyes católicos*, ed. J. de M. Carriazo, Madrid, 1943. Extracts.

Andrés Bernáldez, *Historia de los Reyes Católicos*, in *Biblioteca de Autores Españoles*, Madrid, 1870; vol. 70. Extracts.

Letter of Pope Pius IV, in K.M. Setton, *The Papacy and the Levant*, Philadelphia, 1976–84; IV. Extracts.

Francesco Balbi di Correggio, *La verdadera relacion de todo que el anno de MDLXV ha succedido en la isla de Malta*, Barcelona, 1568. Extracts.

Uberto Foglietta, *De sacro foedere in Selimum*, Genoa, 1587. Extracts.

Venetian report, from K.M. Stetton, op. cit. Extracts.

Leonardo Donà, in *Corrispondenza da Madrid di Leonardo Donà*, ed. M. Brunetti and E. Vitale, Venice/Rome, 1963. Extracts.

Gomes Eannes de Azurara, *The Chronicle of the Discovery and Conquest of Guinea*, ed. and trans. C.R. Beazley, London, 1896. Extracts.

Letter of Christopher Columbus, from *Select Documents Illustrating the Four Voyages of Columbus*, ed. C. Jane, London, 1933. Extracts.

Bernal Diaz, *The Conquest of New Spain*, ed. and trans. J.M. Cohen, London, 1963. Extracts.

MANUSCRIPTS

(b. = bottom; t. = top; r. = right; l. = left)

2 Departure for the crusade (*Statuts de l'Ordre du Saint-Esprit*, French, 14th century. B[ibliothèque] N[ationale], Paris, MS Fr. 4274, f. 6).

6 William of Tyre writing his history (William of Tyre, *Histoire d'Outremer*, French, 13th century. BN MS 2631, f. 1r).

10 A prince in his harem (*The Divan of Havai*, Turkish, 16th century. B[ritish] L[ibrary], London, MS Or, 5346, f. 51v).

18-19 Arab travellers in a village (Al-Hariri, *Assemblies*, Arabic, 13th century. BN MS Arabe 5847, f. 138r).

22/23 Al-Hakim orders the destruction of the Holy Sepulchre (Al-Biruni, *History of Ancient People*, Persian, 14th century. Edinburgh University Library, Edinburgh, MS Arab 161, f. 134v).

27 Men tending trees (Al-Qazwini, *The Wonders of Creation*, Arabic, 13th century. BL MS Or 14140, f. 89v).

37 Men attacking civilians (Marini Sanuti Torselli, *Secreta fidelium crucis*, Italian, 14th century. BL MS Add. 27376, f. 45).

45 Scene from an Apocalypse (*Comentarios al Apocalipsis*, Spanish, 11th century. Biblioteca Nacional, Madrid).

47 Christians and Moors fighting (*Cantigas de Santa Maria*, Spanish, 13th century. Monastery of the Escorial, Madrid).

53 Palermo and its inhabitants (Peter of Eboli, *Liber ad honorem augusti*, 13th century. Burgerbibliothek, Bern, MS 120/II, f. 98).

56-57 Byzantine Emperor bearing the Holy Lance (*Travels of Sir John Mandeville*, English, 14th century. BL MS Add. 24189, f. 10).

58-59 The sack of Jerusalem by Antiochus (Jean de Courcy, *La Bouquechardière*, French, 15th century. BN MS Fr. 20124, f. 331).

62 Urban II preaching the First Crusade at the Council of Clermont (*Livre des Passages d'Outre-mer*, French, 15th century. BN MS Fr. 5594, f. 9).

67 Peter the Hermit leading knights and pilgrims (*Abreviamen de las Estorias*, Provençal, 14th century. BL MS Egerton 1500 f. 45v).

75 The battle of Dorylaeum (William of Tyre, op. cit., French, 14th century. BN MS Fr. 352 f. 49).

77 Citizens of Edessa do homage to Baldwin I (William of Tyre, op. cit., Latin kingdom of Jerusalem, 13th century. BN MS Fr. 9084, f. 42r).

83 The Holy Lance borne in battle outside Antioch (William of Tyre, op. cit., Latin kingdom of Jerusalem, 13th century. BL MS Yates Thompson 12, f. 29).

85 Mongols eating people (Matthew Paris, *Historia Maiora*, English, 13th century. Corpus Christi College, Cambridge, MS 16).

89 The siege of Jerusalem in 1099 (William of Tyre, op. cit., French, 13th century. BN MS Fr. 9081).

90 Map of the world (Higden, *Polychronicon*, English, 14th century. BL MS Roy. 14 C IX, f. 1v-2).

90/91 (Higden, op. cit., detail).

95 Godfrey of Bouillon (William of Tyre, op. cit., Latin kingdom of Jerusalem, 13th century. BN MS Fr. 9084, f. 20v).

96 Coronation of Baldwin as king of Jerusalem (William of Tyre, *Histoire d'Outremer*, French, 13th century. BN MS Fr. 9081, f. 99v).

99 Knights pursuing Arabs (*Les Chroniques de France ou de St-Denis*, French, 15th century. BL MS Add. 21143, f. 90).

103 City of the Apocalypse (*Comentarios al Apocalipsis*, Spanish, 11th century. Biblioteca Nacional, Madrid).

107 Cutaway view of the Holy Sepulchre, Jerusalem (Vicenzo Favi, *Relatione del Viaggio di Gerusalemme*, Italian, 17th century. BL MS Add. 33566, f. 90).

111 Prisoners beheaded by Saracens (*Les Livres du Graunt Caam*, French, 14th century. BL MS Roy. 19 D I, f. 107).

112/113 The fall of Tyre (William of Tyre, op. cit., French, 13th century. BN MS Fr. 2630, f. 111v).

120t. Crossbow mounted in a shield (*Information for the Intellectual* (a treatise made for Saladin's library), Egyptian, 12th century, Bodl[eian Library], Oxford, MS Hunt. 264, f. 117).

120b. Catapult loading device (*Information for the Intellectual*. Bodl. MS Hunt. 264, f. 87).

121 Trebuchet (Information for the Intellectual. Bodl. MS Hunt. 264, 134fv–135r).

134/135 Ship and baggage (Marini, op. cit. BL MS Add. 27376, fol. 4v).

INDEX

ACKNOWLEDGEMENTS

Our thanks to the many museums, libraries and individuals, including those listed below, who provided us with illustrations.

(b. d bottom; t. d top; r. d right; l. d left)

Ancient Art and Architecture Collection, London: 55, 223, 265
Arxiu Mas, Barcelona: 45, 47, 103, 126, 347

Barnaby's Picture Library, London: 130/131, 215, 329, 343, 350/351, 362
Bibliothèque Municipale, Lyon: 143
Bibliothèque Nationale, Paris: 2, 6, 18/19, 75, 77, 96, 150/151, 243, 245, 275, 281, 289, 299, 303, 337, 338/339
Bridgeman Art Library, London: 58/59, 95, 198/199, 282/283, 361, 363, 370/371
British Library, London: 10, 27, 37, 56/57, 67, 83, 90, 90/91, 99, 107, 111, 134/135, 139, 141, 154, 177, 179, 183, 235, 238, 257, 270/271, 279, 287, 301, 306/307, 310/311, 321, 330, 331, 353
British Museum, London: 190/191

Burgerbibliothek, Bern: 53, 175
Corpus Christi College, Cambridge: 85, 158/159, 202/203, 250/251
Edimages/Jourdes, Paris: 224, 319
Edinburgh University Library, Edinburgh: 22/23
Fitzwilliam Museum, Cambridge: 355
John Freeman & Co., London: 365t., 365b., 366, 367, 369
Giraudon, Paris: 160, 167
Elizabeth Hallam: 30/31, 123, 230/231, 263
Sonia Halliday: 62, 70/71, 89, 101, 109, 114/115, 186/187, 291, 314/315
Index, Florence: 42, 43l., 43r., 70, 207, 211, 218/219, 221, 222, 246/247, 259, 269, 334/335
Michael Jenner: 13, 105, 170/171, 197
National Gallery, London: 327
National Maritime Museum, Greenwich: 322/323
David Nicolle: 38/39, 79, 92, 112/113, 118/119, 120t., 120b., 121, 149, 163, 193, 255
Wim Swaan: 232/233
Topkapi Saray Museum, Istanbul: 354t., 354b., 354/355